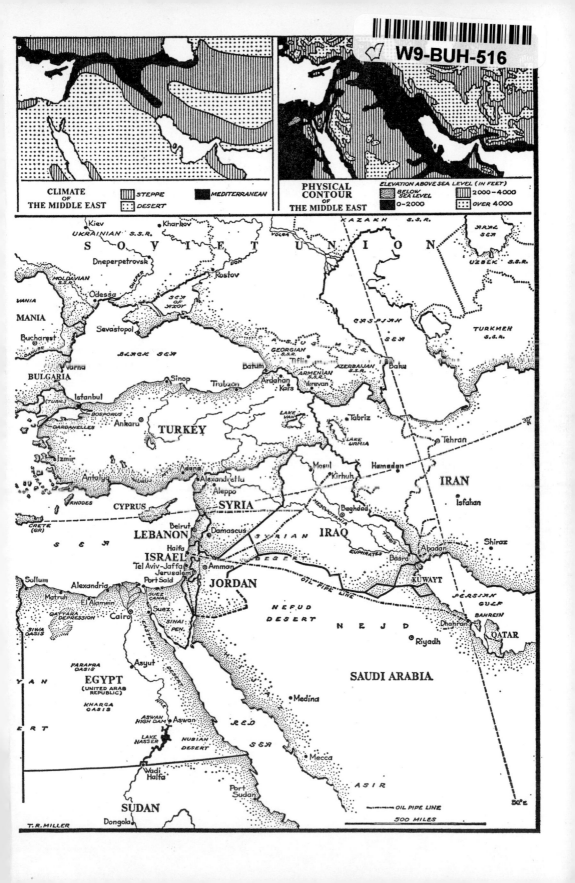

CLIMATE
OF
THE MIDDLE EAST

STEPPE MEDITERRANEAN
DESERT

PHYSICAL
CONTOUR
OF
THE MIDDLE EAST

ELEVATION ABOVE SEA LEVEL (IN FEET)
BELOW SEA LEVEL 2000-4000
0-2000 OVER 4000

Kiev
Kharkov
UKRAINIAN S.S.R.
KAZAKH S.S.R.
ARAL SEA

S O V I E T   U N I O N

Dneperpetrovsk
VOLGA
Rostov
UZBEK S.S.R.
MOLDAVIAN S.S.R.
DON
VANIA
Odessa
DNIEPER
CASPIAN SEA
TURKMEN S.S.R.
MANIA
Sevastopol
SEA OF AZOV
Bucharest
CAUCASUS MTS.
DANU
BLACK SEA
GEORGIAN S.S.R.
Varna
Tiflis
Batum
BULGARIA
Sinop
Trabzon
Ardahan
Baku
Istanbul
(TURK.)
Ankara
Kars
AZERBAIJAN S.S.R.
Yerevan
ARMENIAN S.S.R.
BOSPORUS
TURKEY
LAKE VAN
Tabriz
Tehran
DARDANELLES
LAKE URMIA
Izmir
Adana
Mosul
Hamadan
IRAN
Antalya
Tarsus
Alexandretta
Kirkuk
Isfahan
RHODES
Aleppo
SYRIA
MESOPOTAMIA
Baghdad
CYPRUS
CRETE
(GR.)
Beirut
Damascus
SYRIAN
IRAQ
S E A
LEBANON
DESERT
EUPHRATES
Basra
Shiraz
Haifa
Abadan
ISRAEL
Tel Aviv-Jaffa
Amman
KUWAYT
Jerusalem
Sollum
Alexandria
Port Said
JORDAN
OIL PIPE LINE
PERSIAN GULF
Matruh
SUEZ CANAL
NEFUD
BAHREIN
El Alamein
Cairo
Suez
DESERT
N E J D
Dhahran
QATTARA DEPRESSION
SINAI PEN.
Riyadh
QATAR
SIWA OASIS
Y A N
FARAFRA OASIS
Asyut
EGYPT
(UNITED ARAB REPUBLIC)
SAUDI ARABIA
E R T
KHARGA OASIS
Medina
ASWAN HIGH DAM
Aswan
LAKE NASSER
RED
NUBIAN DESERT
SEA
Mecca
Wadi Halfa
A S I R
50°E
Port Sudan
OIL PIPE LINE
SUDAN
500 MILES
T.R. MILLER
Dongola

The Middle East

A HISTORY

The Middle East

A HISTORY

Sydney Nettleton Fisher

THE OHIO STATE UNIVERSITY

Second Edition

ALFRED · A · KNOPF  *NEW YORK*

THIS IS A BORZOI BOOK
PUBLISHED BY ALFRED A. KNOPF, INC.

FIRST PRINTING

© Copyright, 1959, 1969 by Sydney Nettleton Fisher.
All rights reserved under International and Pan-American Copyright
Conventions. Published in the United States by Alfred A. Knopf,
Inc., New York, and simultaneously in Canada by Random House
of Canada Limited, Toronto. Distributed by Random House, Inc.,
New York.

Library of Congress Catalog Card Number: 68–24673

Manufactured in the United States of America

First Edition, 1959, reprinted six times.

Second Edition, revised and enlarged, 1968.

❧ *Preface* ❧

TO THE FIRST EDITION

For the last two thousand years and more the West has been drawn to, involved in, and fascinated by the culture, religion, resources, and politics of the Middle East. First the Greeks, then the Romans, later the Western Europeans, and now the Americans are discovering the Middle East and its peoples. Historically, the area has been labeled the Orient, the East, the Levant, or the Near East; at present the most widely used term is the Middle East.

The United States, because of her great power and world position since the end of World War II, finds herself concerned with the contemporary problems of the Middle East. In general, Americans of today, many of whom have just become cognizant of the existence of the Middle East, find numerous aspects of its life and affairs quite unintelligible. This is particularly true when these complexities are expressed in the various and often conflicting pronouncements of propagandists for the Arabs, the Israelis and Zionism, the imperialists, the oil companies, the internationalists, the isolationists, the various nationalisms of the Middle East, and all sundry interests.

The attempt of this volume has been to present a brief account of the contemporary Middle Eastern scene so that the beginning college student or general reader can place the area in its proper setting and perspective. Many of the present situations and problems cannot be appreciated or evaluated properly without a knowledge and comprehension of the past, since the contemporary civilization of the Middle East probably has deeper and more significant roots in its past culture and experience than many other civilizations.

With this in mind, it was deemed advisable to begin the story, after a short introduction, with the life of the prophet Muhammad and the revolutionary changes that he made upon the society of his time. From this point the narrative has been carried forward, changing the central locus of the scene from Medina to Damascus to Baghdad to Asia Minor to Istanbul and back to the Arab lands as the fortunes of the area have developed, and at the same time examining each era more in detail as the present is approached.

Certain technicalities have been simplified for the beginner. The titles of many positions, past and present, have been translated into English equivalents in order not to confuse the reader with strange words or tire his eyes with unfamiliar combinations of letters and words. The transliteration of Middle Eastern proper names has always presented difficulties. In Western literature pertaining to the Middle East, one can find the name of the Prophet rendered as Muhammad, Mohammed, Mohammad, Mohamed, Mahomet, Mehmed, Mehmet, Mehemet, and several other ways. In this book, Muhammad has been used for Arabs, Mehmed for Turks, and Mohammed for some others when individuals spelled the name in that fashion. For most words a spelling has been employed that would render them and their pronunciation most easily adopted by American readers. Where names of places or people have acquired a widely accepted Western spelling, those forms have been used.

Since almost every volume concerning detailed or specialized aspects of Middle Eastern life and affairs contains considerable bibliographical material, and because of the excellent and wide coverage provided in Richard Ettinghausen's *A Selected and Annotated Bibliography of Books and Periodicals in Western Languages dealing with the Near and Middle East With Special Emphasis on Mediaeval and Modern Times* (The Middle East Institute, Washington, D.C., 1952 and 1954), the inclusion of an extensive bibliography has not been felt necessary. The bibliographical entries at the end of the chapters have been supplied to indicate to the beginning student where easily accessible additional material on particular subjects may be obtained. These titles are suggested to serve as second steps for inquiring students who wish to dig more deeply into the many topics discussed only summarily in this text.

In gathering material for this volume it has been necessary to refer to a wide range of books, produced after years of diligent research and study by several generations of scholars in various lands. All will recognize my debt to these; students familiar with the literature of the diverse aspects of Middle Eastern history will appreciate my indebtedness to scholars of other years. This text could not have been written without their labors.

Through the years it has been my good fortune to obtain a closer knowledge of many aspects of Middle Eastern affairs and society through personal conversations and correspondence with many individuals concerned with that area of the world. Without mentioning names, I wish to thank them for the contributions they have made, sometimes unknowingly, to this text. Specifically I desire to pay tribute to inspiring teachers and mentors who have given me a better understanding of general and detailed problems and periods of Middle Eastern history. They are Frederick B. Artz of Oberlin College; Dr. Edgar J. Fisher of Amherst, Virginia; the late Albert Howe Lybyer of the University of Illinois; Philip K. Hitti and the late Walter Livingston Wright, Jr., of Princeton University; and Paul Wittek of the University of London.

In addition to these I am under deep obligation to my colleagues Professors William F. McDonald and John R. Randall for their criticism and aid in regard to certain chapters. Also, Dr. Halford L. Hoskins of the Library of Congress and Professor George G. Arnakis of the University of Texas read the entire volume, offered valuable suggestions, and caught numerous errors and slips. Dr. J. Merle Rife, State University, Indiana, Pennsylvania, was most helpful in assisting in the compilation of the bibliographical references.

However, any faults in fact or judgment which remain are my sole responsibility. Further recognition is due The Ohio State University Graduate School for assistance in the preparation of the manuscript.

This text could not have been prepared without the tolerance and co-operation of my entire family, which has lived with the manuscript for several years.

Worthington, Ohio   SYDNEY NETTLETON FISHER

❧ *Preface* ❧
TO THE SECOND EDITION

S ince 1959, when this text first appeared, the Middle East has experienced many events and developments of considerable significance for the world and for the area. Furthermore, new evidence and
information of the past have been revealed by documents, memoirs,
statements, and scholars.

In this revision, an attempt has been made to update the material
since 1958, to include some of the details of the crisis of the summer of
1967, and to change and correct other statements as required by recent
studies and publications.

I wish to thank the various individuals who over the past decade
have pointed out errors and omissions and have offered other views for
consideration. Some of these have been incorporated in the several
reprintings of the first edition and others are included in this revision.
I am especially indebted to Mr. James Saeger of Lehigh University for
aiding in the preparation of additions to the bibliographical references.

Worthington, Ohio

SYDNEY NETTLETON FISHER

❧❧ *Contents* ❧❧

PART II. THE OTTOMAN EMPIRE

✦ List of Maps ✦

BY THEODORE R. MILLER

The Middle East

A HISTORY

CHAPTER 1

Geographic Prologue

GEOGRAPHY

In the mid-twentieth century the term *Middle East* refers to that area of the world comprising the present political states of Lebanon, Syria, Israel, Jordan, Iraq, Saudi Arabia, Kuwayt, Bahrayn, Qatar, Trucial States, Oman, Federation of South Arabia and Aden, Yemen, Egypt, Sudan, Turkey, and Iran. In addition, *Middle East* is employed as a cultural designation for a society and civilization found not only in that region but also to a certain degree in a number of adjacent localities such as Afghanistan, Pakistan, Libya, Tunisia, Algeria, and Morocco.

Two geographic features of the Middle East have been significant in all periods of history. Its location has given it an important, sometimes strategic, position between Africa and Eurasia, and between the Mediterranean world and the Asia of India and the Far East. Nations, tribes, traders, armies, and pilgrims—peoples on the move—have traversed the Middle East, finding the land bridge convenient and along the way discovering the wealth of the area and the civilization of its people.

The second important geographic feature is the relative magnitude of the Middle East. Arabia, the central land mass of the Middle East, embraces an area about the same size as that of the United States east of the Mississippi River plus Texas and California. The southern shore facing the Indian Ocean from Aden to Muscat is as far as from New Orleans to Boston; on the west, the Red Sea is as wide as Lake Erie is long, and the distance from Aden to Port Said is nearly the same as from New York to Denver. Northward from Arabia proper to the Turkish frontier is another 400 miles. If then Egypt, Iran, and Turkey are added, the area becomes equivalent to that of continental United States. Stretching out 2,000 miles westward in a narrow band from the mouth of the Nile River to the Atlantic Ocean lies North Africa, a cultural part of the Middle East since the end of the seventh century. Moreover, this delimitation of the Middle East has omitted Turkestan, Afghanistan, and Pakistan, with such historic cities as Bukhara, Samarkand, Kabul, and Lahore. Thus, the physical size of the Middle East becomes impressive to Europeans and Americans who are accustomed to seeing the area pictured on maps of Asia or Africa, the large continents.

PHYSIOGRAPHY

The geologic characteristics of the Middle East show a wide variety of land features: great areas covered by water; low-lying land and swampy regions creating coal beds; and folds of the earth's crust to form mountains and create faults. In the last six or seven thousand years, however, there is little evidence of any important physiographical change except that the deltas of most of the rivers have grown and extended the land seaward. In western Turkey, for example, camels and cattle now graze on the flood plain of the Meander River in front of the ancient walls of Miletus and Priene, in the exact spot where the Persian fleet vanquished the Greeks five centuries before Christ.

Arabia, in general, is a tilted plateau, slanting upward from the northeast to the southwest with a sharp drop in Yemen from 12,000 feet down to the Red Sea. Central Turkey and central Iran are elevated plateaus, in places reaching an altitude of 8,000 feet. Rugged mountains dominate Middle Eastern geography. From a high center in northwestern Iran in the neighborhood of Mt. Ararat, mountain ranges up to 18,-000 feet in altitude branch out in several chains: the Elburz group running eastward south of the Caspian Sea; the Zagros system, a wide series of ranges protruding in a southeasterly direction to Afghanistan and India; and the famed Taurus Mountains, pushing southwestward to the Mediterranean and separating the Anatolian Plateau from Arabia.

Rivers have played an important role in society and have deeply influenced the development of civilization in the Middle East. Two are fabled and basic in the history of the area: the Nile and the Tigris-Euphrates. Flowing from central Africa and Abyssinia, the Nile passes through a relatively flat region in the Sudan until it reaches the cataract zone north of Khartoum, where a gorge has been cut. Below Aswan, the Nile flows through a well-developed valley about six miles wide to Cairo, where the delta begins. In August the river starts to rise in Egypt, reaching its peak in September, eighteen feet above the low of April and May. Annually some 110 million tons of sediment, rich in mineral substances, are carried into Egypt and more than half of this silt reaches the delta.

The other great river system—the Tigris-Euphrates—rises in the highlands of eastern Turkey. Winter snowfall feeds both streams, which turn and twist through precipitous and narrow defiles emptying out upon the plateau plains of Syria and Kurdistan. Rushing southward, they converge upon Baghdad but meet only about 230 miles farther on where they form the Shatt-al-Arab, which flows gently for about seventy-five miles to the Persian Gulf. The fall in the river beds between Asia Minor and Baghdad is very marked, producing a swift current with strong erosive powers. The rivers are at their lowest in September and October but begin to rise appreciably in December to reach flood stage of about eighteen feet in April for the Tigris and about eleven feet in May for the Euphrates. Within historic times the Tigris and the Euphrates and the former's two Iranian tributaries—the Karkeh and the Karun —filled in the Persian Gulf from near the site of Baghdad to the present shore line. No longer a tributary, the Karkeh is dissipated at the present time in the marshes of lower Mesopotamia.

One of the most renowned and romantic geographic spots of the Middle East has been the Straits—the waterway from the Black Sea to the Aegean Sea. At the northern end is the present-day Bosphorus, a sixteen-mile strait varying in width from nearly two miles to 547 yards at the narrowest point. Everywhere the channel is deep, 400 feet in spots, and the drop off at the edge so sharp that vessels requiring considerable draft may tie up at many places along shore and unload directly upon the road running alongside. On a point of land where the Bosphorus empties into the Sea of Marmara stands one of the great cities of the Middle East—variously known as Byzantium, Constantinople, or Istanbul. Dotted with a number of islands, the Sea of Marmara is sixty miles wide and extends some 125 miles southwestward to the Dardanelles. This historic passage, often called the Hellespont, is twenty-five miles long and is wider than the Bosphorus, varying from 2½ miles to 4½ miles at its southern end, where it empties into the Aegean. These three bodies of water, taken collectively, have been known through the years as the Straits, separating Europe from Asia yet serving as a strong connecting link between East and West. Economically, politically, and strategically, the Straits have been important throughout all history.

CLIMATE

During the Fourth Glacial Period, some 25,000 years ago, when much of Europe and northern Asia was covered with an ice sheet, the Middle East and the Sahara regions were moist and dotted with lakes and seas, a well-watered wooded land abounding with game. As the ice receded, the desert area between the tropic and the temperate zones appeared. Little change, however, has occurred in the climate of the Middle East in the last five thousand years.

Rainfall along the shores of the Mediterranean, Black, and Caspian Seas comes for the most part during the winter months. Many areas receive an average annual fall of thirty inches. As one progresses inland, however, the average drops appreciably; Egypt and the plateaus of Arabia, Iran, and Turkey have a desert climate. Moreover, the rains are not only seasonal but almost capricious. Damascus has an average annual rainfall of about ten inches, but four inches have fallen in one morning. The mountainous areas of eastern Turkey and Iran receive more moisture, but here, too, winter is the wet season, with much of the precipitation occurring in the form of snow. The one exception is the monsoon region of southern and southwestern Arabia, which gets most of its rainfall in the months of July, August, and September.

Temperatures depend upon latitude and altitude, and winter in the mountains of Arabia can be quite bitter. Summer temperatures in Egypt, Arabia, Iran, and the interior of Turkey are hot, over 100° F., during the day, but nights are cool everywhere except in some of the lower valleys where the humidity is high.

FLORA AND FAUNA

For the last 5,000 years a process of deforestation has denuded most of the land in the Middle East. Some stands of oak, beech, pine, juniper, and boxwood remain on the slopes of the Elburz Mountains, in east Asia Minor, and of the Lebanon Mountains. Elsewhere the land would be bare but for cypresses in cemeteries and gardens and poplars along streams and irrigation ditches. In the Middle East wood has been a prized building material and the principal fuel from the beginning of history until the advent of coal and oil.

It has been estimated that unconcern about land conservation over the last 5,000 years has resulted in the destruction of ninety percent of the forest and topsoil resources of the Middle East. But absence of concern cannot be said to exist with respect to the cultivation of edible flora of the area. Wheat, barley, rye, broad beans, lentils, onions, leeks, garlic, figs, grapes, melons, pomegranates, pears, plums, apples, peaches, apricots, almonds, walnuts, olives, and dates are the principal plants and trees developed from the native vegetation of the area.

Domestication of native animals of the Middle East probably began about the same time that the land was beginning to be cultivated. In what order it is difficult to tell, but at some very early time the dog (probably first), sheep, goat, pig, ox, and ass were tamed and made to work or to provide food and clothing for man. Domesticated horses and camels were introduced into the area from farther east in Asia in the second millennium before Christ. As the forests became scarcer, the pig was replaced by more economical all-purpose animals like the ox, goat, and sheep; and the arrival of the camel made habitation in the desert possible and facilitated Middle Eastern nomadism in Arabia proper.

The waters teem with fish. The Caspian has long been noted for its sturgeon and caviar. The Black Sea and the Bosphorus abound in tuna, mackerel, and herring of many excellent varieties. And the eastern Mediterranean, fed by the vegetable matter of the Nile, has continued through the centuries to be an attractive and productive spot for fish of all kinds.

RESOURCES

The significant natural resources of the Middle East have been, and still are, the availability and interrelationship of water, soil, sun, plants, and animals to produce a propitious agricultural life. Other natural resources are the excellent clays with which the bricks, pots, and finer ceramics of many cultures have been fashioned. Mountains, lava extrusions along the geologic faults, and rock formations laid bare by river erosion have provided extensive quarries for basalt, granite, marble, porphyry, sandstone, and limestone.

Gold, silver, copper, and iron occur in easily workable ores, and their ready utilization sounded the death knell of the Neolithic age. The presence of other metals such as tin and nickel with copper led the way to the development of bronze and brass. Deposits of these metals have been worked almost continuously up to the present, and the output has been of considerable value in the economy and life of the area. In the twentieth century other metals have come to the fore. Chromium and manganese are found in sizable deposits; and small amounts of antimony, molybdenum, mercury, and cobalt are available. Coal and lignite exist in considerable amounts in Turkey and Iran, but only in recent years have these beds been exploited.

The greatest of the natural resources of the Middle East of the twentieth century, beyond land and water, is oil. Small fields have been located in Turkey, Egypt, Syria, and Israel, but the large ones are those of Khuzistan in Iran, those of Mosul-Kirkuk in Iraq, and those along the Persian Gulf in Saudi Arabia, Kuwayt, Bahrayn, and the shaykhdoms of the Persian Gulf. No one yet knows the full extent of the oil reserves of the Middle East; but its known reserves alone far outstrip those of any other oil-producing region, and the presence of this natural resource is rapidly changing the world importance of the Middle East.

PEOPLE

The Middle East, therefore, blest with a warm climate, a fertile soil, native animals and plants suitable for food, waters available for controlled irrigation, and varied mineral resources, was an area of the world favorable for the propagation of mankind, for the increase in man's standard of living, and for the growth of an organized society.

Throughout the ages the finest resource of the Middle East has been people—man. Anthropologists, archeologists, and geneticists may yet unravel the twisted and indistinct story of life and the wanderings of pre-historic *Homo sapiens* in the Middle East. It seems quite certain, however, that around 15,000 B.C., as the Fourth Glacial Period terminated, the well-watered regions of Arabia and the Sahara were inhabited by men of the Mediterranean race. Through the ten millennia of the Mesolithic age as the ice cap was retreating to Scandinavia, however, Arabia and the Sahara became desiccated and their inhabitants moved northward and seaward. Some in east Africa became the ancestors of the Hamites of Egypt; others in Arabia clung to the shores of the Persian Gulf or moved to the southern highlands. The latter became known to the world as Semites. Another branch of the Mediterranean race lived on the Iranian plateau, where many of the plants and animals were domesticated. As these peoples moved with their advanced culture into other parts of the Middle East and into Europe, the Neolithic age was born.

With the advent of Neolithic man into the valleys of the Indus, the Tigris-Euphrates, and the Nile our civilization had its beginnings. Because of the annual flooding of the rivers and the annual renewing of the soil and its fertility from the silt deposited, the Neolithic agriculturist could continue to cultivate the same fields year after year, generation after generation. Even a partial nomadism became unnecessary; a stable stationary society evolved. Records accumulated and history in the Middle East began.

REFERENCES: Chapter 1

C. U. Ariens-Kappers, *An Introduction to the Anthropology of the Near East in Ancient and Recent Times:* N. V. Noordhollandsche uitgeversmaatschappij, Amsterdam, 1934. A study of the physical anthropology of the Middle East.

Carleton S. Coon, *Caravan: The Story of the Middle East:* Henry Holt, New York, 1951. An excellent anthropological introduction to the Middle East written in a style easily understood by the layman and the beginning student. The author is an outstanding authority in anthropology, especially as it relates to the Middle East. For many years he has been a curator of the museum of the University of Pennsylvania.

————, *The Races of Europe:* Macmillan, New York, 1939. This is a general study of the peoples of Europe, and it includes the Middle East.

W. B. Fisher, *The Middle East: A Physical, Social and Regional Geography:* Methuen, London, 1952. The only volume of its kind. Authoritative yet easily read by the beginner in the field of geography or Middle Eastern studies.

Norton S. Ginsburg, ed., *The Pattern of Asia:* Prentice-Hall, New York, 1958. Seven chapters on the geography of the Middle East are written by John R. Randall.

Oxford Regional Economic Atlas: The Middle East and North Africa: Prepared by the Clarendon Press and *The Economist,* Oxford University Press, New York, 1957.

R. Roolvink, *Historical Atlas of the Muslim Peoples:* Djambatan, Amsterdam. An excellent collection of historical maps showing events since 612 B.C. Harvard University Press is the American agent.

Pre-Islamic Politics and Society in the Middle East

THE RISE OF CIVILIZATION

Scholars still debate whether Western civilization began first in the Nile Valley or in Mesopotamia along the Tigris-Euphrates River. Whichever came first, it can be shown that each arrived in the area already in a transitional stage from the Neolithic age to the Early Bronze age, that each brought with it domesticated plants and animals (many of which were of common origin), but that each in its new habitat developed an urban civilization largely autochthonous in character.

Somewhat before the year 4000 B.C. the Sumerian people arrived at one of the mouths of the Tigris-Euphrates River. Where they came from has not been determined with any exactitude, but they were an Asianic type of the Mediterranean race and spoke a language wholly unrelated to any known tongue. There in the Tigris-Euphrates Valley, Sumerian city-states evolved with society divided into technological-social classes—nobility, priests, traders, farmers, and artisans—divisions which have persisted as constant factors in all Middle Eastern civilizations. Shortly thereafter other peoples from the shores and watered places of Arabia were drawn to the prosperous Sumerian cities. They spoke a language belonging to the Semitic family, the basic tongue arising in the Arabian peninsula. Thus, very early in history, the Sumerians became a mixed people.

Farther north along the middle Euphrates about the beginning of the third millennium B.C., Semites, probably from the desert, founded the state of Akkad. For a thousand years the Sumerian and the Semitic states were ardent rivals. Cities such as Lagash, Akkad, and Ur, each had its day and then passed the scepter to another. At times, Mesopotamia was united to confront a third force—the Elamites, a non-Semitic ethnic group from Elam (Susa) on the Karkeh River. The Sumerian element in the area, however, was politically submerged by the union of all of Mesopotamia under the Amorite (Semitic) Hammurabi of Babylon about the year 1700 B.C.

At approximately the same time the Sumerians appeared in Mesopotamia, Hamites began to develop a civilization along the Nile. Some came from East Africa, and others from North Africa; the Hamitic tongue of the early Egyptians was a blending of the two. The nature of the land, the annual flooding of the Nile, the local presence of copper (which began to be worked about 3000 B.C.), and the relative isolation of the Nile Valley by the surrounding deserts were conducive to the establishment of an absolute monarchy and a flourishing culture.

Early in the second millennium B.C. Indo-Europeans from eastern Europe and western Asia began a southward movement, exerting population pressures upon the whole of the Middle East. In a succession of thrusts, these intruders with bronze and iron weapons and horses and camels pushed ahead of them into the Middle East such non-Indo-Europeans as the Kassites and the Hyksos. The Kassites came down with horses from the Zagros Mountains to rule Mesopotamia through most of the second millennium B.C.; and the Hyksos came with their horse-drawn chariots to rule Egypt for two centuries beginning about 1800 B.C. Later, genuine Indo-European waves brought Hittites, Armenians, Achaean and Dorian Greeks, Philistines, Medes, Persians, Macedonians, Parthians, Romans, and Sasanids. Between these invasions and conquests of the northmen, Hamite rulers reappeared in Egypt, and Semitic tribes such as Amorites, Assyrians, Arameans, Canaanites, Phoenicians, Hebrews, Nabateans, Palmyrenes, and Ghassanids moved from the Arabian peninsula to establish states in Mesopotamia, Syria, or Palestine.

Each group of invaders, at the time of its arrival upon the Middle Eastern scene and in its first contact with Middle Eastern civilization, was leading a nomadic or pastoral life. The transition to an organized life on the Middle Eastern pattern of greater specialization and division of labor produced turmoil and strains, but the transition was always made successfully within the span of a few generations so that a continuity prevailed and civilization was ever victorious. Each added something in religion, the art of writing, metallurgical skills, political organization, transportation, irrigation, or astronomy, and within a brief period the knowledge became widespread over the entire area.

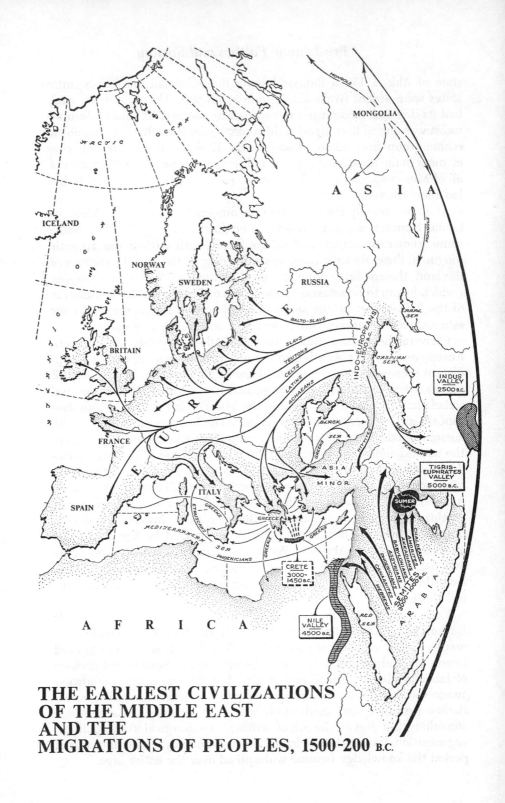

**THE EARLIEST CIVILIZATIONS
OF THE MIDDLE EAST
AND THE
MIGRATIONS OF PEOPLES, 1500-200** B.C.

ANCIENT EMPIRES

By the beginning of the first millennium B.C. the Middle East was rapidly becoming one cultural region, and a number of efforts were made to unite the area politically. Throughout the second millennium B.C., the Egyptian pharaohs sought and from time to time held control of Syria and Palestine. Mesopotamian kings, however, vied with the pharaohs for these provinces; and from that age until the present only when both Egypt and Mesopotamia have been weak or evenly matched has the Syrian coast been able to maintain its independence.

One of the great empires controlling a major part of the Middle East was that of the Assyrians, whose capital was at Nineveh on the upper Tigris in Mesopotamia. Iron weapons, a disciplined army, a tight bu-reaucracy, and iron battering rams mounted on wheels gave the Semitic Assyrians such an advantage in the seventh century B.C. that Nineveh held sway from Sinai to the Caspian Sea and from the Persian Gulf to the plains of central Asia Minor. However, over-extension of the empire and exhausting battles, coupled with luxury, indolence, and unwise tax-ation, weakened the army and the government so that Nineveh with its palace and great library was sacked by Iranians in league with another Semitic group which established its capital at Babylon on the Euphra-tes. Comprising the full Fertile Crescent from Sinai to the Persian Gulf, this new Chaldean empire won fame from the "hanging gardens," from the Babylonian captivity of the Hebrews, and from such names as Nebuchadnezzar and Belshazzar.

Upon the fall of Nineveh the unity of the Middle East was destroyed until the Persians, a small group of Iranians from the southeastern end of the Zagros range, reunited the areas of the previous Assyrian empire and added Greek Asia Minor, Byzantium, Thrace, the Nile Valley to the Sudan, Afghanistan, Baluchistan, the Punjab, Bactria, and Sogdi-ana. With the establishment of the Persian Empire in the sixth century B.C. Semitic rule in the Middle East was crushed for over a thousand years. It was not until the rise of the Arabs under the banners of Islam that the Indo-Europeans lost their hegemony.

Checked at Marathon in 490 B.C. and at Thermopylae a decade later, the Persians maintained their power in the Middle East by an imperial system of government which skillfully combined local autonomy with centralized authority and responsibility. This form of government fash-ioned by the Persians was adopted in most essentials by succeeding rulers for over two thousand years and established a governmental pat-tern which became accepted as a part of Middle Eastern civilization. The twenty-three provinces or satrapies of the Persian Empire were or-ganized along lines of nationalities, and local independence was real to a considerable degree. Taxes and loyalty were the important requirements; a governor (satrap), a general, and a secretary, each reporting independently to the royal residence (Susa, Babylon, or Persepolis), preserved Persian rule.

Another secret of Persian success was the advancement of communications and transportation. Good roads from the frontier to the heart of the empire were kept open under constant repair and surveillance. The old canals between the Nile and the Red Sea were cleaned so that the Phoenicians, the stalwarts of the Persian fleet, could sail directly from the Persian Gulf to the Mediterranean. In the end, however, the old story was repeated: the emperors grew decadent; the traveling inspectors of the empire became careless; and corruption, inefficiency, and incompetence developed.

ALEXANDER AND THE GREEKS

Athens and Sparta, highly civilized states on the fringe of the ancient Middle East, resisted Persian attacks from Thrace and the sea, even though Greek mercenaries by the thousands fought in the Persian armies and participated in Persian civil wars. Although Greek contingents were usually lost in the heterogeneous mob that made up the army of the later years of the Persian Empire, the episode of Xenophon and the Ten Thousand is well known. Greek merchants penetrated most parts of the empire; and the Middle East, including Greece, enjoyed a period of prosperity which came from a century of relative peace and stability.

In the fourth century B.C. a new Indo-European people related to the Greeks began their ascent to power under Philip of Macedon. By the use of heavier armor and the integration of cavalry and the Macedonian phalanx, Greece was subjected to his rule. But Greece captured the mind and spirit of his son, Alexander, perhaps through his private tutor, the famed Aristotle. The campaigns and conquests of Alexander the Great and the creation of his vast Greek empire have been retold through the ages by countless poets, romantics, and historians of many lands and races.

After defeating the Persian army in 334 B.C. the young Alexander, only twenty-two years old, swept all before him. Asia Minor, Syria, Palestine, Egypt, Mesopotamia, Iran, and India to the Indus had been conquered and consolidated into an empire before his death in 323 B.C. Alexander had hoped to unify the entire Middle East into one lasting empire. He married an Asiatic princess and commanded his army officers to follow his example. But his untimely death left only his chief generals to battle for the empire, which they eventually divided: Ptolemy in Egypt, Antigonus in Asia Minor, Antipater and Cassander in Macedonia and Greece, Seleucus in Asia, and a number of lesser officers in scattered corners of the Middle East.

Following the break-up of Alexander's empire, the Middle East fell heir to a century of international political anarchy and intermittent wars; yet it enjoyed a period of vast trade and wealth as well as many decades of important intellectual and artistic activity. It was the apogee of the brilliant Hellenistic Age which persisted for two centuries more until the last vestige of Ptolemaic rule in Egypt had ended with Cleopatra's suicide and the Nile Valley became a Roman province.

THE ROMAN EMPIRE AND ITS SUCCESSORS

At the invitation of Egypt, Rhodes, and Pergamum, Rome became the arbiter of Middle Eastern affairs, and naval disarmament agreements turned the Mediterranean into a vast Roman lake. Except for the Tigris-Euphrates area the Middle East had virtually fallen into a state of vassalage to Rome. Transformed into Roman provinces, the Middle East was subjected to Roman rule until the emperor Constantine transferred his capital eastward to the shores of the Bosphorus. From the establishment of Constantinople in A.D. 330 to the defeat of Emperor Heraclius by the Arab armies in 638 the Roman provinces of the Middle East were important parts of the Byzantine Empire.

The eastern provinces—Mesopotamia and Iran—fell away from the Seleucids, and early in the second century B.C. the great Parthian Empire was established in Iran by Mithridates I. Seleucia-on-the-Tigris was taken; and before the century closed all territory east of the Euphrates had been seized by the Parthian King of Kings, who built his royal palace at Ctesiphon on the east bank of the Tigris opposite Seleucia. The Parthian power rested on its nomadic Scythian cavalry and on the reaction against Hellenism, even though the kings knew Greek and had Greek tragedies performed at their court. The Parthians defeated the Romans and Augustus recognized Parthian dominion over all of Mesopotamia. When Marcus Aurelius destroyed Seleucia, the center of Greek culture in Parthia, any further expansion of Greek influence upon the East was doomed.

Internal weakness, however, brought the downfall of the Parthian kings at the hands of a more national Iranian family, the Sasanids. The founder of the dynasty was a devotee of Zoroaster, and the fire cult was vigorously advanced, becoming the official religion of the empire. Wars with the Romans and Byzantines found the religious differences as important as the rivalries of empire.

From their main residence at Ctesiphon the Sasanids time and again harried the Byzantine provinces of Syria and Asia Minor. After the fifth century when Christianity was tolerated and the Nestorian Church had become widespread in the Sasanid Empire, particularly in Mesopotamia, the conflicts with Constantinople were more imperial in nature. Belisarius, Justinian's general, checked the Sasanids temporarily, but they sacked Aleppo and Antioch and forced upon the Byzantine emperor a peace treaty whereby no Christian proselytizing would be permitted in their empire. Peace, however, was not realized and exhausting campaigns were resumed under Justinian's successors.

A powerful Sasanid army erupted into Syria in 611, destroying the Church of the Holy Sepulcher in Jerusalem, pillaging Damascus, and plundering and massacring everywhere. An Iranian army conquered Egypt in 618, and another captured the cities of Chalcedon and Chrysopolis across from Constantinople. Evil days appeared for the Byzantines, but the tide turned. Between 622 and 628 Heraclius, the new Byzantine emperor, conducted three brilliant campaigns and even succeeded in driving the Sasanids from Egypt and Syria. But the wars and the ensuing destruction left both empires weakened. Syria, Egypt, and Mesopotamia were ripe for picking by the new vigorous Muslim Arabs in the next decade.

PRE-ISLAMIC CIVILIZATION IN THE MIDDLE EAST

For nearly a thousand years the Semitic and Persian Middle East had been subjected to the influence and the forced cultivation of Greek, Hellenistic, Roman, and Byzantine civilizations. Although it would be possible to point out distinguishing characteristics of each of these four civilizations and to show how each evolved from its predecessor, they form one continuous cultural experience and development in the history of the Middle East.

First and foremost among the changes was the adoption of Greek by the educated and by the leaders of society as the language of government, philosophy, literature, and sophisticated communication. Greek colonists—merchants, soldiers, and government officials—settled in most of the Middle Eastern cities and founded many new Greek cities like Antioch in Syria and Alexandria in Egypt. Intellectually and artistically the Middle East appeared as one world. Greek philosophies and Greek science became universal throughout the area, although many leaders were not of Greek stock and much of the philosophy and science was not Greek in origin or inspiration.

Roman rule ended the internecine warfare of the Alexandrian successor states and brought a more bountiful material life to the cities of the Middle East. The remains of the almost countless theatres, temples, baths, and public buildings that dot the Middle East today are silent witnesses of the populous, thriving, and wealthy cities of that age. However, in governing the Middle East the Romans were more crassly materialistic, more ruthlessly extortionate, and more heedlessly arrogant than previous foreign rulers.

Even Roman military might, the Roman genius for efficiency, and administrative skill could not control the Middle Eastern hate for the Romans. On one occasion the population rose in Asia Minor and slaughtered 100,000 Romans. In the states of the Middle East natives who adopted the ways of the Greek and Roman in speech, dress, food, religion, and manners were detested and shunned by the others. Some tried to be two-faced. But as the years passed the Hellenistic states became less and less Greek, conforming more faithfully to the age-old patterns of life in the Middle East. The Ptolemies appeared as pharaohs, and the Seleucids lived as Assyrian and Persian monarchs. Jesus of Nazareth spoke Aramaic, not Greek. St. Paul was a learned Jew with a Greek and Roman education, but his conversion to Christianity exemplified a rejection of foreign ideologies.

For all the show of Greek and Roman civilization in the cities of Syria and Egypt, Hellenism and Romanism rested very lightly on the common peoples of the Middle East. Under the rule of the Byzantine emperors the reassertion of Middle Eastern patterns was accelerated in Syria and Egypt. Asia Minor, with such ancient cities as Miletus, Sardis, Ephesus, and Pergamum, which had participated in Greek cultural development long before the age of Alexander, had not been a part of the empires of the Middle East except that of the Persians. Thus, the Roman province of Asia (western Asia Minor) exhibited a Hellenistic life more Greek and Roman and less Oriental than did Syria or Egypt.

CHRISTIANITY

The new contribution that came to the cultural stream of the Middle East with Byzantine dominion was Christianity, which received recognition as the official religion of the empire. In Hellenistic and Roman periods men were groping for a philosophy of life and a religion that would answer some of the problems of society and man in those rapidly changing and turbulent days. Faith in the power or protection of the Olympian gods had largely disappeared by the time of Alexander. The educated neglected the gods and pursued the philosophies fashioned by Plato and Aristotle. Other philosophic systems followed: Cynicism, Epicureanism, Skepticism, and Stoicism. Each of these had its advocates and its followers, but each was more negative than positive. They were intellectual shelters where sensitive and distressed souls might take refuge from a materialistic and heartless society.

To the masses these philosophies were meaningless. The formation of a world state took from a man his sense of identity with a city-state and its protecting god. As a helpless individual in a large empire he needed a savior. He, therefore, turned to the mystery cults of Asia, which spread widely and had a devoted and numerous following.

Magic and astrology had such a vogue that the latter quite destroyed astronomy for many centuries. By some secret formula a person might force the hand of a god to alter one's fate somehow or open up a short-cut to fortune. But the mystery cults were far more influential. Here the individual, by witnessing and participating in an esoteric ritual, was initiated into the mysteries of life and death, god and immortality. As the savior-god had lived and died and risen again, so the lonely and helpless individual, living in a tumultuous and materialistic world, might win eternal salvation by personal union with the god.

The most important of these religions of the Hellenistic world was that of the triplex of Sarapis-Osiris, Anubis-Horus, and Isis. Sarapis was a Greek Osiris, universal ruler of all mankind, and his son Anubis led the souls of men to immortal life. Isis, however, was above Fate and she freed her adherents from the dominion of Fate and of death. Moreover, being a woman—one who was a wife and a mother and one who had suffered—she appealed to the female half of the population. The ritual of initiation comprised a purification by water, a journey through dark places of the underworld comparable to that of Osiris between the time of his death and resurrection, and a final appearance in holy robes and in a full panoply of light before the whole congregation. From that moment onward the member's soul was godlike and secure from earthly forces.

In the second century A.D. the greatest change in the Middle East came with the rise and spread of Christianity. Taking many of the positive and uplifting tenets of Judaism, of the Greek philosophies, and of the Oriental cults, Christianity added two vital factors which were largely absent in Hellenism and Romanism: Christ offered immortality to all men; and His creed was based on love of humanity.

Early Christianity appealed almost solely to urban Hellenistic society, the language of the church being Greek exclusively. After Christianity obtained official favor and adoption, the Byzantine state rapidly developed into a synthesis of Hellenism, Orientalism, and Christianity and a syncretism of the political power of the state and the religious authority of the church.

The union of autocracy and theocracy in the Byzantine state—the so-called Caesaro-papism of Constantinople—ensured the permanent alienation of the masses in the Middle Eastern provinces. As new doctrines from the Middle East were branded heresies by the state-dominated church councils—Nicaea (325), Ephesus (431), and Chalcedon (451)—separate native Christian churches evolved. Aramaic, its Syriac dialect, and Ethiopic became liturgic languages. Byzantine Constantinople could not force her type of Christianity upon the Middle Eastern peoples.

The Nestorian Church presented a dualism of good and evil not far distant from Zoroastrian doctrines, a fact which may explain its acceptance in Mesopotamia and Iran. Monophysite Christianity certainly embodied some of the Egyptian ideas of the deification of man. Heresies flourished in non-Greek areas of the Byzantine Empire and served as basic factors in the almost complete lack of resistance and even passive co-operation of the Middle Eastern provinces at the time of the conquests by the Muslim Arabs. Links with the Semites from the desert proved stronger than those with Christian Constantinople.

THE ARABS

In the first half of the seventh century the Arabs, another Semitic nation, under the banners of a new religion descended upon Syria, Egypt, Mesopotamia, and Iran—the chief regions of the civilized Middle East. Coming from an area little touched by the main streams of Middle Eastern life, the Arabs seemed to be a new and different force to the peoples of that age.

The Arabs were the last group of Semites to leave the shores and deserts of Arabia. Their chief difference lay in the fact that they did not sever their connections with their past abode as other Semites had done. The Arabs lived along the shores of Arabia, in the southern highlands of Arabia where some rain occurred, and in the scattered oases and around the meager water-holes that remained in Arabia as the Fourth Glacier receded. These desert inhabitants—farmers and shepherds—were numerically small and insignificant until the advent of the camel about 1200 B.C. The peculiar characteristics of this beast made nomadic life in the desert possible and profitable. The camel was as revolutionary to life in Arabia at that time as oil and the motor vehicle have been in the twentieth century. The camel people became lords of the desert. Above all, the camel welded city and desert life in Arabia into one integrated society, each dependent upon the other.

The use of the camel, moreover, eased many difficulties of the transit trade between India and the Mediterranean. Camel caravans began to carry spices and incense along the Hadhramaut to Yemen and thence to Mecca, the Hijaz, Damascus, and the Mediterranean. Cities prospered, small kingdoms were established, and civilization advanced, as demands of the Hellenistic and Roman world expanded.

THE MIDDLE EAST

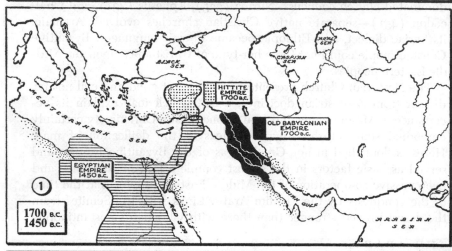

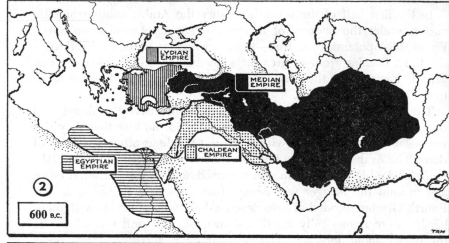

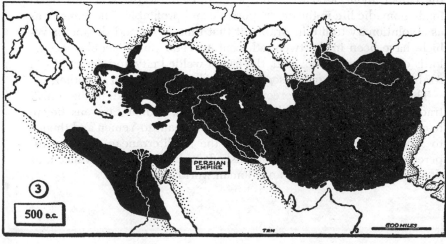

THE MIDDLE EAST

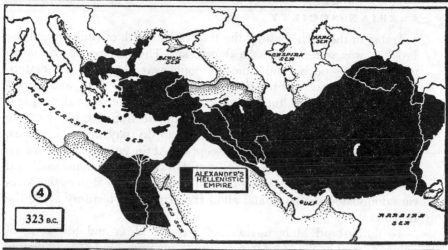

ALEXANDER'S HELLENISTIC EMPIRE

④ 323 B.C.

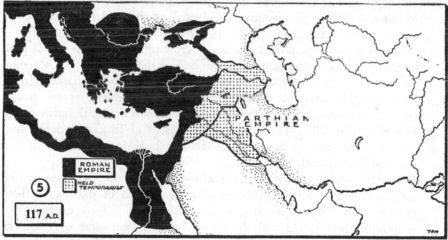

PARTHIAN EMPIRE

ROMAN EMPIRE

HELD TEMPORARILY

⑤ 117 A.D.

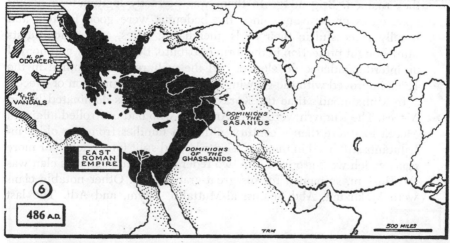

K. OF ODOACER

K. OF THE VANDALS

DOMINIONS OF THE SASANIDS

EAST ROMAN EMPIRE

DOMINIONS OF THE GHASSANIDS

⑥ 486 A.D.

500 MILES

ARABIAN SOCIETY

Arabia in the sixth century, the time of the birth of Muhammad the Prophet, was suffering from a depression. The empires to the north were enjoying peace, and Constantinople was obtaining her eastern luxury goods by way of the Black Sea, the Caucasus, Iran, and Turkestan. Cities and agricultural oases in Arabia became so weakened and disorganized by the loss of revenue from the transit trade that the desert nomads were able to force them to pay tribute. Mecca, Muhammad's native city, was an exception. At the crossroads of caravan routes from Yemen to Syria and from Abyssinia to Mesopotamia and possessing a permanent spring and an ancient sacred shrine, the Meccans dominated the Hijaz and all of the expanse of territory along the Red Sea.

To understand Muhammad's actions and ideas and his sense of values as well as the Meccan response to his preaching, it is profitable to examine briefly the economic, political, social, and religious forces current in his day in the Hijaz and in Mecca.

Mecca was a commercial city and a growing financial center. It had originated as an entrepôt, but by the end of the sixth century Meccan merchants were buying and selling wares in all of the markets from Yemen to Damascus. Mercantile wealth was turning to financial speculation and investment. There is little evidence of local industry in Mecca or the Hijaz. There were orchards at al-Taif, and dates and some cereals grew at the oasis of Medina; but Mecca was set in the midst of barren land.

Nomads—bedouins or desert Arabs—with their herds dwelt in the neighborhood of Mecca. Moving about in search of pasturage, they enjoyed a free, open, precarious existence; yet they were exceedingly jealous of their rights and the ownership of the desert over which they roamed. Brigandage to them was perfectly legitimate, whether upon oases or caravans. Since the bedouins were good fighters and usually successful in their raids, merchants, cities, and agriculturists often bought protection in the form of tribute. Between city and nomad an interdependence developed, and the welfare of the nomad in the Hijaz improved with the growing prosperity and population of Mecca.

In Muhammad's time the Kuraysh tribe of Arabs dominated life in Mecca. The Kuraysh were north Arabians who had controlled affairs in Mecca for more than a century, although families from the older inhabitants still lived in the city. The tribe had split into a dozen or more clans which were grouped into two federations. Muhammad's clan was the Hashim, so named for his great-grandfather. Other notable clans were Makhzum, Abd Shams, al-Muttalib, Taym, and Adi. The last three belonged to the same federation as did the Hashim, while the other two were the most powerful clans of Mecca in Muhammad's day.

Government in Mecca was simple, direct, unorganized, and exceedingly democratic. An assembly of the chiefs and leading men of the clans met as a council, but each clan was independent and could go its own way. Each clan protected and looked out for its own members and any faltering impinged immediately upon the honor of the clan. Unanimity of action had to be achieved by personal negotiation among the leaders who commanded respect because of wealth, wisdom, and strength of character. A few offices possessed privileges, sometimes with profit possibilities, such as control over the water of the sacred well or supplying sustenance to pilgrims.

Political affairs in the foreign field taxed the skill and ingenuity of the Meccan leaders, for the Arabs were buffeted by the contest between the Byzantine and Sasanid empires. Eastern Arabs were satellites of Iran, and such Arabs as the Ghassanids east of the Jordan were on the Byzantine side. Upon the development of a Iranian-sponsored rule in Yemen, Meccan commerce from South Arabia northward to Byzantine Syria became a touchy enterprise. But Meccan neutrality and diplomatic and economic shrewdness consolidated the caravan trade from the south into the hands of the Makhzum and Abd Shams clans. Previously the Hashim clan had operated the caravans north to Syria; the al-Muttalib clan, those from Yemen. Thus, in Muhammad's early life, intense rivalry developed among the clans in Mecca. His own clan was experiencing economic distress in the midst of a situation where international politics, high finance, and foreign trade were creating many uncertain local tensions of a high order.

Society in Mecca was sick. No longer was the Kuraysh tribe a unit; clans had become the units. Membership in a clan was based on kinship through the male line. Security of person and property was a clan responsibility, and to touch either without consent was a cause for reprisal by the clan. An irresponsible member was usually disowned by the clan and consequently became a kind of social, political, and economic outcast.

Manly virtues were still largely those related to desert nomadism—"bravery in battle, patience in misfortune, persistence in revenge, protection of the weak, defiance of the strong." Other admirable qualities were generosity, hospitality, loyalty, and fidelity. The man with honor and moral excellence was the man who exhibited the possession of these characteristics and who with judgment demonstrated his capacity to govern his life by them.

Mecca of that day, however, was moving rapidly from a local nomadic economy to an international commercial and capitalistic economy. The absence of tribal unity was readily accepted, and even individualism within a clan was appearing. Business partnerships were being formed across clan lines. And the leaders and powerful men of Mecca were successful businessmen and capitalists, who did not always live by the long accepted Arab standards of manliness and honor. Common material interests seemed to be replacing common blood in the determination of kinship in the new Mecca. Social maladjustment resulted from the failure of the new economic life to accommodate itself to the old moral values of Arab life.

Pagan Mecca had numerous gods and goddesses, most of whom possessed abstract characteristics. Stones, trees, and other objects were venerated in connection with the worship of these deities, although they were thought only to reside in these objects. The practice of magic and superstition were inextricably interwoven in this paganism, but belief in the gods had begun to fade in Muhammad's time.

A more forceful religion was that which was bound up with the belief in the immortality of the tribe and clan. Honor, bravery, generosity, and the other manly virtues were possessions which ensured the survival of the tribe. Fate was accepted as a fact, but it was believed to govern life in only a few ways, determining, for instance, a man's provisions, the length of his life, his sex, and his happiness. Otherwise man controlled his own destiny. Except for the regulation of sex, life was especially precarious in the desert and therefore seemed to be governed by some unfathomable law or whim of a force beyond man's control or responsibility. There was nothing enduring with the individual, and thus the fate of the individual was unimportant. There was no belief in personal immortality; immortality rested with the tribe.

Finally, in Mecca a conception of monotheism was evolving. The Arab word Allah was derived from the words "al-ilah," meaning "the god." Allah, then, was The God, The Supreme God; and Muhammad in using this word did not have to give his audiences any explanation. The idea, evidently, was in the air at Mecca, though undoubtedly the understanding of monotheism was vague and ill-defined in Meccan minds. The source of monotheism in Mecca and surrounding Arabia is an interesting question for speculation and has been debated by scholars at great length. Judaism and Christianity have had their champions, and certainly the Meccans had had ample opportunities to become acquainted with each of these religions. Evidence from the words of Muhammad would indicate, however, that the sources were laymen rather than learned religious men.

The important point is that Muhammad and Meccan society were not entirely unfamiliar with monotheistic thoughts. Obviously from the course of events which followed they were ready for these thoughts to be organized and marshalled into a systematic religion for them—a religion that was distinctly Arab in its character. That was the great work and accomplishment of Muhammad.

REFERENCES: *Chapter 2*

James H. Breasted, *A History of Egypt from the Earliest Times to the Persian Conquest,* 2nd ed.: Charles Scribner's Sons, New York, 1912. Still the best comprehensive account of ancient Egypt.

Vere Gordon Childe, *New Light on the Most Ancient Near East,* 4th ed.: Routledge & Kegan Paul, London, 1952. A fundamental synthesis of the culture of Mesopotamia and Egypt.

Glanville Downey, *A History of Antioch in Syria, From Selecus to the Arab Conquest:* Princeton University Press, Princeton, 1961.

Nelson Glueck, *Rivers in the Desert: A History of the Negev:* Farrar, Strauss and Cudahy, New York, 1959. A valuable contribution by a leading scholar.

Philip K. Hitti, *History of Syria Including Lebanon and Palestine:* Macmillan, New York, 1951. An excellent portrayal of the development of Syria, particularly of the period preceding the coming of the Arabs.

Ernest Jackh, ed., *Background of the Middle East:* Cornell University Press, Ithaca, 1952. Chapters 7, 8, and 9 by Edgar Alexander are valuable in explaining the development of Christianity into Western, Eastern, and Oriental branches.

Allan C. Johnson, *Egypt and the Roman Empire:* University of Michigan Press, Ann Arbor, 1951. The role of Egypt under the Roman emperors.

Allan C. Johnson and Louis C. West, *Byzantine Egypt: Economic Studies:* Princeton University Press, Princeton, 1949. This volume sheds light on the economic importance of Egypt to the Byzantine Empire and to the entire Middle East in the two or three centuries before the Arab conquest.

James Mellaart, *Earliest Civilizations of the Near East:* Thames and Hudson, London, 1965.

DeLacy O'Leary, *Arabia Before Muhammad:* Kegan Paul, London, 1927. The standard work on the Arabs and Arabia before the birth of Islam.

Albert T. E. Olmstead, *The History of the Persian Empire, Achaemenid Period:* University of Chicago Press, Chicago, 1948. The standard cultural, political, and religious history.

Harry M. Orlinsky, *Ancient Israel:* Cornell University Press, Ithaca, 1954.

E. A. Speiser, *Mesopotamian Origins:* University of Pennsylvania Press, Philadelphia, 1930. A scholarly work.

W. W. Tarn and G. T. Griffith, *Hellenistic Civilisation,* 3rd ed.: Edward Arnold, London, 1952. A profound summary and synthesis of Middle Eastern culture and life in the centuries following the death of Alexander the Great.

A. A. Vasiliev, *History of the Byzantine Empire 324–1453:* University of Wisconsin Press, Madison, 1952. The standard history of the Byzantine Empire.

John A. Wilson, *The Burden of Egypt:* University of Chicago Press, Chicago, 1951. A fine interpretation of Egyptian culture.

PART I

The Rise
and Spread of
Islam

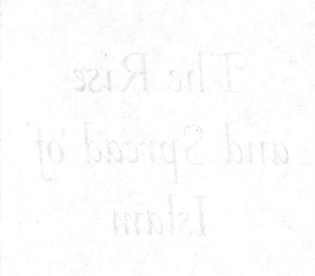

CHAPTER 3

Muhammad:
His Life and Leadership

There is no God but Allah, and Muhammad is His Prophet." The acceptance of this statement as the fundamental truth of life identifies all who follow the teachings of Muhammad. Allah is the God worshipped by Jews and Christians. But who was this man Muhammed? It has been said that Muhammad was the only great Prophet born in the full light of history. Recent investigations, however, have shown that much of his life as traditionally presented is based on numerous biographies that were largely fictionalized.

No biography of Muhammad was written until he had been dead for one hundred years; at least four were compiled during the second century after his passing. From these have come the traditional accounts of Muhammad's life; and although they are not entirely false, fiction and fact are hopelessly, if artfully, intertwined. Thus, Muhammad never emerges completely from the shadows of historical silence. Modern students have, however, been able to sift out some of the stories and have fairly well established many points.

Muhammad was a man; he never professed otherwise and always emphasized this point to his followers, indicating that he would die as any other man. Nevertheless, as the founder of a great religion, he was revered as a most holy man even within his own lifetime. It is not strange, then, to find his biographies, written five or six generations later, full of fabricated and supernatural incidents to show his spirituality and his virtues. Perhaps this traditional figure has been more important than the real in fashioning the culture and civilization of the Middle East from his day to our own.

MUHAMMAD'S EARLY LIFE

In the year A.D. 570 or 571, or perhaps as late as 580, there was born in Mecca to the Hashim family of the Kuraysh tribe a male child who was given the name of Muhammad, meaning highly praised. His family was not one of the wealthier or more powerful of the city; neither was it of the poorest or lowliest class. His father, Abdallah, died before he was born; and his mother died when Muhammad was about six years old. First, as a fatherless boy, and then as an orphan, his lot was not easy. His paternal grandfather, Abd al-Muttalib, cared for and protected him. Upon his grandfather's death Muhammad became the ward of his uncle Abu Talib.

From many of Muhammad's statements it is apparent that his uncle was not a prosperous man and that they lived in very modest circumstances. Evidently there was no opportunity for Muhammad in any of the businesses of his uncles; and without any capital from his father, a job had to be found for him outside the family circle. Such a post was located with the rich widow, Khadijah, of a distantly related family. She had been married twice—once to a Makhzumi—and had children from each marriage.

Khadijah was older than Muhammad, some say as much as fifteen years; and certainly her social position in Mecca was far superior to his. She was an astute businesswoman and continued her husbands' commercial activities. At what age Muhammad began working for her, exactly what he did, and how old he was when she asked him to marry her are uncertainties. The story of her proposal is probably factual. It was not the usual custom for the woman to propose; but in this instance, on account of her wealth, her better social class, and her position as employer, it would not have been unlikely.

This step altered Muhammad's life very greatly, and at this point he becomes a clearer historical personage. They had four daughters who grew to maturity and several sons, all of whom died in infancy or childhood. Khadijah died about A.D. 619, but as long as she lived Muhammad had no other wife, a situation which may have resulted from the differences in their social and economic positions. Although he continued to act as Khadijah's commercial agent, his marriage gave him a security which had been lacking heretofore. Muhammad now had means and a definite position in the society of Mecca.

HIS CALL

In the Middle East from time immemorial it has been the custom for men who have some means and who are troubled intellectually and emotionally by the cares and ills of society to retreat to some lonely

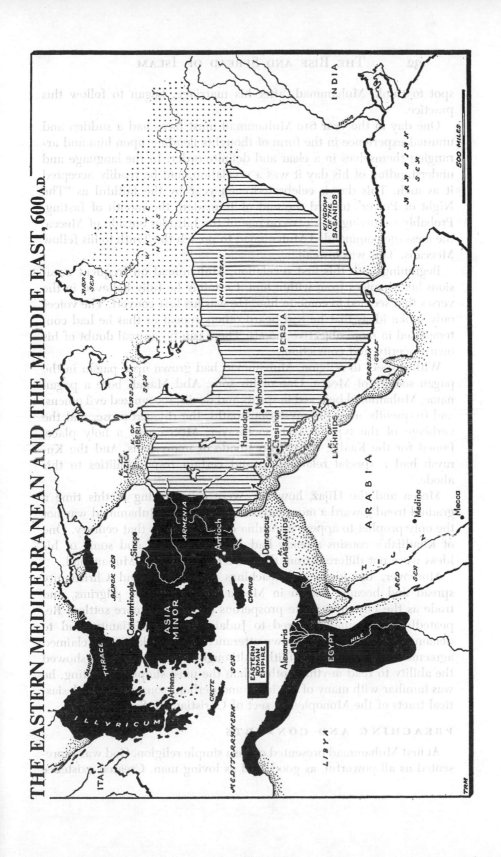

THE EASTERN MEDITERRANEAN AND THE MIDDLE EAST, 600 A.D.

spot to think. Muhammad, after his marriage, began to follow this practice.

One day in the year 610 Muhammad must have had a sudden and unusual experience in the form of thoughts flooding upon him and arranging themselves in a clear and definite order. In the language and understanding of his day it was a revelation, and he readily accepted it as such. This day is celebrated each year by the faithful as "The Night of Power" toward the end of Ramadan, the month of fasting. Probably occurring in a cave on one of the hillsides outside of Mecca, the message commanded Muhammad to preach the Truth to his fellow Meccans. This was his call.

Beginning with this first revelation, Muhammad on frequent occasions heard voices from within him. Certainly he fully believed in the verses that seemed to come to him. He was his first convert. The voices only spoke ideas that he had heard others repeat or that he had contemplated in more objective moods. There can be no real doubt of his own sincerity and conviction.

With respect to religion, Muhammad had grown up a pagan in the pagan society of Mecca. One of his sons, Abd Manaf, bore a pagan name. Muhammad believed in spirits and devils, recognized evil omens, and frequently used the mysterious oaths, the rhymed prose, and the verbiage of the typical Arab soothsayer. Mecca was a holy place, famed for the Kaaba, the earthly abode of many gods. And the Kuraysh had a special relationship and certain responsibilities to this abode.

Mecca and the Hijaz, however, were experiencing at this time a gradual trend toward a more intellectual religion. Muhammad was not the only prophet to appear in Arabia or the Hijaz in that century. One of Khadijah's cousins already had been preaching, and some of his ideas were not different from those later espoused by Muhammad.

Moreover, the ideas and teachings of Judaism and Christianity spread and became known in Mecca through slaves, pilgrims, and trade as the city grew more prosperous and its life more settled. Repeatedly Muhammad referred to Judaism and Christianity, and to demonstrate the truth of his own utterances and revelations he claimed agreement with those older faiths. Although Muhammad never showed the ability to read anything other than the most simple of writing, he was familiar with many of the ideas and perhaps some of the ecclesiastical tracts of the Monophysite sect of Christians in Syria.

PREACHING AND CONVERTS

At first Muhammad presented quite a simple religion. God was represented as all-powerful, as good, and as loving man. Created existence was most transitory; the Creator was permanent. But God in creating man implanted in man a moral responsibility for himself and his fellow men. There would be a final judgment on the day of resurrection. Muhammad really had no idea at that time of founding a new religion. The heavenly truths had been revealed to him and duty compelled him to remind the Arabs of Mecca of these truths in order to save them from divine wrath on the approaching Day of Judgment. The pure man was one who was grateful to God, worshipped Him, appealed to God for the forgiveness of sin, offered prayers frequently, helped his fellow men, avoided all forms of cheating, led a chaste life, and had cleansed himself from love of wealth. Such a man, then, would recognize the goodness and power of God and man's dependence upon God. This was Islam—the surrender to God—and the pious man who thus purified himself became a Muslim.

In the beginning Muhammad's preaching brought no firm opposition and fell on fertile soil. His first converts were in his own household: his wife Khadijah, his cousin Ali, and Sayd, a former slave. The most important of the others were Abu Bakr, Umar, al-Zubayr, Abd al-Rahman, Saad, Talhah, and Uthman. Some of the early converts were younger sons of influential men of the leading families and clans of Mecca. The father of one was the most prominent financier in Mecca; another's father had been a religious leader prior to Muhammad's time; and two were nephews of the head of the Makhzum clan, the wealthiest and dominant family among the Kuraysh. The majority, however, were young men of no great social standing. Some had neither family nor clan ties, and the families of others had ceased for one reason or another to afford them protection.

To characterize this group the terms "young men" and "weak people" are the most appropriate. Early Islam was a movement of young people, mostly well under forty years old and from the middle class of Mecca. They were individuals who felt their inferior positions when they compared their wealth and influence with the fortunes and power of those at the top.

Such a generalization certainly implies that economic, social, and political conditions in Mecca had a hand in fostering the development and growth of Islam. At least for several decades before Muhammad's call life in Mecca had been changing. The rapid growth of commerce and a money economy had widened the gap between rich and poor and between the influential and their dependents. Wealth and the life of a merchant promoted individualism as contrasted to family and clan solidarity. Kinship of money was supplanting that of blood, a substitution which did not satisfy the less "successful." Nomadic manly virtues were hardly those to be esteemed in a mercantile society. The old ideals of generosity and honor were fast dying in the evolving individualistic society. Seemingly, anything could be obtained through money and power.

Muhammad and his early converts, however, were not consciously frustrated men seeking solace in religion. In these first days they were conservatives preaching against the abandonment of the old virtues. Nevertheless, Muhammad did recognize individualism as a permanent aspect of society. The Last Judgment concerned individuals; for it was said that on the Day of the Last Judgment "one shall have no influence on behalf of another."

Muhammad began his public preaching about the year A.D. 613. While his ideas concerning monotheism were still ill-defined, he made a public pronouncement that al-Lat, al-Uzza, and Manat, three goddesses from the old Arab Pantheon, were lesser celestial beings who could intercede for one with God. Traditionally this admission has been called "the satanic verses," for after reflection Muhammad renounced the utterance as the work of the devil. There has been much speculation and contention over this incident. Most likely, Muhammad was attempting to gain a wider following from the more influential Meccans.

PERSECUTION

Upon the denial in 615 of any special powers for these pagan goddesses Muhammad and Islam entered a new period of development. Monotheism evolved and was plainly recognized. Opposition and persecution began. Muslims were subjected to tongue lashing and all manner of verbal insults. Garbage was dumped at their doors. Unprotected individuals were beaten, as were Kuraysh Muslims by their fellow clansmen. Economic pressure was exerted by refusal to pay debts and by a severe boycott that greatly reduced the fortunes of many, including Muhammad's closest friend, Abu Bakr.

Abu Jahl, the head of the Makhzum clan, declared economic war upon the Muslims and asserted that every one of them would be ruined financially. He coaxed and threatened Abu Talib, Muhammad's uncle and the leader of the Hashim clan, to abandon Muhammad. Failure in this approach led to the formation of an alliance of all the Kuraysh clans to pursue an economic boycott of the Hashim clan and its closest ally, the al-Muttalib clan. There were to be no business dealings and no intermarriage with any member of either clan.

This open economic break had long been brewing, and the controversy over Muhammad offered the excuse. Apparently during this break the Hashim maintained their own caravans to Syria and withstood the pressure. After two years the grand alliance was dissolved and the economic sanctions lapsed since they had proved unsuccessful in destroying Muhammad. In fact they had tended to increase the financial and economic hegemony of the Makhzum clan.

More significant was the verbal assault, which indicated the opinions held by those in opposition. They scoffed at the idea of the Day of Last Judgment and ridiculed Muhammad's preaching of the resurrection of the body after it had mouldered in the grave. They kept asking scornfully: "When is the Hour?" Muhammad's conviction that God was One and only One and that all idolatry was evil disturbed Meccan society because to a considerable degree this meant forsaking the religion of their forefathers. Muhammad tried to counter this with the contention that he was following in the footsteps of the religion of Abraham and the prophets of old and thus that Muslims were only regaining the old Arab religion.

The opposition jeered at Muhammad's claim to prophethood, calling him a magician, a soothsayer, a poet possessed by spirits, or, better yet, mad. If God had desired to reveal the Truth, they asserted sarcastically, He would have selected someone more important than Muhammad for this role. And why was not the full revelation made all at one time? How else could Muhammad explain the driblets of revelation except that he and some assistants were busy making up the verses!

Traditionally, the opposition to Muhammad by the leaders of Mecca centered around his preaching of the unity of God and his rejection of the use of all idols. They feared that the adoption and practice of these beliefs would, through the decline of the pilgrimages, ruin Mecca as a flourishing commercial center. To some extent this may have been true, though Mecca at that late date was not very dependent upon the pilgrimage trade. Abu Jahl, the most ambitious financier of Mecca, recognized the threat of Islam and its philosophy to his way of life and realized that widespread acceptance would give the leadership of the city to Muhammad. Other leaders, whose positions seemed beyond jeopardy, regarded Muhammad as an innovator who was disrupting the political and social development of Mecca. Because of the rapid social evolution of Mecca many were cognizant of the disintegration of the old political, social, economic, and intellectual values. Muhammad sought to preserve and adjust these values through religion. Step by step, however, he was led by the opposition to establish a new religion.

The ending of the economic boycott in 619 possibly was interpreted as the harbinger of acceptance and success. One incident after another in quick succession dashed such optimism to the ground and brought Muhammad close to the breaking point. Khadijah died, and then his uncle and protector, Abu Talib, followed her. Abu Lahab, another uncle, who now became the leader of the Hashim, refused to continue the protection. Several years had elapsed since any important person had accepted Islam. Signs indicate that Muhammad began to suffer from a kind of mental depression and fatigue. There was no Muslim in Mecca with sufficient stature to offer him protection. How easily Islam could have perished! The only alternative was to leave the city.

FLIGHT TO MEDINA

Muhammad first visited the neighboring town of al-Taif to explore the possibilities of establishing residence and the headquarters of Islam there. He was met with a quick rebuff and upon leaving was stoned. Several of the nomadic tribes around Mecca were approached but without success.

Some 200 miles to the north and east lay the town of Yathrib—later called Medina by the Muslims. Yathrib comprised an area of twenty square miles of date oases, fertile lands, and scattered settlements. Numerous tribes occupied quarters of the town and had been engaged in bloody and exhausting civil war, undoubtedly over the limited lands of Yathrib. The most important clans were: Aws, Khazraj, Nadir, Kurayzah, and Kaynuka, of which the last three adhered to the Jewish faith.

During the pilgrimage of 620 and following the rebuff at al-Taif, Muhammad discussed Islam with several pilgrims of the Khazraj tribe of Yathrib and raised the question of asylum. Next year additional people from Yathrib participated in the pilgrimage and more discussions occurred. One of Muhammad's trusted supporters returned with them, and converts were obtained from every important family except one. In the pilgrimage of 622 seventy-five Muslims from Yathrib came to Mecca and there made the famous Pledge of al-Akabah to obey and protect Muhammad. Furthermore, there was some understanding relative to the migration of the Muslims, including Muhammad, from Mecca to Yathrib.

Why these pagan Arabs from Yathrib so readily accepted Muhammad and Islam has aroused much speculation, but clearly they took to Islam and welcomed the Muslims and Muhammad on religious grounds. Yathrib was painfully experiencing the evolution of the mores of a nomadic society to those of a settled life. Islam brought a message of one community of people to Yathrib to end the political rivalry and the continual feuding of the many clans.

As soon as agreement had been reached, Muhammad urged all Muslims to go to Yathrib. Over a period of weeks they left in groups until only Muhammad, Abu Bakr, Ali, and a handful remained in Mecca. After all who planned to migrate had gone, Muhammad and

Abu Bakr slipped away at night, hid in a near-by cave for a couple of days until the search for them had been relaxed, and then proceeded to Yathrib. On September 24, 622 they were joyously greeted at the outskirts of the city which has ever since been called Medina—The City.

This migration—Hijrah—was a dangerous move on the part of the Muslims; for they were abandoning the protection of their families and their city for the untested protection of strangers. Almost overnight their position was so changed that the Hijrah came to mark the new era. The Muslim calendar begins with the first of the year—July 16, 622— in which the Hijrah occurred. In Mecca Muhammad and the preaching of Islam had failed to alter society or to break down either the growing individualism or the family ties. In Medina Muhammad immediately became the acknowledged political and social leader as well as the religious head of a compact community.

Residence in Medina placed new demands upon Muhammad's diplomatic and executive talents. He could count definitely on the full support of the emigrants from Mecca—Muhajirun—and the converts of Medina—called Ansar or helpers. Old feuds, however, could be rekindled quickly. The Jews soon began to quiz and mock him because their knowledge of the Old Testament was far superior. Muhammad had expected that they would testify to the validity of his message, but they could not accept an Arab as the Messiah. Upon their rejection Muhammad forsook the older established religions of the Middle East and began to identify Islam as a new faith. By taking over Abraham and the God of the Meccan shrine and by adopting many of the ceremonies with respect to the sanctuary in Mecca, Muhammad moulded his new religious concepts with the old and gave Islam a distinct Arab cultural flavor. This aspect came to be emphasized with the beginning of his Medinese residence.

For protection and sustenance Muhammad created a new kind of brotherhood between every two emigrants. Also, every emigrant was assigned one Medinese as a special brother and protector. The problems and the affairs of the Muslim community were to be brought before God and Muhammad. Their judgments must be obeyed. Herein lay the basis for the establishment of Muslim theocracy. God was Muhammad's Guide and Protector and the disobedient would suffer the agonies of Hell.

In the first days following the Hijrah the Muslims had adopted several of the Jewish rites. One prayed facing Jerusalem; midday prayers and Jewish fast days were observed; and Friday, the Jewish day of preparation, became the Muslim day of public prayer. Later, when relations with the Medinese Jews became tense, Muhammad turned away from some of the Jewish forms. In worship the faithful faced the sanctuary in Mecca; the annual pilgrimage to Mecca was prescribed for Muslims; and a period of fasting—the month of Ramadan—was ordered.

CONFLICT WITH MECCA

During the winter of the first year in Medina Muhammad and his followers were busy establishing their new homes. When spring and summer came and the rich caravans began to pass northward toward Syria, Muslim armed bodies from Medina menaced the Meccan merchants. No booty was taken, and the caravans were so well protected that these incidents served only as reconnaissance missions. However, a livelihood for the ex-patriots of Mecca forced Muhammad to direct attacks upon the passing caravans. It was a normal expediency in Arabia.

Late in 623 a handful of Muslims under orders from Muhammad surprised a small Meccan caravan on the road between Mecca and al-Taif. One Meccan was killed, two were held for ransom, and much booty was captured. Nevertheless, upon their return to Medina sentiment was divided. The emigrants from Mecca had been promised protection from attack, but the Medinese had not agreed to let their city serve as a base of operations against Mecca. The success of the venture, however, invited other and larger expeditions.

Muhammad decided to ambush the main caravan of the Kuraysh upon its return from Syria. Muhammad himself led the band of 305 with over seventy camels and two horses to waylay the caravan under Abu Sufyan, the head of the powerful Umayyad family. At Badr, twenty miles southwest of Medina, Muhammad was challenged by a force of some eight or nine hundred armed Meccans. The fighting was fierce and bloody, but the smaller force of Muslims was victorious. As a battle it was hardly more than a minor fracas. Muhammad lost fourteen men; of the Meccans fifty were killed and fifty captured. The Muslim booty consisted of fourteen horses, one hundred and fifteen camels, coats-of-mail, and other pieces of military equipment. But the significance of the Battle of Badr was such that some have called it one of the decisive battles of history. To the Muslims it was a miracle, positive proof that God was supreme. The armed stores and animals were important in future engagements.

Henceforth Muhammad was a marked man; for the news of this victory traveled quickly over the routes and trails to every tribe and tent of Arabia. Moreover, it set the stage and the pattern of the future. A fifth of all booty was assigned to Muhammad to be allotted to the needy or used by the state. From that moment on there could be no peace until the supremacy between pagan and Muslim Meccans was decided. Within two decades Muslims came to appreciate the momentousness of this battle; those who had participated in it were the "nobility of Islam"; and a cloak which had been worn at the Battle of Badr was a most distinguished robe of honor.

This victory by no means guaranteed to Muhammad a straight and easy path to his now clearly recognizable goal of control over Mecca and the incorporation of all its inhabitants into his Muslim community. The battle showed the Muslims that such a goal was attainable; however, it revealed to the leaders of Mecca the ambition of Muhammad and goaded them into a real effort to annihilate the Muslim community.

Muhammad, taking advantage of his success, moved to consolidate his position. Alliances were made with a number of neighboring bedouin tribes. The Kaynuka tribe, the weakest of those adhering to the Jewish faith, was driven from Medina. In 625, however, Abu Sufyan, the new leader of Mecca since the death of Abu Jahl on the battlefield of Badr, set forth with an army of 3,000 for revenge. Electing to meet the enemy outside the city at the foot of the hill of Uhud, the Muslims were soundly beaten; Muhammad himself was wounded and fled from the field. Torn with dissension as usual, the Meccan army neither pursued the Muslims in rout nor pressed on to Medina. Two years later, Abu Sufyan returned again with an even larger army. Forewarned, Muhammad ordered a wide ditch dug before the less protected sides of Medina. After a fortnight's siege, bad weather, persistent quarrels, and the disaffection of some of the nomad allies led to the withdrawal of the Meccans, who claimed that this trench was a dishonorable artifice to which no Arab would resort. The Battle of the Ditch joined with Badr and Uhud to make the three battles where lines were drawn between the pagan and Muslim Kuraysh. The battles were in some measure part of a civil war. Participants on each side were well known to the other. Old slights and grudges were remembered, and emotions and the spirit of vengeance ran high.

Following each of these failures by pagan Mecca, Muhammad moved quickly to solidify the Medina community. When the Medinese Jews failed to hide their delight over the Uhud misadventure, the Muslims attacked the Jewish Nadir clan and drove them from Medina to Khaybar. After the Ditch affair, the last Jewish tribe of Medina, the Kurayzah, was expelled, and its lands and possessions were seized. Citizens of Medina who, until now, had neither accepted Islam nor recognized Muhammad as their leader joined the Muslim band. This meant that by the end of 627 Muhammad had established Medina as a united community with one religion as its cohesive force.

The next spring Muhammad was advised that some of the men of
Mecca wished to arrange peace with the Muslims. With this information Muhammad called for an advance upon Mecca during the month
of a minor pilgrimage. His bedouin allies would not join him, and
Mecca sent forth an armed force to contest his entry. The compromise,
which stipulated that the Muslims might participate freely in the lesser
pilgrimage the following year, was Muhammad's first success in his
peaceful conquest of Mecca. Later that year the Muslims captured
the fertile oasis of Khaybar, largely inhabited by Jews. This acquisition
made the Muslims wealthy since the lands were most productive. The
inhabitants were not exiled but remained on their lands, paying yearly
taxes to the conquerors and establishing a precedent for the years and
centuries to come.

VICTORY

In March, 629 Muhammad led more than a thousand of his men
into Mecca to perform the rites of the lesser pilgrimage as agreed upon
the previous year. A number of Meccans joined him, recognizing in
Muhammad the coming leader. Two of the most redoubtable military
figures of Islam were among those who joined: Amr ibn al-As and
Khalid ibn al-Walid. Even Abu Sufyan in secret negotiations tried to
adjust to the inevitable.

As more bedouin tribes joined the Muslims, Muhammad began to insist that they accept Islam and become an integral part of the community rather than serve merely as political allies. However, the sense
of completeness and fulfillment of the Muslim community was lacking
so long as Mecca did not recognize Muhammad as the leader and refused to accept Islam. Mecca was the site of the Kaaba, the religious
sanctuary and holy shrine designated by Muhammad. It had also
been the home of the leaders of the Muslim community.

An insignificant incident brought Muhammad and the Muslims with
arms to Mecca in 630. Hardly anyone in Mecca was disposed to fight.
Abu Sufyan came out from the city to pay homage to Muhammad and
received amnesty for all who would submit. Upon entering the city Muhammad gave gifts to all and only demanded the destruction of all idols
in Mecca. He immediately pressed on to al-Taif but failed to take that
city.

Muhammad's astuteness in politics and diplomacy was revealed by
his decision not to settle again in Mecca but to return to his adopted city
of Medina. The Kuraysh were a proud people and it had not been easy
for them to acknowledge Muhammad as the leader. He did not tarry
long to remind them too plainly of their new position. Moreover, the
rapid spread of Islam and the increasing numbers of Muslims were

presenting a multitude of problems. For a time in 631 division and opposition erupted to the point that one group withdrew and established
its own house of prayer. A rather unsuccessful campaign occurred in
Transjordan, and missions went as far as Bahrayn and Oman. There
were small Muslim groups to be found in all parts of Arabia, but many
still denied that Muhammad was God's messenger. In all areas where
Muslim political authority had penetrated, Christians, Jews, and Parsis
were tolerated on condition that they concede political rule to the
Muslims.

Muhammad could now see that Arabia was rapidly becoming one
great united religious community—a community where religion rather
than blood, language, customs, or economics held the people together
and a community where there were no distinctions among the believers
except that of the degree of piety. Muhammad understood that many
Arabs professed Islam, not because they submitted to the will of God,
but because they feared not being a Muslim or because they wanted
its political, social, and economic advantages. Consequently the commandments began to turn more to social and political controls and
stressed to a much lesser degree the forms of worship and the religious
ideas that had been revealed in the Meccan and early Medinese
prophecies.

Although Mecca acknowledged Muhammad as its leader, the great
host of visitors to the Kaaba in the month of the great pilgrimage were
still pagan Arabs. Perhaps because of a possibility of dishonor, Mu
hammad declined to go on the great pilgrimage in 631 and sent Abu
Bakr at the head of 300 Muslims. Ali, Muhammad's cousin and son-in-
law, was deputized to announce that after four months no pagan would
be permitted to participate in a pilgrimage to Mecca and that all alliances of a political nature between Muslims and other Arab tribes
would be revoked if Islam were not accepted. Muhammad's authority
and Muslim power were such that no trouble arose from these pronouncements, although later developments indicated that compliance
was hardly voluntary.

Thus, the stage was set for Muhammad to lead the initial reformed
pilgrimage in March, 632. Only Muslims would be present, and the
veneration for Muhammad would be complete. Since Muhammad died
three months later, this has been called The Farewell Pilgrimage; and
the events of the occasion are buried deeply in later accretion and
tradition. Many of the purely pagan aspects were eliminated from
the ceremonious rites which he performed at the Meccan sanctuary.
Every move and act that he made have been described and followed by
devout pilgrims. He knew the significance of this first solidly Muslim
pilgrimage; and in his address, as leader, he must have said something

to the effect: "Today I have perfected your religion and completed my favors for you and chosen Islam as a religion for you."

Three days later he departed for Medina and in less than three months (June 8, 632) died from an ordinary fever. He had no male heir, and no provision had been made for a successor as leader of the Muslim community-state. Genuine bewilderment reigned in Medina. For a whole day his body lay disregarded. It was finally buried under the floor of Aishah's hut.

The personality and private life of Muhammad remain to be considered. In general his tastes were quite simple. There is no evidence that his standard of living changed greatly upon the successes and the growth of the Muslim community. Perhaps the only significant change was in the number of wives. After Khadijah died, Muhammad married several times. At one time he had nine wives. Without question, his favorite was the daughter of Abu Bakr, Aishah, whom he married soon after the Hijrah while she was still a child. His disposition to all was kindly and gentle, and he made no distinction in his treatment of people. The frailties of human nature were well appreciated, and Muhammad never expected too much from his converts. When he found wrongdoing, he upbraided the culprits for their actions but he was lenient and cautious in his interdicts.

Most outstanding, however, were Muhammad's personality and character. The loyalty and compliance rendered naturally and generously to Muhammad by his companions in Mecca and Medina stemmed from the magnetism of his being. His display of a sense of justice and his revelation of religious truth centered the attention of the citizens of Medina upon him. His converts, from first to last, testified to something special and nigh irresistible in his nature. Lacking this quality, Muhammad's stand as a Prophet of God would surely have been ignored by the worldly citizens of Mecca.

REFERENCES: Chapter 3

Kenneth W. Morgan, ed., *Islam—The Straight Path:* Ronald Press, New York, 1958.

William Muir (T. H. Weir, ed.), *The Life of Mohammad from Original Sources:* J. Grant, Edinburgh, 1923. A full account of the life of the

Prophet including most of the traditional stories and incidents attributed to his life without, however, much sifting or critical appraisal. Yet, it is a useful biography of the traditional Muhammad.

Anthony Nutting, *The Arabs: A Narrative History from Mohammed to the Present:* Potter, New York, 1964.

W. Montgomery Watt, *Muhammad at Mecca:* Clarendon Press, Oxford, 1953. A thorough and scholarly treatment of the life of the Prophet up to the time of his departure for Medina. Based on wide research, the volume discusses the theology and the social milieu in which Muhammad was reared and illuminates the period of his preaching and revelation.

————, *Muhammad at Medina:* Clarendon Press, Oxford, 1956. A sequel to the above. This volume depicts Muhammad as the leader of a community where he served as the religious, political, social, and military head.

————, *Muhammad, Prophet and Statesman:* Oxford University Press, London, 1961. A paperback combining the two preceding titles somewhat revised.

CHAPTER 4

The Establishment of the Muslim State

THE CALIPHATE

Muhammad's position as a Prophet of God precluded the nominating of a successor, even though his other roles as head of the state, chief judge, sole legislator, and commander-in-chief of the armed forces did warrant some such forehandedness. Muhammad had sought counsel and taken advice from his companions as the situations demanded. Within minutes after his death the three most frequent and trusted counsellors agreed that Abu Bakr should be the leader of the Muslims. Muhammad's closest friend, Abu Bakr had led the prayers in the mosque and presided over the gatherings of Muslims in the last days when the Prophet had been too ill to perform these functions of leadership. When news of his death spread through the city, the native Medinese nominated one of their own as head of the community; but the Meccan Kuraysh prevailed upon all to accept Abu Bakr as their commander. The following day in the mosque, even before Muhammad was laid to rest, the assembled citizens swore allegiance to Abu Bakr as the successor of Muhammad.

This procedure or decision was neither unusual nor startling. Chiefs in Mecca and Medina, as well as in Arab tribes, were chosen by the heads of families meeting more or less openly. Leadership often passed to another within the same family, but without any idea of inheritance or of legal claim; the power and prestige of a family prejudiced the decision in its favor. In this instance Abu Bakr commanded the respect and support of the Muslims who had emigrated from Mecca to Medina, and that element was still dominant and won the election for Abu Bakr. Other aspirants would have been from the Makhzumi or Umayyad families of Mecca, from a prominent family of Medina, or perhaps from Muhammad's immediate family; but the election of one of those would have been based on factors other than Islam. Authority passing into the hands of Abu Bakr, one of Muhammad's close companions, meant the survival of the Muslim community.

Khalifat Rasul Allah—Successor of the Apostle of God—was the name frequently used to describe Abu Bakr and his position. Abu Bakr probably used it himself, although not as a title. From this appellation came the title, *Khalifa* (Caliph), used for centuries in the Muslim world. It implied the assumption of all the duties and prerogatives exercised by Muhammad except those connected with his role as Prophet. The Caliph was head of the state, supreme judge, leader in public worship, and commander-in-chief of the army. If he did not actually occupy the pulpit in the mosque the sermon was delivered in his name. His name appeared on coins. And it was he to whom reverence of Muslims was given.

ABU BAKR

Abu Bakr, about three years younger than Muhammad, had probably been the first convert outside the immediate family. A prosperous merchant from one of the lesser Kuraysh families and blindly devoted to Muhammad and Islam, Abu Bakr maintained his position of great respect because of a gentle and genial personality coupled with a clear head in matters of judgment and advice. It was a fortunate election as Abu Bakr pursued Muhammad's ways and thoughts. No innovator, he succeeded in holding together the remarkable and talented men who had risen to prominence in this new society.

The first significant task facing the new leadership was to maintain the degree of centralization in Arabia already established by Muhammad. Except for Medina, Mecca, and a few other near-by places thoroughly controlled by the Muslims of Medina, most of the Arabs renounced the political and fiscal authority of Medina. Some even denounced Islam. The natural Arab proclivity for independent action had led them to seize upon the severing of personal loyalties to Muhammad as an opportunity to cast off the yoke of submission. Abu Bakr met the challenge with the vigor and fire of the Prophet. Khalid ibn al-Walid, a most fortunate choice, subdued the tribes of central Arabia, many of which had not been conquered by Muhammad. Following this encouragement, other Muslim generals suppressed revolts and more thoroughly established Islam throughout Arabia, including Bahrayn,

Oman, Yemen, and Hadhramaut. Treating the vanquished and the renegades with mercy, Abu Bakr in less than a year had subjugated most of Arabia.

Indirectly, the complete Islamization of the Hijaz and the domination of the Arabian peninsula by the Muslims led, in the year 633, to military expeditions into Syria and Iraq. Since fighting among Muslims was contrary to the principles of the new society and since raiding was an economic necessity in Arabia as well as the natural occupation of most Arab tribes, ventures into adjacent lands were inevitable. With little cognizance on the part of Medina, Khalid finished the conquest of northeastern Arabia and then, joined by many of the conquered, spilled over into the Sasanid lands in Iraq, taking Hirah, a city west of the Euphrates and almost on a line with modern Baghdad.

For the men of Mecca and Medina Syria was far more important than Iraq. Their caravans went there; it was more accessible; and to them it was a land flowing with milk and honey. The Syrian expedition was a calculated campaign. Three forces of 3000 men each, led by Amr ibn al-As and Yazid ibn Abu Sufyan, defeated the Byzantine governor of Palestine near the Dead Sea and destroyed his fleeing troops near Gaza in February, 634. To oppose the fresh Byzantine levies Abu Bakr ordered Khalid to cross the desert from Iraq to Syria. Appearing almost miraculously, Khalid, as the supreme commander of the united Arab forces, defeated the Byzantine army in July, 634 in the historic battle at Ajnadayn, thus opening all of Palestine to the Muslims.

The news of this victory reached Abu Bakr on his deathbed. His passing, however, hardly caused a ripple across Arabia; for Umar assumed the power of leadership which he had been exercising behind the scenes. Recognition and fealty were given to Umar publicly and voluntarily by all. But the caliphate of Abu Bakr must not be considered as a brief empty interlude between two glorious periods nor Abu Bakr as a shallow and colorless figure. He made the important distinction between state property and the privy purse of the ruler, even though this action irreconcilably alienated Muhammad's daughter Fatimah. Perhaps most important, when war booty was first coming to Medina from outside of Arabia, Abu Bakr held fast to Muhammad's dictum on the spoils of war—all true believers, whether at the front or at home in Arabia, had equal rights.

UMAR

Umar's accession to the caliphate marked the opening of a ten-year administration of an energetic and brilliant man, then only forty-three years old, whom Muslims consider the second founder of Islam. An early convert, Umar, like Abu Bakr, belonged to one of the less im-

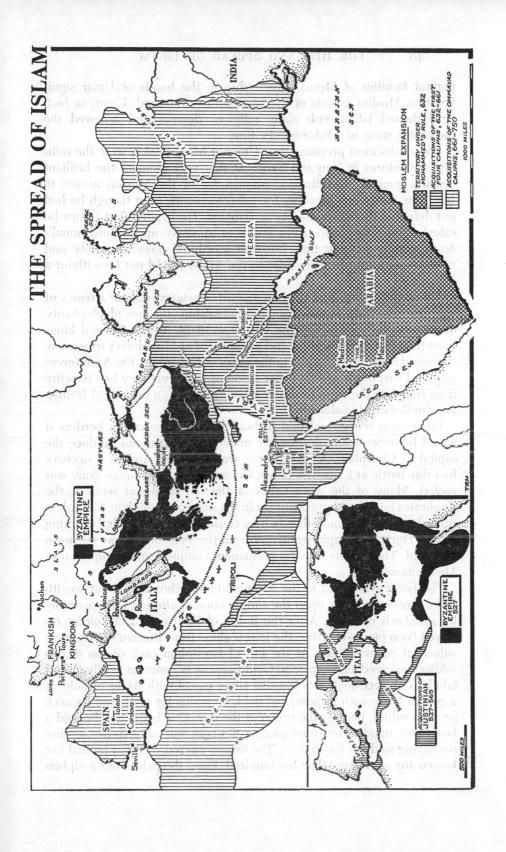

THE SPREAD OF ISLAM

MOSLEM EXPANSION

- Territory under Mohammed's Rule, 632
- Acquisitions of the first four Caliphs, 632-661
- Acquisitions of the Ommayad Caliphs, 661-750

1000 MILES

INDIA

NUBIANS

TURKS

HINDU KUSH

INDUS

OXUS

JAXARTES

PERSIA

NORTHERN TURKS

CASPIAN SEA

CAUCASUS

TIGRIS

Bagdad

EUPHRATES

ARABIA

PERSIAN GULF

Medina

HEGIRA

Mecca

RED SEA

Damascus

Jerusalem

SYRIA

PALESTINE

EGYPT

Cairo

Alexandria

MEDITERRANEAN SEA

Constantinople

BLACK SEA

BYZANTINE EMPIRE

BULGARS

AVARS

MAGYARS

SLAVS

DANUBE

Aachen

FRANKISH KINGDOM

Tours

Poitiers

LOIRE

SAONE

RHONE

GARONNE

PYRENEES

SPAIN

Toledo

Cordova

Seville

ITALY

Rome

Ravenna

Venice

LOMBARDS

ALPS

TRIPOLI

BERBERS

500 MILES

Acquisitions of Justinian 527-565

BYZANTINE EMPIRE 527

ITALY

FRANKS

VANDALS

OSTROGOTHS

VISIGOTHS

MOROCCO

500 MILES

TRM

portant families of Mecca. Leadership in the hands of Umar signified that Muslim aspects of the community continued. Umar, in fact,
strengthened Islam with many religious decrees and renewed the
theocratic state of Muhammad's time.

The affairs most pressing upon Umar at his accession were the military adventures in Iraq and Syria. At that very moment the brilliant
bedouin general al-Muthanna, commander of the Muslim armies in
Iraq, was in Medina pleading for reinforcements, even though he had
just defeated the Sasanid army at Babylon. He begged that troops be
raised among the Arab tribes guilty of apostasy upon Muhammad's
death, rightly judging that, however moribund Sasanid society and
government might be, surrender to the Arabs would not be without a
struggle.

Although the lifting of the ban against apostates brought streams of
warriors into Iraq, superb Iranian generalship, the use of elephants,
the size of the armies, and the wealth available to the Sasanid kings
more than matched the ardor and gallantry of al-Muthanna's tribesmen.
Ravaging far and wide, even to the gates of Ctesiphon, the Arab forces
acquired vast herds and immense stores of grain; yet they had to retire
from Iraq into the western desert when faced by an organized Iranian
army under royal leadership.

Umar soon recognized that to hold Iraq and secure its borders it
would be necessary to destroy the main Iranian army and reduce the
capital at Ctesiphon. A major force was gathered, and in a decisive
four-day battle at Kadisiyah in 635 General Rustem's Iranian army was
routed. Many of the Arab tribes of the Syrian desert west of the
Euphrates joined with the Muslims in the siege of Ctesiphon. Ctesiphon
capitulated in 637, and other battles consolidated the lands bordering
on the Tigris and Euphrates rivers from the Persian Gulf as far north
as Mosul. These years saw the permanent conquest and occupation of
Mesopotamia.

The booty which fell to the Arabs suddenly showered great wealth
and unknown luxuries upon the simple nomad, altering immeasurably
his standards of living. After the Battle of Kadisiyah each soldier received 6000 pieces of silver; the jewels alone from Rustem's body were
valued at 70,000 pieces. At the fall of Ctesiphon each of the 60,000
soldiers received 12,000 pieces. Gold became as common as silver; and
fabulous objects, such as a life-size silver camel with rider of gold or
a golden horse with trappings of gold, emeralds for teeth and its neck
set with rubies, became the prizes of the day. One bedouin who sold a
beauteous maiden for 1000 pieces of silver was chided by another
for having sold her for so little. The excuse offered was that he had not
known any sum larger than ten hundred. From the palace of Ctesiphon

the army sent to Umar the royal banquet carpet, measuring 105 by 90 feet and portraying a landscape. The ground was represented by gold and the paths were silver; meadows were made of emeralds; streams were cascades of pearls; trees, flowers, and fruits were depicted by diamonds, rubies, and other precious stones. Some suggested that the carpet be kept as a trophy; but when many pointed out that earthly goods were but passing things, the carpet was cut into pieces.

Over the next several years Muslim parties raided Khuzistan, took Sus, and advanced toward Isfahan. Iranian forces rallied at Hamadan; but with the removal of Umar's ban on advances into Iran, Muslims overran that land from one end to the other. In the ten years of Umar's caliphate Muslim armies had in an amazing and almost unbelievable sweep conquered Mesopotamia and Iran. Repeatedly they crushed armies that only a few years previously had been able to stand up against the best of Byzantine soldiers. It was even more remarkable considering that other Arab armies at the same time were engaged in conquering Syria and Egypt.

Umar's accession to the caliphate did not change Muslim activities in Palestine or Syria. Several Arab forces converged upon Damascus in 635, and after a siege of more than six months the city capitulated to Khalid. The emperor Heraclius, not willing to cede Syria to the invader, gathered a large army of Greeks, Armenians, Syrians, and Ghassanid Arabs (Christian); but he, too, succumbed to Khalid, in the summer of 636 at the decisive Battle of Yarmuk. Upon receiving the news of this disaster Heraclius left Syria and Palestine to the Muslims; North Syria fell in 637 and Jerusalem surrendered in 638.

Swiftly and conclusively, in only four years, the Muslims had occupied these two fair provinces of the Byzantine Empire. Mountains to the north discouraged further advance into Byzantine lands or the vigorous pursuit of the emperor's armies. Arab generals, however, finding repose most galling, looked for new adventures. Amr ibn al-As, who had traded in Egypt in earlier days, suggested an expedition in that direction. Although Alexandria, the second city of the Byzantines and an important naval base, was strongly tied to Constantinople by sea routes, the loss of Syria and Palestine cut off Egypt from the empire. The chief granary of Constantinople and one of the richest and most populous areas of the Middle East, Egypt was very inviting to an ambitious general like Amr. Umar gave his assent to the campaign, but reluctantly. Amazed at the extent of the territory already occupied by his armies, he was fearful lest they be spread too thinly.

Leaving Palestine by the historic route along the coast, Amr with 4000 men entered Egypt late in 639 and captured Pelusium (al-Farma), not far from the modern Port Said. Amr then moved toward the appex of the Nile Delta, taking Heliopolis, Babylon (near modern Cairo), and most of the eastern delta area before the summer flooding of the Nile submerged the delta and prohibited military operations for the next several months. Joined by a larger Arab contingent under one of the Companions of the Prophet, Amr moved on Alexandria and forced its surrender in the autumn of 641. It was a great and rich metropolis, whose public buildings, harbor facilities, and defense walls and towers were a cause of wonder to the desert Arab.

To protect his position Amr pushed on westward into Cyrenaica and even received tribute from Berber tribes around Tripoli. Egypt, from Alexandria up the Nile to a point well beyond modern Cairo, was now a Muslim possession, thus completing the circle of conquests under Umar. During his caliphate, Iran, Iraq, Syria, Palestine, and Egypt became parts of the Muslim world. They, together with Arabia, are still today the heartland of Islam.

PROBLEMS OF ADMINISTRATION

These conquests alone would have assured Umar the position of second founder of Islam. But Umar's orders regarding the occupation and administration of the new territories were equally important in setting the Muslim pattern which has persisted to the present. Except in a few isolated instances the people of the conquered provinces continued to work and live as they had for centuries, generally with the advantage of paying in tribute less than the former rulers had taxed them. Armies were destroyed and administrators either departed or were employed in similar capacities by the Muslims, but most inhabitants were hardly touched. In Syria and Palestine the urban population had acquired a Hellenistic affectation; but the rural peoples had retained contact with the desert Arab, thus easing the transition to Arab rule. In Iraq Sasanid rule had been a foreign rule; and native tribes, semi-nomadic in their ways and tillers of the soil, rejoiced in the Sasanid defeats. In Iran the Arab was never wholly welcome; and the rapidity of the Muslim conquest can in large measure be attributed to the collapse of the royal government and the momentary inability of the Iranian people to organize a resistance.

In Syria, Palestine, and Egypt heavy imperial taxes and the arrogant, highhanded attitude of officials from Constantinople embittered the provinces. More aggravating and more emotional were the religious persecutions inflicted upon local Christians. The orthodox Council of Chalcedon in the year 451 condemned the Monophysite doctrine of Egypt and Syria according to which divinity and humanity make one compound nature in Christ. This Monophysite heresy was persecuted savagely by many emperors without success, until Heraclius, under whose rule these provinces were lost to Islam, tried to effect a compromise by supporting the Monothelite doctrine—that Christ had two natures in one person with one will. In Syria and Egypt the churches were ardently Monophysite; in Egypt that faith assumed a patriotic coloration which persists today in the Coptic Church. Thus, when it became apparent that Muslim rule meant religious freedom as well as lower taxes, the Arabs had little difficulty in obtaining co-operation from the local peoples. Since at this time Muslims paid no taxes, this toleration of taxpaying Christians and Jews is the origin of the often repeated but little understood Muslim formula of the three-way choice—Islam, taxes, or death—offered to conquered peoples.

Except for Iran the armies of occupation were held aloof from the established urban centers as much as possible. Umar, distressed at the soft appearance and paleness of some of the troops occupying Iraq and quartered in old Ctesiphon, ordered that camps be placed in the open near the desert. Later camp cities were established in each of the newly won provinces—Basrah in lower Iraq, Kufah for central Iraq, Jabiyah in Syria, Ramlah in Palestine, and Fustat (Cairo) in Egypt. Governors were appointed for each province to collect taxes and maintain order. Only a handful of administrators accompanied the governors, and in general bureaus of government were manned by previous officials. Non-Muslims could not bear arms and were subject to their own laws, a practice which established Islamic society as one of the most tolerant of all ages and which developed into the famous millet system of the Ottoman Empire. Outside of Arabia Arabs were not permitted to own agricultural lands. Under the Umayyads this injunction evolved into a system of land ownership and rights of tenancy which still prevails in the Middle East. Considering all aspects of life, the conquered peoples of the Middle East were disturbed very little by Muslim occupation; and civilization proceeded to absorb and modify the new increment.

Many other developments occurred during Umar's caliphate. Arabia was declared a holy land and all non-Muslims were forced to leave, although by this time few remained who did not profess Islam. Even today this decree obtains; and the presence of non-Muslims in Arabia is regarded by the devout as evidence of the forbearance of the rulers of Arabia. With wealth from victories pouring in, the character of Mecca and Medina began to change. There was great building activity, particularly in Medina, where apartments were needed for retired soldiers, administrators, and others who flocked to the capital city as well as for the old inhabitants whose wealth had now greatly increased.

Umar enunciated again the policy that prisoners and movable property belonged to the soldiers who won them, but land and taxes from the conquered people belonged to the whole Muslim community. To facilitate distribution among the Muslims Umar had a census taken in Arabia and a register (*diwan*) made of the sum each was to receive each year from the public treasury. The list included Muslims of all ranks, from Aishah and the Prophet's family down to the lowliest women and children of non-Arab warriors. Aishah received 12,000 dirhams; Companions of the Prophet, 5000; and a child of the lowliest, 200. (A dirham was about the equivalent of thirty cents in United States money.)

Perhaps Umar's regulation of the calendar best showed the belief that a new state and society had been born. Numbering the new era with the Prophet's emigration from Mecca to Medina, Umar decreed that Muslim dating should be counted as so many years after the Hijrah and that he had become caliph in the year A.H. 13.

As the years went by and wealth and power grew, Umar had more and more difficulty with his governors and their administrations. This was especially true in the camp cities of Kufah and Basrah, inhabited by many nomad warriors who were proud, hardy, political Muslims, resentful of Kuraysh rule. Al-Mughirah, Umar's governor of Basrah, was a brilliant, tough, scheming, licentious native of al-Taif, just the sort of rough-and-ready genius that a new city would require. But when caught in adultery, the protests from Basrah were so vociferous that he was recalled to Medina for trial. Although he escaped punishment by slipping through a legal loophole, Umar relieved him of his post. Later al-Mughirah was able to wangle the appointment to Kufah. He retained this appointment for many years, augmenting its power and scope until he became one of the most powerful men in the Muslim world.

In 644 at the very height of Umar's power and prestige he was assassinated at worship in the mosque of Medina by an Iranian Christian slave who had some personal grudge to settle. On his deathbed Umar selected the six leading notables of Medina to choose his successor and directed his own son to wait upon them. Shortly after he had been buried beside Muhammad and Abu Bakr, the notables selected, probably on the basis of seniority, Uthman ibn Affan, who ruled as caliph from 644 to 656.

UTHMAN

Uthman was a member of the very prominent and powerful Umayyad family of the Kuraysh. Noted for his mild manner and his piety, his only distinction as a Muslim leader was having been a respected Companion of the Prophet. His three predecessors had belonged to lesser Kuraysh families, as had most of the emigrants to Medina. Perhaps it was because of this that they had ignored the traditional Arab policy of nepotism and regarded all Muslims as members of one community and one brotherhood. This new social philosophy was one of the revolutionary aspects of Islam.

Although Uthman was seventy when he became caliph and not particularly energetic, he did have at his command a number of vigorous governors and generals who carried forward the banners of Islam. His brother Abdallah was appointed governor of Egypt with financial and civil control, while the conquering Amr was left as commander of the Muslim army. Outraged, Amr immediately repaired to Medina and refused to serve, with the acid remark: "To be over the army and not over the revenue was like holding the cow's horns while another milked her." Abdallah carried on campaigns for booty to the west and south. His armies held Benghazi and Tripoli, ravaged Tunisia, and raided Nubia for slaves. But Abdallah's great contribution was the development of a Muslim fleet, which in 652 repulsed a Byzantine armada before it could attack Alexandria.

As governor of Syria Uthman had his shrewd and aggressive cousin Muawiyah ibn Abu Sufyan, one of the greatest administrators in Muslim history. Umar had appointed him governor of Damascus; and as other governorships in Syria fell vacant they were added to Muawiyah's territory until under Uthman he became the powerful ruler of all of Syria. He rebuffed a large Byzantine army in 647 and in subsequent years sent raiding parties into Asia Minor. He, too, built a fleet, took Cyprus in 649, ravaged the island of Rhodes, and in 655 in conjunction with Abdallah's ships destroyed a large part of the Byzantine navy off the Lycian coast.

Arab armies were active during these years in Iran, ever fanning out eastward. Fars was fully subdued by 650; inroads were made into Armenia in 652; and before the end of Uthman's caliphate raiding expeditions reached Balkh, Kabul, and Ghazna.

Even though the caliph might not be personally aggressive, the valor, might, and leadership of the Muslim army and navy were no longer questioned in the Middle East. The growing problem was the impact of the new empire upon the Muslim community which had so recently emerged from Arab society. Most of the emigrants who still lived were now notables and exceedingly wealthy. One, reputedly, had 1000 slaves and a palace in each of the great cities; another left a fortune of 400,-000 dinars; and many had villas in Mecca and Medina or in the hills near-by.

A second and new generation was coming to full manhood. The amusements and luxuries of Alexandria, Damascus, Ctesiphon, and the camp cities of Basrah, Kufah, and Fustat were tempting. Wine, women, and gambling were the undoing of many. Gone were days when, as

Aishah easily recalled, Muhammad considered wheat bread a rare treat and usually made a meal of dates or milk but never had the luxury of both at the same time. Sumptuous living, however, was neither the sole difficulty nor the root of the other evils. Personal politics, power, prestige, and position began to eat at the vitals of Muslim society, and certainly Uthman was not strong enough to stem the process. Probably no one could have halted it.

MUSLIM POLITICAL PARTIES

Three political parties were developing in the Islamic world. The first considered itself the party of Muhammad. Led by members of the less important families of Mecca, it was composed of those who had established the Muslim community. Abu Bakr and Umar had been members of this party; and in most circles Ali, as the husband of Muhammad's daughter Fatimah, was looked upon as the leader. The strength of the party, legitimists as they are sometimes called, lay in Egypt and Iraq.

Leaders of the second party were members of the Umayyad family and their associates among the Kuraysh. It had been one of the two wealthiest and leading Meccan families in the pre-Islamic period—a family that had bitterly attacked Muhammad and had led the campaigns against the Muslims in Medina. Uthman was an Umayyad, as were Muawiyah, Abdallah in Egypt, and Marwan, who served as Uthman's executive secretary in Medina. Though latecomers to Islam, they possessed great managerial talent and were rapidly surging to the fore in administering the empire. Umar had used them and controlled them; but the legitimists contended that the Umayyads controlled Uthman through their great power and wealth in Syria.

The third party was composed of Arab soldiers who had joined the Muslims just before or after Muhammad's death. They outnumbered the other two parties, but they were unorganized and their leaders did not have the prestige of the Kuraysh. Since, however, their swords had been the instruments responsible for the rapid expansion of Islam and since Islam acknowledged no distinctions among peoples or individuals, they resented the inferior political position forced upon them. The third party had followers everywhere but their forces were concentrated in Arabia and the two great military cities in Iraq.

Having lost the election, the legitimists carped at Uthman for his policies and caviled at his inaction. His one acceptable deed was the standardization of the Koran. Already, different versions had appeared in several provinces and Uthman established one rendition which has remained to the present.

However, he was censured for enlarging the square around the Kaaba in Mecca and for rebuilding and embellishing the mosque in Medina.

Criticism was also leveled at him for appointing so many members of the Umayyad family to high office, for embezzling state properties, and for distributing unjustly the spoils of war. His political opponents claimed that he was reverting to the old order of Arab society where blood ties had ruled. Muhammad had preached earnestly to create a unitary Muslim community wherein all members would be brothers and where social, economic, and political equality would prevail; yet after a dozen years the traditional Arab predilection for the family reasserted its consuming role. From that day to the present it remains as one of the persistent sores upon Middle Eastern society.

Malcontents far and wide across the empire fed on the stories and rumors regarding the sale of positions and the power and wealth of favorites. Supporters of Ali in Kufah first raised the banners of revolt. When a band of revolutionaries from Egypt arrived in Medina and surrounded Uthman's residence, the latter would not permit an army to be raised in his defense and commanded Muawiyah not to come to his rescue. After a siege of several months in 656 the rebels stormed the palace and murdered Uthman, the first dagger being struck by Abu Bakr's son. Anarchy reigned for a week in Medina until a group of notables, under pressure from the rebels from Egypt, elected Ali to the caliphate and restored order.

ALI

Ali, Muhammad's cousin, adopted son, and son-in-law, was a pious and esteemed Muslim, who as an individual soldier in his younger days had shone as one of the great heroes of Muslim battles. He had already been disappointed three times in not being elected caliph, and he knew of the plot to kill Uthman. Generally throughout the Muslim world he was recognized as the caliph; and the new governors appointed by him were accepted everywhere except in Syria, where Muawiyah refused to resign. There were, however, many individuals who did not acknowledge Ali as caliph, largely because of jealousy or shock over the murder of Uthman.

Disgruntled elements among the legitimists led by Aishah, who bitterly hated Ali, hatched a rebellion in Mecca on the pretext that Ali had implicated himself by not punishing the regicides. Ali led his army from Medina, which from that day to the present ceased to be the residence of any caliph, and defeated the insurgents near Basrah in the renowned Battle of the Camel (so-called because the fighting swirled around Aishah on her camel). In this first battle of Muslim against Muslim neither booty nor reprisal against the vanquished was taken. Many illustrious Companions of the Prophet were killed. Aishah was captured but permitted to return to Medina, where she lived on for twenty-two years in her apartment, under the floor of which Muhammad, Abu Bakr, and Umar had been buried.

Denouncing Ali as the confrere of the murderers of the caliph, Muawiyah withheld his fealty and met Ali's forces at Siffin on the banks of the Euphrates in northern Syria in 657. In the midst of battle fighting between Muslims was dramatically halted upon agreement that the contest would be decided by referring to the Koran. Arbitration was unsuccessful; Muawiyah refused to accept Ali as caliph, and Ali would neither abdicate nor consider Muawiyah governor of Syria. Each force, however, retired from the field, and a stalemate ensued.

Following the Battle of the Camel Ali had made his capital at Kufah; and his episode with Muawiyah was, in part, a revival of the age-old and persistent rivalry between Syria and Iraq for dominance in the Middle East. It was also a struggle between the Umayyad Kuraysh and the Arab tribes of the desert for supremacy. At the Battle of the Camel so many of the legitimist party perished that it disappeared from the annals of Islam, leaving Ali, in Kufah, at the mercy of the dominant Arab party. In fact, members of the Arab party took the name of Kharijites (Seceders) and revolted against Ali in protest against his willingness to arbitrate and his propensity for appointing relatives and close Kuraysh friends to high office. Ali destroyed their force in 659, but was assassinated in 661 by a Kharijite in Kufah on the way to prayers in the mosque. Hasan, Ali's eldest son, was declared caliph in Kufah; but Muawiyah was recognized as caliph in Damascus. A few months later Hasan reached an agreement with Muawiyah and retired on a royal pension to the pleasures of his palace in Medina. Muawiyah, thenceforth, was accepted throughout the Muslim Empire as the sole caliph, and the center of the state shifted to Damascus.

Thus ended the republican and democratic era of the caliphate wherein the rulers were elected or chosen for reasons other than birth or military might. Throughout most of this period Medina still served as the capital of the Muslim world, and the leaders of society had known the Prophet personally. It was an Arab state; the conquered provinces had not yet conquered their rulers. With the transfer of the seat of authority to Damascus and the caliphate to Muawiyah of the Umayyad family, a new era was born.

REFERENCES: *Chapter 4*

Ameer Ali, *A Short History of the Saracens Being a Concise Account of the Rise and Decline of the Saracenic Power and the Economic, Social, and Intellectual Development of the Arab Nation from the Earliest Times to the Destruction of Bagdad, and the Expulsion of the Moors from Spain:* Macmillan, London, 1927. Written by a scholar from India, the volume is an excellent exposition of the viewpoint of a schismatic Muslim.

Thomas W. Arnold, *The Caliphate:* Clarendon Press, Oxford, 1924. A careful discussion of the formation and history of the rule of the Muslim state.

Carl Brockelmann, *History of the Islamic Peoples:* G. P. Putnam's Sons, New York, 1947. A general survey of the Islamic period of the Middle East, written by an outstanding German scholar.

Philip K. Hitti, *History of the Arabs from the Earliest Times to the Present:* Macmillan, London, 1953. The standard text of the history of the Arab peoples up to the sixteenth century. The remaining four centuries are treated very briefly. Professor Hitti is a native of Lebanon who was professor of Oriental Languages and Literature at Princeton University for many years.

Bernard Lewis, *The Arabs in History,* Hutchison's University Library, London, 1950. A short but concise account of the rise of the Arab people in the Middle East, emphasizing the broad economic movements in the area through the ages and correlating these developments with the historical processes among the Arabs.

William Muir, *The Caliphate, Its Rise, Decline, and Fall, from Original Sources:* J. Grant, Edinburgh, 1915. Although this volume is outdated in its critical analysis of the sources, it still contains a full and useful running account of the earliest days of the founding of the Muslim state.

❊❊❊ CHAPTER 5 ❊❊❊

Islam

The accession of Muawiyah inaugurated a period of Umayyad and Syrian domination of Islam during which the Hellenistic philosophy and theology of Egypt and Syria rapidly effected a revolution within Islamic thought and practice. Almost immediately the new concepts and dogmas gave birth to numerous Muslim sects; and under the Umayyads the unity of theology, as well as of politics, was forever lost in the Muslim world.

After 660 the various Muslim schools of law, theologies, customs, and practices deviated and multiplied until the simple straightforward conceptualism of Islam was lost and the masses found the exact nature of their religion difficult to determine. Furthermore, rapidity of expansion and multifold conversions admitted to Muslim society many whose knowledge of Islam was limited to a few platitudinous phrases. Throughout all these divergencies and vicissitudes there remained, nevertheless, considerable similarity. The central belief of all variants retained the simple religion preached by Muhammad.

Acceptance of monotheism was the most important facet of religion to Muhammad. To be a Muslim it was sufficient to profess the unity of God and to admit Muhammad as His messenger. God had ninety-nine names and as many related attributes. The mere recitation of these indicates Muhammad's conception of God. He was omniscient, omnipotent, the Judge, the Mighty, the Creator, merciful, compassionate, self-subsistent, forgiving, magnificent, everlasting, most generous, and most high.

Of the infinite qualities of God, Muhammad stressed constantly in his preaching everlastingness. God was the Creator of creation and existed through all eternity. Men were His creatures and He "misleads whom He will and guides whom He will." Fear of God and the Day of Judgment was particularly emphasized in Muhammad's early days to impress materialistic Meccan society; but Muhammad also visualized God as a loving, bountiful, and forgiving Protector of men, "closer to a man than his own jugular vein." A third important attribute of God was mystical in nature: He was termed the Light of the Heavens and of the Earth. In later centuries theologians developed this quality into various organized mysticisms which served as powerful forces in the spread and influence of Islam.

THE KORAN

The basis for Muhammad's views of God and religion and for the central belief of Muslims of every sect rested upon the Koran. Koran, meaning lecture or recitation, was the title given to the collection of Muhammad's revelations. Consisting of 114 chapters, called *surahs*, made up of 6,236 verses (77,934 words), the earliest versions were assembled soon after Muhammad's death. Some of the revelations had been written down in his later years by his secretaries; other revelations were only remembered word for word by his companions. Tradition has it that after a battle where many reciters of the Koran perished Abu Bakr ordered the full Koran to be committed to parchment so that it would not be lost. Later Uthman established the copy held in Medina as the true Koran. In the tenth century the text, as it now stands, was adopted from seven different readings which evolved because of the lack of vowels and diacritical marks in the Arabian script.

Except for the first chapter which is a short prayer, the others were arranged according to length so that the later but longer Medinese chapters are located at the beginning of the Koran. In total length it is about two thirds that of an Arabic version of the New Testament.

Muslims regard the Koran as the word of God, transmitted to Muhammad by the Angel Gabriel; and for many centuries they considered that the Koran contained all knowledge of any value. It furnished the basis for law in the Islamic world for all Muslims; like a modern constitution, it was the skeleton of the legal and judicial systems. It also prescribed a pattern of daily individual and community living which distinguishes Islamic culture from all others. Since no official translation was made until modern times Koranic Arabic served as a common language and a bond for all Muslims from one end of the world to the other. The Koran was the schoolbook and committing it to memory was standard practice for schoolboys everywhere. The very sound of the Arabic words stirs the emotions; read silently, the Koran loses much of its power.

The major part of the Koran is concerned with God: His attributes

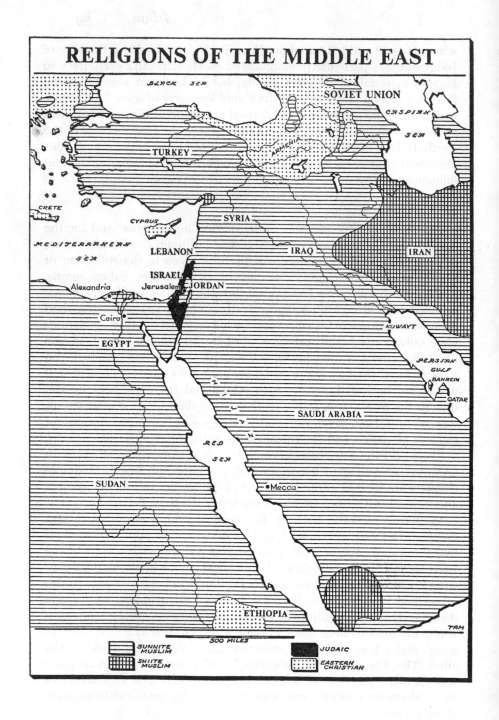

RELIGIONS OF THE MIDDLE EAST

BLACK SEA

SOVIET UNION

CASPIAN SEA

TURKEY

ARMENIA

CRETE

CYPRUS

MEDITERRANEAN SEA

SYRIA

LEBANON

IRAQ

IRAN

ISRAEL

Alexandria

Jerusalem JORDAN

Cairo

KUWAYT

EGYPT

PERSIAN GULF

BAHREIN

QATAR

SAUDI ARABIA

RED SEA

SUDAN

•Mecca

ETHIOPIA

TRM

500 MILES

SUNNITE MUSLIM

SHIITE MUSLIM

JUDAIC

EASTERN CHRISTIAN

are cited, His powers proclaimed, and man's relations to Him defined. Associated with a vivid explanation of the Day of Judgment are portrayals of the Resurrection, Paradise and Hell, and angels and devils. Religious and ethical paths for man to follow in life are sometimes presented directly, almost as codes and commandments; but for the most part they are contained in parables and stories, many of which have been taken from the Old and New Testaments and their associated literature. Adam, Noah, Abraham, Joseph, Moses, David, Solomon, Elijah, Job, Zachariah, John the Baptist, Mary, and Jesus are all set forth, not in any special historical sense but to verify that God rewards the righteous and punishes the wicked.

A perusal of the Torah, the Bible, and the Koran discloses a number of very similar passages. Surah 21, verse 105, is identical to Psalm 37, verse 9: "For evil doers shall be cut off; but those that wait upon the Lord, they shall inherit the earth." The Christians of Constantinople and the West branded Islam as a Christian heresy—a castigation which led to the abhorrence of Muslims and an exaggeration of the differences between Christianity and Islam. In reality, Judaism and its two offshoots, Christianity and Islam, have a great deal in common. The dissimilitude is more in language, style, and form than in substance. Through each of these three religions runs a strong message of personal salvation for righteous individuals. This message of hope gives to the individual a significance and equality that he does not ordinarily have in cultures where other religions prevail.

TRADITIONS

Following the Prophet's death it became obvious that his revelations did not provide an answer to every problem that arises in daily life. Muhammad had recognized, at least after he became the ruler of Medina, that decisions he made publicly were obeyed in the same measure that the revelations of God's will were obeyed. Muhammad always distinguished carefully between spiritual and secular affairs and spoke most explicitly concerning God's word. God's word was law; Muhammad's words were only guides to lead to a wise and holy life. As years slipped by fewer Muslims from their own memories knew Muhammad and what he had said and done, and in order to follow his precedents great collections of his comments and deeds were considered vital. Traditions (*hadith*) by the hundreds of thousands appeared; from these has come much of the common law of Islam, called *sunnah* (custom). Each of the different sects and parties which developed in Islam accepted certain hadith and rejected others as forgeries to prove the correctness of the party's views, no matter whether the contention affected militarism or pacificism, predestination or free will, mysticism or realism, asceticism or worldliness.

By the second or third century after the Hijrah hadith had become very intricate in response to the philosophical and theological demands of the scholars of the time. In the early days of Islam, hadith had comprised the simple, unvarnished ideas and stories that Muhammad had voiced or that his friends had repeated word for word. They are of varied topics, for Muhammad had definite opinions on all types of subjects. On one occasion he said: "God curse the woman who wears false hair and the woman who ties it on." When Aishah acquired a pictured cushion, Muhammad exploded: "Verily, the makers of these pictures will be severely punished on the Day of Resurrection." On slavery he remonstrated: "A slave must not be given a task which he is unable to perform." Muhammad sometimes perceived the difference between legality and righteousness, as when he observed: "Of the things which are lawful the most hateful to God is divorce." In a similar vein he declared: "There is no man who receives a bodily injury and forgives the offender but God will exalt his rank and diminish his sin." Having been an orphan, Muhammad was always concerned with such unfortunates and proclaimed: "The best house amidst the Muslim community is that which contains an orphan who is well treated, and the worst is that wherein an orphan is wronged." Perhaps best known is the attitude Muhammad held toward usury and moneylenders. In commenting on persons paying or charging usurious rates of interest, he averred: "They are equally culpable." Among Muslims one of his oft-quoted commands indicated Muhammad's view that his religion was a matter for everyday life: "No monkery in Islam!"

DOGMAS

Muhammad was not a systematic theologian. But shortly after his death Muslim theologians and philosophers classified Muhammad's faith into three fundamentals: religious beliefs (*iman*), religious duties (*ibadat*), and good works (*ihsan*).

First and foremost, of course, is the belief that God is One and has all of the attributes ascribed to Him by Muhammad. It has never been clear, however, how the attribute of omnipotence ought to be interpreted, and this problem has engendered controversy among Muslims from the days of the first caliphs to the present. In the early unaffected period, God's omnipotence meant without intricate debate that man was completely subordinate to God and could do nothing unless God permitted it. Yet, man was responsible for what he did and would be rewarded or punished as the case might be. Muhammad preached incessantly on this point and declared that a man would fall into evil ways if he did not believe in God.

Muhammad and the first Muslims referred so frequently to the Day of Judgment and the Resurrection that belief in these has become one of the significant aspects of Islam. When the cataclysmic Day comes, each individual's faith and deeds will be weighed, his body will rise, and he will enter Paradise or be cast into Hell. Martyrs for the faith do not wait for the Judgment Day but immediately enter Paradise. Paradise is clearly described as a beautiful garden by a flowing river where the blessed rest on silken couches, partake of heavenly food and drink, and are entertained by dark-eyed maidens and wives of perfect purity. The terrors of Hell are beyond description. Waters are boiling; men's bellies are filled with molten brass. Into this fiery Hell go the unbelieving, the covetous, and those who worship other gods.

Another basic point in the religious belief of Muslims is the role played by angels (*jinn*). Heaven and earth are populated by these invisible spirits who serve as God's messengers and record men's deeds. Gabriel is recognized as the leading angel and the spirit who brought the Koran to Muhammad. Rebellious jinn are devils and like men will be cast into Hell on the Last Day. The leading devil is one who at the time of creation did not worship Adam and who continues to seduce men into evil ways until the Resurrection.

Muslims believe that God has sent many human messengers to teach mankind His ways and that the last and greatest was Muhammad. The Koran specifically mentions twenty-eight prophets: four are Arabs; one is Greek (Alexander the Great); three (Zachariah, John the Baptist, and Jesus) come from the New Testament; and the remainder come from the Old Testament. The most important were Adam, Noah, Abraham, Moses, and Jesus. The last was Muhammad, whom God sent as the "Seal" of all. Prophets did not perform miracles except on special occasions when God gave them these powers. Divine revelation was granted to Moses in the Jewish Torah, to David in the Psalms, to Jesus in the Gospels, and to Muhammad in the Koran, which was his only miracle. All of them preached salvation through the recognition that God is One.

Muslims are to accept and believe all of these scriptures; for they are the word of God and they corroborate each other. The final word of God, the Koran, attests the revelations in the other scriptures, clarifies all previous uncertainties, and brings to man perfect Truth. The Koran is believed to be eternal and uncreated; its earthly reproduction is identical in language and spelling to the heavenly original, every word and letter of which are sacred and divine.

DUTIES

The second essential in Islam as taught by Muhammad comprised the religious duties (*ibadat*) of man. These are actions less obligatory than those of faith; but their performance required and constituted the individual's recognition of the omnipotence of God. These duties have usually been termed the "five pillars" of Islam; they are the easiest to observe and, unfortunately for many uninformed non-Muslims and even for some Muslims, these five pillars have been mistaken for the true religious substance of Islam.

The first and foremost pillar is the open profession of faith. Often reduced to the Koranic formula, "No god but God and Muhammad is the messenger of God," this declaration is used throughout a Muslim's life and suffices to ensure one's acceptance as a nominal Muslim.

Muhammad emphasized prayer as the second obligation for Muslims. The Koran mentions directly no set ritual for prayer, but bids the faithful to pray frequently. Before Muhammad's death it had become customary for Muslims to pray formally five times daily: daybreak, noon, mid-afternoon, sunset, and nightfall. A Muslim prays at these times wherever he may be, although it is preferable to pray in unison with others and in a mosque if possible. One acts as leader and the others stand in rows behind him, all facing Mecca. Each prayer is composed of a certain number of bows: two at daybreak, three at sunset, and four at the others. Each bow consists of seven distinct acts: (1) placing the open hands at each side of the head and repeating: "God is most great"; (2) standing upright with the left hand over the right and repeating the opening prayer of the Koran and at least one other Koranic passage; (3) bending from the hips and touching the knees with the hands; (4) straightening up, saying: "God listens to the one who praises Him"; (5) falling to the knees and prostrating oneself with the forehead touching the ground; (6) sitting on the haunches; and (7) a second prostration. Most Muslim prayers are concerned with God and His attributes, and devout Muslims pray frequently at other times during the day and night. Certain events such as burials, eclipses, serious decisions, and religious celebrations demand specially prescribed prayers. The Friday noon prayer is the great congregational prayer wherein a sermon (*Khutbah*) is usually delivered. At first the sermon was delivered by Muhammad, then by the caliph or his representative, and now by a learned Muslim, who also offers a prayer on behalf of the ruling head of the state.

At the time of prayer one must be in a state of purity, which is determined in various ways. Usually before prayers, simple purity, as defined in the Koran, is achieved by washing the hands and arms to the elbow, the face, and the feet up to the ankles. In the absence of water sand may be used.

Of all the features of Islam, prayer in its public form has been the most constant democratizing force. Side by side in a row at prayer are common soldier and general, prince and pauper, merchant and holy man. No distinction is made and the proudest individual falls to his knees and humbly and reverently prostrates himself in complete obeisance in the presence of the omnipotence and omniscience of God.

The third pillar of Islam is almsgiving. Muhammad at first regarded giving to the poor and needy as a personal atonement and a means of salvation. Sometime in the Medinese period of his prophecy almsgiving was regularized to become a two and one-half percent voluntary tax on all produce and revenue of each Muslim. Termed *zakah*, the proceeds were used to support the poor, to erect religious buildings, and to help defray government expenses. In later years when states were much weaker it was not possible to collect alms on any such basis and it became solely a free-will offering. Alms are also to be given generously for various religious and human charities such as mosques, hospitals, poorhouses, and schools. Likewise, beggars and the destitute are never turned away from the door empty handed. On the Day of Judgment in a Muslim's book of deeds will be recorded the alms he has given.

Fasting, the fourth pillar of Islam, was enjoined upon all Muslims by Muhammad, and in the Medinese era he designated Ramadan (the ninth lunar month) as a month of fasting. From the very first flush of dawn to nightfall food, drink, medicine, and smoke are not to pass the lips; bleeding, application of leeches, and sexual intercourse are also forbidden. At various times and places in history Muslims who have failed to observe Ramadan have been beaten. Fasting is considered the best means of expiating one's sins of the year.

The fifth pillar of Islam, that of the Pilgrimage to Mecca (*Hajj*), stands as the symbol of Muslim unity. In pre-Islamic times there existed a holy month of pilgrimage to the sanctuary in Mecca; Muhammad continued this custom. It was a maxim that each Muslim, man and woman, should participate in the pilgrimage each year if possible. Later, as the Muslim world grew, it became too arduous for many to go from Iraq, Syria, and Egypt; and when Islam had spread to India and Spain the pilgrimage became obligatory only once in a lifetime and only for those who could afford it. Occurring in the twelfth month (*Dhu'l-Hijjah*), the pilgrimage ritual is celebrated on certain days by elaborate and involved rites at the Kaaba in Mecca and at other sacred spots in the neighborhood. Since Muhammad's Farewell Pilgrimage in 632 non-Muslims have not been permitted to be present in Mecca during the pilgrimage; and in general they are forbidden entry into the city at all times.

Throughout the entire course of Muslim history the pilgrimage has been a most valuable unifying force within Islamic civilization. Pilgrims have come to Mecca from the four corners of the Muslim world. There, on the way, and in returning the interchange of philosophical and theological dogmas, the gaining of geographical and economic knowledge, the exchange of seeds and agricultural products, and the interplay of political forces and ideas have been factors in maintaining a common Muslim culture among the diverse peoples embracing Islam.

To some Muslims a sixth pillar of Islam has been added: that of Holy War (*Jihad*). Many consider that every Muslim bears the duty to expand the frontiers of Islam, by force if necessary, until the entire world has been won. At various times Holy War has been an accepted policy of state and a continuous threat to neighboring non-Muslims, although in recent centuries it has not been a vital force among Muslim people.

VIRTUES

It might well be thought that after professing the religious beliefs of Islam and performing the various duties of a Muslim the circle of religion had been completed. In addition, however, the Koran imposes upon all a course of right living, thus giving a religious character to private and public morality. From the virtues extolled Muhammad emerges as a moralist and something of a puritan. The Koran limits the number of wives to four, and then adds: "But if you fear that you will act unjustly among them, then marry only one." There are many other commandments which raised the status of women in Arabian society. Settlements are required to be made upon a woman if she is divorced; a widow can marry whomever she wishes; and the burying alive of daughters is prohibited.

Murderers are promised burning in Hell; and earthly penalties are imposed for homicide, stealing, fraud, perjury, and libel. Injunctions are delivered against gambling, usury, and monopolistic practices. The use of wine and the eating of pork are forbidden. An interdiction is imposed upon making statues, pictures, puppets, and any representation of animate objects, because God is the creator of all things and man should not try to imitate His works. Moreover, idolatry is most sinful and the making of images is only one step removed from worshipping other gods. Most of these declarations of right living are injunctions against practices that were common in the pagan and hedonistic society of Mecca.

In view of the comprehensive scope of Islam with respect to religious beliefs, religious duties, and virtues, Muhammad can only be regarded as a very successful prophet and reformer. Muhammad found Mecca, as one writer has well expressed it, a "materialistic commercial" city "where lust of gain and usury reigned supreme, where women, wine, and gambling filled up the leisure time, where might was right, and widows, orphans, and the feeble were treated as superfluous ballast." Muhammad, practically a nobody in so many of the things that counted in Mecca, brought to his people and those of Mecca a knowledge of God and a way of salvation that changed the life and philosophy of all Arabia. Since Islam required individual belief and morality, the tribal and family morality of pre-Islamic Arabia was replaced by the personal responsibilities of the individual Muslim as a member of the universal Muslim brotherhood.

REFERENCES: Chapter 5

A. J. Arberry, *The Holy Koran: An Introduction with Selections:* Macmillan, New York, 1953. Valuable description of the Muslim holy book and commentary on its contents.

Bayard Dodge, *Al-Azhar: A Millennium of Muslim Learning:* Middle East Institute, Washington, 1961. An excellent and appreciative study of the great Muslim university in Cairo.

H. A. R. Gibb, *Mohammedanism: An Historical Survey:* Oxford University Press, London, 1953. This little volume in *The Home University Library of Modern Knowledge,* #197, is probably the best short account and discussion of Islam in any language. The style is simple and direct, the language is readily understood, and the scholarship is beyond reproach.

Alfred Guillaume, *The Traditions of Islam: An Introduction to the Study of the Hadith Literature:* Clarendon Press, Oxford, 1924. An important monograph on Hadith and its significance in the development of tradition as a part of Islamic belief and ritual.

C. Snouck Hurgronje, *Mohammedanism: Lectures on Its Origin, Its Religious and Political Growth, and Its Present State:* G. P. Putnam's Sons, New York, 1916. Excellent lectures by a Dutch authority who lived in Mecca.

Arthur Jeffery, *The Qur'an as Scripture:* R. F. Moore, New York, 1952. Important for the study of Islam and the Koran.

Henri Lammens, *Islam: Beliefs and Institutions* (E. Denison Ross, trans.): Methuen, London, 1929. A concise summary of the dogmas of Islam by an outstanding French scholar.

D. S. Margoliouth, *The Early Development of Mohammedanism: Lectures Delivered in the University of London, May and June, 1913:* Williams and Norgate, London, 1914. Professor Margoliouth stresses the evolution of Islam in the first few centuries of that era.

Henri Massé, *Islam* (Halidé Edib, trans.): G. P. Putnam's Sons, New York, 1938. A thorough exposition of the rise and development of Islam and some of its intricacies.

A. S. Tritton, *Muslim Theology:* Luzac, London, 1947. The basic principles are well presented in this volume and the variants are explained.

W. Montgomery Watt, *Free Will and Predestination in Early Islam:* Luzac, London, 1948. An excellent presentation of this dichotomy in the philosophy of the Muslim world.

CHAPTER 6

The Spread and Organization of the Muslim Empire under the Umayyads

The death of Ali left no serious rival to Muawiyah and his leadership over all Muslims. Proclaimed caliph at Jerusalem in 661, Muawiyah established Damascus as his chief residence and seat of government. Until his death nineteen years later he managed the provinces through energetic, capable, and forceful governors, who maintained a strong discipline over the proud and turbulent Arab soldiery and over settlers in the garrison cities. At home he ruled confidently and nobly as the first among equals. He discussed policies of state with the notables about him, frequently explaining the course of government publicly from the pulpit of the mosque. More and more he built an administration for the state in the Romano-Byzantine tradition; less and less was he the tribal Arab shaykh governing purely on a personal basis.

Five years before Muawiyah's death he induced the leaders of the empire to recognize his son Yazid as his successor. Thereupon, Yazid was taken to Medina and Mecca to have those holy cities accept him as the next caliph. Neither Arab nor Muslim in tradition, this procedure was definitely a Roman custom; the haughty Muslim aristocracy of Medina declared the step to be a sinful innovation and refused to render the requested homage. This measure tended to make the position of caliph an hereditary one and overtly established the Umayyad Empire, which lasted until 750. Only twice during the period did many question who the next caliph would be; and only once did a serious contender arise outside of the Umayyad family.

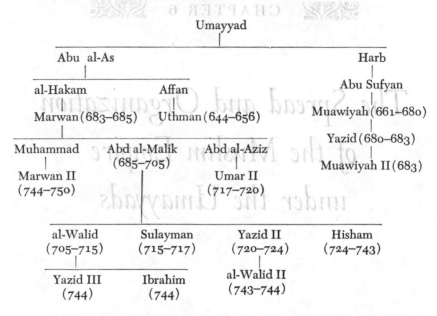

Umayyad

Abu al-As   Harb

al-Hakam   Affan   Abu Sufyan

Marwan (683–685)   Uthman (644–656)   Muawiyah (661–680)

                                              Yazid (680–683)

Muhammad   Abd al-Malik   Abd al-Aziz
           (685–705)   Muawiyah II (683)

Marwan II   Umar II
(744–750)   (717–720)

al-Walid   Sulayman   Yazid II   Hisham
(705–715)   (715–717)   (720–724)   (724–743)

Yazid III   Ibrahim   al-Walid II
(744)   (744)   (743–744)

In general and by comparison with other ruling families the Umayyads produced talented, competent caliphs. They were much maligned by later Muslim historians, who wrote under the patronage of the succeeding dynasty and who depicted the Umayyads as hard-riding, wine-bibbing, luxury-loving, worldly-minded usurpers of the caliphate. But the Umayyads organized the Muslim state into a centralized force that once again carried forward the banners of Islam into distant places. They were hard-hitting realists who to meet existing and evolving situations could not always follow the principles of government and law being formulated by theologians and jurists in the holy city of Medina.

CAMPAIGNS AGAINST BYZANTIUM

The nearest and greatest rival power of the Umayyad state was the Byzantine Empire; the nearest and richest land for the Muslims to raid was Asia Minor. Battles with Byzantine forces were not novel experiences for Muawiyah. As governor of Syria he had driven Byzantine armies from north Syria, twice defeated Byzantine fleets, and occupied Cyprus. Muawiyah's army exploited the weakness of the rule from Constantinople by annual summer excursions through the passes into Asia Minor as far north as Caesarea (Kayseri). After he became caliph his forces roamed far and wide over Anatolia; one Muslim general wintered in 668 at Chalcedon (Kadiköy) across the Bosphorus from Constantinople. That spring Muawiyah sent a fleet to support the land force and attack Constantinople, but the land and sea walls of the city proved too great a barrier for the Arabs. From this campaign has come the legendary hero Abu Ayyub (Eyub), who died and was buried near the walls of Constantinople. The standard-bearer of the Prophet, the now aged Abu Ayyub, had accompanied the soldiers to stimulate their enthusiasm. His remains, discovered in 1453 when the Turks were storming the walls, have been entombed in a mosque-mausoleum near the Golden Horn, where the Ottoman sultans were girded with the sword of their authority.

The raising of the siege of Constantinople did not presage the relaxing of Muslim pressure on the Byzantine Empire. Another assault upon Constantinople was launched by the caliph Sulayman, who subscribed to the legend that Constantinople would be taken by the bearer of a prophet's name. His brother, supported by land and sea forces, occupied both shores of the Bosphorus and held a tight siege of Constantinople for fourteen months. In 717, however, he was foiled by Greek fire and the brilliant defenses of the new emperor, Leo the Isaurian (a Syrian from Marash) and by the ravages of disease, hunger, and an unusually severe winter. Several generations elapsed before the Muslims appeared again before the walls of Constantinople, which always proved too thick and too strong for the Arabs to penetrate without the aid of gunpowder.

Had Constantinople been taken in 717 the subsequent course of European history might well have been greatly altered. The road to Italy and western Europe through the Balkans would have been traversed almost unimpeded; and once in western Europe these Muslim generals would have effected a union with their brothers-in-arms coming by way of North Africa and Spain.

NORTH AFRICA AND SPAIN

The records do not disclose any planned pincers move on Europe by the Umayyads, although simultaneously with their last attacks upon Constantinople the greatest westward movement of Islam was being executed. Amr, governor of Egypt, sent a Muslim force westward into North Africa, the object being Tunisia and Algeria (*Ifrikiyah*), and Morocco (*Maghrib*). A camp city built in 670 at Kayrawan in Tunisia served as headquarters to subdue Berber tribes and the coastal cities dependent upon Constantinople. Toward the end of the century Byzantine rule over the coast was terminated by a co-operative army-fleet maneuver which drove the Greeks from Carthage. Appointed governor of Africa in 708, Musa consolidated North Africa from Egypt to the Atlantic and added greatly to his military force by recruiting new armies from among the Berber tribesmen.

One of Musa's Berber lieutenants led a small reconnoitering band across the Strait of Gibraltar in 710 and returned easily with such valuable booty that Tarik, the fabled Berber lieutenant in command at Tangier, crossed on his celebrated raid in the early summer of 711 with several thousand men, mostly Berbers, and established a base on the strong height which still is called Tarik's mountain—*Jabal Tarik,* or Gibraltar. Crushing the Visigothic forces of Spain, Tarik fanned out northward in all directions at will. Malaga, Cordoba, and Toledo fell; and by winter Tarik found himself master of half of Spain with an almost unlimited amount of booty at his disposal.

Scolding Tarik for acting independently, Musa joined his heroic henchman in 712. Within two years Spain had been overrun by Muslim forces. The highlands of Leon, Aragon, and the Asturias were occupied; and from Galicia Musa looked down upon the waters of the Atlantic and the Bay of Biscay. At this point a messenger ordered Musa to appear before the caliph in Damascus. Accompanied by Tarik, Musa made the long trek overland and presented to the court his trophies and many Visigothic nobles and maidens. A new caliph stripped Musa of his wealth and degraded him, perhaps because of fear or jealousy of Musa's great popularity. Musa died in poverty a few years later in the Hijaz, a strange fate for one who opened Europe to the Muslims.

Within six or seven years the conquest of Spain was completed. The Arabs called the province al-Andalusia (Land of the Vandals) and it, or some part of it, remained a Muslim land for almost eight centuries. The Arab-Berber-Muslim (Moorish) culture left its indelible mark upon Spain, which in turn had a profound influence upon Islamic society. The speed and ease with which Spain was conquered indicated that it was in a state of near anarchy, waiting for a positive force to enter the vacuum. Ruling in a most oppressive and tyrannical fashion and attempting to convert by force all Jews to Christianity, the Visigoths had always been at odds with the Romano-Spanish peoples, who looked upon their Teutonic masters as barbarians.

As in Syria, Iraq, and Egypt, the Muslims did not fight against the inhabitants of Spain, but only against the armies of the rulers. Spain was taken so quickly that in many towns and cities no Arab or Berber forces could be spared for garrison duty; and since Muslim administrators were usually not available, native Jews were left in charge.

One of Musa's successors crossed the Pyrenees in 718 and plundered France as far as Nîmes. Two years later Arab-Berber invaders seized Narbonne on the Mediterranean and established an arsenal and base for operations north of the Pyrenees. Predatory columns rode out of

Narbonne every year, terrorizing the countryside and carrying off rich booty, especially from the treasures of churches and convents. The greatest of these expeditions was the renowned foray of 732 led by the governor of Spain, Abd al-Rahman. Defeating the Duke of Aquitaine near the Garonne, Abd al-Rahman burned churches in Bordeaux and outside of Poitiers. The raiders turned back from their northward course only after the loss of their leader in the determined and bloody resistance put up by Charles Martel in the celebrated but indecisive Battle of Tours.

Never again did an organized expedition of Muslims approach so near to Paris. Yet in 734 they took Avignon and several years later sacked Lyons. Not until 759 was Narbonne abandoned, and attacks upon the French and Italian coasts persisted for centuries. The Arab-Berbers of Spain did not fashion a real hold upon southern France, however, because of their lack of manpower, the distance from Damascus, and the outbreak of civil disturbances in North Africa and Spain.

Bitterness between Berber and Arab led to a running feud and violent insurrection in North Africa and Spain. Conversions to Islam among the Berbers were so extensive as to compromise the relationship between conquerors and vanquished in North Africa. Arabs looked down upon the Berbers, who upon becoming Muslims anticipated equality with the proud Arab. When the expected treatment was not forthcoming, rebellion burst out everywhere. From 734 to 742 North Africa was in flames from one end to the other. Berbers claimed that they were given semi-arid plateau lands in Spain while the Arabs acquired all of the fertile areas.

In addition, factional strife among the Arabs existed at every turn. Political, religious, and family quarrels were at this moment rocking the Islamic world from the Pyrenees to the Indus, making incursions beyond well-established frontiers wholly ineffective. Furthermore, rivalry developed between Arabs from Arabia and the Syrian army sent to subdue Berber uprisings; their bickerings with the Arab governors and lords of Toledo and Cordoba were interminable. From the time of the Battle of Tours to the landing of the Umayyad prince in Spain in 755 the term of the governorship of Spain averaged twelve months. With such turmoil, uncertainty, and anarchy permanent conquests in France were impossible.

EXPANSION IN ASIA

While the Umayyads were extending Islam westward into North Africa and Spain, a similar expansion carried Muslim rule to the Indus river and the frontiers of China. Becoming viceroy of the eastern lands of the caliphate, al-Hajjaj, a school master of al-Taif, gave his governor of Khurasan several thousand Arab troops to establish a strong base at Marw. From there he crossed the Amu Darya (Jayhun—Oxus) and in a series of brilliant campaigns brought Transoxiana under Muslim domination. Balkh (Wazirabad, Afghanistan), Bukhara, and Samarkand in Turkestan (Sogdiana), and Khiva were subdued between 705 and 712 and soon became Islamic strongholds; Buddhist temples and monasteries were destroyed. Native Turkish rulers were left in charge of civil affairs, although Muslim tax collectors and military inspectors represented the imperial authority. In the Syr Darya (Sayhun—Jaxartes) area Buddhist sanctuaries and idols were destroyed and the rulers sent tribute to the caliphs. A generation later another caliph sent an Arab general to Transoxiana as far as Kashgar to reconquer the area and bring the Turkish rulers, some of whom had accepted Islam, again under caliphal authority.

Further south, al-Hajjaj's son-in-law was authorized to lead a column toward India. Taking Makran, he occupied Baluchistan and subdued Sind. Daybul and Haydarabad became Muslim, and Multan in the Punjab was conquered. Muslim control along the Indus was permanent. Steady conversion to Islam soon made this northwestern corner of India an important part of the Muslim world and laid the foundations for the modern Islamic state of Pakistan.

FISCAL DEVELOPMENTS

This second wave of Muslim expansion under the Umayyads brought to a head certain economic and fiscal problems which had been developing at an accelerated pace. From the time of the Hijrah Muslims were subject to a small tax to support their poor and unfortunate brethren, but there was no general taxation. Toward the end of the seventh century, with Arabs scattered over the face of the earth and conversions among conquered non-Arab peoples growing by leaps and bounds, questions of state annuities to worthy Muslims, land ownership, and taxation arose to vex one caliph after another and ignited serious disturbances in Muslim society.

Besides the state's share of booty, which in the Umayyad era was very sizable, the principal source of revenue came in taxes from land and subject peoples. Each free non-Muslim was required to pay for his protection a poll tax (*jizyah*) of four, two, or one dinar, according to his wealth and position. Land taxes were far more complex. In the days of the early conquests Muslims (Arabs) were forbidden to possess land outside of Arabia proper. Domain lands of ousted Byzantine and Sasanid governments and vacant lands fell to the caliph as agent for the Muslim community, and the total income went into state coffers. Ownership of other land was not changed, and in most cases the taxes (*kharaj*) remained the same and were collected by the same agents. As Arab Muslims acquired properties in Syria, Iraq, and other provinces outside of Arabia, freedom from land taxes usually prevailed. The state leased domain land to Muslim Arabs, who bought and sold the rights so that the land had the appearance of private property. Consequently, Arab laws governing landownership and tenure adhered generally to Byzantine, Persian, and more ancient practices and customs, thereby assuring to tillers of the soil throughout the Middle East a continuity which changed only imperceptibly until the great land reforms following World War II.

As the number of non-Arab Muslims increased through conversion, many deserted the land for the city in the expectation of living on state annuities as Arabs did. They paid no taxes on the land left behind in the village and ceased to pay the poll tax. This disastrously affected the treasuries, especially in North Africa, Iraq, and Khurasan. Furthermore, Umar II found it necessary to free Muslims, irrespective of origin or state, from paying poll and land taxes in order to eliminate increasing resentment of non-Arab Muslims and to prevent incipient revolutions in several of the provinces.

Umar's decree, however, by lowering revenues, upset the fiscal system of the government beyond the point of toleration. Caliph Hisham withdrew the order and instituted the policy, generally permanent in Muslim lands ever since, that although poll taxes "fell off" upon conversion to Islam land taxes did not. At that time in the provinces these tax measures were considered by non-Arab Muslims, the principal landowners, to be very inequitable. Great disaffection led to civil war in North Africa and proved to be a major factor in the overthrow of the Umayyad regime by the troops from Iraq and Khurasan.

SOCIAL ORGANIZATION

As the Arabs and the native inhabitants of the conquered territories began to coalesce to form Umayyad civilization, there arose four social classes: Muslim Arabs; Muslim non-Arabs; non-Muslim free persons (Christians, Jews, Zoroastrians); and slaves.

The Arab was the aristocrat of the Muslim world, and the Kuraysh claimed to be the noblest. Wherever Islam spread, Arabs regarded themselves as the rightful leaders of society, and at first only they could live in the new garrison cities such as Kayrawan, Cairo, and Kufah. Although Islam taught the equality of all believers and disavowed family connections in favor of religious ties, Muslim Arabs everywhere retained pride in their lineage; and marriage between an Arab woman and a non-Arab man was considered a serious misalliance. In the Umayyad period all Arabs were enrolled upon the imperial registry, each receiving regular payments from the state treasury on the theory that the receipts of the Muslim community were divided among all its members. In practice the Arabs acted as if it were decreed that the Arab minority would rule the non-Arab majority, Muslims as well as non-Muslims.

By the opening of the eighth century the non-Arab Muslims, often called clients (*mawali*), outnumbered the Arab Muslims in all parts of the Umayyad Empire except Arabia. Moreover, the masses in North Africa, Egypt, Iraq, and Khurasan had been converted so rapidly that revenues in those provinces had dropped very conspicuously. Rarely were these converts accepted as equals by the Arabs and usually they attached themselves to an Arab tribe or family, thus the nomenclature, "clients." Yet the converts were in many instances trained and educated individuals with skills not possessed by many Arabs. Several generations later, because of the universality of the Arabic language and considerable intermarriage, the pure Arab of Arabia who had migrated to conquered territory had been lost in the welter of peoples, all of whom participated in the common culture and practices of that particular section of the Middle East. In Syria and Iraq, where most of the Arabs settled, non-Arab Muslims were absorbed quickly, and the new society became Arab. In more distant lands such as Iran, India, Morocco, and Spain the few ruling Arabs dominated society only temporarily. The non-Arab Muslims soon engulfed their rulers, and Iranian, Indian, and Berber-Moorish characteristics triumphed.

Non-Muslims—Jews, Christians, Zoroastrians, pagan Berbers, and a few scattered others—were called *dhimmis* and were recognized legally as second-class subjects. They were judged almost entirely in their own courts in accordance with their own laws and were permitted to worship in their own way and to live their personal lives as they wished. They were, nevertheless, greatly circumscribed in matters of civil rights and community affairs. Non-Muslims could not bear arms; instead, they paid taxes, as has already been discussed. They were subject to many distinctive regulations concerning dress, styles of coiffures, types of saddles, and manner of riding. Finally, the *dhimmis* could neither hold public office nor give evidence in court against a Muslim.

At the bottom of the social ladder were the slaves. Slavery in the Middle East was as old as time itself; and although Muhammad openly condemned it, saying that manumission was pleasing in the sight of God, he declared the practice legal. In Islamic society no Muslim could be enslaved; acceptance of Islam, however, did not give a slave his freedom. Children of a slave woman remained slaves unless the owner of the slave accepted them as his children. Marriage between master and slave was not permissible, although concubinage was. A concubine who presented her master with children could not be sold, was accorded special recognition as the mother of his children, and gained her freedom upon his death.

Slave trading was a very active and profitable business in the Middle East under the Umayyads. Most slaves were acquired as booty in victorious campaigns and successful raiding expeditions, but many were purchased through regular slave channels. Greeks, Armenians, Turks, Kurds, Spaniards, Goths, Iranians, Negroes, and Berbers predominated; but slaves were of every color and description. Prices rose and fell with the supply. Most Arab Muslims possessed several slaves, and the wealthy frequently counted theirs in the thousands.

POLITICAL ADMINISTRATION

When Muawiyah became sole caliph, his first task was to effect a systematic administration for the empire. Obviously following the example and practices of the East Roman empire current in Syria and even using much of its personnel, Muawiyah organized his government along three main functional or departmental lines: political and military affairs; tax collection; and religious administration, including courts and endowments.

Outside of Syria-Palestine, which was governed directly by the caliph in Damascus, the empire was divided under the Umayyads into five great states, each with a viceroy appointed by the caliph: 1) Kufah, which included all of Iraq and the Muslim lands farther east; 2) the Hijaz, which took in Central Arabia and Yemen; 3) al-Jazirah, comprising the northern lands between the Euphrates and the Tigris, eastern Asia Minor, Armenia, and the Caucasus; 4) Egypt; and 5) Africa, which ran from Cyrenaica to the Atlantic and the Pyrenees.

The army as well as the civil administration in each lesser province acted upon the authority of a governor, and all were directed by and responsible to the viceroy. Local expenses were defrayed from taxes collected in the provinces, only the tax balances being forwarded to Damascus. Toward the end of the Umayyad regime when administration began to weaken, viceroys and provincial governors built up great personal fortunes by neglecting to forward the full balance to the caliph. Viceroys even remained in Damascus, hiring agents to go to the provinces to perform irksome functions. Frequently special officers were sent directly by the caliph to collect taxes and to be responsible solely to him rather than to the viceroy, who always resented the implied lack of confidence. Such a step as this aroused the enmity of Amr in Egypt toward the Caliph Uthman.

As the empire expanded, problems of trained and loyal personnel, of communications, and of money came to the fore. The number of qualified Arabs was too small to fill the positions required to keep the government functioning. In Syria, Iraq, and Egypt Muawiyah retained the services of most of the government employees he found there upon the conquest. These employees used Greek or Persian in their records. Not until the time of Abd al-Malik was the process of supplanting these civil servants with Arabic-speaking officers begun. By the end of the Umayyad era, however, government affairs were recorded in Arabic, and clerks were Arabic-speaking and usually Muslim in faith.

At the time of the conquest the Byzantine and Sasanid empires were largely on a money economy with gold, silver, and copper coins in wide circulation. The Muslims took these over as media of exchange, sometimes with a phrase from the Koran stamped on. True Muslim-Arabic coins, first minted at Damascus in the reign of Abd al-Malik, were similar in value to coins already in circulation. The gold ones were called "dinars" after the Roman denarius; the silver, "dirhams" from the Greek drachma.

Muslim judges (*kadis*) for the various cities of the empire were usually chosen by the provincial governors and were responsible to them. Since these judges were concerned only with the Muslims, there was little occasion for judges in the villages at this time. Caliphs, generals, viceroys, and governors also held court and handed out justice personally in matters pertaining to political and governmental affairs. Judges, who served as guardians for orphans and incompetents and as managers of religious foundations, were selected from those trained in theology and canon law.

As long as Muawiyah lived, his firm hand checked the factious spirit of the Arabs. However, the two great tribal parties of the Arabs, which existed certainly for a century or two before the advent of Islam, persisted even though submerged throughout the period of the first caliphs. Muhammad refused to recognize the differences and Umar was most intolerant of any display of partisanship. Under the Umayyads, party strife touched a high point and influenced every aspect of political life in all parts of the empire.

Reminiscent of the famous Blues and Greens of the Byzantine Empire, the rivalry of the Arab parties was always keen and often bitter. These party rivalries were largely family affairs, and each group went by a variety of names depending upon what particular family was dominant at the time and place under consideration. One main division was called the South Arabian party. Its members argued that the disintegration of economic and political life in the region of Yemen—perhaps capped by the breaking of the Marib Dam—had forced them to migrate northward and settle on the confines of the desert east of the Jordan and the Dead Sea. Claiming common descent from Kahtan (Joktan of the Book of Genesis), they affected a culture superior to others. The other party, North Arabians, was nomadic in character and believed that its families came from the central and northern areas of Arabia. Calling their common ancestor, Adnan, the North Arabians were clearly the Ishmaelites of the Bible.

Between the two parties any differences of language, culture, and physiognomy had long since disappeared; only legend and rivalry remained to perpetuate the factions. Nevertheless, the feuding between the two was very real, as is attested by the oft-repeated incident of the two-year war in Damascus instigated by the stealing of a watermelon from a garden belonging to a member of the other party. Although the Umayyads asserted that they were above party politics, only Umar II conducted affairs of state with a disregard for party affiliations. The other caliphs always had ties closer with one than with the other; four adhered to the North Arabian party whereas the other Umayyads were supported by the South Arabians. Likewise, some cities were party strongholds: Basrah was staunchly North Arabian, whereas Kufah was a rabid South Arabian center.

Under Muawiyah rebellious forces among Muslims never had an opportunity to show their colors. Ali's son Hasan retired on a pension to his harem in Medina, and upon his death his brother Husayn became the head of the house of Ali. Yet, he remained at peace with the Umayyads until Muawiyah's death. Refusing to recognize Yazid as successor and caliph, Husayn along with others from the families of Muhammad's early Companions rebelled openly. Husayn set out for Kufah with a meager force and at Karbala was surrounded and cut down by Umayyad supporters on the tenth of Muharram, A.H. 61 (October 10, 680). Although at the time it caused hardly a ripple across the Muslim body politic, his death was later celebrated by the Shiite sect of Muslims, which came to regard Husayn and his brother Hasan as martyrs for the faith. Karbala has become a most holy spot, and frequently a kind of passion play is enacted on the tenth of Muharram.

Husayn's martyrdom left opposition to the Umayyads in a most weakened position. When Medina surrendered, Yazid's army proceeded to Mecca, where the rebels sought the protection of the supposed inviolability of the Holy City. In the midst of siege operations which shattered the Kaaba and broke the mysterious Black Stone news of Yazid's death led the Syrian army to withdraw. The North Arabian party in Mecca thereupon openly supported a certain Ibn al-Zubayr, who was recognized as caliph throughout Arabia, Iraq, and Egypt, and even in parts of Syria. Had he been willing to transfer his residence to Damascus, it is probable that all Muslims would have accepted his rule. The contest came on the field of Marj Rahit in Syria; Ibn al-Zubayr's followers were defeated by the South Arabians who placed on the throne Marwan, Muawiyah's cousin and formerly executive secretary to Caliph Uthman.

This civil war of the Umayyads with Husayn and Ibn al-Zubayr was more than a personal or dynastic struggle; it was even more than a violent outbreak of political party rivalry. In the first instance, the lesser families and clans of the Kuraysh of Mecca still resented and begrudged the power and dominance which the Umayyad clan had possessed in the decades just prior to the Hijrah. Added to this bitterness was indignation over the fact that Umayyads had opposed Muhammad almost to the very end; in fact, Muawiyah's father had driven Muhammad and the Muslims from Mecca. That Abu Sufyan's sons and family should inherit Muhammad's mantle was more than the Prophet's Companions could stomach.

More serious in the long run was the moving of the center of the state to Syria. It was inevitable that the wealth and worldliness of that Roman province would effect a marked transformation of the simple Arab life. Visitors from Arabia were shocked at the elegance and pomp of the Damascus court and were scandalized by the flow of wine, the singing girls, and the devotion to the chase exhibited there. All these seemed far removed from the teachings of Muhammad. As the wealth and power of the ruling society increased, idleness, pleasure-seeking, and disregard for Muslim virtues multiplied. It was often told, for example, that Caliph Yazid drank wine daily and had a pet monkey which would become drunk along with him. Caliph al-Walid drank only every other day, whereas Hisham drank wine only on Fridays. The prize went to al-Walid II who enjoyed swimming in a pool of wine, drinking as he swam.

Such antics and the neglect of strict Muslim precepts fanned the fagots on the propaganda fires of all malcontents of Islam. Shiite and Kharijite parties flourished in Iraq, Iran, and Khurasan. Iraq took umbrage over Syrian rule. In a sense it revived the old enmity between East and West exemplified in the wars of the Sasanid and Byzantine empires. Shiites, who held the view that the mantle of the Prophet rightfully belonged to the family of Ali and objected to the idea that might makes right, formed the nucleus of the opposition At this time they were joined by the Kharijites, Muslim anarchists, who objected to all authority and maintained that a council of state rather than any caliph should rule over Muslims.

The third subversive party was that of the Abbasids, led first by Muhammad, a great-grandson of al-Abbas, who in turn was an uncle of the Prophet. This Muhammad circulated the story that one of Ali's grandsons transferred upon his deathbed the rights of the Alids to the Abbasid family. Beginning about the year 740, Abbasids from their headquarters south of the Dead Sea posed as the leaders of the House of Hashim—Alid as well as Abbasid—and gathered under their standard all anti-Umayyads of Islam.

The most valuable support to Alids and Abbasids came from non-Arab Muslims of Iran and Khurasan, who in a restored national vigor objected to an inferior position and demanded the equality preached in Islam. The organizational structure of the Umayyad Empire was decaying rapidly. An atmosphere of vicious, petty, and murderous rivalry surrounded the court; and in every corner of the empire there was strife between the two Arab parties. Such violent partisanship, coupled with the Sybarite life of so many Arab leaders, invited rebellion everywhere and played into the hands of non-Arab Muslims. The Abbasids utilized these factors to the full in their propaganda in the east and gathered Iranians, Khurasanians, Shiites, Alids, and all of the malcontents around their banner, for which they chose the Prophet's color of black. The Umayyad's and Alid's banners were white; that of the Kharijites, red.

In June, 747 Abu al-Abbas, a great-great-grandson of al-Abbas, raised the standard of revolt, and under his Iranian agent a band of Iranians, Khurasanians, and South Arabians took the city of Marw. Iraq fell in 749, and Abu al-Abbas was recognized in Kufah as Caliph. Marwan II met the rival force early in 750 on the bank of the Zab, a tributary of the Tigris. The great Abbasid victory opened all Syria, and Damascus surrendered in April, 750. At an infamous banquet near Jaffa some eighty Umayyads were murdered, and members of the family were hunted from one end of the empire to the other in an Abbasid attempt to extirpate the entire Umayyad tribe. Among the few who escaped was Hisham's grandson, Abd al-Rahman, who made his way to Spain and established the great Umayyad caliphate of Cordoba.

Abu al-Abbas moved the capital of Islam from Damascus to Kufah, establishing Iraq as the center of the Abbasid Empire. The East had been triumphant over the West.

REFERENCES: Chapter 6

Volumes cited at the end of Chapter 4 are pertinent to this chapter.

Alfred Joshua Butler, *The Arab Conquest of Egypt and the Last Thirty Years of the Roman Domination:* Clarendon Press, Oxford, 1902. The best account of the subject.

D. C. Dennett, *Conversion and the Poll Tax in Early Islam:* Harvard University Press, Cambridge, 1950. This volume deals with one of the most vexatious problems of the Umayyads.

Nabih Emin Faris (ed.), *The Arab Heritage:* Princeton University Press, Princeton, 1944. A collection of essays that covers the growth and expansion of the Muslim world.

John B. Glubb, *The Great Arab Conquests:* Prentice-Hall, Englewood Cliffs, 1964. A military history by an English general with long experience in the Middle East, especially in Jordan.

Gustave E. von Grunebaum, *Medieval Islam: A Study in Cultural Orientation:* University of Chicago Press, Chicago, 1946.

————, *Muhammadan Festivals:* Abelard-Schuman, New York, 1951.

Stanley Lane-Poole, *A History of Egypt in the Middle Ages* (600–1500): Methuen, London, 1901. Still useful and authoritative.

————, *The Mohammedan Dynasties:* Constable, London, 1894. A standard work which gives a brief account of each ruling family and lists the members and the date of their lives.

CHAPTER 7

The Flowering of the Muslim World under the Abbasids

The destruction of the Umayyads marked the opening of a new era
in Muslim development. With the establishment of the Abbasid
family in the caliphate the center of Islam shifted eastward to the
Tigris-Euphrates Valley. Since Arabia proper had become insignificant in power and wealth, Damascus with its interior lines of communication and transport no longer held an advantage as the capital of
such an empire. Iraq was more productive than Syria or Egypt and
profited from extensive trade with India, China, the Indies, and central
Asia, whereas commerce languished in the Mediterranean and Europe.
The markets of India and China were fabulous and their industry was
varied; the decaying economy of the West, except for Spain and
Constantinople, was yielding rapidly to the demands of a self-subsistent
agricultural life.

The Abbasids shrewdly capitalized on the obvious worldliness of
the Umayyads and their rapid drift toward the role of a Byzantine
succession dynasty. The Umayyads were weakened further by deep-
seated opposition from the followers of Ali, by hereditary tribal feuds
among the Arabs, and by the resentment of the non-Arab Muslims over
their inferior political and social status. In an adroit propaganda campaign throughout Islam the Abbasids posed as the champion of each
disgruntled group, thereby benefitting from the shifting sands of Arab
politics and establishing themselves as the royal family in possession of
the caliphate.

Hardly was Abu al-Abbas, the first of the line, seated on the throne than he openly showed the insincerity of Abbasid promises. Though he surrounded himself with theologians and pretended to take their advice, positions of authority and power were filled by Abbasids or by trusted family agents. A new governmental official, the chief executioner, always stood near the caliph's throne. Alids (followers of Ali) were ignored; other Arabs received little consideration; viceroys, generals, and ministers who became too wealthy or too popular were executed; and Abbasid rulers governed more imperiously than their predecessors. Heads fell with little compunction. In the inaugural speech Abu al-Abbas referred seriously to himself as "the bloodletter," *al-saffah,* a nickname which has clung to him through the ages. But the true installation of the new empire occurred when his brother Abu Jafar ascended to the caliphate in 754. This ancestor of the next thirty-five caliphs took the sobriquet al-Mansur, meaning rendered victorious, setting the precedent of honorific titles or surnames for Abbasid rulers.

Like many of the Abbasids that followed, al-Mansur pursued and destroyed rival caliphs from the Alid or Shiite party. On one occasion, when his troops had gone to Medina to disperse disloyal Shiites, al-Mansur discovered his personal safety was in question, especially since his residence lay so close to hostile Kufah. The danger led him to build a new capital at the village of Baghdad, where a personal bodyguard of several thousand was on hand at all times. This new circular fortress-palace of al-Mansur grew within a few decades into the fabled luxury-filled city of Baghdad which thrilled the imagination of peoples from the Atlantic to the Pacific.

In the first years of Islam leaders of the Arab community had elected their rulers, while in Roman and Byzantine society emperors had inherited their power and positions. A satisfactory synthesis of these conflicting practices was never achieved in the Muslim Middle East, and the eternal question of succession to the throne sapped the strength and effectiveness of the Abbasid government. To obtain the recognition for al-Mahdi, al-Mansur gave prodigious bribes to his cousin, who had been named to the line of succession by al-Saffah. None the less, al-Hadi was almost passed over by the generals and court ministers in favor of his more popular brother, al-Rashid. The court intrigues involving the accession of later caliphs grew more direct and perfidious as time passed. By the close of the ninth century the question of the succession overshadowed every act of the caliph and dominated the thoughts of the court. By the tenth century caliphs were removed, blinded, and turned out into the streets to beg.

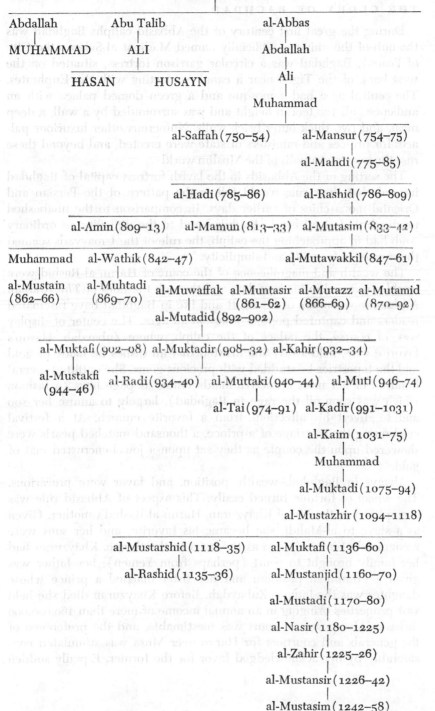

Hashim
|
Abd al-Muttalib
|

Abdallah	Abu Talib	al-Abbas
MUHAMMAD	ALI	Abdallah
HASAN	HUSAYN	Ali
		Muhammad

al-Saffah(750–54)   al-Mansur(754–75)

al-Mahdi(775–85)

al-Hadi(785–86)   al-Rashid(786–809)

al-Amin(809–13)   al-Mamun(813–33)   al-Mutasim(833–42)

Muhammad   al-Wathik(842–47)   al-Mutawakkil(847–61)

al-Mustain   al-Muhtadi   al-Muwaffak   al-Muntasir   al-Mutazz   al-Mutamid
(862–66)   (869–70)   (861–62)   (866–69)   (870–92)

al-Mutadid(892–902)

al-Muktafi(902–08)   al-Muktadir(908–32)   al-Kahir(932–34)

al-Mustakfi   al-Radi(934–40)   al-Muttaki(940–44)   al-Muti(946–74)
(944–46)

al-Tai(974–91)   al-Kadir(991–1031)

al-Kaim(1031–75)

Muhammad

al-Muktadi(1075–94)

al-Mustazhir(1094–1118)

al-Mustarshid(1118–35)   al-Muktafi(1136–60)

al-Rashid(1135–36)   al-Mustanjid(1160–70)

al-Mustadi(1170–80)

al-Nasir(1180–1225)

al-Zahir(1225–26)

al-Mustansir(1226–42)

al-Mustasim(1242–58)

THE GLORY OF BAGHDAD

During the great first century of the Abbasid caliphs Baghdad was the hub of the universe. Officially named Madinat al-Salem (the City of Peace), Baghdad was a circular garrison fortress, situated on the west bank of the Tigris near a canal connecting with the Euphrates. The central area had a mosque and a green domed palace with an audience hall 130 feet in height and was surrounded by a wall, a deep moat, and two thick outer brick walls. Numerous other luxurious palaces for princes and ministers of state were erected, and beyond these rose the busy metropolis of the Muslim world.

The setting of the Abbasids in the lavish fortress capital of Baghdad insured that their rule would follow the pattern of the Persian and Oriental monarchies of earlier days. In comparison to the unabashed prodigality of royal life in Baghdad and to the difficulty an ordinary Arab had in approaching the caliph, the rule of the Umayyads seemed the essence of frugality and simplicity.

The wealth and magnificence of the court of Harun al-Rashid were world renowned in his own day, and through the tales of *The Arabian Nights* the splendors of his court and life in Baghdad have fascinated readers and captured popular fancy in all ages. The center of display was, of course, the palace of the caliph, where Zubaydah, Harun's favorite wife, held sway. She insisted that all dishes be made of gold and the tapestries be studded with precious gems. She outfitted several hundred of her most attractive maidservants as page boys (a fashion which was soon all the rage in Baghdad), largely to amuse her son and to divert his affections from a favorite eunuch. At a festival celebrating the marriage of a prince, a thousand matched pearls were showered upon the couple as they sat upon a jewel-encrusted mat of gold.

Always in Baghdad, wealth, position, and favor were precarious. The wheel of fortune turned easily. This aspect of Abbasid rule was exemplified in the life of Khayzuran, Harun al-Rashid's mother. Given as a slave to al-Mahdi, she became his favorite; and her sons were recognized at an early age as the heirs to the throne. Khayzuran had her family brought to court (perhaps from Yemen); her father was given a prominent position; and her sister married a prince whose daughter was the famous Zubaydah. Before Khayzuran died she held vast properties bringing in an annual income of more than 160,000,000 dirhams. Her power at court was inestimable, and the preference of the generals and courtiers for Harun over Musa was stimulated considerably by her acknowledged favor for the former. Equally sudden and precipitous could be one's fall as the lives of many favorites and advisers attested.

About the court any word or act of flattery, a song or poem that pleased, or a deed well done was rewarded most handsomely: 60,000 dinars tossed to the singer of a pleasant tune with complimentary lines; 100,000 dirhams to a poet who beguiled at the right moment; a landed estate to an entertainer or a dancer! For a sonnet extolling Harun al-Rashid on a trivial occasion a poet was given 5,000 gold pieces, a robe of honor, ten Greek slave girls, and a horse from the imperial stables.

From the four corners of the known world came royal embassies bearing gifts and seeking the caliph's favor. Most publicized of these, at least in the West, was the mission sent by Charlemagne in 797 to secure greater safety for Frankish pilgrims to the Holy Land, to get Abbasid aid against Umayyad Spain, and to seek co-operation against the Byzantine Empire. No mention of this embassy has been found in Eastern sources, and there is little evidence that it ever accomplished any of its aims. Still, the trophies from the journey, the most fantastic being an elephant, so magnified and embellished the incident for the West that Baghdad and Arabia became romantic, incredible, and fabulous places and Harun al-Rashid a person in some far-off never-never land.

Intellectual interests of the Abbasids, hand in hand with imperial munificence, produced a great cultural flowering. The learning of the Greco-Romans, the Iranians, and the Hindus was translated into Arabic and assimilated into Muslim culture. Arabic became the common language not only for theology and jurisprudence but for philosophy, science, and the humanities. History, political treatises, literature, poetry, and etiquette came largely from Iran; astronomy and mathematics, from India; philosophy, medicine, and science, from Greece. By the middle of the ninth century the main works of Aristotle, Plato, Euclid, Ptolemy, Hippocrates, and Galen had been translated into Arabic and were well known the length and breadth of the Islamic world. Royal patronage set the stage for translations and the expansion and dissemination of knowledge. Every prince, governor, and high official followed the same course and became, on a lesser scale, a patron of scholars.

ADMINISTRATIVE ORGANIZATION

The Khurasani soldiery was the power that had raised the Abbasids to the caliphate; and for several generations a Khurasan bodyguard maintained imperial authority in Baghdad and elsewhere. Eastern or

Iranian influences grew apace at the court. After the building of Baghdad Iranian dress, manners, and techniques spread quickly throughout the empire, especially in fashionable society. Foremost among the Iranian introductions was the rank and office of vizir (*wazir*). The Umayyads had had advisers and ministers heading various departments of the government. Under the Abbasids, however, there arose the office of chief minister, the vizir, who became the *alter ego* of the caliph. The vizir's power was almost unlimited and the office was frequently handed down from father to son.

The first family of vizirs was the famous Barmakids of the last half of the eighth century. Khalid ibn Barmak, son of a Buddhist chief priest of Balkh, held the confidence of al-Saffah and al-Mansur. Although a Shiite in faith, Khalid served as minister of finance and then as governor, became a general, and acted as guardian of Harun. Khalid amassed a great fortune; on one occasion he was forced to pay 3,000,000 dirhams of taxes which as governor he had not forwarded to Baghdad. His son Yahya served al-Mahdi as vizir but fell into disfavor and was imprisoned by al-Hadi.

The apogee of Barmakid fortunes was reached under Harun al-Rashid. Yahya became the first true grand vizir, issuing orders and managing the empire with great skill and profit. His sons al-Fadl and Jafar also exercised unlimited power. The son al-Fadl followed in his father's footsteps as governor and vizir, while Jafar became Harun's boon companion and confidant. The Barmakids lived in a sumptuous manner, and their generosity to their own favorites and clients became proverbial throughout the Arabic-speaking world. Yahya, however, was distressed by Jafar's personal and intimate relationship with al-Rashid, fearing that it would bring disaster. The family was after all Iranian and Shiite and could not hope for social, political, or religious equality with the Abbasids. In 803 without warning Jafar was beheaded, undoubtedly because he used Harun's friendship to impinge too far upon royal prerogatives; Yahya, al-Fadl, and two others were imprisoned; and the Barmakid fortune—palaces, lands, and some thirty million dinars in cash—was confiscated.

Other families of vizirs rose and fell, and with them rival generals and armies. Under the Abbasids generals were always a significant factor in obtaining the throne. Again following al-Rashid, intense rivalry arose between the voluptuous al-Amin, son of the famed Zubaydah, and the more serious and steady al-Mamun, son of an Iranian slavegirl. The latter had the better generals; and marching from his base in Marw with the full support of the Iranian army, he attacked Baghdad and beheaded his caliph brother. Although al-Mamun ruled illustriously for twenty years, generals henceforth decided the succession to the throne. The rulers al-Mamun and al-Mutasim, Harun's son by a Turkish slavegirl, brought Turkish slaves to Baghdad and Samarra (al-Mutasim's capital) in such numbers that the chief of the Turkish bodyguard became the actual ruler of the state and acquired the title *Sultan* (he-with-authority).

Rapidly after the middle of the ninth century the Abbasid caliphs receded into the background as puppet rulers. Powerful captains in the eastern and western provinces seized authority and established independent Muslim states. The unity of Islam, which had already been cracked in the 750's by the establishment of the Umayyad state in Spain, was completely shattered with the advent of the ruling military bodyguard of the Abbasids.

ECONOMIC LIFE

The bases of Abbasid wealth rested upon agriculture and a century of relatively capable, honest, and stable administration of the provinces. Caliph al-Mansur established such a vigilant and judicious system of government throughout the empire and enforced such thrift that it took more than a century of profligate largesse to dislocate the economy of the state. In Iraq the ancient canal system was operated so efficiently and extended to such an extent that productivity rose to a peak never matched in any period of its long history. In that same century imperial revenues from Egypt, Syria, and Iran showered great wealth upon the ruling circles and the inhabitants of the capital cities.

As a natural corollary to this organized agriculture and governmental stability, a flourishing commerce and, for that age, an advanced technical industry arose. The great preponderance of Islamic commerce was in the nature of "domestic" trade. Caravans plied the trade routes from the Indus to the Pyrenees, distributing the wares of each province throughout the empire and exchanging manufactures of Iran for those of Egypt, carpets of Tabaristan for paper of Baghdad. Handsome profits were realized, but great fortunes were as easily lost.

The bulk of Muslim "foreign" trade was with the Far East. From Baghdad and Basrah Muslim merchants carried their goods by sea to China, India, and the Archipelago, but the main route to China lay overland through Samarkand. Trade with Italy, France, and Germany, or with Constantinople, Russia, and Scandinavia was undoubtedly profitable. It seemed so trivial, however, that Muslim traders left it for the most part to Christian and Jewish itinerants. Goods from the Middle East were too expensive and too refined for barbarous Western tastes, and the West had little to offer in exchange.

Concurrent with the rich agriculture and brisk commerce of the Abbasid Empire, there developed an active industry in every province.

Artisan traditions of the ancient Middle East had never perished, and under a relatively secure political system these industries revived and expanded. Textiles of linen, cotton, silk, and wool were the most important. Although each area produced high-quality fabrics of many types, every city or province excelled in some particular pattern or technique; carpets from Bukhara, silk kerchiefs from Kufah, linens from Egypt, damask from Damascus, and brocades from Shiraz gained world renown. Special skills were often localized and families guarded trade secrets, which were passed as prized possessions from father to son through the centuries.

The science of paper making was acquired from China, and by the tenth century paper mills existed in Iran, Iraq, and Egypt. In the twelfth century one was built in Spain. Fine glass was produced in Egypt, and the glass industry of old Phoenicia still survived along the Syrian coast. The ceramic industry in the Middle East reached back into the most distant past, and the Abbasid era created some of the finest potteries and glazed tile. Samarkand, Rayy, Baghdad, and Damascus won fame for their decorated porcelains and their fine blues, greens, and turquoise shades. Middle Eastern artisans were equally skilled in the shaping, working, and hammering of metals: iron, steel, copper, brass, silver, and gold. Other industries of great note manufactured fine soaps, dyes, perfume, jewelry, leather, inlaid and decorated wood, and enamel work on wood and metal.

The Middle East in the eighth and ninth centuries utilized many arts, skills, and techniques of the handicrafts of China, India, Iran, and the East Roman empire, and those of the early civilizations of Greece, Egypt, and Mesopotamia. The synthesis of these gave great life to Muslim industry, which was regarded in Europe as the marvel of the ages. The slow movement of Middle Eastern know-how across the Mediterranean and over the Pyrenees gave rise to the development of similar handicrafts in Europe.

The Abbasid championing of non-Arab elements within the Muslim empire promoted a rapid Arabization of the empire. Iranians, Berbers, Syrian Christians, Copts, and others began to speak Arabic in their daily living. Science, philosophy, literature, and books of knowledge from other cultures and tongues were rendered into Arabic. And an Arab civilization evolved in which poets, scholars, musicians, merchants, soldiers, viziers, and concubines considered themselves cultural Arabs and little heed was given to parentage or birthplace.

Although Arab civilization came to prevail in the Abbasid era from the borders of China to the Pyrenees, there was never more than a fleeting political unity. The theological views of the followers of Ali were never modified, and as time passed more and more religious sects arose to battle against authority. Social and economic ills disturbed the empire periodically. Ambitious and not too loyal soldiers sought to carve out their own principalities. Centered upon a land area, communications and transportation over most of the empire were costly, slow, and tedious. Distant provinces were difficult to control; and, as caliphs grew less and less concerned with the gruelling task of governing, even nearer provinces flaunted the wishes of the Abbasid rulers. When Abbasid caliphs degenerated into mere puppets in the hands of generals of the bodyguard, governors and soldiers in the provinces readily declared their independence.

Local rulers, however, followed the common patterns of Abbasid government and administration so that Muslim-Arab civilization continued to prevail. Political loyalties might differ, and even sometimes religious doctrines; but artists, men of letters, scientists, merchants, and travelers were as much at home in Cordoba as in Cairo, Baghdad, or Samarkand. Provincial governors, even those who were not independent, imitated as sumptuously as they could the court at Baghdad. From India to Spain were built artistic palaces and impressive mosques where petty princes lived in the grand manner among poets, scholars, artists, soldiers, dancing slaves, and fawning courtiers.

SPAIN AND NORTH AFRICA

Abd al-Rahman, grandson of Caliph Hisham, escaped from Abbasid vengeance, and, making his way in disguise through Syria, Egypt, and North Africa, reestablished the Umayyad dynasty in Spain in 756. First as amirs and then in the tenth century as caliphs the rulers maintained at Cordoba a court which enjoyed an eminence that rivaled its contemporary in Baghdad. Many distinguished scholars, scientists, and literati of the Muslim world flourished under their patronage. At its zenith in the tenth century Cordoba had half a million inhabitants, seven hundred mosques, three hundred public baths, and a royal palace comprising four hundred rooms which ranked second only to those at Baghdad and Constantinople in size and splendor.

Umayyad power, however, commenced to deteriorate toward the middle of the tenth century. As with the Abbasids in Baghdad the palace guard seized control; and Muslim Spain disintegrated into smaller states (Seville, Malaga, Toledo, Saragoza, and Granada) under the leadership of various families. In the eleventh century resurgent Christian Spain began a drive which ended in 1492 with the capitulation of the sultan of Granada, the last Muslim ruler in Spain. Though Muslim law and government were terminated, the deportation of the Spanish Muslims (Morescos) was not enforced until a special edict was issued in 1609 by Philip III.

In 788 Idris ibn Abdallah, a descendant of Ali, established an independent Shiite regime in Morocco. From their capital at Fez the Idrisids ruled Morocco for two centuries, firmly implanting Islam in that corner of Africa before succumbing to the Umayyads of Cordoba. In the middle of the eleventh century a religious military brotherhood, the Murabits (Almoravides), swept out from an island in the Senegal, conquering Algeria, Morocco, and southern Spain and establishing Marrakesh and Seville as their capitals. But the luxuries, vices, and complexities of civilization prepared the way for the submission of the Murabits in the twelfth century to the Muwahhids (Almohades), a band of Muslim reformers originating in the Atlas region of Morocco. Spain toppled, too; and within a decade the Muwahhids overpowered Algeria, Tunisia, and Tripoli. They were driven from Spain in 1212; and when their capital, Marrakesh, was taken a half century later by Berber tribes, the Muwahhids disappeared from the scene.

Harun al-Rashid appointed Ibrahim ibn al-Aghlab governor of Africa in 800. The latter, however, declared his independence, and for a century the Aghlabids ruled as free amirs from Kayrawan in Tunisia. Their fleets ravaged the coasts of Italy and France, seizing Malta, Sicily, and Sardinia. The great mosque of Kayrawan was built by the Aghlabids and soon became for western Muslims a venerated shrine, next in importance and holiness to Mecca, Medina, and Jerusalem. But in 909 the Aghlabids were engulfed by a Shiite uprising which placed on the throne one who claimed to be a descendant of Fatimah, the Prophet's daughter.

Meanwhile, beginning with the middle of the ninth century, a succession of clever governors and two short-lived Turkish dynasties, Tulunids and Ikhshidids, ruled Egypt independently of Abbasid dominion. In the last half of the tenth century Egypt was conquered by the Fatimids of North Africa, who took the title of caliph and transferred their capital from Kayrawan to the newly constructed city of Cairo.

Under the Tulunids and Ikhshidids and to a greater extent under the Fatimids the Egyptian court and its society experienced a prosperity and a great burst of accomplishment in commerce, art, letters, and learning. No longer did even a part of the produce or taxes of Egypt flow to Baghdad. Though Shiite in faith, Fatimid Egypt participated greatly in the artistic and intellectual endeavors of the Muslim world; most of the great works of medieval Muslim art and architecture still extant in Egypt date from the Tulunid and Fatimid periods.

The Tulunids added Syria to their realm and established a naval base at Acre. The Ikhshidids had been given the Hijaz and Yemen by the Abbasids so that at their height about the year 1000 the Fatimids ruled all of the western Muslim world except Spain and the Fatimid caliph's name was mentioned in the Friday prayers from the Atlantic to the Euphrates. However, because of idle rulers and foreign slave armies the Fatimid Empire began to break up early in the eleventh century. To a considerable degree it was this disintegration which permitted the handfuls of Western knights called Crusaders, to penetrate, capture, and hold the Christian Holy Land and the Syrian littoral in the twelfth and thirteenth centuries.

THE EASTERN PROVINCES

East of Baghdad, the Abbasid Empire was likewise succumbing to the laxity of the caliph's rule and falling into the hands of aggressive soldiers and politicians who founded ephemeral dynasties. In the ninth century the Tahirids and Saffarids extended their sway from Marw to the frontiers of India. In the tenth century the Samanids seized all of Khurasan, but settled in Transoxiana, establishing Bukhara as their capital and Samarkand as the leading city of the state. Culture and civilization, however, did not perish and the new forces were quickly assimilated. This was illustrated by the Samanid ruler who invited the young Ibn Sina (Avicenna) to Bukhara and gave him free run of the state library. Under the Samanids Firdawsi wrote his first poetry, marking the rebirth of Persian literature. From the Muslim conquest to the Samanid period Arabic had been the language used everywhere by scholars and men of letters; this new era signaled the advent of the brilliant works of Muslim Iran.

From the bodyguard of the Samanids a Turkish slave Alptigin rose through the ranks to govern Khurasan. Fleeing from the Samanid domain, he captured Ghaznah and established the famed Ghaznawid empire of Afghanistan and the Punjab. The most eminent of the family was Alptigin's grandson Mahmud, who led nearly a score of expeditions into India and in the eleventh century laid the foundations of the permanent Islamization of north and northwest India. Loot from Hindu temples gave him the material strength to destroy the Samanids and extend his state to include most of the eastern provinces of the Muslim world. Although a vestige of the Ghaznawid empire remained at Lahore until 1186, decline followed rapidly upon the death of Mahmud in 1030. Muslim independent states in India broke away, and Buwayhid Iranians and Seljuk Turks appeared in western areas of the Ghaznawid empire.

In Baghdad itself the authority of the Abbasid caliph vanished almost completely. Only the idea remained. Turkish captains of the bodyguard deposed caliphs at will; at one time three blind ex-caliphs were beggars on the streets of Baghdad. Taking the title *amir al-umara* (literally, commander of commanders, but better, prince of princes) the *de facto* ruler imprinted his name on coins and insisted that his name be coupled with the puppet caliph in the Friday prayers.

Toward the middle of the tenth century a Shiite Iranian, Ibn Buwayh, entered Baghdad with a strong army and was recognized by the caliph as the commander of commanders. Making and un-making caliphs openly, the Buwayhids of Shiraz took various titles such as king (*malik*) or king of kings (*malik al-muluk* or *shahanshah*) and ruled over what remained of the Abbasid state. They beautified their city and brought to it many learned men. For a century Shiraz rivaled Baghdad, Ghazna, Bukhara, Cairo, and Cordoba in culture and splendor. But in the eleventh century Buwayhid fought against Buwayhid for the position of king and in the end fell easy prey to the Turks riding in from the east.

THE TURKS

Turkish nomads from the Kirghiz steppes of Turkestan wandered into the Transoxiana region and became partially settled there toward the middle of the tenth century. Their chieftain or khan under the Samanids was Seljuk, and for three centuries his dynasty played such an outstanding role in the Muslim world from Syria eastward and so dominated the Turkish elements of society that even today all Muslim Turks of that age bear the name of Seljuk Turks.

The true founder of the dynasty, Seljuk's grandson Tughril, ascended to power rapidly in Khurasan. Defeating the Ghaznawids and ejecting the Buwayhids from Iran, Tughril entered Baghdad with an army in 1055; he was recognized King of the East and the West and *al-Sultan*. Henceforth, Seljuk rulers adopted sultan as their official title.

Tughril's nephew Alparslan followed as sultan and succeeded in gathering within his domain the vast lands of the Muslim world from the frontiers of China to the Mediterranean. Having expanded into Armenia and taken the Byzantine emperor prisoner in the decisive Battle of Manzikert in 1071, Alparslan opened Asia Minor to his Turkish nomads. His horsemen camped on the shores of the Sea of Marmara and lay astride the commercial and pilgrim routes of Asia Minor. His son Malikshah pushed westward and southward, taking Damascus and Jerusalem and threatening Fatimid Egypt. When he made Baghdad his capital, the old imperial city of the Abbasids became once again the hub of the eastern Muslim universe and recaptured much of its abandoned glory.

The political genius through the reigns of Alparslan and Malikshah was Nizam al-Mulk, their principal vizir. A cultured and versatile Iranian, Nizam al-Mulk founded the renowned Nizamiyah Academy or university in Baghdad and wrote the *Siyasatnamah,* a scholarly monograph on the science of government. Nizam also revised the calendar and is perhaps best known in the Western world as the patron of the Persian astronomer-poet Umar Khayyam.

Any semblance of unity among the Seljuks vanished in 1092 upon the death of Malikshah and the assassination of Nizam al-Mulk. In prior years there had been numerous civil wars among members of the family; upon the demise of these two leaders the breakup into petty Seljuk states was immediate. One son succeeded to the sultanate in Baghdad. A brother held Damascus and Aleppo, although these cities were soon seized by different sons. A cousin ruled Asia Minor from Konya; others possessed Jerusalem, Edessa, Mosul, Diyarbakir, and Amasya. Soon afterward the appearance of the Crusaders from the West disrupted Seljuk rule in Syria even further, though the main branch of the dynasty maintained its hold upon Baghdad until 1194.

The death of Malikshah and the collapse of the Seljuk state definitely heralded for medieval times the end of a Muslim political entity strong enough and sufficiently organized to dominate the Middle East. Under the rule of Malikshah a merchant could travel alone unmolested with his goods from Samarkand to Aleppo. But within a few years intraregional political anarchy and its disastrous social and economic chaos lured eastward the Crusader. Not until the appearance of the Turks from their strong base on the Bosphorus in the sixteenth century did the Middle East again experience a stable political existence.

REFERENCES: *Chapter 7*

Titles mentioned at the end of Chapters 2, 4, and 6 contain material significant for this chapter.

Nabia Abbott, *Two Queens of Baghdad: Mother and Wife of Harun al-Rashid:* University of Chicago Press, Chicago, 1946. Not only does this volume detail the lives of Khayzuran and Zubaydah, but it is full of the color and life of Baghdad in the eighth and ninth centuries.

A. J. Arberry, *Shiraz: Persian City of Saints and Poets:* University of Oklahoma Press, Norman, 1960. A colorful story of a city of artists and intellectuals.

F. W. Buckler, *Harunu'l-Rashid and Charles the Great:* Mediaeval Academy of America, Cambridge, 1931. An account of the mission from Charlemagne to Baghdad and its return.

Richard N. Frye, *Bukhara: The Medieval Achievement:* University of Oklahoma Press, Norman, 1965. An authoritative account of one of the great cities of Central Asia.

John B. Glubb, *The Course of Empire: The Arabs and Their Successors:* Hodder and Stoughton, London, 1965. An emphasis on the military aspects.

George E. Kirk, *A Short History of the Middle East from the Rise of Islam to Modern Times:* Praeger, New York, 1955. Although covering the entire period, it brings out the main points of each age.

Edward William Lane, *Arabian Society in the Middle Ages: Studies from the Thousand and One Nights:* Chatto and Windus, London, 1883. Although an old book it still contains much of value for this period.

Guy Le Strange, *Baghdad During the Abbasid Caliphate:* Oxford University Press, London, 1924. An interesting description of the great city at its height.

Reuben Levy, *A Baghdad Chronicle:* Cambridge University Press, Cambridge, 1929. A survey of the city from the eighth to the thirteenth century.

H. St. John B. Philby, *Harun al-Rashid:* Appleton-Century-Crofts, London, 1934. An important biography by a British Orientalist who became a convert to Islam and served as an adviser for many years at the court of the kings of Saudi Arabia.

Percy M. Sykes, *A History of Persia,* 2 vols.: Macmillan, London, 1930. A standard volume for the medieval period of Iran.

CHAPTER 8

Muslim Theology and Law

THEOLOGY

The uncomplicated, direct, and ethical religion preached by Muhammad appealed to the untutored Arab of Mecca and Medina and to the unlettered nomad of the desert. In general it was easily adjusted to the needs of the theocratic state under Muhammad and the Companions who immediately followed him at Medina.

Upon the spread of Islam and Muslim rule beyond Arabia and the establishment of regimes based on military power, Muhammad's theocracy faced unforeseen conditions. Succeeding generations of Muslims were exposed to the intellectualized philosophies current in the acquired provinces and developed a finely drawn Islamic theology.

Though the political capital of Islam was transferred to Damascus and then to Baghdad, Medina maintained for several centuries its ascendancy as a center of Muslim theology. Opinions not subscribed to by the doctors of Medina were declared to be in serious error. Divergent views led to the formation of groups branded as heretical by the orthodox of Medina. At the time of the disputation between Ali and Muawiyah the Kharijites broke away, rejecting the concept of compromise which Ali proposed. Shortly thereafter the Kharijites hardened into a sect which held that good works are the measure of faith and the only path to salvation. They also insisted upon pursuing openly and literally the commandment to preach to all men a righteous life and to restrain them, by the sword if necessary, from doing evil. Laxity of life in Damascus induced others to uphold belief in the adequacy of inherent faith in attaining personal salvation. Rebuked by Medina, these Murjiites, as they were termed, eased their ethics to political accommodation under the Umayyads and found their redemption in the doctrine of predestination.

In the formative period of Muslim theology those between these two extremes were known as Mutazilites. By the time of Harun al-Rashid, however, Mutazilites were entangled in Aristotelian and Hellenistic Christian philosophies and engaged in adjusting Islam to Greek logic. Adhering to rationalism in the ninth century, they lost acceptance when the orthodox creed was pronounced in the tenth century by al-Ashari of Baghdad and fixed in the following century by al-Ghazzali (Algazel) of Khurasan.

Three theological arguments stood out above all others. Foremost was the question of God's omnipotence in relation to man's responsibility or, as it devolved to the religious plane, the problem of predestination and free will. The second great problem related to the nature of the Koran: Was it uncreated and eternal or was it created? The third troublesome subject centered upon the nature of God and His attributes. If God could hear, see, and speak, was not His unity in doubt?

According to al-Ashari the apparent contradiction embodied in the concepts of predestination and free will was explained by the doctrine that man did acquire responsibility for his actions but only because God willed it. For al-Ashari the Koran was pre-existent and eternal; the words or expressions were created and revealed by the angels to the Prophet only as guides to the eternal Word. The apparent contradiction between the unity of God and His other, more human attributes referred to in the Koran was explained by the dogma that God was One and Eternal, but that His existence was not the same as existence in the world. Thus, these attributes were real but were divested of all anthropomorphism.

Many other points in orthodox theology were established by al-Ashari such as: right and wrong were what they were because God declared them to be so; and God could inflict pain on man in this world or in the next without being unjust.

Even al-Ashari, however, was cursed by the religious men of Medina, because they considered his theology too rationalistic and too far removed from the Islam of Muhammad. Asharite scholastics remained unpopular in Baghdad for many years until the advent of al-Ghazzali, whose writing and teaching united the modified Greek logic and philosophy of al-Ashari with Muhammad's religion to create a faith which has remained the basis of orthodox Islam to the present day.

THE SCIENCE OF TRADITION

When the word of the Koran did not appear to give the answer to some specific problem, the divines of Medina and the pious throughout Islam looked for guidance in the words and actions of Muhammad or in those which he had allowed. Arab tribes were devoted to traditions, and custom (*sunnah*) was a powerful force in their lives. In the new community established by Muhammad and severed from many tribal customs, the life of Muhammad served as the touchstone for proper Muslim thought and conduct.

Early in Muslim history great collections of these statements and deeds of Muhammad were made. Aishah was the source of several thousand; and Medina, where so many Companions resided, became the center of the compilations. Each saying was called a *hadith*, or a tradition; and the whole body of these traditions was known as the *hadith*. When forgeries appeared, each *hadith* acquired an introduction giving its full pedigree of transmission. Scholars developed a science with respect to these traditions to establish which were authentic and which spurious. Each sect of Islam, each lawyer, and each theologian chose the most suitable traditions on which to base some contention or press a point.

The first written collections were instigated for judicial ends, but by the ninth century the collections and literature on the subject grew so voluminous that the science of *hadith* evolved. The author al-Bukhari, who died in 870, published his collection under the title, *al-Sahih* (*The Genuine*). Containing over 7,000, it was pronounced by the orthodox as the most authoritative source of tradition. One of the largest collections was that of Ibn Hanbal, who assembled nearly 30,000 to form a corpus of tradition that served as the basis of his law code.

Acceptance of a body of traditions in time established for Islam a Muhammadan *sunnah*, a new customary or common law. Attachment to these traditions by the orthodox Muslim community identified them as following the Islamic *sunnah* and thus gave them the name of Sunnites.

MUSLIM LAW

Early Muslims, pious and devout, perceived hardly any difference between law and religion. Only God knew the perfect law and co-existing with Him was natural law, comprising right and justice. Islam, then, was the ideal system and its law pointed the "path" (*Shariah*) to an individual's salvation; divine law recognized good and evil. Law preceded the state, which only existed to enforce the law. If the state failed to enforce the law, the state's validity ceased. The caliph as head of the state was charged principally with the enforcement of law. Divine law was inexorable and unchanging, allowing no consideration for time or place. Muslims living beyond the pale of Islam still were bound by the law. Law upheld the common good of the community and only served individual interests when these conformed to those of the Muslim community as a whole. Islamic law had to be observed in good faith and sincerity; duplicity and dissimulation were repudiated.

The Muslim system of law grew largely from two roots: the Koran and the traditions. At an early date, however, three other sources—analogy, consensus, and opinion—had a profound effect upon the *Shariah*. Caliphs and their judges, even in Medina, discovered that the Koran and the traditions were not explicit with respect to many situations with which they had to deal. In the absence of a definite statement, judges and lawyers resorted to the use of analogy (*kiyas*) to some instance in the Koran or the traditions in deciding a case brought before them. Although the strictest judges did not practice analogy on the grounds that it allowed too much to human judgment, it was, nevertheless, adopted widely in the eighth century as a legal aid and from precedent to precedent became an integral part of the *Shariah*.

In the same century Malik ibn Anas, a jurist-theologian of Medina, compiled a book of traditions which incorporated many of the local juridical customs and practices. This procedure introduced the element of public consensus (*ijma*). At first it was reserved to Medina, but in the following century it was widened by al-Shafii to include the consensus of the Muslim community at large. Although criticized by many who believed that it was too difficult to secure unanimity among widely scattered Muslim scholars, consensus enabled Islam through the centuries to adapt its institutions to a changing world.

A third additional source of Muslim law has been private opinion (*ray*). Private opinion was never quite accepted as a fifth principle of the *Shariah*, but it was widely practiced. Early caliphs employed it extensively until bitter complaints that legislation by man corrupted divine law forced its abandonment. Nevertheless, most caliphs and later rulers were compelled by administrative necessity to issue laws and decrees which were sanctioned almost wholly by opinion. Such laws and regulations were later termed *Kanuns*, from the Greek and Latin word. Thus, Muslim canon law meant civil and secular law, whereas Islamic divine law was the equivalent of Western canon law.

FOUR ORTHODOX SCHOOLS

The orthodox jurists accepted the five roots of the *Shariah* but differed as to which traditions were genuine and as to the weight which ought to be allowed to analogy, consensus, and opinion in establishing a viable Muslim code of law. At the time of al-Mansur it was suggested that he codify and enforce the diverse laws in the empire. Local particularism, however, won the day, and numerous systems prevailed among the Muslims. Since the eleventh century four principal schools of legal practice have been recognized as permissible by the orthodox, and law schools such as the al-Azhar in Cairo have carried instruction in all four of the rites.

In point of development the earliest school was the Hanafite. Abu-Hanifah, legal scholar of Kufah and Baghdad, held a tolerant view on the use of analogy and consensus and particularly emphasized the value and necessity of private opinion and judgment on the part of those administering the law. By the eleventh century, however, a strong conservative movement closed the door on further innovations in the matter of juridical opinions. Judges, henceforth, could allow only opinions previously rendered and were required to adhere closely to the Hanafite teachings. The Hanafite rite was the established procedure followed in the Ottoman empire, parts of India, and central Asia.

Historically, the second orthodox school was the Malikite. Malik ibn Anas of Medina, who died in 795, codified the traditions of Islam and acknowledged the authority of the consensus of the Medina community. Malikite jurists, however, never equivocated in their stand against general consensus, private opinion, and the broad use of analogy. The Malikite school was accepted in Spain, and still prevails in North Africa and eastern Arabia.

Next to the Hanafite school in general acceptance has been that of the Shafiite. The jurist al-Shafii studied under Malik in Medina and taught in Baghdad and Fustat (Cairo), where he died in 820. The Shafiite rites permitted wider use of consensus than did those of the Malikites, and al-Shafii asserted that consensus was the safest and highest legislative authority in Islam. The Shafiite school dominates legal practice in Palestine, Lower Egypt, eastern Africa, western and southern Arabia, parts of India, and the East Indies.

The Hanbalite school was the fourth and smallest among the orthodox schools. Its founder, Ahmad ibn Hanbal, a student of al-Shafii, rebelled against the teachings of his master. The Hanbalites accepted neither private opinion nor analogy and scorned the use of consensus. The only valid basis of Muslim law, besides the Koran, were the traditions. They would not accept public office, and Ibn Hanbal was beaten and persecuted by al-Mamun and al-Mutasim. Although more than 500,000 attended Hanbal's funeral when he died in Baghdad in 855, Hanbalism was too rigid to be popular or practical over the centuries and had only scattered followers in Syria and Iraq. After the Ottoman conquest the doctrine perished, to be revived in the eighteenth century by the Wahhabis in central Arabia, where the Hanbalite rites are still observed.

In addition to the four principal codes of law, another body of law evolved from a court practice of submitting the summary of involved and important cases to a learned jurist, as a consultant, for an opinion. Such a consultant was called a *mufti;* and his reply, which presented the legal issues and indicated the proper decision, was a *fatwa. Fatwas* were later collected and served as guides to the courts in rendering judgments. Until the advent of the Ottoman empire *muftis* more or less remained free from control or restraint by the government.

RATIONALISM

In essence all of these jurist-theologians were attempting to fashion a system of law by a synthesis of Islamic truths and the highly refined and developed rationalism of the Greek philosophers. In the Umayyad period those favoring the introduction of Hellenistic logic into Muslim theology were called Mutazilites. The arguments respecting the nature of God and the Koran rocked the empire. The debates lasted for several centuries, and the particular views of each caliph determined which opinion flourished at any given time. Hisham put to death several who preached the doctrines of the created Koran and of free will. Caliph al-Mamun persecuted all but Mutazilites and ruthlessly suppressed all who did not support free thought. Caliph al-Mutawakkil ousted the Mutazilites. Eventually, theologians under al-Ashari and the learned founders of the schools of religious law brought the controversy to rest and orthodox dogma was established.

The great philosophic efforts, however, had the effect of taking Islam away from the people and ran the danger of destroying it as a practical religion. Man desired a living experience of God, not a metaphysical or conceptual discussion of religion. To the simple Muslim God was a Personage always near at hand. One could talk to God as a bedouin's prayer in a time of drought attested: "O God of the devotees, what is the matter with us and You? You used to give us water—What has possessed You? Do send rain down on us. Exert Yourself!"

ASCETICISM AND MYSTICISM

In the first years after Muhammad piety in Islam took the form of asceticism. In a manner similar to the practices of holy men in Christian Syria and Mesopotamia pious Muslims seeking knowledge of God and salvation for themselves adopted and preached asceticism. Prayer, fasting, solitary meditations, and prolonged vigils would lead the soul to God. Poverty, humility, patience, repentance, and silence in this world for the believer who was seeking godliness would save him from eternal chastisement and permit him to come into the presence of God, to taste the unalloyed and unabated joys of Paradise, and to abide therein to eternity.

In spite of a waning of ascetic tendencies in the Abbasid period the traits and virtues of asceticism remained strong forces among Muslims across the centuries. Sultans, generals, rich merchants, judges, and scholars might not adopt ascetic practices themselves; but they usually paid open deference, sometimes approaching veneration, to those who did.

Toward the end of the eighth century mysticism entered into Islam with a great impetus. Theology and philosophy had never affected the masses; and after the first half of the ninth century the majority of the literate community found little of interest in the hairsplitting of the scholastics. For religious experience they turned to mysticism. Knowledge of God was to be achieved by the inner light of the individual soul, not by the intellectual methods of the philosopher.

Mysticism spread over Islam, bringing into the creed of the Koran and the preaching of Muhammad all of the quietism and occult practices and beliefs of the East: Buddhist stories, Hindu monism, Zoroastrian dualism, Gnostic ideas from Iraq, and miracles from the Gospels. The second coming of Christ became the doctrine of the coming of the Mahdi, the rightly-guided one, who would bring complete victory to Islam.

The essence of mysticism was love, an ecstatic communion with the divine, and final absorption into the godhead. Nothing existed but God. To know and love God and to be united with Him, without any thought of reward or salvation, was an emotional means of purifying the soul. God was Eternal Beauty and the path leading to Him was love. The mystic sought to lose the self in life with God. The process of comingling self with God could best be achieved by love and thought of God and a unifying of the senses which might be exercised as one. A mystic poet has expressed the thought in the lines:

> *My eye conversed whilst my tongue gazed;*
> *My ear spoke and my hand listened;*
> *And whilst my ear was an eye to behold everything visible,*
> *My eye was an ear listening to song.*

Until the twelfth century popular preachers who based much of their message and won their wide appeal upon mysticism were despised by philosophers and theologians and were frequently adjudged guilty of heresy. As al-Ashari made rationalism and Islamic theology compatible, so al-Ghazzali led the orthodox doctors and jurists to accept mysticism.

Appointed professor at the Nizamiyah at Baghdad in 1091, al-Ghazzali had the court and the scholars at his feet; and for four or five years his fame spread far and wide. Apparently secure for life, some sort of personal admonition flashed through him; he abandoned it all to become a mendicant mystic. After about a decade of wandering, writing, and contemplation, he returned to society and taught at the Nizamiyah at Nishapur. His great contribution, largely through his writings, vitalized Islam by making personal experience and emotion a part of religion. Islam began to live again for the ordinary man.

FRATERNAL ORDERS

At the time of the appearance of mysticism a holy man was called a *sufi*, meaning one garbed in wool. *Sufis* preached to the masses, and as pious men, mystics, and often occultists lived a life of example for those to whom they were appealing. Evidently, al-Ghazzali forsook the world and as a *sufi* travelled to many of the Muslim lands. Without question the conversion to Islam of the Berber tribesmen of North Africa, the fellaheen of Egypt, and the masses in many of the Muslim lands of today was the accomplishment of the *sufis*.

For several centuries *sufism* was an unorganized movement throughout Islam. Only individuals pursued its doctrines and preached its way of life. Certain *sufis* obtained a devoted following but partisanship was usually personal. Before the end of the tenth century, however, groups of *sufis* formed compact brotherhoods. The master *sufi* (a shaykh, *baba,* or *pir*) was the teacher and initiated disciples into the order. The members (dervishes) by study, ritual, and piety proceeded up the ladder of the order until they were ready to leave to establish a branch center.

A master's residence was called a *ribat, khangah,* or *tekkeh,* and by the thirteenth century thousands of such lodges dotted the Muslim landscape from Morocco to India. Each order had its own peculiar ritual and liturgy (*dhikr*). Some were elaborate and others simple; but all were mystical efforts to reach God. In addition to the master and the dervishes most fraternities had hundreds, sometimes thousands, of lay members, who went about their normal occupations in city or town. At stated times they met at the lodge to observe their ceremonies. A few of the orders increased the mystical stimulus by an accompaniment of music or by dancing or whirling.

It was not possible to know how many different orders existed at any one time; for new splinter fraternities were springing into being and others disappearing at regular intervals. One of the strongest and best known was the Kadiriya, which had its center in Baghdad and spread throughout Islam. More orthodox than most, its members have been noted for their philanthropy and humility. Morocco, parts of Spain, and North Africa yielded to the grip of the militant and strict Murabit and Muwahhid orders. The fanatical Rifaiya have been famed for glass-eating, fire-walking, and self-mortification. In Turkey the two best known orders were the Bektashi, to which most of the Ottoman janissaries belonged, and the Mevlevis, whose members because of certain aspects in their ritual were popularly called "Whirling Dervishes." In eastern Anatolia and Iran there was the Nakhshandiya order, and in India the Chishti and Kalandari orders were established.

As a great social and religious development the significance of the fraternal orders lay in the wide member participation in the spread and popularization of Islam. With *sufi* and dervish becoming nearly synonymous, the majority of the people in North Africa, Sudan, Asia Minor, central Asia, certain parts of India, and Indonesia were converted to Islam. In this process, much to the horror and disapproval of Muslim theologians and lawyers, local beliefs and religious customs were grafted upon the original doctrines to form a popular Islam. In most instances therefore, popular Islam in different parts of the world became exceedingly diverse in form and practice and far removed from the teachings of either Muhammad or Muslim theologians. Only the barest fundamentals and the simplest of externals were retained.

SHIISM

Differences of opinion and belief have always been accepted in Islam. Heresy has not been easy to achieve. Variations in practice and doctrine among the four orthodox legal systems, the many conflicting interpretations of tradition in vogue throughout the Muslim world, and the confusing welter of exotic ideas rampant in popular orthodox Islam have made a definitive imputation of heresy difficult to verify on purely theological grounds.

Until comparatively recently a ruler usually persecuted subjects whose religion was at marked variance with his. None the less Islam was exceedingly tolerant, as the treatment of Christians and Jews testifies; and the caliphs permitted many types of religious deviation. In general deviation became a serious matter only when religious doctrines denied to the caliph the right of his position and his power. Therein lay the true seeds of heresy.

With the defeat and death of Ali at the hands of the Umayyads and the obvious triumph of might, die-hard Alids contended that caliphs were usurpers and that the imamate, as they called the caliphate, should be lodged in the house of Ali and Fatimah. For more than two centuries intermittent political and military attempts were made by the Shiites (partisans or sect of Ali) to unseat the caliph. Failing in this, the Shiites developed an intricate theology, engendering many dogmas repugnant to orthodox Islam.

The Shiite faith held that Ali had been the legitimate imam and that the imamate was rightfully transmitted to his descendants. Ali had been given an esoteric power to interpret the Koran, a knowledge which was handed in turn on to his sons and grandsons. Later some extremists even professed that God's revelations had been intended for Ali but that the Angel Gabriel mistakenly gave them to Muhammad. Ali's descendants, therefore, ruled by a divine right which was handed down to them from Adam; they were infallible, impeccable, and certainly beyond human censure.

The Shiite heresy has been divided into numerous sects since the eighth century. The majority, the Twelvers, adhered to the faith that there was a succession of twelve imams to Muhammad al-Muntazar

1. Ali　d. 661
|
2. Hasan　d. 669　　　　　　3. Husayn　d. 680
|
4. Ali Zayn-al-Abidin　d. 712
|
Zayd　　　　　　5. Muhammad al-Bakir　d. 731
|
6. Jafar al-Sadik　d. 765
|
Ismail　　　　　　7. Musa al-Kazim　d. 799
|
8. Ali al-Rida　d. 818
|
9. Muhammad al-Jawad　d. 835
|
10. Ali al-Hadi　d. 868
|
11. Hasan al-Askari　d. 874
|
12. Muhammad al-Muntazar　d. 878

(The Expected), who disappeared in a cave to return as the savior (Mahdi) of mankind. In his absence the law and the creed were interpreted by scholars who acted only as agents of the hidden imam. Thus, in law, the Shiites accepted only the Koran, those traditions narrated by a recognized imam, and a scholar's or judge's personal opinion when it could be upheld by tradition or precedent established by an imam. Analogy and consensus were rejected.

Aside from petty ritualistic differences which through the centuries were greatly exaggerated in the minds of all Muslims, the chief peculiarities of these schismatics—Twelvers, or Imamis—were the allowance of temporary marriage and the practice of dissimulation. The former virtually legalized prostitution. The latter permitted the Shiite to deny his faith to avoid persecution when caliphs and Sunnites attacked Shiites for disavowing caliphal authority. In the twentieth century the majority of Muslims in Iran and southern Iraq are Shiites of the Twelver persuasion.

The most orthodox of the Shiites are found in Morocco and Yemen. In its political organization Morocco became Shiite; yet her theology and law were strictly Sunnite. In Yemen is the sect called Zaydi, which has recognized the series of imams. The Zaydis, however, allow for no supernaturalism in their theology and have no esoteric dogmas. The founder of their sect was Zayd, a grandson of the martyred Husayn.

On the other extreme of the Shiite sect there have been a score or more of divergent heterodoxies. Of these the sect of the Ismailis, or Seveners, has had the greatest following. They regarded Ismail as the rightful seventh and last imam. At first Jafar al-Sadik named Ismail, his eldest son, as successor; but because Ismail imbibed wine freely, Jafar designated another son, Musa, as successor. The Seveners rejected this substitution as impossible, arguing that the imam was incapable of erring and that drinking wine did not therefore affect him or the succession. Seven became a sacred and mystical number as in the Pythagorean system. The emanence of the universe came in seven steps: God, universal mind, universal soul, matter, space, time, and earth and man.

The Ismailis were masters of organization and tactics. Sent out by the true founder, Abdallah ibn Maymun, from Salamyah in northern Syria, missionaries traveled through the Muslim world preaching that the language of the Koran was an occult veil covering an inner and true meaning which could be revealed only to the adept. Initiation of the novice proceeded in seven graded degrees, wherein was divulged secret knowledge such as transmigration of souls, the divinity of Ismail, and the coming of the Mahdi. The son of the real founder of the Ismaili sect established his rule in North Africa early in the ninth century. His successors, the Fatimids, ruled much of the western portion of the Muslim world.

CULTS AND SECTS

Two effluences of the Ismailis in medieval times were the communistic Karmatians and the notorious Assassins. Led by Hamdan Karmat in the ninth century, the former sect was a revolutionary group which supported itself from a common fund contributed to by all, practiced the community of property and wives, and considered proper the shedding of the blood of any opposition, even Muslim. A Karmatian state was established on the western shore of the Persian Gulf and kept the whole area in bloody turmoil. In 930 the Karmatians raided Mecca and carried off the sacred Black Stone from the Kaaba.

The Assassins were founded in Iran by Hasan ibn al-Sabbah, who studied Ismaili rites and doctrine in Fatimid Egypt and then returned to his home as a missionary. In 1090 he established near Kazwin in the Elburz Mountains his fortified monastery of Alamut, which became the residence of the grand master of the order. Below him were priors and propagandists; at the lowest rank stood the *fidais*, who risked death for the faith. Their familiar name, Assassins, was derived from their use of hashish in their fearless raids from mountain fortresses. Adopting values based vaguely on Ismaili theology, the Assassins freed themselves from dogmas and prophets and were encouraged "to believe nothing and dare all." Exact information is lacking, however, because their records and books were destroyed in 1256 when Hulagu razed Alamut.

Spreading westward, the Assassins converted the Turkish prince of Aleppo in the twelfth century and held numerous castles in north Syria. The most famous Assassin master was Rashid-al-Din Sinan of Masyad, who as the *shaykh al-jabal* became for the Crusaders and thence to the West "The Old Man of the Mountain." The assassination of the famous vizir Nizam al-Mulk in 1092 was the first in a series of assassinations of prominent individuals which struck terror through Islam. The western branch of the order was eliminated by Baybars, the Mamluk Sultan of Egypt in 1272.

Other Ismaili sects were the Nusayris, or Alawites, of northern Syria and the Druzes of Lebanon, Syria, and Jordan. The Nusayris were devotees of the eleventh imam but nevertheless adhered to the main tenets of the Seveners. They looked upon Ali as the incarnation of God and possessed a liturgy with many Christian borrowings. The Druze sect was an eleventh-century splinter group from Fatimid Egypt. Its members settled in the Lebanon mountain region, where they developed an elaborate ritual and a pattern of life distinctive even in minor detail. Both the Druze and the Nusayri maintained strict secrecy with respect to their faith and practices; even today mystery shrouds their beliefs and ceremonies.

Probably the best known Ismaili in the twentieth century was the incomparable Agha Khan III of Bombay, London, Paris, and the Riviera, who traced his descent through the last grand master of the Assassins at Alamut to the seventh imam. Regarded as infallible and impeccable by his followers in Syria, India, Oman, and Zanzibar, he received a tenth of their revenues.

In addition to the sects and divisions of the orthodox and heterodox branches of Islam already described, there have been and are at least forty or fifty more. Perhaps the most curious are the Yazidis of Syria, who follow much of the theology of the Ismailis but assign the divine attributes to the Umayyad caliphs Yazid and Marwan.

Thus, the plain unvarnished revelations of the Prophet Muhammad and the simple direct philosophy of his preaching passed through the fires of Greek logic, Hellenistic Christianity, and Persian dualism to evolve a finely drawn legalistic and intellectual theology, a highly-charged supernatural recondite religion, or a semi-ascetic mysticism. The apocryphal words of Muhammad have apparently been fulfilled: When told that there were seventy-two varieties of Christianity, the Prophet was supposed to have said that Islam would have seventy-three!

REFERENCES: *Chapter 8*

References for Chapters 1, 3, and 5 relate to the subject matter of this chapter.

Soheil M. Afnan, *Avicenna, His Life and Works:* George Allen and Unwin, London, 1958.

A. J. Arberry, *An Introduction to the History of Sufism:* Longmans, Green, London, 1943. Comprehensive.

Thomas Arnold and Alfred Guillaume, eds., *The Legacy of Islam:* Oxford University Press, London, 1931. Two chapters, "Philosophy and Theology" by Alfred Guillaume and "Law and Society" by David de Santillana, contain valuable material on the subject discussed in this chapter.

Dwight M. Donaldson, *The Shi'ite Religion: A History of Islam in Persia and Irak:* Luzac, London, 1933. A history and compendium of the dogma of this important sect.

H. A. R. Gibb, *Studies in the Civilization of Islam:* Beacon Press, Boston, 1962.

Majid Khadduri, "Nature and Sources of Islamic Law," *The George Wash-*

ington Law Review, 22 (October, 1953). This article gives a clear and concise summary of many of the fundamental concepts of Muslim Law.

————, *The Islamic Law of Nations: Shaybani's Siyar:* Johns Hopkins Press, Baltimore, 1966. An insight into an eighth century treatise on international law.

————, *War and Peace in the Law of Islam:* Johns Hopkins Press, Baltimore, 1955. The fundamental nature of the Islamic state and law is explored; and the classical Muslim attitudes toward foreign policy, international trade, warfare, treaties, and neutrality are examined.

Majid Khadduri and Herbert J. Liebesny, eds., *Law in the Middle East:* Middle East Institute, Washington, 1955. The various chapters are authoritative and cover a wide field of Islamic law.

Bernard Lewis, *The Origins of Isma'ilism:* Cambridge University Press, Cambridge, 1940. An authoritative study.

Duncan B. Macdonald, *The Development of Muslim Theology, Jurisprudence, and Constitutional Theory:* Charles Scribner's Sons, New York, 1903. Origin, history, and theory of Muslim law.

R. A. Nicholson, *Studies in Islamic Mysticism:* Cambridge University Press, Cambridge, 1921. An excellent introduction.

E. I. J. Rosenthal, *Political Thought in Medieval Islam:* Cambridge University Press, Cambridge, 1958. A first-rate book in paperback.

J. J. Saunders, *A History of Medieval Islam:* Barnes and Noble, New York, 1965.

Joseph Schacht, *An Introduction to Islamic Law:* Oxford University Press, New York, 1964.

W. Montgomery Watt, *Muslim Intellectual: A Study of al-Ghazali:* University of Edinburgh Press, Edinburgh, 1963.

CHAPTER 9

Muslim Culture

The Arabs burst from the cities of the Hijaz and the deserts of Arabia into the complex Greco-Roman civilizations of Syria and Egypt, into the cultured valleys of India, and into the refined society of Mesopotamia and Iran. Everywhere they demonstrated a remarkable genius for assimilating the diverse attributes of these native cultures and blending them with their own to form a new and varied Muslim culture. Belief in the Oneness of God, acceptance of Muhammad as His Prophet, and the Arabic language became the three significant distinguishing characteristics of Islamic culture. After a few centuries even Arabic did not remain universal.

Although Muhammad's teachings, the Koran, and the solidarity of the new Islamic community had created a theocratic state, the shrewd Arab mind quickly assimilated a number of features of the religions, theologies, and legal systems with which it came into contact. In the preceding chapter the fruition of this fusing was described. In other facets of Muslim culture the Arabs also took ideas from the older Middle Eastern civilizations which they found about them to create the great Muslim culture that shone so brilliantly for centuries. Indeed, for several centuries, Muslim society alone carried the torch of human progress.

PHILOSOPHY

The emergence of the Mutazilites indicated that Greek logic was studied during the Umayyad era. Not until the reign of al-Mamun, however, was the bulk of Hellenistic thought and science translated into Arabic. Beginning with a majority of the works of Aristotle and Plato, translators soon rendered almost the whole of Hellenic and

Hellenistic philosophies into Arabic. It was upon this base that Arabian philosophy was erected.

The earliest of the prominent Arab philosophers was al-Kindi (Alkindius), born in Kufah in the first half of the ninth century. He excelled in the study of optics, chemistry, medicine, and music; but above all he was a philosopher. A Neo-Platonist of the school of Plotinus and Porphyry, al-Kindi also imbibed the ideas of Aristotle and Plato. He intermingled philosophy and theology, holding that the world of intelligence was supreme. Immortality resulted from having the correct knowledge of God and the universe. A century later al-Farabi (Alpharabius), a Turk from Transoxiana, blended Aristotelian, Platonic, and Sufi thought. He presented his philosophy in a political science treatise by describing a model city where the ruler was a moral and intellectual being and the happiness of all was the governing force. However, al-Farabi shocked Muslims by claiming that the world was not created and had no beginning.

Arabian philosophers better known to the Western world were Ibn Sina (Avicenna) and Ibn Rushd (Averroes). The former, called by the Arabs "the shaykh and the prince of the learned," was born in 980 in a village near Bukhara. An Ismaili Iranian Ibn Sina lived as a young man at the Samanid library of Bukhara, where he acquired an encyclopedic knowledge of medicine, mathematics, astronomy, and philosophy. Since he was able to write concisely, yet in a popular style, Ibn Sina's numerous works on these diverse subjects had a wide vogue among Muslims and greatly influenced the advancement of philosophic thought in medieval Europe. Pursuing Aristotelian philosophy, Ibn Sina developed and passed on to the Western schoolmen the notion that there are two intelligibles—the concept of an object such as a chair, and the pursuant or logical concept of a chair in relation to its abstract universal concept. He taught that the idea of a chair existed before the chair was created, that in each chair existed the idea of chair, and that from many chairs came the idea of chair. Such logic resembled the later thoughts of Abélard and were in part taken over by Albertus Magnus and his pupil Saint Thomas Aquinas.

Ibn Rushd, the Malikite Muslim judge and philosopher, lived in Cordoba, Seville, and Marrakesh during the Muwahhid regime. He wrote in the fields of philosophy, medicine, mathematics, law, and theology. As the last of the classical Muslim philosophers of Spain, he built on the systems of al-Farabi, Ibn Sina, and his fellow countrymen Ibn Bajjah (Avempace) and Ibn Tufayl. He declared that active human reason and possible reason or knowledge were one and present in all men. Although differing considerably on this point, Ibn Rushd and Aquinas advanced philosophies that were remarkably parallel. Ibn

Rushd's commentaries on Aristotle were more popular in Christian Europe than they were in the Muslim world.

From Aristotle, Plato, and other Greek philosophers the Muslim scholars, writing in Arabic, created an Arabian school of philosophy which had a profound and recognized influence upon Christian philosophers of medieval Europe. More significant to the Middle East, however, was their permanent popularity throughout the Muslim world. Summaries, treatises, and commentaries on these philosophers and scores of others less well known were widely read and discussed; public and private libraries bulged with books on metaphysics, cosmology, and philosophy.

MEDICINE

Muhammad supposedly declared that there existed two sciences: the science of God and the science of man—theology and medicine. Consequently throughout the period of medieval Islam most Muslim philosophers and scientists were students of medicine; frequently they were also practicing physicians. Muslims first became aware of medical knowledge at the Damascus court of the Umayyads, through their Greek, Syrian, and Iranian physicians, whose skills were based almost exclusively on works of Greek scientists. A few Greek or Syriac treatises were translated into Arabic, and the Alexandrine medical school was transferred, part to Antioch and part to Harran in Iraq.

The great strides in medicine, however, were taken under the Abbasid rule in Baghdad. Medical works of Galen, Hippocrates, and Paul of Aegina and the *materia medica* of Dioscorides were translated into Arabic. Seven of Galen's books, lost in the original Greek, were preserved in Arabic. Several schools of medicine developed, and a physician took state examinations to obtain a license to practice his profession. In the year 931 eight hundred and sixty physicians were registered in Baghdad; they swore to work for the benefit of humanity and for the relief and cure of the sick and not to give deadly medicines. Jails as well as traveling clinics for the poor were supported by the state. Hospitals, an Iranian innovation, were introduced into the Muslim world by Harun al-Rashid. The Seljuk Turkish Sultan Malikshah had with him on most of his campaigns a traveling hospital, carried on forty camels. Pharmacists were also examined and licensed, and schools of pharmacy and drugstores were established. In 776 Jabir ibn Hayyan compiled the first Arabic pharmacopoeia.

In 765 the Nestorian Jurjis ibn Bakhtishu, dean of the academy of medicine of Jundishapur (Shahabad in southwestern Iran), came to the court of al-Mansur to cure the caliph's stomach ailment. Fortunes were made by court physicians, who passed on their professional skills and practices as valued possessions from father to son for generations.

Ibn Bakhtishu's grandson understood psychiatry; he cured one of al-Rashid's slavegirls of hysterical paralysis by the pretense of public disrobing. Descendants of Ibn Bakhtishu served the Abbasid court for nearly three centuries.

The arrival of physicians from Jundishapur opened the way for medical investigations beyond the works of the ancient Greeks, and the ninth century in Baghdad was a period of many advances in medical knowledge. Ibn Masawayh dissected apes and wrote a monograph on ophthalmology. The compendium by Thabit ibn Kurra of Harran discussed general hygiene. It stated causes, symptoms, and treatment for diseases of the skin and every part of the body from head to foot. Infectious diseases were classified; fractures and dislocations were described; and the importance of climate, food, diet, and sex was explained.

The most ingenious Muslim physician was al-Razi (Rhazes), chief of the Baghdad hospital during the first quarter of the tenth century. Considered the best original mind and clinician of the Middle Ages, he developed the use of seton in surgery, treated bladder and kidney stones, and presented the first clinical report on smallpox. He had some one hundred and twenty monographs on medicine and surgery to his credit. His *al-Hawi*, a comprehensive medical encyclopedia, was translated into Latin in 1279 and first printed in 1486 under the title *Continens*. A contemporary, al-Majusi (Haly Abbas), wrote on childbirth, the capillary system, and dietetics, and also compiled a materia medica.

The most famous of Muslim medical works was *al-Kanun*, written in the eleventh century by Ibn Sina (Avicenna) of Bukhara. Encyclopedic in character, it showed the advances of Muslim knowledge and the originality of Ibn Sina in this field. He explained the contagious nature of tuberculosis and understood that disease could be spread through water. Pleurisy was recognized, and a diagnosis was made of bilharziasis. Seven hundred and sixty different drugs were described. Largely replacing the works of Galen and al-Razi, *al-Kanun* was the chief medical book of the Middle East and Western Europe from the twelfth to the seventeenth century. Gerard of Cremona translated it into Latin, and it ran through sixteen printed editions before the end of the fifteenth century.

Muslim Spain possessed superior physicians and surgeons. The ablest surgeon was Abu al-Kasim (Abulcasis) of Cordoba. He practiced the art of crushing bladder stones, cauterized wounds, and advocated dissection and vivisection. His surgical writings were translated by Gerard of Cremona and became the surgical manual at the medical schools of Salerno, Montpellier, and other European centers. In Seville, Ibn

Zuhr (Avenzoar), vizir and court physician to the Muwahhid rulers, carried on the family profession and found time to write six medical works, of which the most valuable is on therepeutics and diet. At the time of the Black Death in the middle of the fourteenth century the Muslim physicians of Granada, Ibn al-Khatib and Ibn Khatima, recognized its contagious character; and in their treatises they noted that a patient's symptoms were identical to those of the person from whom he had been infected. Although religious law denied contagion, Ibn al-Khatib held that "experience, investigation, the evidence of the senses and trustworthy reports" established without a doubt the reality of infection from the afflicted.

Building on Greek and Persian sources, the galaxy of Muslim physicians pushed the frontiers of medicine forward. Their practice, monographs, and compendiums demonstrated originality and ingenuity. The diversity and number of their works, translated into Latin and eventually printed, further established the place of Muslim physicians in the history of medical science. Evidence of their actual skill was attested by the eagerness with which the Crusaders sought the services of Muslim doctors. Part of the progress originated in the popularity and fashionable reputation enjoyed by medical knowledge. Since the chief avocation of countless leading Muslims was medicine and the study of its lore, every medical genius was encouraged to reach the pinnacle of his ability and capacity.

MATHEMATICS

Arab scholars also found mathematics an attractive and useful science, especially in company with astronomy and astrology. By far the greatest achievement of the Arab mathematicians was the adoption and wide use of "Arabic numerals." It is not known whether they were brought from India or developed locally. In any case the use of these numerals, including the use of zero and the placing of the digit in a series to denote units, tens, hundreds, etc., made "everyday arithmetic" possible and simplified calculations so that Arabs were able to take the square and cube roots of numbers. The word "cipher" was taken directly from the Arabic "*shifr*," meaning empty.

Building on Indian and Greek works, Middle Eastern scholars advanced mathematical knowledge very considerably. In the ninth century al-Khwarizmi of Khurasan did a study on numerals which later circulated in the West. Through his name came the word "algorism." He wrote on the solution of quadratic equations; and from part of the title of one of his books was derived the word "algebra" (*al-jabr*—integration).

In the same century three sons of a Baghdad astronomer worked on the measurement of plane and spherical surfaces, while the geometrician Thabit ibn Kurra developed new propositions and studied irrationals. The Iranian al-Battani (Albategnius), converted to Islam from pagan Sabanian beliefs, was the first to present ideas on trigonometric ratios. Toward the end of the tenth century another Iranian, Abu al-Wafa of Baghdad, established the formula in trigonometry for the addition of angles. Through a simple geometric process al-Karaji was able to determine the sum of successive numbers raised to the third power $(1^3 + 2^3 + 3^3 \cdots n^3)$; with great skill al-Kashi of Samarkand did the same for successive numbers raised to the fourth power $(1^4 + 2^4 + 3^4 \cdots n^4)$. By using the intersection of a hyperbola and a circle, Sijzi gave the solution to the problem of the trisection of an angle.

One of the most distinguished mathematicians was the Iranian poet Umar al-Khayyam. He advanced far beyond al-Khwarzimi, establishing procedures for the solution of cubic and quadrinomial equations and developing analytical geometry in numerous ways to the same level achieved much later by Descartes. The last great medieval mathematician of the Middle East was the Iranian Nasir-al-Din al-Tusi, who assembled his laboratory at Maraghah in northwestern Iran under the patronage of Hulagu Khan. Here he wrote his famous *Treatise on the Quadrilateral* and carried on his brilliant studies in the field of spherical trigonometry.

Thus, besides assimilating and transmitting to posterity the mathematics of the ancients, Middle Eastern savants made many original contributions in the practical and theoretical branches of the subject. The widespread use of numerals gave arithmetic an everyday value. Algebra became an exact science, and solid foundations were laid in the fields of analytical geometry and plane and spherical trigonometry. Through Spain and Sicily most of these ideas passed at an early date to the Western world, where they contributed to the scientific advancement of Europe.

ASTRONOMY

From mathematics it was an easy step to astronomy, especially since in the construction of any mosque it was always necessary to fix the *kibla* (the prayer niche) in the direction of Mecca. Furthermore, since astrology and horoscopy were much pursued and the latitude and longitude of one's birthplace determined one's horoscope, the movement of the stars was significant.

When al-Mansur decided to build his new palace in Baghdad, the Iranian astronomer Naubakht was employed to draw the plans. Shortly thereafter, Mauka, an Indian astronomer, introduced the court to

Sindbind, an Indian treatise on astronomy. This treatise was translated into Arabic by al-Fazari, who was also familiar with the Pahlawi astronomical tables compiled in the Sasanid period. A few decades later Ptolemy's *Quadripartitum* was translated. Muslim astronomy thus started from Greek, Iranian, and Indian contributions.

Many palaces in Baghdad had private observatories, where the planets, stars, and constellations were studied. The main observatories were at Jundishapur and Baghdad; and from the latter at the time of al-Mamun went forth the scientists to the plain of Sinjar to determine the length of a degree of latitude. Walking north and south until the pole star rose or sank a degree and thus assuming the earth to be round, they took the mean distance for one degree. From this they calculated that the earth's diameter was about 6500 miles and its circumference roughly 20,400 miles. This made the Mediterranean 52° in length, improving upon Ptolemy's 62°. The precession of the equinoxes was well understood. Rather exact astronomical tables and calendars with a compendium were prepared by al-Farghani (Alfraganus) of Transoxiana in the ninth century. These were translated into Latin in the twelfth century and were still used and valued by Regiomontanus and Melanchthon.

Thabit ibn Kurra determined the altitude of the sun and computed the length of the solar year, while al-Battani (Albategnius) recorded his observations on the appearance of the new moon, the inclination of the ecliptic, the length of the tropic and sideral year, and eclipses of the sun. Abu Mashar (Albumasar) of Baghdad, although chiefly concerned with astrology, wrote on the relation of the moon's rising and setting with the laws of the tides. The astronomer al-Biruni at Ghaznah in Afghanistan proposed the idea that the earth rotated on its axis and reckoned quite accurately latitudes and longitudes for every important city in the Middle East. Umar al-Khayyam, who was a better astronomer than poet, arranged for Sultan Malikshah at the Naysabur observatory a calendar with an error of only one day in 5,000 years.

In the west al-Zarkali (Arzachel) of Toledo invented an astrolabe, on which he wrote a treatise later used by Copernicus. Near Cordoba a century later lived the great astronomer al-Bitruji (Alpetragius), who computed the length of the Mediterranean and found it to be 42° of longitude, a nearly correct measurement. He advanced the idea of diurnal movements of the earth and explained the movement of the stars by the turning of the earth on its axis as well as by its circling about the sun.

One of the finest observatories was established by Hulagu at Maraghah, where the scientist Nasir-al-Din al-Tusi developed the most precise instruments in medieval times. He greatly perfected the armillary sphere and constructed a mural quadrant and a solstitial armil. Because of his excellent equipment his *Ilkhanian Tables* were long regarded as the most exact of astronomical tables.

The Arabic names of many stars and constellations and the Arabic origin of such words as azimuth, nadir, and zenith vouch for the brilliance of the Middle Eastern astronomers and the acceptance of their contributions by the West. One can only wonder if Columbus would have had the courage to set sail westward for India and Cathay had he known the size of the earth as determined by al-Bitruji.

SCIENCES

In addition to medicine, mathematics, and astronomy, the medieval Middle Easterners investigated all of the basic physical and natural sciences. It is not possible here to detail the various advances made in each science. Works on botany existed, chiefly in connection with drugs for the pharmacist and physician. Zoological studies were made, some for use by veterinarians. (Arabs were always interested in horses.) The Arab al-Masudi, who died about 957 in Cairo, discussed earthquakes, described windmills, and advanced a theory of evolution. In his book on geology Ibn Sina suggested several postulates about earthquakes, winds, climate, and geologic sedimentation.

However, the greatest strides in the other sciences were taken in chemistry and physics. Chemistry was studied mostly in connection with alchemy. Even the word affirms the Arabic origins of that science. The Arabic term is *al-kimiya,* which was probably derived from an ancient Egyptian word meaning "black." Even in antiquity the science had a reputation as "black magic."

Alchemy was founded on the belief that all metals were basically the same and that it was possible to transmute one to another. Further, it was believed that gold was the purest form of metal and that some substance existed which could transform baser metals into gold. In the search for this substance and the technique of its use countless individuals were engaged in every corner of the Muslim world. Celebrated philosophers and physicians gave their time and genius to the quest. One of these men, al-Razi, distinguished volatile and nonvolatile bodies and classified all matter as vegetable, animal, or mineral. Others in their research determined the specific weights of stones and metals.

The greatest chemist, or alchemist, was Jabir ibn Hayyan (Geber), who lived in Kufah toward the end of the eighth century. Jabir advocated experimentation and recognized the importance of confirming by careful observation theories resting only on previous writings and hypotheses. He was able to prepare arsenious oxide, lead acetate, sulphide of mercury, and sal-ammoniac, the last of which had been unknown to the Greeks. Jabir presented new and improved methods of evaporation, filtration, sublimation, melting, crystallization, and distillation. Jabir's works were translated into Latin in the twelfth century by Robert of Chester and Gerard of Cremona and proved to be the foundation of Western alchemy and chemistry. The Arabic origin of such words as alkali, alcohol, antimony, and alembic and aludel (parts of the older typical apparatus for distilling) gives an inkling of Western dependence upon Middle Eastern discoveries in this branch of science.

In physics the widest interest lay in theoretical and applied mechanics as related to problems of irrigation and the flow of water. Water wheels and clocks were built in many cities of the Middle East, some of the water clocks being exceedingly ingenious in design. In the twelfth century al-Khazine of Marw observed the greater density of water when it was nearer the center of the earth.

The most significant developments in physics, however, were in the field of optics. Many prominent scientists of the age investigated the subject. The most outstanding was al-Hasan ibn al-Haytham (Alhazen), who flourished in Cairo at the time of the Fatimids. In his book *On Optics* he refused to accept Euclid's and Ptolemy's theory that the eye emits visual rays; instead he advanced the theory that vision is due to the impact of light rays. Experimenting with reflection and optic illusions, he studied refraction through spherical segments filled with water. In another work, *On Light,* he proposed that light is fire reflected at the spheric limit of the atmosphere; and from observing phenomena at twilight he reckoned the atmosphere to be about ten miles high. During eclipses he noticed the semi-lunar shape of the sun's image on a wall opposite a fine hole in a window shutter, probably the first recording of the *camera obscura.* Ibn al-Haytham's studies greatly influenced, through translation, the works of Roger Bacon, Vitellio, Kepler, and Leonardo da Vinci.

GEOGRAPHY

The religious precept of a pilgrimage to Mecca once in a lifetime undoubtedly led to a persistent urge to travel and see the world, an urge especially prevalent in the medieval Islamic world. Geographic data were needed by these travelers; and they in turn, sometimes after twenty years of travel, wrote detailed books on where they had been and what they had seen. Muslim traders did likewise. The result was that geography became one of the most popular pursuits of the Middle Ages.

Before the end of the ninth century Ptolemy's *Geography* had been translated into Arabic, and Muslim geographers always had difficulty in freeing themselves from some of the ancients' concept of the world. The scientist al-Khwarizmi, at al-Mamun's command, prepared a great map of the earth and a companion text which was used by geographers until the fourteenth century. Largely following Ptolemy, al-Khwarizmi pictured the world encircled by a continuous ocean from which the Sea of Rum (Mediterranean) and the Sea of Fars (Indian Ocean) branched to separate the land of the earth, which was divided into seven climate zones. The western prime meridian of longitude ran through the Canary Islands, and all east and west directions came from the "world cupola" located in India at Arin (Ujjayini).

Fortunately, travelers and sailors ignored the orthodox and classical geographers, whose views were sanctioned by the Koran. The former recognized irregular coasts strewn with gulfs and peninsulas and stated that the Indian Ocean in certain directions had no limit. The tales of these voyagers came down through the ages as the stories of Sindbad the Sailor. They described China in the ninth century and Russia in the tenth. Their road books were a mine of historical topography and economic and political geography. The tenth-century scholar was frequently on the move. The greatest globe-trotter was al-Masudi, who visited every country of Asia, Zanzibar, and most of North Africa. His thirty-volume work became one of the two recognized geographical encyclopedias of the medieval period. Other travelers and geographers left numerous works, many with special merit for their colored maps of separate countries and areas. One of the last discerning voyagers was Ibn Battutah of Morocco. Living in the fourteenth century, he was on the move for nearly three decades. He made four pilgrimages to Mecca and visited China, Ceylon, Constantinople, and central Africa.

The most noted geographer of the Muslim world was al-Idrisi (Edrisi), born in Ceuta in 1100 and for many years the chief geographer for King Roger II at Palermo in Sicily. In his writings and discourses (in Arabic) he summed up the ideas and contributions of Ptolemy, al-Khwarizmi, and al-Masudi. Using silver, al-Idrisi constructed for his patron a celestial sphere and a disc-like map of the earth. It is interesting that the latter distinctly showed the source of the Nile to be a lake in central Africa.

The last eminent Muslim geographer was Yakut ibn Abdallah al-Hamawi, a Greek slave from Asia Minor who was educated and given his freedom by his Hamawi owner. Before his death at Aleppo in 1229 Yakut compiled his famous *Mujam al-Buldun*, a vast encyclopedia of geographical information. Arranged alphabetically, it summed up the whole fund of knowledge to his day in this field and thus became an invaluable source book for all scholars.

AGRICULTURE

The Arabs were not farmers, and to engage in agricultural work was beneath the dignity of free men in Arabia. But moving into the rich agricultural lands of Iraq, Syria, and Egypt, they quickly learned the value of efficient cultivation of the soil. As the native populations of these provinces and other fertile areas, such as Spain and Sogdiana, were converted to Islam, Muslims were engaged directly in agriculture. Accordingly, the governing classes, the landowners, and the actual farmers were concerned with agricultural progress.

In the Middle East in historic times the prime factor in agriculture has been water. Problems of irrigation and canal-building were not private affairs and everywhere rulers paid strict attention to digging, reopening, and repairing water channels. Under Muslim governments gardens flourished and many different plants, vegetables, and fruit trees were propagated. The Arabs had known numerous varieties of dates, and families treasured their own species with favored qualities of flavor, sweetness, and moisture. The same interest and care was given to all produce of the land as Islam spread into new areas and new crops were grown. The Middle Easterner usually took keen pride in his garden and his land. His own peaches or apricots, cotton or sugar cane, melons or squashes were always something quite special. He was interested in improving their quality, and he took them wherever he went. On pilgrimages to Mecca he usually carried seeds and cuttings to exchange for others from distant lands. Thus, the best varieties were distributed far and wide. Into Spain on the distant edge of the Islamic world was introduced the cultivation of cotton, sugar cane, oranges, apricots, peaches, and rice. One of the best known gardens of the world was that of the Generalife (*jannat al-arif*—the inspector's paradise) near the Alhambra.

With the date palm and fruit trees, the technique of controlled pollenization was known and frequently practiced with special and prized varieties.

The Crusaders learned to value Middle Eastern agriculture and acquired a taste for many of its products. Yet, it was largely through Sicily and Spain that agricultural knowledge and skills passed to Christian Europe.

POETRY

In pre-Islamic Arabia poetry was a favorite vehicle of expression. Epic and lyric poetry abounded. A talented poet was highly esteemed, and the cultured man was one who appreciated fine poetry and could recite an endless quantity of verse. Muhammad found much of this poetry distasteful, since the virtues extolled and the way of life suggested were not those of Islam. But Islam was unable to eradicate the love of verse inherent in Middle Eastern peoples.

The advent of the Umayyad regime set the stage for the return of poetry to its pre-Islamic popularity. The poet Umar wrote with charming grace of free and erotic love, and his directness and simplicity influenced generations of Arab poets. Singers and entertainers found his style well suited to their ballads. His contemporary Jamil, however, wrote of platonic love and honored chaste and faithful passion. Lyric poetry reached its height in the Majnun-Layla romance. The author-hero of the Layla tribe became mad (*majnun*) because of his burning passion for a lady whose father compelled her to marry another. The deranged lover roamed the world seeking his beloved. Ever after, Majnun Layla was the typical hero of unrequited-love poems throughout the Middle East.

In addition there reappeared in the Umayyad period many writers of eulogistic and epic poetry of the pre-Islamic style. Noted for their dissolute language and political invective, these panegyrists pleased their patrons; but their poetry was more revealing of the life and morals of the age than worthy of a niche in world literature.

With the coming of the Abbasids and the court's move to Iraq and Baghdad the poets followed. Persian influence and rich caliphal patronage introduced an elegance and a licentiousness unknown in Umayyad poetry. One of the first poets in this period was Bashshar ibn Burd, whose paeans of love were so popular and so apt for singing that al-Mahdi had him executed in 783 for endangering public morals. The boon companion of Harun al-Rashid was the sparkling and lusty Abu Nuwas, whose libidinous poetry was well shown by his verse:

> Ho! a cup, and fill it up, and tell me it is wine.
> For I will never drink in shade if I can drink in shine!
> Curst and poor is every hour that sober I must go,
> But rich am I whene'er well drunk I stagger to and fro.
> Speak, for shame, the loved one's name, let vain disguise alone:
> No good there is in pleasures o'er which a veil is thrown.

Poetry, however, was not all wine, women, and song. Abu al-Alahiyah raised his voice against the lascivious and frivolous verses of his contemporaries and sang the praises of a moral and ascetic life. Unmindful of the reproaches, al-Rashid pensioned him generously.

At the court and in wealthy society poetry was on the lips of all, and every elegant household had its poet. The immediate material rewards were great and much of the verse was ephemeral doggerel or limerick eulogizing the patron or adorning the moment. Since the golden days of Baghdad the poetry of that classical age has retained its favored position among educated Arabic-speaking Middle Eastern peoples.

In the West the best known poet was Ali ibn Hazm of eleventh-century Cordoba. His platonic love verses, collected in an anthology called *Tawq al-Hamamah* (*The Dove's Necklace*), have been much translated into Western tongues. Much more significant was the indigenous development of the *zajal* and the *muwashshah* (the ballad and folk song) of Muslim Spain, which were popularized and spread by wandering minstrels. The epoch of the troubadour in northern Spain, Italy, and France was largely dependent upon this Spanish development; the idealization of the lady and love found in the troubadour songs was a Christian characterization of themes prevalent in Arabic lyrics of the Muslim world.

At the other end of the Muslim world in the province of Fars and especially in Shiraz, there arose the school of Persian poets. As an outgrowth of national feeling Firdawsi, who died in 1020, presented his *Shahnamah,* or great national epic, to Mahmud of Ghaznah. No poetry has ever stirred the soul of the Iranian people as has Firdawsi's *Shahnamah;* even today one can hear illiterate camel-drivers reciting with great emotion national legends and history from Firdawsi's poetry.

The Persian poet best known outside of Iran is, of course, Umar al-Khayyam, whose *Rubaiyat,* through FitzGerald's unrivaled translation, has come in the West to be regarded as the epitome of Middle Eastern poetry. His quatrains expressed the cultured hedonism of twelfth-century Nishapur and were only the product of the idle moments of this illustrious mathematician.

Besides Firdawsi, the other poets regarded as truly gifted by Iranians were: Nizami, whose romantic *Five Treasuries* were exceptionally popular and whose rendition of the Majnun-Layla theme was depicted in countless miniatures; Jalal al-Din al-Rumi, the mystic poet who founded the Mawlawi (Mevlevi) dervish order and died at Konya in Asia Minor in 1273; Sadi of Shiraz, another mystic whose *Gulistan* (Rose Garden) and *Bustan* (Orchard) were among the most favorite poems of Iran; and the fourteenth-century Hafiz, the master of Persian lyricists, a materialist yet a mystic, whose love for the shady gardens, the wine and women, and the laughter-loving people of Shiraz was shown in his *Diwan* or *Collection of Odes.*

LITERATURE

For the most part the classical literature of the medieval Middle East consisted of the writings of famous philosophers, theologians, geographers, historians, and men of like interests. Belles-lettres, prose fiction, and drama were not so highly regarded among the Arabs; not until the tenth century did Persian contacts influence the general taste to produce Arabic literature of this type. Affected and ornate to the Westerner and embellished with philological curiosities, rhymed prose emphasized elegant form over substance. In Muslim Spain a type of anecdotes, frequently introducing a moral lesson through the adventure of some dashing hero, became the prototype of the Spanish picaresque novel. In his rhetorical tales al-Hariri of Basrah (1054–1122) criticized rather subtly the existing social order.

Superb, howevever, was a set of delightful anthologies—half composed by the author-collector, and half a treasury of poetry, literature, and history. Today they serve as invaluable sources for the study of Muslim civilization. Two outstanding examples are the twenty-volume *Kitab al-Aghani* (*Book of Songs*) gathered by Abu al-Faraj al-Isfahani, who died in 967 in Aleppo, and *al-Iqd al-Farid* (*The Unique Necklace*) by Ibn Abd Rabbih, who died in 940 in Cordoba.

Of all the literature of the Middle East the most colorful, fanciful and noteworthy through many centuries has been *The Arabian Nights*. Taking the core of the stories and names of leading characters from an old Persian collection, al-Jahshiyari in the first half of the tenth century in Iraq blended local color and current episodes and romances of the courts of Harun al-Rashid, al-Mamun, and the other spirited caliphs to produce the great *Alf Laylah wa Laylah* (*One Thousand and One Nights*). Its present form was achieved in the fourteenth century in Mamluk Egypt. In the nineteenth century excellent English translations were made by Edward W. Lane, John Payne, and Sir Richard F. Burton.

HISTORY

Middle Eastern peoples have always been mindful of their own history, the Muslims not excepted. The epic poetry of pre-Islamic days related the history of the tribes and families of Arabia, and the collecting and arranging of the traditions (the *hadith*) so soon after the death of Muhammad definitely preserved a great deal of historical material. To the early Muslims the break with their immediate past appeared so sharp and complete that several generations passed before they began the process of examining their own chronicles. The caliph Muawiyah in Damascus commanded one Abid to prepare a *Book of Kings and History of the Ancients,* but this was desired so that Muawiyah might pursue kingly ways.

By the middle of the eighth century historical works began to attract the attention of Muslim scholars. The first known biography of the

Prophet was composed by Ibn Ishak, who died in 767 in Egypt. In the ninth century accounts of the early battles of Islam, tales of the astonishing Arab expansion, and biographical dictionaries of historical figures appeared. The two best were al-Hakam's (an Egyptian) story of the conquest of Egypt, North Africa, and Spain and al-Baladhuri's (an Iranian) full narrative of Muslim expansion.

The lengthy and more formal histories of the Middle East produced in the medieval era were numerous and varied. Every century and court had professional chroniclers. One of the more noted was al-Tabari (838–923), who traveled widely and studied at many important Muslim centers. A most prolific writer for more than forty years, al-Tabari left a monumental historical chronicle incorporating data sifted from innumerable monographs. His contemporary from Baghdad, al-Masudi, dealt with the same material but treated the unfolding of civilizations topically instead of chronologically as al-Tabari had done. The historian al-Masudi traveled everywhere; but before his death in 956 he settled down in Egypt, where he composed his thirty-volume work.

Probably the best known of Muslim historians has been the Tunisian Ibn Khaldun (1332–1406). A citizen of the Muslim world, he studied and held important political positions in Fez, Granada, Algeria, and Cairo. His history of the Muslim states and peoples was a significant contribution to knowledge, especially the sections regarding North Africa. But Ibn Khaldun's fame rested on his history's first volume, entitled *Mukaddamah* (*Prolegomena*), in which he presented his philosophy of the development of civilization and explained how the historian should record and study the interrelated forces of society. Since he considered the factors of climate, geography, economics, and culture, Ibn Khaldun can be called the first modern historian.

EDUCATION

In the early days of the Muslim empire the ruling Arabs held that a man was educated if he learned to read and write, to use the bow and arrow, and to swim. A man should be taught courage, endurance, justice, hospitality, honesty, manliness, generosity, and respect for women. Among the conquered peoples schools of various types and grades existed, and in general they attained high proficiency in their intellectual skills. By the opening of the eighth century most leading Muslims employed tutors or owned slaves to teach their children. The only education available for the masses was that which could be obtained from Koran readers in the mosques.

In the Abbasid period the number of elementary schools increased, so that many children were taught to read and write. The curriculum centered upon the Koran and allied religious texts, and memory achievement was the goal. Children of wealthy and prominent families continued to get rigorous and comprehensive private instruction. It was still not easy to acquire an advanced education, although to make one's way about the Muslim world in quest of the great teacher was less arduous than in earlier days. Various academies existed, some with endowments; but they were unorganized and did not furnish any systematic education.

The first university to be established under Islam was the University of Cordoba, founded by Abd al-Rahman III in the middle of the tenth century. Enlarged and placed upon a more solid financial basis by al-Hakam, Cordoba gathered professors and attracted students from every Muslim land. Professorial chairs were endowed, and fellowships were granted to advanced students. One of the most famous of the Islamic universities was the al-Azhar University in Cairo, founded by the Fatimid Caliph al-Aziz in the latter part of the tenth century. Through the centuries al-Azhar maintained a reputation for scholarship and a high quality of education, especially in the fields of theology and law. Still today it draws thousands of students from every quarter of Islam.

A bureau for translation, a library, and an observatory in al-Mamun's House of Wisdom in Baghdad served as a kind of collegiate institution; but the honor of creating the first university in the east fell to Nizam al-Mulk, the ingenious eleventh-century vizir. His Nizamiyah in Baghdad was duplicated within a few years throughout the Muslim world by other nizamiyahs called *madrasahs*. In the leading cities of Islam each of the larger mosques included a *madrasah*, where theology, law, philosophy, history, and the sciences were taught. Memory work predominated as in most educational establishments in all civilizations throughout the ages. But the need for thinking and the obligation to correlate the ideas imparted in the process of education to ethical and social requirements of society were recognized by noted Muslim teachers.

ARCHITECTURE

One feature of Muslim civilization that has always impressed visitors has been the mosque and its accompanying minaret. The house of the urban Arab in Muhammad's time was almost invariably a simple enclosure, usually square, with a few huts placed in a rather haphazard way along the edge. The first mosque was none other than the house of Muhammad. Before he died it assumed a public character; for here the followers congregated to pray with Muhammad and to hear his revelations, sermons, and instructions. Along one side palm trunks were set up and covered with palm leaves as a protection from the sun. Muhammad first used to lean against a trunk when he spoke; later he stood on a piece of a palm trunk. Some pointer indicated the direction of Mecca so prayers could be made facing that holy city. Bilal stood on some roof top to call the Muslims to prayer or to a community meeting. Thus were established the essentials of a mosque.

As the Arabs and Muslims expanded into other lands, they employed local masons, carpenters, stonecutters, and other craftsmen in the building of mosques, so that skills, techniques, and materials differed from place to place. But the fundamentals of a congregational mosque remained unchanged. A large part of the mosque area was an open courtyard, usually with a fountain where ablutions could be performed and sometimes with a narrow covered arcade on three sides. On the fourth side was the mosque proper. In most mosques in Syria, Egypt, North Africa, Spain, and Iraq the mosque proper consisted of a system of arches supported by piers or columns arranged in series of parallel aisles and upholding domes, vaults, and either a flat or a gabled wooden roof. Where the dome covered a square chamber or area, the transition from the arch was made by the use of squinches or spherical triangular pendentives. Stilted and horseshoe arches appeared early in the development of Islamic architecture, largely because the available cut columns taken from older structures were not long enough to hold the roof at the desired height. At Cordoba that problem was met by a series of columns and arches superimposed upon another series.

At one or more of the corners of the enclosure there stood a minaret. First appearing at the mosque in Damascus, it was a square tower-like structure from which the call to prayer was given. Round or pencil-shaped minarets did not develop until late in the medieval period, although circular ziggurat-type minarets are known to have existed in ninth-century Iraq and Iran.

In the wall of the mosque on the side toward Mecca a niche (*mihrab*) was usually constructed to indicate the exact direction of the Holy City. This was particularly helpful in converted churches, as they were often not correctly oriented. A wooden or marble pulpit (*minbar*) was a necessary piece of furniture of a congregational mosque so that the imam who delivered the Friday sermon could be seen and heard by all. The façade encasing the main portal of the mosque enclosure as well as the inner façade around the doorway to the mosque itself came in time to be elaborately decorated, taking on the appearance of an external *mihrab*. Semidomes, vaults, arcatures, stalactite corbeling, marble paneling, and molding surrounded these entrances and made peerless approaches for the mosques. In Iran and the east some mosques had lofty and imposing portals showing an unmistakable influence of ancient structures of Persepolis and Ctesiphon upon Muslim architecture.

The exterior and interior decoration of the mosques was based upon matched and quartered panels of marble, porphyry, and other types of stone, different colored stones being used in alternate courses in the walls or in alternate voussoirs in the arches. Capitals, spandrils, and other spaces were often covered with finely carved geometric and floral patterns; and in many instances the walls were given color, warmth, and depth by the use of plain or figured tiles. One of the most frequent and pleasing patterns employed in stone, wood, or ceramics was that composed of highly stylized Arabic letters, almost invariably a verse from the Koran. Human and animal figures were forbidden by the Koran and their use in decoration rarely appeared in a mosque, although the prohibition was often disregarded in objects of secular use.

Some of the imposing mosques of the Middle East which date from the early medieval period are: the Umayyad mosque of Damascus, begun in 705; the Mosque of Ibn Tulun in Cairo, finished in 879; the Great Mosque of Kayrawan, built about 743; the Mosque of Karawiyn of Fez, begun in 859 and finished in 1135; the Great Mosque of Cordoba, begun in 785 (now the cathedral); the Friday Mosque of Isfahan, built about 760; and the Mosque of Sultan Ala-al-Din of Konya, built in 1220.

Although mosques and great mausoleums have been the most permanent of Middle Eastern edifices of the medieval period, various books contain descriptions of numerous libraries, hospitals, bazaars, palaces, forts, shrines, and palatial public baths in Baghdad and other cities. Probably the most widely known sacred building in the Muslim Middle East is the revered *Kubbat-al-Sakhra* (The Dome of the Rock), often popularly referred to as The Mosque of Umar. An annular structure, it was begun in 685 by Caliph Abd al-Malik to cover and enshrine the spot from where according to legend Muhammad made his nocturnal journey to heaven. Termed the oldest extant Muslim place of worship, it comprises an octagon surmounted by a dome which rests upon an interior circle of piers and columns. The space between the inner circle and the octagonal wall was too wide to be spanned by beams, so that an intermediate octagon of arches borne by piers and columns was necessary. Thus was formed two rings which were used for ceremonial circumambulation. Originally the upper part of the exterior was covered with marble and gold mosaics, but these were replaced with the decorated tiles which are now there. The style of the building was a composite of Syrian, Roman, and Byzantine traditions and contained a number of novel adaptations. The style, however, was followed in later Muslim architecture only in technical and decorative details and not as a general model for other structures.

THE MINOR ARTS

In the whole field of the so-called minor arts Muslims in the medieval period carried on the skills and techniques of antiquity in a most notable fashion. Far ahead of western Europe in each of the minor arts, at least until the High Renaissance of the fifteenth century, the Middle East produced outstanding rugs, silk and cotton textiles, leather work, fine glass, highly glazed ceramics of many types, shapes, and varieties, and exquisite pieces in gold, silver, copper, brass, and bronze, many of the pieces heavily inlaid with other metals or encrusted with precious gems. The illumination of manuscripts and the painting of miniature pictures developed into a fine and precise art, while skill with the pen produced a calligraphy so graceful and so pleasing that later Western artists frequently employed strips of Arabic script in their own decorations. The expertness of the Middle Eastern artist in the medium of enamel inlay upon metal was manifest to the Crusaders, so much so that many terms used in describing color (enamel work) in armorial bearings and in heraldry were derived from Arabic words.

One striking evidence of the real unity of the Muslim world between the seventh and thirteenth centuries was the ease and extent of exchange of knowledge and movement of individuals. Such a circulation dictated a considerable universality of Muslim civilization, and the minor arts are an excellent illustration. From Marrakesh and Toledo on the west to Samarkand in the east each of the great cities boasted reputable craftsmen and artists in all of the arts. Each may have professed a slight difference and some were acknowledged to excel in a particular skill; yet, for centuries Byzantine Constantinople was the only comparable center outside of the Muslim world.

THE SECLUSION OF WOMEN

By the tenth century the role of wealthy, middle-class, and urban women in the family and in society had undergone a marked change. The veil, seclusion, and segregation of the sexes were practiced by Muslims and by many non-Muslims in the Middle East. Their origin and the reasons for their introduction are not certain, but the best indications point to Byzantine civilization as the main influence. With the general and wide acceptance of concubinage and its excesses, the rank of the actual wife was greatly elevated. Slavegirls might sing, dance, and entertain quite openly and freely for the guests of their masters; wives never. Thus, the veil and seclusion grew as a protection and a mark of distinction. However, the freedom and the public life of women such as enjoyed by Aishah, Khayzuran, and Zubaydah disappeared, not to return to the Muslim world until the twentieth century.

RECREATION

The great mass of people in the medieval Middle East, as in all other regions and in other periods except for the present, had neither time nor energy for recreation and entertainment. People of moderate means as well as the wealthy and the leaders of society in the Middle East enjoyed poetry and music. Although Muhammad had castigated music as one of the devil's handmaidens, song and music from various instruments were exceedingly popular. Accomplished musicians were praised, highly rewarded, and accepted as companions in high society. Slaves with musical talent and training commanded high prices. The elite themselves sometimes performed, and al-Rashid's brother Ibrahim was regarded as a truly accomplished musician.

The Middle Eastern gentleman relaxed at home or at a public bath which served as his club. Baghdad in its heyday boasted several thousand such establishments. After soaking and steaming and a vigorous massage the patron might sip cool sherbet, listen to music, and engage in a game of dice, backgammon, or chess. Chess was an ancient Indian game which came to Christian Europe by way of Iran and the Muslims. The word "chess" is a corruption of the Persian *shah*, "checkmate," of *shah mat* (the king is dishonored). The "rook" is the Persian *rukh*, or the dreaded "roc" described by Sindbad the Sailor. In Spain, the piece known in English as "bishop" is called *el alfil* from the Arabic *al-fil* (the elephant). And the modern "queen" has evolved from a piece which Chaucer called "fers," which was the Arabic *al-firzan* (the counselor).

Outdoor sports were many; favorites were archery, javelin-throwing, fencing, polo, and a ball game that may have been the ancestor of tennis. Hunting with its allied sports of hawking and falconry was much in vogue in the Umayyad and Abbasid eras. Caliphs and generals organized great hunts in which thousands participated in driving the game into confined quarters where the hunters could shoot the quarry without much effort. Wild game at close range frequently provided a dangerous and exciting sport, sometimes depicted in painting and ceramic decoration. The art of falconry was greatly refined, and there were numerous books on the subject.

The most royal of all sports in the Middle East was horse racing. In ancient Iran, in Greece, and in Roman and Byzantine times racing was the sport of kings and the favorite of the masses. The Arabs loved and prized horses; and the Muslim rulers quickly took to racing their horses in Syria, Iraq, and Egypt, as the Byzantine and Sasanid governors were doing when the Arabs appeared on the scene. Caliphs had their own stables, and it is related what pleasure Harun al-Rashid evidenced when his horses won their races. Betting, though unlawful by Koranic injunction, accompanied horse racing, as it did all sports for that matter, and made the races and games more exciting. Pedigrees and an interest in the breeding of horses advanced to the point where eastern horses were recognized and valued everywhere as Arabian horses.

From the foregoing survey of the many aspects of Muslim culture and its development in the medieval period it can be adduced that the permanence of Muslim culture must be credited to the wisdom of Muhammad and the Islamic leaders during the formative years of their empires. They appropriated and adapted from other civilizations and societies valuable ideas, experiences, and skills of man to create the new Muslim civilization. No civilization has been able to endure for long or to pursue any dynamic course when isolated, either geographically or intellectually. Progress has been accelerated by the exchange of knowledge among men and cultures; the greater the exchange the faster the acceleration. Although the Muslim empires were always politically unstable, any investigation of Muslim society reveals a continuing progress until the havoc and chaos following in the wake of the Mongol invasions of the thirteenth century brought upon the whole Middle Eastern society a penury and a despair from which it is only now in the twentieth century escaping.

REFERENCES: Chapter 9

Among volumes already cited, those of particular value for this chapter are in Chapters 4, 5, 7, and 8.

Arthur J. Arberry, *Classical Persian Literature*: Macmillan, New York, 1958.

Tjitze J. de Boer, *History of Philosophy in Islam* (E. R. Jones, trans.): Luzac, London, 1903.

Martin S. Briggs, *Muhammadan Architecture in Egypt and Palestine*: Clarendon Press, Oxford, 1924. A thorough survey of the field.

E. G. Browne, *Arabian Medicine*: Cambridge University Press, Cambridge, 1921. Excellent.

————, *A Literary History of Persia*, 4 vols.: Cambridge University Press, Cambridge, 1928. The standard work on this subject.

K. A. C. Creswell, *Early Muslim Architecture: Umayyads, Early 'Abbasids and Tulunids*, 2 vols.: Clarendon Press, Oxford, 1932–1940. An essential work for a study of the subject.

H. A. R. Gibb, *Arabic Literature: An Introduction:* Oxford University Press, London, 1926. Contains a good bibliography of available translations.

Gustave E. von Grunebaum, ed., *Unity and Variety in Muslim Civilization:* University of Chicago Press, Chicago, 1955. A symposium by sixteen specialists showing the impact certain well-established cultures had upon Muslim culture when the latter was forcefully imposed upon the former.

Reuben Levy, *Persian Literature: An Introduction:* Oxford University Press, Oxford, 1923. Excellent for the beginner.

————, *The Social Structure of Islam:* Cambridge University Press, Cambridge, 1957. A thorough study and analysis of all aspects of society in the Islamic world from the earliest times to the present.

D. S. Margoliouth, *Lectures on Arabic Historians:* University of Calcutta, Calcutta, 1930.

R. A. Nicholson, *A Literary History of the Arabs:* Cambridge University Press, Cambridge, 1930. Gives the reader an excellent view of the many types of Arab poetry and prose before 1000 A.D.

Arthur Upham Pope, *An Introduction to Persian Art Since the Seventh Century* A.D.: Charles Scribner's Sons, New York, 1931. Well-written and amply illustrated by an authority for the beginner, but interesting also to the specialist in the field of Middle Eastern studies.

Ernest Tatham Richmond, *The Dome of the Rock in Jerusalem: A Description of Its Structure & Decoration:* Clarendon Press, Oxford, 1924. A complete description of this historic shrine.

————, *Moslem Architecture, 623 to 1516: Some Causes and Consequences:* Royal Asiatic Society, London, 1926. A good, inexpensive introduction to the field.

CHAPTER 10

The End of Medieval Islam

THE CRUSADES

In preaching the crusade in 1095 at Clermont, France, Pope Urban II was unquestionably governed by religious spirit and motivation. Pilgrims returning from the East brought tales of woe which recent Seljuk conquests inflicted upon them in Asia Minor and Syria. They also reported that disunity and internecine warfare among the petty Muslim states of Syria and their leaders made possible a victorious assault by Christian knights of Europe. Furthermore, the desperate appeal sent by Alexius Comnenus, Emperor of Constantinople, promised the co-operation of the Byzantine army and fleet.

Western feudal Christendom had developed economically, socially, politically, and psychologically to a degree that it could outfit and send a temporary expeditionary force overseas. Its success stemmed from the power vacuum and political chaos which descended upon the Middle East after the death of Sultan Malikshah.

Gathering at Constantinople as an advance base, the Crusaders, almost always called Franks by Middle Easterners, departed for the Holy Land in the spring of 1097. Taking by force Iznik (Nicaea) in June and Eskishehr (Doryleum) in July, the main Frankish army won Antakya (Antioch) after many heroic and emotional incidents and a nine-month siege. By an inland route the Crusaders began the investing of Jerusalem on June 7, 1099 and successfully stormed the walls on July 15. Later that year the first victory on the coast was scored at Ascalon, and in the ensuing decade one after another of the coastal cities of the Levant fell to the merchant fleets of Pisa, Venice, and Genoa.

Shortly after the conquest of the Holy City Godfrey of Bouillon became the Baron and Defender of the Holy Sepulchre and the titular head of the Kingdom of Jerusalem. Other prominent Crusaders scattered along the coast to become the Count of Edessa, Prince of Antioch, and Count of Tripoli, these newly created principalities being held as fiefs of Jerusalem. Merely extensions of feudal Europe, these four little crusader states along the Mediterranean littoral were the so-called Latin kingdoms of the East. Most of the Crusaders returned home as soon as the first victories were won, and those who stayed on were hard pressed continuously to retain their possessions. In fact, they would have been lost at an early date had not an uninterrupted stream of knights appeared from the West and had not the merchant cities of the western Mediterranean maintained fleets in the Levant.

Eventually the Kingdom of Jerusalem was extended eastward across the Dead Sea and southward in a narrow tongue of land to touch the Gulf of Akaba. In the north the County of Edessa reached eastward to the headwaters of the Tigris. Elsewhere, the Franks clung close to the coast, in some places holding a strip barely ten to fifteen miles wide. They never gained possession of such cities as Aleppo, Homs, or Damascus.

The great majority of Western successes sprang from the complete disunity of the Muslim rulers. The amirs of Syria were delighted by the Crusaders' defeat of the Seljuks in Asia Minor; and during the siege of Antioch emissaries from Egypt proposed a combination of the Crusaders and the Fatimid caliph against the Turks. It becomes tiresome to record the alliances made by Muslim princes with the Latins against fellow Muslims, or alliances made by Franks with Muslim amirs against fellow Crusader feudal lords.

Before a decade had passed only a newly arrived naïve Crusader carried the religious spirit and fervor that had launched the First Crusade. In the Middle East the Latin knight reverted to the search for fiefs and the constant fighting which he had known in the West. That he could do this and feel at home in Syria and Palestine in the twelfth century was a result of the political chaos already present at his arrival. Nevertheless, the more advanced civilization of the Middle East began to influence the more barbarous Westerners. Latin nobles emulated the ways and adopted the higher standard of living of Middle Eastern ruling classes, thus opening the way for some of the knowledge of the East to find its way to Western Europe and hasten the coming of the Renaissance.

Baghdad and the eastern Seljuk sultans were hardly perturbed by the inroads of the Crusaders, especially since the latter succumbed within a few years to the general pre-existing political pattern of the Middle

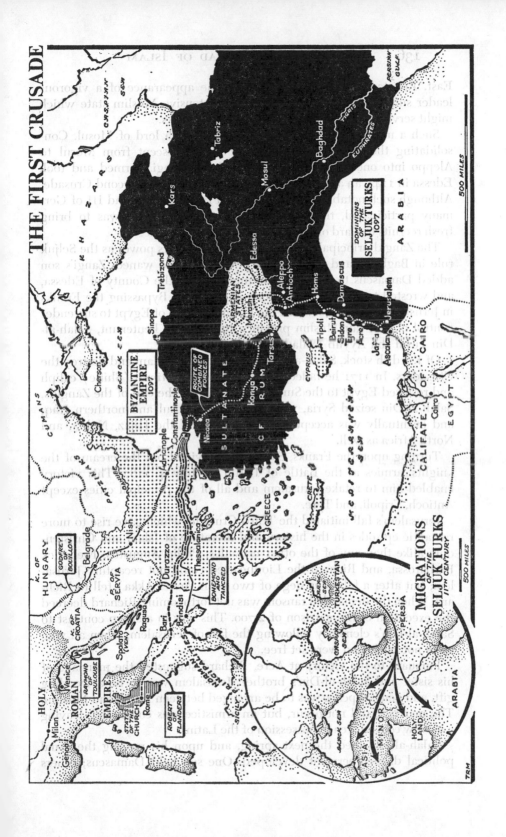

THE FIRST CRUSADE

DOMINIONS
OF THE
SELJUK TURKS
1097

BYZANTINE
EMPIRE
1097

ROUTE OF
COMBINED
FORCES

MIGRATIONS
OF THE
SELJUK TURKS
11TH CENTURY

East. Resistance to the West awaited the appearance of a vigorous leader sufficiently capable to create an extensive Muslim state which might serve as a base for an attack upon the Franks.

Such a man was the blue-eyed Zangi, Turkish lord of Mosul. Consolidating the northern arc of the Fertile Crescent from Mosul to Aleppo into one Muslim state, Imad-al-Din Zangi stormed and took Edessa in 1144, an act which touched off the so-called Second Crusade. Although such notables as Louis VII of France and Conrad III of Germany participated, the chief effect of this expedition was to bring fresh recruits to ward off other blows and hold the line.

The Zangid principality, however, augmented its power as the Seljuk rule in Baghdad and the Fatimid power in Cairo waned. Zangi's son added Damascus to his state, conquered all of the County of Edessa, and wrested territory from Antioch and Tripoli. Bypassing the Franks in Jerusalem, his armies forced the Fatimid caliph of Egypt to surrender control of that fair Muslim province to a Zangid lieutenant, Salah-al-Din Yusuf ibn Ayyub (Saladin).

Of Kurdish stock, Salah-al-Din sought to unify Islam and destroy the Crusaders. In 1171 he failed to recognize the Fatimid (Shiite) caliph and restored Egypt to the Sunnite creed. Upon the end of the Zangids, Salah-al-Din seized Syria, went on to take Mosul and northern Iraq, and eventually was accepted as the sultan of the Hijaz, Nubia, and North Africa as well.

Turning upon the Franks, Salah-al-Din wiped out the cream of the knights' armies at the Battle of Hittin on July 4, 1187. This victory enabled him to retake Jerusalem and all of the principal cities except Antioch, Tripoli, and Tyre.

Jerusalem's fall initiated the Third Crusade, which gave rise to more romantic episodes in the history and literature of Islam and Christendom alike than any of the other crusades. Philip Augustus, Frederick Barbarossa, and Richard the Lionhearted could not recapture Jerusalem; but after a fabulous siege of two years Acre (Akka) fell to Richard. When the demanded ransom was not forthcoming Richard decreed the execution of the garrison of 2,700. This was in a sharp contrast to Salah-al-Din's clemency following the fall of Jerusalem, when all who were not ransomed were set free.

Pursuant to the victory at Acre, Richard suggested the marriage of his sister and Salah-al-Din's brother. Jerusalem was to be a wedding gift, and general peace was to be arranged between Frank and Muslim. The marriage did not occur, but an armistice was concluded, leaving a narrow coastal area in possession of the Latins.

Salah-al-Din died the next spring, and upon his passing the usual political dismemberment developed. One son held Damascus; others governed at Cairo and Aleppo. A brother, the Saphadin of Western chroniclers, ruled Transjordania and conquered Syria and Egypt. Upon his death division and anarchy again ruled the Ayyubids until their own slaves and the Mongols destroyed them.

The recurring Muslim turmoil played into the Westerners' hands, enabling them to retake Beirut, Tiberias, Ascalon, and Jerusalem (1229). However, quarrels of Venetian against Genoese, Templar against Hospitaler, and baron against baron prevented lasting achievements. Salah-al-Din's nephew forced the Latins to abandon Damietta in Egypt, where they had landed in realization of the significance of Egypt and the Red Sea in their commerce with India and the East. Nevertheless, he made friendly treaties with the Italian city-states, entertained and discussed theology with St. Francis of Assisi, and gave Jerusalem to Frederick II.

Jerusalem fell in 1244 to a band of Turks; Louis IX's crusade to Egypt fell victim to the plague in 1249; and in that same year the Ayyubid family in Egypt was supplanted by Turkish generals from its slave army. A new era in Muslim history was emerging—the Mamluk (slave) period. Baybars, the fourth Mamluk sultan, captured Palestine and moved northward along an inland route to take Antioch. His successor continued the drive against the Latin state, and in 1291 another Mamluk took Acre. This was the signal for the remaining crusader towns of Beirut, Sidon, and Tyre to surrender. An episode in the history of the Middle East had ended.

As significant events influencing the development of civilizations and the destiny of mankind the Crusades have been greatly overrated. Nineteenth-century romanticists dramatized them and enlarged their role far beyond the actual facts. Most of the Crusaders remained in the Middle East such a short time and were so poorly prepared psychologically and educationally that they profited little from the experience. Of the few who resided in the Middle East for any length of time only the rare knight was fain to exchange the rich and interesting life in his new abode for the dull monotony on his former estate in the West.

Trade between East and West in the Mediterranean did, however, increase markedly. Italian merchants had now for the first time a paying eastbound cargo: Crusaders. This reduced the cost of Eastern goods in Western markets. Furthermore, returning Crusaders created an expanded Western market for Eastern goods, since even those who remained in the Middle East only a brief time did acquire a taste for Oriental foods and a preference for its superior manufactured goods such as textiles, cutlery, metal wares, and leather goods. However, the main channels of Muslim influence upon Western Europe were Sicily and Spain. Perhaps the flow through those areas was accelerated as a result of the Crusades and the returning Crusaders' awakened consciousness, if not appreciation, of a foreign civilization obviously richer than their own.

The effects upon the Middle East were much less significant. Its people became convinced that the Westerner was a ruthless soldier, semi-barbarous in nature, ignorant, and uncivilized. Even today Syrian mothers frighten their children when they misbehave by threatening them with "Richard the Lionhearted will get you." For centuries, Crusaders' castles dotted the landscape, but these never altered in any measurable degree the architecture of the Levant. The Middle East was politically disunited when the Crusaders arrived; it was still in fragments when they departed. In the interim, to be sure, the Ayyubids united the Muslims from the Nile to the Tigris. But this had no relationship to the Crusades; it was only an example of the recurring pattern of centralizing and decentralizing political forces continually at work in the area. In general it can be said that the Crusaders were more destructive than constructive, and that the Middle East was poorer because of the experience.

THE MONGOL INVASIONS

In the thirteenth century as the Crusades were waning, devastation rode in upon the Muslim world from the east. Born about 1160 in the neighborhood of Lake Baikal, Genghiz Khan, ruler over Mongol nomads and the self-styled "Scourge of God," consolidated in his hands the military might of the tireless Mongol warriors. Shortly after the opening of the thirteenth century Genghiz and his hordes moved westward to Iran, conquering all lands in their path. Bukhara, Samarkand, Marw, Nishapur, Hamadan, Maraghah, and many other centers of civilizations were stormed and sacked. Inhabitants were slain by the hundreds of thousands, perhaps millions.

Iraq, Syria, and provinces in the west were spared by Genghiz's death in 1227 and by the subsequent division of the empire among his sons. But his sons and grandsons and other Mongol khans maintained the great empire. Pressure continued upon the Middle East. The Seljuk Turks in Asia Minor were defeated in a ruinous battle in 1243, and the Mongols levied tribute upon them. Under Mangu, the third successor to the position of Supreme Khan, a great expedition moved westward under the direction of Mangu's younger brother Hulagu. Starting from Karakorum in 1252 to rid the world of the Assassins and to destroy the Abbasid Caliphate, Hulagu Khan razed Alamut, the Assassin headquarters. Baghdad's turn came in 1258. Following a siege of several months, the city fell and was given over completely to the troops for a week. Destruction continued for a month. The Mongols then proceeded westward as far as Damascus but were halted by Baybars, the Mamluk sultan of Egypt, in an historic battle in 1260 at Ayn Jalat, near Nazareth. Egypt was spared Mongol violence; and Baybars pressed his victory, freeing Syria from Mongol control.

The Mongols in their conquests helped themselves to whatever they wanted and destroyed the rest, not knowing what to do with it. They could not garrison the cities adequately; they were pagans; and they neither understood nor appreciated the cultures and civilizations of the peoples they conquered. The devastation wrought by the Mongols is only now in the twentieth century being mended. Millions of peoples perished; cities vanished; canals silted full and irrigation ceased; lands became barren and deserted; government disintegrated; civilization foundered; and life returned to the bare essentials. Through the previous ages conquering armies and peoples had come and gone—Medes, Persians, Sasanids, Greeks, Romans, Byzantines, and Arabs—and customs, religions, knowledge, and culture had been modified, developed, and altered. But through all this time the Middle East had never suffered such a cataclysmic and paralytic shock as it received from the Mongol invasions.

MAMLUK RULE IN EGYPT

Cairo, Alexandria, and the land of the Nile were spared the sound of the hoofbeats of the horses of the Mongol nomads. Untouched by devastation, Egypt suddenly became the great stronghold of Muslim civilization, even though she herself had just entered into the strangest epoch of her long history.

Upon the death of the Ayyubid sultan in 1249 one of his widows seized power with the support of a Turkish slave general whom she married. Later when she had him murdered in his bath she was beaten to death by his slaves. The rule of Egypt then passed briefly to his son and then to other slave generals, one after another until 1517 when Egypt was conquered by the Ottomans. This long period of two and a half centuries of Egyptian history was termed the Mamluk (slave) era. Until 1390 the Mamluks were mostly Turkish and Mongol in origin, and they went by the name of Bahri (river) Mamluks. Between 1390 and 1517 they were generally Circassians and were known as the Burji (citadel) Mamluks.

Begun by the later Ayyubids as a slave army and bodyguard of foreign origin, the Mamluks evolved into a self-perpetuating slave military oligarchy. The recruit was purchased, usually in an eastern slave market, by a slave general or officer and rigorously trained in the arts of war. As he developed and progressed toward the top, he in turn made new purchases. A score of generals or amirs at the summit intrigued and battled for supremacy, though nominally electing the successor to the late Mamluk sultan. Many never bothered to learn Arabic and were Muslims in name only. Aloof from the native Egyptians, whom they despised, the Mamluks oppressed their subjects unmercifully. Frequently illiterate, always crafty, the life of the Mamluk sultan was fearfully uncertain, the average reign of the forty-seven Mamluk sultans being less than six years.

Some of the Mamluk sultans were capable organizers and redoubtable generals. The most resourceful, Sultan Baybars, not only turned back the Mongols in Palestine but also cracked the strength of the Crusaders in Syria. Understanding diplomacy and statecraft, he established friendly relations with Sicily, Aragon, and Seville, sent envoys to the Byzantine emperor, and made an alliance with the Kipchak Turks of the Volga River basin (his own birthplace) against the Mongols of Iran and Mesopotamia. Bringing from Damascus a refugee scion of the Abbasid family, Baybars originated the practice of having an Abbasid in Cairo as titular caliph without actual power. Such caliphs resided there up to the time of the Ottoman conquest, and their presence gave to Mamluk rulers a mark of legal recognition throughout Islam.

Under the Mamluk regime feudalism spread in Egypt. Since late Roman rule in the Middle East certain practices of feudalism were already present, and many of these were accepted by the Muslim conquerors. But in the tenth and eleventh centuries as the power of the Abbasid governments declined army generals, captains, and cavalrymen were assigned provinces and estates from which they collected taxes which they retained for their own support. For these privileges and benefits they were expected to serve the caliph or sultan, usually in a military capacity. Gradually all of the land of Egypt was granted to Mamluk officers who had to support, equip, and assure the service of a number of soldiers, the number depending upon their rank and the size of the grant.

DESTRUCTION OF THE MEDIEVAL MUSLIM WORLD

Simultaneously with the development of Middle Eastern feudalism came the spread of a self-subsistent manorial economy. As the uncertainties of government mounted and the difficulties of transportation and communication increased, industry and commerce were depressed and the money economy was greatly weakened. Political anarchy and civil wars destroyed the controls over the nomads within the Middle East and the perpetual battle between the Desert and the Sown was resumed, hastening the advent of a manorial economy. The Middle

Eastern Muslim lands entered into this new era piecemeal over a long period of time. In the middle of the eleventh century the Beni Hillal and the Beni Sulaym, Arab tribes transplanted to Upper Egypt, ravaged Libya and Tunisia, and sacked the Holy City of Kayrawan, leaving that part of North Africa in the desolate state which in large part persists today.

The major portion of the Middle East under the Mongol Empire was split into a variety of provinces. Government and wealth moved eastward. From time to time in the century following the conquests of Hulagu peace among Genghiz Khan's descendants allowed for passage of traders and travelers such as Marco Polo and Ibn Battutah. But the persistent threat of military violence and its repeated harassment stunted the growth of a middle class. Moreover, in 1368 the founder of the Ming Dynasty in China conquered the Mongols and closed the trade routes from central Asia into China, diverting all commerce with the Mediterranean to the route through the Arabian Ocean, the Red Sea, and Egypt.

The final blows to the highly developed Muslim culture and civilization of the medieval period in Mesopotamia, central and eastern Asia Minor, and parts of Iran were administered by the Mongolian Turks. For a quarter of a century, 1380–1405, the east was in turmoil because of the eruption of the Mongolian Turks led by Timur Leng (Timur the Lame—Tamerlane). Son of a Turkish chieftain who revolted against a descendant of Genghiz Khan, Timur first won control of Transoxiana, which served as a base for expansion, both eastward and westward. In 1380 his hordes began the conquest of Afghanistan, Iran, and Kurdistan. In rapid succession he captured Baghdad, Isfahan, Delhi, Aleppo, Damascus, Ankara, and Smyrna. Timur's death in 1405 and the subsequent anarchy among his heirs brought relief to the Middle East; but the majority of the middle class had disappeared, and much of the desolation wrought at his hands was never repaired. His most notorious custom was the construction of pyramids of human heads after the sacking of cities; at Aleppo twenty thousand heads were built into such markers. Schools, mosques, and libraries were destroyed, and only the walls of the famed Umayyad mosque in Damascus were left. Skilled artisans and theirs families were deported to Samarkand; many ancient skills which had survived through the ages were now lost forever.

In the wake of this barbarian tide three states remained in the Middle East: a fragmentized Iran; a broken and reduced Ottoman state; and the wealthy, firmly organized, corrupt Mamluk state of Egypt. Fifteenth-century affairs in the Middle East revolved around the economic, political, and international problems and interrelationships of these three powers.

THE OTTOMAN TURKS

The fortunes of the Ottoman state are considered in more detail else-where in this volume. In this connection it is sufficient to point out that the Ottoman state was reunited by Sultan Mehmed I within fifteen years after the debacle of his father at Ankara. The process of building an empire by adding provinces in the Balkans and Asia Minor was resumed, with Constantinople falling to Sultan Mehmed II in 1453. Following that world-renowned event, the Ottomans in their expansion southward and eastward came into conflict with Iranians and Mamluks. Mehmed II in 1473 turned back Uzun Hasan of Iran, and Selim I soundly trounced Shah Ismail, clearing Anatolia of most of the Iranian sympathizers and fellow heretics. Under Mehmed II border disputes flared between Turkey and Syria and between the satellites of the Mamluks and the Ottomans. In the 1490's Bayezid II was engaged in seven campaigns against the Mamluks. The latter won technical deci-sions in each case; but twenty years later (1517) Selim I and his army marched victoriously into Cairo, reducing the Mamluk state to an Ot-toman province and carrying off the last puppet Abbasid caliph to Istanbul.

IRAN

Iran in 1409 came under the rule of Timur's son Shah Rukh, who at-tempted to rebuild Herat and Marw and to establish a peaceful and prosperous regime. The succeeding Timurids, however, battled among themselves to such an extent that they were unable to control the Turkish nomadic tribes of the area. New groups and families appeared to divide Iran and to render her impotent in the struggle for power in the Middle East. Raids by Uzbeg tribes in Transoxiana and the absence of trade to the east led the center of population and importance to shift westward.

In the Caucasus and the highlands of eastern Anatolia Turkish tribes under the leadership of the Kara Koyunlu (Black Sheepmen) seized control of Armenia and Azerbayjan. For a time after the death of Timur the Kara Koyunlu ruled Baghdad and established Tabriz as their capital, building the famous "Blue Mosque" there. Other Turkish tribes in an Ak Koyunlu (White Sheepmen) federation were established in Armenia and northern Mesopotamia with Diyarbakir as their capital. The pinnacle of Ak Koyunlu power came under Uzun Hasan, who ruled all of Iran from 1467 until his death in 1478. Married to a daugh-ter of the Greek emperor of Trebizond, Uzun Hasan was approached through his in-laws by Venice to induce him to fight Venetian battles against the Ottomans. The envoy, Caterino Zeno, successfully persuaded Uzun Hasan. However, he found Mehmed II a formidable foe, especially since Venice made no move to engage the Ottomans in another quarter.

After the death of Uzun Hasan the Ak Koyunlu state rapidly disintegrated, preparing the ground for the rise of the more native Safavi dynasty under Shah Ismail. From this strictly Iranian rule the modern and contemporary state of Iran emerged.

EGYPT

The trade of the Far East and India passed to Europe through the Red Sea and to the Mediterranean either by way of Egypt or by the historic caravan routes in the Hijaz to Transjordan, Damascus, Beirut, Aleppo, and Alexandretta. The Mamluk empire, therefore, possessed a strong, almost monopolistic, control over east-west trade. The steady growth of this trade in the fifteenth century together with the natural productivity of the Nile Valley and the skilled artisan manufactures of Egypt gave to the Mamluk-Arab society a brilliance unrivaled in any other Arab land. What cultural life and quest for knowledge remained in the Arab world found refuge and patronage in Cairo and Alexandria. Although originality had passed, science and literature were cultivated by students and supported by the court and the wealthy. The greatest activity was in the construction of mausoleum-mosques. Of these the most outstanding was that of Sultan Kaitbay, who died in 1495. Noted for its alternate red and white stone courses, the mosque-tomb-school has a stately high dome over the tomb chamber. The exterior of the dome is covered by an elaborate geometric pattern interspaced with intricate floral designs. The minaret, in several stories, is one of the most handsome in Cairo. The arched gallery of the second floor of the school reminds one of the arched loggias of Venice.

Yet, despite all the trade and wealth and the escape from invasion and devastation, society and civilization in Egypt were sick and decadent. Government was uncertain. Mamluk sultan succeeded Mamluk sultan with frequency and violence. In the fifteenth century there were twenty-two changes of sultan; on one occasion there were three sultans in a single year. The system of training Mamluk officers and soldiers broke down, and the quality of new slaves deteriorated as the difficulty of purchasing slaves in the Volga and the Black Sea areas increased. Law became the whim of the ruler, and the ruling class was beyond the law. Graft, corruption, and inefficiency within the Mamluk order mushroomed. As land revenues declined, government officials grew more venal.

Between native Arab-Egyptian and Mamluk the chasm widened; the community of interests ceased. Personal insult was heaped upon exploitation and civil degradation until the Mamluk, although a core-ligionist, was loathed by the native Egyptian. Nevertheless, rich merchants flourished in Cairo. In the middle of the fifteenth century there were reported to be at least two hundred merchants worth a million ducats each and over two thousand worth one hundred thousand ducats each. The presence of such wealth gave Cairo an aura of prosperous strength that misled most European visitors.

The Mamluk Empire included the Hijaz and Syria as well as Egypt, the outlying provinces being held through semiautonomous amirs. These satellites to the north were tied to Cairo loosely when the sultan was weak; and frequently at such moments the amirs played the dangerous game of flirting with the reviving Ottoman state or with whatever prince ruled in Iran. Border disputes were inevitable, and in 1485 when a war broke between rivals for the throne of Dhu-al-Kadr, Ottoman Sultan Bayezid II backed one while Mamluk Sultan Kaitbay supported the other. Six campaigns followed. At one time the Ottomans occupied Aleppo; at other times Mamluk generals penetrated Anatolia as far as Kayseri. Before the war ended, the commanding Ottoman general was twice captured and carried in chains to Cairo. The Mamluks won the battles but could not achieve victory, and in 1491 peace was arranged through the efforts of an envoy from Tunisia.

Within a decade after this successful defense of the distant frontiers of the state Mamluk good fortune was irretrievably lost. The Portuguese rounded Africa and strongly established themselves in the Indian trade, since they could afford to pay higher prices for goods than the Arabs could. In 1502 the Portuguese attempted to block the Gulf of Aden to prevent ships from entering the Red Sea. Portuguese ships threatened the port of Jidda on the Red Sea, and in 1506 the Portuguese occupied and fortified the Island of Socotra near the entrance to the Gulf of Aden. Syria alone had spices to export, and the Mamluk Sultan Kansawh al-Ghawri began the construction of a fleet on the Red Sea. His efforts, however, were too little and too late. The small Mamluk fleet was destroyed in 1509 by the Portuguese under their able Admiral Albuquerque. Bayezid II of Turkey sent timber and armament for thirty ships, but to no avail. The trade was lost, and the Egyptian economy collapsed. The coinage was debased as revenues declined. Living standards fell, and the Mamluk government disintegrated.

It was upon such a hopeless scene that the Ottoman Sultan Selim I appeared when he arrived in Syria. The Mamluk sultan brought his army to Aleppo to threaten the rear and flank of Selim, who was engaged with Shah Ismail of Iran. Selim turned quickly, crossed the Taurus Mountains, and routed the Mamluk rabble at Marj Dabik in August, 1516. Twenty years previously the Mamluk army was well paid and well equipped, but the force before the Ottomans here was a sullen, dispirited, and unpaid mob using obsolete armament. Selim proceeded southward taking all of Syria with ease; cities such as Damascus, Tripoli, and Beirut surrendered peacefully.

Cairo was taken by assault in January, 1517, and the last Mamluk Sultan, Tumanbay, was seized and hanged. Egypt became an Ottoman province; and the puppet caliph, al-Mutawakkil, was taken to Istanbul. With Selim I's departure from Egypt the center of the Middle East politically, economically, and culturally shifted to Istanbul and the Ottoman Empire. An age had wearily come to an end. Although Turkish sultans, Turkish generals, and Turkish slaves had been ruling in Arab countries for several centuries, the future now belonged to a Turkish rule that identified itself as Turkish and based its power on Turkish people.

REFERENCES: Chapter 10

Many volumes already cited bear upon this chapter, including several in Chapters 4, 6, and 7.

David Ayalon, *Gunpowder and Firearms in the Mamluk Kingdom:* Valentine, Mitchell, London, 1956.

V. V. Barthold, *Turkestan Down to the Mongol Invasion*, Luzac, London, 1928. The standard work on Central Asia from the seventh to the thirteenth century.

Bayard Dodge, *Muslim Education in Medieval Times:* The Middle East Institute, Washington, 1962. An unusual and scholarly work.

H. A. R. Gibb, *The Arab Conquests in Central Asia:* Royal Asiatic Society, London, 1923. Readable and based on original sources.

————, *The Damascus Chronicle of the Crusades, Extracted and Translated from the Chronicle of Ibn al-Qalanisi:* Luzac, London, 1965.

Ira Marvin Lapidus, *Muslim Cities in the Later Middle Ages:* Harvard University Press, Cambridge, 1967.

Bernard Lewis and P. M. Holt, eds., *Historians of the Middle East:* Oxford University Press, New York, 1962. A most important work.

Steven Runciman, *A History of the Crusades,* 3 vols.: Cambridge University Press, Cambridge, 1951–58. Thorough and readable. Largely from the Western point of view.

Robert Lee Wolff and Harry W. Hazard, eds., *A History of the Crusades,* Vol. II, *The Later Crusades (1189–1311):* University of Pennsylvania, Philadelphia, 1962.

Nicola A. Ziadeh, *Damascus under the Mamluks:* University of Oklahoma Press, Norman, 1964.

The Ottoman Empire

CHAPTER 11

The Byzantine Empire

ESTABLISHMENT OF THE STATE

A prominent student of Byzantine history has defined the Byzantine empire as "the Roman Empire in its Christian form." If this is true, then its history must begin with the era of the Emperor Constantine and his building of the city of Constantinople on the site of ancient Byzantium.

Except for a period in the thirteenth century when Latin knights of the Fourth Crusade occupied it, Constantinople was the hub of the Eastern Empire until its fall to the Turks in 1453. Thus, the Roman Empire under Christianity endured for more than eleven centuries—centuries which witnessed, especially in Constantinople: the preservation and propagation of the Christian faith and its theology; the knowledge of the Hellenistic and Roman ages; the art and architecture of the ancient world; the artisan skills of Greece, Rome, and the Orient; and many techniques of government discovered through centuries of Roman rule.

In establishing a new capital for the empire Constantine placed his chief residence closer to the populous part of the empire and in a better situation for the defense of the Balkan provinces. Moreover, he was able to break more completely with obsolete paraphernalia of government in Rome. His reforms, and those of Diocletian before him, were easier to sustain in a new location.

In Constantinople the emperor was the accepted absolute monarch with power strictly centralized in his hands. Except in a very few provinces civil and military powers were separated, and a regular civil service system for the various bureaus of government was expanded on a basis of merit and seniority. The University of Constantinople was created to further the dissemination and advance of Hellenistic culture.

Finally, but perhaps first in significance, was Constantine's recognition of Christianity, his participation in Christian affairs to the extent of calling the first general council of the Christian Church at Nicaea in 325, and his use of the emperor's power to try to achieve uniformity in Christian doctrine. Constantine's action resulted in the union of Church and State and the interdependence of emperor and patriarch which is known as the Caesaro-papism of the Byzantine Empire.

From the first days, therefore, the Byzantine state embodied imperial tradition, Christian orthodoxy, and Hellenistic culture—forces which gave direction to government, religion, and literature in Constantinople for a thousand years.

POLITICAL HISTORY

Following Constantine, more than seventy emperors or empresses graced the imperial throne of Constantinople before its fall in 1204 to Fourth Crusaders. A relatively large number of these rulers were capable leaders, and many were outstanding. Theodosius I (r. 379–395) made Christianity the official and sole religion of the empire. Theodosius II (r. 408–450) published the code of Roman law bearing his name and constructed the storied land walls of Constantinople, which stretch from the Sea of Marmara five miles to the Golden Horn. Without a doubt this formidable barrier saved the imperial city, and therefore the empire, from northern barbarians and the Arabs on countless occasions.

Justinian I (r. 527–565), an Illyrian, and his empress Theodora (r. 527–548) have enjoyed fame through the ages. Many of their buildings still stand in Istanbul, the noblest of which are the incomparable Church of Hagia Sophia and the majestic aqueducts north of the city. Equally celebrated were the Justinian codes of laws, compiled and digested by a commission of leading jurists and law professors. Remaining the foundation of law through the years in the Byzantine Empire, these codes appeared in Italy in the twelfth century and served as the basis for the reintroduction of Roman law in the West. Probably the main reason for publication of the laws was Justinian's need for rigorous control of the empire and efficient collection of taxes to provide funds for his western military campaigns.

The next gifted emperor, Heraclius (r. 610–641), an Armenian and son of the governor of Carthage, is often called the creator of the medieval Byzantine period. He was the first to use officially the title Basileus, and it was under him that Greek became the official language of the empire. Upon his accession he found the empire in a disturbed and debilitated condition, with Slavs and Sasanids threatening its existence. By reuniting Church and State, by revitalizing the army and navy, and by reinstituting strict economy, Heraclius defeated the Iranians in a series of brilliant campaigns and freed Syria and Egypt from Sasanid control. However, the financial strain of these wars and the cost in manpower left the Basileus unable to meet the Muslim Arabs in a favorable posture, and the recovered provinces were lost to Islam in Heraclius' last days.

During the remainder of the seventh century the frontiers contracted and the economy of the state materially weakened. Muslim armies ravaged Asia Minor, camped on the shores of the Sea of Marmara, and took to the sea in the eastern Mediterranean. But the empire was preserved by the accession of Leo III (r. 717–740), an Isaurian from Marash in the region of the Taurus Mountains. Besides shielding the empire from Eastern onslaughts, the Isaurian advanced Heraclius' administrative system of themes, which were provinces where the military general (*strategos*) was also governor. Thus, they were military districts, although judges and other civil officials did submit their accounts directly to the central administration. At first only a few were organized in this manner, but by the time of the Fourth Crusade thirty-eight provinces had been transformed into themes, the most important of which were in Asia Minor facing the Muslims.

A contemporary of Charlemagne and Harun al-Rashid, the Empress Irene (r. 797–802) captured the imagination of many ages. The Greek wife of Leo the Isaurian's grandson and the power behind the throne of her son for twenty years, Irene blinded her son and ruled alone as *emperor* until overthrown by a revolution. She recognized Charlemagne as Holy Roman Emperor, paid tribute to Harun al-Rashid, and gave her support to factions in the capital that opposed Isaurian iconoclastic policy. The first two points were indicative of the decline of Byzantine power. The third disclosed the deep-seated religious division which persisted in the empire. Many with Monophysite tendencies, especially those from eastern reaches of the empire, objected to icons, images, pictures, and in particular representations of the Virgin Mary in church services and decorations. Leo III, over the objections of many bishops and monastics in Constantinople, forbade the use of icons, an act pleasing to the soldiery of his eastern themes. Irene made a political alliance with orthodox churchmen, and for their favor in her struggle for imperial position and power she pursued orthodox doctrines of anti-iconoclasm.

Evil days again fell upon the Byzantine Empire until the ascent of Basil the Macedonian (r. 867–886). Maintaining its supremacy until 1056, the Macedonian dynasty led the empire during one of the more brilliant periods of its long life. Basil, of humble origin, rose from the imperial stables, where his superb physique and feats of prowess attracted the attention of the emperor. Soon co-ruler, Basil I took the next step and had his patron murdered. Nevertheless, he and his successors, particularly Basil II (r. 976–1025), were capable emperors, republishing old codes of laws, restoring harmony in the Church, and pursuing a vigorous defense of the state against Arabs and Bulgarians.

Between the Macedonians and the fall of Constantinople in 1204 three dynasties—the Ducas, the Comneni, and the Angeli—ruled the empire. Of these the Comneni (r. 1081–1185) were the most illustrious, perhaps because they held the throne throughout most of the period of the Crusades. Alexius I found himself between Turk on the east and Frank on the west, hardly knowing which to fear the more. His daughter Anna Comnena has left a most interesting account of the arrival of the First Crusade at Constantinople; the contrast in culture and civilization of the two Christian societies of her day was sharply drawn.

Unfortunately for the Comneni, during their last days there was a large influx of Latins into Constantinople. Many influential government positions were given to them, much to the displeasure of the Constantinopolitan citizenry. A French noblewoman, Mary of Antioch, served as regent for her son Alexius II (r. 1180–1183) and became so much the target of public hatred that a pleasing scoundrel, Andronicus I, stirred up the capital to murder Latins quite indiscriminately and to sell others into captivity. As one author says: "the seed of the fanatic enmity between West and East, if not planted, was watered." Two decades later Constantinople did fall to Venetians and Fourth Crusaders, an act which brought an end to the true Byzantine Empire. What later passed for that empire proved to be only a shell of her former power, grandeur, and significance.

THE CHURCH

Before discussing this later phase of the empire, it may be well to study a few institutions of society as they were at the height of Byzantine glory; for their forms persevered into the weak last days and even beyond into the Ottoman period. The strongest and most vital arm of the emperor was the Christian Church. After the demise of paganism in the fourth century the capital, the Balkans, Greece, and Asia Minor were devoted in their support and loyalty to the Church. Its tight organization with the Patriarch at its hierarchical apex gave powerful support or presented determined opposition to the emperor and government. Consequently, the emperor always tried to control the selection of the Patriarch and reckoned with his views. As many as one hundred monastic or holy orders had cloisters in Constantinople, and the members had a profound influence upon the religious views of the populace. Frequently the government found it necessary to follow doctrines espoused by the populace, even though other dogmas were preferable for reasons of imperial policies. Whenever an emperor compromised with heresy to mollify a distant province or the army in some Asiatic theme or entered into an understanding with the Papacy regarding the universal Christian Church, the orthodox voice of the capital was heard.

In a way the Church resembled an administrative department of the government, and the Patriarch acted as a minister of state in charge of religion. A dynamic emperor chose, appointed, and dismissed Patriarchs; an energetic Patriarch bent weak emperors to his will. It was this interrelationship that has been called Caesaro-papism, but at most times the emperor was supreme and the Church was subordinate to the State.

THE GOVERNMENT

It could hardly have been otherwise; for the emperor was an autocrat, modified by the legal right of revolution against him. Strength of government, beyond the unity created by an absolute emperor, resided in highly educated and well-trained civil servants who administered the departments of the central government as well as those of the provinces. Jealous of their position and rank, they made the government function during palace revolutions and reigns of incompetent emperors. They also resisted inroads of reform and innovation.

A further strength of government resulted from the division of power and responsibility in the provinces. Even after the evolution of theme government judges, publicans, and managers of state lands had access to their respective bureaus in Constantinople so that theme governors never had full and irrevocable authority.

AGRICULTURE AND INDUSTRY

After the loss of Egypt to the Arabs Constantinople and cities of the empire were supplied with necessary sustenance by Asia Minor, Thrace, and the Balkans. The lot of the peasant was hard and few envied him his life. Yet, he seldom lacked food, clothing, or shelter, and famines were rare. Land was fundamental to the economy, and livestock such as oxen greatly increased productivity of the land and peasant. Monasteries in the capital and elsewhere possessed numerous estates which provided monks with their living. This would indicate that agriculture in the Byzantine Empire was not at the low level of a subsistence economy. One bought and held land for the money income which it produced.

Although agriculture was the mainstay of the empire, industry and commerce gave it wealth and luxury. In the great cities of the empire compact populations were engaged to a considerable degree in manufacturing articles of everyday use. Many, too, produced luxury goods of great value which were used in rituals and services of thousands of churches and monasteries and which were vital to the pageantry of the imperial court. Sumptuous living was much enjoyed; and the wealth of silk fabrics, gold brocades, jewelry, reliquaries, enameled wares, fine glassware, and all the precious and refined luxury of the medieval age dazzled Western visitors. Crafts and skills of Roman and Hellenistic artisans prevailed for a thousand years in the Byzantine world, making it almost as much an industrial society as it was agricultural.

TRADE

The most active commercial city of the Byzantine empire, Constantinople was filled with warehouses, depots, caravansarais, banks, moneychangers, and all aids and agents for promotion of foreign and domestic commerce. Trade from the Black Sea area and most of Russia centered upon Constantinople. Goods from the Far East and western Asia passed down the Bosphorus to quays on the Golden Horn. Surplus produce—manufactures and raw materials—of the empire gravitated to the capital for exchange and transshipment. Ships plied regularly between Constantinople and Cherson, Trebizond, Salonica, Venice, Amalfi, and Genoa. A standard tax of ten percent, levied on all imports and exports, brought to the imperial government a large part of its revenue. Italian cities, however, found it possible to obtain tariff concessions from the emperors; Basil II permitted Venetian merchants a reduction in taxes on goods exported from Constantinople in return for their "policing" the Adriatic, which they already controlled, and for carrying imperial cargoes if requested. The Comneni granted a concession of six percent in the export-import tariff for Venetian, Genoese, and Pisan merchants trading in the empire.

Commerce in certain goods was forbidden: soap could not be imported; and gold, raw silk, court ceremonial robes, unsewn fabrics, and salt fish could not be exported. Industry and commerce were strictly regulated by the government. Controls were exercised over prices, quality and quantity produced or imported, profits, locations of business, labor conditions, and movement of workers.

GUILDS

Implementation of these controls was effected by individual guilds—industrial, commercial, and financial—which were highly organized and fully developed before the year A.D. 900. Most guilds were granted special privileges and certain monopolies so that membership in the respective guild was a prerequisite to engage in any business or trade. To some extent guilds were restrictive in character. At times they were repressive, and they were always conservative. Yet, they prevented speculation and collusion, protected rights of individuals in local and distant markets, and performed many social and legal functions for members.

Through the ages and up to the present writers have maligned the Byzantine Empire, its civilization, and particularly its rulers. Intrigue, court politics and so-called palace revolutions, the sharp business acumen of the merchants, and the mercenary character of some aspects of its life have led historians to use the word "byzantine" in a most malicious and derogatory manner. Nevertheless, a close and objective study of Byzantine records reveals a fully civilized society which possessed an efficient government and excellent public services, which was managed and directed by an educated and sophisticated bureaucracy, and which was protected by an army of high tactical ability. At a time when Western Europe was semibarbaric inhabitants of the Byzantine Empire were enjoying literature, philosophy, urban social culture, and a much higher standard of living.

THE CRUSADES

In 1071 when Emperor Romanus IV Diogenes was defeated by Alp-arslan at the Battle of Manzikert near Lake Van in eastern Asia Minor, the rout was so complete that Asia Minor became overrun with Turkish bands. Within a few years they were encamped on the shores of the Bosphorus across from Constantinople. Food supplies and raw materials, revenues, commerce, trade routes, and man-power supplies were lost; this further contraction of the empire spelled its doom.

A desperate call went out to Western Christendom for aid. The Crusades were the response; but they did more harm than good. Italian merchants traveled in the Crusaders' vanguard and, as soon as the Latin states were founded, they arranged to carry their Oriental trade through Syria, frequently bypassing Constantinople. The West expended little sentiment over the Byzantine Empire, as the infamous Fourth Crusade demonstrated. The fall of Constantinople to Venetian merchants and soldiers in 1204 terminated abruptly the Byzantine Empire, and its society and civilization collapsed. The Orthodox Church was latinized; monasteries disappeared; wealth of the churches was carried off; the University closed; learning and literature vanished; books and libraries were lost; and works of art were destroyed. Original works of Praxiteles, Aristotle, Aeschylus, and others, known to have existed in Constantinople in 1204, were never found or heard of after that catastrophe.

The flight of the Byzantine court and ruling classes from Constantinople in 1204 had the immediate effect of producing several independent Greek principalities in the Byzantine provinces. Shortly, the fragmentation was reduced to three: Trebizond on the Black Sea coast in eastern Asia Minor; Nicaea in Bithynia in northwestern Asia Minor; and Arta and Salonica in Epirus and Thrace. At Nicaea Theodore Lascaris, husband of an Angeli princess, gathered many of the old aristocracy and had the Patriarch crown him emperor, thereby gaining a prestige never enjoyed by his two rivals. Meanwhile, the Latin empire of Constantinople hardly had a chance. Fraught with internal feuding and largely deserted by the West, the Crusaders were hemmed in by the Bulgarian Kingdom and the Greeks of Epirus and Nicaea. Finally in 1261 Michael Palaeologus, a general who usurped the Lascaris throne, overthrew the Latins and re-established the Byzantine Empire in Constantinople.

THE END OF BYZANTINE RULE

From 1261 to 1453 Byzantine rule held in Constantinople; but it cannot justly be regarded as a restoration of the Byzantine Empire. It was never more than a Greek kingdom, and for the final half century nothing more than the capital city itself. The old empire was broken beyond repair. Furthermore, simultaneously with the expulsion of the Latins from Constantinople the invasions of Genghiz Khan and his grandson Hulagu destroyed the Seljuk Empire of Asia Minor. Thus, this sector of the Middle East was groping for new leadership, and adjustment of the balance of power to new conditions became inevitable. Upon the ruins of these two empires a new Ottoman state arose.

The Palaeologi tried to maintain a style of imperial government unjustified by the extent of their actual domain. Only a small part of northwestern Asia Minor remained in their hands, and the Balkans were held by Bulgarian and Serbian rulers. Land revenue was extremely low; and with so much of Far Eastern trade passing to western Europe through Mamluk Egypt the imperial crown jewels had to be pawned in Venice.

One mediocre ruler succeeded another; palace poverty and intrigue spawned civil wars and revolutions. Interminable squabbling marked the history of the Church. The Palaeologi, in their desperation for aid, repeatedly made and accepted bids to subordinate the Orthodox Church to the Pope and his authority. Monks, churchmen, and the people always objected so that religious unity with the West was postponed or abandoned. Toward the middle of the fourteenth century the poor rose in Constantinople and Adrianople and massacred the aristocracy and the rich. In Salonica the populace had a peoples' republic for seven years.

In foreign affairs, the Greek state of Constantinople, in addition to negotiations and agreements with the Papacy over church matters, was confronted with the rising dynamic Ottoman Turks in Asia Minor and the Bulgars and Serbs in the Balkans. In 1355 Stefan Dushan, at the head of an extensive Balkan Serbian empire bounded by the Aegean, the Adriatic, and the Danube, seized Adrianople. Perhaps only his sudden death saved Constantinople.

Foreign and transit trade of Constantinople fell into the hands of Venetians and Genoese. The latter from their docks and counting-houses of Galata, a suburb across the Golden Horn from Constantinople, yearly grew more powerful and more insolent in their dealings with the Palaeologi. Since the Genoese possessed numerous ports and stations on the shores of the Black Sea and the Sea of Azov, many old Greek trading families of Constantinople found themselves excluded from their traditional haunts.

The most spectacular group of foreigners that came to the Byzantine state was the mercenary Catalan Grand Company of soldiers under the leadership of Roger de Flor. No longer could the state afford a regular standing army; only when a crisis arose or a threat appeared could an army be supported. Roger, a German by birth, and his Spanish company of ten thousand, including wives, mistresses, and children, were hired in 1302 to combat the mounting aggression of the Turks. The emperor, however, was soon more terrified of the Catalans than he was of the Turks and successfully plotted Roger's murder.

In the century and a half preceding the fall of Constantinople international politics in the Byzantine area consisted almost entirely of constantly shifting alliances and realignments among the Byzantine successor states, of which the Greek state was only one. Greek emperors made friends with Turkish princes of Asia Minor against the Ottomans. However, when Venetians and Serbs banded together to seize Constantinople, Orhan, the Ottoman ruler, obtained the hand of the emperor's daughter as partial inducement to bring his forces across the Dardanelles into Europe to defend Thrace from that combination. A rival emperor in alliance with the Genoese drove the Ottomans back to Asia and sent his predecessor to a monastery to spend the rest of his days writing his brilliant memoirs. Deposed by his own son and the Genoese, the new emperor called for Ottoman support, which returned him victoriously to Constantinople in 1379.

From that time on Ottoman sultans were deeply involved in Byzantine affairs. Emperors frequently recognized sultans as their suzerains, sent their sons as hostages to the Ottoman court, and sometimes led the Turkish fleet on adventures into the Black Sea. Sultans plotted palace revolutions in Constantinople, and emperors sponsored rivals to the sultan's trone and intrigued with Turkish principalities against the Ottomans. Manuel II and Mehmed I personally discussed affairs from their respective galleys on the European shores of the Bosphorus and then crossed to the Asiatic side for a picnic, although the emperor did not descend from his galley. When an emperor died childless in 1448, Murad II approved the selection of Constantine XI, whose niece married Mehmed II.

Genoese, Venetians, Serbs, Bulgars, Greeks, and Ottomans were the active groups in the Straits area of the Middle East in that epoch; and the religious and linguistic differences among the six protagonists proved an insufficient barrier to political or economic partnerships. A blending of social patterns and institutional structures was proceeding so naturally that contemporary observers who were familiar with the situation showed no burning concern over the thought that the Ottomans might take Constantinople and the Straits. Little fear was evidenced that an Ottoman society and government on the Golden Horn would be very different from the Greek state. Life, trade, government, and religion would go on much the same. The Ottomans showed every indication of being as much Europeans as they were Asiatics.

From a Byzantine point of view the debacle in Asia Minor following the Mongol invasions nurtured a new Turkish principality under the leader Osman. Within a few decades the northwestern section of Asia Minor came under Ottoman control. (Ottoman was an Italian corruption of Uthman, just as Osman was a Turkish corruption of Uthman.) And for the remainder of the century Ottoman activity was centered in Europe. At first the Ottomans were invited and hired by Byzantine emperors to fight in battles against Serbs, Bulgars, and Italians or for one faction of Palaeologi against another. Later they settled in Europe, and before the close of the fourteenth century they had become masters of Thrace, Macedonia, Bulgaria, and parts of Serbia. Constantinople was isolated but obtained a fifty-year reprieve from Timur's crushing defeat of the Ottomans at the Battle of Ankara in 1402.

For fifty years Constantinople was all that remained of the Byzantine Empire. That it did not fall to the Ottomans after their state was re-created under Mehmed I can be credited almost wholly to its superb defensive position. With water on three sides and the marvelous Theodosian Wall between the Golden Horn and the Sea of Marmara making the fourth side, the inhabitants of Constantinople felt secure. Any attacker had seemingly insurmountable obstacles to overcome.

By building the famous castles on the European shore of the Bosphorus in 1452 Mehmed II could blockade Constantinople by sea. Control of the Balkans gave him complete freedom to mass an army equipped with heavy artillery before the land walls in the spring of 1453. The plight of the city was obvious to all. When the walls were breached and his army transported from the Bosphorus over the hills of Pera to the Golden Horn, the fate of Constantinople was sealed. Constantine XI died vaingloriously on the walls; Muslim prayers were said in Hagia Sophia; and bells tolled in Europe. The once great and vigorous Byzantine Empire finally succumbed of old age after a long and painful illness. The young Ottoman Empire ushered in a new day for the great imperial site on the Bosphorus.

REFERENCES: Chapter 11

G. Georgiades Arnakis, "Captivity of Gregory Palamas by the Turks and Related Documents as His Historical Sources," *Speculum*, Vol. 26, pp. 104–118 (January, 1951). A short but illustrative picture of the early relationship between the Turks and the Byzantines.

Ernest Barker, ed., *Social and Political Thought in Byzantium, from Justinian I to the Last Palaeologus:* Oxford University Press, New York, 1957.

Norman H. Baynes & H. St. L. B. Moss, eds., *Byzantium: An Introduction to East Roman Civilization:* Clarendon Press, Oxford, 1948. Fourteen essays by a group of international scholars.

Charles Diehl, *Byzantium: Greatness and Decline* (Naomi Walford, trans.): Rutgers University Press, New Brunswick, 1957. The first English translation of the French classic. It is also the first volume in the Rutgers Byzantine Series and contains a fine bibliographical essay by Peter Charanis.

———, *History of the Byzantine Empire* (George B. Ives, trans.): Princeton University Press, Princeton, 1925. An important work by the great French Byzantinist.

Jack Lindsay, *Byzantium into Europe:* Bodley Head, London, 1952. Emphasizes the relationship of the Byzantine Empire to Western Europe.

George Ostrogorsky, *History of the Byzantine State* (Joan Jussey, trans.):
Rutgers University Press, New Brunswick, 1958. The best one-volume his-
tory of the Byzantine Empire. This is the second volume in the Rutgers
Byzantine Series. Translated from the Russian.

Alexander Van Milligen, *Byzantine Churches in Constantinople, Their History and Architecture:* Macmillan, London, 1912. Detailed and well illustrated.

————, *Byzantine Constantinople: The Walls of the City and Adjoining
Historical Sites:* John Murray, London, 1899. Out of date, but still the best.

CHAPTER 12

Early Turkish States of
Asia Minor

TURKISH PENETRATION OF ASIA MINOR

The Battle of Manzikert in 1071, wherein Alparslan completely routed the Byzantine army, ranks as a decisive historical event: it opened Asia Minor to Turkish settlement. Suleiman, one of Alparslan's distant cousins, was assigned responsibility for the Seljuk frontier facing the Byzantine Empire. Within ten years Turkish forces fanned out over Asia Minor and established themselves so solidly that Suleiman could choose Nicaea, a western city, as his capital. Smyrna was taken, and Turks occupied towns and villages along the Asiatic shore of the Sea of Marmara.

The ease with which the Turks invested Asia Minor suggests that a vacuum existed and that some Turks were conditioned already to exploit the opportunity. Emperors of the Ducas dynasty taxed the Anatolian provinces heavily and withdrew financial support and governmental privileges from frontier districts. March-warriors (*akritoi*) and Armenian areas were disaffected, and gave the emperors little aid. After the humiliation of Manzikert these groups deserted the empire. Furthermore, during the eleventh century there took place a rapid expansion of large estates in Asia Minor with a corresponding growth of a sizable serf-peasant class working lands of wealthy aristocrats and clergy of Constantinople. When Suleiman entered Asia Minor, he found numerous Armenian principalities asserting their independence. To the serfs he gave freedom from all dues. Many *akritoi* had already joined their arms with those of Turkish frontier-warriors (*ghazis*) in overrunning Asia Minor—in effect opening Anatolia for the entry of Suleiman and his Seljuk cohorts.

Alparslan never expected to conquer Asia Minor; his victory at Manzikert was a maneuver to guarantee his right flank while he subdued Syria and Egypt. Suleiman, whose father had been guilty of treason, was sent partially as an exile; but he looked upon the post as a fortuitous opportunity to gather a loyal army and following with which he might return victorious to the main Seljuk state. But Suleiman and his Seljuk organization did not conquer Anatolia; many Turkish tribes and bands infiltrated the provinces and settled upon the land. The Seljuk family only systematized the conquest.

Since the seventh-century era of great victories and Muslim expansion the Taurus Mountains and Armenian highlands of eastern Asia Minor served as an effective boundary between Christendom and Islam. Armies of each raided and penetrated across frontiers into lands of the other; but no extensive change in the line occurred. On each border arose semiautonomous provinces to attract adventurers, outcasts, heretics, fanatics, and the unemployed from each society. Muslims called them *ghazis*, "warriors of the faith"; to the Byzantines they were *akritoi*. But together they comprised a typical body of freethinkers and freebooters, forming one society with one culture, even though nominally part were Christian and part were Muslim.

Prior to the Battle of Manzikert Turkish bands plundered Asia Minor, even such cities as Sivas, Kayseri, and Konya. Afterwards Anatolia was fully opened to the ghazis, who for more than a century had been chiefly Turkish in origin and language. As they scattered over the land, great numbers of Turkish nomadic tribes found the roads and passes inviting. These peoples, traditionally called Turkomans or Yuruks, were identical in blood, and nearly so in dialect, to Seljuks and their Turkish adherents or to Turkish ghazis. In fact, nomadic Turks were staunch allies of organized Turkish forces. One day a Turkoman would be peacefully tending his flocks or threshing his grain, and the next he might be lending his sword to Seljuk or ghazi in furthering the conquest of Asia Minor.

SELJUK TURKS OF RUM

The First Crusade infused Byzantine forces with a new strength to stem the Turkish tide. Nicaea was retaken, and western sections of Asia Minor were restored to Byzantine control. Central and eastern Anatolia remained Turkish, and ghazi Turkish at that. Ruling in Baghdad, Syria, and Iran, the Seljuk family took cognizance of this new province of Islam and sent Suleiman to reign over that land. Since little power ac-

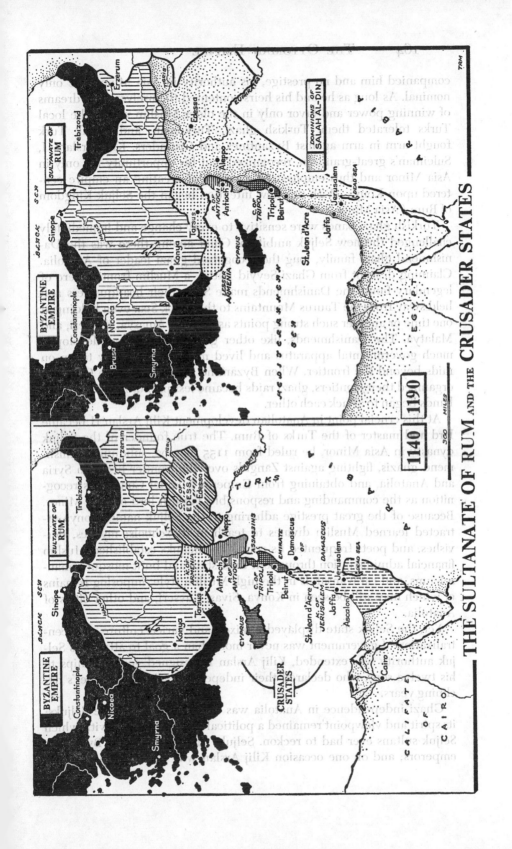

THE SULTANATE OF RUM AND THE CRUSADER STATES

companied him and no prestige, his authority in Asia Minor was only nominal. As long as he and his heirs contented themselves with dreams of winning power and favor only in the older Muslim world, the local Turks tolerated them. Turkish ghazi, Turkoman, and Seljuk Turk fought arm in arm against Byzantines and Crusaders. Kilij Arslan II, Suleiman's great-grandson, recognized that his opportunity lay only in Asia Minor and thus emphasized a policy of creating an empire centered upon Konya. With this new intention began the Seljuk Kingdom of Rum (Asia Minor).

Turkish ghazi bands were sensitive to every change and immediately challenged the new Seljuk ambition. Chief among these was the Danishmend ghazi family, long the recognized ghazi leader of Anatolia. Claiming descent from Ghazi Seyyid Battal, a Muslim frontier hero of legendary fame, the Danishmends made Sivas their headquarters and held sway from the Taurus Mountains to the Black Sea, even holding at one time or another such strong points as Ankara, Amasya, Kayseri, and Malatya. The Danishmends, like other ghazi states, never developed much governmental apparatus and lived mainly from booty taken on raids beyond the frontier. When Byzantine forces under the Comneni organized their frontiers, ghazi raids became less profitable and Turkish bands began to attack each other.

At this crucial point in Anatolian development Kilij Arslan II became lord and master of the Turks of Rum. The true founder of the Seljuk dynasty in Asia Minor, he ruled from 1155 to 1192, subduing Danishmend ghazis, fighting against Zangids over the frontier between Syria and Anatolia, and obtaining from Emperor Manuel Comnenus recognition as the commanding and responsible Turkish lord of Asia Minor. Because of the great prestige adhering to the Seljuk name, Konya attracted learned Muslim divines to teach in its schools; mystics, dervishes, and poets frequented its court. The Seljuks established Muslim financial administration throughout their state and built mosques, mausoleums, and caravansarais in the high Muslim style, imposing remains of which may still be seen in Konya, Sivas, Kayseri, and other cities of Anatolia.

Yet, the Seljuk state displayed a mixed and varied culture, and centralization of government was never more than a goal to attain. As Seljuk authority was extended, Kilij Arslan II assigned governorships to his twelve sons, who declared their independence in their father's declining years.

Ghazi independence in Anatolia was never crushed by the Seljuks; its spirit and viewpoint remained a political and social force with which Seljuk sultans ever had to reckon. Seljuks made peace with Byzantine emperors; and on one occasion Kilij Arslan was welcomed and enter-

Seljuk Dynasty of Rum

Arslan
|
Kutlumish
|
Suleiman I
|
Kilij Arslan I (d. 1107)
|
Masud I (d. 1155)   Malikshah
|
Kilij Arslan II (d. 1192)
|

Kaikhusraw I (d. 1210) Malikshah (1188–1191) Suleiman II (d. 1204)
| |
Kaikaus I (d. 1219)   Kaikobad I (d. 1237)   Kilij Arslan III (d. 1204)
|
Kaikhusraw II (d. 1245)
|

Kaikobad II (d. 1257) Kilij Arslan IV (d. 1266) Kaikaus II (d. 1280)
| |
Kaikhusraw III (d. 1283) Masud II (d. 1302)
|
Kaikobad III (d. 1302)

tained royally by Emperor Manuel I in Constantinople, much to the
consternation of the ghazi element. To receive Christian renegades at
the court in Konya and give them responsible positions or to possess
Christian women in the harem and have a Christian mother were understandable, but to fraternize with Christian potentates was unthinkable. Everywhere Christian churches and monasteries remained, even
owing their allegiance to the patriarch in Constantinople. The mixed
culture prevailed in rural areas, in former ghazi districts, and definitely
at the frontiers toward the Byzantine Empire. In certain Turkish circles
criticism of Kilij Arslan's soft policy was so significant that a small success over Manuel was trumpeted as proof of the Seljuk ardor in extending Islam.

Through the century from A.D. 1150 to 1250 the Seljuk sultanate of
Konya, or Rum, shone brightly. Muslim and Christian traders frequented its markets, and a considerable share of Far Eastern trade
passed through the area to enrich various treasuries. Schools were
crowded and the arts flourished. Armenian stonecutters, Iranian tile
decorators, Persian poets, and Arab calligraphers practiced their crafts
and were much appreciated. Ghazis settled down, Turks became villagers, communities were established, and life and people in central

and eastern Asia Minor in the course of one hundred fifty years grew increasingly homogeneous in every aspect.

Nevertheless, frontier marches were never fully consolidated within the culture of the central provinces of the Seljuk state. Brothers, cousins, and nephews of sultans were in continual rebellion and usually found support or refuge among frontier warriors, from whom the Seljuk sultans never commanded complete obedience. Unreformed ghazis could not comprehend Seljuk peace treaties with Christian emperors and did not accept the idea of coexistence in Asia Minor.

Peace and a more settled life quickly produced many effects of population pressures. Another blow to ghazi life and economy fell when Seljuk sultans ceased sending out raiding parties. More and more warfare in Anatolia was only among contestants for the sultanate of Konya. Then, early in the thirteenth century Turks, nomadic families and tribes, soldiers, princes, bureaucrats, dervishes, artisans, and scholars began drifting into Anatolia in swelling numbers. Mongols, under the leadership of Genghiz Khan, drove them westward, and Seljuks encouraged these displaced persons to settle on the frontiers.

A complicating factor of significant proportions for the Seljuks and the frontier marches resulted from the fall of Constantinople to the Fourth Crusade. With their capital moved to Nicaea, Byzantine emperors gave full attention to Anatolia and its defenses. Ghazi aggressions suddenly met sterner resistance; frontier lines became rigid; and the growing Turkish population was ready to burst its bounds.

That the land was in a state of ferment was demonstrated by a movement in 1239 against Kaikhusraw II led by Baba Ishak, a holy man who protested against the luxurious life of the sultan and his court. The sultan suppressed unmercifully this socio-religious outbreak, but in so doing forever alienated the allegiance of ghazi Turks and Turkomans of Anatolia. Martyrdom of the holy Baba at the hands of Christian and Norman mercenaries insured the wide and permanent acceptance of his heretical doctrines throughout Asia Minor.

MONGOL INVASION

No sooner was Baba Ishak's resistance movement driven underground than Kaikhusraw II was confronted by Mongol invasions. Erzerum was taken, and at the fateful Battle of Kozadagh in 1243 the Seljuk armies were crushed. Sivas fell, Kayseri was sacked, and its population slaughtered. Upon the sultan's sudden death two years later, Seljuk independence was extinguished. Kilij Arslan IV journeyed eastward to Karakorum, where he observed the election of Kuyuk as the Great Khan of the Mongols and where his position as Seljuk Sultan of Rum was confirmed. All Seljuk rulers, thenceforth, were only puppets or vassals of the

Mongols. At the time of Kilij Arslan IV's appointment the amount of yearly tribute was set, and from its size the fiscal extortion of the Mongols became apparent. Later the Mongol Hulagu divided Muslim Anatolia in two, giving all east of the Kizil Irmak to Kilij Arslan IV and assigning the land west of that river to his brother Kaikaus II. The latter conspired with the Mamluks of Egypt and fled to Constantinople to to the home of his uncles. (His mother was the daughter of a Greek priest of that city.)

In the face of such actions and because of obvious weakness any respect for Seljuk rulers by other Turks of Anatolia vanished. Since Mongol rulers never had the time or interest to establish their authority firmly in Asia Minor, their invasion, followed by an immediate withdrawal, politically fragmentized Turkish Anatolia. Each Turkish prince was suddenly on his own. Almost simultaneously the Byzantine emperors regained Constantinople and became involved immediately in Balkan affairs. Their Asiatic provinces were neglected. Turkish ghazis and Turkoman tribes discovered not only that the restraining hand of the Seljuk sultan could be ignored but also that Byzantine resistance had disintegrated and the frontiers easily penetrated.

FRAGMENTIZATION OF ASIA MINOR

Within a few years Asia Minor except a small northwestern corner was overrun by Turkish forces in much the same fashion and speed as their ancestors had occupied eastern and central Anatolia after the Battle of Manzikert nearly two hundred years earlier. The eastern half of the Seljuk state remained for many decades under Mongol authority and continued to render tribute to the Great Khan. In the western half, however, and in the newly acquired more westerly areas Turkish independence was openly declared and easily maintained.

Although each Turkish principality had different and individual characteristics, two general types appeared: Turkoman, and ghazi. Few of the former left much of a mark on the pages of history. The Torgud and Warsak tribes of the Taurus Mountains maintained their independence until the sixteenth century, but never had more than nomadic states and governments. Other Turkoman groups from Malatya to Antalya on the Mediterranean formed principalities which with the passing of time assumed the way of life of ghazi states. The leaders, for whom the states were named, however, never adopted the title of ghazi. The more permanent of these states were Teke-eli at Antalya, Ramazan at Tarsus and Adana, and Dhu-al-Kadr (Sulkadr) at Diyarbakir, Malatya, and Elbistan.

From the ghazi states arose the pattern of political and social life that dominated Asia Minor and Turkish life for several centuries. Countless ghazi leaders created independent baronies in the wake of the Mongol demolition of the Seljuk state. Gradually, energetic leaders consolidated numerous petty holdings into sizable ghazi principalities, or amirates. At the time the one founded by Osman near Eskishehir was quite insignificant. Other more important and more extensive amirates were: Menteshe at Milas and Mughla; Sarukhan at Manisa; Aydin at Aydin; Karaman at Laranda, Karaman, and eventually Konya; Karasi at Bergama; Isfendiyar at Kastamonu; and Hamid between Antalya and Konya. Another principality of considerable importance in connection with the development of the Ottoman state was that of Kermian (Germian) at Kutahya. Never calling themselves ghazis, Kermian rulers were more typical of the Seljuk rulers, but they were allied with the ghazi states about them. Eventually the state founded by Osman conquered or annexed all the others.

TURKISH GHAZI STATES

Since records are scanty, the political evolution in this period of Anatolian history has remained confused and uncertain. Perhaps the oldest of these states was established in the extreme southwestern corner of Asia Minor by Menteshe, who came there by sea from the Seljuk winter residence and naval base at Antalya. Menteshe, his sons, and followers took to sea raids and could be called ghazi pirates. Dismantling of the Byzantine fleet for economy reasons led many Byzantine sailors to join the Menteshe forces, which were then able to take the Island of Rhodes and raid coastal areas almost at will. The Knights of St. John, however, expelled the ghazi corsairs from Rhodes about 1310 and denied them easy access to the Aegean Islands.

Soon the Menteshe amirate was eclipsed by that of Aydin, built on the site of the ancient Greek city of Tralles on a tributary of the Meander River. Ensconced in the hinterland around Smyrna, Ghazi Aydin combined the strength of land and sea ghazis. He took Smyrna—Turks called it Izmir—and led his raiders to Greek and Thracian coasts, returning richly laden with booty. His fame spread, and volunteers appeared in camp from amirates far and near. In 1344 an active alliance of Venice, Cyprus, Rhodes, and the Pope defeated the Aydin ghazis and retook Smyrna. The Aydin amirs, however, remained independent until the end of the fourteenth century, when Ottoman forces subdued the amirate.

Karamania, situated in the foothills of the Taurus Mountains southwest of Konya and originally a ghazi state, offered the most persistent opposition to the Ottomans. Arising among the partisans of Baba Ishak, Karaman was the son of a sufi mystic. The demise of the Seljuk state, nevertheless, encouraged the Karamans to assume Turkish leadership and to move to Konya as the Seljuk heirs. In so doing they lost many ghazi characteristics and acquired qualities of older and more catholic Muslim governments. These latter qualities gave greater stability and permanence to the organization of the state, and enabled the Karamans to maintain their independence from the Ottoman Empire until the beginning of the sixteenth century.

Other ghazi amirates of Anatolia were similar to these three, and that established by Osman at Sögüt had few attributes different from usual ghazi traditions upheld in these principalities. Ibn Battutah, a fourteenth-century Moroccan globetrotter, visited Asia Minor and left a record of his impressions of these amirates. Entertained at the courts of many, he reserved no special tribute for Orhan, Osman's son, and in no way singled out the Ottomans for the fame that was to be theirs.

GHAZI SOCIETY

One may well ask: What were these ghazi traditions and attributes? Foremost, a ghazi state possessed as the reason for its existence a duty to battle against the infidel. It consisted of a band of dedicated warriors who rode out on raids beyond the frontiers of Islam, bringing back rich plunder which in most instances gave economic viability to the group. Although ghazis held fiefs of land, the state collapsed when raids were unsuccessful. Ghazis were equal socially and politically; aristocracy was derived from actions and leadership rather than from blood. It was a typical frontier society. To become a ghazi, however, was not an automatic step. One had to prove his worth by deeds and by evidence of character. In a ghazi state society was organized into several classes or corporations, the ghazi group being the highest.

Another feature of ghazi life was recognition and acceptance of the *futuwwa*, a set of rules by which the virtuous life should be lived. In fact, ghazi brotherhoods were organized on this moral and ethical base. Mutual fidelity among the membership was particularly emphasized. Likewise, almost every ghazi brotherhood recognized a spiritual leader; in most cases this leader was a mystic, dervish, or sufi, so that ghazis usually adhered to some dervish order. Frequently a badge or special headgear would be worn to distinguish ghazis from other individuals.

A ghazi, then, was one who had a sense of belonging to a separate and distinct corporation of individuals whose main occupation was military conquest. In a world of confusion and a period of political disintegration the ghazi movement flourished. But ghazi states found that raids eventually ceased, whereupon the states withered since life was not devised on a solid internal economy. To make the transition required more administrative apparatus than ghazis possessed. This problem ever confronted the Ottomans in their meteoric path across Anatolia and the Balkans. The success with which they solved this continuing problem determined, in considerable measure, the permanent or ephemeral character of Ottoman conquests. This theme is more or less central in the understanding and explanation of the rise and spread of the Ottoman state.

REFERENCES: Chapter 12

Unfortunately the number of works on this period of Middle Eastern history is few. Material can be found in Chapters 2, 4, 7, 10, and 11.

John K. Birge, *A Guide to Turkish Area Study:* American Council of Learned Societies, Washington, 1949. An indispensable bibliography.

Herbert A. Gibbons, *The Foundation of the Ottoman Empire:* Clarendon Press, Oxford, 1916. The first book to tackle the problem; still useful.

William L. Langer and Robert P. Blake, "The Rise of the Ottoman Turks and Its Historical Background," *American Historical Review,* Vol. 27, pp. 468–505 (April 1932). An important article.

Guy Le Strange, *Mesopotamia and Persia under the Mongols in the Fourteenth Century* A.D.: Royal Asiatic Society, London, 1903.

Tamara Talbot Rice, *The Seljuks in Asia Minor:* Praeger, New York, 1961. An architectural history.

Behçet Ünsal, *Turkish Islamic Architecture in Seljuk and Ottoman Times, 1071–1923:* Alec Tiranti, London, 1959.

Paul Wittek, *The Rise of the Ottoman Empire:* Royal Asiatic Society, London, 1938. A masterful work by the most eminent authority in the field.

CHAPTER 13

Ottoman Origins and Early Institutions

OTTOMAN ORIGINS

Osman, founder of the Ottoman state, was the son of Ertogrul, a
Turkish frontier warrior who possessed the land of Sögüt as a
fief, given by one of the later Seljuk sultans. An insignificant place and
an extreme outpost on the frontier, Sögüt was neither a rich fief nor
particularly desirable. Ertogrul must not have been very outstanding or
he would have commanded a more important assignment; and nothing
of certainty is known about his ancestry or background.

Ertogrul, like any other frontier warrior(*ujbey*), led raiding excursions into Byzantine territory; but he bequeathed to his son Osman little more than the original fief of Sögüt. Moreover, the conquest and
absorption of neighboring villages and fortified places began only in the
1280's. This was presumably after Osman had married Malkhatun, the
daughter of a certain Shaykh Edebali, who adhered to one of the mystical or sufi sects common to those frontiers. It was probably he who introduced Osman to the ghazi corporation and gave him the moral and
ethical ideas of the *futuwwa*.

In any case, Osman as a leader of ghazis began to acquire by capture
or alliance a number of small towns such as Eskishehir, Inönü, Bilejik,
and Yenishehir. Between 1300 and 1320, using Yenishehir as a base, Osman and his ghazis seized the countryside west of the Sakarya River
as far south as Eskishehir and the Kermian amirate, and west and north
to Uludagh (Mt. Olympus) and the Sea of Marmara. Yet, they were
not strong enough or sufficiently well equipped to take the walled towns

of Brusa, Nicaea, and Nicomedia. Not until Osman was on his deathbed in 1326 did his ghazis under the leadership of his son Orhan (Orkhan in old Turkish spelling) take Brusa, which surrendered without a struggle after several years of siege.

The fall of Brusa was the signal for Byzantine collapse in that corner of Asia Minor. Orhan occupied Nicaea in 1331; Nicomedia, in 1337. Later he dispossessed the quarreling sons of the amir of Karasi and placed Ottoman rulers over Bergama (Pergamum) and other towns of that amirate. Thus, by 1345 the Ottoman state included the entire northwestern corner of Asia Minor from the Aegean to the Black Sea.

Several factors prepared the way and assisted in this accelerating growth of the Ottoman state. No doubt, the personality and spirit of Osman counted heavily in forging a firm and successful band. Certainly, his men and his lieutenants were loyal and devoted to him. At first, Osman was placed in an exposed position between and near fortified areas within one day's sail from Constantinople. Even though emperors were weak and consumed with constant intrigues, they possessed sufficient determination to resist Ottoman attacks until the fourteenth century. Thereafter, Byzantine force weakened rapidly, and such towns as Brusa and Nicaea were summarily abandoned to their fate.

A most important element in the growth of Ottoman forces was the policy of welcoming any and all fighting men who would join in advancing the ghazi cause. Köse Mikhal, a Greek renegade, became one of Osman's favorite comrades, and his descendants, as the Mikhaloglu, held prominent positions through centuries of Ottoman history. In 1305 some of the Catalan Company joined the Ottoman camp; defeated Mongol raiders, given clemency, fell in with the men under Orhan; and many disillusioned Greek soldiers defending Brusa became Muslims and fought as Ottomans after that city capitulated. Fighting men from Kermian, Karasi, and other Turkish and ghazi amirates flocked to the Ottomans as their successes multiplied.

However, in the first half century under Osman and Orhan, Ottoman expansion was gradual enough to permit the organization of some governmental administration. Moreover, the Muslim world was in such disorder that Muslim artisans, merchants, bureaucrats, theologians, jurists, fiscal experts, teachers, and scribes were attracted by seemingly unlimited opportunities in this new frontier Muslim state. Schools of theology were built in Bursa and Iznik (Turkish names for Brusa and Nicaea) soon after their capture, and Bursa long remained the center of learning and philosophical discussion for the Ottomans.

Furthermore, the immigrant artisans and merchants formed corporations known as *akhis*. Somewhat like European guilds, these akhis were closely knit bodies subscribing to specific *futuwwa* very similar to the ghazi code of honor. A close alliance and understanding between ghazi and akhi gave to Ottoman society an economic strength lacking in other ghazi states. But the early arrival of Muslim lawyers and theologians (*ulema*) tempered the ghazi crusading fervor, so that Orhan accepted the older Muslim practice of allowing Christians and Jews to live in a Muslim land by paying taxes and special tribute. Thus, at an early date social and economic disturbances in towns passing into Ottoman hands were largely minimized. Life went on in much the same way with considerable intermingling of people. Orhan himself married Nilufer, a daughter of the Greek lord of a captured town. Taronites, Orhan's Greek physician, felt very comfortable and much at home among the Ottomans.

By the middle of the fourteenth century Orhan had become amir of a sizable state facing the historic Straits and Europe beyond. Silver coins were minted, and a lively trade developed in such prosperous towns as Bursa, Iznik, Izmid (Nicomedia), and Bergama. The Ottoman state assumed a place as an important powerful component in the political, diplomatic, and military turbulence concomitant with the decline of an obsolete empire.

Ghazis were long accustomed to raiding parties in Thrace and Macedonia. Orhan and his men became allies of Emperor John VI Cantacuzenus in 1345 to fight against his rival Emperor John V Palaeologus. Part of Orhan's bargain was the privilege of plundering; another part was the hand in marriage of Theodora, Cantacuzenus' daughter. Six thousand Ottomans ravaged the hinterland of Constantinople and the Black Sea coast and were instrumental in taking Adrianople. Similarly, every year thereafter Ottoman soldiers practiced their profession in Thrace and the Lower Balkans, amassing fortunes in booty.

OTTOMANS IN EUROPE

In these same years the Black Death struck. Reaching Constantinople first in 1347, it spread in following years through the Balkans and to the maritime towns and cities of the Aegean and the Straits and on to Europe, leaving dislocation and terror everywhere. It ended all talk of a crusade to crush the Ottomans or to regain Constantinople again for the Franks. No soldier would go to the East! The Black Death made victories for the Ottomans much easier in Europe.

In 1354 a severe earthquake demolished the walls of Gallipoli on the European shore of the Dardanelles. Ottoman forces in Europe rushed into Gallipoli, asserting God had given it to them. Orhan refused to return it to his father-in-law and set Ottomans there to colonize the city, much of whose population had been carried off by the Black Death.

From this first bridgehead in Europe Ottomans stormed over Eastern

Thrace, seizing all areas between the Aegean and the Black Seas except, of course, the imperial city of Constantinople. Adrianople opened its gates in 1362 to Murad, third in the Ottoman line of rulers, and for nearly a century that city (which the Turks call Edirne) stood as the Ottoman European capital.

Murad I, the younger son of Orhan and Nilufer, followed in his father's footsteps, vigorously pushing one campaign after another northward and westward into the Balkans. Rival emperors of Constantinople, Serbian and Bulgarian tsars, independent princes of Greece, the city-states of Venice and Genoa, popes, and Crusaders kept the Balkans in such a constant turmoil and confusion that Murad in his expeditions never had to worry about facing a consolidated offensive and usually had several Christian allies in his camp.

Under Murad's leadership (r. 1360–1389) Ottoman armies and raiders succeeded in conquering most of Bulgaria, Macedonia, and parts of Serbia to Lake Ochrida, including Widin, Sofia, Monastir, and Nish. At the decisive and crushing Battle of Kossovo over the Serbs in 1389 Murad lost his own life, but sealed the doom of independence for any Christian Balkan state and securely established the Ottoman position in southern Europe.

Likewise, Murad made extensive advances in Asia. He took Ankara and by a combination of prestige, power, money, and diplomacy nearly doubled his Anatolian possessions. Marriage of his son Bayezid to the daughter of the Kermian amir brought the town of Kutahya as a dowry. Murad forced the amir of Hamid "to sell" most of his domain and will the balance to the Ottomans. Campaigns were launched against Karamania and Teke, but with little success; for ghazis were unwilling to fight against those whom they considered to be "warriors of the faith." In these Anatolian campaigns Murad's most loyal supporters were contingents of his Slavic allies and mercenaries.

When Bayezid I succeeded to the Ottoman sultanship on the field of Kossovo, he inherited a state which stretched from the Danube to the Taurus Mountains and which had grown from a petty principality to a dominant power in a brief span of two generations. The Black Death, political anarchy in Europe and Asia, religious fervor, and a search for booty on the part of ghazis may have accounted for some of the rapidity of the development. Credit, however, should also be given to the dynamic personalities, the administrative talents, and the driving genius of Orhan and Murad.

OTTOMAN ARMY

Among the Ottomans the army, its organization, and its recruitment were matters of prime importance. Under Osman criers went through

the villages announcing that anyone who wished to fight and to participate in a raid should meet at a given place at a specified time. Orhan,
however, organized the army. Traditionally he did this on the counsel
and under the supervision of his brother Ala al-Din Ali and a maternal
relative Kara Khalil Chendereli. The latter was probably of akhi membership and has usually been considered to have had some formal education. Moreover, in the wars of Orhan and Murad closer contacts with
the Byzantine military provided examples from which the Ottoman
army obtained useful suggestions.

The army was organized on a basis of units of 10, 100, and 1000 men,
with a responsible officer over each group. This was as true of irregular
infantry(*azab*) and volunteer horsemen and cavalry scouts(*akinji*)
as it was of regular feudal cavalry(*sipahi*) and the newly formed jan-
issaries(*yeni cheri*). Officers of the immediate family and entourage of
the Ottoman ruler were placed in over-all charge of the armies. Evrenos
Bey, a Greek from Karasi, became chief of the European frontier and
always led the feudal sipahi, while Köse Mikhal was responsible for
the scouts. Suleiman Pasha, Orhan's eldest son, was the first to be com-
mander-in-chief(*Beylerbey*) of the troops in Europe.

The institution of the janissaries held a special place in Ottoman annals. The origin of this corps has been much debated. Their role in innumerable Ottoman victories through several centuries was so prominent that many authors have sought for some special beginning or at
least for the name of their brilliant innovator. In a Muslim state, even in
the time of the Prophet, the ruler as the embodiment of the state usually received one fifth of the booty of war. Since human beings had long
been valuable prizes of successful campaigns and since their lot was invariably one of slavery, Ottomans under Orhan and Murad found more
slaves on their hands than they knew how to employ in customary tasks.
Moreover, the market for slaves in surrounding areas was slack. The answer was to turn them into soldiers to fight for their captors.

Caliphs and sultans in the past had slave bodyguards, and in contemporary Egypt the ruling cliques, the Mamluks, were slaves. Youths
captured in battle, therefore, were kept as slaves by the Ottoman sultans, nominally converted to Islam, and banded together and trained as
special corps in the army about the sultan. Their name, *yeni cheri*(new
soldier), was corrupted to "janissary" by Europeans, who learned to
fear these soldiers and stand in awe of their discipline, their *esprit de
corps,* and their prowess with arms. Many younger captives were
"farmed out" for a number of years to Ottoman feudal officers as ap-
prentices. During these years they learned some Turkish, which became
the Ottoman *lingua franca,* and they grew, were toughened, and became adept in the skills of fighting. To assimilate the janissaries into the

Ottoman ranks as soldiers and as people was not difficult. Most of these captives were Greeks, Serbs, and Bulgars, and were hardly different, socially, racially, or culturally, from many of those free renegades who voluntarily became ghazis and Ottomans.

Probably not exceeding 3,000 in number in the days of Murad I, the janissaries were paid a small daily wage and did not marry while active as soldiers. Living together in barracks, drilling, training, and being garbed alike gave the janissaries the status of a standing army more than a century before standing armies became the European practice. Some were cavalry; most were infantrymen; others were members of a specially honored left-handed guard. Many rose through the ranks and became high officers and trusted civil officials; and a few were beheaded for dishonesty or disobedience. Before a century passed, only those who became regular infantrymen were known as janissaries. Other ranks and other corps had their own special designations.

Another important factor contributing to Ottoman successes was the development of sipahis, who answered the need for regular cavalry, for colonization of newly won lands, and for local provincial administration. Adapting Seljuk, Arab, and Byzantine feudal practices, Ottoman rulers rewarded ghazis and fighting men with grants of land from which they derived their living. Actual dispensation of land was made by the commander on the field. Greater valor resulted in larger fiefs. The smallest unit granted was a *timar*, to which additional fields were joined as more service was rendered. When lands held were sufficient to produce revenue to outfit more than five horsemen, the *timarji* became a *zaim* and his holding was termed a *ziamet*. Still larger grants were called *khass*, but these were reserved for special officers such as governors and commanding generals.

Each year when a campaign was announced, sipahis left their estates and appeared equipped to fight under the immediate leadership of a local officer whom they elected. This feudal cavalry not only was the main force of the Ottoman armies but also was engaged almost continually in raids beyond the frontier. Sons went along on campaigns with their fathers and learned the profession of arms. They were eligible to inherit his trade and were usually awarded at least a part of the family fief. By settling and rearing families on the land, the feudal cavalry served as the first Ottoman colonizers and administrators of new territories.

Running strongly through the ranks of the Ottoman feudal cavalry until the end of the sixteenth century was the ghazi spirit and ideology. In certain areas where the frontier was long a battleground as in Bosnia, northern Epirus, the Albanian mountains, Macedonia, and Thrace, a ghazi society emerged similar to those of earlier ghazi frontier areas in

Anatolia. A thorough admixture of Ottoman warriors with local populations occurred, giving rise in the Balkans to Greek-, Serb-, and Albanian-speaking Muslims.

BAYEZID I

Seizing the reins of government on the field of Kossovo in 1389, Bayezid I avenged his father's death with victory over the Serbians. Then, even before nightfall, he consolidated his position by ordering that his only brother, Yakub, be strangled. Yakub had fought valiantly at Kossovo and had served his father well and loyally not only in battle but also as governor of several provinces. Having the example of bitter and destructive rivalries of the Byzantine imperial family ever present before him, however, Bayezid judged that bowstringing his brother was for the best. He attempted to legalize this action by Koranic reference, with such success that practices of this kind became standard and legal procedure for a new sultan to take upon accession to the throne and prevailed in the Ottoman family for 250 years.

Years later upon the rise of modern nationalism Kossovo became the symbol among the Serbs for lost national identity and for subjection, but at that time no great ill-feeling seemed to be generated. The Serbian royal princess Despina was married to the victorious Bayezid, who became devoted to her; and Serb levies and contingents remained most loyal to Bayezid throughout his reign. In succeeding years Ottoman forces raided Bosnia and Hungary, even crossing the Danube and Bayezid brought greater numbers of Ottomans into Europe, especially into Thrace.

All of Thrace up to the very walls of Constantinople was occupied so that, beginning in 1391, the city was virtually blockaded from the land side. A full investiture of Constantinople was outlined and a full blockade planned. On the Asiatic side of the Bosphorus at Anadolu Hisar fortifications were constructed in 1393. Bayezid attempted to close the Bosphorus and the Dardanelles to ships destined for the imperial city. But attacks, first in Europe and later in Asia, saved Constantinople for half a century.

Sigismund, later Holy Roman Emperor but then only King of Hungary, was concerned over successful Ottoman aggressions. He, therefore, invaded Bulgaria in 1392 and captured the fortress of Nicopolis, only to withdraw within a few months before a large Ottoman force. The following year Bayezid judged it necessary to eject his Bulgarian vassal, whose capital, Tirnovo, fell before the onslaughts of Bayezid's son Suleiman. Suleiman followed the victory by fortifying Silistria, Widin, and Nicopolis. These actions, in addition to the creation of an

Ottoman navy which began depredations in the Adriatic, led Europe to heed Sigismund's loud cries for a crusade.

The romantic and fateful crusade of Nicopolis of 1396 was the result. Nobles from England, France, Germany, Flanders, and Burgundy, laden with wine and women, joined as if on a picnic. Leadership went to Jean de Nevers, grandson of the king of France, who appeared with Sigismund and Hungarian and Wallachian armies before Nicopolis. They foolishly charged the center of the Ottoman forces, commanded personally by Bayezid, who had left the siege of Constantinople to meet the knights of Europe. Utterly outmaneuvred, the flower of Western nobility fell on the battlefield of Nicopolis, and thousands were captured. Those under twenty years of age were taken for the janissary corps or the sultan's court. One of these—Johann Shiltberger—after twenty-five years returned to his German home and wrote a most valuable historical account of his experiences. Many, like Jean de Nevers, were held for ransom. And others as ordinary slaves were impressed to row in the galleys. This first serious encounter between Europeans and Ottomans brought disaster to the former and vetoed for several decades any thought of a crusade on their part.

A follow-up campaign deep into Europe was feared by Venice, but Bayezid turned his attention instead to Greece. Ottoman armies overran Thessaly, penetrated the Peloponnesus, and captured towns and smaller cities. Ottomans were settled in the northeastern corner of the Peloponnesus, then called Morea, and fiefs were handed out in northern Greece. But fortified cities such as Athens, Salonica, Nauplia, Coron, and Modon that could still be supplied from the sea were, like Constantinople, beyond Ottoman reach.

Conquests and crusades from Europe and the investment of Constantinople did not deter Bayezid from campaigns in Asia Minor. Without question, one of his burning ambitions was to unite under his rule, contrary to ghazi tradition, all Muslim lands of Asia Minor and perhaps of the entire Middle East. Although this idea paralleled naturally the common phenomena of expansion and unification attendant upon the rise and growth of a new state, Bayezid's haughty manner and ruthless tactics spelled his ruin.

In rapid succession between 1390 and 1397 Ottoman forces, frequently led by Bayezid in person, captured and annexed old ghazi and Turkoman amirates such as Aydin, Sarukhan, Menteshe, Teke, Karaman, and Isfendiyar and seized the areas of Kayseri, Sivas, Samsun, and Sinope. The dispossessed princes, instead of being commissioned with Ottoman responsibilities to weld them into the Ottoman people, fled with revenge in their hearts to the court of Timur Leng (Tamerlane).

Acquisition of Aydin and Menteshe brought experienced ghazi sailors to the Ottoman state, and in 1390 the first Ottoman navy was formed. Ships harried the coasts of Greece and descended upon various islands of the Aegean, and an embargo was declared on grain ships destined for Rhodes, Lemnos, Lesbos, and Chios.

With Bayezid engaged in subduing Bulgaria and in besieging Constantinople, the Karaman leaders judged a revolt might be successful. Bayezid, however, with amazing speed transferred his troops to Asia and destroyed the Karamans in front of Bursa. He did this so completely and so quickly that his soldiers dubbed him *"Yilderim"* (Lightning).

Except for a few walled towns like Constantinople and Athens, Bayezid Yilderim was now lord and master of the land from the Adriatic and the plains of Hungary to the Euphrates. In barely a decade he doubled his Asiatic possessions and gained recognition as lord of the Balkans. In 1395 he held court at Serres; Serbian princes and Byzantine emperors rendered homage. The uncomplicated Ottoman state of Osman and Orhan had vanished, and the rulers were no longer humble and unaffected.

POLITICAL AND SOCIAL DEVELOPMENT

In the time of Murad I the government began to grow; under Bayezid expansion was rapid and very noticeable. Its organization by religious leaders and graduates of the theological schools of Bursa and Iznik introduced more efficiency and rigidity in administration. At the same time evolution of the post of grand vizir in the hands of Kara Khalil Chendereli, later known as Khair al-Din Pasha, aroused considerable opposition and much unhappiness among ghazi feudal soldiers, accustomed for generations to great freedom.

This dismay also stemmed from Bayezid's dreams of empire. In 1394 he sent an embassy to the caliph in Egypt requesting to be invested with the title Sultan of Rum. Even Bayezid's grandfather used that title, and evidently it fell from every tongue. Yet, he wished recognition from the older Muslim world. Numerous Turkoman amirates of Asia Minor which were engulfed looked upon him as a tyrant and spread treasonable ideas at every turn. Few true ghazis participated in his Asiatic campaigns; Bayezid learned that in operations against fellow Muslims he could be sure only of his personal slaves (janissaries) and contingents sent by his European Christian vassals. Many Muslims in Asia could hardly escape questioning Bayezid's own faith when he led Christain soldiers against Muslim soldiers.

There were other ways in which Bayezid's actions alienated his subjects. The ghazi cultural background of Ottoman leaders left them open for many innovations, and with a medley of individuals appearing among them eclecticism developed. Discussions among religious leaders of various sects within the Ottoman state led to proposals for a common religion from a composite of Islam, Judaism, and Christianity. Undoubtedly this trend can be seen in the names of Bayezid's younger sons—Musa (Moses), Isa (Jesus), and Mehmed (Muhammad). Other sons were: Ertogrul (Turkish name), Mustafa (Muslim mysticism), Kasimir (Balkan Christian), and Suleiman (Solomon).

Even more objectionable were Bayezid's personal habits. More and more he took on the ways of life of Balkan and Byzantine rulers and nobles. Manners and dress changed; court ceremony became more elaborate. Many ghazis still remembered the ease with which they could approach Orhan and contrasted the simplicity of Orhan's establishment to the complexity of Bayezid's. Bayezid, though brilliant and energetic at first, fell under the spell of grandeur and sumptuous living. He became addicted to wine and sodomy, both of which scandalized the Ottomans. His harem was large and he began to follow in the footsteps of the caliphs of old. Even the increase in the number of his sons (Osman had only two, Orhan three, and Murad three) would indicate a devotion to his harem, an institution not mentioned in connection with either Osman or Orhan.

DEFEAT AT ANKARA

This dissatisfaction and unrest among Bayezid's subjects, especially the Muslims, and the presence of many Anatolian émigré amirs in the entourage of Timur induced the latter to lead an incursion into Anatolia. In addition, Bayezid had invaded territory beyond the Euphrates to the Tigris and given indications of ambitions in Syria, thereby threatening Timur's vassals. After Bayezid ignored letters from Timur inviting him to mend his ways, Timur marched into Asia Minor.

Surprisingly overconfident, Bayezid moved leisurely to meet the threat. In the face of so great a danger he organized a huge hunting party, wasting valuable time and tiring his men. The contest came in 1402 at Ankara, where only the janissaries and the Christian vassals of the Balkans stood fast. Bayezid, a prisoner, was brought before Timur, who honored him until his haughtiness became insufferable. Within a few weeks he died of humiliation, and his body was returned to Bursa, the chief Ottoman burial site.

Following the great victory, Timur marched across Anatolia to Smyrna on the Aegean. He showed, however, little desire to hold Anatolia directly. Ottoman conquests in Europe and the early holdings of Osman and Orhan in Asia were divided among Bayezid's remaining sons: Suleiman, Musa, Isa, and Mehmed. Kasimir for some reason was never considered; Ertogrul had been tortured to death earlier by Timur; and Mustafa disappeared at the Battle of Ankara. Anatolian amirates taken by Murad and Bayezid were restored to their previous hereditary families.

Bayezid had a dream of empire, but it was shattered at Ankara. The Ottoman family was left in possession of those of its holdings which were considered legitimate. His sons and all other amirs of Anatolia swore allegiance to Timur and became his vassals. Three years later when Timur died, the amirs of western Asia Minor renounced all dependence upon the Timurids, and Anatolia was left as it had been before the invasion except for the breakup of the Ottoman domain among Bayezid's four heirs. If there was to be an Ottoman empire, it was yet to be fashioned.

REFERENCES: Chapter 13

Volumes cited at the end of Chapter 12 are important for this chapter.

A.D. Alderson, *The Structure of the Ottoman Dynasty:* Clarendon Press, Oxford, 1956. An important volume on the Ottoman family and the lives of the individual sultans.

Edward S. Creasy, *History of the Ottoman Turks: From the Beginning of Their Empire to the Present Time:* Richard Bentley & Son, London, 1877. Based on the many-volume history of the Ottoman Empire by Joseph von Hammer-Purgstall, which though uncritical and out-of-date is still one of the most extensive works in any language.

G. J. S. Eversley and Valentine Chirol, *The Turkish Empire from 1288 to 1922:* T. F. Unwin, London, 1923. A standard work.

Stanley Lane-Poole, E. J. W. Gibb, and Arthur Gilman, *The Story of Turkey:* G. P. Putnam's Sons, New York, 1888. Still a fine one-volume work.

CHAPTER 14

The Winning of the Ottoman Empire

MEHMED I REUNITES THE STATE

The capture of Sultan Bayezid I at the Battle of Ankara in 1402 left the remaining Ottoman provinces to be apportioned among his sons. Timur recognized Mehmed, probably the youngest, as governor of Amasya, his residence under his father. Isa was designated as lord of Bursa. Suleiman, the eldest and formerly governor at Manisa, went to Edirne and ruled the Ottoman possessions in Europe. Musa, taken prisoner by Timur, was placed on parole to the Kermian family at Kutahya. Shortly afterwards, he was authorized to take his father's body to Bursa for burial and was then sent to the court of his brother Mehmed.

The transitory character of Timur's conquest permitted the four sons to quarrel among themselves over their patrimony. At first Mehmed and Musa teamed up against Suleiman and Isa, striking their first blows in Asia. With Mehmed's compliance Musa drove Isa from Bursa. Fleeing to Constantinople, Isa was encouraged by Suleiman, himself under pressure from Musa, to make a bid to regain his city. He was, however, beaten by Mehmed and vanished from the scene.

Meanwhile, having escaped from the Ankara disaster with Ali Pasha Chendereli and the leader of the janissaries, Suleiman arrived at Edirne, European headquarters for the Ottoman family. With the richest part of the state in his hands and supported by his father's chief ministers, Suleiman in 1403 claimed to be ruler of the Ottomans. But Mehmed and Musa refused to acknowledge his supremacy.

Rivalry among the three brothers endured for a decade. Its genesis was the act of Bayezid I in killing his own brother on the field of Kossovo. But competition among Suleiman, Musa, and Mehmed also arose from the factionalism in Ottoman politics which emerged from their father's attempts to consolidate and centralize the state.

The imperial clique found its candidate in Suleiman. Supported by the Chendereli and Evrenos families, by the governmental machinery in Edirne, and by the janissaries who survived the rout at Ankara, Suleiman reigned until 1411. Treaties with the Venetian doge and the Byzantine emperor recognized him as Ottoman ruler and facilitated trade and commerce in Europe, affairs in which the Chendereli family was personally interested. Suleiman failed, however, in his campaigns to dislodge Musa and Mehmed from Bursa.

With the aid of discontented Serbs and Wallachians Musa carried the struggle against Suleiman to Europe in 1410, engaging him in battle between Edirne and Constantinople. Unsuccessful in the first attempt, Musa caught Suleiman the next year in a surprise raid upon Edirne and killed him as he was fleeing to Constantinople. Ibrahim Chendereli, the Evrenos family, and the court immediately transferred their loyalty to Musa, who was now recognized as lord of Europe. Mehmed remained supreme in Asia Minor.

Besides Balkan vassals and Ottoman European officialdom, Musa was supported by a freethinking religious coterie pursuing a theological eclecticism popular at that time. As chief judge in Ottoman European territories he appointed Shaykh Bahr al-Din Mahmud ibn Kadi Simawna, who held views leading toward a socialistic society and a union of Judaism, Christianity, and Islam. Some years later Shaykh Bahr al-Din led an unsuccessful socialist rebellion against the state.

Musa was an energetic individual and sent out raiding parties into Greece and as far into Europe as Carinthia. The siege of Constantinople that had been lifted upon the coming of Timur into Anatolia was resumed. Strangely, Mehmed aided the emperor against his brother. Musa's revolutionary tendencies and his open favoring of the common people drove many of his supporters among high officials and the wealthy such as Ibrahim Chendereli over to Mehmed, who carried on an active campaign for allies among high-placed Ottoman feudal lords in Europe. Most of these went over to Mehmed; and in 1413 Edirne fell to Mehmed, who caught up with Musa near Sofia. Musa perished, and his body was returned with honor to Bursa to be buried beside his grandfather.

Mehmed now reigned alone and all Ottomans paid him homage. Having first governed in Amasya, heartland of the old Danishmend ghazi district, Mehmed professed the ghazi way of life and throughout remained its champion. With the favor of this powerful faction, essentially the military foundation of the state, propaganda for him among frontier raiders and Ottoman colonists in Europe took root easily. Mehmed in their eyes represented the "good old days" of Osman and Orhan.

In looking for factors in the success of Mehmed, the role of his tutor (*lala*), Bayezid Pasha, cannot be disregarded. As was customary, Mehmed was sent as a boy to govern a province and learn the art of ruling. A high state dignitary accompanied the prince "to advise" in all matters. In this instance the tutor was Bayezid Pasha, an Albanian by birth and a war captive retained by Murad and raised at court. Bayezid Pasha proved to be an outstanding general and a devoted slave to Mehmed, winning battles, organizing campaigns, and above all leading Mehmed to the task of reuniting the Ottoman state. Bayezid Pasha was one of the very first of a new type of high Ottoman official who in his attachment to his masters, the Ottoman family, showed his proclivity for a strongly centralized state.

Most important, Mehmed avoided the mistakes of his father and his brother Suleiman in their European and Balkan manners. He strongly identified himself with Anatolia and the old ghazi way of life. He chose for his wife a daughter of the amir of Dhu-al-Kadr, a Turkoman amirate of the Syrian frontier. Known as Chelebi (Gentleman), Kurushji (Wrestler), or Pahlevan (Champion), Mehmed grew to be revered by the Ottomans for his gentleness, integrity, and modesty.

EXPANSION IN ASIA

There were, however, in Asia Minor many Turks who were not considered Ottomans and who did not accept the idea of one united state or acquiesce in its rule. Although forces from Karamania and Dhu-al-Kadr fought with Mehmed when he ousted his brother Isa from Bursa, the Karaman prince, always the prime Ottoman rival in Anatolia, besieged Bursa when Mehmed was destroying Musa in Rumeli. (The European part of the Ottoman state was always Rumeli—the land of the Romans, i.e. Byzantines.) The Karamans were defeated in 1414, but their state was not conquered. In the same year Mehmed dealt with an adventurer from Izmir by name of Junayd, who had in turn supported Bayezid I, Isa, Mehmed, Suleiman, and Musa. Junayd gathered strength from Aydin and the coastal areas around Izmir, but recognized his defeat before any battle occurred. According to the standard practice of assigning European positions to dispossessed Anatolians, Mehmed magnanimously gave Junayd the governorship of Nicopolis on the Danube.

Except for the states of Karaman, Dhu-al-Kadr, and Isfendiyar, Turkish families recognized the dominant position of the Ottomans in central and western Anatolia. The disruption of society resulting from the invasion of Timur and continued by the civil wars of Bayezid's sons generated many religious and mystical sects in Asia Minor. Many dervish orders founded by holy men from Iran date their origin from this period. Social disorders, too, were not unknown. In 1416 Bayezid Pasha had to raise levies from most of Anatolia to quell in the peninsula north of Izmir a socio-religious revolutionary movement led by Bahr al-Din, one-time European army judge under Musa.

As a genuine ghazi, Mehmed could not ignore Europe and the great conquests there. Furthermore, the manner in which the Balkans were acquired made Rumeli produce far greater revenue for the Ottoman government than did Anatolia. Any slackening of the sultan's activity in Europe always brought on financial repercussions. Mehmed intervened in Wallachia, built fortresses north of the Danube, and encouraged ghazi raids in Hungary, Bosnia, and Styria.

After Junayd's defeat Mehmed gathered a fleet to clear Venetian pirates from the Aegean Islands and the Izmir coast. Venice sent her ships to protect her vassals, and Admiral Loredano broke Mehmed's fleet off Gallipoli in 1416. Peace, however, was soon negotiated, and Mehmed refused to resume the attack which his father and brothers had begun upon Constantinople.

One other episode marred the peace and harmony of Mehmed's rule. In 1419 one who claimed to be the Mustafa who disappeared at the Battle of Ankara arose in Europe, obtaining immediate support from the Wallachians and the scoundrel Junayd in Nicopolis. When Mehmed defeated them, they received asylum in Salonica. Later they were sent by the governor to the emperor in Constantinople, who held them for Mehmed.

Unquestionably Mehmed re-established Ottoman unity, approximately to the extent that it existed in his father's time. But an Ottoman empire was not yet created. There remained Constantinople, geographic and economic center of the area. Without the power emanating from its position, an empire could not be. Mehmed made no attempt upon it. Friendly relations with the emperor in times of distress induced him to refuse to entertain any designs upon the city. None the less, his early death from a stroke in 1421 may have saved the city from attack.

MURAD II

The idea of the continuity of the state and the sultan's relationship to governmental power had so grown that Mehmed's closest advisers, of whom Bayezid Pasha was one, concealed his death for forty days until his son and successor, Murad II, arrived in Edirne from Amasya to take charge. Nearly eighteen years old, Murad with his advisers and tutors

had resided at Manisa before being moved to Amasya and had participated in the campaign against Bahr al-Din. Mehmed had three other
sons. Two, who were hardly more than infants, were consigned to the
care and protection of Bayezid Pasha. They lived for a number of years
in Bursa, but while still mere boys died from one of the numerous
plagues that visited the land every few years. The third, Mustafa, was
thirteen years old when his father died. Afraid that Murad would destroy him as Bayezid had strangled Yakub, he fled from his Anatolian
governorship with his tutors to the protection of the Karaman family in
Konya.

Murad surrounded himself with representatives of old Ottoman families such as Chendereli, Evrenos, Timurtash, and Mikhaloglu and with
leaders of the new courtiers like Bayezid Pasha, although this latter
group was less numerous. At the very outset of Murad's reign the perfidious Byzantine emperor freed the old pretender Mustafa, who circulated
in Rumeli gathering supporters, chief among whom was none other than
Junayd, again governor of Nicopolis. Mustafa and his supporters defeated and killed Bayezid Pasha, seized Gallipoli with the emperor's
aid, and invaded Anatolia. Murad rallied and drove them back to Europe. In 1422 Genoese co-operation in transporting his troops across the
Straits permitted him to catch and kill the pretender and the rebels in
Edirne.

Murad raged at the emperor for his duplicity and ordered resumption
of the siege of Constantinople. With prodigious effort, much enthusiasm,
and the use of breaching cannon for the first time in Ottoman history,
Murad and his soldiers stormed the walls. After two months of failure
Murad lifted the siege to meet a new threat in Asia Minor. Byzantine
diplomacy with the Karamans brought Murad's brother Mustafa from
his refuge in Konya to an unsuccessful attack upon Bursa.

Though Mustafa was caught and hanged, Murad never resumed the
attack upon Constantinople. The emperor agreed to pay the Ottomans
a yearly tribute of 30,000 ducats and surrender all territory outside the
walls except for areas which fed the aqueducts of the city. In Anatolia,
Murad judiciously alternated between diplomacy and force. A slight
engagement with the amir of Isfendiyar ended when Murad married
the amir's daughter and obtained possession of the copper mines in that
region. The Karaman amir sued for peace, and Menteshe and Teke recognized Murad's suzerainty. Peace with Karamania, however, was
never sure; and whenever Murad became deeply engrossed or embarrassed in Europe war with the princes of Konya became imminent and
sometimes necessary.

Murad's greatest efforts were expended in Europe, and there lay his
greater gains. In 1430 Salonica was taken after a long struggle from

Venice, which had purchased the city from the Byzantine emperor. Ottoman pressure was maintained in the Morea, northern Epirus, Albania, Bosnia, Serbia, Hungary, and Wallachia. Upon the accession of Ladislaus, King of Lithuania and Poland, to the throne of Hungary, dissident elements—Serbs, Wallachians, Hungarians, and Bosnians—banded their arms together and invaded Ottoman territory. In 1443 under the leadership of John Hunyadi, Sigismund's illegitimate son, the invaders won numerous strongholds, were victorious at Nish and Sofia, and brought Murad to the edge of ruin. The Karamans chose this moment for an attack, and it is important to note that Murad himself fought the enemy in Asia and sent trusted generals to the European front.

Nevertheless, Murad concluded an honorable peace with King Ladislaus in 1444 at Szeged, each promising not to invade the other's territory for ten years. Murad had defeated the Karamans, and Hunaydi realized that the Ottoman army, with Murad at its head and the janissaries included, would be quite a different body from the feudal army that he had met the previous year. Murad gave up suzerainty over Wallachia and Serbia and ransomed his son-in-law for 60,000 ducats.

OTTOMAN SOCIETY AND CULTURE

Evidently Murad felt that he had made peace with the world in Europe and Asia and that the time was propitious for retirement from active rule. He was forty years old and had been sultan for twenty-three years. Murad's eldest son, Ahmed, had died some years before. And after the sudden death of his second son, Ala al-Din, Murad abdicated in favor of his fifteen-year-old third son, Mehmed, who went to Edirne with Khalil Pasha Chendereli as grand vizir and Molla Khusraw of the Warsak Turkoman tribe as chief judge.

Murad himself withdrew to his favorite residence in Manisa, where he intended to live in ease and peace with poets, mystics, theologians, and men of letters. He wished to pursue the *futuwwa*, the ideal life of man, modestly studying and writing in quiet contemplation. It was an age of the beginning of a Turkish renaissance. The Turkish language, as spoken at the Ottoman court and in western Anatolia, became a medium of cultured expression. Konya, Kutahya, and Bursa in Asia Minor and Edirne in Europe were its centers; its patrons were the Karaman, Kermian, and Ottoman families and their courts. Heretofore, Persian and Arabic were the languages of poetry, records, and education. But Turkish was growing more popular. Umur Bey, a son of Timurtash Pasha, instructed a poet in writing for him to use as many Turkish words as possible.

Many Persian and Arabic works were translated into Ottoman Turkish, and such poets as Shaykhi, Kemal Ummi, Eshrefoglu, Rumi, Husami, Shemsi, and Nedimi were held in high esteem. Sufis, mystics, and holy men (or *shaykhs* as they were known in Anatolia) were numerous and earnestly venerated. The most revered in Bursa from the time of Bayezid I until his death in 1430 was Amir Sultan, a native of Bukhara in Turkestan. The shrine built over his tomb indicated his popularity and the honor rendered him by the Ottomans.

Ottoman history was first cultivated under Murad, when a "romantic" movement arose. Until this time Ottoman chronicles were sagas of ghazis and their great deeds. Under Murad there developed a new and formal Ottoman history, which included illustrious ancestors going back to the most noble of Turkish tribes—the Oghuz tribe. Beautiful tales were written of Osman's ancestors riding with 400 horsemen into Asia Minor from Turkestan and plunging into a battle they witnessed. Naturally turning the scales in favor of one side, they were richly rewarded with fiefs. In this manner the Ottomans received their start! It must be remembered that at the time of Murad's retirement one hundred and fifty years had passed since Osman began his first conquests, and that in a new and rapidly evolving society not many men could relate the exploits of their great-great-great grandfathers.

Above all, Murad was concerned with the education of his children. He employed as teachers for the princes the most enlightened and distinguished scholars of the state. Many had important army or administrative positions. Included with the princes in the palace school were other boys, some of whom were captives of war or sons of distinguished vassals of the sultan. Murad desired not only to educate his own sons to their responsibilities but also to train other youths in discipline, integrity, and moral values that might serve state and sultan intelligently and faithfully. Proof of the value and thoroughness of this school was first demonstrated visibly in the education and ability of Murad's son Mehmed.

MILITARY DEVELOPMENTS

For a few months all went well in the Ottoman state. Murad had retired to Manisa, and the boy Mehmed II was surrounded by advisers and teachers at Edirne. But the Hungarians broke the peace of Szeged in the autumn of 1444, perhaps thinking that the treaty with Murad was invalidated by his retirement and that victory would be possible against a boy ruler. Murad was recalled from his retirement and crushed the invaders near Varna. King Ladislaus and Cardinal Julian, who had insisted upon breaking the treaty against Hunyadi's admonitions, lost their lives.

Ottomans now easily overran Serbia and Bosnia. Since Ottomans were tolerant of all forms of Christianity whereas Hungarians in their brief sway had begun to impose Latin rites upon Serbian and Bosnian churches, many fortresses opened their gates to Murad.

With this affair apparently settled, Murad abdicated a second time in 1445 and returned to Manisa. It was not long, however, before an open demonstration of rebellion against Mehmed II by the janissaries brought Murad back from the pleasures of retirement to active rule in Edirne. The ringleaders were executed, imprisoned, or exiled from the capital, and the sultan's authority fully restored.

This episode was a harbinger of future difficulties of grave proportions that Ottoman sultans would experience with janissary and other imperial troops. They were becoming hardened ruthless professional soldiers, reared and trained exclusively for warfare and not too well paid because of the expectation that they would be richly rewarded from plunder won on campaigns. Simply educated and disciplined to give supreme loyalty to the sultan, the janissaries felt their power and importance and were easily induced to demand favors of many kinds. Between them and older Ottomans—feudal cavalry and old family administrators like those closest to Murad—rivalry was keen and often bitter.

In this connection Murad about 1430 reinstituted for the janissary corps a draft (*devshirmeh*) procedure originated in the reign of Murad I. Every five years army officers toured the Balkan districts, conscripting Christian boys of ages from ten to fifteen. These youths from Greece, Macedonia, Albania, Serbia, Bosnia, Herzegovina, and Bulgaria were brought to Edirne. As slaves of the sultan they were parceled out among court officers, the feudatory of Asia Minor, and the sultan himself. After a few years of growth, toughening, Islamization, and Turkification in language and customs they returned to Edirne, where they received military training and were assigned to a janissary barracks. The more favored were attached to the palace; and the very best attended the princes' school, whereupon any position in the state was open to them. At first employed to augment the ranks of the janissaries when wars and raids failed to yield sufficient captives, the draft was justified as another form of taxation for the subject communities, analogous to poll taxes except they paid taxes in boys! More significant was the fact that the most vigorous and capable Balkan youths were removed from their villages, were raised as Ottomans, and served the state faithfully and well. Some observers remarked that this policy helped to keep the Balkans in subjection by drawing away future leaders. Other families turned to Islam rather than lose their sons.

It was also the custom for vassal Christian princes to send a son or two as hostages to the sultan's court. Various defeated Balkan leaders were permitted to retain their lands, but sent their sons to be reared as Ottomans. Such was the case of George Kastriota, who with his three brothers was sent to Murad II. Renamed Iskender (Alexander), he was educated in the princes' school, served in various responsible posts under Murad, but deserted in 1443. Skanderbeg, as he was now called, returned to his native Albania; and there for twenty-five years he led resistance movements and guerilla warfare against Murad and Mehmed II, with whom he had gone to school.

After the janissary revolt of 1445 was put down, Murad did not again retire but engaged in campaigns in Europe. Twice he entered Albania in pursuit of Skanderbeg. In 1448 he drove Hunyadi out of Serbia, defeating him on the plains of Kossovo. Murad also campaigned in Greece and the Peloponnesus, seizing Corinth and Patras. The aged warrior (about fifty years old) died in Edirne early in 1451, having twice tried to retire to peace and contemplation but finding himself caught in the web of state responsibilities and the dynamics of the Ottoman military machine. He was finally laid to rest in Bursa. The young Mehmed, now grown to manhood, when apprised in Manisa of his father's death, supposedly leaped on his horse and raced to Edirne to take charge.

MEHMED II

Mehmed II possessed a character entirely different from that of his father. Since he had the benefits of the princes' school, his mind was well trained. He knew literary Turkish, Arabic, Persian, and Greek and was able to converse in ordinary Serbian and Italian. He enjoyed poetry and was familiar with the classical poetry of Iran, Greece, and Rome. Mehmed was an accomplished poet himself and gathered about him poets from the four corners of the Muslim world.

As a student he read philosophy and was much taken with writings of the Stoics and the Peripatetics. He loved history, particularly biographies of Alexander the Great and the Caesars. The study of war and of everything associated with war such as strategy, supplies, munitions, and topography, aroused his interest greatly. Every Ottoman, even of the royal family, had a trade—perhaps because of the *akhi* heritage—and Mehmed was an accomplished gardener. Later, between campaigns and for relaxation, he worked in the gardens of the royal palace.

Thoroughness and efficiency combined with great energy and promptness became the order of the day whenever Mehmed was present. Delay and procrastination were foreign to his nature. In many respects Murad was not very businesslike in his administration, and Mehmed spent the first year of his reign reorganizing governmental departments. The treasury, in particular, was tightened up; many tax

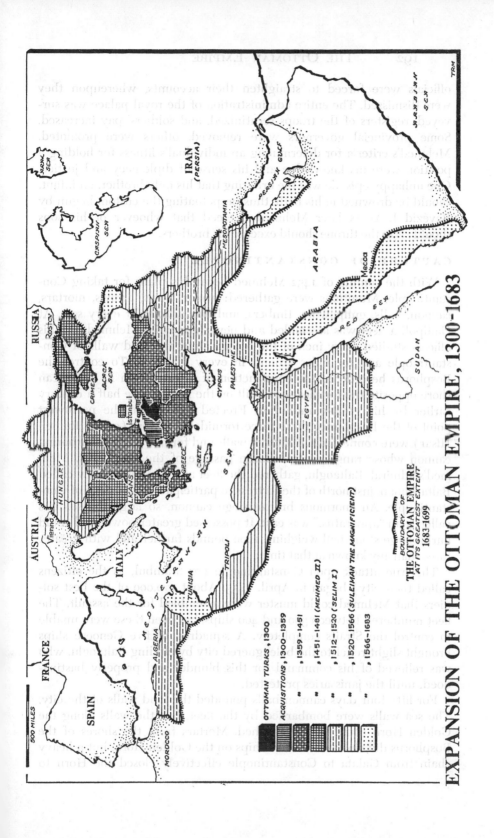

EXPANSION OF THE OTTOMAN EMPIRE, 1300-1683

officials were forced to straighten their accounts, whereupon they were dismissed. The entire administration of the royal palace was surveyed, registers of the troops scrutinized, and soldiers' pay increased. Some provincial governors were removed, others were promoted. Mehmed's criteria for determining an individual's fitness for holding a position were his knowledge and his sense of diplomacy and justice. One unhappy episode was the ordering that his only brother, an infant, should be drowned in his bath, thus perpetuating the custom begun by Bayezid I. Years later Mehmed decreed that whoever of his sons should seize the throne should execute his brothers.

CAPTURE OF CONSTANTINOPLE

With the coming of 1452 Mehmed began his plans for taking Constantinople. Munitions were gathered: armor, bows, arrows, mortars, cannon, balls, gunpowder, timbers, and war articles of every sort. At Gallipoli a fleet was assembled and new ships built. Mehmed and his officers studied every inch of the terrain along the land walls of Constantinople and for miles around in every direction. To control the Bosphorus he ordered the construction of a fortress on its European shore opposite the fortifications built on the Asiatic side half a century earlier by his great-grandfather. Erected just above the narrowest point of the Bosphorus, these three formidable towers (called Rumeli Hisar) were connected with heavy walls and formed a castle harboring cannon whose range controlled the passage of the Bosphorus. Mehmed's admiral, Baltaoglu, gathered the fleet at a small inlet, now called Balta Liman, just north of the fortress to participate in the siege of Constantinople. An enormous bronze siege cannon, so large the soldiers called it an "apparatus," was cast. It possessed greater power and could hurl a large stone ball weighing 1200 pounds farther and with greater force than any known at that time.

The true attack upon Constantinople (or Stambul, as the citizens called their city) began in April, 1453. About 170,000 of the best soldiers that Mehmed could muster were assembled for the assault. The fleet numbered between 300 and 400 ships, but even these were unable to control the Straits completely. A squadron of five Genoese ships brought slight relief to the beleaguered city by eluding Baltaoglu, who was relieved of his command for this blunder and properly bastinadoed, until the janissaries protested.

For fifty-four days cannon balls pounded the land walls of the city. The sea walls were bombarded by the fleet, but the walls along the Golden Horn could not be reached. Mortars from the shores of the Bosphorus did sink some Greek ships on the Golden Horn, but a heavy chain from Galata to Constantinople effectively closed the Horn to

Mehmed's ships. Not to be thwarted, Mehmed constructed a greased wooden runway from the shore of the Bosphorus at Dolma Bakche up the hill of Beyoglu (Pera) and down the slope to the Golden Horn at Kasim Pasha. Sixty-seven ships of the Ottoman fleet were hauled up over the incline and slid down to the Golden Horn, from where they threw their stone cannon balls on the city walls.

Cut off completely and bombarded from every side, the defenders of Constantinople resisted the attacks valiantly. The Genoese and other Italians in Galata and Pera gave no assistance, and most of the 50,000 inhabitants of the once great city acted supremely indifferent to their fate, perhaps because Emperor Constantine in desperation called for aid from the West and announced submission to the Pope in exchange for promises of soldiers. A few came, but help was entirely inadequate. The citizenry preferred Ottoman to Latin rule and Muslim tolerance to Roman intolerance.

A stupendous assault near the Gate of St. Romanos (Top Kapu) was launched on May 29, 1453, and the city was taken. Following the universal custom of that age, the troops had full rein and complete license in the city, except that no public buildings could be touched. When on the third day Mehmed entered the city, the plundering ceased. He went to Hagia Sophia, where prayers were said. He then quickly turned to the problem of the city which the Ottomans have always called Istanbul. A governor was appointed; inhabitants were encouraged to remain by exempting them from taxes and by giving back to them their houses; the sultan ransomed many on condition that they would stay; the army was disbanded; and Mehmed returned to Edirne, his capital.

The capture of Constantinople had more psychological repercussions than economic, military, or cultural effects upon the world. For a century it was an island in an Ottoman sea, isolated and largely cut off from the West. Later centuries developed a myth that the Fall of Constantinople blocked the trade routes to the Far East, thereby forcing the Age of Discoveries and the voyages of Columbus. According to another legend, at the Fall of Constantinople Greek monks and manuscripts found their way to Italy, thus initiating the Renaissance. One story has related that the Fall of Constantinople removed the Balkan bastion, at once enabling the Ottoman Turks to conquer the whole peninsula of southeast Europe. All three of these myths have been exploded by careful examination of historical development. Yet, even today, these tales are repeated and found in modern books.

Nevertheless, the emotional impact of the Fall of Constantinople on the people of the fifteenth century should not be minimized. To Christian Europe, and especially to the West, the great imperial city had fallen. In a sense the Roman Empire had come to an end. Heretofore the Turks had been raiding "unknown and uncertain" areas, but Constantinople was a real place in Western thinking. Everywhere there was talk of a crusade; but of course, it was only talk.

To Muslims the Fall of Constantinople was a great and glorious achievement. Islamic rulers and armies had attempted it many times in the past. To them Constantinople was the majestic city of imperial tradition, whose conquest had always been a goal of the great caliphs. Now a new Muslim state had accomplished the impossible, and consequently Mehmed II received great acclaim and respect throughout the East.

To the Ottomans it was the conquest of the natural capital and center of their state. Since the time of Bayezid I its incorporation in the state had been a logical and necessary step, but it had been long in coming. Its acquisition served as the keystone in creating the Ottoman Empire.

REFERENCES: Chapter 14

References in Chapters 12 and 13 are important for this chapter.

Barnette Miller, *Beyond the Sublime Porte: The Grand Seraglio of Stambul:* Yale University Press, New Haven, 1931. The most accessible account of this great, historic monument.

——, *The Palace School of Muhammed the Conqueror:* Harvard University Press, Cambridge, 1941. A thorough and well-written exposition of this important institution of the Ottomans.

Kritovoulos, *History of Mehmed the Conqueror* (Charles T. Riggs, trans.): Princeton University Press, Princeton, 1954. A contemporary account by a Greek in the service of the Ottomans.

Edwin Pears, *The Destruction of the Greek Empire and the Story of the Capture of Constantinople:* Longmans, Green, New York, 1903. Carefully written from Greek and Western sources.

CHAPTER 15

CHAPTER 15

Building the Ottoman Empire

CONSOLIDATION OF THE EMPIRE

Beyond taking Constantinople Mehmed II, always called *Fatih* (The Conqueror) by his subjects, extended the periphery of his empire only moderately. Campaigns and wars were scheduled almost every year, but in the main they consolidated the Ottoman possessions, rounded out frontiers, and built the empire. Operations were conducted in the Balkans and Asia Minor and from Venice and southern Italy to Iran and the Crimea. Affairs and relations with any one area always involved those of others; and Mehmed never was able to isolate his many international and domestic problems to deal with one at a time. Moreover, Venetian envoys were plotting at every court to swell the number of his enemies and bring his downfall.

Ottoman campaigns, colonization, and government had been proceeding in the Balkans for a century. None the less, Ottoman rule was still not effective in several regions, and many provinces which were tied to the Ottomans by a kind of vassalage or alliance were not integrated units of the state. Bosnia and Serbia remained under local rulers who were subservient to the sultans. Whenever opportunity arose, rebellion was in the air. Mehmed set his campaign in 1456 for the stronghold of Belgrad, hoping that its fall would give him a tighter grip on central and lower Danube regions and lessen the danger of Serbian revolt.

The heroic effort failed, however, just as the walls were breached and as victory seemed in his grasp. Since vast quantities of munitions, especially cannon, were abandoned in the hasty retreat, no major campaign could be undertaken anywhere the following year. Instead, colorful festivities to celebrate the circumcision of his two older sons, Bayezid and Mustafa, were arranged in Edirne; distinguished visitors and envoys from many countries attended. Pressure on the Balkans, however, was maintained continuously. In the next decade Serbia and Bosnia were subjected to Ottoman rule and organized as regular imperial provinces; while Wallachia and Moldavia were forced to become allies. Skanderbeg was checked in Albania, and the fortresses of Elbasan, Kroia, and Skodra taken. After Skanderbeg's death in 1478 Albania and Herzegovina became provinces of the empire. Greece and the Peloponnesus, except for a few Venetian ports of call such as Coron and Modon, were conquered, and some of the lands were parceled out as fiefs.

In Asia Minor Mehmed also pursued a vigorous policy. The most resistant foe had always been the Karaman dynasty. In 1464 Mehmed directed a large force against them, and in 1466 at the Battle of Larenda Karaman opposition was broken. Later Cilicia was acquired; and as his reign closed Mehmed became involved in family quarrels of the Dhu-al-Kadr of Diyarbakir. The entire Mediterranean coast of Asia Minor was now in Ottoman hands.

Since Istanbul and the Straits were now Ottoman, Mehmed moved eastward, hoping to control the Black Sea shores. Sinop with its adjacent copper resources was taken from the last of the Isfendiyar, who received fiefs in Europe. That same year (1461), with the co-operation of the navy from Gallipoli, Mehmed forced the surrender of the Greek emperor of Trebizond, thus obliterating the last remnant of the Byzantine Empire.

These activities led the Ottomans into conflict with Ak Koyunlu, who dominated Iran, Armenia, and eastern Asia Minor. Venetian ambassadors traveled to the court of Uzun Hasan at Tabriz and encouraged war against Mehmed. Although Venice was concerned with Eastern trade, the main consideration was to lessen Ottoman pressure upon Venice and her European territory. Mehmed collected a mighty army including his two sons, Mustafa and Bayezid, his grand vizir, and Gedik Ahmed Pasha, a burly general who had risen from the ranks of the ordinary janissaries. He defeated Uzun Hasan in 1473 near Erzinjan in eastern Asia Minor. Next the Crimea, which was ruled by Turkish khans, came under Ottoman aegis, and the important commercial city of Kaffa (the modern Feodosiya) on the Straits between the Black Sea and the Sea of Azov was taken from the Genoese. Except for the coast between the Crimea and the Danube, the Black Sea was now an Ottoman lake.

Although Venetian envoys professed friendship for Mehmed, conflict between Venice and the Ottoman Empire was almost inevitable. To insure control of the Aegean coast of Anatolia and safeguard Ottoman ventures into the Morea it was necessary to incorporate into the empire the Aegean Islands, particularly Chios, Lemnos, Lesbos (Mytilene), and Euboea (Negroponte). This was particularly important since Venetians and pirates used these islands and their numerous harbors as bases to harry the Ottoman coast and hold up trade. Mehmed's fleet, therefore, captured these islands along with Cephalonia in the Ionian Islands; and for fifteen years (1463–1478) he was at war sporadically with Venice. Pressure on Venetian outposts along the Dalmatian coast was constant, and ghazis from Albania and Bosnia kept alarms sounding on St. Mark's Square. In 1477 Ottoman raiders overran Friuli and descended to the Italian plain north of Venice. At night Venetian senators from the roof of St. Mark's could see Ottoman camp fires and burning villages as far as the banks of the Piave. When autumn came the Ottomans returned home laden with booty. Venice concluded peace with Mehmed and recognized his island acquisitions.

In 1480 an Ottoman army under Gedik Ahmed Pasha crossed the Adriatic from Epirus and took Otranto on the heel of the Italian peninsula, thus establishing a bridgehead for the conquest of Italy. Gedik Ahmed wintered there; but upon Mehmed's sudden death in May, 1481 the expedition to Otranto was withdrawn, never to be launched again. Simultaneously (1480) Mesih Pasha led an unsuccessful attack upon the Knights of St. John on the Island of Rhodes. In the spring of 1481 Mehmed gathered an army in Anatolia, but he died suddenly in camp in May before he or his line of march had divulged his destination. The conqueror was dead. Bells pealed in Europe when the news arrived. Secrecy was maintained in the Ottoman Empire until a successor could mount the throne. There was no doubt anywhere but that a great man had died.

SETTLEMENT OF ISTANBUL

When Constantinople fell in 1453, it was only a half-populated city at most; it had been depressed and dying slowly for more than two centuries. The city never recovered from the devastation wrought by the Fourth Crusade; and since the first Ottoman crossing to Europe gradual economic strangulation had reduced the population. Many buildings were empty and in various stages of decay. From the very outset Mehmed was concerned with repopulating the city. For twenty days he tarried in Istanbul, freeing many prisoners allocated to him, encouraging others to remain, and exempting many from taxation for various lengths of time. The Christian population was never subjected to the *devshirmeh*. In almost every conquest in later years inhabitants of this town and that were ordered to move to Istanbul, frequently settling old vacant districts and giving their names to sections of the city such as Aksaray and Karaman.

When Mehmed "Fatih" entered the city, he learned that the patriarch was dead. Appreciating the need for the election of a new patriarch and understanding the security and stability that such a move would give the Greek community of Istanbul, Fatih indicated confidence in George Scolarius, who had long been popular with the Greeks of the city and in disfavor with the last Byzantine emperor because he headed the anti-Roman faction. Duly elected, Scolarius took the name Gennadius. Mehmed feted him, recognized him as patriarch and leader of the Christians in Istanbul, and ordered the vizir and officers to accord him proper respect. Gennadius was also charged with responsibility for the obedience, conduct, and life of the Greek people and their relationship to the Ottoman government. Thus, in many ways Greek Christians were encouraged to reside in Istanbul and allowed to live according to their own ways and laws as long as they did not infringe upon or come into conflict with the administration of the government and the lives of Muslim subjects.

Public buildings were reserved for the state, and many churches were converted into mosques. The outstanding example was Justinian's great church Hagia Sophia which became the Muslim Aya Sofya. Since the decline in population had left many empty churches and chapels, the conversion of the churches worked little hardship upon the Greek inhabitants. Another site was designated for the erection of a new mosque; and a series of surrounding structures, for schools, hospitals, and poor relief. The new mosque was badly damaged by an earthquake in the eighteenth century, and the present Fatih Mosque is of later construction and design.

Fatih chose as his residence the Monastery of the Pantocrator in the old Forum of Theodosius, the most populous part of the city and today the site of the University of Istanbul. Various additions were made to the monastery, which he occupied for about twelve years whenever in Istanbul. In 1459 he chose a new spot for his quarters, and here in 1465 was completed a new palace which remained the chief domicile of sultans until the nineteenth century. The old palace, Eski Saray, became the abode of the harem until the time of Suleiman I; thereafter for three centuries it was a home for wives, daughters, and harems of previous sultans. The new palace, Yeni Saray, was erected on the site of the fortress of ancient Byzantium on the point of land between the Golden Horn and the Sea of Marmara. Facing the entrance to the Bosphorus, it was the most natural and beautiful spot in the city for an imperial residence. It was soon called popularly Top Kapu Saray

(Cannon Gate Palace), because of the heavily fortified gate at the tip of the point of land. The whole area enclosed by walls was soon known everywhere by its Italian name, Seraglio; it was famed for its many splendid buildings and large number of inhabitants. Yet, Fatih passed winters, summers, and many seasons at the palace in Edirne or at family lodges in Bursa, Demotika, and other cities of the empire. Edirne remained the favorite summer headquarters of sultans until the eighteenth century.

THE PALACE SCHOOL

In the years of Mehmed's reign full integration of the empire with governors for all provinces appointed by the sultan, along with expansion of the state, its growing complexity, and diversity of population, augmented the need for trained personnel to operate the government. Murad II had faced a similar problem and had resolved it by placing the most promising of his young slaves in the school beside his own sons. Mehmed met the crisis by creating the Palace School of Istanbul. It was first established at the old palace, but was later transferred to the Seraglio, where it maintained continuous operation until the twentieth century. Students, called pages, were either selected after a most careful screening from the boys of ten to fourteen years old among war captives or drafted from Christian provinces. At the Palace School they received a thorough secular education in languages, literature, music, law and theology, military science, mathematics, philosophy, governmental administration, taxation, finance, physical training, personal conduct, sports, and manual training. Only the very best lasted through the ten to twelve rigorous years of the course; those unable to continue drew governmental positions commensurate to their abilities.

Graduates were appointed to administrative posts in various departments of the government. They were pledged to secrecy about the school and life of the inner palace where they had lived for such a long time. The instructional staff was drawn from the finest teachers in mosque schools of Bursa, Edirne, and Istanbul and from high administrative offices of the government. Physique was considered important, weight-lifting and carrying heavy loads were practiced so that many developed the strength to carry seven or eight hundred pounds for as many paces. It was thought fitting that each should learn a trade in case that one should some day have to earn a living as a craftsman. All in all, a tremendous spirit was induced into the students; graduates of the Palace School formed a firmly knit group that stood apart in their conduct and loyalty to the sultanship. Trained by one sultan, they often served his son or held the government together until a successor was determined. These "courtiers," as Western observers and envoys termed

them, were reported to be more cultured, more faultless in their cour-
tesy, more devoted to their master, and more skilled in their operation
of the government than the courtiers and advisers of any Western king
or emperor. At the time of the great success, efficiency, and strength of
the Ottoman government, the entire system was based on merit. Merit
alone brought appointment to government office and subsequent promotions and favors. When factors other than merit began to have
weight, the government stagnated.

BAYEZID AND JEM

Mehmed II left two sons. Bayezid, aged thirty-three, was governor
of Amasya, the old ghazi center. Jem, aged twenty-one, was governor
of Konya, the former Seljuk capital. Since Amasya was eight days' ride
from Istanbul whereas Konya was only four, the younger son had an
advantage in obtaining control of the central administration. But the
janissaries, the pages of the palace, and the government officials who
were slaves of the sultan and graduates of the Palace School preferred
Bayezid. Mehmed's last grand vizir, however, belonged by birth to
the old Muslim aristocracy of Anatolia and was partial to Jem. He tried
to conceal Fatih's death, secretly dispatched couriers to Jem, and
moved to isolate Istanbul until Jem's arrival. However, Mehmed's death
became known, whereupon the slave officials and the janissaries seized
control, murdered the grand vizir, impaled his messengers to Jem, and
awaited Bayezid's appearance. They chose the latter because they considered his residence of twenty-five years or more at Amasya as wedding him to the ghazi tradition, of which they were fast becoming the
heirs. Moreover, recognizing the so-called Law of Fratricide, Bayezid
attached cleverly through marriages and political friendship several
potent figures of the government hierarchy to his candidacy. Jem was
supported by the conservative Muslim community of Asia Minor. His
chief difficulty was his comparative youth; Bayezid for years had been
gathering his party for the eventual day, and Bayezid's eldest son was
already, with his preceptors, governor of Manisa.

To break through the cordon of officers blocking the gate to the palace, Bayezid pledged a handsome gift of money to every janissary, declared an amnesty for all plundering and crimes committed in the
period of interregnum, and most significantly agreed to appoint to the
vizirship only men from the soldier-palace-slave group.

Jem with forces from Karaman and Konya occupied Bursa and challenged Bayezid for the throne. Gedik Ahmed was recalled from Otranto
and with the army that Mehmed had gathered defeated Jem, who fled
to Egypt whence he made the holy pilgrimage to Mecca. Bayezid of-

fered him a princely income if he would live peacefully in Jerusalem, but Jem returned in 1482 and made a second vain attempt at the throne. Escaping to the protection of the Knights of St. John of the Island of Rhodes, he was held in custody by them and used to obtain a favorable treaty of peace with the Ottomans. Bayezid agreed to pay 40,000 ducats a year as long as Jem remained in captivity. The Knights subsequently moved him to their castles in France, where he fell into the hands of Charles VIII. Later Jem was presented to the pope; and in 1494 Charles borrowed him from Pope Alexander VI, ostensibly to participate in a crusade against the Ottomans. Jem, however, died of a fever in Naples early the next year. His body was finally obtained by Bayezid and interred at Bursa.

WARS OF BAYEZID II

Between 1482 and 1495 Bayezid's fear of his brother's return some- what restricted him in foreign activities. Yet, the organization of the Ottoman state was conditioned to aggressive expansion. When cam- paigns were not in progress, feudal sipahi, janissaries, and the court became uneasy. During these years, therefore, a number of expeditions along the Dalmatian coast and into Hungary, Styria, and Carinthia were undertaken. Although these raids were usually indecisive, they were rewarding in plunder. Akkerman on the Black Sea at the mouth of the Dniester River was taken and Wallachia and Moldavia were subdued.

In this early period of Bayezid's reign war broke out with the Mamluk sultans of Egypt. Dynastic difficulties among the Dhu-al-Kadr involved Egyptians and Ottomans in a border dispute. In 1484 after the aid and asylum had been given to Jem open war broke out.

Despite six sizable campaigns wherein the Ottoman army and fleet participated, Bayezid was not able to retain Adana; and his leaders were captured repeatedly by the Mamluks. The peace concluded in 1491 left Egypt in possession of the disputed border areas; but since Turkoman and non-Ottoman forces in southern Anatolia were sup- pressed by Ottoman armies, no difficulties appeared for two decades.

Following Jem's death Bayezid pursued a more aggressive policy in the west. The tempo of Ottoman raids along the Dalmatian coast in- creased; Sinop, Gallipoli, Lepanto, Valona, and Preveza rang with the noise of carpenters, coopers, and caulkers constructing war galleys and ships of all kinds. When war broke out with Venice in 1499, Ottomans took Modon and Coron in the Peloponnesus and defeated the Venetian fleet in a great sea engagement at Navarino. Peace was not concluded until Andrea Gritti and Bayezid's vizirs came to terms in 1503. The war further eclipsed Venetian power in Greece and the eastern Mediterranean, and Ottoman sea power became strongly established. Thereafter in Bayezid's reign contingents of the Ottoman navy raided every Mediterranean shore, and Ottoman admirals and captains followed the pattern of the old ghazi corsairs.

The end of the war with Venice marked the rise of a new figure on the Ottoman frontier. Shah Ismail of Iran kindled a religio-national enthusiasm in the breasts of the peoples of Iran and eastern Asia Minor. Claiming descent from the Prophet Muhammad, Ali, and the Seventh Imam on the paternal side and from Ak Koyunlu Turks and Byzantine emperors on the other, Ismail united Iranians, Turks, and heterodox followers of Ali in devotion to his mystical being. Ismail (often called the Great Sufi) became shah in 1502 and pronounced Shiism as the official doctrine of his realm. Political agents—sufis and shaykhs—permeated Asia Minor, concentrating in mountainous areas of the east, south, and southwest. Ismail's propaganda was effective in the provinces of Teke, Karaman, and Dhu-al-Kadr, and among the Warsak and Torgud tribes of the Taurus regions. His followers in Anatolia were called *Kizilbash* (red head) from the red hats which they wore.

Muslims of the Ottoman Empire were not thoroughly orthodox; Bayezid was a philosopher by nature and enough of a mystic that one of his nicknames was Sufi; and the janissaries as well as Bayezid and many court officers belonged to the Bektashi dervish order which entertained many heretical creeds. Despite or perhaps because of these facts the Ottomans could not permit the subversive ideas of a foreign monarch free rein within their state. Minor skirmishes occurred near Diyarbakir in 1502, and Ismail protested that his followers were prevented from visiting him. Although envoys traveled back and forth, Bayezid kept Ismail's ambassador isolated and under strict surveillance for fear the janissaries might be corrupted. Armies were assembled in 1508 and stationed in Anatolia to face Ismail in Harput and Diyarbakir, but no battle ensued. Difficulties arose in eastern Iran compelling Ismail to transfer his attentions, whereas Bayezid had no taste for war because Ismail had so many sympathizers.

Shah Ismail's doctrines, however, proved popular; and open revolt developed in 1511 under the leadership of Karabiyik, an eastern shaykh using the pseudonym of Shah Kuli. Starting in Antalya and Teke, Shah Kuli besieged and took Konya, seized Kutahya, Ottoman Anatolian army headquarters, and impaled the Ottoman commander-in-chief. An army including 4,000 janissaries under the grand vizir and three Ottoman princes caught Shah Kuli near Kayseri, where both he and the grand vizir fell. Since the leader was gone, the heretics scattered and the rebellious problem subsided, only to come to a violent head a few years later under Bayezid's successor.

SELIM'S SUCCESSION

Since the end of the Venetian war Bayezid suffered poor health and was often carried on a stretcher so that the troops might see him. With each illness his sons and grandsons became exceedingly nervous and concerned about the future. Of his eight sons, only three remained in 1511: Korkud at Manisa; Ahmed at Amasya; and Selim, the youngest, at Trabzon. Each was jockeying for advantages and seeking favors and strategic appointments for friends and sons. The janissaries and the soldiers preferred Selim, since he was the most energetic and devoted to warfare. Bayezid and the high officials advanced Ahmed as the solid administrator. The poets, philosophers, and theologians supported Korkud; for he was one of them.

From Trabzon Selim moved his forces to Kaffa, where his son Suleiman was governor. Then with the support of the khans of the Crimea he brought his army toward Edirne. Assuaged with appointment over Semendra in the Balkans, Selim held his hand for immediate action should Bayezid suddenly die as his French doctors were predicting. When Bayezid and his close advisers began granting vast authority and prodigious sums of money to Ahmed, Selim seized Edirne. Bayezid could find no officer to drive Selim from his prize. Meanwhile, to gain friends in Anatolia Ahmed had turned heretic and donned the red hat of the *Kizilbash*. Upon this development the staunchly orthodox Bayezid called Selim to Istanbul in 1512 and abdicated in his favor. A month later Bayezid died while en route to retirement in the palace at Demotika, where he had been born.

For thirty-one years Bayezid, a peace-loving, scholarly, and contemplative philosopher, governed the Ottoman Empire. Never attacking a neighboring state without provocation, he spent years in organizing the administration of the government for the well-being of the state, and incidently its inhabitants. He took great interest in the Palace School, often quizzing the students himself. Trade flourished; merchants from Venice, Genoa, Florence, and Ragusa thronged to Istanbul. Bayezid was exceedingly tolerant of other religions, and more than 100,000 Jews came to Istanbul, Izmir, Edirne, and Salonica when they were driven from Spain in 1492. Yet, he was strict with Muslims. His father's unorthodox ways disturbed him, and one of Bayezid's first acts as sultan was to clear from the palace the pictures of his father and court officials painted by Gentile Bellini. He sold them in the bazaar.

Selim I (nicknamed *Yavuz*, which means stern or inflexible) gave a munificent bonus to each soldier, as had become the custom in securing the throne. But he entered the palace by a side gate in order not to bow openly to their demands. The facts were that he held only Rumeli with Istanbul, Ahmed controlling most of Anatolia from his seat at Amasya. When in the previous year Selim marched his army to Edirne, Ahmed occupied Bursa and camped not far from the Bosphorus. He went back to Amasya only upon the insistence of Bayezid, who pointed out that Selim had returned to the Crimea and Kaffa.

Upon Selim's enthronement Ahmed sent his son to take Bursa. Selim instantly crossed to Asia and carried the attack against Ahmed. Ahmed resisted with political guile and force until the following spring, when he was defeated and strangled. Meanwhile five of Selim's nephews and his brother Korkud were taken and strangled. Ahmed had obtained considerable support from the heretics of Anatolia who belonged to the Shiite sect that had participated in the rebellion of 1510 and 1511 against Bayezid and had joined the camp of Shah Ismail of Iran before that. Selim decided to curb the growth of the *Kizilbash* sect, particularly as it was popular in the difficult mountainous and frontier areas of Teke, Karaman, and Diyarbakir. Late in 1513 Selim stationed troops and agents in all parts of the empire. Lists of active heretics were drawn up, and at a given notice about 40,000 were cut down. By transporting others to Europe, Selim hoped that he had settled the religious problem of Asia Minor.

WAR AGAINST IRAN

In this ferocious act Selim came face to face with the role of Shah Ismail in Asia Minor. Two of Ahmed's sons were at his court, and many people in Anatolia looked to Ismail as a holy saint. When, however, he began to interfere in affairs of Dhu-al-Kadr, and along Ottoman frontiers, Selim acted. He sent the fleet with his commissariat to Trabzon. And with several thousand janissaries, the grand vizir, and feudal troops of Rumeli and Anatolia, supported by batteries of cannon, he marched eastward in quest of Shah Ismail. The latter scorched the earth as he retreated, and Selim's soldiers murmured as they were driven on. But Selim would not turn back. In August, 1514 at Chalderan, northeast of Lake Van not far from the foot of Mt. Ararat, Selim's cannon turned the tide. Ismail fled, even leaving his harem to be captured.

Following the battle the Ottoman army captured Tabriz, Ismail's capital, where Selim expected to spend the winter. But the janissaries objected and returned to Istanbul. Selim, however, wintered at Amasya, from where he organized new conquests of Diyarbakir, Kurdistan, north Iraq, and Syria east of the Euphrates.

THE CONQUEST OF EGYPT

With Shah Ismail's defeat, Selim began to use the title shah and sometimes shahinshah (king of kings), or padishah (father of kings). More important, the balance of power among the three eastern Muslim states—Iran, Egypt, and the Ottomans—was fully upset in favor of the last. Ismail wrote to Kansawh al-Ghawri, the Mamluk sultan, for aid against Selim. In 1516 the Mamluks, though feigning peace, marched into Syria in full force. Ottoman agents kept Selim well informed. As usual Selim took the offensive, crushing the Mamluk army at Marj Dabik, north of Aleppo. Again it was a victory of artillery, muskets, bullets, and powder in the hands of a well-disciplined, well-paid, and well-supplied army over swords, spears, and bows and arrows in the hands of an undisciplined, unpaid, and disloyal motley force. Aleppo, Damascus, Beirut, and other cities opened their gates to the Ottomans. Ottoman governors were appointed everywhere, but little else was changed. Taxes continued to be farmed; the amirs of the Lebanon mountains became only nominal vassals; and Jews and Christians were well treated. Tariffs were reduced from twenty to five percent; pilgrim fees in Jerusalem were cut to an insignificant sum; and Selim established an annual grant of 500 ducats to the Franciscan Brothers of the Holy Sepulchre in Jerusalem.

By January, 1517 Selim and his army were on the outskirts of Cairo, which they stormed and took after several days of fighting. Selim was now sultan from the Danube to the cataracts of the Nile. Shah Ismail hastened to congratulate him on his new territories, and from every side of the Middle East the Ottoman Empire was recognized as the dominant power.

A quarter of a century earlier the Mamluk power had defeated the Ottomans in several campaigns over successive years. Now Selim took their measure with little difficulty and captured the Mamluk Empire in one campaign. Between these two events the Portuguese rounded Africa and cut the trade routes that passed through Syria and Egypt. The Mamluk government was impoverished and could no longer meet its commitments or protect the state. Evidence of this condition began to appear late in the reign of Bayezid II and progressed rapidly in the years before the conquest. Yet it is not certain that Selim would have attacked had not the Mamluk sultan attempted to interfere in Ottoman affairs with Iran.

Back in Istanbul by midsummer 1518 after an absence of two years, Selim faced the question of the Caliphate. At Aleppo the puppet Abbasid Caliph al-Mutawakkil, whom the Mamluks brought along on the expedition, fell into Selim's possession. Selim took the caliph to

Istanbul, where he was charged with embezzlement of trust funds and confined to Yedi Kuli—the state prison. Much later, in 1543, he was permitted to return to Cairo, where he died. It has been claimed that he transferred his caliphal authority to the Ottoman ruling family before he departed; and in later years the Ottoman sultans based their use of the title of caliph and the exercise of its power on this incident.

In Selim's long absence his only son, Suleiman, wielded power in Edirne; Piri Pasha, the great admiral, managed Istanbul; while Bursa was governed by Hersekoglu Ahmed Pasha, several times grand vizir and cavalry officer under Mehmed II and Bayezid II. Even under such able guidance the affairs of state suffered and the treasury was depleted. Selim remained in Edirne and Istanbul, straightening out accounts, collecting back taxes, and preparing a navy adequate for an attack upon Rhodes. However, cancer struck him in the spring of 1520 and he died that autumn.

SELIM I

Selim Yavuz was a controversial figure. *Yavuz* means good, just, stern, inflexible, ferocious; and he was all of those. He massacred 40,000 heretics in his land. Vizirs and generals lost their heads at seemingly the slightest failure. A standard curse came to be: "May you become Selim's vizir!" He was an excellent general, a brilliant poet, and a skillful administrator. His court supported philosophers, historians, theologians, and literary figures of many kinds. His tastes were simple; he read widely, slept little, and was uninterested in his harem. Some attributed his moods to an addiction to opium, but there is no assurance that he used the drug before cancer troubled him.

In Selim's brief reign of eight years Ottoman territory increased greatly—almost exclusively in Asia at the expense of other Muslim states. Dominating the Middle East, the Ottoman Empire became the outstanding Muslim empire of the area, heir of the medieval Umayyad and Abbasid empires and ruler of the Muslim Holy Lands. These acquisitions were a determining factor in the process of orientalizing the Ottoman Empire. Selim's sole male heir was his son, Suleiman, who reigned over the Ottomans for forty-six years. Longer than any heretofore among his forefathers, Suleiman's rule brought the Ottoman Empire and the life of its people to the pinnacle of power and luster. The fabric of society and the sources of power and wealth, however, were well fixed by the time of Selim's death; and the eminence of Suleiman's period rested on the firm building of his ancestors.

REFERENCES: *Chapter 15*

Works mentioned at the end of Chapters 13 and 14 relate to this chapter.

Sydney Nettleton Fisher, *The Foreign Relations of Turkey, 1481–1512:* University of Illinois Press, Urbana, 1948. Deals with the period of the reign of Bayezid II.

Charles Grey, trans. and ed., *A Narrative of Italian Travels in Persia in the Fifteenth and Sixteenth Centuries:* The Hakluyt Society *Works,* Vol. 49, London, 1873. A collection of many interesting voyages, two important ones being those of Caterino Zeno and Giovan Maria Angiolello.

Bernard Lewis, *Istanbul and the Civilization of the Ottoman Empire:* University of Oklahoma Press, Norman, 1963. A brilliant survey of the city at its heyday.

William Miller, *The Latins in the Levant: A History of Frankish Greece (1204–1566):* J. Murray, London, 1908. The standard work by the master of the field.

Gertrude Randolph Bramlette Richards, ed., *Florentine Merchants in the Age of the Medici. Letters and Documents from the Selfridge Collection of Medici Manuscripts:* Harvard University Press, Cambridge, 1932. An excellent view of the economic relations between Turkey and the Middle East and Italy, especially Florence, and an insight into some of the problems of doing business in the Ottoman Empire of that day.

E. Denison Ross, "The Early Years of Shah Ismail, Founder of the Safavi Dynasty," *Journal of the Royal Asiatic Society,* n.s., Vol. 28 (1896). An important work.

George William Frederick Stripling, *The Ottoman Turks and the Arabs, 1511–1574:* University of Illinois Press, Urbana, 1942. Although published earlier, this is a sequel to the reference by Fisher, above, and covers the reigns of Selim I, Suleiman, and Selim II and the conquests of Syria, Egypt, and Iraq.

CHAPTER 16

Institutions of the Ottoman Empire

THE SULTAN

At the head of the Ottoman Empire and at the pinnacle of the various social strata stood the sultan. In the West his government was called "The Sublime Porte," presumably because edicts and decisions emanated from the principal gate of the palace. The sultan's authority was derived from the military power which he controlled, from the reverence and obedience which his subjects gave him, and from the constitutional position of caliph which was held after Selim I's conquest of Egypt.

All military power was under his command. Whether slaves, feudal cavalry, irregular infantry, or sailors of the fleet, all were supposed to obey his orders. Not that they always did! Feudal cavalry groups frequently went on unauthorized raids into Christian lands, often to the embarrassment of the sultan. On numerous occasions the army insisted upon abandoning long and arduous campaigns which took them from the pleasures of Edirne and Istanbul during winter months. And the janissaries always demanded bonuses and concessions from the sultan upon his accession to the throne.

Nevertheless, the armed services were generally loyal, and certainly they were more obedient than similar forces in Western Europe were to their kings and emperors. Upholding the sultan was the long ghazi tradition of his leadership; no other family possessed the prestige of the Ottoman dynasty. Moreover, the slave status of most of the officers and the nature of their rearing gave the sultan such a hold over their lives that deviation from his wishes was risky.

Although Ottoman sultans avoided use of the title caliph, those following Selim I wielded the powers of that position. The sultan was head of the Islamic state, defender of the faith, and executor of Sacred Law. Muslims rendered obedience to him. Indirectly Christians did likewise, since the sultan appointed and invested the Greek patriarch and ordered church officials and laymen to obey him.

In general Ottomans followed the law and jurisprudence of Muslim Arabs. Four distinct bodies or sources of law existed. Foremost and supreme over the other three stood Sacred Law (*Shariah*). (The Ottoman interpretation of Sacred Law followed that of the orthodox Hanafite school.) Sultan, judges, and lawyers were bound by Sacred Law, and to ignore it invited disaster. Second stood *Kanuns*, or published decrees of sultans, which were either administrative in character or supplementary to Sacred Law. Kanuns, for example, dealt with intricate ceremonial law of the Ottoman government and with feudal, military, financial, criminal, and police law. Last in the strata of law were *Adet* and *Urf*. Adet was customary law as observed by Turks from time immemorial, by Ottomans, and by peoples conquered by them. Thus, adet in Bosnia might be different from adet in the Morea, and both might be different from adet in Ankara. Urf was the sovereignty or will of the ruling sultan and might contravene adet. Kanuns could change adet and urf and could annul or amend other kanuns. Sacred Law was inviolable.

The great institutions of the state, established either by Sacred Law or kanuns, were accepted as emanating from God or from the sultan's supreme will; in no sense were they considered to flow from the desires of the people. In examining governmental institutions of the empire, two categories are disclosed: the Ruling Institution and the Muslim Institution.

THE RULING INSTITUTION

The Ruling Institution was composed of: the sultan and his family; officers of his household; executive officers of the government; the standing army made up of infantry, cavalry, engineers, artillerymen, and sailors; boys and pages in training for these positions; and feudal lords and knights and their administrative officers. The Muslim Institution included educators, theologians, officials of mosques and pious foundations, lawyers, judges, and dervishes. War captives, tribute boys, and renegades were invariably members of the former group. Members of the latter were always freeborn Muslims, although freeborn Muslims were not necessarily excluded from the Ruling Institution. Sons of first-generation Ottomans were freeborn Muslims, but they usually served in the Ruling Institution; and many top-echelon bureaucrats and feudal lords were descended from old Ottoman Muslim families.

Technically, individuals of the Ruling Institution with the exception of the feudatory enjoyed membership in the sultan's court and were expected to be a part of his retinue on ceremonial occasions or in camp. More specifically, the court consisted of the harem, the inside service, and the outside service.

Until about 1540 there were relatively few in the harem, which was quartered in the Old Palace in Istanbul or in the palaces in Edirne and Demotika. It included consorts of the sultan, female servants of the court, and girls in training. When the last reached the age of twenty-five, they were married to court officers. The greatest lady of the harem was the sultan's mother (*sultana valideh*); after her the mother of the sultan's first-born son, and then mothers of other sons. Numbering about two hundred and guarded by forty black eunuchs, the harem was transferred to the Great Palace in 1540; the Old Palace housed elderly and retired women of the harem.

Functionaries who took care of the sultan's personal affairs comprised the inside service, which was divided into five groups, chambers, or halls: Inner (Royal Bedchamber); Treasury; Commissariat; Great; and Small. Chief of the entire inside service was the General of the Gate, a white eunuch. He was invariably a high state dignitary, who served also as grand master of ceremonies for the palace, director-in-chief of the Palace School, and confidential agent of the sultan. Chief administrators of the halls and their immediate assistants were white eunuchs, who numbered about fifty in the sixteenth century.

Aside from the white eunuchs, members of the halls were called pages and were young men chosen from the elite of the captives and tribute children. The Great and Small Halls were divisions of the Palace School; and pages in the other halls were serving a kind of post-graduate internship in administering affairs of the sultan and his palace. Once a page was promoted to a position outside the inner palace, he never returned; and the tight-lipped silence on life in the inner court maintained through the years by ex-pages was remarkable.

The outside service included learned associates of the sultan, the kitchen service, the personal bodyguard, palace-guards, gardeners, tent-pitchers, masters of the hunt, equerries, and officers of supply. The caliber of men and the inherent prestige associated with the various positions differed greatly. The learned associates of the sultan were members of the Muslim Institution, constituted by the sultan's religious teacher and adviser, preachers, muezzins, chanters, readers, astrologers, physicians, and surgeons. The bodyguard was drawn from sons of high officials, choice graduates from the inner service, and veteran janissaries—in all about four hundred men. Many palace-guards were responsible officials and to that group belonged ambassa-

dors and executioners. Others tended the palace gardens or rowed the
sultan's caïques on Bosphorus excursions. Boys destined for the ordinary
ranks of the janissaries frequently served as helpers in the outside service.

The sultan's court with its three branches numbered in the neighborhood of ten thousand persons at the time of Suleiman I. Earlier Ottoman sultans lived more simply; several accounts of public ceremonies in mosques and other places report that it was difficult to distinguish the sultan from his attendants. Probably with the court of
Murad II and certainly in that of Mehmed II, magnificence in ceremony appeared. After the conquest of Constantinople Mehmed II introduced into his bodyguard a company of one hundred halberdiers,
copied in arms, costumes, and manners from the Byzantine emperor's
bodyguard. By the middle of the sixteenth century rituals and functions
of each section of the services became so elaborate and rigid that a Law
of Ceremonies was drawn and observance of details involving procedure equaled in importance the fulfilling of duties.

Until the reign of Suleiman I the court and its personnel seldom
trespassed upon the direct field of government and administration.
The court served the personal needs of sultan and palace. Insofar as
court officers and chamberlains had direct access to the sultan they
could be influential persons whose favor was eagerly sought. To have a
friend highly placed at court was a precious asset. The administrators
who ran the government were usually members of the Ruling Institution. From the fifteenth century on they were chiefly recruited from
the tribute and captive children. At the top was the vizir, or chief
minister; when later four ministers had the title of vizir, one was designated first vizir, or under Suleiman I grand vizir. The vizirs made up a
council, or Divan, with whom the sultan conferred on matters of state.
Other members of the Divan, often called vizirs, were: two *kadiaskers*,
or chief judges—one for Anatolia and one for Rumeli; two *defterdars*,
or treasurers, again one each for Anatolia and Rumeli; and the chief
nishanji, or secretary of state. Since judges were members of the Muslim Institution, their responsibilities will be described later.

The two principal treasurers were charged with accounting for all
receipts and expenditures of the central government. Until the time of
Mehmed II collection of taxes was administered directly by the treasury, but difficulties and leakages in collections led to a system of
tax-farming. The Ottoman empire was greatly decentralized financially;
provincial governments collected and spent their own funds; and the
religious establishment was supported by revenues from properties
granted as endowments and not always funneled through the treasury. Total revenue for the central government in the 1520's has been

estimated at from six to eight million ducats, a sum which compared favorably with incomes of contemporary governments of Western Europe. The secretary of state recorded all ordinances and commands of the sultan and his government, affixing the seal of authority and the sultan's signature to official documents.

The Divan met with the sultan for several hours every Saturday, Sunday, Monday, and Tuesday to discuss and decide all matters of government. It was analogous to a modern cabinet meeting but also had some resemblance to a supreme court. In fact, it served as a kind of union and capstone to the two branches of the Ottoman government.

By the middle of the sixteenth century the core of the Ottoman army was the janissary corps. The janissaries numbered over ten thousand in the sixteenth century. They were commanded by an Aga (General) who was usually an officer trained in the palace, although sometimes he rose from the ranks like other janissary officers. One hundred and fifty of the best bowmen formed the *Solak* guard, which marched with the sultan on a campaign; other superior janissaries were regularly advanced to other posts in the sultan's service.

The regular cavalry, generally called *Sipahi of the Porte* to distinguish it from the feudal cavalry or *sipahi,* was drawn principally from the ordinary janissaries and the pages of the palace. A few of the feudal cavalry, however, were rewarded with admission to the regular cavalry. One special battalion was a kind of Foreign Legion, consisting of non-Ottoman Turks, Kurds, Arabs, Christian renegades, and horsemen from sources outside the sultan's court.

The Ottomans gave special attention to the technical services; and all European observers at that time marveled at the equipment, food, transport, and roads provided for Ottoman armies. Most important were the artillery corps and ordnance services which cast cannon and manufactured gunpowder. These branches more than any other brought victory after victory to Ottoman arms.

Beginning with Murad II, the navy became an effective division of the armed services. Development of sea power advanced reign by reign until under Selim I and Suleiman I the navy applied its force in all corners of the Mediterranean. Ships were built at many different ports from the Black Sea to the Adriatic. Venetian master shipbuilders along with Greek and Turkish builders, frequently working by flares at night, kept the navy in fighting trim. Commanded by the Kapudan Pasha, who ranked with the vizirs, the navy was manned by experienced seafaring men from North African coasts and the eastern Mediterranean area.

Fleets of three and four hundred ships, as large and as well armed as those of Spain, France, or Venice, were maintained at all times. In peaceful years Ottoman sea captains, many of them Greek or Italian renegades, sailed on their own responsibility and often turned to piracy against Christian Europe in much the same fashion as ghazis on land raided Carinthia and Styria.

One of the superior segments of the Ottoman army came from the provinces and from fief-holders. Whenever a campaign was announced, the governor of each province assembled the feudal cavalry, which until the end of the sixteenth century matched any cavalry of Western Europe. Each *timar* and *ziamet* holder came with a predetermined number of knights in his entourage. They elected their own immediate leaders, although their provincial commander (*sanjakbey*) was an appointee of the sultan (frequently after the time of Murad II a graduate of the Palace School). Prior to the period of Suleiman I supreme command of the feudal cavalry rested on the shoulders of two generals —the Beylerbey of Anatolia and the Beylerbey of Rumeli. (At a later time additional beylerbeys were designated for areas such as Syria, Hungary, and Baghdad.) These two generals acted as vizirs, attended meetings of the Divan when convenient, and commanded the wings of the army in battle. They rewarded the brave directly with fiefs and meted out punishment to laggards.

Other branches of the armed forces were the *akinjis* and the *azabs*. The former were irregular, unpaid, volunteer cavalrymen who answered the call to arms in hopes of booty or the gift of a fief for valor rendered in fighting on the frontier. *Azabs* were similar to *akinjis* except they were foot soldiers. Usually on a military campaign and in any battle *akinjis* and *azabs* were used as front-line troops to absorb the first shocks of contact with the enemy.

THE MUSLIM INSTITUTION

Parallel with the Ruling Institution stood the Muslim Institution. The sultan joined the two at the top, and they touched each other at almost every level in governmental and economic relations. Functionally, the Muslim Institution had three categories: religion, education, and law. An important facet of the Institution was its financial support.

Since Islam has no priesthood, no clergy, and no monks, it has always been difficult to describe Muslim religious groups in Western terms. Teachers in all schools and others who had passed through schools beyond the primary grades were classified as the learned (*ulema*). Other purely religious members of the Muslim Institution were preachers, mosque caretakers, muezzins, professional leaders of prayers in mosques, dervishes, and Sharifs and Sayyids. Mosque endowments provided for regular attendants and leaders in mosque activities on a full-time basis. Dervishes were for Islam what monks, hermits, and begging friars were for Christianity; they preached holy wars, spread heresies, and led in emotional public demonstrations. Sharifs and Sayyids traced their descent from Hasan and Husayn, grandsons of the Prophet, wore green turbans, and had numerous personal prerogatives. One was always the sultan's standard-bearer (*mir-alem*) and ranked above all officers of the army.

Every mosque, large and small, had a primary or reading school, where pupils studied reading, writing, Arabic, and the Koran. Advanced schools were called *medressehs* (colleges) and taught grammar, logic, metaphysics, rhetoric, geometry, and astronomy. Advanced *medressehs* gave courses in law and theology. Students in *medressehs* were partially supported by religious endowments; those in law were completely subsidized. *Medressehs* were numerous throughout the empire, and in Istanbul every sizable mosque had one or more attached to it. Fatih's mosque had eight; Suleiman's, five. Those who studied and finished a *medresseh* belonged to the learned class, and each stage was rigidly graded. A graduate received a degree, called *Danishmend* (*Talisman*), and became qualified to teach in a primary school. Further study raised the *Danishmend* holder to higher ratings which permitted him to be a professor in a *medresseh* or a jurist or judge.

The learned who completed law courses of *medressehs* usually received appointments as a judge (*kadi*), as a legal counselor (*mufti*), or as an assistant in the office of one of these. In every city and large town the sultan appointed a judge who exercised juridical control over the surrounding territory. Slaves of the sultan, Sharifs, and Sayyids had their own judges and courts. In cases which did not concern Muslims foreigners and non-Muslims lived according to their own laws. Sanjakbeys, beylerbeys, and vizirs also administered justice in their courts except in cases involving Sacred Law. The hierarchy of judges was based on five carefully classified grades, and advancement proceeded from one grade to another.

At the top of the system of judges were two *kadiaskers*—one for Europe and one for Asia—who nominated all judges of the empire. Appeals progressed from court to court, and sentences were executed by the civil authorities. Although each judge had a special title, all were generally referred to as *kadis*, and *molla* was the title of respect enjoyed by all.

Associated with the judge of every city was a *mufti* who had finished the regular law course of a *medresseh* and who was assigned to interpret Sacred Law for the judge and high government officials. Appointed for life, the muftis remained private citizens; in legal and juridical matters they had no initiative of action. When a judge, or even a private citizen, was faced with a legal problem, he submitted the question in point to the *mufti* for legal opinion. The *mufti* examined the law and gave his answer, a *fetva,* which usually settled the case for the judge or helped the private citizen in his pending lawsuit. In Istanbul the *mufti* ranked above the judge; and since the sultan and vizirs might pose important questions vital to the life of the whole empire, he became a very significant official. Mehmed II added to the *mufti's* dignity by conferring upon him the title *Shaykh al-Islam,* Leader of Islam.

The Muslim Institution within the Ottoman Empire, from the Shaykh al-Islam and the sultan's personal *Hoja* (teacher) to the lowliest *naib* (village judge) and teacher in a mosque primary school, welded the empire together under one type of education and one body of law. Any Muslim child, if he studied hard and passed the various examinations, might rise in the ranks of the Institution, just as fighting men and the sultan's slaves advanced on merit in the Ruling Institution.

Poverty was no barrier in the Muslim Institution. Perhaps one third of the land of the empire was set aside as endowment for various religious activities. These endowments, or *vakf,* were gifts of sultans and private individuals for support of some specific mosque, library, school, hospital, bridge, or fountain. The imperial treasury actually handled the funds; but the Shaykh al-Islam, the grand vizir, or an official close to the sultan was usually designated as trustee. The donor often stipulated in the deed of transfer that his own descendants should be administrators of the endowment. Slaves of the sultan found this method a convenience in providing perpetual and inalienable income for their sons and descendants. Furthermore, since official members of the Muslim Institution were exempt from taxation and since their properties were not subject to confiscation, families of the Muslim Institution had many financial advantages and formed a kind of privileged class.

NON-MUSLIM SUBJECTS

Following the arrival of Muslim *ulema* in the Ottoman state at the time of Sultan Orhan, Ottomans grew tolerant of non-Muslims in the fashion of the older Muslim world. Christian and Jewish groups were given their religious and cultural freedom; many Balkan communities preferred such autonomy under the Ottomans to religious and cultural restrictions and persecutions suffered under Hungarian and Hapsburg rule.

When the settlement of Istanbul was made in 1453, Mehmed II, in recognizing the election of Gennadius as patriarch of the Orthodox Church, pursued the custom of Byzantine emperors in confirming the election of patriarchs. He also acknowledged the practice, already well established in the Ottoman state, of permitting Christians to retain the independence of their religious community. Likewise, Mehmed II recognized Jewish and Armenian Gregorian communities.

These three separate religious groups were called *millets*, which meant "a community or nation of people with a particular religion within the Ottoman Empire." Each *millet* or nation had the legal right to use its own language, develop its own religious, cultural, and educational institutions, collect taxes and render them to the imperial treasury, and maintain courts for trying members of the nation in all cases except those involving public security and crime. Each *millet* had a leader who was responsible to the sultan for the payment of taxes from the *millet* and for the good behavior and loyalty of members of his community. To some degree, therefore, these three *millets* stood alongside the Ruling and the Muslim Institutions to which Ottomans belong.

FOREIGNERS

Further paralleling these Institutions and subject nations as part of the empire were groups of foreigners, chiefly merchants residing in Istanbul. Each group lived under provisions of a formal treaty drawn up between the sultan and the foreign authority. Even Bayezid I, Mehmed I, and Murad II had agreements with Ragusa, Venice, and Genoa. Mehmed II, Bayezid II, and Selim I had regular treaties with Ragusa, Hungary, Genoa, Milan, Venice, Florence, the Pope, Naples, and the Knights of St. John on the Island of Rhodes. Suleiman I had one with France.

The general tenor of these treaties was exemplified in the Treaty of 1503 between Bayezid II and Venice. Among other things, the sultan agreed that a Venetian consul (*bailo*) might come to Istanbul with his family and reside there for three years. Although Venetians could live in certain designated cities of the empire for one year and although the sultan agreed to be reasonable in extending their residence, they could travel about only with the consul's permission. The consul should settle all cases and disputes between Venetians; and Venetian testimony was recognized as valid in courts of Christian and Jewish Ottoman subjects. In criminal cases Venetians were guaranteed justice in regular Ottoman courts. That same year in a similar treaty with the King of Hungary, an article provided that commercial clauses would be valid for subjects of certain other states, including the Holy Roman Empire, France, England, Spain, Portugal, and Poland, upon proper ratification of the treaty by the king of the respective state.

These treaties recognizing certain rights and obligations for European residents in the Ottoman Empire were based on the assumption that since Christians could not avail themselves of Muslim Sacred Law they would have to live by their own Christian laws. However, in later years when the balance of power between Western Europe and the Ottoman Empire shifted to favor the former, such arrangements evolved into the famous Capitulatory Treaties, which gave nationals of other governments an apparent privileged position in the Ottoman Empire and frequently allowed foreign governments untold influence over vital policies of the Sublime Porte.

REFERENCES: Chapter 16

In addition to general studies on Middle Eastern history and Muslim institutions, references in Chapters 12, 13, 14, and 15 are of particular importance.

John Kingsley Birge, *The Bektashi Order of Dervishes:* Hartford Seminary Press, Hartford, 1937. A significant work by a careful scholar on the origin and development of this order and its relationship to the leaders and various strata of Ottoman society.

Ogier G. de Busbecq, *Turkish Letters* (Edward S. Forster, trans.): Clarendon Press, Oxford, 1927. De Busbecq was imperial ambassador to the Porte for many years; his observations were singularly objective and discerning.

H. A. R. Gibb and Harold Bowen, *Islamic Society and the West: A Study of the Impact of Western Civilization on Moslem Culture in the Near East,* Volume I (in two parts): *Islamic Society in the Eighteenth Century:* Oxford University Press, London, 1950 and 1957. A detailed and penetrating study of Ottoman institutions as they existed in the eighteenth century and as they had evolved from earlier forms in the fourteenth century.

Richard Knolles, *The Generall Historie of the Turkes, from the First Beginning of that Nation to the Rising of the Othoman Familie: With all the Notable Expeditions of the Christian Princes Against Them. Together with the Lives and Conquests of the Othoman Kings and Emperours . . . :* London, 1603. This is still the most extensive and longest Ottoman history in the English language, written by an Englishman, long resident in Turkey. There are many later editions.

Albert Howe Lybyer, *The Government of the Ottoman Empire in the Time of Suleiman the Magnificent:* Harvard University Press, Cambridge, 1913. A thorough examination of the institutions of the Ottomans. A pioneer study in this field.

CHAPTER 17

The Ottoman Empire
as a World Power

SULEIMAN I

The government of the Ottoman Empire was so well organized, regulated, and staffed under Mehmed II, Bayezid II, and Selim I and the number of intelligent, trained, and disciplined officers, pages, and students in the palace was so great that the government could function well without much direction from the sultan. And since Selim I left only one son, the transfer of authority in 1520 generated no stress and no factious activities at the Porte. His son, Suleiman, moreover, was born in the year A.H 900, the opening year of the tenth century of Islam, and was the tenth of his dynasty. Because of these portentous beginnings his subjects believed that he was destined to rule over a great part of the world.

In this favorable setting the youthful Suleiman appeared as a magnificent sovereign, certainly the match of his equally youthful contemporaries Charles V, Francis I, and Henry VIII. Suleiman reigned for forty-six years. During those years the Ottoman Empire, built on solid foundations by his predecessors, reached its height in power, wealth, and brilliance. Accordingly, Suleiman, called "The Magnificent" by Europeans and *"Kanuni"* (The Lawgiver) by his own people, has been regarded as a majestic figure among the galaxy of distinguished rulers of all ages.

During the latter years of Bayezid II's reign Suleiman, then a lad of fifteen or so, was assigned as governor of Bolu. But after strong protests by his uncle Ahmed he was transferred to Kaffa in the Crimea, where his mother, daughter of a Tartar khan, was reared. After his father seized the throne Suleiman was called to govern Istanbul, while Selim fought against brothers and nephews in Asia Minor. Suleiman governed Edirne again during his father's long wars in Iran and Egypt. Only upon Selim's return to Istanbul in 1517 was Suleiman sent to rule the province around Manisa in western Anatolia. Thus, Suleiman attended the pages' school in Istanbul and resided for more than five years at the palaces of Istanbul and Edirne. In addition, he had nearly six years of experience as provincial governor, surrounded by teachers, advisers, and graduates of the famous Palace School. No prince of his time had better training or more practical preparation for the responsibility of ruling a great empire. He was a refined gentleman of the Renaissance.

BELGRAD AND RHODES

Suleiman passed the first winter of his reign becoming acquainted with his elevated position; and since Piri Pasha continued as grand vizir, no sharp break in governmental personnel occurred. When spring came Suleiman met the demand for action by choosing Belgrad for the campaign of 1521. At Sofia he gathered his army and supplies, including three thousand camels carrying ammunition and thirty thousand laden with grain. Ten thousand wagonloads of grain were requisitioned locally, and three hundred cannon were brought up the Danube from Istanbul.

Little opposition was expected from Europe. Charles V was not only busily engaged preparing for war against Francis I but also deeply involved with Luther and imperial problems, whereas the cream of Hungarian nobility was at Bratislava celebrating the marriage of King Louis to Mary of Hapsburg, Charles V's sister. Nevertheless, Belgrad offered a valiant defense, its garrison holding out for three weeks. Ottoman cannon, implanted on an island in the Danube, demolished a part of the inner fortress and ended all resistance late in August. Many Serbs were transplanted to the outskirts of Istanbul, where the Belgrad Forest still remains as testimony to this important victory which opened the Hungarian plains and the upper Danube basin to the Ottomans.

The following year Suleiman assembled his forces in Asia for the heralded attack upon the Island of Rhodes. Rhodes lay six miles off the coast of Asia Minor astride the sea route from Istanbul to Alexandria, and since the conquest of Egypt the Knights had continually harassed Ottoman trade. Frequently Ottoman prisoners were slaughtered contrary to the provisions of the treaty concluded with Bayezid II, who regarded the Knights as professional pirates and cutthroats.

Rhodes was a highly fortified port, and large contingents of knights from many European commanderies of the Order arrived to defend the citadel. Venice sent her fleet, but to protect Cyprus! Massing 300 ships and 100,000 men, Suleiman led the attack. It lasted from July until December. Thousands of stone cannon balls of prodigious size bombarded the walls, and a few rudimentary explosive shells were hurled into the town. Effective attacks were launched in conjunction with sapping and mining operations against the walls, but the cost in men on each side was beyond reason. Since Pope Adrian VI's finances and Charles V's victory that spring over Francis I precluded any aid from reaching the Knights, they surrendered on Christmas Day, 1522. They were allowed to depart with all mercenary soldiers and towns-men who desired to leave. Those who remained were unmolested, were guaranteed full civil rights, and were freed from taxation for five years.

SULEIMAN'S COURT

The fall of Rhodes and Belgrad consolidated fully into Ottoman hands the Middle East, or the Levant as it was called in the West. For the following three summers Suleiman remained in Edirne, Istanbul, or their environs enjoying peace. He loved the gardens of the palace, and one of his greatest pleasures was boating on the Bosphorus and the Sea of Marmara. Frequently he would be rowed across to the Asiatic shore to walk in his gardens there.

It was also during these years that a Russian slave girl named Khurrem caught his fancy. Known generally to posterity as "Roxelana," meaning "the Russian," she soon captivated Suleiman completely, became his legal wife, and dominated him until her death in 1558. Suleiman's mother ruled his harem until her death in 1533; after that date Roxelana forced her way into political affairs. Her chief rival, Gulbahar, a Montenegrin slave girl and mother of Suleiman's oldest living son, Mustafa, departed to Manisa in 1534 in the company of her son when he was established there as governor. Roxelana bore Suleiman three children: Selim, Bayezid, and a daughter, Mihrimah. Suleiman had two other sons who grew to manhood: Mehmed, who was older than Selim; and Jihangir, a hunchback. Competition in the harem for Suleiman's affections and intense rivalry among the mothers for the advancement and protection of their sons brought dismay and affliction upon Suleiman and the government in later days.

At this same time Piri Pasha, the grand vizir, retired on a handsome pension, and Suleiman advanced to the grand vizirate his favorite and boon companion, Ibrahim. Ibrahim was the son of a Greek sailor of Parga on the Adriatic coast. He was captured by pirates and sold to a lady of Manisa, who gave her slave an excellent education. As a prince in Manisa, Suleiman recognized Ibrahim's talents, enjoyed his playing on the violin, and brought him to Istanbul as chief falconer and head of the pages of the Inner (Royal Bed) Chamber. Instead of advancing the second vizir who fully expected the promotion because of his meritorious conduct during the siege of Rhodes, Suleiman appointed the youthful Ibrahim to the post vacated by Piri Pasha, and also to the office of Beylerbey of Rumeli. For the following thirteen years Ibrahim governed the empire, year by year relieving Suleiman of more of the tiresome duties of ruling. He even took the title of Seriasker-Sultan (Commander-in-chief of the Armies with the power of Sultan). He dined with Suleiman, was with him at all hours, and even slept in the sultan's apartments. Between 1523 and 1536 no policy of state was reached without Ibrahim's consideration and approval.

Unfortunately, Ibrahim's rapid advancement to chief of the Royal Bedchamber and then to grand vizir ran counter to the system of promotions based on merit and service. There could be no question but that Ibrahim was a brilliant and successful administrator and adviser. Still, others who proved their abilities through service were passed over by the sultan's personal favorite. Thus, early in Suleiman's reign the personalities of Roxelana and Ibrahim and their roles at the palace sowed the seeds of harem influence and personal favoritism which proved so disastrous in succeeding centuries.

The first demonstration of Ibrahim's genius came in Egypt. The second vizir in 1523 asked and received as a consolation the governorship of Egypt. Within months after his arrival in Cairo he was deeply involved in treason and was murdered in his bath by loyal Ottomans. Other revolts by Arab tribes and Mamluks led Suleiman to commission Ibrahim to go to Egypt for six months to inaugurate a more stable regime. Finances, administration, law, and trade procedures were thoroughly overhauled. The Ottoman pasha was also given more responsibility, although landholders still had direct access to the sultan and considerable local autonomy. The arrangement cleverly tied Ottoman authority to Egyptian independence, producing a system that worked for nearly four centuries.

THE SIEGE OF VIENNA

But the janissaries and palace troops grew restless under the long inactivity and the paucity of booty which Suleiman's repose enforced upon them. Stringent measures in 1525 along with a few well-placed executions were required to quell a janissary riot that could easily have grown into a serious rebellion. Immediately, preparations for a major campaign were unfurled. Following the disastrous Battle of Pavia in

1525 the French begged Suleiman to join in a war against Charles V. All summer Suleiman and his viziers debated whether a campaign up the Danube beyond Belgrad or one into Transylvania would be better.

In April, 1526 the choice fell on the former. And Suleiman, Ibrahim, and other viziers set out from Istanbul with 100,000 men and several hundred cannon. In July Peterwardein was taken by Ibrahim. Early in August the Ottomans crossed the Drava unmolested at Osijek and moved toward Mohacs, where a crushing victory opened all of Hungary. Early in September Buda surrendered to Suleiman, and two weeks later Pest on the east bank of the Danube was burned. The following day Suleiman and his army began the long trek homeward, reaching Istanbul in the middle of November.

But the expedition into Hungary, even with its exciting battles, ended only as a magnified raid. Suleiman did not possess adequate manpower to garrison such distant cities as Budapest and Mohacs. No lands were handed out as fiefs to Ottoman officers; and Hungary remained a political vacuum. John Zapolya, Duke of Transylvania, occupied Budapest and was crowned king of Hungary. However, Ferdinand of Hapsburg, Archduke of Austria, defeated Zapolya at Tokay in 1527 and became Hungarian king.

In desperation Zapolya turned to the Ottomans. Through the suave diplomacy of the Venetian-Ottoman Ludovico Gritti, Ibrahim's business partner, Suleiman moved in 1529 to punish Ferdinand by ousting the Austrians from Hungary. Not until the middle of May did the army leave Istanbul, and drenching and continuous rains impeded its march. The larger cannon were abandoned along the way. Mohacs was reached only in mid-August; Budapest, a month later. Soon afterward *akinjis* penetrated into Austria like swarms of locusts, and the attack upon Vienna opened on September 29th. Although Ferdinand had all summer to meet the threat, forces to defend Vienna assembled less than a week before the siege began.

Mining operations, assaults, countermining, and sorties raged day after day. On October 12, 1529 mines seriously damaged the walls, and infantry attacks almost succeeded. Both sides grew weary, however, and on the fifteenth the Ottomans retired. To the defenders of Vienna it seemed miraculous; for they were on the point of surrender. In truth, the retreat was forced by the grumbling of the janissaries, who wished to reach Edirne and Istanbul before winter. Ferdinand, unable to pursue the retiring Ottomans, recognized Suleiman's hold upon Hungary in a peace treaty in 1533.

Vienna had not been taken by Suleiman because his communications were so extended that his forces could not be effective. Incessant rains in the Balkans and in Austria made the long marches arduous and the hauling of the heavy cannon which took Belgrad almost impossible. The army left Istanbul only after the mud dried late in April and insisted upon returning before the winter rains began in December. Neither the janissaries nor the feudal cavalry would campaign in the winter. Vienna was beyond Ottoman reach, although Christendom failed to appreciate the full facts of the sultan's limitations.

NAVAL ACTIVITIES

While Suleiman was engaged in Hungary combating the Hapsburgs, the French looked to him as a useful ally in their struggle against Charles V. Two French embassies reached Istanbul in 1525, both pleading for aid against the king of Spain. But the wily Francis called upon Suleiman only as a last stratagem in war against Charles. In 1530 he quickly dropped the Ottomans and co-operated with Charles against them, sending a dozen French galleys with Andrea Doria's fleet to attack Algeria. But again in 1535, with the vagaries of political and diplomatic fortunes, French envoys pursued Suleiman to the Caucasus to secure Ottoman aid against Charles. No commitments were made; but ambassadors were exchanged on a more permanent basis, and in the following year a treaty was signed giving the French recognition and status similar to that accorded Venice and other Italian city-states for the residence and trade of their nationals in the Ottoman Empire.

Relations with the French and Hapsburgs inevitably led the Ottomans to extend their interests to the entire Mediterranean. Ottoman navies had existed before the fall of Constantinople and had grown in competence. Mehmed II was able in 1480 to support an expedition across the Adriatic to the heel of Italy. Under the great sea captain Kemal during the reign of Bayezid II Ottoman sea power became of age, controlled the eastern Mediterrean, and repeatedly plundered the shores of Spain. Under Suleiman the navy occupied and added much of North Africa to the empire.

While Selim I was conquering Egypt, Aruj Barbarossa and his more famous brother Khair al-Din appeared in Tunis to lead the fleets against Christian Europe. Their father was an Ottoman fiefholder from Rumeli who settled on the Island of Mytilene following its conquest by Mehmed II, and they followed the sea-ghazi tradition prevalent along that coast for more than two centuries. After retaking Algiers, Aruj lost his life in an assault upon Tlemcen. Thereupon Khair al-Din, who inherited his brother's sobriquet Barbarossa, sent word that he would consent to Selim's overlordship in exchange for aid and official position. Appointed Beylerbey of Algiers and North Africa with absolute authority to rule those provinces and to raise and organize a janissary army, Barbarossa exercised Ottoman power in the Mediterranean until his death in 1546. His ships raked the coasts of Spain and maintained unceasing pressure upon Charles V. Barbarossa's men were of all nationalities, thus truly Ottoman; but his personal bodyguard was composed exclusively of Spanish renegades.

As a diversionary tactic in 1532 when Suleiman was campaigning in Austria, Andrea Doria in a dashing raid with the Spanish retook Coron on the Peloponnesus. Two years later they evacuated this advanced position, because their weakness did not permit a steady supply line and the possession of Coron was only a minor irritant to Ottoman sea power. Nevertheless, Suleiman summoned Khair al-Din to Istanbul, where with much fanfare he was reappointed Beylerbey of Algiers and given a fleet of eighty-four ships, many of which were built under his supervision. He regarded himself as a veritable sea-ghazi, and on this occasion visited the tomb of Jelal al-Din Rumi in Konya to obtain the blessings of this patron saint of all ghazis. After ravaging the coast of southern Italy in a manner long remembered, Barbarossa descended upon Bizerta and became master of Tunis.

Such a victory could not be left unchallenged. The following year Charles V and Andrea Doria, employing a large fleet and a powerful army, dislodged the Ottomans from Tunis. But Barbarossa escaped with a score of his ships to Algiers to pillage Minorca and the coast of Valencia. Thence he proceeded with his loot, which included six thousand prisoners and two rich Portuguese caravels, to Istanbul—where Suleiman appointed him Kapudan Pasha and made him responsible for all naval activities.

No important naval conquests graced the remainder of Suleiman's reign. Spanish attacks upon Algiers were beaten off, and Ottoman sea captains-ghazis-pirates raided and plundered from one end of the Mediterranean to the other. They visited the Canary Islands, and the English ambassador in Spain complained to Queen Elizabeth in 1562 that North African pirates seized three English ships near Cadiz, making off with more than 100,000 ducats. After the treaty with France in 1536 French ships frequently co-operated with Ottoman fleets in the western Mediterranean. In the winter of 1543 the harbor and town of Toulon were given over entirely to Barbarossa, his ships, and men; the inhabitants gladly moved out to avoid unpleasant incidents. After Khair al-Din died in 1546 his role was admirably filled by Turgut (Dragut), Piale Pasha, Uluj Ali (a Calabrian by birth), and Khair al-Din's son Hasan. Tripoli was stormed and became the headquarters of Turgut who was named its beylerbey. The strategic Island of Jerba off the eastern coast of Tunisia fell to Piale Pasha, who had sailed out to prevent Philip II's fleet from recovering Tripoli.

In 1565 Suleiman sent Piale with 200 ships and a landing force of nearly 30,000 men to take the Island of Malta from the Knights of St. John whom he had driven from Rhodes more than forty years earlier. After several months of costly and fruitless assaults upon the island fortresses, the Ottomans withdrew. Curiously, the Christian forces made no attempt to follow up this failure. Ottoman supremacy upon the Mediterranean continued for many years after Suleiman's death.

EASTERN CAMPAIGNS

On several occasions in the early years of Suleiman's reign there were difficulties with the shah of Iran. The Ottoman court, being Sunnite, looked with contempt upon the Shiites of the east. They also feared any successes of these heretics; for devotees lived in various parts of the Ottoman Empire. Although Selim I had beaten Shah Ismail and destroyed thousands of heretics in Anatolia, border chieftains in eastern Asia Minor vacillated in their loyalty from Tabriz to Istanbul and back to Tabriz again as advantages shifted from one to the other. Such changing allegiance brought conflict between the two great empires and perpetuated minor border engagements.

The first eastern campaign conducted personally by Suleiman was in 1534. Ibrahim led the advance contingents into Tabriz, Suleiman reaching the Iranian capital weeks later. Not being able to come to grips with Shah Tahmasp, they moved southward and captured Baghdad. There Suleiman passed the winter, arranging the administration of this new addition to his empire. The sacred bones of the revered Muslim legalist and theologian Abu Hanifa were discovered, and Suleiman constructed an appropriate shrine to the founder of the legal school followed by Ottoman courts. Suleiman then sacked and fired Tabriz. He returned to Istanbul early in 1536, having been gone for eighteen months.

A decade later Shah Tahmasp's brother appeared at the Porte, seeking help in a bid for the Iranian throne. Suleiman left Istanbul in 1548, recaptured Tabriz, wintered in Aleppo, and spent all of 1549 pillaging cities and pursuing the elusive Tahmasp, who never dared risk a battle.

Again, in 1553 Tahmasp, perhaps believing that the Ottomans were fully engaged in Europe, adopted an aggressive policy towards the Porte and seized Erzerum. Rustem Pasha, the grand vizir, headed a large army to halt the Iranians. The army, however, particularly the janissaries, disliked him; they began to mutter that if Suleiman were too old to lead them his eldest living son, Prince Mustafa, should. Egged on by Roxelana, who was plotting for the favored position for one of her sons, Suleiman took the field. Mustafa was summoned to meet his father at Eregli, where three mutes strangled him with a bowstring at Suleiman's command. Suleiman again wintered at Aleppo and spent 1554 in subjugating the lands east of the Euphrates. Recognizing, however, the futility of trying to hold these eastern conquests, the Porte arranged a peace which allowed the Ottomans to retain Iraq, including Baghdad, and a port on the Persian Gulf.

Suleiman also took an interest in developments in the Red Sea area and along the shores of the Arabian Sea. Salman, an ex-pirate, led an Ottoman force that plundered Yemen and Aden in 1525. Thirteen years later an Ottoman admiral sailed from Suez, installed loyal governors in Aden and Yemen, and then passed on to the Malabar coast, where he landed and unsuccessfully besieged Diu. Suleiman also found that the Portuguese blocked the exit from the Persian Gulf, in part nullifying his capture of Baghdad and Basrah. When the famous geographer-sea captain, Piri Pasha, failed to oust the Portuguese from the Straits of Hormuz, he was beheaded for cowardice. His successors were likewise unsuccessful in driving them from Hormuz. None the less the Ottomans retained control over the Persian Gulf, Aden, Yemen, and the Red Sea.

HUNGARY AGAIN

Suleiman, like other rulers of his time, had too many irons in the fire to press vigorously his eastern campaigns. In the latter half of his reign he became involved again in Hungary. His vassals quarreled continually, so that in 1541 he led his army into Hungary. He occupied Budapest and for the first time merged Hungary directly into his empire. His officers were installed in all territories between the Danube and the Theiss. Some twenty-five provinces were formed, each with a governor under the Beylerbey of Budapest (Ofen). As always in the Ottoman state, the Magyar people continued to live and worship as they had in the past.

Ferdinand of Austria tried to retaliate but his siege of Budapest failed. He succeeded only in enticing Suleiman into a campaign which extended the empire to include Gran and Stuhlweissenburg. Peace treaties were signed in 1547; each party retained the lands in his possession, and Austria paid a tribute of 30,000 ducats a year to the Porte. The Hapsburgs, however, violated the peace; and in 1552 Suleiman's second vizir captured fortress after fortress and incorporated the Banat of Temesvar into the empire. Only a minor fortress of Sziget in Hungary remained. Busbecq, the noted commentator on Suleiman's court and the Imperial ambassador at the Porte, arranged a renewal of the peace in 1561.

Maximilian II succeeded his father, Ferdinand, in 1564. He, too, refused to pay the tribute and attacked Ottoman territory. When governors clamored for support in 1566, Suleiman set forth on his seventh campaign into Hungary. He was over seventy years of age; and since he could no longer ride a horse, he traveled in a carriage. Pointing for Erlau, the troops were deflected to reduce the fortress at Sziget, where a Croatian count had killed one of Suleiman's favorite officers. Situated on lowlands near the Danube, Sziget was surrounded by marshes and lakes. Dry weather, however, prevailed, and Sziget fell on the evening of September 5 with the explosion of a huge mine under the walls. That same night Suleiman died. Hungary was consolidated and Suleiman expired at the fulfilment of the conquest which had begun with the fall of Belgrad in his first year of campaigning.

SULEIMAN'S FAMILY AND FRIENDS

Mehmed Sokolli, the grand vizir, kept Suleiman's death a secret for over three weeks, while a messenger went to Kutahya to summon Selim to the succession. Suleiman had eight sons, but only one outlived him. Three died as small children in the first years of his reign. Mehmed, who was Suleiman's favorite, died in 1543 at the age of twenty-one. The fate of Mustafa, the son of Roxelana's chief rival, has already been narrated; and his brother, Jihangir the hunchback, committed suicide upon learning of Mustafa's death. The remaining two, Selim and Bayezid, were Roxelana's sons. Selim, the elder, drank too much and was given to intrigue. The soldiers preferred Bayezid, who resembled Suleiman and who was probably the choice of Suleiman and Roxelana.

Rivalry between the two was intense, and each had a following at court. Selim and his friends employed every means to advance his power, even daring to risk forging and intercepting letters between Bayezid and his father. Especially after Roxelana's death in 1558, Selim's fortunes were watched over by Rustem Pasha. The latter was the husband of Roxelana's daughter Mihrimah, who had as much power over her father as her mother. Civil war between the two broke out in 1559. Suleiman ordered the provincial governors in Asia Minor to give active support to Selim, who was then victorious in a battle near Konya. Bayezid asked to be forgiven, but the letter never reached his father. Fleeing to the court of Shah Tahmasp, Bayezid became the source of much diplomatic correspondence. Eventually on the payment of 400,000 ducats he was turned over to Suleiman's agent, who executed him. Thus, when Suleiman died, there remained of his sons only Selim the Drunkard—a fat, gay, and debauched person.

Another unhappy personal incident of Suleiman's reign involved his companion and grand vizir Ibrahim. After he was appointed to office in 1523, Suleiman grew to depend upon him for nearly every important decision. Before Suleiman designated Khair al-Din Barbarossa Beyler-bey of Algiers, Barbarossa had to proceed to Aleppo to secure the blessing and approval of Ibrahim. For the first Iranian campaign Ibrahim was named seriasker and at times appropriated the title "sultan" (one who commands). Presumably, Suleiman came to feel that Ibrahim was amassing too much power. One evening in 1536 Ibrahim dined as usual with Suleiman and retired for the night to his customary place in Suleiman's apartments. The next morning his strangled body was found outside the palace. No reason was ever given. His immense wealth reverted to the crown as he was Suleiman's slave. In later years Suleiman tried to avoid promoting officers too rapidly or elevating them too obviously over the heads of their seniors.

IMPERIAL PROBLEMS

The relationship between Suleiman and Ibrahim and its calamitous end were symptomatic of the rapidly changing scene in and about the government. The expansion into eastern Asia Minor, Syria, and Egypt by Selim I was followed without much breathing space by Suleiman's conquests in Serbia, Hungary, North Africa, and Mesopotamia. The result was that in two decades the empire experienced an astonishing increment not only of power and wealth but also of responsibilities.

More and more provinces were created with a proportionate increase in the number of governors, judges, tax collectors, and clerks. The janissary corps was doubled in size. Wealth poured into Istanbul; and high officers of the court, personally interested in money even in the days of Murad II, adopted a life of sumptuous pomp and splendor. To celebrate the circumcision of Mustafa, Mehmed, and Selim in the summer of 1530 high dignitaries gathered in Istanbul for festivities which lasted three weeks. At their termination Suleiman asked Ibrahim which had been the more splendid affair, this fete or that of his marriage to Suleiman's sister. Ibrahim readily replied that the latter had been more august because at his wedding he had been honored by Suleiman, the noblest guest that one could expect! Each vizir had a magnificent court of his own, modeled after that of his master. Each had his own slaves, whom he trained and employed for his own interests. Ibrahim even established a school. Mehmed Sokolli, the grand vizir at the time of Suleiman's death, had become Suleiman's slave when Iskender Chelebi, the chief treasurer, was executed and his property confiscated in 1534. Ayas Pasha, Ibrahim's successor as grand vizir and a slave of Albanian origin, lived in the grand manner. At his death from the plague it was cryptically noted that there were forty cradles at one time at his palace and that he left 120 children!

As governmental administration became vaster and more complex, favoritism, corruption, and intrigue multiplied. The situation was abetted by the haphazard growth of Ottoman law and legal procedures. Suleiman, therefore, issued numerous new laws and revamped and codified old laws in a vain attempt to regularize his administration. On the basis of this legal activity he has been known in Ottoman history as Suleiman Kanuni—the Lawgiver. Many laws related to matters of inheritance, salary, rank, and ceremony for officers of the Ruling Institution. Market and guild regulations were modified; criminal laws were developed; and in 1532 a full Egyptian law code, almost a constitution, was arranged based on the decrees and settlements made by Ibrahim while he had been there in 1524. One of the greatest collections of laws was that fashioned in 1530 for the feudal class to eliminate confusion and end the growing corruption. The granting of all fiefs was changed from the hands of the beylerbey to those of the sultan. A sipahi or a prospective sipahi received a note from the beylerbey, but had to appear at the Porte to obtain his confirmation.

Suleiman's revenues were greater than those of any of his contemporary monarchs in Europe. Income was derived from many sources. Since the Ottomans usually followed the customs which were practiced in a province before its conquest, the sources varied from province to province. Tithes on land, poll taxes, special taxes on lands of non-Muslims, trade, animals, produce, markets, mines, confiscations, escheat, and booty annually brought Suleiman about twelve million ducats. (A ducat in gold content was equal to $3.93.) It is hard to estimate what the relative purchasing power would be for modern times, but there was no doubt about the power and splendor which this income commanded. Even so, Suleiman, like each of the European monarchs, was often hard pressed for funds; and in his later years he forced gifts from his officers upon their appointment to a higher position, a practice which unfortunately opened the door to venality.

SELIM II

Throughout his reign of eight years Selim II retained his father's last grand vizir, Mehmed Sokolli, who administered the government and might well be called the actual ruler. Selim was a truly gifted poet and surrounded himself with men of literary tastes and talents. He was highly emotional and sensitive, but lived in the company of fawning courtiers and adventurers. Virtually afraid of his grand vizir, Selim respected him and other high officials of proven abilities. He always rose to greet Abu Saud, Shaykh al-Islam and author of many laws under Suleiman, and otherwise demonstrated esteem and affection for him. Yet, Selim was self-centered. He was unaware of how the court and the soldiers felt toward him and was easily influenced by unscrupulous adventurers, of which there was a goodly number at the Porte.

Since Mehmed Sokolli continued as grand vizir throughout Selim's reign and on into that of his successor, there was no break in governmental procedure or policy. There might have been difficulty at the onset. Selim and his personal friends erred in not comprehending the power and fearlessness of the janissaries; and at first they declined to give the customary accession donations to the soldiers. Murmurs, demands, and a show of force followed until Selim promised the money.

The course of events proceeded as it had under Suleiman. Piale Pasha took the Island of Chios from the Genoese; Bosnian sipahi raided Carniola; ambassadors came and went; peace was signed with Austria and Poland; and Yemen was subjected. An ambitious project was undertaken in 1569: an officer was sent with ships and troops to Azov, whence they departed to conquer Astrakhan at the mouth of the Volga River. Engineers and excavators started digging a canal to connect the Don and the Volga at a point where they are only about thirty miles apart. The purpose was to enable ships and military supplies to be sent to the Caspian Sea and to support attacks upon Iran. The garrison at Astrakhan withstood the storm, and Prince Serebinoff led an army which drove away the workmen on the canal. Thus, the enterprise was abandoned and peace between Muscovy and the Porte re-established.

Sokolli had a similar dream of cutting a waterway across Suez, but affairs in Yemen and Arabia and then Selim's insistence upon war against Venice for the conquest of Cyprus postponed the work. Lala Mustafa, Selim's adviser who had intrigued and plotted so successfully to destroy Bayezid, obtained command of the war against Venice. The Beylerbey of Anatolia and many governors were ordered to support him. Three naval contingents assisted when the attack began in 1570. The ports fell and the whole island of Cyprus was subdued at heavy cost by midsummer of 1571. Cyprus became a unified part of the empire; and Selim could now command the entire output of Cypriote wine of which he was so fond.

The fall of Cyprus and the extraordinary naval preparations of the Ottomans not only alarmed Venice but instigated the formation of a redoubtable naval league which included Spain, Venice, Savoy, the Pope, and the Knights of Malta. Commanded by Don Juan of Austria, the Christian fleet met the Ottomans under the leadership of the Kapudan Pasha at the Gulf of Lepanto in October, 1571. A furious battle ensued with the Ottomans losing over 200 ships and many men. The allied fleets suffered less, and victory was theirs. To the Ottomans and the East the Battle of Lepanto was a severe loss in a long series of naval engagements. However, a new fleet was built that winter in the naval yards of Gallipoli and Istanbul; and by the spring of 1572 the Ottoman naval position was largely repaired. To the Christians, however, it seemed a notable victory; it gave them courage and proved that the Ottomans were not invincible upon the sea. Nevertheless, they failed to follow up the victory, and their combined fleets were scattered. By spring of the following year it was too late. A new Ottoman navy was in being.

Peace between Venice and the Porte was never officially broken, and in 1573 a new treaty was signed in which Venice not only recognized the loss of Cyprus but agreed to pay the Ottomans the cost of the war. Don Juan did, however, act to drive the Ottomans from the harbor and city of Tunis, part of which was occupied by Uluj Ali while the conquest of Cyprus was underway. Uluj Ali, as Kapudan Pasha, returned in 1574 and was renamed Kilij Ali. Tunis now joined Algiers and Tripoli as Ottoman strongholds on the north shore of Africa and remained an Ottoman possession until the nineteenth century.

Whether the decay and weakening of the Ottoman Empire would have become noticeable under Selim had he lived longer is difficult to determine. In any case, late in 1574 Selim was inspecting a new bath at the palace; and to protect himself from any dampness of the fresh plaster drained an entire bottle of Cypriote wine. Being slightly unsteady, he fell on the damp floor and died a few days later from a brain concussion. His death, followed a year later by the assassination of Mehmed Sokolli, terminated an era in Middle Eastern history. The glory of the empire and its augmentation soon turned into stagnation and decline. The powerful and dynamic Ottoman Empire rapidly gave way to the weak and corrupt state which the rising centralized monarchies and nation states of Europe found so tempting.

OTTOMAN ARCHITECTURE

In this illustrious period of Ottoman history the most visible and lasting evidence of its greatness and magnificence was the galaxy of majestic mosques which still silhouette the skyline of Istanbul from every quarter and every angle. Sultans, grand viziers, kapudan pashas, princes and princesses, ladies of the harem, and *validehs*—all built impressive mosques and tombs to memorialize themselves. Most of the prominent mosques of the empire, and of Istanbul in particular, date from the sixteenth century. A few Byzantine churches were converted at the time of the conquest or shortly thereafter, but of these only Hagia Sophia was outstanding. A few mosques were erected before the close of that century, but the score of great ones comprised a series which began with the Mosque of Sultan Bayezid II (completed about 1500), and ended with the Blue Mosque of Sultan Ahmed I (1617).

The simplest style and form, exemplified in the Mosque of Sultan Selim I in Istanbul, consisted of a plain square building carrying one large dome. The transition between square and circle was accomplished by flat and spherical triangular pendentives.

The second type of imperial mosque was evolved in the Mosques of Bayezid II and Suleiman I. These mosques showed that Ottoman architects studied Hagia Sophia, saw its grandeur, and appreciated its solution of the problem of building an open square or rectangular structure suitable for congregational worship which was none the less covered by a dome. In these two mosques, the great rectangle was roofed by a large dome on spherical pendentives which effected the transition from the dome to the four broad pointed arches resting upon four piers. The dome was abutted longitudinally by semidomes fitted to their rectangles by pendentives or small semidomes, which in Suleimaniyeh were anchored to their corners by stalactite pendentives. The pendentives confused the eye so that the awkwardness was hidden, serving much the same function as the colored mosaics of the Byzantines. The strong buttresses in the lateral walls were admirably concealed by building external porches. In some details the influences of Italian Renaissance architecture were also evident.

The architect Sinan was the master of the age and he contended that his Shahzade Mosque in memory of Suleiman's son Mehmed was the work of an apprentice; Suleiman's Mosque, the work of a journeyman, and Sultan Selim II's Mosque in Edirne, the work of a master. In Shahzade Sinan presented a new style aimed at opening the entire edifice into one congregational hall so that every worshipper could see the mihrab. The great Mosque of Sultan Ahmed I followed the same principle and achieved its goal by replacing the small domes of the lateral aisle by one large semidome. The central dome at Ahmed was supported by large circular piers. Upon entering Ahmed, one noticed immediately that the whole area was unified and that the central space was vaster than in Hagia Sophia, where the vision into the side aisles was partially obstructed by arcades that led the imagination on and on quite indefinitely to create an illusion of far greater space.

At the Mosque of Sultan Selim II in Edirne Sinan developed another type of imperial mosque. The dome, thirty-one meters across, was supported by an octagon of arches, pendentives of stalactite corbels, and eight sturdy paneled piers which Sinan called "elephant feet." Again, as in Suleimaniyeh, the buttresses were hidden by external porches.

The internal centers of the domes were usually decorated with flowered and calligraphic frescoes, and the walls were embellished by panels of colored and veined marble or colored ceramic tiles. The Ottomans were more conscious of esthetic external lines and composition than Byzantine builders, and this accounts for the evolution of the pencil-like minarets with their one, two, or three muezzin balconies which gave to the Istanbul horizon its splendor of domes and slender minarets.

OTTOMAN LITERATURE

The sixteenth century led in architectural achievement; but it was also a brilliant period of Ottoman literary activity. Suleiman had a strong historical feeling; he emphasized the parallelism of Mehmed II and Constantine and equated himself to Justinian. Like Justinian, Suleiman was lawgiver and law codifier, builder of remarkable religious edifices and aqueducts, leader of armies, and generous patron of scholars and men of letters.

A quarter of the eminent Ottoman poets and writers belonged to the period of Suleiman and Selim II. Poetry and history were the outstanding forms of literary effort. Suleiman kept a historical diary which has proved of unique value in studying his reign; and both sultans were accomplished poets, Suleiman writing under the *nom de plume* of Muhibbi. The shining lyric poet of that age and perhaps of the Turkish language of all ages was Abd al-Baki. Others were Khiali, Sati, Deli Birader, Yahya Bey, and Shemsi.

Historians flourished. Their works were sometimes general in scope and sometimes specific, describing only one phase or incident of the period. Ramazan wrote of the capture of Rhodes; Kemalpashazade narrated the victorious campaign of Mohacs. One of the most revered of Ottoman historians appeared late in the sixteenth century in the person of Saad al-Din. Tutor of Suleiman's grandson Murad III, he wrote and compiled a work, *The Crown of Histories*, which covered in numerous volumes the gamut of Ottoman history. Continued by Saad al-Din's son, for several centuries it dominated concepts of Ottoman development from the earliest times to his own day.

Progress in the Ottoman Empire in the sixteenth century was typical of that in other Mediterranean and European countries. Selim I was a harsh, brilliant, demanding, energetic tyrant, who set the governmental machinery in motion toward momentous conquest. Suleiman was a dignified, orderly, just, conscientious, and artistic soldier and gentleman, who gave the Ottoman Empire a sense of distinction and cultural urbanity. Selim II was a talented, irresponsible, emotional, dissolute drunkard, who hastened the decay of the state.

REFERENCES: Chapter 17

Most titles already cited for the chapters discussing the Ottoman Empire are relevant to this chapter. Especially noteworthy are those in Chapters 12, 13, 14, and 16.

Stephen A. Fischer-Galati, *Ottoman Imperialism and German Protestantism, 1521–1555:* Harvard University Press, Cambridge, 1959.

E. J. W. Gibb, *A History of Ottoman Poetry,* 6 vols.: Luzac, London, 1900–1909. This is the standard work.

Peter Holt, *Egypt and the Fertile Crescent, 1516–1922:* Cornell University Press, Ithaca, 1966.

Preben Liebetrau, *Oriental Rugs in Colour:* Macmillan, New York, 1963.

R. B. Merriman, *Suleiman the Magnificent, 1520–1566:* Harvard University Press, Cambridge, 1944. An adequate summary of the life of the great sultan. Largely written about the year 1900 by Professor Archibald Cary Coolidge, the manuscript was only slightly revised by the author.

John Stoye, *Siege of Vienna:* Holt, New York, 1965.

Unesco World Art Series, *Turkey, Ancient Miniatures:* New York Graphic Society, New York, 1961.

CHAPTER 18

A Century of Stagnation and Decay

PRIVILEGE, INDOLENCE, AND CORRUPTION

The death of Selim II in 1574 ushered in a century and a quarter of disgraceful and despicable Ottoman history. A dozen sultans ruled during the period. Four were under sixteen years old when they succeeded to the throne, and most of the rest were undisciplined young men. The wealth, splendor, and ease of the court sapped their energy and morals. The Ottoman political system, which had developed with an absolute sultan as the keystone of the arch of power, sagged badly and began to crumble.

The causes of this obvious change are difficult to pinpoint. The character of Selim II or the influence of Ibrahim and Roxelana has frequently been described as a cancerous development that brought the downfall. Others have ascribed the collapse to an evolving process discernible for a number of years. Certainly, seeds of decay were nurtured for several decades and the causes of the decline were varied and profound. Since its earliest days the Ottoman state supported itself in considerable part from raids and conquest. As frontiers in Europe were extended, the enemy increased in number and campaign costs became staggering. The booty obtained hardly met expenses, and little was left for palace extravagances.

The shift in world trade from the Mediterranean to the Atlantic permitted the Ottomans to take a weakened Egypt. But in the end, this shift brought a marked decline in Ottoman revenues from international trade. Simultaneously, Europe and the Mediterranean world were experiencing a continuing monetary inflation. Government income never quite met expenditures, and most contemporary monarchs were plagued with unbalanced budgets.

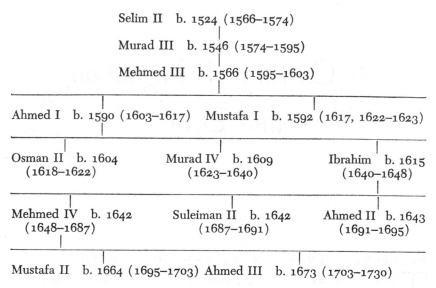

Selim II   b. 1524 (1566–1574)

Murad III   b. 1546 (1574–1595)

Mehmed III   b. 1566 (1595–1603)

Ahmed I   b. 1590 (1603–1617)   Mustafa I   b. 1592 (1617, 1622–1623)

Osman II   b. 1604   Murad IV   b. 1609   Ibrahim   b. 1615
(1618–1622)   (1623–1640)   (1640–1648)

Mehmed IV   b. 1642   Suleiman II   b. 1642   Ahmed II   b. 1643
(1648–1687)   (1687–1691)   (1691–1695)

Mustafa II   b. 1664 (1695–1703) Ahmed III   b. 1673 (1703–1730)

In the last two decades of Suleiman's life and in the reigns of Selim II and his successors finances were always straitened. Without loot from beyond the frontiers coming into Istanbul it was difficult to maintain the magnificence to which all had grown accustomed. To make up for this loss of revenue officials were obliged to give liberal sums to the sultan upon promotions. With the reign of Murad III the sultan obtained bribes for appointments, and by the time of Sultan Ibrahim there was open trafficking in offices at the Porte. Such corruption quickly filtered down to the lowliest official.

As a result of the conquests of Selim I and Suleiman I and the doubling of the empire's size, administrative problems became more and more difficult. As the paper work increased to irksome and unbearable proportions, the sultan left more affairs of state to the grand vizir. Suleiman threw over most of the work to Ibrahim and began to defer to him in policy decisions. Later sultans were unwilling to perform any onerous duties as head of the state and gave themselves up to a life of total voluptuousness and frivolity. Meanwhile, vizirs, beylerbeys, and leading officers drew unprecedented power into their hands. Beginning with Selim II's son Murad III, the sultans gave high office and substantial authority to their favorites, who were usually ill fitted for the jobs to be done. As long as Mehmed Sokolli lived, he tried unsuccessfully to prevent this trend, but after his assassination in 1579 the favorites held full sway.

Equally damaging to affairs of state were the influence and even the actual formulation of policies by women of the palace. Murad III was controlled by his mother and his favorite, Sultana Safiye Baffo. The latter actually ruled the empire while her son Mehmed III occupied the throne. Daughter of the Venetian governor of Corfu and from the noble Baffo family, she was captured by corsairs and presented to Suleiman, who in turn gave her to his grandson. For a time Murad was so faithful to Safiye that his mother and sister, the wife of Sokolli, fretted over her undue power and made presents of pretty and clever slaves to distract Murad's attention. They were obviously successful; Murad fathered over one hundred children, of whom twenty sons and twenty-seven daughters survived him.

Another enervating and corrupting practice developed upon the accession of Ahmed I in 1603. Unlike his father, who strangled his nineteen brothers, Ahmed allowed his insane brother, Mustafa, to live closeted in the palace. Henceforth, the usual practice was to immure brothers and sons in the palace, the eldest male of the dynasty succeeding upon the death or abdication of the sultan. Ibrahim, for example, was so frightened when the viziers came to announce his accession that he barricaded the doors and refused to let them enter until they brought the dead body of his brother.

The sultans were surrounded by fawning officials and courtiers, truckling women and slaves, jugglers, wrestlers, musicians, buffoons, dwarfs, eunuchs, soothsayers, astrologers, and servile literati. They usually found it impossible to differentiate the important from the petty and frequently bordered upon mental derangement. Mustafa I was quite mad, and Ibrahim's reign of eight years was one long series of wild caprices. The latter disrupted divan meetings and once called out the grand vizir to purchase some carts of firewood for the harem kitchens. Ibrahim had a great passion for furs and commanded that the floors and walls of his apartments be carpeted and covered with sable.

In such an atmosphere intrigue flourished. Personal spies, agents, forgeries, intercepted letters, perjury, and malicious gossip became acknowledged techniques of government. Apparently the executions of Suleiman's sons, Mustafa and Bayezid, resulted from machinations in the palace. Another evil of Ottoman society sprang from the slave system in the army and government. Separated from family and country at an early age, soldiers and officials of the court were trained and educated to be loyal to the sultan and to serve him. Wealth, high office, and the sultan's favor were the rewards; the irresolute found the emoluments irresistible and were governed by mercenary motives. Earlier

Venetian envoys remarked at the eagerness of Bayezid II's vizirs for rich presents and pouches of ducats. When the sultans could no longer command true respect from their slaves and officers, venality ruled, the power and services of the state degenerating rapidly.

The degradation of sultans, high officers of the state, and the military invited insubordination and rebellion from the rank and file of the armed forces. By the time of Mehmed II the janissaries and sipahi of the palace were already headstrong and willful bodies that had to be placated by monetary donations at festivals and, especially, at accessions of new sultans. The janissaries ordered the retirement of Bayezid II and frequently dictated policies in Suleiman's time. Beginning with the reign of Murad III, soldiers often stormed the palace to demand the head of a particular official, usually one who was obnoxious or corrupt and whose rapacity or incompetence inflicted hardship and injury upon them. Once this type of action proved successful, ambitious officials through clever propaganda for their own ends instigated movements among the troops to remove rivals.

Equally debilitating were civil wars between different branches of the services and open revolts of garrisons or local forces in the provinces. Bad blood developed between the janissaries and the sipahi of the court. In the reign of Murad III warfare broke out in the streets of Istanbul. Under Mehmed III the janissaries, at the bidding of Safiye Baffo, broke the insubordination of the sipahi. Osman II was deposed and later murdered, because he sought to weaken the power of the janissaries. He had entered into war against Poland with the purpose of reducing the number of janissaries and had intended to set out later for Anatolia to gather an army of Kurds and Turkomans to fight the janissaries. It was this latter project which led to his dethronement and death.

The saddest chapter in seventeenth-century Ottoman history was the sixteen-year period embracing the reign of Ibrahim and the minority of Mehmed IV. Ibrahim, a voluptuary of the lowest type, commissioned a trusted woman of the harem to make the rounds of Istanbul baths to seek out special beauties and describe their charms. Her master then contrived to install the more comely in his harem. He even seduced the daughter of the Shaykh al-Islam; no person and no property were secure against seizure by Ibrahim. In 1648 the janissaries and ulema, led by the Shaykh al-Islam, deposed Ibrahim as unfit to rule and placed his seven-year-old son on the throne. Ten days later when the sipahi rioted in his favor, the executioners were sent to his cell. For eight years the Ottoman Empire was the scene of "court intrigue, military insubordination and violence, judicial venality, local oppression and provincial revolt." Ibrahim's mother was murdered, and chaos descended upon Istanbul. Sultana Tarkhan, Mehmed IV's mother, saved the day for her son by appointing an old, experienced, and honest official (Mehmed Köprülü) as grand vizir with absolute power and authority.

With all the evil developments appearing in the Ottoman Empire there persisted beneath the surface of high-level debauchery a remarkable devotion to the government and a substantial body of capable, trained, and right-minded officials. Even before the advent of Köprülü flashes of old Ottoman vigor crossed the horizon. Murad IV was cast in the same mold as his ancestor Selim I, the conqueror of Egypt. At Murad's accession the treasury was empty, the coinage debased, and the soldiery of Istanbul unruly and lawless. His mother had talent and energy and preserved the sultan's authority for several years until he became of age. In 1632 the sipahi rose in revolt, camped for three days in the hippodrome, and called for the heads of seventeen high officials, including the Shaykh al-Islam and the grand vizir. The sipahi were appeased, but more heads were demanded. For two months terror reigned at the Porte. Murad perceived that his own turn might easily come, unless he acted swiftly to quell the disorder. Gathering a few faithful officers and obtaining the full support of the janissaries and the judges, he seized and executed the leaders of the rebellious sipahis and through vigorous measures restored a semblance of order and government to Istanbul and the provinces.

Twice, Murad in person led expeditions eastward in Asia Minor. The second time, in 1638, he reconquered Baghdad from the Iranians, personally performing prodigious feats with his sword. As the years progressed, however, he grew hardened to the presence of the executioner. Frequently through mere caprice he removed someone's head, perhaps just for crossing the road before him. Furthermore, he took to excessive drinking bouts which undermined his rugged physique and carried him to the grave at the age of twenty-eight.

Even though there were occasional upsurges of reform and governmental strength and even though Europe was engaged in bitter struggles such as the Thirty Years' War, the external affairs of the empire fell to a moribund state. Venetians and Maltese plundered Ottoman ships in the Mediterranean and captured Lemnos and Tenedos in the Aegean. Transylvania and Hungary were repeatedly the scenes of incursions into Ottoman territories. And cossacks from southern Russia raided the shores of the Bosphorus. Defection was just as extensive in Asia Minor and Syria. Power ebbed so low that the weakened shahs of Iran encroached upon the eastern Ottoman provinces and temporarily seized Baghdad.

RESURGENCE UNDER THE KÖPRÜLÜS

The problems of state seemed beyond solution. But Mehmed Köprülü assumed office in 1656 with a ruthless determination to cleanse the government of officials who faltered in their duties. In five years of his grand vizirate some thirty thousand officers, officials, judges, theologians, and others were executed for acts contrary to the interests of the sultan. His son Ahmed Köprülü succeeded to the post and remained grand vizir until his death in 1676. Restoration of law and order under these two vizirs revealed that the strength of the state had not been sapped beyond repair.

Although Mehmed IV gave himself up completely to hunting and to the harem, he remained steadfast in his support of the Köprülüs. In 1663 an army gathered at Edirne to settle the Hungarian frontier. Mehmed placed the battle standard in the hands of Ahmed Köprülü, who then led the largest force assembled since the campaigns of Suleiman I to Belgrad and beyond. Victories were obtained over the Austrians that year and well into the next. However, Ahmed Köprülü was repulsed at the renowned Battle of St. Gothard in Austria. The peace settlement with the Hapsburgs discontinued tribute to the Porte and elevated the Austrian emperor to a rank equal to that of the Ottoman padishah (emperor).

Ahmed Köprülü then turned his attention to the Island of Crete. In 1645 Ibrahim ordered its conquest, because Maltese pirates seized several Ottoman ships and took them to Crete under the shelter of the Venetian rulers. But Candia, the ancient Knossos, resisted sporadic Ottoman assaults for twenty years; to the Porte it became like a running sore. Köprülü conducted a three-year siege of Candia until it fell in 1669; and Crete, which had been in Venetian hands since the Fourth Crusade, became an Ottoman possession.

Next, the scene shifted to Galicia, Podolia, and the Ukraine. Cossacks of the Dneiper and the Bug threw off their Polish yoke; joining the Tartars of the Crimea, they sought protection of the Porte. When he came to Istanbul in 1672, the cossack *hetman* received a two-horsetail standard from Köprülü and was named sanjakbey of the Ukraine. Poland protested; and the grand vizir led an army which captured Kamenets and Lvov (Lemberg), forcing Poland to surrender Podolia and the Ukraine and to pay an annual tribute of 220,000 ducats. Several more campaigns followed when the Poles failed to pay the tribute. The Ottomans were able to maintain their army in strength, and a treaty in 1676 incorporated Podolia and the Ukraine into the empire.

Three days after the signing of this treaty Ahmed Köprülü died. Unfortunately, Mehmed IV filled his place with his court favorite, Kara

Mustafa. Within two years he lost the Ukraine to Russia. In 1683 there followed the last attack upon Vienna. Early in the spring the ambitious Kara Mustafa gathered at Edirne an army of more than 200,000 men and marched north through Belgrad, reaching Vienna in the middle of July. For two months the army mined and bombarded the walls of Vienna, which were defended by Count Starhemberg and a force of only 11,000 men. As September approached, the weakness of Vienna and the depletion of its garrison were obvious. The janissaries felt confident that Vienna would fall and fretted that the grand vizir did not order a full assault upon the walls. But Kara Mustafa was hoping for its surrender, in which case the wealth of the city would be his whereas if the soldiers took it by storm it would be theirs to loot. Kara Mustafa ignored the information that King John Sobieski of Poland, who had considerable experience fighting against the Ottomans in Podolia, was approaching with an army of 70,000 to relieve the city. When Sobieski encamped on the Kahlenberg, no move was made to face him or to hinder his descent, made difficult by many sharp ravines. The debacle occurred on September 12, 1683. Only a small portion of the Ottomans escaped to return with Kara Mustafa, who was executed by the sultan for incompetence.

RETREAT FROM VIENNA

In the next four years one calamity after another descended upon the empire. Venetians under Generals Morosini and Otto von Königsmarck captured the Morea, Corinth, and Athens. In the siege of Athens the Ottoman defenders made their last stand on the Acropolis, which von Königsmarck shelled, exploding the Parthenon which was serving as a powder magazine. The Austrian forces pursued the victory at Vienna, took Gran and Budapest, and seized Hungary. In 1687 the loss of Mohacs so infuriated the Ottoman soldiers against their discredited leaders that they forced Mehmed's deposition and placed his next younger brother on the throne as Suleiman II. The new sultan, who had been incarcerated in the palace for forty-five years and had passed his time in reading and study, did not know how to cope with the situation. Janissaries and sipahi rioted in Istanbul, partially sacked the city, and completely dislocated the administration. Belgrad fell in 1688; Widin and Nish, in 1689.

Previously when Ottomans suffered reverses they recouped their losses quickly, regrouped their forces, and returned to fight in strength. This was notably true before Vienna in 1529 and at Lepanto in 1571. But the calamities of the seventeenth century left their mark upon the institutions of Ottoman society, especially upon the military. Governorships were given to court favorites; their domestic servants obtained fiefs; and other estates were left vacant so the income would devolve upon the governor. Nonfighting men acquired fiefs, and all were squeezed by the financial rapacity of superior officers. Governorships were sold to new courtiers every two or three years, and a succession of inexperienced, unqualified, and grasping rulers led to desolation in the provinces. When the call for a campaign was sounded, the feudal sipahis hid in their estates or bribed the commanding officer to be excused. Only the poorest and weakest appeared for duty. At one time a census was ordered, compelling all sipahis in Europe to register in Edirne in order to expose all unfit and fraudulent fief-holders. Unfortunately, the inspectors were so incompetent that they could not distinguish a soldier from a pastry cook, and no one was caught. The number and quality of sipahis so declined that by the eighteenth century there were only 25,-000, most of whom came unattended and armed only with baskets and shovels to move earth and stone or to dig trenches and haul cannon.

The degeneration of the janissaries, the sipahi of the court, and palace soldiers was no less deplorable. Captive boys and renegades diminished in numbers as the seventeenth century progressed; and the drafting of Christian boys from Balkan villages ceased entirely during the reign of Murad IV. Ahmed Köprülü in his attempt to restore the vigor of the state reinstituted the program and collected 3,000 boys in 1675, but the policy was dropped after his death. Sons of janissaries and court officials joined the ranks; even jugglers, acrobats, and other unsuited persons were rewarded by membership in the privileged bands. Worst of all was the ignoring of merit in questions of promotion; for it meant that officers were not necessarily skilled in military affairs. European commanders in the seventeenth century observed the mediocre and foolish leadership of Ottoman armies and outmaneuvered them time and time again. By the beginning of the eighteenth century the janissaries had become an ill-disciplined, oddly-equipped, turbulent gang, more dangerous at the palace and on the streets of Istanbul and Edirne than against aggressors at the frontiers.

After the loss of Nish in 1689 Suleiman II recognized the desperate plight of his empire and appointed as grand vizir Mustafa Köprülü, brother of the late Ahmed Köprülü. The genius of the Köprülü family ran strong in the new grand vizir. He instituted financial measures which made it possible to assemble an army and regain Nish, Semendra, and Belgrad. Köprülü attempted again the following summer to drive the Austrians further back but lost his life in battle.

The energy of Mustafa II brought a series of minor Balkan victories; but when faced by Prince Eugene of Savoy in 1697 at Zenta the Ottoman companies were crushed, and Hungary and the lands north of

Belgrad were lost forever. Meanwhile, the city of Azov surrendered after repeated attacks in 1696 to Peter the Great of Russia.

TREATY OF KARLOWITZ

In the face of these reverses Mustafa called to the vizirate Husayn Köprülü, who listened to the offers of mediation advanced by Lord Paget, English ambassador to the Porte. For a number of years prior to 1697 Austria was engaged with France in the War of the Palatinate, but the Peace of Ryswick freed the Hapsburgs to press their advantage over the decaying Ottoman state. Nevertheless, the courts and armies of Europe were nervously awaiting the momentarily expected death of the childless king of Spain and the anticipated war between the Hapsburgs and Bourbons for that throne. The English, who wished to free their Austrian ally from any possible distraction from the Ottoman quarter, pressed Husayn Köprülü for peace.

After much sparring and preliminary correspondence negotiators met at Karlowitz north of Belgrad in modern Yugoslavia. Under the chairmanship of Lord Paget. Mehmed, Ottoman minister of foreign affairs, and representatives of the Netherlands, Austria, Venice, Poland, and Russia agreed on a general principle that each power should retain what it possessed. Peace was signed in 1699. In addition, the sultan reiterated that he would give his Christian subjects consideration and protection, as he always had and as the ancient capitulations stipulated Venice gave up Athens, but retained the Morea and Dalmatia. Austria obtained Transylvania and Hungary with the exception of the Banat of Temesvar. Poland received the provinces of Kamenets and Podolia. As for Russia, only a two-year truce was signed; England wished to keep the Porte occupied with Russia to prevent Ottoman arms from supporting the French in the forthcoming struggle over Spain. Russian envoys, however, came to the Porte and agreed to the Treaty of Istanbul in 1700, drawn up on the basis of the Karlowitz Armistice.

Karlowitz marks a definite period in Middle Eastern history, especially in the relations of the Porte and Europe. First, it was a treaty with European states arranged by and participated in by one or more nonbelligerent powers, thereby acknowledging that all European states were rightfully concerned with questions of the Middle East. It recognized the interest and importance of the tsars with respect to the Ottoman Empire and the Middle East. The treaty and the negotiations preceding it indicated the entrance of the sultan's Christian subjects into the diplomatic pouches of European foreign offices.

At the Peace Conference of Karlowitz European emissaries carried on their negotiations largely through the Ottoman minister's Greek interpreter and assistant, Alexander Mavrocordatos and carried away the erroneous impression that he was chief of the delegation. But his presence and evident role signified the change that was transpiring in the Ottoman government and its civil service. For several decades the great majority of Ottoman officials were Turks of the second and third generations. Many were not educated in the palace and their schooling was less secular than in previous generations. To be sure, they called themselves Ottomans, were proud of that distinction, and had a background and training quite different from most Turks living in Asia Minor. Yet, more and more they became dependent upon Christian subjects, chiefly Greeks residing in Istanbul, for secretaries, interpreters, and counselors. After Karlowitz it was not incorrect to speak of the Ottoman Empire as the Turkish empire.

As for Europe, Karlowitz ended the fear of an Ottoman invasion of central Europe and opened an avenue for further aggressions toward Istanbul and the Straits. When Europe was engaged in her own internal struggles, Turkish forces were able to win victories, but from the beginning of the eighteenth century Ottoman armies and navies were no match for first-rate European soldiers. No longer was the Ottoman Empire a grave military question. As one writer aptly put it, her importance became diplomatic.

REFERENCES: Chapter 18

Works important to this chapter are also found in Chapters 12, 13, 14, 16, and 17.

Uriel Heyd, *Ottoman Documents on Palestine, 1552–1615:* Oxford University Press, London, 1960. Valuable source material by an outstanding Israeli scholar.

Lawrence Lockhart, *The Fall of the Safavi Dynasty and the Afghan Occupation of Persia:* Cambridge University Press, New York, 1958.

Harry Luke, *The Making of Modern Turkey from Byzantium to Angora:* Macmillan, London, 1936. Important for the position of the subject peoples.

Paul Rycaut, *History of the Turkish Empire, 1623–1677*, 2 volumes in 1: Clabell & Roper, London, 1680. A detailed account by an eyewitness.

————, *The Present State of the Ottoman Empire*: Clabell & Roper, London, 1686. Really a third volume to the reference cited above.

Walter Livingston Wright, Jr., *Ottoman Statecraft, The Book of Counsel for Vezirs and Governors of Sari Mehmed Pasha, the Defterdar, Turkish Text with Introduction, Translation, and Notes*: Princeton University Press, Princeton, 1935. This is the translation of a book written by a Turkish ex-official pointing out the weaknesses and evils in the Ottoman system and the sources of its corruption.

CHAPTER 19

The Decline and Retreat of the Ottoman Empire

WEAK SULTANS

The sultans of the eighteenth century were weak figures. They were not vicious, but they lacked the strength to meet the vicissitudes facing the empire. To cope with the corruption, inefficiency, incompetence, harem intrigue, vested interests, and indolence of the court, will power was required; to comprehend the policies of state, training and education were important. Each one of the sultans, however, came to the throne after decades of confinement; none had opportunity to learn the art of statecraft or to develop an effective personality. Usually his mother or the harem favorite dominated the government; and, though clever and forceful, these women lacked the experience to conduct the business of government.

Ahmed III was gay and frivolous, interested in birds and his tulip gardens. Fortunes were spent on festivals and illuminations for the women of the court. Mahmud I loved literature and surrounded himself with second-rate poets and men of letters. The rest of his energy was devoted to building mosques, palaces, kiosks, and other structures of questionable utility. Osman III, Mustafa III, and Abdul Hamid I were well along in years when they ascended the throne; and they proved to be mild, ineffectual rulers. The last may at least be commended for the freer life he permitted his nephew Selim, the heir apparent; for with Selim's accession in 1789 the more vigorous attempts at reform which marked the nineteenth century began.

WARS WITH RUSSIA AND AUSTRIA

Austria and Venice contested the power of the Ottomans in the seventeenth century; and the latter's role fell in the eighteenth century to Russia. Although Karlowitz ceded Azov and about eighty miles of hinterland, Peter was not satisfied. The Black Sea, the Straits, an outlet to the Mediterranean which would mean freer commerce with the West, and, most important, Tsargrad (Constantinople)—all beckoned the Russians on against the Ottomans. In one sense Russia could never be fully admitted to the polity of Europe as long as control over these waterways and the seat of empire were denied to the tsars.

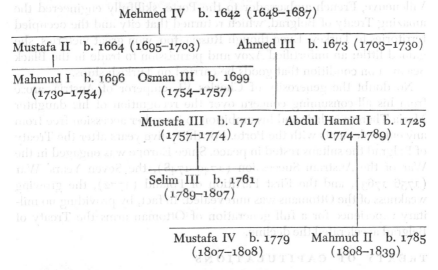

Mehmed IV b. 1642 (1648–1687)

Mustafa II b. 1664 (1695–1703)   Ahmed III b. 1673 (1703–1730)

Mahmud I b. 1696   Osman III b. 1699
(1730–1754)   (1754–1757)

Mustafa III b. 1717   Abdul Hamid I b. 1725
(1757–1774)   (1774–1789)

Selim III b. 1761
(1789–1807)

Mustafa IV b. 1779   Mahmud II b. 1785
(1807–1808)   (1808–1839)

After the defeat at Pultava in 1709 Charles XII of Sweden fled to Turkey, where he induced Ahmed III to heed the pleas of the Crimean khan for an expedition against Russia. When Peter led his army across the Pruth in 1711, he fell into an Ottoman trap. To escape he accepted the famous surrender of the Pruth, which returned Azov and surrounding areas to the sultan, razed all fortresses in the neighborhood, and relinquished the right to have Russian ships in the Black Sea. Ahmed III dismissed the grand vizir for agreeing to such easy terms when the Ottoman army might have destroyed Peter and crushed the Russians for decades.

Peace with Russia and Austria freed the Ottomans to regain their possessions lost to Venice at Karlowitz. Using some naval clashes as a pretext, the grand vizir swept Venice from the Peleponnesus and the islands of the Archipelago in 1715 and proceeded to attack Venetian towns along the Adriatic. These victories enticed Austria to break with the Porte. Prince Eugene won several smashing engagements, capturing Temesvar and Belgrad. Britain, as eager as ever to mediate peace, arranged the Treaty of Passarowitz of 1718, which ceded all the territory won by Austria but permitted the Ottomans to retain the lands taken from Venice.

Further aggression against Turkey rested for more than a decade, until Austria and Russia formed an alliance and acted together. The latter overran the Crimea, captured Azov, and demanded the sultan's lands from the Danube to the Caucasus. Refusal by the Porte brought Austria into the fray, and Nish fell to her arms. When a Turkish resurgence in 1739 pushed the fighting back to the walls of Belgrad, the Marquis de Villeneuve, French ambassador to the Porte, skillfully engineered the amazing Treaty of Belgrad, which returned that city and the occupied territories to Turkey. Even though Russia, too, won great victories, she gained little: an unfortified Azov and permission to trade in the Black Sea area on condition that goods be carried on Turkish ships.

No doubt the generosity of Charles VI, emperor of Austria, arose from his all-consuming concern over the recognition of his daughter Maria Theresa as heir and his ambition to leave her accession free from any entanglements with the Porte. For thirty-five years after the Treaty of Belgrad the sultans rested in peace. Since Europe was engaged in the War of the Austrian Succession (1740–1748), the Seven Years' War (1756–1763), and the First Partition of Poland (1772), the growing weakness of the Ottomans was unrevealed. In fact, by providing no military experience for a full generation of Ottoman arms the Treaty of Belgrad accelerated the decline.

TREATY OF CAPITULATIONS

As reward for the brilliant mediation of the Marquis de Villeneuve at Belgrad and through his continued representations at the Porte, France obtained in 1740 the renowned Treaty of Capitulations. France and England, and to a lesser extent the Netherlands, had valuable commercial interests in the Middle East. Ottoman wars with Venice, Austria, and Russia disturbed their trade, a factor which animated English and Dutch mediation at Karlowitz and Passarowitz.

The trading privileges which the French enjoyed under the Mamluk sultans in Egypt since the treaty obtained in 1251 by St. Louis were reconfirmed by Suleiman in 1528; and a regular treaty with France was concluded in 1536 similar to those made with Venice, Florence, Naples, Hungary, and other powers by Mehmed II and Bayezid II. The French treaty was reaffirmed in 1569, 1581, 1597, 1604, and 1673. Again in 1740 the new treaty of eighty-two articles obtained by de Villeneuve reiterated the chief points of previous treaties.

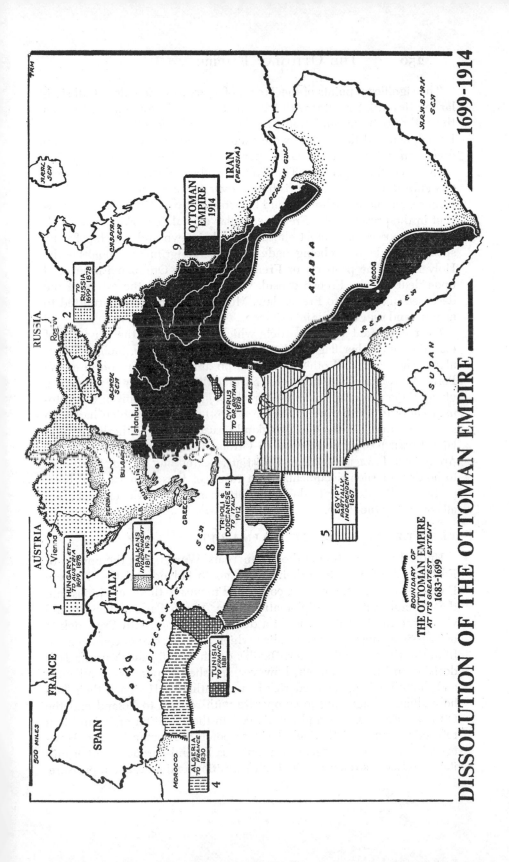

DISSOLUTION OF THE OTTOMAN EMPIRE

1699-1914

OTTOMAN
EMPIRE
1914
9

IRAN
(PERSIA)

BOUNDARY OF
THE OTTOMAN EMPIRE
AT ITS GREATEST EXTENT
1683-1699

1 HUNGARY, ETC.
TO AUSTRIA
1699, 1878

2 TO RUSSIA
1699, 1878

3 BALKANS
INDEPENDENT
1817, 1913

4 ALGERIA
TO FRANCE
1830

5 EGYPT
PARTIALLY
INDEPENDENT
1867

6 CYPRUS
TO GR. BRITAIN
1878

7 TUNISIA
TO FRANCE
1881

8 TRIPOLI &
DODECANESE IS.
TO ITALY
1912

9 OTTOMAN EMPIRE
1914

FRANCE

SPAIN

AUSTRIA
Vienna

ITALY

RUSSIA
Rostov

SERBIA

BULGARIA

RUMELIA

ALB.

GREECE

Istanbul

BLACK SEA

CRIMEA

CASPIAN SEA

ARAL
SEA

PALESTINE

ARABIA

Mecca

SUDAN

RED SEA

PERSIAN GULF

ARABIAN SEA

MEDITERRANEAN SEA

AEGEAN SEA

MOROCCO

500 MILES

The significant points of the Treaty of 1740, to which almost all similar treaties of later dates with foreign states refer, granted Frenchmen the right to travel and trade in any part of the Ottoman Empire. Frenchmen and their goods were exempted from all forms of taxation except *ad valorem* import and export duties which were set in Article XXXVII at three percent. The French ambassador and consuls were recognized as having full jurisdiction over Frenchmen in the Ottoman Empire, and no Frenchman could be arrested by an Ottoman officer except in the presence of a French consular official. The French were allowed to possess and erect churches of their own and worship freely, special considerations being made for French pilgrims and monks in the Holy Land. The property of Frenchmen in the Ottoman Empire fell upon death to the French consul, who administered the estate of the deceased according to French law. Moreover, heirs were permitted to acquire and remove their inheritance.

Most important was the article which gave France the privilege of enrolling under her flag and her protection Portuguese, Sicilians, Catalans, Anconans, and others who had no ambassador or consul at the Porte. All Roman Catholics were considered and treated as Frenchmen, giving them a very special consideration among Christians in the Ottoman Empire. Furthermore, France and other nations which had such an article in their treaties (England, Austria, the Netherlands, and later Russia) could sell *barats* to Ottoman subjects—usually Greeks, Armenians, Jews, and Balkan Christians—extending trading privileges to holders of such documents. As a result of these provisions a large portion of the exterior trade of the Ottoman empire was exempt from all control by the Porte.

TREATY OF KUCHUK KAINARJI

Upon the termination of the Seven Years' War in 1763 the powers of Europe were free to turn their attentions to Poland and the Ottoman Empire. They were, however, compelled to weave these ambitions into the general European diplomatic fabric. Ragib Pasha, ablest grand vizir since the Köprülüs, sought a defensive alliance with Frederick II of Prussia against Austria, a policy which found active encouragement from the English ambassador. Ragib's death in 1763 and Mustafa III's decision to rule for himself, however, quashed hopes for an alliance; and the following year Frederick II and Catherine II signed their "unholy alliance," agreeing to co-operate with respect to Poland and the Ottoman Empire. England acquiesced in the Partition of Poland and refused to oppose Catherine's designs upon the Ottoman Empire. However, Louis XV sent Vergennes as ambassador and Baron de Tott as military adviser to strengthen the Porte's position against Russian pressure

Upon the advice of Vergennes, Mustafa III unwisely rushed headlong into war against Russia in 1768, when his demands with respect to Poland were not met. Since the Turkish armies were quite unprepared, the Russians occupied Jassy and Bucharest and within two years held all of Moldavia and Wallachia.

Meanwhile a Russian fleet, directed by John Elphinston, sailed from the Baltic to the Aegean unmolested by the French or Spanish, who were immobilized by British threats. Upon arrival off the Morea, Count Orloff assumed command. His raids upon the coasts aroused Greek hopes and speculations, but eventually left the inhabitants at the mercy of the Turkish soldiers and disillusioned with the Russians. Orloff proceeded to win a victory at Chios and destroyed the Ottoman fleet. None the less, Elphinston's plea to force the Dardanelles and storm Istanbul was ignored, until Baron de Tott repaired the fortifications sufficiently to thwart Orloff's later attempt to sail the Straits. Foiled, Orloff seized Lemnos, only to be driven off by an Ottoman admiral commanding a crew quickly mustered from the streets of Istanbul. Orloff sailed off to Egypt to threaten the Porte from that direction.

Russian successes in the Danubian provinces excited the Austrians in 1771 to sign a secret treaty of assistance with the Porte, pledging military support if the Russians crossed the Danube. Informed of this maneuver by the English ambassador, Berlin prevented war between Austria and Russia by speeding the partition of Poland among the three neighbors and simultaneously inducing Catherine to relinquish her conquests on the Pruth and the Danube. Partition of the Ottoman Empire was saved by the sacrifice of Poland! Desultory fighting came to a halt in 1774 upon the signing of the Treaty of Kuchuk Kainarji.

This famous treaty was a landmark in Russo-Ottoman relations for nearly a century and a half. The sultan gained possession of Bessarabia, Moldavia, Wallachia, and the Greek Islands, and Catherine's hold on Azov and the independence of the Crimean Tartars were confirmed. Navigation on the Danube was freed, and the Black Sea was opened to Russian shipping. A permanent Russian ambassador was accepted at the Porte; and Russian consuls could be stationed wherever the tsar thought necessary. The right of Russian pilgrimages to holy places was admitted, and permission to build a Russo-Greek church in the Galata section of Istanbul was granted.

Of particular significance for the future were Articles XII and XIV, which stated in vague terms that the sultan promised to protect the Christian religion in his empire. More important, Russia as a "neighboring and sincerely friendly Power" could offer the sultan representations in behalf of his Christian subjects and could speak in favor of Bessarabia and the Danubian provinces. These two articles served Russia in the nineteenth century as useful wedges in her ambitions in the Balkans and the Straits.

PEACE OF JASSY

The actions and diplomacy of Austria were pursued to prevent Russia from gaining an advantageous position over the Ottoman Empire. As soon as the sultan agreed to the terms of Kuchuk Kainarji, Austria delivered her demand for the province of Bukovina as a reward for non-belligerency during the Russian war. When Vienna ordered the occupation, the Porte recognized its helplessness and ceded Bukovina to the Hapsburgs.

For a decade and a half the sultan was left in peace, while Russia and Austria discussed the problems and possibilities of further Ottoman disintegration. By the Treaty of Ainali Kavak in 1779 Russia's role in selecting the Khan of the Crimea for the "independent" Tartars was conceded and the fate of the Crimea established. Yet the "Greek Project" of Catherine II and Joseph in 1782 marked the first specific design for partitioning the Ottoman Empire. Austria would obtain Serbia, Bosnia, Herzegovina, Dalmatia, and various fortresses on the Danube; Venice's share was to be the Morea, Crete, and Cyprus; France was to be rewarded with Egypt and Syria; and Russia would be favored by a Christian kingdom of Dacia under Prince Potemkin to include Bessarabia, Moldavia, and Wallachia. And if Istanbul were taken, a Greco-Russo-Byzantine empire would be re-created under the emperorship of Catherine's grandson, appropriately named Constantine. War broke in 1787. Austria and Russia won initial victories; but international complications in Europe and serious internal disorders in the Hapsburg realm enabled the Porte to obtain the Peace of Sistova with Austria (1791) and the Peace of Jassy with Russia (1792). The former returned the frontier to the *status quo ante,* but the latter allowed Russia to advance her frontier to the Dniester River.

The Second (1793) and Third (1795) Partitions of Poland, the death of Catherine II (1796), and the outbreak of the French Revolution gave Selim III (1789–1807) a relief from European aggression. Napoleon's rise naturally implicated the Ottoman Empire in the wars and diplomacy of that era. Incidents and circumstances of those affairs, however, fall more into the pattern of nineteenth-century European imperialism in the Middle East. The radical upsetting of the balance of power in the world, especially in Europe after 1815, was reflected in European intrigue and activities at the Porte. Meanwhile, significant changes transpired in the Ottoman Empire to weaken the state still further and to sweep the entire Middle East to the brink of complete disintegration into petty political units.

THE PHANARIOTES

One of the more baneful developments at the Porte was the insidious avarice of the so-called Phanariotes. In the seventeenth century the residence of the patriarch was established in a district bordering the Golden Horn, taking its name *Phanar* from the Greek word meaning "lighthouse." Earlier most Greeks who served the sultan became Ottomans, but by the end of the seventeenth century it was no longer necessary for Greeks to adopt Islam to hold office and participate in state affairs. Out of this circumstance grew the term *Phanariot,* used to designate a Greek or Hellenized Christian in Ottoman service.

The ascendancy of the Phanariotes took place gradually in the last half of the seventeenth century. Alexander Mavrocordatos, who studied law at Bologna and medicine at Padua and who published learned works in Italian, became attached to the Köprülü family as a secretary. He then moved to the position of chief interpreter (*terjumeni*) of the Minister of Foreign Affairs (*Reis Effendi*). As such, he became known in the West as Dragoman (*Terjumeni*) of the Porte. Alexander served as principal negotiator in drafting the Treaty of Karlowitz, and his descendants held high posts in the Ottoman service for more than a century. In fact, all Phanariotes of distinction in the eighteenth century either had Mavrocordatos blood in their veins or had wives of that family. From the Phanariotes came patriarchs, bishops, Dragomans of the Porte, ambassadors, and governors of Moldavia and Wallachia from 1714 to 1821.

Of these posts, the most lucrative and therefore the most expensive to purchase were the governorships of Moldavia and Wallachia. Consequently, Phanariot governors (*hospodars*) found it necessary to sell every office and favor, ruling over their subjects in a fashion identical to that of the sultan in Istanbul. By the end of Phanariot rule Rumanian peasants had fallen to an estate lowlier than any in the Balkans. Certainly, the tone of society in Bucharest and Jassy was more corrupt and cynical than in Belgrad, Sofia, or Athens.

Yet the Danubian principalities remained the larder of Istanbul. Wheat, butter, cheese, honey, wax, lumber, horses, and livestock of every sort were sent to Istanbul. More than 500,000 head of sheep moved every year. As the production of Anatolia became less available and after the loss of the Crimea, the Danubian provinces assumed even greater importance as an imperial granary. Certain portions were requisitioned by the palace; and trade remained in the hands of Armenians, Jews, and Greeks. The evils of Phanariot rule were augmented by the frequent wars of the eighteenth century fought on Danubian soil and by four Russian occupations which increased the misery of the peasants by wholesale requisitioning, epidemics, plague, pillage, and the presence of ill-disciplined troops.

Perhaps because Rumanians under Phanariot rule were governed by Christian princes, the Danubian principalities were much freer from the political and financial control of the Porte than most provinces of the empire. However, other governors also enjoyed considerable independence of action since Suleiman's reorganization in 1530 failed to centralize the authority. Seventeenth-century vizirs and sultans were already confronted with numerous recalcitrant pashas. But by the middle of the eighteenth century the process of disintegration arrived at a point where any energetic and ambitious governor could build up his own independent military, political, and economic power and defy or ignore the commands of the sultan.

REBELLIOUS PROVINCES

To describe each one of these petty lords and to relate the incidents of his rise to power and his local tyrannies would be monotonous and repetitious. In Europe the best known were Ali Pasha of Janina, who ruled Epirus from 1788 to 1822, and Osman Pasvanoglu of Widin, who terrorized the lower Danube from Belgrad to the sea. Both recognized the Porte's suzerainty and occasionally sent tribute to the sultan; yet each regularly defied the central government and entered into diplomatic relations with European powers.

The most famous of the quasi-independent lords in other parts of the empire were the beys and deys of the Barbary states of North Africa. Even in the sixteenth century at the heyday of the sultan's power, the authority of the Porte in Algiers, Tunis, and Tripoli was never very positive. In the eighteenth century North African corsairs recognized the sultan's overlordship only to the extent of sending him an annual token gift.

With respect to the weakening of central government and the Porte's loss of revenue, the more significant developments of the eighteenth century occurred in Egypt, Syria, Iraq, and Anatolia. The Mamluk system was never fully eradicated by Selim I or Suleiman's Ibrahim Pasha, and once the reins from Istanbul were loosened it flourished again. Under Ali Bey Egypt followed an independent course, and Count Orloff made overtures to him following the Russian fiasco in the Greek Islands. From 1749 to 1831 Iraq was in the hands of another Mamluk dynasty, and Mosul was held for more than a century by the Jalili family. The al-Azm family ruled in Damascus; other families held Jerusalem; and Aleppo was so torn with strife, civil wars, and depredations that between 1765 and 1785 hundreds of villages disappeared.

The most adventurous career was that of Ahmed al-Jezzar (Ahmed the Butcher). Of Bosnian origin, he obtained his nickname from his ruthless tactics against nomadic Arabs in the Nile Delta when he was employed by Ali Bey of Egypt. Although appointed commander of Beirut by the Druzes of the Lebanon, he was driven away with Russian co-operation when he ceased to be subservient. Regaining the favor of Istanbul, he became Pasha of Sidon and Acre, augmenting his territory later to include Damascus. Ahmed al-Jezzar Pasha maintained a private army of Albanians, Moroccans, and fellow Bosnians, built a fleet, established monopolies, made commercial agreements with Western merchants, and created an efficient governmental organization.

Even in Anatolia an identical situation prevailed in the eighteenth century. Called *Dereh Beys* (Valley Lords), leaders of local families seized power; and the central government was compelled to appease their whims in order to obtain any recognition of authority or any compliance with respect to law, taxes, and military support.

SEARCH FOR REFORM

Beset by foreign powers and enfeebled and embarrassed by internal political dissolution, the empire hung together miraculously. In Istanbul and other cities the several trade and craft guilds served as a powerful coagulant, giving individuals a sense of security and a definite place in society. The average male subject found his life ordered and regulated by his guild, experienced his social life in the guild, and had his contacts with government almost exclusively through guild leadership. In the countryside landowners avoided political association as much as possible, and peasants were only concerned with their landlords. Simple village life was the chief aim of the majority.

Nevertheless, many Ottomans perceived that the state was stagnating and predicted that the future of the empire was surely doomed unless political, economic, financial, military, and social reforms were undertaken. Ex-officials of the government wrote treatises deploring practices which inevitably led to corruption, inefficiency, and decay. Notable essays on these points appeared in 1632, 1657, 1725, and 1777; each of them condemned most emphatically the practice of selling offices and recounted specific abuses by every official from the sultan down to the lowliest scribe. In a book written in 1725 a former imperial treasurer prescribed as a remedy return to the higher ethical and moral values which prevailed two centuries earlier in the reign of Suleiman.

No changes or reforms could be initiated with any hope of success unless supported by the sultan. In fact, it was necessary that reforms should come from the hands of the sultan himself! Many sultans of the eighteenth century desired reforms but did not know how to inaugurate them. Selim III, who succeeded to the throne in 1789, introduced many innovations and hoped to change the course of affairs from further decay to progress and growth. But a reorientation of the government demanded the labors of many dedicated souls who understood Ottoman conditions in relation to the developments and advances unfolding in other parts of the world. There were still many devoted patriots in the Ottoman Empire, but the Enlightenment in Western Europe failed to touch them. Selim III was too far advanced for his compatriots and died a martyr for the cause of reform and progress.

REFERENCES: Chapter 19

Important for this chapter are books cited in Chapters 12, 13, 14, 16, 17, and 18.

Ahmad Mustafa Abu Hakima, *History of Eastern Arabia, 1750–1800: The Rise and Development of Bahrain and Kuwait:* Khayats, Beirut, 1965. An understanding and thorough work.

M. S. Anderson, *The Eastern Question, 1774–1923: A Study in International Relations:* Macmillan, London, 1966. Follows in the tradition of Marriott's work, cited below.

James Burrill Angell, "The Turkish Capitulations," in *Selected Addresses:* Longmans, Green, New York, 1912. A good introduction to the problems involved.

Gabriel Baer, *Egyptian Guilds in Modern Times:* The Israel Oriental Society, Jerusalem, Israel, 1964. An important contribution.

J. C. Hurewitz, *Diplomacy in the Near and Middle East,* Vol. I. *A Documentary Record: 1535–1914:* D. Van Nostrand, Princeton, 1956. An indispensable volume for the treaties of the decline of the Ottoman Empire and the imperialism of the nineteenth century.

J. A. R. Marriott, *The Eastern Question: An Historical Study in European Diplomacy:* Clarendon Press, Oxford, 1917. A biased but serviceable outline.

William Miller, *The Balkans: Roumania, Bulgaria, Servia and Montenegro With New Chapter Containing Their History from 1896 to 1922:* T. F.

Unwin, London, 1923. A fair summary of the histories of each of these peoples.

————, *The Ottoman Empire, 1801–1913:* Cambridge University Press, Cambridge, 1913. The introduction contains a summary of the decline of the Ottomans.

Mary Wortley Montagu, *Letters:* Jonathan Cape, London, 1934. Lady Mary accompanied her husband to Turkey on a diplomatic mission in 1717–1718. Her letters, though sometimes doubtful as to accuracy, are interesting reading and give a valuable record.

Alexander Pallis, *In the Days of the Janissaries:* Hutchinson, London, 1951. A good account of the janissaries in their later days.

Abdul-Karim Rafeq, *The Province of Damascus, 1723–1783:* Khayats, Beirut, 1966. A detailed work that reveals the decline of the Ottoman regime.

G. Bie Ravndal, "Capitulations," in *Modern Turkey, A Politico-economic Interpretation, 1908–1923, Inclusive, With Selected Chapters by Representative Authorities:* Macmillan, New York, 1924. Written by an American consular officer, this work reflects the operations of the capitulations during the twentieth century.

Avedis K. Sanjian, *The Armenian Communities in Syria under Ottoman Dominion:* Harvard University Press, Cambridge, 1965.

R. W. Seton-Watson, *A History of the Roumanians from Roman Times to the Completion of Unity:* Cambridge University Press, Cambridge, 1934. A good summary of the history of the Danubian provinces under the Phanariotes.

Stanford J. Shaw, *The Financial and Administrative Organization and Development of Ottoman Egypt, 1517–1798:* Princeton University Press, Princeton, 1962. The most significant study of Ottoman imperialism in the Arab world.

Mary Lucille Shay, *The Ottoman Empire from 1720 to 1734 as Revealed in Despatches of the Venetian Baili:* University of Illinois Press, Urbana, 1944. A study of diplomacy.

B. H. Sumner, *Peter the Great and the Ottoman Empire:* Blackwell's, Oxford, 1949.

Shirley H. Weber, *Voyages and Travels in the Near East to 1801:* American School of Classical Studies at Athens, Princeton, 1953. Dr. Weber was librarian at the Gennadion in Athens where he had access to a wide variety of travel books.

PART III

European Imperialism in the Modern Middle East

European
Imperialism in
the Modern
Middle East

CHAPTER 20

The Era of the French Revolution and Napoleon

SELIM'S REFORMS

In the month preceding the convening of the Estates General at Versailles which ushered in the French Revolution Selim III was girt with the sword of Osman, and a new era in Ottoman history opened. Selim took his position seriously and desired to restore the power of court and governmental authority. Whether he thought of himself as a reformer in a modern sense or regarded the changes which he sought in terms of progress is doubtful. But he did understand that techniques pursued in Russia and the West had unquestionably placed great power in the hands of the ruler and his government.

In 1789 Selim was about twenty-seven years old and had studied and read more widely than most of his immediate predecessors. At first, wars with Austria and Russia tied his hands. The French Revolution, however, dissipated the attention of the European powers, gave the Ottoman Empire a few years of respite from Western imperialism, and offered Selim an unexpected opportunity to show his true character.

In the central government Selim sought to curb the arrogant powers of the grand vizir by reorganizing the Imperial Divan to consist of twelve ministers and by commanding that it be consulted on all important measures. Selim encouraged the founding of schools and aided them in many ways. Printing establishments were reintroduced; and books, some translated from Western authors, appeared in Istanbul. Permanent Ottoman embassies were accepted at London, Paris, Vienna,

and Berlin, where a number of young Turks were sent to learn about
Western society and diplomacy and to improve Turkish foreign policy.

In the provinces the sultan's authority had been rapidly declining for
decades. Selim found that his word received little heed and foresaw
that reforms would prove ineffectual unless a thorough transformation
could be carried out in the army. The janissaries and standing cavalry
had degenerated into virtual worthlessness; the training and weapons of
all were hopelessly obsolete. Following the Peace of Jassy Selim discovered Omar, a Turk who had served as a lieutenant in the tsar's army.
The sultan commissioned him as an aga and gave him a corps of six
hundred men, who were outfitted in the current European military
garb and trained and drilled in European tactics and maneuvers.
When Selim suggested to the Divan that the janissaries should adopt
similar uniforms and be drilled in the same manner, he was able to appease mutineers only by withdrawing the request.

The historic interest which French governments had shown in the
commerce and diplomacy of the Ottoman Empire since the days of
Francis I did not evaporate with the French Revolution and its nationalism. In 1796 the Directory sent General Dubayet as ambassador to
the Porte, presenting as the customary gift to the sultan several of the
latest pieces of artillery and munitions. In his suite were artillerymen
and army engineers to advise in the use and manufacture of the new
pieces and drill sergeants from French infantry and cavalry regiments
to reorganize and train a new Ottoman army. The janissaries refused to
adopt any of the "Christian" devices, but the other advisers had some
success. Unfortunately, the direction of these activities lapsed entirely
when General Bonaparte invaded Egypt.

NAPOLEON INVADES EGYPT

The sultan's authority in Egypt had been only nominal for nearly a
century. Selim I and Suleiman had exercised considerable power in
Cairo, Alexandria, and the Delta, but they had not destroyed the
Mamluk bands. In fact, lands in Egypt were parceled out to Mamluks
to control and manage for the state. As the power of the Porte waned,
Mamluks grew wealthy and independent. At various periods in the
eighteenth century Mamluk groups in Egypt defied the sultan's orders
and refused to remit taxes to Istanbul. Ali Bey achieved a predomi-
nance over other Mamluks in 1769, when he became governor of Cairo
and declared his independence from the Ottomans. When Ali was murdered, other Mamluks seized power. At this point an Ottoman fleet and
army occupied Alexandria and Rosetta. However, even more rapacious
Mamluks rose to rule when the Turks departed; and Europeans openly

disparaged any hope of maintaining residence much longer in Egypt.

Ostensibly, General Bonaparte invaded Egypt to destroy the Mamluks, who were proving so troublesome and rebellious to his ally Sultan Selim III. Bonaparte's real objectives are even today shrouded in mystery. Claims have been put forward that the French looked upon the campaign as an attack upon Britain and her route to India, which the French had so recently surrendered to England, and that the possession of Egypt would widen the French sphere in the Mediterranean and offset the loss of India. In view of Napoleon's known regard for the importance of Istanbul, perhaps he intended to take Egypt and thence move upon Istanbul, the Balkans, and Austria.

In any case, Bonaparte gathered his army at Toulon; and accompanied by engineers, historians, archeologists, architects, mathematicians, chemists, and Egyptologists, he set sail in May, 1798 to take Malta and Egypt. He landed on July 1, took Alexandria on July 2, and defeated the Mamluks at the famous Battle of the Pyramids outside of Cairo on July 21. His fleet, however, was destroyed by Lord Nelson at Aboukir Bay, thus cutting his line of supply and impeding his freedom of action.

Since Egypt was a province of the Ottoman Empire, the attack brought a declaration of war from the Porte, which joined with England and Russia in a coalition against France. Selim gave Ahmed al-Jezzar command of the army in Syria, and a fleet and army were collected at Rhodes for the relief of Egypt. Napoleon, having decided to carry the battle to the Turks, marched on Syria in 1799 in the hope that discontented Muslim Arabs, Druzes in Lebanon, and Christians in Syria would rise against the Turks. He took Gaza and Jaffa, where in cold blood he murdered two thousand Turkish prisoners. But at Acre al-Jezzar, with reinforcements landed by an English squadron, held off Napoleon's attack. Repulsed there, Napoleon hurried to Egypt to meet a landing of Turkish infantry and cavalry at Aboukir Bay. These he drove into the sea, regaining mastery of Egypt. He then deserted his troops and sailed for France, where he executed his famous *coup d'état*.

The French forces remaining in Egypt were not conquered or evacuated until 1801. Several Turkish expeditions, in collaboration with an English army and naval squadron, forced the surrender of the French and gave them a guarantee of safe-conduct home. British forces held Egypt and prevented the several local competing factions from open warfare until the Peace of Amiens in 1802 required the departure of the British. At that point Muhammad Ali, leader of one of the Ottoman factions, took advantage of the prevailing political and military anarchy and set the course of his meteoric ascent. His rise was of great significance for the Middle East, but it separated to a very marked degree the affairs of the Nile from those of the Straits and the Porte.

At the time that the Peace of Amiens was concluded, agreement was reached between Selim III and Napoleon. The capitulations were restored for Frenchmen; and Napoleon sent General Brune and, later, General Sebastiani as ambassadors to the Porte. Selim was also at peace with England, Russia, and Austria. Trade revived in Ottoman ports, and shipping was brisk on the Black Sea and the Bosphorus. The Russians and British, however, used every device to offset French influence and to gain the Porte as an ally for their European policies.

UPRISING IN SERBIA

Upon the general establishment of peace in Europe Selim expected to proceed with his reforms, but calamity befell him in Serbia. The Treaty of Sistova provided for the return of Belgrad and its environs to the sultan; but it also provided that the janissaries, who previously ruled the area in a most ferocious manner, would not be permitted to return. Selim's new governor gave Serbia the most peaceful, prosperous, and enlightened rule she had known for nearly a century. However, to appease Pasvanoglu Pasha of Widin, Selim agreed to the return of the janissaries to Belgrad in 1799. Murdering the enlightened governor, four janissary leaders defied Selim's orders and authority and divided Serbia among themselves. Outrage upon Christian and Muslim people followed outrage, until there occurred the famous uprising of 1804 against the janissary rule, not against the sultan.

Aided by Austrian arms and led by Kara George, Serbian insurgents were successful in destroying the janissaries. Selim sought to re-establish Ottoman rule in Belgrad, but the Serb leaders insisted that the terms of settlement be supervised by an Austrian commissioner. The Serbs looked to the Hapsburgs for assistance; but Selim declared he could not consent to foreign interference in domestic affairs, and Austria refused to break the Treaty of Sistova. When the Serbs then turned to Russia for recognition, the Porte sent troops against the rebels. Victorious, the Serbs organized a provisional autonomous regime and again defeated the Turks. In 1806 the outbreak of war between Turkey and Russia induced the latter to aid Serbia, clearing Ottoman arms from the entire province. Thereupon Serbian affairs became a part of the European tangle of international diplomacy and power politics.

In the midst of this uprising realignment in Europe had its repercussions on the Golden Horn. When England formed the Third Coalition against France in 1805, General Sebastiani succeeded in obtaining Selim's sympathy for the French. But the Porte renewed the peace with

Russia upon threats of war and invasion. It was only after Austerlitz and Jena that Selim felt able to declare openly for the French. At this time he removed the two pro-Russian governors of Wallachia and Moldavia, replacing them with pro-French officials. When Russia invaded the Danubian provinces in 1806, the Turks declared war and closed the Straits to Russian ships. Britain co-operated with her ally by assembling a squadron near the mouth of the Dardanelles and insisted that Selim expel Sebastiani from Istanbul and open the Straits. Upon Selim's refusal Admiral Duckworth led the fleet through the Dardanelles into the Sea of Marmara to lie near Istanbul. With Russian troops invading Moldavia, the Porte considered a pre-emptory rebuff of Admiral Duckworth unwise. While the sultan's ministers spun out the negotiations, Sebastiani and military engineers hurriedly repaired the defenses of the Straits. Duckworth's intelligence advised withdrawal before escape became impossible, and the British retired from their foolhardy venture.

OVERTHROW OF SELIM

Napoleon's victories in central Europe and the defeat of the Russians at Friedland in 1807 strengthened the Turkish position. Meanwhile the appearance of five hundred French cannoneers to defend the Straits from further escapades served to bring Selim closer to an open alliance with the French. However, a change of equipment for the garrisons on the Bosphorus incited the janissaries to demand the dismissal of the Divan. And since payments to the janissaries were in arrears, their soup kettles were overturned, the traditional sign of revolt. Misinterpretation of the arrival of the French cannoneers precipitated Selim's deposition and the elevation of his cousin Mustafa IV in May, 1807. Formal charges against Selim were that he incited revolution by military innovations and that he had fathered no children after more than seven years of rule.

Mustafa IV was a mild and ineffectual person, the puppet of those who had overthrown Selim. Although the French officers and technicians were dismissed, the new sultan sent Napoleon a present of ten fine horses to indicate friendship for France—an amity which led to a truce between Russia and Turkey. The truce, however, was disastrous for Mustafa and the rebellious janissaries, since it freed the Ottoman armies on the Danube. An Ottoman army of Bosnians and Albanians, commanded by Bayraktar, governor of Ruschuk, marched on Istanbul and camped near the capital. Bayraktar called many leaders to his camp and in July, 1808 moved upon the city and the palace. Before Bayraktar's men could force the gates, Mustafa executed Selim and gave orders for the strangling of his own brother Mahmud. The insurgents, however, imprisoned Mustafa and placed on the throne Mahmud II, who was hidden in an empty furnace of the palace.

MAHMUD II AND THE NAPOLEONIC WARS

Mahmud II gave the office of grand vizir to Bayraktar, and the movement for reform proceeded along the lines drawn by Selim. After the organization of a new Europeanized army Bayraktar permitted his Bosnians and Albanians to return home. Thereupon, the janissaries rose up and destroyed Bayraktar. Civil war endured a week in the streets of Istanbul with serious fires, explosions, and chaos, during which Mustafa was executed. Mahmud, now the sole surviving male of the Ottoman dynasty, was fairly safe; but friends of the janissaries controlled the government, and military reforms were out of the question.

Shortly after Admiral Duckworth fled to the more open seas of the Aegean in 1807 Turkey adhered to Napoleon's Continental Blockade and the Straits were closed to English commerce. But Russian failure to withdraw from Moldavia, as promised, incited the Hapsburgs to mediate the breach between the Porte and England, since England was most likely to withstand the advances of a Franco-Russian combination. These maneuvers resulted in 1809 in the famous Treaty of the Dardanelles between the Ottoman Empire and Great Britain. Turkey withdrew the decrees against British commerce, and England recognized the ancient orders with respect to the Straits. Until the Napoleonic invasion of Egypt the Straits were always closed to all warships when the Ottoman Empire was at peace. The new treaty only restated the ancient principle.

The French and Russians were furious; and the tsar sent his troops to the Danube, taking Silistria, Ruschuk, Nicopolis, and Sistova. These victories were valueless, however, because in 1811 the break with Napoleon was foreseen and operations in the Balkans came to a halt. Luckily for Russia, the Treaty of Bucharest was signed a month before the French attack on Russia was launched. If this had not been the case, the Porte might have obtained better terms. Mahmud II dismissed the grand vizir and executed the negotiators for giving Bessarabia to the tsar.

The Treaty abandoned the Serbs to the sultan who, pledged that Serbs could manage their own internal affairs. The Russian regiment left Belgrad and the Turks attempted to rule the province. Although Kara George departed, a new leader, Milosh Obrenovitch, continued the Serbian revolt. The Congress of Vienna in 1815 allowed the Serbs to retain their arms and gave them a voice in the management of their own government through an elected parliament. The sultan's suzerainty over Serbia was hardly more than a legal fiction, as most of the taxes which the Serbs collected remained in Serbia. At the Congress, Turkey urged that Bessarabia be returned; but Vienna was unconcerned and the Treaty of Bucharest stood. This indicated that the relations between Russia and Turkey with respect to the use of the Straits returned to the ancient rule and that the Treaties of 1798 and 1805 were indirectly rescinded. Likewise, no contrary stipulation was raised at the Congress concerning the Treaty of the Dardanelles, which established the relations of Turkey and England and which, curiously enough, recognized that Turkey might be simultaneously a belligerent in the Black Sea and a neutral state in the Mediterranean.

From all appearances, therefore, the Ottoman Empire in 1815 successfully weathered the wars and cataclysms of the French Revolution and Napoleon. Bessarabia was lost; a semiautonomous regime was legalized in Belgrad; and two sultans were slain by military revolts. But little change resulted in the internal organization of the empire. None the less, the seeds of nationalism and reform were sown by wide movements of men and ideas, and a growth in commerce raised incentives to a new high.

The Ottoman Empire was on the threshold of a new century and a new life.

REFERENCES: *Chapter 20*

Among volumes already cited, those of particular value for this chapter are in Chapters 12, 13, 16, and 19.

A. J. Arkell, *A History of the Sudan to 1821:* The Athlone Press, University of London, London, 1961.

Gabriel Baer, *A History of Landownership in Modern Egypt, 1800–1950:* Oxford University Press, New York, 1962. A most important work.

Huseyn Efendi, *Ottoman Egypt in the Age of the French Revolution:* Harvard University Press, Cambridge, 1964.

William Eton, *A Survey of the Turkish Empire:* T. Cadell & W. Davies, London, 1799. An interesting contemporary account.

Shafik Ghurbal, *The Beginnings of the Egyptian Question and the Rise of Mehemet Ali; a Study in the Diplomacy of the Napoleonic Era Based on Researches in the British and French Archives:* Routledge, London, 1928. By an Egyptian scholar.

✓ Andreas M. Kazamias, *Education and the Quest for Modernity in Turkey:* University of Chicago Press, Chicago, 1966. Especially important for the twentieth century.

William L. Polk, *The Opening of South Lebanon, 1788–1840:* Harvard University Press, Cambridge, 1963. A detailed and comprehensive study.

Vernon J. Puryear, *Napoleon and the Dardanelles:* University of California Press, Berkeley, 1951. A comprehensive work on the diplomacy of the Middle East during the period of the French Revolution and Napoleon.

Paul F. Shupp, *The European Powers and the Near Eastern Question, 1806–1807:* Columbia University Press, New York, 1931. Based on English and French archival material.

Harold W. V. Temperley, *England and the Near East,* Vol. I, *The Crimea:* Longmans, Green, London, 1936. An indispensable work covering the years from 1808 to 1854.

Shirley H. Weber, *Voyages and Travels in the Near East, XIX Century:* American School of Classical Studies at Athens, Princeton, 1952. A continuation of his volume cited in Chapter 19.

CHAPTER 21

Mahmud II—Nationalism and Reform

THE GREEK REVOLUTION

One of the exciting legacies of the French Revolution to the Middle East was the rise of the Greek nation. Eighteenth-century liberal Europeans wished to emulate ancient Greek society and culture; they particularly admired Greek political ideas. When, therefore, Greeks came into contact with Europeans at the turn of the century, they were impressed with their own heritage and fostered an intellectual and literary renaissance of significant proportions in all Greek communities from Odessa to Marseilles. Before 1820 over three thousand different books had been published in modern Greek. These included not only translations of the important works of Voltaire, Schiller, Goethe, Alfieri, and Montesquieu but also renditions of the ancient Greek classics into a form which modern Greeks could read and understand.

The two outstanding Greek intellectual patriots were Rhegas and Adamantios Koraes, each of whom traveled and studied in Europe. Rhegas, in his Greek version of the *Marseillaise*, roused his countrymen to arms and aided them in forming a society to raise money and munitions to cast off the Turkish yoke. Following Plato and Rousseau, Koraes held that every form of bad citizenship was an injustice. He also asserted that every bad citizen was a Turk at heart. In addition to hating Turks and carrying Western ideas to the Greeks, he glorified the heroic deeds of ancient Greeks and advanced the reconstruction of modern Greek by condemning foreign words and abandoning colloquialisms and barbarisms that had crept into the ancient tongue.

The labors of these patriots would have been fruitless had it not been for the Greek Church, which preserved the identity of the Greek community, and for Greek schools, everywhere present to train churchmen and incidentally to teach many to read and write Greek. As Greeks became prosperous, they founded more schools and many pursued advanced studies in Italy and France. After the fall of Venice in 1797 the Greek cultural center moved to Vienna, where a Greek press published books and newspapers that circulated wherever Greeks went.

The decay of the Ottoman government gave rise to many outlaw bands in the mountains of Greece. Known as *klephts,* these brigands posed as Robin Hoods attacking Turks and helping Greeks. They fired the Greek spirit and created a nucleus of Greeks familiar with the handling of weapons. Also, the islands and coastline of the area led many Greeks, as in antiquity, to the sea and foreign commerce; and their knowledge of the ways and languages of the Middle East proved extremely beneficial in trade between Ottoman and Mediterranean ports. During the Napoleonic wars they reaped enormous profits flying the Turkish or Russian flag in the Black Sea and the Turkish or other flags in the Mediterranean as conditions demanded.

In 1814 a group of Greeks in Odessa founded a secret band named *Philike Hetaeria* (Friendly Society) to organize a rising against the Turks. Similar to contemporary European secret societies, the *Hetaeria* grew so rapidly with the commercial depression after 1815 that over two hundred thousand were initiated by 1820. Its members could not be restrained; and in 1821 Alexander Ypsilantis, a distinguished Phanariot Greek and a general in the Russian army who had lost his right hand at the battle of Kulm, unfurled the banner of revolt.

He crossed the Pruth River from Russian Bessarabia into Turkish Moldavia. This was not the most propitious spot to launch a Greek Revolution, since the native Rumanians hated Greeks far more than they did Turks. Turks in Galatz and Jassy were impaled. Bankers were blackmailed. The Powers, at that moment convening at Ljubljana (Laibach) to suppress a Neapolitan uprising, induced Russia to strike Ypsilantis' name from Russian army rolls and disown the adventure. When a Turkish army drove him from Bucharest, he shamelessly deserted his followers and fled to Hungary.

Within a few weeks of the crossing of the Pruth, the Revolution was in full swing in the Peloponnesus. From Kalamata to Patras to Corinth, Turks—men, women, and children—were massacred and the population of surrendered towns put to the sword. When Tripolitsa, the Turkish capital, fell, over eight thousand Turks were butchered. (Many modern wealthy Greek families acquired their fortunes in the sack of the city.) Athens, except for the Acropolis, fell, as did Mesolonghi and other towns on the northern shore of the Gulf of Corinth. Immediately the Turks fought back; on Crete and some of the Aegean islands reprisals and counter-reprisals were common.

The rebellions in the Danubian provinces and the Peloponnesus led Mahmud II to take action against suspected *Hetaeriaists* in Istanbul. A number of leading Phanariotes were executed, and on Easter Sunday the Greek Patriarch was hanged from the gate of his residence. Of all the Aegean islands, Chios with its famous mastic gardens was the most wealthy, and its inhabitants showed no interest in the uprisings on the mainland. Early in 1822, however, Greek adventurers took over the island against the wishes of the Chiotes. Thereupon, a Turkish admiral landed. Greek sailors counterattacked in vain. The Turks leveled villages, put Chios to the torch, and massacred nearly twenty-five thousand Greeks, scattering the rest to all parts of the world. Shortly thereafter, Turks surrendered the Acropolis in Athens on the pledge that their lives would be spared. The promise was not kept.

Ottoman forces were weak, and Mahmud had dispersed his military might. When Mahmud withdrew the best of his soldiers to subdue Ali, the rebellious pasha of Janina, the Peloponnesus and certain Greek areas were almost invited to revolt. For thirty years Ali ruled as a benevolent tyrant, corresponding with Napoleon and negotiating with British governors of the Ionian Islands. He was a strange mixture of eighteenth-century European enlightenment, Oriental splendor, and devotion to ancient Greek literature which captivated the imagination of Europe. In 1820 Mahmud decided to settle many a score with Ali. An army was sent to Epirus to bring in his head. During this campaign the Turkish garrisons in Athens, Tripolitsa, and other Greek towns were reduced to the barest minimum, leaving the towns defenseless against a popular uprising. When, however, Ali Pasha's head and those of his sons and grandsons were exhibited on a silver platter outside the sultan's palace in Istanbul in 1822, Mahmud's forces had better success against the Greeks. The sultan's forces were considerably spent, but the Greeks were torn already with dissension.

INTERVENTION BY EGYPT AND THE POWERS

The Powers looked upon the Greek activities with uncertainty and considerable misgivings, but philhellenic committees in England and France compelled their governments to take an interest in Greek affairs. Furthermore, the Greek provisional government obtained in 1824 the first of a series of loans from British bankers, a move which guaranteed a continuing interest from London. Considerable romantic publicity accompanied the enlistment of veteran European soldiers, especially philhellenes. The most famous of these was Lord Byron, whose death in 1824 at Mesolonghi created more sentiment for the Greek cause than any other single event in the long Greek struggle.

In 1824 Mahmud commissioned his powerful vassal of Egypt, Muhammad Ali, to aid in suppressing the insurrection. His son Ibrahim was appointed governor of the Peloponnesus and set out to subjugate his new charge. He landed at Modon in 1825, captured Navarino, and proceeded to establish his authority by fire and sword. Meanwhile an Ottoman army subdued western Greece, took Mesolonghi, and recaptured Athens. Greek independence seemed very doubtful.

The victories of Mahmud's lieutenants hastened the intervention of the Powers. Various preliminary discussions suggesting local Greek autonomy led to the Treaty of London, signed in 1827 by England, Russia, and France. In this treaty the three demanded an armistice from Turkey and Greece and the mediation of any differences. Since Mahmud refused to declare an armistice, Admiral Codrington was ordered to intercept, with cannon balls if necessary, all supplies and reinforcements destined for Ibrahim. The famous Battle of Navarino on October 20, 1827 completely shattered Ottoman naval forces, and a French army compelled Ibrahim to withdraw.

Russian interests in Greece were tied to the affairs of Serbia and the Danubian provinces. Even before Nicholas I agreed to the London treaty, an ultimatum had been delivered to the Porte demanding: cession of Kars and other eastern provinces; evacuation of Moldavia and Wallachia, whose governors would be elected for seven-year terms by the native aristocracy and could be removed only upon Russian consent; and immediate autonomy for Serbia. On the last day of grace Mahmud accepted the terms, which were incorporated in the Convention of Akkerman of 1826.

After the destruction of the Ottoman navy at Navarino Russia could not resist taking advantage of Turkish weakness. A peculiar kind of war was declared in 1828: Russia became a belligerent in the Balkans and the Black Sea but remained a neutral in the Mediterranean. One army advanced in the Caucasus with considerable success, taking Ardahan, Bayezid, and Erzerum; another under General Diebitsch took Varna and Burgas on the Black Sea, crossed the Balkans, and entered Edirne.

TREATY OF ADRIANOPLE

Upon the advice of Prussian and British envoys Mahmud sought peace. Diebitsch was in collaboration with the Russian fleet, which was divided between the Black Sea and the Aegean; and it appeared that nothing could prevent him from occupying Istanbul. The Treaty of Adrianople (Edirne) of 1829 re-established the frontiers much as they were before the war. The Straits were open again to Russian trade. The Danubian provinces no longer had to supply corn, wood, and mutton to the sultan's government; only the annual tribute to the Porte was continued. Governors held their posts for life and ruled in consultation with native assemblies. The ties with Turkey were reduced to a minimum, and Russia moved into the vacuum.

Other provisions of the treaty stipulated that the articles of the Convention of Akkerman should be put into immediate effect. Another article declared that Turkey adhered to a second Treaty of London which England, France, and Russia had concluded earlier in 1829 and which established a Greek state. In consequence of its inclusiveness the Treaty of Adrianople was an important landmark in Balkan development as well as in the relationship of the Ottoman Empire to the great European states.

DESTRUCTION OF THE JANISSARIES

Although the Duke of Wellington erred in thinking that the treaty foretold the imminent collapse of the Ottoman Empire, the treaty did materially change the balance of power in the Balkans and in the Middle East. An event of vaster proportions and ramifications, however, preceded the treaty and was in part responsible for it. In 1826 Mahmud destroyed the janissaries. For more than three hundred years sultans found the janissary corps unruly; and since the beginning of the seventeenth century these soldiers frequently vetoed policies of state and grand viziers were beheaded at their behest. Through the eighteenth century several of the sultans contrived to modernize the army and equip the janissaries with more efficient weapons, but each scheme was successfully rebuffed. Since the sultan's authority in the provinces was continually snubbed by recalcitrant governors, a reliable standing army had to be created before he could reassert his power. The modernization of the army became even more urgent as Ottoman units met with Austrian and Russian regiments, to which they compared adversely.

Selim lost his life in the attempt to modernize the army. Mahmud plotted more warily. Although Ali Pasha of Janina, Ahmed al-Jezzar of Syria, and Muhammad Ali of Egypt possessed competent standing armies, the sultan depended upon janissaries and feudal levies. The lesson of Murat, who cleared the streets of Madrid in 1808 with cannon and grapeshot, was not lost upon Mahmud. Ottoman artillery was carefully improved, and more than fourteen thousand artillerymen were gathered in Istanbul. When the blow was readied, Mahmud had the loyalty of the artillerymen, the grand vizir, the Shaykh al-Islam, the chief of the janissaries, and a sizable force of Anatolian levies stationed at Uskudar across the Bosphorus.

In 1826 Mahmud forced the Divan to order some janissaries to drill in European fashion. The revolution broke, as was expected. The artillery mowed down the janissaries as they charged the palace and then shelled their barracks into a mass of ruins, burying four thousand beneath the rubble. Victory was followed up in the provinces, where janissaries were hunted down and either exterminated or completely scattered. New troops were ordered to be assembled, and Mahmud planned to organize and train an army of forty thousand. Although the Russian attacks in 1828 and 1829 were launched before the new troops were trained and weakened them permanently as the Russians had hoped, Mahmud rid his state of an anachronism which considerably retarded the process of change in the empire. It was a first step in destroying the power of the governors in outlying provinces and in rebuilding the centralized control which proved so effective in the fifteenth and sixteenth centuries. Other reforms could now come forward.

MUHAMMAD ALI AND MAHMUD II

But there was hardly any time for sound reform. Peace was no more than established when Mahmud faced rebellion and serious attack by Muhammad Ali, his vassal in Egypt. The following chapter relates the development of Egypt and other parts of the Middle East under Muhammad's leadership. For Mahmud, however, the actions of this dynamic newcomer effected his empire profoundly, particularly in its relationship to the great Powers.

For lending aid to the sultan Muhammad Ali was given an outright promise of Crete and of the governorship of the Peloponnesus for his son Ibrahim. The latter did not materialize, however, because the Powers established the Kingdom of Greece; and the former was totally inadequate. Muhammad Ali, therefore, turned his eyes on the Barbary Coast. But French action in Algeria in 1830 diverted his attention to Syria, which he requested for Ibrahim in lieu of the Peloponnesus. Since some reward in Syria was originally offered for the Greek adventure, this request seemed appropriate.

Mahmud refused, and Muhammad Ali began his march into Syria in 1831. He first assembled his army to answer Mahmud's call for help against a rebellious pasha in Albania. Later he announced that the invasion of Syria would coerce Abdallah of Acre to subserve the sultan and chastise him for harboring Egyptian conscript dodgers and practicing the arts of extortion upon Egyptian merchants.

Ibrahim waged a combined land and sea attack upon Acre, which finally fell in 1832 after a prolonged siege and several bloody assaults. Mahmud hardly lifted a finger to aid Abdallah; Ibrahim easily routed a Turkish army collected near Homs; and in rapid succession Damascus, Aleppo, Adana, and Konya were occupied by the Egyptian army. Up to this point the Powers were unconcerned; France even looked with favor upon the expansion of Muhammad Ali's territory. When Ibrahim defeated the main Turkish army near Konya and pushed on to Kutahya, however, Mahmud grew frantic and begged the Powers to rescue him. Metternich refused; England was involved in parliamentary reform and Belgian affairs; France had strong ties with Muhammad Ali; only Russia responded. Early in 1833 a Russian fleet anchored in the Bosphorus and fourteen thousand Russian marines landed to protect Mahmud from his vassal and to guarantee the concessions and treaties the Russians had obtained from the Porte since 1774.

Meanwhile Russian and Ottoman envoys in Cairo were discussing peace terms, while French diplomatic and consular agents were pressing Mahmud to accept some of the Egyptian demands. Compromises were effected, and the Convention of Kutahya was signed. Syria, including Damascus and Aleppo, was assigned to Muhammad Ali upon condition that he pay an annual tribute. Ibrahim's troops were recalled from Anatolia. The Russian fleet and troops, however, postponed their departure from the Bosphorus. Two days before they re-embarked from the Bosphorus village of Hunkiar Iskelesi, where they had encamped, a treaty was signed which shocked the other European Powers and achieved for Russia a long-sought goal. The Treaty of Hunkiar Iskelesi of 1833 was a straightforward alliance between Russia and Turkey, providing for perpetual friendship, peace, and mutual assistance. The provocation lay in a secret article, which did not remain unknown very long, stating that the sultan would upon Russian request close the Straits to the extent of "not allowing any foreign vessel of war to enter therein, under any pretext whatsoever." Although diplomats and writers questioned the significance of the secret article, the value of Hunkiar Iskelesi to Russia and the objection of the Powers rested on the right of Russia to interfere in Turkish affairs "to the exclusion of the alliance and intervention of the Powers."

MAHMUD'S REFORMS

Whereas England and France recognized immediately the advantage won by Russia and initiated action to recoup their losses, Mahmud used the peace he so dearly purchased to carry forward the reform of his government. Destruction of the janissaries and the formation of new troops, termed Muslim Soldiers, were only publicized aspects of his military innovations. The abolition of feudalism ruined the cavalry and levies upon which sultans greatly depended and which had proved extremely valuable for Mahmud. Although income from fiefs now went directly to the treasury, and officers of the sultan enlisted recruits from these areas, the central government was not as thorough or efficient in these functions as local notables. However, real progress was made. Helmuth von Moltke and a group of Prussians participated in training Turkish officers; other Turkish officers studied at Woolwich in England. Military and medical colleges were opened in 1830; and a national militia was organized in 1834 to give rudimentary training in the provinces.

Since the religious leaders, the *ulema,* opposed previous attempts at reform, Mahmud silenced the more irresponsible of them. Dervish orders were attacked. Bektashi leaders were exiled and the order's buildings and properties confiscated. Actually this latter decree was never fully executed; dervish houses remained in the possession of Bektashis in most parts of the empire, even in Istanbul, until the twentieth century. The fez was adopted as the headgear for governmental officials. The frock coat was also adopted. And within a few years the fez and the frock coat became the standard dress in urban centers. When the Shaykh al-Islam objected, Mahmud removed him, giving public notice of his earnestness in these matters.

Changes in the military were the means to strengthen and reorganize the government. The independent local lords (*dereh beys*) in Anatolia were checked, Iraq was subdued in 1831, and other governors began to feel and respect the sultan's authority. To a certain extent the war with Egypt resulted from Mahmud's desire to project his power into every corner of the realm. As a further curb on local rulers, governors were forbidden to execute anyone without referring the case to Istanbul. This removal of the death sentence from a governor's whim gave people throughout the empire a deeper sense of security.

Every department of government was staffed by better-trained civil servants. Better salaries lessened bribery, and more attention was given to promotion on merit. The use of passports for travelers was adopted, and in 1832 Mahmud devised a postal system. More modern methods of quarantine were prescribed; and in every way European techniques of government were studied and employed. Many sinecures were abolished and much governmental "red tape" eliminated.

The end of the wars with Russia and Egypt left Turkey almost bankrupt. Foreign observers commented on the great wealth and bountiful produce of the country but inefficiency in the collection of taxes reduced the sultan to penury. Under new procedures the central government assumed direct responsibility and sent out its own agents or tax farmers, thereby reducing the number of hands through which the taxes passed. New roads improved trade, and Muslims were encouraged to enter business by the abolition of the Court of Confiscations in which the government seized the property of an exiled or condemned individual. Creditors henceforth felt less personal danger in pressing the government and its high officials for the payment of debts. In general these measures were effective. By the end of Mahmud's reign European consular officials were reporting that the empire had progressed remarkably in the preceding twenty years.

Mahmud also recognized the stimulus to reform which a general circulation of books and newspapers would generate. Presses were established in Istanbul and Izmir, which with those of Muhammad Ali in Egypt published several thousand books in Turkish and Arabic between 1830 and 1840. The military and medical colleges introduced many young Turks to French and German and opened to them the eighteenth- and nineteenth-century liberal ideas contained in the literature of those languages. French newspapers were founded in Izmir in the 1820's; and in 1832 the first Turkish newspaper, *Takvimi-Vekayih*, appeared in Istanbul with official support from Mahmud.

The Ottoman Empire found in Mahmud a sultan whose high ability in the craft of ruling broke the conservative and reactionary grip held by special interest groups upon the government and society. In later decades of the nineteenth century the progress of reform might seem slow and uncertain. Yet after Mahmud's changes a return to the old order was impossible and a liberalizing forward-looking movement prevailed.

REFERENCES: Chapter 21

Works containing material pertinent to this chapter are cited in Chapters 12, 13, 18, 19, and 20.

Frank Edgar Bailey, *British Policy and the Turkish Reform Movement: A Study in Anglo-Turkish Relations, 1826–1853:* Harvard University Press, Cambridge, 1942. Written largely from the British point of view.

Stephen George Chaconas, *Admantios Korais: A Study in Greek Nationalism:* Columbia University Press, New York, 1942. A thorough study of this famous Greek patriot.

C. W. Crawley, *The Question of Greek Independence:* Cambridge University Press, Cambridge, 1930. An instructive monograph on the Greek revolution.

Z. Y. Hershlag, *Introduction to the Modern Economic History of the Middle East:* E. J. Brill, Leiden, 1964.

Charles Issawi, ed., *The Economic History of the Middle East, 1800–1914:* University of Chicago Press, Chicago, 1966. A fine collection of essays.

Fuat Koprulu, *On the Way to Democracy:* Mouton, The Hague, 1964.

Vernon John Puryear, *France and the Levant from the Bourbon Restoration to the Peace of Kutiah:* University of California Press, Berkeley, 1941. A history of diplomacy in the Middle East for the period.

Helen Anne B. Rivlin, *The Agricultural Policy of Muhammad Ali in Egypt:* Harvard University Press, Cambridge, 1961. An outstanding work.

William Yale, *The Near East: A Modern History:* University of Michigan Press, Ann Arbor, 1958. Good for the nineteenth century.

CHAPTER 22

Muhammad Ali and the Development of Modern Egypt

RISE OF MUHAMMAD ALI

Nineteenth-century Egypt was the creation of Muhammad Ali, who must be recognized as one of the great rulers of his age. In 1798 when Selim III raised an army to send to Egypt against Napoleon, the governor of Kavalla in Thrace supplied three hundred men, the second in command being Muhammad Ali, probably of Albanian descent and then about twenty-nine years old.

He had been engaged in the tobacco trade, but his latent political talent was soon manifested in Egypt. The Peace of Amiens in 1802 and the British evacuation of the Nile found Muhammad Ali responsible for several thousand Albanian and Bosnian troops. At the moment three major powers existed in Egypt: the Ottoman Pasha, who ruled in the name of the sultan; the Mamluks, who held landed estates and were hopelessly split in jealous factions; and the Albanians. The people of Cairo constituted a weak fourth.

Muhammad Ali played his cards extremely well. When the British left Egypt in 1803, he sided with the Mamluks and drove the Turkish governor from Cairo. Muhammad Ali then played one Mamluk faction against another. Finally, with the aid of the Cairo populace, he chased the Mamluks into the desert, deposed the new governor who had just arrived from Istanbul, and was recognized as governor by the citizens of Cairo. When in 1806 Muhammad Ali accepted the honor and asserted his full submission to Selim, the latter appointed him Pasha of Egypt.

Affairs in Europe in 1807 pushed Turkey into the French camp; since Muhammad Ali persisted in his loyalty to the Porte, a British expeditionary force landed at Alexandria. In league with Mamluk remnants, the British occupied Alexandria, but were defeated at Rosetta and withdrew. After the Treaty of Tilsit, which threw England and Turkey into each other's arms, Britain renounced all designs upon Egypt, leaving the Mamluks to shift for themselves. Muhammad Ali was now the actual as well as the titular ruler of Egypt.

Finances cramped him severely. On several occasions Muhammad Ali's own Albanians, their pay considerably in arrears, shot at him as he passed in the streets of Cairo. War and the successive passage of troops in Lower Egypt reduced the Delta to barrenness. In previous administrations taxes and levies supported an Egyptian army, but Muhammad Ali found little to levy upon and taxes quit insufficient. Consequently, in 1808 he ordered a survey of all landholdings and confiscated properties with irregular titles. Later he seized land grants upon which payments to the state were in arrears, abolished the ancient system of land tenure, and expropriated the remaining fiefs (*multazim*). Even exemptions for lands belonging to religious institutions were rescinded and their lands surveyed to be sure none escaped.

As land taxes increased, Muhammad Ali turned his attention to commerce and established a government monopoly on the export of grain. In several of these years the Nile Valley possessed the only exportable surplus available to the British fleet and Wellington's army in Spain. Demand was brisk, and profits in the grain trade often reached five hundred percent. Frequently, Muhammad Ali accepted cotton goods and small manufactures in exchange for grain, thus gaining from a two-way trade as well as improving his relations with the British.

Muhammad Ali's power and the loyalty of his troops rose in direct proportion to his improved finances. One long-standing score remained to be settled, not only for himself but for the authority of his suzerain, the Ottoman sultan. The Mamluks had never been fully subjected, particularly those holding fiefs in Upper Egypt; and they defied one Ottoman governor after another. For several years Muhammad Ali threatened, cajoled, and attacked them. His entreaties induced many to settle at Giza across from Cairo; and at the ceremonies of the investiture of his son as Pasha of Jidda in 1811 they were tricked into entering the Citadel of Cairo, where the Albanian soldiers slaughtered them. A year later another thousand were executed in Upper Egypt.

ARABIA AND THE SUDAN

Organization of the finances of Egypt and destruction of the Mamluk power enabled Muhammad Ali to consider widening his rule. For many decades the Porte was troubled by attacks and depredations of the Saudi tribe of Arabia. In the middle of the eighteenth century Muhammad ibn Saud became converted to the teachings of Muhammad ibn Abd al-Wahhab, a native of Nejd who had studied in Damascus and Baghdad. Returning home, the latter grew convinced of the necessity of eliminating from Muslim practices the pagan superstitions which had become prevalent among the desert Arab tribesmen. He also felt compelled to destroy the philosophic subtleties and the worldly deviations which had crept into Islam over the ages and to restore Islam to the pure, original, and simple form as pronounced by the Prophet.

Muhammad ibn Saud and his descendants, armed with the Wahhabi faith, spread their rule over many tribes in Arabia, pillaging Shiite and Sunnite shrines. Their seizure of the Hijaz during the Napoleonic wars disrupted Meccan pilgrimages, and the Porte entreated Muhammad Ali to drive them from Medina and Mecca. In 1811 his son Tusun headed an expedition to annex the Hijaz. Not until 1818, however, under the firm and courageous leadership of Muhammad Ali's able son Ibrahim did the superior equipment and discipline of the Egyptian troops turn the scales against the Saudi-Wahhabi forces.

Ibrahim was named governor of the Hijaz and Ethiopia, the latter consisting then of a few Red Sea ports which served as outlets for the Sudan as much as for Abyssinia. Muhammad Ali looked upon the Sudan as a boundless area full of gold, precious stones, and slaves. He also believed that he could develop a fine army from stalwart negro slaves from the Sudan, thereby securing independence from his unruly Albanians. An expedition went southward in 1820 under Ismail, another of his sons. Sennar and El Obeid were taken; and within six years the country was pacified and the modern city of Khartoum founded.

GREEK EXPEDITION

The experiment with regard to an army of Sudanese slaves proved a total failure. An attempt was made at Aswan under the direction of a French officer, Colonel Séve, who as Suleiman Pasha served Muhammad Ali loyally for more than twenty years. But disease and fatalities among the Sudanese constrained him to build an army around Egyptian soldiers and Turkish and European officers. Over thirty thousand Egyptian peasants were sent to Aswan, where in a short time they were drilled into effective soldiers. Meanwhile, Muhammad Ali assembled a fleet. One ship mounting sixteen guns was built at Suez; he bought others in Bombay, Genoa, Venice, Marseilles, and the Greek Islands.

While these developments were in process, the Greek Revolution turned the eastern Mediterranean into a nest for Greek pirates. In 1822 Mahmud II offered the governorship of Crete to Muhammad Ali, if he would subdue it. After Muhammad Ali had taken Crete, Mahmud bestowed upon him the overlordship of the Peloponnesus on like terms. Under Ibrahim's command sixteen thousand men and a sixty-three-ship navy left Alexandria in 1824 to clear the Aegean of the Greek pirate-nationalist navy. Various islands were attacked and plundered, Muhammad Ali replacing his losses with new ships from France and Italy; he even bought some from Greek shipbuilders. Ibrahim and Suleiman Pasha landed in Greece in 1825; their successes and losses have been related in another chapter. The Greek adventure was extremely costly for Muhammad Ali: his fleet was ruined, and his trained and disciplined army returned to Egypt starved and crippled.

CONQUEST OF SYRIA

But Muhammad Ali was not a ruler to be discouraged easily. For a time he dallied with French suggestions to co-operate in the destruction of the Dey of Algiers, but he tired of French indecision and came to realize that such an excursion would render him a French vassal. Syria was far more inviting, especially since its four districts were pledged to him as payment for his undertaking in Greece. Using a variety of excuses, Muhammad Ali sent Ibrahim against Acre, which fell in May, 1832. He then turned upon Turkish forces, speedily entered the Beylan Pass south of Alexandretta, and marched northward to the outskirts of Konya. Ibrahim's devastating victory at Konya carried him on to Kutahya, where peace between Mahmud and his rebellious viceroy was concluded in 1833. Crete, Egypt, Syria, Adana, and Tarsus were assigned to Muhammad Ali, for which he agreed to pay £150,-000 a year tribute to Istanbul.

Ibrahim governed Syria for eight years. A distinguished Syrian has written that these years "may be regarded as the beginning of the modern age for the country." Taxes were regularized, justice was more sure for people of all religions, commerce was encouraged, privileges for foreigners were less abused, education was stimulated, law and order were more prevalent. Ibrahim proved to be more of an Arab than he was a Turk, and ideas of a revival of an Arab state to include all Arabs were circulated.

The resolute rule which Muhammad Ali created in Egypt was also attempted in Syria. Had it been given a longer period of trial, it might have succeeded. Conscription, however, was hated, and rebellion faced Ibrahim on several occasions. A strong army was an absolute necessity for Muhammad Ali and Ibrahim; and Mahmud was rebuilding an army while European officers were training new Turkish regiments. Since the governorships of Egypt, Syria, and Crete were granted for only one year at a time and since there were constant disputes over tribute, Muhammad Ali considered maintenance of an ever-ready army a prime requisite for his own safety. When, therefore, European governments urged abandonment of conscription in Syria, reduction of his armaments by half, and withdrawal of his troops from Syria, Muhammad Ali gladly agreed, but on condition that Mahmud grant him hereditary title to his territories and that the Powers guarantee him against aggression.

Receiving no agreement to such conditions, Muhammad Ali decided to declare his independence. Before this could be done, however, Ottoman forces invaded Syria and were destroyed at Nazib by Ibrahim in June, 1839. Five days later Mahmud II died, and before July was out the Turkish fleet deserted to join the Egyptians at Alexandria. Muhammad Ali was now master of the situation, and the Porte prepared to surrender to his demands of hereditary vassalage for all territories then in his possession. However, a joint note from Austria, England, France, Prussia, and Russia informed the sultan that they were concerned with developments within the Middle East and recommended that no action be taken on Muhammad Ali's claims without their approval. The British feared that Russia would call into operation provisions of the hated Treaty of Hunkiar Iskelesi or that France through Muhammad Ali would dominate Syria and Egypt and control all routes from the Mediterranean to India. The British, therefore, preferred a united action to Russian or French unilateral steps. Fortified with this backing, the Porte informed Muhammad Ali of European concern and awaited the decision of the Powers. In the end Lord Palmerston prevailed upon Russia, Prussia, and Austria to sign the Treaty of London in 1840. This treaty was a diplomatic defeat in the Levant for Louis Philippe's government. It allowed Muhammad Ali the hereditary governorship of Egypt if he agreed to the settlement within twenty days, and a lifetime rule over south Syria if he agreed in ten days. Otherwise, the four powers would blockade Egypt and defend the integrity of the Ottoman Empire.

Since Muhammad Ali refused to budge, the only recourse was force. British agents in Lebanon and Syria raised a rebellion against Ibrahim, while a combined British-Austrian fleet landed troops at Beirut and captured Acre. Muhammad Ali was forced to recall Ibrahim from Syria and accept British terms. Egypt was left as a hereditary province to Muhammad Ali and his heirs. Since communications were slow and the arrangements complex, it was not until July, 1841 that the Porte confirmed him in the hereditary position in Egypt and granted him authority to make military appointments below the rank of general. France agreed to the terms and returned to the concert of European powers in their concern with affairs of the Middle East.

ORGANIZATION OF EGYPT

The defeats of 1840 and the diplomatic negotiations of 1841 gave Muhammad Ali full power in Egypt, but left him an old and broken man. He lived on until 1849. In his declining years Europe learned to appreciate his numerous accomplishments. Ibrahim visited France and England, where he was feted. Muhammad Ali was invited to London, but the old man ventured only to Istanbul and his birthplace, Kavalla. He lapsed into senility in 1847. Ibrahim died in 1848. And the government passed to Muhammad Ali's grandson Abbas.

For forty years Muhammad Ali ruled Egypt, and every phase of life and society interested him at one time or another. A new government was created; and a cabinet with ministers of war, navy, agriculture, finance, commerce and foreign affairs, education, and security developed. Real power, however, never slipped from the hands of the Pasha, as Muhammad Ali was always known. In the 1830's Councils of Notables were appointed to discuss governmental affairs. Western travelers were greatly impressed, but the Pasha never intended that his rule be other than that of a benevolent despot.

The trade monopoly for grain was extended to include cotton, tobacco, and indigo, although the British attempted to terminate the system in 1838 when a new commercial treaty for the entire Ottoman Empire was concluded with Mahmud II. Since taxes were paid in kind, the Pasha's government continued to be the principal participant in the export trade; and most foreign merchants in Alexandria did not object after Muhammad Ali agreed to offer his goods at public auction to export houses. Corn and rice were introduced. In many areas steam pumps and better canals allowed summer irrigation, enabling the fellaheen to double the yield by growing two crops a year. Great attention was given to the science of irrigation. Swamp lands were drained, old canals opened, and new ones built. North of Cairo a great barrage was constructed to raise canal levels, especially in years of scanty floods. However, since the engineering work was not too sound, it proved ineffective until rebuilt in the 1880's.

The age of Muhammad Ali in Egypt coincided with the first industrial surge in western Europe and the Pasha became convinced of the value of such a program for his land. He imported textile plants and built sugar factories. But knowledge to keep them in operation, suitable labor, and supplies of coal and iron were lacking; and even before Muhammad Ali died, the failure to industrialize Egypt was apparent.

Two of his successful endeavors were sanitation and education. Great plagues raged every year; and annual deaths from cholera and bubonic plague sometimes rose to ten percent of the population. A more effective quarantine was organized and Muhammad Ali appointed the foreign consuls in Alexandria to a Board of Sanitation, which was given ample funds and absolute authority. After 1840 visitations of these diseases were restricted, and health conditions improved. The marked increase in the population (4,500,000 according to the census of 1847) was largely attributed to improved agriculture and the absence of epidemics.

The first schools established were for the military—infantry, cavalry, engineers, marine, and artillery. Most of the instructors in these schools were French; and boys were often sent to study in France and England. In 1833, however, the Polytechnic School was founded with all Egyptian teachers, except two. Soon, preparatory schools to feed the Polytechnic were organized in Cairo and Alexandria. A medical college was established by Clot Bey, a French doctor long in the Pasha's service. In connection with the schools a government press was set up at Bulaq near Cairo; most of its publications were translations of European technical works. Newspapers printed in both Arabic and French, not only gave urban society a vehicle by which Western ideas were circulated but also made Egypt a leader in the intellectual life of the Arab world.

Muhammad Ali was impatient and tried to change society rapidly without a sufficient supply of sympathetic officials. His innovations were too hurried and too shallow to endure. He once commented toward the end of his life that he had found Egypt "utterly barbarous" and that he tried to make some improvement. Alexandria was transformed into a Mediterranean city resembling Marseilles, Genoa, and Naples. Construction of the great Mahmudiyah Canal brought all Nile trade and traffic from Cairo to Alexandria and turned the latter into a boom town. Its population increased from 15,000 in 1805 to 150,000 in 1847. Since many of its inhabitants were Europeans, Alexandria became one of the most cosmopolitan cities of the world. When Muhammad Ali died, he had given Egypt the first constructive leadership in centuries and sown the seeds for the establishment of a national state. Incredibly, this was done without incurring any debts.

Abbas Pasha, the new ruler, had headed an army in Syria under Ibrahim. He was a conservative old-fashioned Turkish gentleman who believed his interests paralleled those of the British. He shunned Frenchmen and permitted many of his grandfather's innovations to lapse. Factories were abandoned, trade monopolies abolished, and schools closed. Aggressive policies were curtailed, and the army was halved. Although a British firm constructed the first railway between Alexandria and Cairo, French agents seeking to build the Suez Canal were unable to receive a hearing. Upon his murder in 1854, authority passed to his uncle Said, Muhammad Ali's favorite son, who surrounded himself with Frenchmen.

THE SUEZ CANAL

In Said's youth he had formed a friendship with Ferdinand de Lesseps, son of the French Political Agent in Egypt, and within four months after his accession Said granted his friend a broad concession to construct the Suez Canal. Officially promulgated in 1855, the news touched off a long diplomatic imbroglio. The British government opposed the scheme, believing that it would impair British commercial advantages with the Orient and that it would inevitably create an Egyptian question for European diplomacy. Because it was involved at the moment in the Crimean War, the Porte could ill afford to antagonize England and thus did not accord the project the necessary ratification.

In 1856 an international commission of engineers surveyed the land and reported on the proposal, setting an estimate of £6,000,000 as a maximum cost. In a detailed concession given to the *Compagnie Universelle du Canal Maritime de Suez*, three types of shares of stock were authorized. Preference shares, which enjoyed fifteen percent of the net profits of the company, went to Said for granting the concession and for furnishing the labor required to dig the canal. Founder shares, which received ten percent of the net profits, were held by the organizers or were given without cost to influential personages. And 400,000 ordinary shares sold for 500 francs each.

Until 1858 Napoleon III seemed unconcerned, but when the subscription lists were opened for the ordinary shares, his views changed. It is believed that de Lesseps gave a substantial number of founder shares to influential members of his court, if not to the emperor and empress themselves. When in November, 1858 the books were closed, 207,111 shares had been bought in France, and 96,517 in Egypt (92,136 by Said). Some 85,500 shares reserved for nationals of England, Russia, Austria, and the United States remained unsold. Although Said warned that construction of the canal should not begin until approved in Istanbul, digging started in April, 1859. The British protested vigorously over the use of forced labor and were able to keep the sultan from ratifying the concession. Notwithstanding the fact that Said took up the balance of unsubscribed shares, little work had been accomplished when Said died in 1863 and Ismail, Ibrahim's oldest living son, became governor.

Ismail was thirty-three years old. He had been educated in Paris at the *École d'État-Major* and had gone for Said on missions to Turkey,

France, and the Vatican. At his accession the American Civil War had inflated prices of Egyptian cotton to such an extent that the crop in 1863 sold for £25,000,000 instead of the normal £5,000,000, giving Ismail a revenue of unaccustomed proportions. Ismail accepted the commitments concerning the canal, and by 1866 the British no longer opposed it. Under pressure from Napoleon III the Porte gave its authorization. Ismail paid an indemnity for not supplying forced labor and the construction proceeded rapidly. When it was finished in 1869, Ismail spent £1,000,000 on the opening ceremonies. The Empress Eugénie was the guest of honor among six thousand guests including the Emperor of Austria and the Crown Prince of Prussia.

For the first several years the canal operated at a loss, and the company was perilously close to bankruptcy. However, traffic increased and profits showed continuously after 1875. Ismail and Egypt, nevertheless, did not benefit from it. The cost of the canal to Said and Ismail was estimated at £11,500,000, for which Egypt received no return. To a considerable extent this was because Ismail was a spendthrift and impractical.

From the beginning two questions confronted the company. The original concession authorized a charge of ten francs a ton for passage. To settle how a ship's tonnage should be calculated an international conference was held in 1873 at Istanbul. The conference also set a higher schedule of rates until traffic and profits should warrant a reduction. Increasing commerce gradually reduced the dues, and by 1906 the charge per ton was only 7¾ francs. The concession also stipulated that the canal would be open, without any preferential treatment, to merchant vessels of every flag. During the Egyptian crisis of 1881 and 1882 the British closed the canal for four days, and navigation by warships was debated. A conference in Istanbul in 1888 attended by Austria, France, Germany, Great Britain, Italy, the Netherlands, Russia, Spain, and Turkey agreed to the Constantinople Convention, which declared the canal should "always be free and open, in the time of war as in time of peace, to every vessel of commerce or of war, without distinction of flag." Britain signed with reservations which she did not relinquish until 1904.

ISMAIL'S RULE

From the moment of Ismail's accession in 1863 until his deposition in 1879 life at the court in Egypt was sumptuous and money flowed like the waters of the Nile. Ismail showered munificent gifts upon all, and his trips to Europe and Istanbul were lavish in every detail. Presents to the sultan on the order of £1,000,000 and a diamond-encrusted solid gold dinner service were not unusual. Ismail possessed a charming personality which dispelled all opposition; and his use of flattery and urbane suavity earned him the acclaim of Europe. In 1866–67 he visited Istanbul, where through princely gifts he won the title Khedive and recognition of the succession to the Egyptian throne by the law of primogeniture. In 1869 he visited the capitals of Europe, where he was received, entertained, and decorated by the crowned heads of Europe. However, Ismail was rapidly falling into the clutches of unscrupulous moneylenders and European bankers.

EUROPEAN INTERVENTION

At Ismail's accession Egypt had a foreign debt of £3,000,000 and a domestic debt of £4,000,000. Thirteen years later it had a foreign debt of £68,000,000 and a domestic debt of £30,000,000. Of this, nearly thirty-five percent was incurred in the form of discounts and commissions so that the rates were on the "verge of fraudulence." Interest charges mounted to £5,000,000 per annum, half the total annual revenue of the government. Ismail flogged the fellaheen to increase taxes and sought new sources of income for new extravagances. In 1874 Ismail sold his 176,602 ordinary shares of Canal stock to the British government for nearly £4,000,000. (He had previously sold 1040 shares to French capitalists.) But this only delayed the day of reckoning, which came in 1876 when Ismail ceased payment on his bills and debts.

To extricate himself from bankruptcy Ismail conducted a losing battle against European bondholders, bankers, "unofficial" government officials, commissions of inquiry, and consuls general. In a pretense at constitutional government Nubar Pasha was installed as prime minister, Mr. Rivers Wilson as finance minister, and M. de Blignieres as minister of public works. Threats of action on the part of Bismarck in 1879 led England and France to join in obtaining the Porte's deposition of Ismail in favor of his son Tawfik.

On the surface this interference appeared auspicious. Dual controllers were appointed: M. de Blignieres for the French and Major Evelyn Baring for the British. The controllers could attend cabinet meetings, demand information, give advice, and report to their diplomatic representatives in the event advice was ignored. They became the real rulers of Egypt. On the findings of an International Commission of Liquidation (British, French, German, Austrian, and Italian), the Law of Liquidation was enacted, squeezing the debt down to £85,000,000 and reserving £4,500,000 of the annual government income for the budget. All excess income, then estimated at £4,000,000, was to be employed to retire the debt. Unfortunately for the future development of Egypt, expanding revenues resulting from increased productivity and hard work or from inflation would not benefit Egyptians or improve services of the government. Since the controllers were duty bound to guard the revenue and pay off the debt, they could hardly fail to be unpopular with the Egyptians, to whom their regime appeared unduly oppressive.

The Egypt of 1880 was a far cry from the Egypt of 1840. Ismail's reign, because of his love of European ways and even because of his grandiose manners, went a long way toward Europeanizing Alexandria and Cairo and their leading citizens. Ismail loved to say that "Egypt was a part of Europe." Sons were educated in Europe; many Europeans lived in Egypt. Considerable transformation in Egyptian outlook also resulted from the building of railways, telegraph lines, 4500 schools, and a sugar and tobacco industry as well as from the construction of the Suez Canal and the introduction of many European forms in government and society.

Establishment of the mixed courts, however, weakened the government and frequently frustrated its operation. As a part of the Ottoman Empire Egypt was subject to the Capitulatory Treaties with other states, chiefly European. Abused by traders and all foreigners, the treaties practically assured that law cases were settled by diplomatic pressure rather than on a basis of merit or justice. The number (100,-000 in 1875) and the variety of foreign nationals residing in Egypt made cases of one foreigner against another difficult to adjudicate. In 1873, therefore, a conference in Istanbul authorized mixed courts. Judges, Egyptian and foreign, were appointed by the khedive, although foreigners were nominated by participating governments which agreed to recognize judgments of these courts. (Judge Farman of New York was nominated by President Grant and served for many years.) Inaugurated in 1875, the courts had a majority of foreign judges, used French as their language, and employed a code based on French law.

Naturally the Anglo-French Dual Control cut expenditures to the bone. The size of the army was reduced; many officers were retired; civil budgets and personnel were pared. Yet, a sizable number of foreign administrators came in at inordinate salaries. Opposition quickly formed in Egypt. The evolution of society under Ismail brought four parties to the fore: a weak reactionary party led by Riaz Pasha; a vigorous Islamic modernist party developed by Muhammad Abdu; a Constitutional party of wealthy Europeanized Egyptian landowners organized by Sharif Pasha; and an army group composed of pure Egyptians in the lower officer echelons and inspired by Colonel Arabi. Only the reactionary party acquiesced in the foreign Dual Control, which it preferred to any of the other Egyptian groups. The army was the most violent in its opposition, because high-ranking officers were Turks or

Circassians and the Dual Control did not remove these officers to the extent it curbed the rise of native Egyptians.

BRITISH OCCUPATION

When in January, 1882 England and France presented a joint note to the khedive protesting the formation of a constitutional government, the army party gained control of the cabinet. England and France had to occupy the country or give up the Dual Control. Nationalist excesses in Alexandria served as the pretext. A change in the French government, however, altered French policy; and England alone intervened. The English occupied Egypt in July, 1882 to overthrow Arabi and re-establish European control. Alexandria was shelled; the British navy occupied Port Said, Ismailia, and Suez; and in September British troops won the Battle of Tel-al-Kebir and took Cairo. At this point rebellion in Egypt collapsed.

Control of Egypt was now solely a British responsibility; and the British army remained the source of power for many decades. British administration presumed that occupation would be temporary and of short duration. Thus, an attempt was made to return Egypt to her position before the shelling of Alexandria. Arabi Pasha was exiled to Ceylon, and a Legislative Council of thirty members—fourteen nominated by the khedive and sixteen elected—was established. All other financial, judicial, and commercial controls were restored. In 1883 Sir Evelyn Baring returned to Egypt as British Agent and Consul-General. Elevated to the peerage as Lord Cromer in 1892, he ruled Egypt autocratically until his retirement in 1907.

The British rule in Egypt under Lord Cromer and his successors up to the outbreak of World War I was very real. Early in Lord Cromer's regime a policy was formulated whereby Egyptian ministers and governors either followed the advice of the British Agent or forfeited their posts. Several prime ministers served under Cromer: Sharif Pasha, until he refused advice on the Sudan; Nubar Pasha, who held office several times but always quarreled over internal administrative affairs and local government; Riaz Pasha, a strong administrator who resigned over control of the Egyptian courts; and Mustafa Pasha Fahmi, who served the longest continuous period and who was so subservient to the British that promising Egyptians joined societies and political parties whose first principle was nationalistic and anti-British.

In the course of these years Lord Cromer and British advisers and officials determined and administered finances, the army, trade policies, agriculture, communications, irrigation, health, and foreign affairs. Egyptians retained control of local justice, national courts, internal administration, and local police. Education fell between the two and consequently failed to fit into any program. Illiteracy of the masses was hardly touched; yet the number receiving a secondary education without any technical or proficient skill was so far beyond the need that many became dangerously frustrated.

Egyptian finances were straightened out; and the foreign debt, though remaining large, became manageable. Irrigation was improved, and considerable land was subjected to perennial irrigation which greatly increased yields per acre. The Delta Barrage was reconstructed, and the Aswan Dam built. As imports and exports doubled and trebled, national income rose appreciably. The population jumped from 6,800,000 in 1883 to 12,300,000 in 1914. The army demonstrated its improved condition at the Battle of Omdurman in the Sudan in 1898.

In technical and purely administrative services British occupation generally brought improvement. Exceptions could be found, however. An example was the shocking spread of bilharzia among the fellaheen as a result of intensive cotton culture, perennial irrigation, and the increasingly soggy condition of the land of the Delta. In the field of politics and international relations, deterioration was marked. Lord Cromer became more imperious as the years progressed; and his successors, Sir Eldon Gorst in 1907 and Lord Kitchener in 1911, did not improve the situation. Little was done to Egyptianize governmental services, and British were more and more employed at all ranks and levels in the government. Under Lord Kitchener even the quality of British officials declined; for he was unable to brook any differences of opinion from his staff.

The Islamic modernist Muhammad Abdu was modestly nationalistic and quarreled with the excessive Europeanizing influences that surrounded Ismail. Returning from the exile to which he was sent upon the collapse of the Arabi movement in 1882, he became one of the important teachers at al-Azhar University. Aggressive nationalism, common in nineteenth-century Europe, advanced in Egypt under the leadership of Mustafa Kamal and his *Hisb al-Watani* (National Party). Educated in French politics, Kamal was anti-religious and succeeded in keeping the developing nationalism free from religious fanaticism. However, his early death in 1908 permitted his party to fall under the spell of Shaykh Shawish and a low brand of chauvinistic and abusive nationalism.

Sir Eldon Gorst attempted to stem the rising anti-British tide by establishing a more representative legislative council where cabinet ministers could be questioned, but he soon discovered that the council was chiefly interested in preventing government rather than in determining it. In 1910 Butros Ghali, the prime minister, was assassinated by a member of *Tadaman*, a secret terroristic society of a type prevalent among the half-educated and underemployed secondary-school students and graduates. Lord Cromer had tried to quiet these groups by appointing Mustafa Fahmi's nationalist son-in-law, Saad Zaghlul, as minister of education. Kitchener rebuffed Zaghlul by refusing him a simple appointment, but in 1913 found him president of the newly created Legislative Assembly. By 1914 the efficiency of British officials in Egypt could be legitimately questioned, and certainly what skills they possessed had long ago become fully dissipated by the fact that they were not Egyptians. General resistance and non-co-operation should have led British policy makers to realize that a more effective rule could have been maintained by Egyptian personnel. But Lord Kitchener hated politics and politicians and bravely faced a difficult task which he believed could be accomplished only if done under his orders. The problems which the British experienced in the post-World War I period were coming rapidly to the fore even before 1914. Only the outbreak of war and subsequent strong military occupation prevented Egyptian nationalists from openly attacking the British position. Such action was reserved for the time when the war would be over.

THE ANGLO-EGYPTIAN SUDAN

Throughout the nineteenth century the governing forces in Egypt maintained a lively interest in the Sudan. Muhammad Ali sent his expedition into that area in 1820, and in 1842 the sultan recognized him as governor-general of the Sudan. During the middle of the century the chief activities with regard to the Sudan were along the Red Sea and involved conflict with Abyssinia over ports like Massawa. Ismail was Europeanized to the extent of considering Egypt as a participant in the partitioning of Africa, and he devised grandiose schemes of expanding Egypt to the equator and including all of the basin of the White Nile. In 1869 he declared that steps were being taken to end the slave trade in the Sudan and sent a British explorer, Sir Samuel Baker, to govern equatorial Sudan. Baker's successor, Charles Gordon, so reduced the slave trade that Muslims of northern Sudan, for whom the slave trade was a principal preoccupation, came to resent his presence and Egyptian interference.

In 1881 Muhammad Ahmad of Dongola proclaimed himself to be the Mahdi, the religious leader sent to complete the work of the Prophet. When revolt broke out about 150 miles south of Khartoum in the province of Kordofan, affairs in Egypt were so chaotic and finances so desperate that the Sudan was left to herself. However, in 1883 Khedive Tawfik sent Colonel Hicks to head the Egyptian army in the

Sudan. He and his rabble conscript army were cut to pieces by the forces of the Mahdi, and Sir Evelyn Baring upon his arrival in Egypt insisted upon complete withdrawal from the Sudan, largely for financial reasons. Gordon was then sent in 1884 to arrange for the evacuation of Khartoum, but he delayed the operation and received almost no direct aid from Cairo. In 1885 Khartoum fell to the Mahdi, and Gordon and his men were slain.

For the following decade the Sudan was abandoned to the Mahdi, and Wadi Halfa became the frontier post of Egypt. In the 1890's the Italian war in Eritrea and French pressure upon Abyssinia led the British to consider the reconquest of the Sudan. Sir Herbert Kitchener, commander-in-chief of the Egyptian army, took Dongola in 1896. Two years later with the support of some Indian troops, two English brigades, a cavalry regiment, and an artillery battery he won the famous Battle of Omdurman, completely routing the Mahdi's forces. In 1899 the Sudan Convention was pronounced in Cairo, establishing what soon came to be known as the Anglo-Egyptian Sudan. Theoretically it was a Condominium, but the Egyptian voice in ruling the Sudan remained only nominal. Military and civil power was vested in a governor-general chosen by the British. Egyptian law was not valid in the Sudan, nor were the mixed tribunals extended there. Import duties were not levied on goods coming from Egypt, and the slave trade was prohibited. Firearms and spirituous liquors were outlawed following the Brussels Act of 1890, which governed the traffic of such items in certain parts of Africa. Consular agents of other powers could be accredited in the Sudan only upon the consent of the British government. Although the British and Egyptian flags were flown side by side over all public buildings, no one ever doubted what power ruled the Sudan.

REFERENCES: Chapter 22

Readings for this chapter are also found in Chapters 7, 13, 19, 20, and 21.

C. C. Adams, *Islam and Modernism in Egypt:* Oxford University Press, London, 1933. An analysis of one of the great problems of Egypt.

Osman Amin, *Muhammad 'Abduh* (C. Wendell, trans.): American Council of Learned Societies, Washington, 1953. A short biography of the great reformer.

Wilfrid S. Blunt, *Secret History of the English Occupation of Egypt*: T. F. Unwin, London, 1907. Not really secret, but contemporary!

Wendell Cleland, *The Population Problem in Egypt: A Study of Population Trends and Conditions*: Science Press, Lancaster, 1936. An analysis of births and deaths over thirty years and an inquiry into the Malthusian theory as it pertains to Egypt.

Evelyn Baring Cromer, *Modern Egypt*, 2 vols.: Macmillan, London, 1908. The account of his rule of Egypt.

Henry Dodwell, *The Founder of Modern Egypt: A Study of Muhammad 'Ali*: Cambridge University Press, Cambridge, 1931. Lacks much that has been presented by recent scholarship, but still serves as a good summary.

Halford L. Hoskins, *British Routes to India*: Longmans, Green, New York, 1928. A masterful study of the Middle East from the mid-eighteenth century to the twentieth century, particularly as it related to European interests.

E. W. Lane, *Manners and Customs of the Modern Egyptians*: E. P. Dutton, New York, 1923. A significant work.

George Ambrose L. Lloyd, *Egypt Since Cromer*, 2 vols.: Macmillan, London, 1933–1934.

John Marlowe, *A History of Modern Egypt and Anglo-Egyptian Relations, 1800–1956:* Archon, Hamden, Conn., 1965. A useful survey.

Vernon J. Puryear, *England, Russia and the Straits Question, 1844–1856:* University of California Press, Berkeley, 1931. A thorough study.

——, *International Economics and Diplomacy in the Near East, 1834–1853:* Stanford University Press, Stanford, 1935. The relationship of these topics is discussed with a wealth of material.

Frederick S. Rodkey, *Turco-Egyptian Question, 1832–41:* University of Illinois, Urbana, 1924. A diplomatic account.

Arthur E. P. Brome Weigall, *A History of Events in Egypt from 1798 to 1914:* W. Blackwood & Sons, London, 1915. Still a useful outline.

George Young, *Egypt:* Charles Scribner's Sons, New York, 1927. A valuable survey.

❧❧ CHAPTER 23 ❧❧

European Ambitions and Diplomacy in the Middle East

EUROPEAN INTERESTS

Throughout the nineteenth century Russia, England, Austria, and France maintained a continuing interest in affairs of the Ottoman Empire. Toward the end of the century Germany joined them to make a fifth major European power involved in imperialism in the Middle East.

Dynastic aggrandizement at the expense of the Ottomans motivated Austrian and Russian conquests in the eighteenth century. The Hapsburgs desired Hungary, Transylvania, Dalmatia, and Serbia; and at the turn of the century they would have pushed southward in the Balkans, had not the Napoleonic wars absorbed their full strength. Metternich recognized the importance of Istanbul and the weakness of the Ottoman Empire, but advocated the preservation of its integrity, since Austria was unable to expect a major portion from any partition scheme. He opposed rescuing the Greeks for fear that even a modicum of Greek independence would redound in more freedom for Serbs and other national groups within the Austrian Empire. Austria was also apprehensive lest Russia gain advantages in the Balkans, control Istanbul and the Straits, and flank Austria dangerously from the south.

France thought of the Ottoman Empire in terms of commerce, imperial geopolitical strategy, diplomacy, military and naval alliances, culture, and tradition. The merchants of Marseilles, who were engrossed in trade in every port of the Levant, were most instrumental in obtaining the great Treaty of Capitulations from the Porte in 1740.

France was interested in empire and commerce in India and farther Asia in addition to her interests in North Africa and the Mediterranean. The land mass of the Middle East lay astride the routes to the Orient. Since England rivaled France in the East, whichever power gained secure access to Middle Eastern routes could threaten and block the communications of the other. For this reason Muhammad Ali of Egypt appeared to be an excellent ally, and the French cultivated him and his successors assiduously.

In the realm of diplomacy the French endeavored to sway the Porte toward a course amicable to France and tried to get the sultan to view international affairs through the eyes and words of the French ambassador. The heroic age of the Crusades and the mighty deeds of their ancestors in the Levant and the Holy Land gave most Frenchmen a historic interest in the Middle East. The French king was still His Most Christian Majesty and possessed the right to defend the Holy Places. Broadly interpreted, this right meant the privilege of interfering in all events of the Middle East. As a kind of corollary to these interests, Frenchmen believed fervently that penetration of their culture and use of their language in the Middle East would indissolubly tie the people to French views and create a sympathetic and understanding bond of everlasting friendship.

British interest in the Middle East began during the reign of Elizabeth I, but remained almost exclusively commercial until the Napoleonic era. In the nineteenth century, especially after the Treaty of Adrianople (Edirne), a changing emphasis in trade and empire and a shifting European balance of power won over Britain to the maintenance of Turkey as a means of blocking Russian egress into the Mediterranean. This policy impelled England to oppose partition of the Ottoman Empire and to pursue a positive course to strengthen the sultan's government. Moreover, profitable markets in the Middle East stimulated the British to cultivate the friendship of the Turks. Sir Stratford Canning—later Viscount de Redcliffe—combined these varied British interests into a unified approach to the Porte. His words and instructions had a statesmanlike quality, respected and esteemed by the Turks. The populace of Istanbul referred to him as "The Great Ambassador."

Russia proved the most consistent and persistent enemy of the Ottoman Empire in the eighteenth and nineteenth centuries. The tsars and tsarinas dreamed of gaining Istanbul and re-establishing a Christian empire in the city of Constantine. Joined to this ambition was belief that control of navigation through the Straits for commerce and war was an absolute necessity to complete the full sovereignty of Russia. Means to these ends, but eventually ends in themselves, were: interests in the Holy Land; concern over the welfare, security, and friendship of all Christians in the Ottoman Empire; and creation of friendly Christian satellite states in the Balkans and the Caucasus.

Although war and peace recurred intermittently between Russia and the Ottoman Empire, the first notable landmark pointing to the broad characteristics of their relationship in the nineteenth century was fixed by the famous Treaty of Kuchuk Kainarji of 1774. A number of subsequent treaties concluded between the two states—Ainali Kavak in 1779, Jassy in 1792, Istanbul in 1798 and in 1805, Bucharest in 1812, and Akkerman in 1826—confirmed the concessions granted by the Porte but without greatly augmenting them. The Treaty of Adrianople, however, *date* ? altered the *status quo*. It gave Russia an increased role in the Balkans and served definite notice to the European powers that Russian policy might not be averse to an immediate dissolution of the Ottoman Empire. But the dangers for Russia in such a policy alarmed Count Nesselrode and Nicholas I, who advocated the presence of a weak Turkish neighbor as a safer course. Partition would mean certain prizes for England and France in the Middle East, a development that could only be hostile to Russian interests.

Nicholas, therefore, accepted in 1833 the invitation to protect the Ottoman Empire against attack by Muhammad Ali and sent Count Orloff with a fleet and marines to the Bosphorus to defend the helpless Mahmud. Orloff was a superb diplomat, and after thwarting Muhammad Ali but before the armed forces departed he obtained the famous Treaty of Hunkiar Iskelesi. Important territorial concessions might have been wrung from Mahmud at this time; possibly even a protectorate could have been established. But Nicholas did not presume that Russia was strong enough to face the certain hostility of England, France, and Austria to such a unilateral action. Hence, he preferred a weak independent Ottoman Empire.

Diplomats and political leaders immediately sensed the gravity of Hunkiar Iskelesi. Even with one secret clause, it was a simple short treaty proclaiming a defensive alliance between the two states and promising aid to each other in case of need. In particular, Turkey declared anew the "ancient rule of the Ottoman Empire" and the closing of the Straits to all warships. Its chief import, however, lay in its affirmation of friendship, which indicated the direction in which the weathervane of Ottoman diplomacy turned.

COMMERCE AND TRADE

Lord Ponsonby, British ambassador, set about immediately to redress the balance and win the favor of the Porte, a task in which his success was demonstrated in 1838 by the signing of the important and advantageous Commercial Convention of Balta Liman, a significant blow to Russian favoritism. British traders were permitted to import goods upon payment of five percent *ad valorem* duty; upon the export of Turkish goods a duty of twelve percent was charged. Furthermore, monopolistic practices were abolished on goods exported from the empire. This provision specifically included Egypt. The most important result of the arrangement was the ability, henceforth, of British merchants to carry on foreign trade at the same rates as applied to Ottoman nationals. Since British firms had a wider organization and were not subject to Ottoman taxation, the Convention soon proved to be a blow to Turkish traders.

Again, articles of the Balta Liman Convention did not in themselves bestow upon Great Britain any marked position in the Middle East. France, the Netherlands, and other nations were accorded identical treatment before the year was out. In the following years, however, when Muhammad Ali reasserted his position against the sultan, the British were instrumental in removing the unilateral approach to the Straits question as contained in Hunkiar Iskelesi. They substituted the concerted five-power settlement of the Straits and Middle Eastern problems contained in the London Conventions of 1840 and 1841. The earlier of these dealt with the affairs of Muhammad Ali, Syria, and Egypt. Even that Convention, however, contained articles emphasizing that any occupation within the Straits by foreign armed forces to protect the sultan from Muhammad Ali must be only temporary and "not derogate in any degree from the ancient rule of the Ottoman Empire."

The following year the Convention among Great Britain, Austria, France, Prussia, Russia, and Turkey reaffirmed the ancient rule, mentioning the Bosphorus as well as the Dardanelles. Each European signatory was thus committed to defend the sultan's sovereignty over the Straits and to prohibit warships from entering those waters while the sultan was at peace. With the expiration of Hunkiar Iskelesi that autumn no European state had any special privilege which others did not possess. Europe recognized that the Treaties of Kuchuk Kainarji, Akkerman, and Adrianople were still valid and that Russia enjoyed specified rights in the Balkans and among certain Christian groups throughout the empire. But, in the Straits and at the Porte none had a treaty advantage or position of favor over another.

The Convention of Balta Liman marked a definite upsurge in commerce between Turkey and western Europe. After 1846 and the repeal of the corn laws in England, the grain trade with the Ottoman Empire and especially with the Danubian provinces rose to unprecedented heights. Within a few years Britain was obtaining as much grain from Turkey as she was from Russia (a development which should not be ignored in considering the factors leading to the Crimean War). In addition to grain, general trade between Turkey and England increased. Opium, raisins, currants, figs, olive oil, silk, mohair, wool, cotton, sheep, carpets, and a variety of goods were bought by British merchants in Istanbul, Izmir, Beirut, Alexandria, Aleppo, Trabzon, Salonika, and many lesser markets. Britain sold textiles and manufactured goods in increasing volume as her purchases mounted. In 1827 British exports to the Ottoman Empire were about £500,000; by 1845 they had jumped to £2,210,000; in 1849 they were £2,400,000. British imports from the Middle East were in this period nearly as great as her exports and were expanding no less rapidly.

The trade of France, the Netherlands, Prussia, and Austria in the Middle East also developed, though not as markedly as that of Britain. Marseilles remained an important trading city with the Levant, and Austrian trade with the Balkan provinces improved as transport developed along the Danube. Growing industrial areas in Western Europe found in the Middle East a source of foodstuffs and raw materials that could be obtained in exchange for the products of the new machines of the West. The trade, however, seriously affected handicraft industries in the Middle East, largely substituting machine-made textiles of Western Europe for local homespun cloth. Many an Eastern village suddenly experienced an economic crisis from which it never recovered.

Use of machines and new types of power made it possible for the West to forge far ahead of the Middle East in matters of material welfare and wealth; and the imbalance of power and prestige of Western industrialized states over the agricultural Middle Eastern areas became more preponderant with each decade. The Ottoman Empire speedily developed into an economic colony of Western Europe. The privileges known as Capitulations hastened the process and fastened the bonds more securely.

THE CAPITULATIONS

Originally given to foreign merchants in the fifteenth century in order to encourage commerce with Christian states, the Capitulations indicated procedures, laws, regulations, and responsibilities of nationals of a state residing and trading in the Ottoman Empire. With great increases in trade in the nineteenth century and shifting power relationships, the Capitulations became exceedingly onerous for Turkey. With the support of their governments foreigners took advantage of every loosely worded phrase, and all significant trade within the Ottoman Empire devolved into foreign hands. Any Turkish subject who wished to enter the field sought means by which he could become a foreigner in his own country. This step was done by securing from a consul or ambassador, for a consideration, a document called a *barat*, which conferred upon the holder the rights of a national of that country as expressed in the capitulatory treaty. Since *barats* were frowned upon in the nineteenth century, outright sale of citizenship and passports was practiced openly by the unscrupulous and winked at by the punctilious ambassadors. Consequently, in Ottoman ports Greeks, Jews, Armenians, and Levantines were often nationals of some European state even though they or any of their ancestors had never set foot on their "native land." Furthermore, their children and their children's descendants, though born within the Ottoman Empire, retained foreign citizenship.

Three facets of the Capitulations were particularly important: law, taxes, and tariffs. Foreigners had the right to be tried in their own consular courts, where laws of their own country prevailed. Since Turkish government officials frequently relied upon the advice of powerful European ambassadors, consuls could usually have criminal cases against their nationals dropped. No foreigner could be arrested or held by Turkish police, unless an official from his consulate was present. This regulation meant that most misdemeanors by foreigners were ignored or glossed over by the Turkish authorities to avoid difficulties, arguments, and awkward situations.

Foreigners were exempt from local taxes and were thus able to conduct local business with less interference from the government and at a lower cost than Turkish subjects. The sultan found it impractical to increase many business taxes, since the result was only deleterious to Turkish nationals.

Important export tariffs were established by the Capitulations and could not be changed except by consent of each party in a specific treaty. Since each treaty also contained a "most favored nation" clause, it was necessary to change all treaties in concert to make any successful change at all: to get all to agree was virtually impossible. Because Turkey was not strong enough to defy all Powers at once and denounce all Treaties simultaneously, tariffs in Turkey in the nineteenth century moved only in the direction of free trade. Such a situation made possible the commercial exploitation of the weak Middle East by the powerful Western nations. No relief could be expected until the Capitulations were abrogated; and to this the Powers would not give their consent because of the benefits their nationals derived with respect to residence, law, and taxes, as well as to trade.

RELIGIOUS ISSUES

Into this picture of the Capitulations the powers injected an additional feature: religion. Oddly enough, the reasons for many of the so-called Capitulatory articles were religious. Mehmed II, after conquering Constantinople, recognized the native Orthodox Greek religious community and soon thereafter the Armenian and Jewish communities as special legal entities, called *millets*. In a parallel way, various foreign national communities such as Venetians, Florentines, Genoese, and French, each under a designated representative, were recognized by the Capitulations as "national *millets*." Frequently a treaty, like the French treaty of 1740, permitted a foreign community to adopt other nationals whose governments possessed no treaty with the Porte.

The most extraordinary extension came with assertions in the French treaty of 1740 and the Treaty of Kuchuk Kainarji in 1774 that Roman Catholics were under the protection of the French and Orthodox Christians under the aegis of the tsar. In subsequent negotiations the Porte pressed for its understanding that only the respective clergy were included, but France and Russia held that the entire communities were embraced. The extension of foreign interest, therefore, had a widening concern in Ottoman domestic affairs; and, coupled with the ancient *millet* system, it led to an identification of creed with nationality, making nationalism synonymous with religion.

Prior to the Treaty of Adrianople and the recognition of Greek independence there were still only three *millets* in the Ottoman Empire. But by 1914 there were seventeen, and almost all enjoyed the sponsorship of a foreign government. Not entirely responsible for this movement but certainly encouraging it were the foreign missionaries and Bible societies. Christian missionaries from Europe labored in the Middle East for many centuries; and Roman Catholic churches, convents, hospices, and missions were well established in the Levant before the nineteenth century. The great drive in the Middle East, however, began during the Napoleonic wars and carried through to the present. Russian, Polish, Austrian, Prussian and German, Danish, Dutch, French, Italian, British, Canadian, and American mission groups of many denominations established schools, churches, hospitals, printing presses, orphanages, and a variety of other service groups to carry the Christian message and Western concepts of society to Middle Eastern peoples. Completely unsuccessful in converting Muslims, they concentrated their efforts upon the indigenous Christian groups. With respect to the Muslims they philosophized that they might Christianize them by first Westernizing them.

Individual missionaries and home societies supporting them were entirely sincere in their goals and made many noble sacrifices in their work. Their governments, however, often subsidized them for ulterior aims and gave direction to their work for political ends. Russia and England, for instance, competed for the Armenians, and neither wished to see American missionaries enter the field. Missionaries always were regarded as an advance guard in the process of imperialism—political and economic—and the *millet* system lent itself wonderfully to the business of expanding a national influence.

The European powers quarreled and competed for the minds and souls of the Christian population of the Middle East and the expected advantages of religious and missionary patronage. Through the efforts of Sir Stratford Protestants in the Ottoman Empire were recognized as a *millet* in 1850. This move was certainly warranted; yet it could hardly do other than favor British interests, since the French had the Roman Catholics and Russia the Orthodox.

The greatest rivalry occurred in the Holy Land between the Russians and the French. Since medieval times Latin monks and clerics attended the shrines and Holy Places in Bethlehem, Jerusalem, and Nazareth. The Capitulatory Treaty of 1740 confirmed the right of the French government to protect these churchmen and accorded them certain privileges, one of which was possession of the key to the main door of the Church of the Nativity in Bethlehem. Since almost every treaty or convention signed by the Porte with any European state contained equal recognition, the true legal situation was entirely confused by the middle of the nineteenth century.

Orthodox churchmen dated their rights to control and protect the Holy Sepulchre from the seventeenth century. They protested against the French rights, claiming that they were false and had been wrung from the sultan when Orthodox support had been weak. Whatever the rights may have been, few Latin pilgrims visited the Holy Land in the eighteenth and nineteenth centuries, whereas crowds of Orthodox traveled thousands of miles to pray at the Holy Sepulchre or the Grotto of the Holy Manger in Bethlehem. Russian pilgrims, Russian monks, and generous monetary gifts from the Russian tsar and his government descended upon Palestine. Only a few Frenchmen evinced any interest, and most of these were moved by romanticism and visited Jerusalem to paint pictures or write poetry. Latin privileges, therefore, lapsed through neglect and default. In 1808 the Church of the Holy Sepulchre was ruined by fire. The Orthodox under the direction of the patriarch of Istanbul rebuilt it, levying a tax on all Orthodox Christians in the Ottoman Empire for the purpose. Even Mahmud II made a generous donation.

Beginning about 1840, there was a rising crescendo in France over the Holy Land and the position of the Latin Church therein. Nurtured by the ultramontanists, Latins complained that Greeks had stolen a silver star engraved with the arms of France and infixed over the Holy

Manger, protested that Latins were permitted to enter only by a side door, and alleged that Latins were discriminated against in all Holy Places. In 1842 when the cupola of the Church of the Holy Sepulchre needed repair, a great commotion arose over which sect should enjoy that privilege. Actual fighting broke out in 1847, and at Christmastime in Bethlehem Latin and Greek monks attacked each other with candlesticks and crosses at the Church of the Nativity. The pasha of Jerusalem posted sixty soldiers inside the Church of the Holy Sepulchre to prevent disorders and bloodshed. The Greek patriarch of Jerusalem usually resided in Istanbul; but in 1843 the newly elected Cyril, who had been Bishop of Lydda and the Russian candidate, chose to live in Jerusalem, where he received callers and entertained with dignity and great splendor. Likewise, Pope Pius IX in 1847 ordered the Latin patriarch of Jerusalem, who for centuries never resided in his See, to live there and combat the influence and prestige of the Orthodox.

THE CRIMEAN WAR

With the election of Louis Napoleon as president of France and then his *coup d'état* in 1852, rivalry between Russia and France at the Golden Horn and in the Holy Land became acute. Each insisted upon historic rights over the Holy Places; and in the process Nicholas insulted Napoleon by addressing him as *bon ami* instead of *mon frère*. The Porte confounded the issue by a note to the French acceding to their demands and by a royal decree given to the patriarch in Istanbul which affirmed that no changes would be made. It then stood as a matter of personal and national honor and a question of religion upon which compromise was difficult. Since the royal decree was never publicly read and thus never fully legal, Russians felt that they had been duped by the sultan and the French. Consequently, it was the tsar who took the initial overt action.

Prince Menşikov arrived at the Porte in 1853 with explicit instructions to deliver Russia's demands. As drawn up by Nesselrode, points to be insisted upon were: full restoration and public recognition of Orthodox privileges and prerogatives in the Holy Land; Russian right to repair the cupola of the Church of the Holy Sepulchre (which meant the construction of a Russian-type bulbous dome which Latins would never countenance); special treaty or convention with Russia again guaranteeing for an indefinite future full privileges for all Orthodox Christians in the empire and reacknowledging the tsar's obligations to protect them as recorded in previous decrees and treaties (Kuchuk Kainarji, Jassy, and Adrianople); rejection of French ascendancy and restriction of other Christian communities that worked to damage Russian influence; and conclusion of a secret defensive alliance with Russia in case the sultan hesitated over other points for fear of French displeasure and aggression.

For weeks, Mensikov intrigued, threatened, bullied, and bribed to obtain the Russian program. Settlement was reached on the first two items. Both Orthodox and Latins received concessions at the Holy Places. And the sultan would repair the Church of the Holy Sepulchre, following the plans of its original construction. But ultimatums, Mensikov's threatened departures, and mobilization along the Pruth did not intimidate the sultan's government. Gestures were made to placate Mensikov, but Abdul Mejid refused to accede to the demands regarding protection of Orthodox Christians. To do so was in the view of the imperial divan tantamount to giving Russia the right to govern ten or twelve million inhabitants of the Ottoman Empire.

Undoubtedly, the Porte was encouraged in this stand by the known attitude of Napoleon and by the confidence held for the British ambassador Lord Stratford de Redcliffe, who was reappointed to his post and returned early in 1853. His appearance in the midst of the crisis and his revelation to Abdul Mejid that the British cabinet had authorized him to call up the British fleet from Malta stiffened Turkish resistance. But accusations hurled by authors and statesmen at that time and ever since that Lord Stratford de Redcliffe desired and engineered the outbreak of the Crimean War cannot be substantiated.

Nicholas ordered the crossing of the Pruth and occupation of the Danubian provinces. The British and French sent their Mediterranean squadrons to Besika Bay, just outside the Dardanelles. Still there were no declarations and no intention of war. The Porte sent a note to European diplomats convening at Vienna, stressing the sultan's peaceful sentiments. He also forwarded copies of recent decrees granting anew in perpetuity the ancient privileges to Orthodox Christians. Turkish feelings now ran high; and this note was regarded as the final appeasement. At Vienna, however, the Powers substituted their own version of a settlement, which stated that France and Russia would guarantee the *status quo* regarding Christians in the Ottoman Empire. Stiffened and excited by the recent arrival of a large Egyptian fleet at the Golden Horn, the Turks rejected the Vienna Note. Meanwhile the war party in Istanbul fanned the emotions of the populace by calling for the ousting of the Russians from Moldavia. Thereafter, events moved rapidly, and Lord Stratford de Redcliffe was unable to prevent a Turkish declaration of war.

Nevertheless, Europe and the leading statesmen did not want war. Although Nicholas pledged Russia would not interfere in Ottoman in-

ternal affairs, the British cabinet instructed Stratford to acquiesce to
French insistence on bringing the fleets to the Bosphorus, in part because the autumn gales made Besika Bay an impossible anchorage.
Stratford with supreme effort obtained a promise from the Ottoman
council of ministers to abstain from any hostile act for two weeks. Unknowingly, however, Omar Pasha attacked the Russians on the Danube,
and war began. Inconsequential Turkish successes were obtained on
the Danube and in the Caucasus; but real victory was won by the Russians when the Turkish navy was destroyed off Sinop on the Black Sea
coast. Nicholas was satisfied; but the British and French governments
sent their combined fleets into the Black Sea to inform Nicholas that
all Russian ships must withdraw to the harbor at Sevastopol. This was
more than Russian honor could accept, and the British and French ambassadors in St. Petersburg were handed their passports.

No European power was prepared to participate in, much less to allow, the partition of the Ottoman Empire. Russia and England had an
entente to that effect ever since Nicholas's verbal agreement with Lord
Aberdeen in 1844. Russia, however, blundered into a difficult position
over the religious controversy. Since neither Nicholas nor Nesselrode
ever bothered to read the Treaty of Kuchuk Kainarji, they never understood how much they were demanding of the Porte. Not mollified, Russia followed her time-honored procedure of occupying the Danubian
provinces, a step which sent the British and French fleets to the Bosphorus to ensure the security of Turkey. In the spring of 1854 Austria
and Prussia joined in the concert against Russia by requesting assurances of the integrity of Turkey. When Austria mobilized her forces, the
tsar's army retired behind the Pruth; Nicholas was not prepared to face
all Europe, and war should have terminated then. Disturbances in
Serbia were quelled, and British and French troops occupied Athens to
"put some sense in the heads of King Otto and his Queen" and force
the Greeks to abandon their attack upon Turkey. But sentiment in England and France, on the streets and in the governments, was for further
war.

Since a treaty of alliance was already consummated by Britain,
France, and Turkey, the sultan followed suit. There is no need to relate
the episodes of the Crimean War here, as it was a European rather than
a Middle Eastern war. About seven thousand Turkish soldiers, nearly
ten percent of the allied army, fought before Sevastopol. Ottoman monetary debts to English and French bankers mounted as costs mushroomed. Cholera weakened the armies more than did battles, but the
will to fight persisted. Nicholas died in February, 1855; peace overtures
failed; and war continued until the fall of Sevastopol to the allies in

September and the fall of Kars to the Russians in November. Austria suggested peace, which was speedily concluded at Paris in March, 1856 after less than five weeks discussion.

RESULTS OF THE WAR

The Treaty of Paris with two additional Conventions solemnly declared that the Ottoman Empire was a European power. In a separate treaty England, France, and Austria agreed to respect, defend, and guarantee its independence and integrity. Special vassalage status was conferred upon Wallachia and Moldavia; and navigation upon the Danube and Black Sea was to be free and unrestricted under the administration of a commission composed of the signatories. The Black Sea was neutralized and demilitarized; except for small defined coastal police vessels for Russia and Turkey warships were banned. Equally important was European acceptance of a new reform edict already promulgated by Abdul Mejid, guaranteeing many reforms for Christians.

The peace treaty returned the Middle East, broadly speaking, to the *status quo ante bellum*. But the war had profound effects upon the Middle East and its development. Moreover, war brought the Middle East to the attention of a great many Europeans; for the battles and incidents of the Crimean War were discussed in the newspapers more vividly than those of any previous war. For the first time Europe became fully conscious of the Near East, as it was then called; and events there were regarded by the general public as of prime importance.

The modern state of Rumania was born at Paris in 1856. The victors decided that a stronger and more independent rule for the Danubian principalities would serve as a better buffer between Turkey and Russia. Britain feared the breakup of the Ottoman Empire and secured the establishment of an anomalous fiction called the United Principalities of Moldavia and Wallachia. Eventually the natural desire of the two peoples for union was permitted, and in 1866 Rumanian leaders chose young Prince Charles of Hohenzollern as their Prince Carol. Rumania had taken a further step toward independence, and thereafter her development touched only indirectly the course of Middle East affairs.

THE LEBANON

While issues on the Danube were testing the friendship of the recent allies of the Crimean War, a series of bloody events in Syria and Lebanon furnished another pretext for forging the pattern of European intervention in internal problems of the Middle East. After the ejection of Ibrahim from Syria a political vacuum arose in Lebanon, or the Mountain as it was usually called. Since the time of Napoleon Amir Bashir Shehab ruled the Mountain from his palace, Bayt-al-Din, with ruthless calculation. His staunch loyalty to Ibrahim, however, compelled the Porte to replace him in 1840 with an incompetent nephew. Maronites and Druzes soon fell to fighting. European pressure elicited from the sultan in 1843 a pacification: the northern regions of the Mountain were governed by a Maronite, supported by the French; the southern portion was left to the Druzes, who were favored by the British.

An uneasy peace and prosperity reigned for a decade in Lebanon. However, a new and weak governor in the Maronite district, installed in 1854, permitted feudal lords to abuse villagers; and population pressures were felt keenly. In 1857 a kind of social upheaval was effectively crushed; but in 1860 a similar phenomenon in the Druze district, where many of the peasants were Maronites, so roused French anxieties that the Powers, under a protocol, permitted Napoleon to send a force of six thousand to restore order to the Mountain. The Porte, however, had the situation in hand before the French arrived; and a European commission under Lord Dufferin drew up a Statute at Beirut for autonomous rule in Lebanon. Signed by Abdul Mejid in 1861, it provided for an Ottoman Christian governor appointed with consent of the Powers. He was to have full executive power and was to be assisted by a central administrative council composed of members of all important religious groups. Feudal law ended, and a separate police force and judiciary was created. The first governor, Daud Pasha, an Armenian Catholic, proved exceptionally able as a diplomat and administrator; and the rule under the Statute, redrawn in 1864, remained in effect until modified by the French mandate in 1920.

OTTOMAN FINANCES

While better government was being established in the Mountain of Lebanon, the same could not be said for the central government on the Golden Horn. One of its most unfortunate developments, which concerned the Powers and which they both condoned and abetted, was the contracting of foreign loans. Beginning with the Crimean War, the Ottoman government contracted loans to meet extraordinary expenses of the army and navy. The financial structure and tax system were antiquated even before the war; and for years the sultan had borrowed locally to satisfy current expenses. Tax anticipations were, therefore, hopelessly inadequate for a loan of the size needed in 1854. Guaranteed by the Egyptian tribute, a £3,000,000 loan was handled in London at six percent interest with the issue price set at 80. Another loan the next year for £5,000,000 was floated in London at only four percent interest with an issue price of nearly 103, the interest being guaranteed by the British and French governments.

Once the habit was fixed, loans were contracted almost every year, with Istanbul customs duties, tobacco and salt taxes, sheep taxes, and various revenues pledged as security. By 1875 Ottoman foreign debts had risen to £200,000,000 bearing annual charges of £12,000,000. The total revenue of the government stood at £22,000,000. Either bankruptcy or government reorganization was in order, but European moneylenders could not bring themselves to terminate such a golden bonanza. Even in 1874 there was a loan of £40,000,000 issued at 43½!

Although these loans were made chiefly in London and Paris, no idea or intention of annexing the Ottoman Empire to the British or French empire was entertained. Money was seeking investment, and issue prices ran interest rates well over ten percent. As long as confidence could be maintained, bankers had little difficulty in floating bonds; and profits were enormous. When one grand vizir balked at taking a loan, Palmer, a British banker, used his influence to replace him for a more willing borrower. Bankers in Galata, the commercial district of Istanbul, made current loans to the government or discounted its bills at ruinous rates. When a sizable amount accumulated, the debt was consolidated into a bond issue and sold to greedy small investors in England and France with the approval of their embassies and governments. Furthermore, the Russian ambassador encouraged the growing indebtedness, perhaps as a development rushing headlong toward the dissolution of the empire.

The theory of the right of European governments to intervene in Ottoman affairs grew with the series of loans in the 1860's and 1870's. Commissioners were appointed to investigate spending of the funds and financial feasibility of the loans and to supervise the collection of the moneys designated as security for the loans. But there is ample evidence that intervention remained only theoretical. On October 6, 1875 the Ottoman government announced, in face of a large budget deficit, that only half the amounts due on foreign bonds would be paid in cash. The balance was to be met by five-year bonds bearing five percent interest. The end had come.

The growing financial crisis affected every part of the empire. The burden of the foreign debt left the treasury a diminishing sum to meet expenses of government. Officials who went unpaid resorted to corrupt practices, while the government adopted harsher methods of taxation to keep the treasury in funds. Peasants everywhere were squeezed, and provinces stirred with an uneasy patience. The most serious rebellion burst in Bosnia.

BALKAN PROBLEMS

From their mountain retreats descendants of Muslim Slavic *ghazis* of earlier days resisted innovations of a new age. In 1831 they fought

Mahmud's reforms. European disturbances in 1848 and unrest among the Serbs again provoked the Bosnians to rebel. This time they were subdued in 1850 by Omar Pasha, a Croat by birth, who established a new Bosnian capital at Sarajevo. Financial difficulties called for rigid collection of taxes in Bosnia in 1875, even though there was a scanty harvest the previous year. Revolt throughout Herzegovina and other Balkan areas erupted from the stringent measures. Montenegrins and Serbs sympathetically transformed the revolt into an open declaration of war in July, 1876.

Before formal hostilities began, the insurgents tasted considerable success; and pan-Slavs in Russia, Serbia, and Austria were jubilant. Russian Red Cross units appeared in Bosnia, and General Chernayeff of Russia turned up in Serbia as a newspaper correspondent. Austria sent a note to the Porte and then to the Powers, hoping reforms in Bosnia would isolate the revolt and forestall Russian intervention. Failure carried the problem to Berlin in 1876. Bismarck, Andrassy, and Gortchakov, faced with the murder of the French and German consuls in Salonika and riots in Istanbul, proposed an armistice for two months, a commission, relief, and sundry other measures. Upon Britain's refusal of the Berlin Memorandum, Alexander II and Franz Josef discussed at Reichstadt division of Ottoman territories in Europe, should Turkish arms be defeated by the Balkan peoples, as everyone expected.

Disraeli, however, was still the enigma, and the presence of the British fleet at Besika Bay added to the uncertainty about his intentions. At this juncture news of Bulgarian massacres jolted European governments, newspapers, and peoples. The Balkan revolt was spreading to Bulgarian districts; and an irregular militia perpetrated a horrible massacre upon the villagers of Batak, who were preparing to join in the uprising. Perhaps five thousand individuals out of seven thousand in Batak were killed. Reports from newspaper correspondents, describing many shocking incidents, appeared in London papers. Disraeli, without any official conformation, set them aside as "coffeehouse babble." When reports were verified by the British Embassy and by Schuyler of the American Legation, who went into the area upon the insistence of Dr. Washburn of Robert College, Gladstone and the Liberal opposition took Disraeli severely to task. For the next two years the Eastern Question was subjected to the most partisan politics witnessed in England in many decades. The controversy seemed to preclude any possibility of British objectivity on the subject.

Because of the high emotion aroused in British politics by the Bulgarian atrocities, Russia and Austria considered the moment propitious for a change in the Balkan *status quo* and perhaps for a fulfillment of their Reichstadt Agreement. The Porte still declined the proffered armistice; and Turkish armies defeated the Serbs, especially when the latter were led by Russians. Annihilation of Serbia was imminent. Serbia asked the Powers to intervene, and Russia gave the Porte forty-eight hours to arrange an armistice. When this was granted, a conference of the Powers met upon British suggestion to discuss peace between Serbia and the Porte and to review the future of European Turkey. A distinguished assemblage of statesmen convened at Istanbul two days before Christmas, 1876. Lord Salisbury, secretary of state for India, represented England and followed the instructions of Beaconsfield (Disraeli had accepted an earldom) and Lord Derby, advocating the *status quo* in Serbia and Montenegro, similar regimes for Bosnia and Herzegovina, a reorganization in Bulgaria, and general reform everywhere. But Sir Henry Elliot, British ambassador at the Porte, encouraged Midhat Pasha, the grand vizir, to resist by assuring him that public sentiment in England would never permit the Russian will to be imposed upon Turkey.

The Constantinople Conference, as Europe termed it, was rudely shocked on its opening day by the sultan's proclamation of a full-drawn Constitution, providing for a bicameral legislature, a responsible cabinet, freedom of the press, compulsory education, and a reformed judiciary. Midhat Pasha and Sir Henry Elliot had been discussing the Constitution for more than a year, and this moment was regarded as most appropriate for its announcement. With a Constitution in hand and the friendship of the British, the Porte refused to accede to the Powers, and the conference broke up in January, 1877. Peace was signed directly between Serbia and Turkey in February upon the basis of the *status quo*, and the Powers signed in London a puerile protocol stating they would watch the enactment of proposed Turkish reforms and act in concert for the protection of Balkan Christians.

RUSSO-TURKISH WAR

Russia had several hundred thousand men mobilized along the Pruth. Either she would obtain a firmer promise for the Balkans and Turkish demobilization or war would follow. Russian demobilization without diplomatic success would be humiliating, and private conversations with Beaconsfield caused Russians to believe he would not object to a small Russo-Turkish war which did not threaten Istanbul and the Straits. At first, Turkish resistance softened, since Sir Henry Elliot's recall was interpreted as a repudiation of his Turkophil views. Elliot, however, was replaced by Sir Henry Layard of Nineveh fame, who much earlier had been confidential agent and "outrider" for the great Lord Stratford de Redcliffe; and the Porte quickly regained its aplomb and hardihood toward Russian demands. Russia declared war on April 24, 1877.

Russia believed she had squared herself with Austria and Germany and reasoned from Beaconsfield's public utterances that Britain would protest only if the Straits were threatened. Bismarck rightly opined that Russia would find Turkey tougher than supposed. No one expected the war to last very long, because neither contestant had any ready cash and loans did not materialize. The Turkish navy dominated the Black Sea. But Rumania deserted Turkey, declared her full independence, and aided Russia. Crossing Rumania, the Russians passed the Danube and appeared to be on their way to Edirne and Istanbul. Then Osman Pasha dug in near Plevna in Bulgaria, resisting the Russian siege from July until December. Meanwhile, Ottoman arms were defeated at Kars by a Russian general, in Herzegovina by the Montenegrins, and at Nish by the Serbs. Turkey threw herself upon the mercy of the European concert. Russia, Rumania, Serbia, and Montenegro, however, continued the war, occupying Edirne on January 20, 1878. Muslims fled before the advancing armies since cossacks and Balkan armies were as brutal in their atrocities as Turkish irregulars had been at Batak.

The Russian lines approached Istanbul, and Grand Duke Nicholas placed his headquarters at the village of Yeshilköy (San Stefano), only ten miles from the Turkish capital. Part of the British fleet was ordered up from Besika Bay to Istanbul and anchored off Buyuk Ada (Principo). Excitement ran high and London music halls rang with the song:

> *We don't want to fight:*
> *But, by jingo, if we do,*
> *We've got the men, we've got the ships,*
> *And, we've got the money too.*

Sultan Abdul Hamid begged the British to withdraw their fleet to Besika Bay, since the Russians threatened to counter by an entry into Istanbul. After the fleet left, the Treaty of San Stefano was signed on March 3, 1878, recognizing the independence of Montenegro, Serbia, and Rumania, each of which received considerable territory at Ottoman expense. Bosnia and Herzegovina obtained autonomous rule; and Russia acquired Batum, Kars, and eastern Anatolia up to Trabzon and Erzerum. Bulgaria was created as a large self-governing Christian principality from the Aegean to the Black Sea and westward to Albania, including Edirne but not Salonika. As a final blow 300,000,000 roubles (roughly £30,000,000) was set as an indemnity for Turkey to pay to Russia.

THE CONGRESS OF BERLIN

Almost before the ink dried, objections arose. Rumania and Serbia felt slighted, and Austria was apparently ignored. However, the creation of "Big Bulgaria" produced a storm. Greece, Serbia, Rumania, and Montenegro protested, and representatives of Albanian groups petitioned to be heard. British and Austrian opposition demanded a settlement of the Eastern Question by the concert of Europe. At Berlin there gathered on June 13, 1878 a galaxy of statesmen, foreign ministers, and diplomatic stars such as had not met since the Congress of Vienna. Bismarck, Beaconsfield, Salisbury, Gortchakov, Shuvalov, Andrassy, Waddington, Corti, and many lesser lights vied for personal prestige and popularity while advancing the interests of his own particular state. The main policy, however, was settled between Shuvalov and Salisbury in London in May, and only the details remained. A month later the Treaty was signed. At the same time the Anglo-Turkish Convention of June 4, 1878, ceding the administration of Cyprus to Britain, was announced.

The Treaty of Berlin reduced the "Big Bulgaria" of the Treaty of San Stefano to a small autonomous principality, where the prince would be chosen by an assembly of Bulgarian notables and confirmed by the Porte. A province of Eastern Rumelia was constructed, where the governor-general was appointed by the sultan with consent of the Powers. Although Turkey could maintain troops and erect fortresses there, the police force was drawn from the native population. Commissions and constitutions were to be enacted for the remaining Ottoman provinces in Europe. Rumania, Montenegro, and Serbia became independent kingdoms; and Austria-Hungary occupied and administered Bosnia and Herzegovina. Navigation of the Danube was to be supervised by a commission. Ardahan, Kars, and Batum were given to Russia, and the provisions of the Treaty of Paris of 1856 regarding the Black Sea and the Straits were preserved. Finally, Turkey pledged religious liberty, civil equality, and access to all courts for the sultan's subjects in Europe and Asia alike.

The dignitaries rejoiced when they signed the Treaty, because a troublesome question had been handled without a major war. Although each official felt he had done reasonably well for his country, special interests at home attacked him for having compromised on their points. As he defended his position and claimed diplomatic victories for himself, opposing statesmen in other countries claimed greater successes lest their people believe that they had been defeated or worsted in the bargaining. Soon no one was satisfied, and Bismarck who posed at the

Congress as "the honest broker" complained that his role was not an enviable one.

Because of recrimination and jealous rivalry generated among the Powers as an aftermath, a number of the clauses of the Treaty were not carefully followed by the Porte. Nevertheless, European ambitions and diplomacy with respect to the Near and Middle East were momentarily less rampant. Soon, however, an epoch opened when a new and modern European imperialism discovered with consternation the rising nationalism of many Middle Eastern peoples—Arabs, Armenians, Iranians, and Turks, each with many variants.

REFERENCES: Chapter 23

All of the references in the preceding chapter relate to this chapter. In addition to these, others already cited are in Chapters 19 and 20.

Donald C. Blaisdell, *European Financial Control in the Ottoman Empire: A Study of the Establishment, Activities and Significance of the Ottoman Public Debt:* Columbia University Press, New York, 1929. The most complete picture of this extraordinary episode of the Ottoman history.

Clara Boyle, *Boyle of Cairo:* Titus Wilson, Kendal, England, 1965. Biography of Lord Cromer's Oriental secretary.

Maybelle K. Chapman, *Great Britain and the Bagdad Railway, 1881–1914:* Smith College, Northampton, 1948. A late reappraisal of the diplomatic rivalries and the complications in the Middle East with special reference to the railroad.

Edward Mead Earle, *Turkey, the Great Powers and the Baghdad Railway: A Study in Imperialism:* Macmillan, New York, 1923. A classic.

Rose Louise Greaves, *Persia and the Defense of India:* Oxford University Press, New York, 1959. British and Russian policy in the nineteenth century.

Harry N. Howard, *The Problem of the Turkish Straits:* Department of State, Washington, 1947. A thumbnail survey by an outstanding scholar. Very useful.

Philip Magnus, *Kitchener, Portrait of an Imperialist:* Dutton, New York, 1958.

John Marlowe, *World Ditch: The Making of the Suez Canal:* Macmillan, New York, 1964.

A. O. Sarkissian, *History of the Armenian Question to 1885:* University of Illinois Press, Urbana, 1938. A thorough investigation and study of diplomatic and political issues involved.

R. W. Seton-Watson, *Disraeli, Gladstone, and the Eastern Question: A Study in Diplomacy and Party Politics:* Macmillan, London, 1935. Important for the English interests during the latter half of the nineteenth century.

James Thomson Shotwell and Francis Deak, *Turkey at the Straits: A Short History:* Macmillan, 1940. A concise diplomatic account.

N. Sousa, *The Capitulatory Regime of Turkey, Its History, Origin, and Nature:* Johns Hopkins Press, Baltimore, 1933. A survey from 1535 to 1923.

A. L. Tibawi, *American Interests in Syria, 1800–1901:* Oxford University Press, New York, 1966.

————, *British Interests in Palestine, 1800–1901:* Oxford University Press, London, 1961.

Robert L. Tignor, *Modernization and British Colonial Rule in Egypt, 1882–1914:* Princeton University Press, Princeton, 1966. A very fair evaluation.

Arnold T. Wilson, *The Persian Gulf: An Historical Sketch from the Earliest Times to the Beginning of the Twentieth Century:* George Allen & Unwin, London, 1928. A commercial and political history.

————, *The Suez Canal, Its Past, Present and Future:* Oxford University Press, London, 1939. Interesting and useful.

CHAPTER 24

From Tanzimat to the Constitution

HATT-I SHARIF OF GULHANEH

The reforms of Mahmud II were conceived not so much in the spirit of the French Revolution and eighteenth-century European Enlightenment as in the pattern of governmental changes enacted by Louis XIV and Napoleon Bonaparte to strengthen and widen the authority of the central regime. Destruction of the janissaries had been the primary requirement. Upon their abolition a more effective and responsive army was developed, and other changes introduced. Disobedient and unmanageable provincial governors succumbed one after another to the force of the new Mahmud. From his desire to enforce the subservience of Muhammad Ali, however, issued the disastrous defeats of 1832–1833 and 1839. In the latter struggle Mahmud's reconstituted army and navy were lost. He died on July 1, 1839, leaving his sixteen-year-old son, Abdul Mejid, to face military defeat and to be saved by the colloquy of the Powers.

The new sultan had only a scanty informal education and felt most at home in the company of eunuchs and women of the palace. Yet he apparently had a kindly disposition toward his subjects and wished for their well-being. Since his view of the world, his own country, and human society hardly extended beyond the palace walls, his understanding of the problems of his empire and their solution was extremely rudimentary. His misconceptions, uncertainties, and personal whims led to constant shifts of grand viziers and other ministers, frequently at the instigation of powerful ambassadors at the Porte.

Four months after Abdul Mejid's accession a most solemn ceremony was accorded to the declaration of a Hatt-i Sharif (Noble Words) by the sultan, ushering in a new political era for the Middle East. Before all of the notables, dignitaries, and grandees of the empire and the ambassadors gathered in the Gulhaneh (Chamber of Roses) at the palace, Rashid Pasha, foreign minister, read this imperial decree. It abolished capital punishment without a trial; guaranteed justice to all with respect to life, honor, and property; and established a Council of Justice to frame laws and a new penal code against which no infringements would be tolerated because of personal rank or influence. The second reform measure of the Hatt-i Sharif of Gulhaneh ended the system of tax-farming and instituted the collection of taxes by government officials. Lastly, methods of army recruitment and length of service were to be reviewed by the imperial military council, and new procedures were promised to insure regularity and impartiality for all parts of the state. It was also embodied in the decree that its provisions pertained to all subjects, irrespective of religion or sect.

The Hatt-i Sharif was the Porte's demonstration to Europe that the Ottoman Empire was capable of self-preservation and reorganization to withstand pressures from non-Turkish groups for independence or autonomous rule. Its issuance made enactment of the London treaties of 1840 and 1841 concerning the Straits and the integrity of the Ottoman Empire appear more reasonable and just, thus easing British adherence to the settlement. Whether Rashid, who had served as ambassador for four years in London and Paris, recognized the value and appeal that statements in the Hatt-i Sharif would generate in European capitals and brought them forth as a brilliant diplomatic coup or whether he had drunk deeply of the liberal political philosophies current in Paris has been much debated. In any case, Rashid in this act committed himself to a more liberal regime. Though sometimes weak in holding to a course and often personally corruptible, he became the advocate of reform and was thoroughly pro-British in his leanings.

Though the Hatt-i Sharif was endorsed by the grand vizir, the Shaykh al-Islam, and the sultan, the new spirit was soon curbed. As soon as the Powers decided to drive Muhammad Ali back to Egypt and preserve the Turkish Empire, reaction set in. Rashid had introduced a new penal code, based somewhat on French models, but fell from office in 1841 over discussions of the new commercial code. With Rashid out, the course of reform took a different direction. Under Riza Pasha, a conservative court favorite and commander-in-chief of the army, a more rigorous conscription among Muslims was effected and some foreign officers hired. (Christians were excluded from the conscription.) The regular army, *nizam*, and the reserve, *redif*, were increased to nearly half a million; regulars served from three to four years. The currency situation was greatly improved by withdrawing most of the paper money in circulation and introducing a silver coinage, of which the twenty-piaster piece came popularly to be called a "Mejidiyeh." Government officials who went out to collect taxes proved so incompetent that peasants, Muslims and Christians alike, complained, clamoring for a return to tax-farmers as the lesser of two evils. As a result the new commercial code was suspended.

TANZIMAT

Rashid returned to office as foreign minister in 1845 and became grand vizir the following year. Immediately, he set about to re-establish the forward movement initiated in 1839 and called for reorganization along the lines of old, pure, and tolerant Muslim practices—*Tanzimat,* the movement was termed. His friends and supporters, Ali and Fuad, drove ahead to organize education on a more formal and widespread basis. The University of Istanbul was created in 1846 to co-ordinate the various colleges of medicine, agriculture, naval science, government administration, and veterinary medicine launched earlier by Mahmud and Abdul Mejid; but many delays and difficulties postponed its effective organization. Appointed to study needs of secondary education, a special council recommended universal, compulsory, and free education with free textbooks. Six schools of this type were operating by 1851, but the drive collapsed upon lack of funds and the return of reactionary leaders.

Sir Stratford Canning returned to England in the autumn of 1846, not to resume his post in Istanbul until 1848. While he was absent, Rashid fell from office. When, however, Sir Stratford invited the sultan to reappoint his reforming minister, he regained power. There was no question about the influence of the "Great Ambassador," and some of Rashid's successes and the developments in the government revealed Sir Stratford's hand. The Tanzimat period, however, resulted not from foreign intervention but from internal pressures and growth. With the great increases in British commerce in the Middle East occurring in the 1840's, Rashid, who was friendly with the West and who pushed changes at the Porte favorable to England and France, naturally found an eager ally in the British ambassador.

The truer Tanzimat spirit was manifested in the growing number of Turks who were educated in the West or in a Western manner and who thus became Europeanized in their outlook. The best evidence of this growth was the plethora of newspapers, journals, and books that appeared in the decade preceding the Crimean War. Politics, history, biography, and philosophy were popular subjects; and new ideas awakened the younger generation. Everywhere in Europe revolts against conservatism and the old order were stirring; and Turkey, on

the edge of Europe, felt some of this movement. Ever-growing nationalist sentiment among Greeks, Armenians, Bulgarians, and others
could not fail to arouse some Turkish patriotism, too. But a nationalist
drive among the Turks existed only in an embryonic form in Istanbul
and not at all in the provinces.

Some of Rashid's reforms were extended beyond the capital and appeared in measures regarding equal justice, withdrawal of capital
punishment from the hands of local governors, and creation of local assemblies elected to advise the governor and give their consent before
he could take action. Since assemblies were usually composed of
wealthy influential notables with a Turkish majority, they prevented
changes from being adopted and were frequently in collusion with the
governor. They did, however, check the prevalence of arbitrary local
government.

In 1851 Sir Stratford Canning reported from Istanbul that he had
abandoned all hope for reform and development of a modern Euro-
pean-type state in Turkey. The following year he left for England, never
expecting to return. (His elevation to the peerage was little solace for
his depressed feeling.) About him he saw venal government officials
and recognized that his favorite Rashid had himself become corrupt,
appointing incompetent and notorious persons to high office.

The Great Ambassador did not, however, comprehend the slowness
and stealth by which society changes. Communication with Western
Europe was affecting an ever-widening circle of Turkish people, especially the youth. As their number increased they found encouragement in one another and resisted pressures from older generations to
conform to accepted political, social, and intellectual norms.

HATT-I HUMAYUN

The process of change was accelerated greatly by the Crimean War.
The presence in Istanbul of large numbers of British, French, and Italian soldiers, government officials, merchants, journalists, and tourists
had a marked sociological repercussion upon the Turks. Contacts between East and West had not been so widespread in many generations,
and the quantities of money expended by the Allies in Turkey gave to
many Turkish families the opportunity of satisfying their desire for
European travel, study, books, and ideas. A European education became the fashion; and every young man of a good or ambitious family
was sent to Paris, Geneva, London, or some other center to assimilate
as much Western culture as possible. The movement eventually transformed the Ottoman Empire but the results were not immediately evident.

England, France, and Sardinia were allied to the Ottoman Empire

during the Crimean War and were ostensibly fighting for its preservation. Before the Treaty of Paris could be completed and the public in
Western Europe satisfied that the Turkish state was worth saving, a new
reform document had to be issued. This was the Hatt-i Humayun (Imperial Words) of February 18, 1856, which re-endorsed the Hatt-i
Sharif of Gulhaneh and the Tanzimat. But it was far more specific in
its details and certainly more extensive in scope than previous reform
measures.

The imperial decree was in the main concerned with the Christian
population of the empire and granted them the rights and privileges
which the Muslim community possessed or, at least, imagined that they
enjoyed. Patriarchs and heads of communities (*millets*) were appointed
for life, and through self-chosen assemblies each community controlled
its own temporal administration. Freedom of worship was declared,
and no one could be compelled to change his religion. No disability
with regard to holding public office, employment by the state, entry
into a school, or service in the army was countenanced because of distinction of religion or nationality.

In matters of justice and court procedures, commercial and criminal
cases between Muslims and non-Muslims and among non-Muslims of
different sects were referred to mixed tribunals whose proceedings
were open to the public. Corporal punishment was outlawed and reform of the penitentiary system pledged. Equality of taxes and army
service among the various religious groups within the empire was pronounced, and a full new law regarding military service was promised
"with as little delay as possible." Foreigners were, henceforth, permitted to own, purchase, and dispose of real property in the sultan's
realm.

A budget for the state would be drawn up each year; banks and other
financial institutions, formed; and concrete steps to reform the monetary and financial systems of the empire, guaranteed. Roads and canals
were envisaged. Commerce and agriculture were to be encouraged by
positive means. Schools for every community were authorized. And
every means was to be sought for the empire "to profit by the science,
the art, and the funds of Europe."

On paper the Hatt-i Humayun contained the essentials necessary for
a strong revival. To put the decree to work, however, required the
backing and valiant service of more men than were available. The
Hatt-i Humayun ignored the rising tide of nationalism among non-
Muslims and failed to appreciate the effect of foreign residents upon
the millet system. The Capitulations in the Ottoman Empire, including
Egypt, gave political, social, and economic privileges to foreign nationals as individuals and as groups. Similar status was the ambition

of non-Turkish Ottoman nationals, who wanted all privileges and en-
joyments of living in the Ottoman Empire with none of the responsibilities. Through their schools and literature these nationalists accepted
the dictum that people could only enjoy the greatest happiness when
governing themselves. Thus the Hatt-i Humayun, in spite of the efforts
of such men as Fuad, Ali, and Midhat Pashas, was doomed to failure
almost from the beginning. Moreover, with the wars in Europe from
1859 to 1871 accompanying the unification of Italy and Germany and
the reforms and reorganizing plans which were engrossing the days of
Alexander II of Russia, the Ottoman Empire was allowed to follow
her own political course. This meant preserving the *status quo*.

BANKRUPTCY

Since there were not enough men sincerely and deeply dedicated to
a new order, the last days of the broken Abdul Mejid and the entire
reign of his weak brother, Abdul Aziz (1861–1876) were marked by
disappointment. The few men who preached modernization and the development of the natural resources were almost completely silenced by
those who mismanaged affairs of state, lived on corruption, and assured
the political stagnation of the realm. In 1867 Abdul Aziz visited Paris
and London in the company of his nephews Murad and Abdul Hamid
and his Foreign Minister Fuad Pasha. He returned home full of the
desire for reform. But he was so lacking of perspicacity that he only
reorganized his court to follow the etiquette witnessed in Europe and
constructed more palaces and triumphal arches in the style seen in the
West.

Instead of reform, Turkey rushed precipitously into bankruptcy. Between 1854 and 1875 one billion dollars was borrowed from Western
Europe, and at the end of that period almost nothing remained to
show for such a vast sum except debts. The tax system grew antiquated, and the increasing national income hardly augmented the tax
income. To meet the rising cost of everything and to pay for the extravagances of Abdul Mejid and Abdul Aziz more loans were contracted and bonds floated in the money markets of the West. At the
same time Turkey had a yearly surplus of imports over exports. Since
the 1830's the balance was met by shipments of bullion; and hard
money in Turkey was being rapidly debased or replaced by paper
currency. After the Crimean War unfavorable trade balances were
largely offset by loans, since much of the governmental expenditures
directly responsible for the loans was made internally. The great bulk
of Turkish imports were consumer goods, however, and loans did not
bring in the capital goods which in the end might have expanded
Turkish productivity and facilitated repayment of the loans. Although

the Porte recognized the need and right of British and French supervision over the spending of loans, the commissions and councils remained ineffective, supinely watched the "supreme operation rathole,"
and frequently encouraged it by reporting on the basic wealth of
Turkey and the financial soundness of the country!

Obviously, the process could not continue indefinitely. In October,
1875 the grand vizir, Mahmud Nedim, perhaps influenced by the Russian ambassador, announced insolvency by declaring obligations could
not be honored in full. This statement was the first signal for a new
era of wide European control of the Ottoman Empire to be ushered
in a few years later. The approaching bankruptcy had served to tighten
the tax screws upon the provinces and brought open revolt in Bosnia
and Herzegovina. The general European repercussions and consequences of these disturbances have been discussed in the preceding
chapter. But it should not be considered that these events had no
effect upon internal Turkish affairs.

MIDHAT PASHA AND THE CONSTITUTION

The widening influence of Western European books and ideas upon
political affairs was more and more noticeable in Ottoman circles after
the Crimean War, as more Turks visited and studied in Western centers. Young Ottoman Turks aped French poetry, art, philosophy, and
social forms; nationalism was discussed instead of religion; and Persian
elegance of phrasing was outmoded. French manners, liberalism, urbanity, and sophistication became the fashion. The effect, however,
that this group had upon Ottoman society and the state as a whole
was at this moment almost nil. Its day came a generation later.

Another group of men in Turkey did find in their study of the West
political institutions and practices which, in their eyes, would greatly
benefit Turkey. Of this latter group, the most outstanding and the
eventual leader was Midhat Pasha. A first-rate administrator, devoted
to reform and an open enemy of corruption, Midhat made his mark in
provincial government. After his success in quelling two different outbreaks of brigandage in the Balkans, he was appointed governor of
Nish. Conditions became relatively so salutary in Nish that Midhat
was recalled in 1864 to Istanbul, where with Fuad and Ali Pashas he
drew up a new law of the provinces. Reorganizing the empire into
twenty-eight large provinces (*vilayets*), the law provided for mixed
tribunals for cases involving Christians and Muslims and for assemblies
of notables to counsel the governor. Yet, since final authority and the
power of appointing the governor rested in the hands of the sultan or
his advisers, the quality and type of administration enjoyed by a province depended almost wholly upon the governor's personality. One

foreign observer bitingly remarked that it seemed to him as if the sole reason for the existence of the Ottoman Empire was to enable forty or fifty wealthy Turkish families and a like number of wealthy Armenian, Greek, and Jewish bankers to wring from the peasants the product of their toil.

For a few years the energetic Midhat returned to Bulgaria as governor of the new Province of the Danube. He built roads, bridges, railroads, orphanages, schools, hospitals, banks, agricultural co-operatives, and stagecoach routes. Even more important was his establishment of law and order and his just treatment of the Christian population. On the other hand, Midhat Pasha refused to condone revolutionary action and ruthlessly suppressed several outbursts of nationalism aimed at self-government and independence. In rapid succession following the Bulgarian assignment Midhat served on the imperial council of state, governed the province of Iraq, became grand vizir for three months in 1871, held the governorship of Salonika, and then retired to private life in Istanbul. But the financial collapse under Mahmud Nedim Pasha and violent uprisings in the Balkans with their corollary of European intervention heartened Midhat Pasha to engineer the deposition of the incompetent Abdul Aziz and install his nephew, Murad V, on May 30, 1876. In August Murad had a nervous breakdown and was replaced by his unpopular brother Abdul Hamid II.

Nine years before, Abdul Hamid had accompanied his uncle and the liberal Fuad Pasha on their European tour; and it was generally believed from the impressions he made and from the knowledge he supposedly acquired that his accession to the throne augured well for a liberal progressive regime. Midhat Pasha's designation as grand vizir was also interpreted throughout the Ottoman Empire and in Europe as an indication of the new governmental steps to be taken.

Midhat Pasha disappointed very few; for on December 23, 1876 Abdul Hamid proclaimed a constitution which Midhat and others had been formulating since the deposition of Abdul Aziz. Accepted with great rejoicing among the liberals of Istanbul, the constitution provided for a cabinet and an elected parliament and gave proportional representation to all nationalities according to the European form. It reaffirmed that all subjects of the sultan were equal, regardless of race or creed. Freedom of religion, education, and the press and equality of taxation were guaranteed.

Parliament held two sessions in a chamber in the Ministry of Justice. But the outbreak of war with Russia enabled Abdul Hamid in February, 1878 to prorogue parliament and quietly ignore the constitution. A year before, in February, 1877 Midhat Pasha had been summarily placed aboard a ship in the harbor and exiled to Europe. By the end of the war and the settlement of the Congress of Berlin, Abdul Hamid and his reactionary cabal had the government well in hand. In 1883 Midhat and several of his liberal compatriots were strangled in the dungeons of al-Taif, near Mecca, in Arabia. Modernization through parliamentary action died quietly, and stagnation continued for another generation.

REFERENCES: Chapter 24

Almost all volumes concerned with the Middle East in the nineteenth century relate to subjects discussed in this chapter. Of special significance are those found in Chapters 8, 12, 13, 18, 19, 20, 21, 22, and 23.

Roderic H. Davison, *Reform in the Ottoman Empire, 1856–1876:* Princeton University Press, Princeton, 1963. First-rate study of ideas and forces in the Ottoman Empire.

Robert Devereux, *The First Ottoman Constitutional Period: A Study of the Midhat Constitution and Parliament:* Johns Hopkins Press, Baltimore, 1963. This work with those by Roderic H. Davison and Şerif Mardin makes a fine trilogy.

Ahmed Emin (Yalman), *The Development of Modern Turkey as Measured by Its Press:* Columbia University Press, New York, 1914. An excellent work, which surveys advances since 1830.

William Foster, *England's Quest of Eastern Trade:* A. C. Black, London, 1933. Although this book reaches back to the seventeenth century, it is strong on the trading developments of the nineteenth century.

Cyrus Hamlin, *Among the Turks:* Robert Carter & Bros., New York, 1878. Dr. Hamlin was the founder of Robert College and lived in Turkey from the 1830's until the 1870's.

Uriel Heyd, *The Foundations of Turkish Nationalism:* Harwell Press, London, 1950.

Stanley Lane-Poole, *The Life of the Right Honorable Stratford Canning, Viscount Stratford de Redcliffe,* 2 vols.: Longmans, Green, London, 1888. In any study of the Middle East of the nineteenth century the life of this great ambassador cannot be disregarded.

Şerif Mardin, *The Genesis of Young Ottoman Thought: A Study in the Modernization of Turkish Political Ideas:* Princeton University Press, Princeton, 1962. Most significant.

Ali Haydar Midhat, *The Life of Midhat Pasha:* J. Murray, London, 1903. A fine biography of the great Turkish statesman written by his son.

Edwin Pears, *Forty Years in Constantinople, 1873–1915:* Appleton, New York, 1916. Sir Edwin was a British lawyer in Constantinople and corresponded with several London newspapers. He was a keen observer and often knew inside details of events.

E. D. G. Prime, *Forty Years in the Turkish Empire; or, Memoirs of Rev. William Goodell, D.D., Late Missionary of the A.B.C.F.M. at Constantinople:* Robert Carter & Bros., New York, 1876. The life of one of the first American missionaries, who came to Constantinople in 1831 and remained there until 1865. The volume was written by his son-in-law from material in journals and letters.

E. I. J. Rosenthal, *Islam in the Modern National State:* Cambridge University Press, New York, 1966.

George Washburn, *Fifty Years in Constantinople:* Houghton Mifflin, Boston, 1909. Dr. Washburn was the second president of Robert College and retired in 1903. He was influential in Ottoman affairs in Bulgaria.

✥ CHAPTER 25 ✥

Abdul Hamid II and Despotism

BULGARIA

The strange events of the summer of 1876 which brought the deposition first of Abdul Aziz and then of his nephew Murad V and
resulted in the accession of Abdul Hamid II were symptomatic of the
general unrest pervading the entire empire. Nowhere was this uneasy
state of affairs more evident than in Bulgaria. So thoroughly was the
Bulgarian area dominated by the Turkish government, Ottoman feudal
lords, and Greek clergy that many travelers in passing through that
region were not even aware that a Bulgarian people existed. By the
1830's, however, enzymes of nationalism took effect; and Bulgarian
schools, history, language, folklore, and national consciousness developed rapidly. Not least in importance in this growth were the opening of the area commercially, the marketing of wheat, flour, lumber,
and attar of roses in Western Europe, and the migration of Bulgarians
to Odessa, Istanbul, Moscow, and the West.

Without discussing every facet of the progress of Bulgarian nationalism, recognition must be given to important advancements and indirect
encouragement which resulted from Midhat Pasha's benevolent rule.
Education, economic prosperity, and personal security improved mark
edly in the 1860's to culminate in 1870 in the first official notice of
Bulgaria by the creation of the Bulgarian Exarchate, which included
most of the Province of the Danube. Headed by an autonomous Exarch,
the Bulgarian Church stimulated the nationalist movement and turned
Macedonia, still a part of the Ottoman Empire, into a battleground
between Bulgars and Greeks. The Turks stood over the two parties and
tried to preserve peace and order. Bulgarian political nationalists or-

ganized revolutionary societies in Bucharest and sustained a steady influx of agents and literature into the province to maintain the nationalist spirit at fever pitch. Further unrest and agitation arose in the Bulgarian province by the forced settlement in the 1860's of ten thousand Crimean Tartars and many more Circassians from Russia. The latter, in particular, terrorized peasants and kept villagers in a state of perpetual siege.

The situation in Bulgaria became tragic in 1876. Discontent in Bosnia and Herzegovina burst into a revolution, and Russian volunteers streamed across the Balkans to join the rebels. In the autumn of 1875 the Porte announced interest payments on its bonds could not be met in full. Apparently being pressed to the wall, the Ottoman government reacted desperately against an incipient uprising in Bulgaria by sending wild Circassians and ill-disciplined militia to pacify the area. Massacres followed; villages were destroyed; and the world was informed by British newspapers.

International events set in motion by these disturbances have been discussed: the Constantinople Conference of Ambassadors, the Russo-Turkish War, the Treaty of San Stefano, and the Congress of Berlin. Equally important for Europe and far more significant for the Middle East were domestic events in the Ottoman Empire. In May, 1876 theological students, *softas*, demonstrated on the streets of Istanbul against Abdul Aziz, obtaining as had been done so frequently in preceding centuries the dismissal of the grand vizir and the Shaykh al-Islam.

ACCESSION OF ABDUL HAMID II

Two political parties were in process of formation. One was distinctly liberal, progressive, and Western in its desire for constitutional government, fiscal reforms, and economic progress looking toward industrial and commercial development. The other was conservative, corrupt, and composed of self-seeking, ambitious, ruthless, and narrow-minded men. The former was led by Midhat Pasha and Husayn Avni Pasha, since Rashid, Fuad, and Ali Pashas were dead; the latter soon fell under the sway of Damad Mahmud Jelal al-Din and Redif Pasha.

The populace of Istanbul awoke on the morning of May 31, 1876 to find a new sultan on the throne. Midhat and Husayn Avni, with a handful of followers and the co-operation of the fleet and a few soldiers, deposed the extravagant Abdul Aziz and enthroned Murad V. The liberal ministers were retained; and two immensely popular liberal journalists, Ziya and Namik Kemal, became the sultan's private secretaries. The reactionary party held its fire; and Midhat proceeded to draft a constitution which would introduce responsible parliamentary and cabinet government to the Ottoman Empire.

Unfortunately for the Middle East, Murad proved mentally unstable. The suddenness and circumstances of his accession quite unnerved him, since any hitch in the plot on that fateful night or a subsequent reversal of the *coup* meant his execution. A few days later Abdul Aziz committed sucide. Ten days later a crazed officer broke into a cabinet meeting and assassinated four officials, including two ministers. These incidents turned the scales and Murad became incapable of governing. Affairs of government stood still, until in August Midhat deposed Murad in favor of Abdul Hamid II.

The latter promised to support the liberal party and retain Ziya and Namik Kemal as his private secretaries. Abdul Hamid, however, had much more sympathy for the party of Damad Mahmud Jelal al-Din. Although he never appointed the liberals as his secretaries, Midhat did become grand vizir and the constitution described in another chapter was promulgated. As soon as the conference of Powers adjourned from Istanbul, Midhat was called to the Palace, placed aboard the sultan's yacht, and carried away to Italy and exile. Parliament met in March, 1877; but Abdul Hamid prorogued it after a few weeks and completely shelved the constitution. Until 1908 the constitution was printed each year in the official register, but remained ignored in every respect. The war with Russia served as the excuse for its suppression and Abdul Hamid ruled as the complete autocrat.

OTTOMAN PUBLIC DEBT ADMINISTRATION

The suspension of the payment of half of the interest due on Ottoman bonds in 1875 was a potent factor in producing the accession and removal of Murad in 1876. It is not clear whether bankruptcy was the cause or only a symptom of the failure of the Ottoman government to keep pace with the changing society of the Middle East. But in any case bankruptcy, followed so closely by the Russian war and defeat, compelled Abdul Hamid and his ministers to resort to measures not consonant with complete sovereignty.

On December 20, 1881 Abdul Hamid issued an imperial decree (Decree of Muharram) legalizing an arrangement with bondholders' groups whereby about £191,000,000 of the external debt of the empire was consolidated and reduced to £106,000,000. Furthermore, revenues from salt and tobacco monopolies, stamp taxes, excise taxes on fish, spirits, and silk, and other income from Bulgaria and Cyprus were assigned for debt liquidation. The Council of Administration of the Ottoman Public Debt was devised as an authorized body to collect and disburse revenues and taxes on behalf of the bondholders. The Council consisted of seven members: five represented British and Dutch, French, Italian, German, and Austrian bondholders; one was nominated by the Ottoman Bank, which was British- and French-controlled; and one was appointed by the sultan. Largely the work of the British ambassador Goschen, an international banker, this Decree of Muharram regularized Ottoman finances and re-established the sultan's credit. Without the Ottoman Public Debt Administration the considerable economic progress of Turkey in the period between 1880 and 1914 could not have transpired.

Within a few years after the inception of the Ottoman Public Debt Administration it became more than a collecting and banking agency. Under its direction great improvements were made in silk culture and tobacco smuggling decreased. Meanwhile, more efficiency and less corruption in the collection of taxes augmented revenues. Slowly debts began to be liquidated; and, even more important, Ottoman credit was rehabilitated so that railways could be built and many Western innovations installed. In almost every case where Ottoman credit or public operation was involved, an agreement provided that the Ottoman Public Debt Administration should act for the government. Thus, by 1900 many railways in Turkey were supervised by the Public Debt Administration and railway bonds were its obligations. It was so successful and in such good repute that the government itself used the organization to collect various unassigned taxes, such as those on valona and opium.

In the beginning foreigners staffed the branches of the Debt Administration, establishing its procedures and its good reputation; but as the years passed, more Ottoman subjects were employed. In 1912 only 169 agents were foreigners, whereas Ottoman nationals in the Administration numbered 5,625 full-time and 3,250 part-time employees. The scale of pay was better in its service than in governmental departments and certainly more regular. Not only did the Debt Administration attract a much higher caliber of personnel than the government, but the training and experience acquired proved exceedingly valuable in later years when many Debt Administration employees offered their talents to the Ottoman government and its successors. In 1903 a supplemental decree was issued reconsolidating several old series of bonds and distributing some new series. Important for the Ottoman government was the injection of a stipulation that two thirds of all revenues above a fixed point were to be transferred to the government. This provision meant that improved economic conditions in Turkey would be reflected in the receipts of the public treasury, permitting better services by the government.

In some aspects the Ottoman Public Debt Administration served as an instrument of economic imperialism and, by its strength, sometimes as a political force. However, by and large, it was characterized by its restraint. It recognized that interests of the bondholders would be best served by an improved economy. That its existence impinged upon Ottoman sovereignty, however, there could be no doubt, and Turkish nationalists found it particularly offensive. The Young Turks in their revolt in 1908 were not strong enough to force its demise. The Kemalists, however, although they never denied the validity of the Ottoman debts, refused categorically to entertain even the idea of foreign intervention as indirectly implied in the Debt Administration. It died quietly when the Treaty of Lausanne omitted all reference to it.

SUPPRESSION OF THE CONSTITUTION

Through the early decades of the life of the Debt Administration, when it was proving its value and maintaining the credit of the empire, Abdul Hamid was rapidly destroying the reputation and strength of his realm by his tyranny and ignorance. Any apparent disposition for the liberals of Midhat Pasha's stripe was simulated. When informed that a constitutional sovereign followed the dictates of his ministers his natural predilection for absolutism surged to the fore. Midhat was strangled in the dungeons of Arabia, and illustrious Turks died in exile or in inhospitable spots to which they were consigned. Surrounded by adventurers and sycophants, Abdul Hamid lived constantly in mortal terror of his subjects. He refused to occupy the splendid palaces of his predecessors and took refuge at Yildiz, which he enhanced and rebuilt and then protected by a double encircling wall.

In many quarters Abdul Hamid gained a reputation for astuteness. He was cunning and suspicious and had spies everywhere. He was intolerant and failed to understand the world development of his time. General von der Goltz of Germany was employed to train the army. Colonel Baker of England was engaged to organize a police force for the empire. Fine new ships for the navy were ordered in England, France, and the United States; but they rusted in the Golden Horn. Suggestions were ignored; and any Turk with an idea for governmental improvements was more than likely to be found in a weighted sack in the Bosphorus.

In such an atmosphere the press had a difficult time. In the 1860's several Turkish newspapers were launched, most of which were liberal in their attitudes toward government. Shinasi, Ziya, Namik Kemal, and Ali Suavi were the most noteworthy and capable editors and writers. But newspaper work meant "patriotic martyrdom," since editors and popular authors were almost invariably exiled and newspapers were suspended with regular frequency. Ziya died a broken man in 1880 in Adana; Namik Kemal followed in 1887; and Ali Suavi was executed for his part in a plot against Abdul Hamid in 1878. Many writers lived and published their works abroad and sent them into Turkey through the protection of the various foreign post offices established under the Capitulations by the states of Europe.

Yet the work of the press went indefatigably on, educating the literate population to the developments and thoughts of the outside world. Ebuzzia Tevfik, one of Namik Kemal's close friends, published a host of European classics and many valuable works by Turkish authors. He also edited a fortnightly magazine which copied the style and general content of the *English Fortnightly Review* and brought a Western point of view on many subjects. Other newspapers carried in serial form translations of European books. Many books appeared as single publications. Over three hundred were published in 1890, many of them being exciting French novels which introduced Turks to a very different world. Abdul Hamid controlled the press and suspended opposition papers as they appeared. But he did not have enough spies to police the entire empire; consequently, the verbal and printed attacks upon him could not be wholly suppressed. Wherever Turks gathered in the absence of Abdul Hamid's agents, the discussion gravitated quickly to bemoaning the tyrannical state of affairs and the apparent helplessness to do anything about it.

Liberalism among the Turks was not crushed, but the greatest public expression of it came from Turks living safely in Europe. Among the better known of these were: Ahmed Riza, who edited a newspaper under the title of *Meshveret (Deliberation)* and later became president of the Assembly in Turkey; Halil Ganem from Beirut, who first published *La Jeune Turquie;* Murad, a history teacher from the Civil College and one-time employee of the Ottoman Public Debt Administration who established in Paris a newspaper *Mizan (Balance)* which became very popular in Turkey; and Prince Sabah al-Din, a son of Abdul Hamid's sister, who organized a congress of Turkish patriots and exiles to overthrow his uncle and then to re-establish a constitutional regime.

The spreading of Western thought in Ottoman schools swelled the ranks of the discontented, most of whom fled as exiles to western Europe. Strangely enough, Abdul Hamid founded many schools and even supplied the students with pocket money in hopes they would remain loyal to their patron. Such, of course, was not the case; for thrown together from every class of society, they became militant and dissatisfied. Perhaps because the teachers in the medical and military schools had had European experience, their students were the most unsettled of all. In pursuing their studies many were exposed to French or German, which immediately opened to them the ideas of nineteenth-century Europe. As a result, army officers and medical men from 1900 until recent times held positions of political leadership in Turkey out of all proportion to their numbers in society.

THE ARMENIAN QUESTION

Abdul Hamid became odious to most Turks. Many Europeans and his non-Turkish subjects knew him as the "Red Sultan," or "Abdul the Damned." In large measure such appellations resulted from his treat· ment of the Armenians. As national aspirations stirred Serbs, Greeks, Rumanians, and Bulgars, so Armenians were moved in the latter half of the nineteenth century. Encouraged by the Russian government and stimulated by European and American missionaries, the three Armenian religious communities—Gregorian, Catholic, and Protestant—and their respective educational institutions generated the development of national consciousness. Perhaps because confidential representations at the Congress of Berlin for Armenian cultural autonomy within Turkey were allowed, political societies flourished. Visions of an independent Armenia were also provided by revolutionary committees in Russia and the United States. The tsars promoted these hallucinations but steadfastly refused to become involved, since similar experiences in Bulgaria had not proved remunerative.

Abdul Hamid became frightened of the Armenian situation. He feared that six or more eastern provinces forming the Armenian highlands, where most of the Armenians were concentrated, and Little Armenia, or Cilicia, might become separated from the empire. To subdue the people, break their spirit, and destroy the possibility of an Armenian state, violent attacks upon the villages and shocking massacres were perpetrated intermittently from 1894 to 1897. Outrages occurred in Yozgat, Erzinjan, Kharput, Sivas, Marash, Urfa, and many other places, even in Istanbul. In all, perhaps one hundred thousand Armenians lost their lives.

These atrocities had a very deep effect upon Turkey. The few revolutionary societies were wiped out, and Armenians were entirely cowed. Emigration appeared as the only solution. Economic life in many areas was disrupted, and most knowledgeable Turks were genuinely depressed by their government's action. Charitable foreign aid societies provided relief; but the British, French, Italian, and Ameri· can governments protested in vain. Newspapers, magazines, churches, and lecture halls told and echoed to stories of the "Terrible Turks," so that Western governmental and diplomatic actions in Turkey were controlled to a considerable degree for several decades by an unfriendly public opinion.

CRETE

The regime's despotic nature was also exposed in Crete. Quality of government on Crete varied greatly, since the distance of the island and remoteness of certain parts of it left governors considerable autonomy. A small uprising occurred in 1841, and demands by local assemblies for reforms multiplied after the Hatt-i Humayun was issued. In the 1860's the better educated subscribed to Greek nationalism, the first outburst for union with Greece taking place in 1866. Desultory fighting and Ottoman countermeasures persisted until 1870. Although emotions aroused in Athens affected government policies, Athens recognized that lack of preparation for war forbade overt actions against Turkey.

In 1885, when the union of Eastern Rumelia and Bulgaria occurred, concentration of European naval units at Suda Bay in Crete placed a damper on Greek preparations for war against the Ottomans and discouraged Cretan enthusiasts for union with Greece. None the less, disorders of various origins and intensities continued to maintain the tensions. In 1896 and 1897, after bloody battles on the streets of Canea between Greeks and Turks brought matters to a head, Prince George of Greece cut off Turkish reinforcements and the Powers occupied Canea. Boiling national sentiment in Athens compelled the king to initiate a war against Turkey. Although the king hoped the Powers would prevent it, they did not act. The "Thirty Days' War," better known as the Greco-Turkish War of 1897, was a series of Greek disasters. Only intervention of the Powers saved Athens from a Turkish occupation. The Peace of Istanbul, which restored the boundaries, placed a heavy indemnity upon Greece. Not until the end of 1898 did Europe effect a settlement in Crete by recognizing Prince George as High Commissioner under suzerainty of the sultan. The Turkish minority emigrated gradually; and by 1908, when union was finally achieved, less than ten percent of the population was Muslim.

MACEDONIA

Armenia and Crete were enough to keep the Porte embroiled with the European Powers and stampede Abdul Hamid into innumerable unwise and bloody decisions. The complex affairs of Macedonia, however, sealed his fate and substantiated the charge that the Balkans were the powder keg of Europe. Populated by Turks, Bulgars, Greeks, Serbs, Albanians, Rumanians, and many other groups, Macedonia became the chief bone of contention of the chauvinistic nationalism rampant in the Balkans for several decades prior to World War I. A proviso of the Bulgarian Exarchate, permitting churches in Macedonia a choice between Greek and Bulgarian affiliation, touched off the explosion. Balkan nationalism erupted at its worst. Schools, scholarships, newspapers, books, raids, village burning, kidnapping, and assassination were among the tactics employed to achieve nationalist ends.

A Macedonian committee purporting to advance a movement of "Macedonia for the Macedonians" was formed in Sofia. It suggested the organization of an autonomous Macedonia with its own government at Salonika. The obvious intention was a repetition of the Eastern Rumelia episode and the union within five years of Macedonia and Bulgaria. The proposition was rejected by all except the Bulgarians; and Macedonia was assigned to disorder and chaos. Turkish police forces and martial law were unable to cope with the situation. And in 1903 the Mürzstag Program, suggested by the Powers, went into effect. Accordingly, the British, French, Italians, Austrians, and Russians each policed an area. Although some regions were excluded from the agreement, European control was sufficiently successful to induce the Powers to extend the Mürzstag Program in 1908 for another six years.

BERLIN TO BAGHDAD RAILWAY

It should be noted that Germany did not participate in the pacification of Macedonia. Until this era German imperial interests in the Ottoman Empire were negligible. Bismarck regarded the area as worthless to Germany, and his exertions were designed only to keep Russia and Austria from fighting each other. One German banking firm was involved in the Ottoman bankruptcy in 1881 and was duly represented as a minor interest on the Council of the Ottoman Public Debt Administration. But with the accession of William II Germany's role changed. General von der Goltz began to advise the Ottoman army in 1883, and the army was equipped with good Mauser rifles. In 1888 Baron Hirsch's Oriental Railway was completed through to Istanbul, while a newly-formed German syndicate, the Anatolian Railway Company, was granted a concession to construct a railroad from the Bosphorus to Ankara. These last two events marked the full-fledged entry of the Germans upon the Middle Eastern scene.

Supported by the *Deutsche Bank*, the line to Ankara was in operation by 1893. Another contract assured a branch from Eskishehir to Konya, which was completed in 1896. Energetic German penetration of Anatolia flowered handsomely, as German exports to Turkey increased 350 percent in value and Turkish exports to Germany jumped over 700 percent. German salesmen were everywhere. The *Deutsche Levante Linie* established direct steamship service between Hamburg, Bremen, and Istanbul. In 1889, and again in 1898, William II paid official visits to Istanbul; on the latter trip he went to Jerusalem and Damascus, where he uttered the famous speech promising Muslims that the German emperor would be their friend. Oriental studies became popular in Germany; and Dr. Kiepert, the famous cartographer, surveyed Anatolia. But above all else, German interests focused upon railroad concessions, which blossomed into the much-publicized Berlin-to-Baghdad venture.

Abdul Hamid, the Porte, army leaders, and officials of the Ottoman Public Debt Administration favored building railroads and used every available means to extend lines in every direction and to all parts of the empire. They fancied that railroads would unify the empire and bring the central government more effective power and authority over outlying regions. More of the untold mineral resources of Anatolia and Arabia would be developed and a burgeoning prosperity guaranteed. The military posture of the state would be improved and independence protected. Although railroads were costly enterprises it was believed that the advantageous results would amply repay the effort and monies expended.

The fondest dream encompassed building a railroad from the Bosphorus to the Persian Gulf. In 1886 Abdul Hamid proposed such an undertaking to Stanford of the United States; but Stanford was too engrossed in building American transcontinental railroads to agree. Already British and French companies had built and were operating several lines connecting Izmir with the Anatolian hinterland, when in 1888 the Anatolian Railway Company took over the British railroad from Haydar Pasha on the Bosphorus to Izmit and extended it to Ankara.

These railroad concessions usually called for a Turkish subsidy to the construction firm, a guarantee of a minimum annual revenue, or both. In extending the line to Ankara, the sultan assured the Anatolian Railway Company at least 15,000 francs per kilometer annual revenue, for which the taxes of several provinces were granted as collateral, the collection of these taxes being assigned to the Debt Administration. In 1896, when the German line reached Konya, other railroads in Asiatic districts were the Izmir-Aydin, the Izmir-Kassaba-Afyon-Karahisar, the Mersin-Adana, the Jaffa-Jerusalem, and the Beirut-Damascus-Aleppo lines. The government naturally desired to link these together and push on to Mesopotamia and the Persian Gulf. Austrian, Russian, French, British, and German capitalists and entrepreneurs were all anxious to obtain the concession, and each presented plans and offers for its construction. But only the German plans met the requirements of the Porte and the Ottoman Public Debt Administration.

For strategic reasons Abdul Hamid insisted that the line traversed should not approach the Mediterranean, where gunfire from enemy fleets could interrupt traffic. The Germans, therefore, proposed to proceed from Konya to Adana, then through the Amanus range eastward to the valley of the Tigris near Mosul, and down the river to the Persian Gulf. This plan was more expensive than others, but militarily more secure. Actually, British and French capitalists accepted the idea that the concession would be awarded to the Germans, and their governments were fully satisfied. Agreements were reached among the three groups in 1899. In that year Lord Curzon arranged for Britain to conduct all foreign relations for the Shaykh of Kuwayt; this permitted England to block the railroad's best terminus on the Persian Gulf.

On March 18, 1902 Abdul Hamid issued an imperial decree giving the concession for the Baghdad road to the Anatolian Railway Company; a year later a revised convention established the Baghdad Railway Company as actual builder and owner, arranged the financing, and enabled engineers to start construction of the first two hundred kilometers. The Ottoman Empire paid 275,000 francs per kilometer for building the railroad, guaranteed 4,500 francs per kilometer annual gross operating receipts, granted mineral rights twenty kilometers on each side of the right of way, exempted from taxation all articles imported, and gave numerous minor benefits to the company.

When British capitalists refused because of adverse public sentiment to participate equally with German and French interests, ten percent of the Baghdad Railway Company stock was subscribed by the Ottoman government, ten percent by the Anatolian Railway Company, and the remaining eighty percent by a syndicate (French, German, Austrian, Italian, and Swiss) formed by the *Deutsche Bank.*

The necessary bonds were floated and construction began. In October, 1904, the first section was opened. The terrain crossed was not difficult; building cost less than was expected; and profits were high. In 1906 the Porte arranged with the Powers for a slight increase in tariffs to pay for further extensions. New loans were provided in 1908; but because of the Young Turk Revolution, it was not until December, 1909 that a construction company was organized to undertake the second leg across the Taurus and Amanus ranges. Certain bridges and tunnels in the Taurus Mountains were still not finished at the outbreak of war in 1914. Thus, a through-route to northern Iraq or Syria was not opened to traffic until the post-World War I period.

Railways to Ankara and to points beyond Konya, however, brought an agricultural revolution to Anatolia. In districts penetrated by these roads new settlements were formed, produce marketed, and new lands cultivated. The companies initiated irrigation projects and agricultural training centers to stimulate traffic on their railroads; in these details the Germans were the most efficient and thorough. By 1910 mileage guarantees for annual receipts were no longer necessary; and railroads were paying profits into the Ottoman treasury. Simultaneously, German business and banking penetration between 1899 and 1908 was facilitated and encouraged by railroad interests.

For the Middle East the building of railroads was most important. By opening up vast areas to world commerce they improved local economic conditions and gave many Middle Eastern districts their first touch with the West. There was a distinct possibility that these developments might effect a real recuperation for the "sick man" of Europe. The railroads brought German imperialism, which the Middle East found to be a relief from British and French colonialism. Usually Germans were more tactful and considerate of Turkish feelings and were more willing to do things in a Turkish fashion. Unfortunately, German inroads into the Middle East frightened the British, who in turn after 1904 and 1907 drew the French and Russian governments to co-operate with them in trying to block German aspirations for a *Drang nach Osten*. Without question the Baghdad railway project and its ramifications were significant factors in developing the European climate that led to World War I.

REFERENCES: Chapter 25

Many readings touch upon this chapter. Those cited in Chapters 12, 13, 19, 20, 22, 23, and 24 are of particular value.

Metin And, *A History of Theatre and Popular Entertainment in Turkey:* Forum Yayinlari, Ankara, 1964. An important paperback on a little-known subject.

J. N. D. Anderson, *Islamic Law in the Modern World:* New York University Press, New York, 1959.

Niyazi Berkes, *The Development of Secularism in Turkey:* McGill University Press, Montreal, 1964. The most profound and stimulating book on this subject to appear and one that no student can overlook.

Charles R. Buxton, *Turkey in Revolution:* T. F. Unwin, London, 1908. Written by a man who was in Turkey during the Revolution of 1908.

Halidé Edib, *Memoirs:* Century, New York, 1926. The life of a Western-educated Turkish woman.

Charles N. E. Eliot, *Turkey in Europe:* E. Arnold, London, 1908. Particularly strong on the Balkans and Macedonia.

David S. Landes, *Bankers and Pashas, International Finance and Economic Imperialism in Egypt:* Harvard University Press, Cambridge, 1958.

Eliot Grinnel Mears, ed., *Modern Turkey:* Macmillan, New York, 1924. A collection of essays on a variety of topics written by excellent observers who were long resident in Turkey. One entitled "Levantine Concession-Hunting" by Mears is most revealing of this type of financial imperialism.

Edwin Pears, *Life of Abdul Hamid:* Constable, London, 1917. A good biography by an English barrister who was resident in Istanbul throughout the reign of Abdul Hamid II.

Richard Peters, *The Story of the Turks from Empire to Democracy:* C. S. Publishing Co., New York, 1959.

Ernest E. Ramsaur, Jr., *The Young Turks:* Princeton University Press, Princeton, 1957. The best volume in any language on this topic. Based on many letters and communications from leading Young Turks.

CHAPTER 26

The Young Turks

SECRET SOCIETIES

The Young Turk Revolution of 1908 was a natural reaction to oppression, absolutism, and corruption in the regime of Abdul Hamid II. Added to this was the development and growing Westernization of certain portions of the empire and the consequent effect of contemporary European ideas upon Turkish youth. At various times in the nineteenth century dissident Ottomans lived in exile in Europe and dreamed of governmental reformation at home. Many saw a temporary fruition of these hopes in the ousting of Abdul Aziz and in Midhat's constitution of 1876. When Abdul Hamid's true nature was divulged, hardy characters plotted revolution.

In 1889 at the Istanbul Imperial Military Medical College a group of students led by an Albanian, Ibrahim Temo, organized a secret society, The Committee of Progress and Union. Membership spread to the Military Academy, the Naval Academy, the Artillery and Engineering School, the Veterinary School, and the Civil College. Similar to the Carbonari societies in Italy of which Temo had learned in Brindisi, Progress and Union subscribed to nationalist ideas and reforms suggested in the zealous writings of Namik Kemal, Ziya, and Shinasi.

Abdul Hamid heard of the Committee through his secret agents and took reprisals against school officials and students. None the less, the Committee flourished, gathering new recruits from each succeeding class at the various schools. By 1896 more important elements of Ottoman society dominated the Committee, and it attracted members from earlier groups of rebellious spirits known as New Ottomans and Young Turks.

Committee members who escaped to Europe made common cause with other Ottoman malcontents. The best known of these was Ahmed Riza, whose *Meshveret* (*Deliberation*) became the Committee's official organ. At the same time Murad Bey, a history teacher of the Civil College, fled to Paris and published a more popular newspaper, *Mizan* (*Balance*). These two papers obtained easy entrance into the empire through foreign post offices and gathered a considerable following.

Membership in Progress and Union became widespread, but rumor exaggerated its number to the point where Abdul Hamid took fright and the Committee members believed a *coup d'état* possible. Its program denounced violence or any thought of overthrowing the reigning family. It preached reform, rejected slavish Westernization, advocated Ottoman nationalism, and opposed intervention of European powers as a substitute for Ottoman authority. But a series of arrests nipped in the bud the society's *coup* planned for August, 1896. Abdul Hamid, curiously enough, only sent the leaders to remote parts of the empire, whence they slipped away to Paris and Geneva. The latter city became the headquarters of the Committee under the presidency of Murad Bey. The program was reduced to the simple formula that all evils of the Middle East stemmed from Abdul Hamid. Remove him, restore the constitution, and all would be well. But the wily sultan, promising a general amnesty and agreeing to listen to reform, enticed Murad Bey to Istanbul, and shattered the Committee of Progress and Union.

Triumph was only fleeting; for Abdul Hamid's nerve was badly shaken by the escape to Paris of his brother-in-law and two nephews in 1899. Prince Sabah al-Din convened in Paris in 1902 the first congress of Ottoman Liberals, which held as its high objective the restoration of the constitution of 1876. Prince Sabah al-Din championed a nationalist idea which included all peoples of the empire—a federation of Turks, Arabs, Greeks, Armenians, Kurds, Macedonians, Albanians, Jews, and others. In the pages of *Meshveret*, on the other hand, nationalism meant an Ottomanization process in which all divergent groups would become Ottoman Turks.

Turkish or Ottoman dissidents and exiles in Paris and Geneva kept hopes alive for a thorough change in the Ottoman government and a consequent revitalization of the Middle East. But they could hardly produce a revolution, not even a mild *coup d'état*. That had to come from within; and in 1897 Abdul Hamid cleverly crushed the Committee of Progress and Union. The state of society, however, remained constant, and new revolutionary groups sprang up faster than he could cut them down.

Every class at the Military Academy was infected, and at the General Staff Academy in 1905 Mustafa Kemal was arrested as a revolutionary agitator on the very day he was commissioned. Later when released and stationed in Damascus, he organized *Vatan* (Fatherland), a secret revolutionary society which spread among officers of the Fifth Army Corps in Syria. Since Macedonia and its cosmopolitan center of Salonika were susceptible to revolutionary propaganda, Kemal journeyed surreptitiously to Salonika to organize branches of Fatherland among officers of the Third Army Corps. His work developed into a society, Fatherland and Liberty, which merged with another before Kemal arranged his transfer to Salonika in 1907.

Another association, Ottoman Society of Liberty, was founded in Salonika; included in its earliest membership were Talat Bey, Rahmi Bey, Fethi Bey, and Colonel Jemal Bey. Absorbing Fatherland and Liberty, it spread rapidly throughout European Turkey with major centers at Monastir, Uskub, Drama, and Edirne. Ismet Bey was the leader at Edirne. Pledged to overthrow Abdul Hamid and establish a just government, the Ottoman Society of Liberty drew to its ranks all liberal and freethinking Turks—Bektashis, Melamis, and Freemasons. When army officers fraternized with their European colleagues stationed in Macedonia, pursuant to the Mürzstag Program of 1903, they compared their own unfavorable lot and arrears in pay with the pleasant life of European officers.

And in 1907 fugitives from Salonika won over Ahmed Riza in Paris to accept the possibility of armed revolution. Abdul Hamid's enemies joined then in a second congress of Ottoman Liberals, at which even an Armenian revolutionary society was represented. After this meeting the Paris and Macedonia groups merged under the name, Society of Union and Progress, and set up a permanent committee of the Society to implement the program adopted by the Congress—opposition to the Ottoman government in every way possible.

THE REVOLUTION

But the real revolution began in the Middle East, not in Paris. Army mutinies became frequent in 1906, largely because of arrears in pay and miserable conditions. When rebellions were shown to bring immediate improvements, many more occurred in 1907, with civilians joining to protest against corrupt officials, in Erzerum, Bitlis, Izmir, and even in Istanbul. In the spring of 1908 mutinies broke out in Macedonia; officers whom Abdul Hamid sent to investigate were shot. Various Turkish officers of the Society of Union and Progress took to the hills, and rebellion spread everywhere. Late in July, 1908 came the fateful telegram from Serres announcing that the Third Army Corps would march on Istanbul to enforce the reproclamation of the constitution which the Society of Union and Progress had demanded the preceding day.

The army threat was the telling blow. On that evening, July 24, 1908, Abdul Hamid restored the constitution and ordered elections for members of the Chamber of Deputies. A liberal grand vizir was appointed; and on the 25th, the Istanbul press and citizens rejoiced over the good, though unexpected, news. Abdul Hamid bowed to the force of the demands and rode with the popular tide. But he did not surrender.

The summer of 1908 was spent in preparing for the elections and readjusting government ministries to the wishes of the committee of the Society of Union and Progress. The program called for the sultan's deposition; but the Society had never cultivated the masses, and the popular cries in the capital were: "Long Live the Constitution," "Long Live the Sultan," and "Down with the Spies." Abdul Hamid went to Aya Sofya for his public prayers on the first Friday after the Revolution and received much adulation from the throngs that gathered. He was fostering the view that he was happy over the turn of events! The committee was not fooled, but recognized that it did not have the force or following to depose him.

On December 17, 1908, in the chambers near Aya Sofya where Midhat's parliament had met thirty-one years earlier, Abdul Hamid, accompanied by five of his sons and in the presence of the notables of the empire and foreign representatives, opened parliament and gave his speech from the throne. Major religious and national groups of the empire were represented, and various political views were in evidence: 142 Turks, 60 Arabs, 25 Albanians, 23 Greeks, 12 Armenians, 5 Jews, 4 Bulgars, 3 Serbs, and 1 Vlach. The best-organized group was the Macedonia-Salonika branch of Union and Progress, but it was far from having complete control of the situation. Ahmed Riza, their distinguished publicist from Paris, was chosen president of the Chamber of Deputies and served as a valuable figurehead for the anonymous members of the committee of the Society.

Members of parliament coalesced into three political groups. In addition to Union and Progress, there were the Liberal Unionists of Ismail Kemal, Prince Sabah al-Din, and Hassan Fehmi. The Liberal Unionists believed the solution of the ills of the empire could be found in creating a loosely federated state of locally autonomous nationalist provinces. The third party was the conservative and reactionary Muslim Association, which supported ideas of Pan-Islamism and firm adherence to religious law. Union and Progress, however, showed its power in February, 1909 by engineering the downfall of the grand vizir on a motion of no confidence when he refused to appoint two of its members as minister of war and minister of marine.

FAILURE OF THE COUNTER-REVOLUTION

The counterrevolution struck April 13, 1909, and leading members of Union and Progress went into hiding. Developing spontaneously among soldiers of the First Army Corps in Istanbul, the cries were: "Down with the Constitution," "Down with the Committee," and "Long Live the Sacred Law." Abdul Hamid gave his blessing to the counterrevolution, and a new grand vizir took office. The Young Turks of the Revolution, as they were called, were inexperienced in government and few in number. Moreover, they harbored the illusion that the proclamation of the constitution and announcement of just, efficient, honest, and rational government would solve all evils of the Middle East. All good people would rise up and usher in the promised day. But it did not happen. Soldiers' pay was no better, and general conditions remained about the same. The people of the Middle East were not prepared to destroy the mental attitudes of the millet system or tolerate equality among Turk, Greek, Armenian, Bulgar, Jew, Arab, Albanian, and the other peoples of the empire. "Under the same blue sky we are all equal; we glory in being Ottomans." These oft-quoted words of Enver, one of the committee members who later rose to fame, stirred emotions but were not accepted as fact.

The committee of Union and Progress, however, acted decisively. Mahmud Shevket Pasha, commander of the Third Army Corps in Macedonia, was invited to march on Istanbul and defend the constitution. When he arrived at Yeshilköy on April 23, he proposed to parliament, which was holding a rump session there, the declaration of martial law, punishment for mutineers, and full obedience to him. His terms were accepted, Istanbul was occupied, and order restored in five hours on the 25th. In an executive session of April 27, Parliament deposed Abdul Hamid, having obtained a favorable *fetva* from the Shaykh al-Islam. The new sultan, Mehmed V, was born in 1844. He was a mild gentleman, who declared he had not read a newspaper in the last twenty years. He had been completely surrounded by his brother's spies and minions—even the ladies of his harem—and had lost all initiative. He was the perfect constitutional monarch for the Young Turks.

ITALIAN WAR

The task before the Young Turks would have staggered the most experienced administrators. Internal problems commanded the highest priority, but foreign affairs and war rose to occupy the minds of the committee and consume the meager funds available. Europe feared that the Young Turk regime would restore vigor to the empire. Contemplated acts of aggression should be made at once. On October 5, 1908

Prince Ferdinand of Bulgaria cut all ties with the sultan and took the title of Tsar. On October 7 Austria-Hungary announced annexation of Bosnia and Herzegovina. On October 12 Crete revolted and declared union with Greece. None of these acts was surprising or momentous for the Ottoman government; they had been all but written off several years previously. Politically, however, they were hard blows against the prestige of the Young Turks and were factors in the counterrevolution of April, 1909.

A far greater shock was delivered by the Italian ultimatum of September 28, 1911 demanding that Turkey not object to an Italian military expedition to Libya. War was declared immediately. Although the Turks were driven from the coastal towns of Tripoli and Benghazi, guerilla warfare continued in the interior. Italy then occupied Rhodes and the Dodecanese Islands, and shelled the Dardanelles. Sentiment ran high in Turkey. People refused to eat macaroni, and the Young Turks closed the Straits. When England and Russia protested, the Straits were reopened; but peace seemed difficult to arrange. Enver Bey and Fethi Bey, both prominent members of Union and Progress and military attachés in Berlin and Paris respectively, along with other officers of later distinction like Mustafa Kemal, made their way with difficulty to Libya, where they organized and for a time led a resistance movement among the Sanussi tribes.

Ottoman victory was hopeless; and when it appeared that the Balkan states were plotting a common war against Turkey, the Ottomans hastily signed the Treaty of Ouchy on October 18, 1912. Under the terms of the treaty Turkey withdrew from Libya; Italy, from the Aegean Islands. Italy agreed to assume a share of the Ottoman debt and authority of the caliph was recognized in Libya. Italy, however, refused to evacuate her island conquests, claiming Turkey continued to incite Arab warfare in Libya.

THE COMMITTEE OF UNION AND PROGRESS

Shortly after the deposition of Abdul Hamid in 1909 the Society of Union and Progress held a party congress in Salonika and established a central executive committee which remained active until the party was dissolved at the end of World War I. From its headquarters in Salonika it ruled the party, the government, and the ministers when the party was in power. After 1912, when the Balkan wars broke out, the central executive committee sat in Istanbul and there dictated to the membership.

But the many activities of the Union and Progress party began to tell on its popularity. Even before defeat by the Italians, parliamentary control weakened, and to forestall a defeat in the Chamber of Deputies the Young Turks had Mehmed V dissolve the Chamber and call for a new election. This new Chamber was also closed, in August, 1912, when radical young leaders of Union and Progress attacked a cabinet composed of men of more experience and prestige. Two ministries largely representing the Liberal Unionist party followed. The latter, however, succumbed to a *coup d'état* by the Union and Progress in January, 1913, when extremists rebelled at surrendering Edirne to the Balkan states. From that moment until the end of World War I leaders of Union and Progress maintained a firm control over the government.

The desires of the Young Turks flowed out in every direction. Their intention was to examine all institutions of their society, changing any which had become anachronistic. Javid Bey, Young Turk minister of finance, reorganized his department, with the aid and advice of Charles Laurent of France. Sir Richard F. Crawford of England advised the customs bureau. General Liman von Sanders headed a German mission to transform the army under the direction of Enver Pasha. British Admirals Gamble and Limpus reformed the navy. French Count Roubilant formed a new gendarmery. And Count Ostorog, a French Pole, was employed for a short time to suggest means of introducing secular law without prejudicing the Sacred Law. In education and social services Young Turk reformers took the helm. Ziya Gökalp, Tevfik Fikret, Mehmed Amin, Halide Edib, Fuad Köprülü, and many others devoted their energies and talents to improving education.

Stimulated by their studies in the West or by their reading of Western books in the original or in translation, these Young Turks sought to raise the well-being and ameliorate the life of the great mass of Ottoman subjects. They deplored the poor existence in Turkey, suffered in their souls with the people, and wished to give pride, dignity, and an energetic determination to the nation. They wanted to create a national consciousness. They were nationalists! But in the Middle East society appeared to lack homogeneity. Racial origins were many, but the ages had mixed them completely. There were religions by the score. Languages and dialects were so diverse that young British consular officers coming to Istanbul took lessons in Turkish, Greek, Persian, Arabic, Armenian, and Russian! And rural and urban cultures and manners were so foreign, one to the other, that no common group appeared to be possible.

NATIONALISM

Ziya Gökalp and his friends debated these problems in their budding nationalism, and at various times emphasized one factor over another. Because of these complexities three main types of nationalism developed: Ottomanism; Pan-Islamism; and Pan-Turanism. Ottomanism possessed the greatest attraction in the earlier days of the Revolution.

It was recognized that origins were mixed, and as good nineteenth-century European liberals and radicals they minimized and scoffed at religion. Language was less of a barrier as Turkish had long been the *lingua franca* of the Ottoman Empire. It was easy to note that Turkish gentlemen had manners similar to Greek and Armenian gentlemen and that peasants and artisans were alike in many respects. Ottomanism was fashionable; thus, the bold rejoicing of all groups and nations when the Revolution came in 1908.

But fundamental views and historic feelings soon triumphed. Usually most non-Turks in the Chamber of Deputies voted as a bloc in opposition to the Turks. So-called programs for Ottomanization were branded as attempts to Turkify all others. Such moves eventually provoked a revolt in Albania, where the tribes resisted fiercely. Equality in the army, holding government posts, and paying taxes went against the customs and views of too many groups in the empire to be accepted voluntarily very long. As soon as one began to advocate and practice Ottomanism overtly, differences were highlighted and proved insurmountable.

The next move was toward religion and Pan-Islamism. Throughout the nineteenth century there were drives to seek rapport among Muslim states and peoples and to strengthen the position of the Porte by means of wider support for the caliph. Missions were sent to Kabul, and Abdul Hamid subsidized Jemal al-Din al-Afghani in his work in Egypt and Syria in preaching for a reform in Islam. Many Young Turks in their nationalist enthusiasm found great satisfaction in Pan-Islamic dreams. Unfortunately these reveries, when translated into reality, encouraged all manner of harshness, discrimination, and persecution for non-Muslims and freethinkers. Full responsibility for the atrocious massacres of Armenians in Cilicia in 1909 was never ascertained; but the blame should probably be shouldered by the Young Turks and reactionary elements, each of whom had strong Pan-Islamic tendencies. The stringent and reactionary measures of a Pan-Islamic nature adopted by the Union and Progress party from April, 1909 to July, 1912 led, at least in part, to its downfall.

The third form of nationalism appeared in Pan-Turanism, which espoused the union or federation of all Turkish peoples as far eastward as Central Asia and recognized kinship to Finns, Hungarians, Tartars, and many Turkish tribes in Russia. Enver, one of its chief advocates, eventually died in 1922 pursuing the policy in Turkestan. The main efforts of Pan-Turanists, however, were devoted to the policy of Turkification of all non-Turks and to the arduous task of instilling a national feeling among all classes of Turks within the Ottoman Empire, especially in Istanbul and Anatolia. To accomplish the latter task Union and Progress created an institution called *Türk Ojak* (Turkish Hearth), where lectures on diverse subjects were sponsored as a program of adult education aimed at developing a national consciousness.

ALBANIA AND THE BALKAN WARS

In the end the policy of Turkification produced the downfall of the Young Turks. Although educational drives were commendable, non-Turkish communities bitterly resisted. In several districts in Asia Minor trouble arose with Greeks and Armenians, whose boycotts and attacks caused serious dislocations of commerce. Many Arabs became disillusioned. Revolts broke out in Yemen and Asir; and purely Arab nationalist societies were formed in Baghdad, Damascus, and Beirut. In part these Arab societies were made up of Arab members of Union and Progress, Fatherland, and other Young Turk revolutionary societies.

The most violent storm broke in Albania, when in the process of Turkification the government took steps to enforce a decree forbidding the possession of arms. Albanians also objected to a census, taxes, and the drafting of young men to serve in Yemen (which was always called the graveyard of Ottoman armies). The Albanian rebellion was quelled early in 1911 after diplomatic intervention by Montenegro and a grant of considerable local autonomy.

Concessions to the Albanians, however, aroused hopes among other nationalities; the Macedonians particularly hoped for the establishment of a regime similar to the one in Eastern Rumelia. These concessions also excited the ambitions and jealousies of officials in Greece, Bulgaria, Serbia, and Montenegro. The Young Turks, nevertheless, pushed their policies of centralization of government, keeping the provinces at the boiling point. Although the Liberal Unionists achieved an ascendancy in Istanbul during the last half of 1912, they came too late with proposals of decentralization. The Balkan states declared war on the Turks in October.

The Powers, sensing that a Balkan League was being formed to attack Turkey, had previously notified the Balkan governments that no aggrandizements won as a result of aggression would be countenanced. Ignoring the warning, Bulgaria, Greece, Serbia, and Montenegro agreed on the division of Macedonia; and within a month after the start of war the Allies overran all of European Turkey north of the Chatalja lines protecting Istanbul, except for Edirne, Skodra, and Janina. The effects of the reorganization of the Balkan armies in the preceding decade surprised the Great Powers, which accepted the fact that the *status quo* could not be enforced.

In December an armistice was signed, and the five belligerents met in London to negotiate peace. Cession of Edirne was demanded as the price. When it became apparent that Kiamil Pasha, the grand vizir, and the Liberal Unionists were willing to pay the price, Enver Bey and about two hundred members of Union and Progress staged a successful *coup d'état*. They assassinated the minister of war, Nazim Bey, and returned the radical party to power. In February, 1913 war was resumed. In rapid succession Janina, Edirne, and Skodra fell to Greek, Bulgarian, and Montenegrin forces. Meanwhile, the Greek navy defeated the Turkish forces outside the Dardanelles and occupied a number of the Aegean islands.

In April a second armistice was arranged, and peace was signed in London on May 30, 1913. Turkey ceded to the victors all European possessions north of a line from Enos on the Aegean to Midia on the Black Sea and consigned to the Powers financial, judicial, commercial, and nationalist questions arising from the transfer of territory and the division of the loot among the Balkan states. Establishment of Albania upon the insistence of the Great Powers goaded Greece and Serbia to demand a revision of their previous understandings with Bulgaria. Failure brought war between Bulgaria and Serbia on June 30, 1913. Greece, Montenegro, and then Rumania entered the war against Bulgaria. And on July 15, 1913 Turkey invaded Thrace. Enver Bey reoccupied Edirne. The Treaty of Bucharest ended this Second Balkan War in August, although a separate settlement in Istanbul between Turkey and Bulgaria, which restored Edirne to Turkey, was not drawn up until September.

THE TRIUMVIRATE

The Balkan Wars were over, and the Young Turks had lost almost all Ottoman possessions in Europe. From a long-range point of view this was probably a happy development, as it withdrew a heavy drain upon Turkish resources and manpower. At the moment it gave power to the radical wing of the Young Turks. Following their *coup d'état* in January, 1913, Mahmud Shevket Pasha became grand vizir. But his assassination in June and the grand vizirate of Said Halim Pasha, a mild and weak Egyptian prince, permitted the reins of government to fall into the hands of a triumvirate of Young Turks: Talat, Enver and Jemal.

Talat Bey was born of a poor family near Edirne and started his rise as a telegraph operator in the government office at Salonika. Possessed of a brilliant mind, he was one of the organizers of the revolutionary movement in Macedonia and served as minister of interior in several cabinets of the Young Turks. He was a dedicated man who remained poor and modest in his character and habits throughout his career. Ruthless in his tactics, he made a distinction between personal and national morality, believing that many acts which would be entirely immoral and cruel if perpetrated by and for an individual were perfectly moral if performed in the interests of the state. Polite and exceedingly considerate, he never forgot his humble origin.

Enver came from a lower-middle-class family and received a military education. Catapulted to public attention by his defiance of Abdul Hamid and his flight to the Macedonian hills in the first stage of the revolution in 1908, Enver loved the heroics of nationalism and won fame in the war in Libya against Italy. He was a man of action and quick decisions. Imbued with strong Turkish nationalist feelings he held to that course throughout his life. As an attaché in Berlin, Enver fell under the spell of Prussian militarism and thoroughly believed in the superiority and invincibility of the German military machine. He, more than any other, brought Turkey into World War I as a German ally. As he rose to power, he became vain and more distant—a development which many of his former friends and admirers deplored. As one remarked: "Enver Pasha has destroyed Enver Bey."

Jemal Pasha, who became minister of the navy, was an early member of the Society of Union and Progress, if not one of its founders. He came from an old Ottoman family and had been a Pan-Islamist; but in the days of the triumvirate he became an ardent Turkish nationalist. The weakest of the three, Jemal served as a kind of policeman for the Young Turks, maintaining discipline and holding the faltering in line.

To the day of the entry of Turkey into World War I, or more properly until the arrival of the *Göben* and the *Breslau* in the Bosphorus, the triumvirate ruled Turkey with a strong hand. Disobedient party members were punished; opponents were eliminated; and uncertainty and terror returned to Turkish government circles.

REFERENCES: Chapter 26

Many references mentioned for the four preceding chapters are important for this chapter; in addition those of particular note are in Chapters 12, 13, 18, 19, and 20.

G. F. Abbott, *Turkey, Greece and the Great Powers:* R. Scott, London, 1916. A lengthy report on the problems of the Balkans and Turkey during the first decade of the twentieth century.

Niyazi Berkes, trans. and ed., *Turkish Nationalism and Western Civilization: Selected Essays of Ziya Gökalp:* Columbia University Press, New York, 1959. An important source.

Leonard Binder, *The Ideological Revolution in the Middle East:* Wiley, New York, 1964.

Norman Daniel, *Islam and the West: The Making of an Image:* Edinburgh University Press, Edinburgh, 1960.

John A. DeNovo, *American Interests and Policies in the Middle East, 1900–1939:* The University of Minnesota Press, Minneapolis, 1963. A thorough work that includes all aspects of American interests.

Leland J. Gordon, *American Relations with Turkey, 1830–1930, An Economic Interpretation:* University of Pennsylvania Press, Philadelphia, 1932. Particularly good on the period before World War I and American dollar diplomacy in Turkey.

E. C. Helmreich, *The Diplomacy of the Balkan Wars, 1912–1913:* Harvard University Press, Cambridge, 1938. Basic for this topic.

Walter Z. Laqueur, ed., *The Middle East in Transition:* Praeger, New York, 1958. A collection of important essays by well-known scholars.

Bernard Lewis, *The Middle East and the West:* Indiana University Press, Bloomington, 1964. A provocative essay.

R. W. Seton-Watson, *Rise of Nationality in the Balkans:* Constable, London, 1917. Important for the Balkan Wars.

Telford Waugh, *Turkey, Yesterday, To-Day, and To-Morrow:* Chapman & Hall, London, 1930. A useful work incorporating many facts of the prewar period.

Wilbur W. White, *The Process of Change in the Ottoman Empire:* Chicago University Press, Chicago, 1937. Discusses the impact of the West on this area in the nineteenth century, country by country.

CHAPTER 27

Arab Nationalism

THE ROLE OF EDUCATION

At the opening of the twentieth century the twin questions of Arab nationalism and formation of an independent Arab nationalist state were hardly considered. But the movement and feeling were already reaching a degree of development that could burst at any moment into the full light of world attention. The activities and speeches of Muhammad Ali and his son Ibrahim stirred a few to think in terms of a truly Arab state. During the years of Egyptian occupation of Syria a few sparks of nationalism were struck; and upon Ibrahim's withdrawal and the return of Ottoman rule Beirut and Damascus became centers of nascent Arab nationalism.

In Syria the leading role was played by Western educational penetration. Although Jesuit fathers arrived in the seventeenth century to teach in Maronite and Catholic communities, little rejuvenation occurred until 1820 when American Presbyterian missionaries landed in Beirut. The latter organized schools almost immediately. Catholic fathers now increased their energies to compete with the American Protestants; and Ibrahim furthered the educational drive by establishing many elementary schools for boys on the model of those in Egypt. Girls' schools were also opened. And in 1834 Americans set up a printing press in Beirut.

Education advanced by leaps and bounds. A training college for teachers was founded in Lebanon. In 1866 the Syrian Protestant College of Beirut opened its doors. Later becoming the American University, it played an important role in training the youth (Muslim and Christian alike) from every corner of the Arab world. Almost simultaneously Catholic missionaries, largely from France, settled in Syria in greater numbers, and schools spread from Beirut to Damascus, Aleppo, and many other towns. In 1875 the opening of the University of St. Joseph in Beirut marked a forward step of great significance, for here were educated many outstanding leaders of Syrian national and cultural life.

The stimulation from these activities affected many circles. Two individuals, Nasif Yaziji and Butrus Bustani, came forward to guide the local movement. In 1847 the Society of Arts and Sciences was established to engender a spirit of inquiry into the sciences and a literary revival of the Arabic tongue. The Jesuits, not to be outdone, organized the Oriental Society in 1850. Because of missionary participation in these two groups, Muslim Arabs refused to join. However, upon the exclusion of the foreign influence in 1857 the Syrian Scientific Society was born. Its members included Muslims and Christians of all sects. They all took pride in being Arabs. From this society came Ibrahim Yaziji's famous *Ode to Patriotism,* a secret revolutionary incitement to Arab insurgence.

In Egypt a similar educational renaissance was under way. Muhammad Ali and his successors maintained close relations with Europe and employed numerous British, French, and Italian advisers who brought ideas of European education. Egyptian boys were sent to Europe to achieve a Western education, and the numerous schools opened in Egypt to train civil servants changed the outlook of society in Cairo and Alexandria. The famous Bulaq Press, started in Cairo in 1822, printed over 300 books in Arabic, Turkish, and Persian before 1850. It gave to Cairo the distinction of being a literary center and drew there many intellects from every part of the Arab world. Without the printing press Arab nationalism and the regeneration of the Arab people would have progressed very slowly. Books were emitted in ever-growing volume, and newspapers sprang up in the leading cities. An incomplete tally in 1913 showed 118 newspapers in the Arabic language within the Ottoman Empire, excluding Egypt.

With the advent of Abdul Hamid and his varied persecutions, clandestine societies multiplied in the Arab provinces. A Beirut secret society posted placards preaching patriotism and declaring the aims of the society to be: independence of Syria, including Lebanon; Arabic as the national language; end of censorship and freedom of expression; and exclusive use of locally-recruited units on local military service.

EGYPTIAN NATIONALISM

In Egypt local autonomy freed Arab nationalism from the sultan's surveillance. Arab nationalism and Egyptian xenophobia were also aroused by the privileged position of foreigners, especially in Alexandria; by the building of the Suez Canal; and by the numerous Turkish families, who held a disproportionate number of positions under the khedive and owned a large part of the cultivated land of Egypt. The uprising of Arabi Pasha in the 1880's was an outburst of this feeling, and after the British occupation Arab refugees from Abdul Hamid's anger flourished in Egypt.

One of these exiles was Abd al-Rahman Kawakibi of Aleppo, who wrote _Umm al-Kura,_ a humorous yet penetrating symposium on the future of Islamic society, and _The Attributes of Tyranny,_ naturally published anonymously in Cairo. Together they analyzed the decrepit society of Islam, especially Arab society. Kawakibi attacked the ignorance of the masses and the obscurantism of the theologians who dominated the educational field. He was also one of the first to separate Arab national revival from Pan-Islamism.

Another eminent leader who stirred the imagination of the Arabs appeared in the teacher and preacher Jemal al-Din al-Afghani. He resided in Egypt from 1871 to 1879 and became so influential that the government asked him to leave. The remainder of his life was spent in Iran, France, England, and the Ottoman Empire. He died in 1897. Jemal al-Din al-Afghani desired to reform Islam progressively by means of education and to adapt Islam to the conditions of modern life. He did not see how this could be done without revolution, political unity of the Muslim world, and freedom from foreign domination.

Perhaps al-Afghani's most illustrious pupil was Muhammad Abdu, a peasant from Lower Egypt who had a distinguished career as a mystic, journalist, judge, and teacher. Differing from his mentor, he deplored the use of violence and believed that true reforms came only by a gradual process. Abdu advocated a reform of Islam which would return Islam to its earliest purest dogma, permitting a more flexible interpretation of its precepts than was allowed in the Cairo of his day. Muhammad Abdu, like Arabi Pasha, wished to free the people of Egypt from despotic rule and institute a more democratic society. He also worked for the development of Arabic into a more unified tongue, attempting to draw newspaper Arabic and the spoken vernacular together and bring both nearer to classical Koranic Arabic.

The ambitions of Khedive Ismail to make Egypt equal to the nation states of Western Europe, which he admired so much, instigated his wild extravagances. But they also fostered the rapid advance of education, expansion of the means of disseminating information, and growth of a class of intellectuals. Because of the British occupation, however, the primary objective after 1882 was liberation from British rule; and from this time on the quest for an independent nationalist Arab state centered more and more upon Beirut and Damascus.

THE YOUNG TURKS AND ARAB NATIONALISM

The program of the Young Turks before the counterrevolution in 1909 appealed to many Arab leaders, who saw in it only the destruction of Abdul Hamid's tyranny. As a positive force they fully subscribed to the Ottoman program of the Society of Union and Progress because they translated it to mean decentralization of the empire, as proposed by Prince Sabah al-Din, and equality of Arab with Turk. Abdul Hamid exiled many Young Turks to Damascus, Jerusalem, and Baghdad. And like many unhappy Turkish army officers languishing in these remote parts the rising Arab nationalists looked upon the Turkish liberal struggle as their own fight, too.

In the early days of the Revolution there was every co-operation. The Young Turks insisted that Abdul Hamid designate Sharif Husayn of the Hashimite family Governor of the Hijaz, Keeper of the Holy Places, and Prince of Mecca. Although Husayn had resided quietly for fifteen years in Istanbul as a kind of hostage, Abdul Hamid astutely judged the man to have ambitions to rule an independent Arab state. He, therefore, warned the Young Turks of the folly of their recommendation; but in September, 1908 he acquiesced and appointed Husayn to the post. In the same month Istanbul witnessed the inauguration, with much ceremony and fanfare, of The Ottoman Arab Fraternity—an Arab society to defend the Ottoman constitution, promote the welfare of Arabs, and "foster the observance of Arab customs."

Hardly had the society been started when it was suppressed by a decision of the Union and Progress party. After the counterrevolution of 1909 centralization of government, Turkification, and disallowance of all local customs and tradition contrary to Turkish practice became veiled objectives of the Young Turks. As non-Turkish political societies were suppressed, the Arabs, among others, went underground. Here, then, was the birth of passionate and uncompromising Arab nationalism.

ARAB SECRET SOCIETIES

As usual, a welter of societies and parties sprang into being not only among the Arabs in Istanbul, but also among those in Damascus, Beirut, Baghdad, Aleppo, and other Arab cities. An important one was the Literary Club, which almost immediately took the place of The Ottoman Arab Fraternity in Istanbul. The successor disavowed political activities; it posed as a meeting place, library, and clubhouse for Arabs living at the capital and a center for Arab travelers. Within a short time its membership reached thousands, and branches were located throughout Syria and Iraq. This was open testimony of growing Arab consciousness; but it was impossible to prevent Arabs, sitting relaxed in the club-house, from discussing political philosophy as it pertained to the Arab situation.

The second important open group was The Ottoman Decentralization party established in Cairo in 1912 by experienced Arab public figures. The objectives were to mobilize Arab public opinion and impress upon the Young Turks the need to organize the new Ottoman Empire on a more federal basis. Headquarters remained safely in Cairo, although branches were located in Iraq and Syria and close contact was maintained with the Literary Club in Istanbul. The Decentralization party stressed party machinery and enjoyed partial success during the last half of 1912 when the Union and Progress party was out of power.

One interesting secret society was called al-Kahtaniya. (Kahtan was a legendary ancestor of the Arabs.) It advocated the creation of a dual Turko-Arab empire, much like the Austro-Hungarian Empire, where "unity" of the two peoples could be attained by "separation." More and more as the Turkish leaders of Union and Progress showed their hands and guided affairs definitely along paths of Turkification, aspirations for a Turko-Arab accommodation died. With these hopes went al-Kahtaniya.

Suppression by the Turks drove many Arabs abroad. Like Turks a decade earlier, they flocked to Paris. Already Arabs were active there. In 1904 Najib Azuri had founded the League of the Arab Fatherland, and in 1907 he had set up his paper, Arab Independence. In 1911 the Arab refugees formed The Young Arab Society, better known as al-Fatat (Youth). A secret society, al-Fatat rejected the idea of any integration within the empire and worked for full Arab freedom and independence. It became the most widespread and effective force among Arabs, moving its headquarters to Beirut in 1913 and to Damascus in 1914.

In view of these activities and the general Arab enthusiasm they evinced, the Young Turks adopted more stringent measures. A committee of reform, which gathered in Beirut in 1913, publicly announced a program for Arab home rule and won such wide acclaim that the Young Turks suppressed it. Shops and offices in Beirut closed, and newspapers went into mourning. Thereupon, the leaders were arrested. The crisis appeared to be coming to a head, and under the leadership of al-Fatat a congress of Arabs was held in Paris. Attended by twenty-four delegates representing many Arab parties, the congress adopted the platforms of the Decentralization party and the committee of reform. The results of the congress were ostensibly accepted by the Young Turks; and an imperial decree in August, 1913 incorporated the declarations as stated policy in Arab provinces. However, the reforms re-

Aziz Ali al-Masri

mained unenforced, and the Arabs believed they had been duped. Partially in reply, an Arab, Major Aziz Ali al-Masri of the Ottoman general staff, initiated a new society called The Covenant (*al-Ahd*). The Covenant was comprised exclusively of army officers and became for the military what The Young Arab Society was for civilians. It had many members in Beirut, Damascus, and Baghdad. Perhaps getting wind of the action, the Young Turks without warning arrested Aziz Ali in 1914. He had been a member of Union and Progress in Salonika before 1908 and had won honors during the march on Istanbul in 1909, during a military mission to Yemen in 1910, and during the war against Italy in Libya. Charged with treason in Libya, Aziz Ali was tried, found guilty, and condemned to death. Public opinion became so indignant, especially in Egypt, that the British protested to the Porte. He was pardoned and sailed for Egypt as a public hero to lead The Covenant from Cairo. Any hope that the Young Turk leaders had for Arab co-operation and participation was now completely dispelled. Ottomanism and Pan-Islamism for Arab leaders disintegrated in the face of an obvious and understandable drift to Turkish nationalism shown in actions of radical Young Turks.

THE ARAB PRINCES

Not only did the Turks have difficulty with Arab nationalists and their many patriotic societies, but also they discovered that Arab governors and semi-autonomous rulers employed every means to gain independent positions. Unsuccessful expeditions were sent to bring Imam Yahya of Yemen and Muhammad ibn al-Idrisi of Asir to heel. Tiring of the continual drain on resources, the Young Turks reached an accord with the two, granting them many powers and a liberal subsidy. In eastern Arabia they found their support of the Rashid family unavailing against Abd al-Aziz ibn Saud, who drove the Turks and their allies from the rich province of al-Hasa in 1913.

Had it not been for the Hijaz Railway which connected Syria with Medina, the Young Turks' authority over Sharif Husayn would also have vanished. A Turkish garrison stationed at Mecca rendered overt revolution foolhardy without considerable strength and careful planning. Early in 1914 Prince Abdallah, Husayn's second son and an Arab member of the Ottoman parliament, hinted vaguely to the British as he passed through Cairo that his father would be open to suggestions and assistance from them for rebellion against the Turks. These overtures, very discreet in nature, indicated that Husayn was considering a treaty similar to that which the British had with Arab princes and shaykhs in the Persian Gulf area. Such treaties provided for British recognition of the Arab ruler's independence from the sultan, protection, and a pen-

sion in exchange for British conduct of all foreign relations, friendship
for Britain, and permission for a British resident minister to live at the
court.

Suspicion of Husayn's harboring of these intentions drifted back to Istanbul where the Young Turks acted to limit his authority. Governorship of the Hijaz was assigned to another, who arrived in Mecca to destroy the Prince. In the spring of 1914 the Turks understood that Husayn had consolidated his position with the tribes of the Hijaz, and to
forestall a violent insurrection the new governor was ordered to make
peace. At a public ceremony in Mecca the unfortunate governor hum-
bled himself and kissed the hem of Sharif Husayn's robe.

It was not clear that any connection existed between the actions of
Husayn, al-Idrisi, Imam Yahya, and Ibn Saud on the one hand and the
revolutionary societies of the Ottoman Arab world on the other. Foreign
governments were friendly to the Arabs; and partly to counter the
growing influence of the Germans with the Young Turks, British and
French officials in Beirut and Egypt gave encouragement to Arab societies. British and French consuls general received delegations of Arab
nationalists. A delegation from Damascus which visited Lord Kitchener
in Egypt suggested that Britain annex Syria to Egypt, giving it a separate administration.

In 1913 an Arab conference was held at Mohammerah in Iran to advance the independence of Iraq. Attended, among others, by the
Shaykhs of Kuwayt and Mohammerah and Sayid Talib Pasha of Basrah, it exhorted Arabs to work together to drive out the Turks. Another
conference was called for 1914 at Kuwayt, with additional invitations
going to Sharif Husayn, Abd al-Aziz ibn Saud, Ibn Rashid of the Shammar tribes, and Shaykh Ajaymi of the Muntafik tribes. It never met,
however, because of rivalries and jealousies among these Arab leaders.
Therein lay the weakness of the Arab movement in the days before
World War I.

When the conflict opened in 1914 the Young Turk triumvirate realized that defection in Arab provinces was likely and that loyalty of
Arab officers was highly questionable. Yet Enver, Talat, and Jemal
hoped that the natural Arab proclivity for dissension would save the
day. Their hope was justified. The secret societies of officers and nationalists in the urban centers were opposed to the autocratic rule of kings
and suspected them of princely ambitions. Equally apprehensive were
the various princes, one of each other. Sayid Talib, for example, was believed by other Arabs to be working against the Ottoman regime not for
the independence of Iraq or the local autonomy of Basrah but to carve
out an independent principality on the order of Kuwayt. When such
fears were prevalent, united action from all groups and factions was un-

likely. The Ottoman Empire was saved for the moment. But it was only a question of time before Arab nationalism would flare into the open. World War I and the disturbances, confusion, and promises it brought hastened the day of Arab revolt.

REFERENCES: Chapter 27

Works cited at the end of Chapter 20 are valuable for this chapter. In addition there are those in Chapters 4, 7, 19, 23, 25, and 26.

Khaldun S. al-Husry, *Three Reformers: A Study in Modern Arab Political Thought:* Khayats, Beirut, 1966.

George Antonius, *The Arab Awakening: The Story of the Arab National Movement:* Hamilton, New York, 1938. This is the fundamental work on this topic.

Gustave E. von Grunebaum, *Modern Islam: The Search for Cultural Identity:* University of California Press, Los Angeles, 1962.

Manfred Halpern, *The Politics of Social Change in the Middle East and North Africa:* Princeton University Press, Princeton, 1963.

Albert H. Hourani, *Syria and Lebanon, A Political Essay:* Oxford University Press, London, 1946. The earlier chapters give a clear picture of the rise of Arab nationalism.

Nejla Izzeddin, *The Arab World, Past, Present and Future:* Henry Regnery, Chicago, 1953. The sections on the awakening of the Arabs in modern times are exceedingly well done.

Elie Kedourie, *Afghani and Abduh, An Essay on Religious Unbelief and Political Activism in Modern Islam:* Frank Cass, London, 1966.

Malcolm A. Kerr, *Islamic Reform: The Political and Legal Theories of Muhammad Abduh and Rashid Rida:* University of California Press, Berkeley, 1966.

Hans Kohn, *A History of Nationalism in the East* (Margaret M. Green, trans.): Harcourt Brace, New York, 1929. An understanding work.

————, *Western Civilization in the Near East:* Columbia University Press, New York, 1936. Philosophical.

John Marlowe, *Arab Nationalism and British Imperialism:* Praeger, New York, 1961.

Mohammed Rifaat, *The Awakening of Modern Egypt:* Longmans, Green, London, 1947. Although it covers the period since 1798, it is strong on the development of nationalism.

Hassan Sa'ab, *The Arab Federalists of the Ottoman Empire:* Djambatan, Amsterdam, 1958.

Zaki Saleh, *Mesopotamia (Iraq), 1600–1914:* Albert Daub, New York, 1958. Mostly British foreign affairs.

Zeine N. Zeine, *Arab-Turkish Relations and the Emergence of Arab Nationalism:* Khayats, Beirut, 1958. A basic study by an eminent scholar and professor at the American University of Beirut.

————, *The Struggle for Arab Independence: Western Diplomacy and the Rise and Fall of Faisal's Kingdom in Syria:* Khayats, Beirut, 1960.

PART IV

The Contemporary Middle East

CHAPTER 28

Impact of World War I upon the Middle East

TURKEY ENTERS THE WAR

The shot at Sarajevo which killed Franz Ferdinand of Austria rico-cheted around the world. Its blows upon the Ottoman Empire proved fatal. Sentiments in Turkey were mixed regarding the war. The great majority of influential men desired neutrality and believed that therein lay the best interests of Turkey, already torn, defeated, and impoverished by mediocre governments, revolutions, and the Balkan wars. Another group, trained in the liberal traditions of French and British political and university circles, inclined toward the Entente, although the inclusion of Russia, traditional Ottoman enemy, disturbed these men very considerably.

A hard core of army leaders, however, dominant in the committee for Union and Progress, had come under the spell of German military genius in their schooling under men of the type of von der Goltz Pasha. Guided by Enver Pasha, minister of war, and spirited by Baron von Waggenheim, German ambassador, the triumvirate of the Turkish cabinet signed a secret alliance with Germany on August 2, 1914. Each engaged to assist the other, and Germany agreed not to withdraw her military mission from Turkey. Although known to only five Turks, the alliance was reinforced a week later by the entry into the Straits and "purchase" of the German cruisers *Göben* and *Breslau*. Purportedly, this purchase was made to replace two Turkish ships built and ready for delivery in England but sequestered by Britain on the outbreak of war. Renamed the *Sultan Selim Yavuz* and *Midilli* (*Mytilene*) but still manned by their German officers and crews, these warships with their guns pointing at the palace and the ministry of war commanded the situation.

During the following eleven weeks military and diplomatic events in Europe and at the Porte moved rapidly. Turkish conversations with the Entente for an alliance raised questions about the Capitulations, Turkish mobilization on her eastern borders, and German concessions in Anatolia, Thrace, and the Aegean Islands. The Turkish price was too high. Russia, England, and France held the military strength of the Ottomans in low esteem and believed that a push through would be comparatively easy. They, therefore, decided that it would be more convenient to have Turkey join the Central Powers and once and for all settle her partition upon victory. How else would Russia ever obtain her coveted Constantinople and the Straits?

The policies of extremists and adventurers in high Turkish circles prevailed, even though they were a small minority and completely out of touch with the masses. No action was taken against the Germans in Turkey, and by October German officers were in full command. Colonel Weber closed the Dardanelles; and after the German defeat at the First Battle of the Marne the German High Command brought Turkey into the war by sending German Admiral Souchon with the *Yavuz* and *Midilli* to shell Sevastopol and Odessa (October 28, 1914). Enver, who had given permission, was determined to have war so that he could "liberate Egypt" as Napoleon had done. The press was subsidized and in readiness! Russia formally declared war on November 4; England and France followed the next day. The sultan pronounced a "holy war" on November 14. In the estimation of many Turkish leaders, the Ottoman Empire had begun to dig its own grave.

The great mass of Turks—Anatolian villagers—would fight for and support the sultan and his government with or without a "holy war" declaration. But Muslims under the French in North Africa, under the British in Egypt, the Sudan, and India, and under Russia in central Asia might be induced to rebel. Moreover, the war party of the Society of Union and Progress held illusions of recapturing Egypt and Libya and recognized the need of active Arab co-operation in the venture. But the holy war fell upon unreceptive ears. Revolts of even the slightest significance did not materialize and outright hatred generally felt among the Arabs for the Turks more than counterbalanced any Islamic tie which a holy war might have mustered. Furthermore, since the caliph was allied with the Christian powers of Germany and Austria-Hungary, the cynicism involved in the declaration of a holy war against the infidels escaped no one.

The immediate Arab reaction was twofold. One group looked upon the outbreak of war involving Turkey and the imperialistic European states as a God-given opportunity to obtain a united and independent Arab national state. The other group, consisting of princely Arab families and their clients, regarded the war as a time to rebel against the Ottoman sultan and establish independent Arab kingdoms—each for himself and heaven protect the others.

With the formal entry of Turkey into the war German domination over Turkish actions and affairs became paramount. General von Sanders directed the army, and Admiral Souchon, the navy; British Admiral Limpus was, of course, "recalled." Transportation, food supplies, finance, and many other highly important wartime problems were frequently left in Turkish hands, though German policy usually dictated the course pursued and German officials regularly acted as they pleased. Turkey swarmed with Germans, and as the war progressed she became more and more a German protectorate.

GALLIPOLI CAMPAIGN

A few days after the Turkish naval expedition into the Black Sea a British contingent bombarded the entrance to the Dardanelles. In January, 1915 the British War Cabinet acquiesced to the views of Winston Churchill and agreed to send a force to break through the Straits, take Turkey out of the war, and open a first-rate munitions supply route to Russia. The British army command, however, sabotaged the venture and greatly lessened its chances of success. After unsuccessful attacks in February and March by naval forces, an Anglo-French army began landing operations on the Gallipoli Peninsula in April, 1915. The army met withering fire and stubborn defense by Turkish forces and some German officers under the command of General von Sanders. Suffering outrageous losses, the Anglo-French force was joined by the Italians in August, clung on, and twice nearly succeeded in a break-through. Lack of co-operation by the Russians at the Bosphorus end of the Straits, skillful tactics on the part of the Germans and Turks, and faulty intelligence work by the offensive led first to a stalemate and then to Allied withdrawal from the Straits in January, 1916. The withdrawal was accomplished without any losses.

TURKISH WAR PLANS

The Russians were perturbed over the Dardanelles campaign for fear the British and French would take the Straits, capture Istanbul, and fail to relinquish them to the Russians. None the less, they made the first overtures for some kind of a campaign to relieve them of Turkish pressure in the Caucasus. The over-all Ottoman war plan called for an attack upon the Russians in the east and an expedition to drive the British from Egypt. In the last months of 1914 Turkish forces moved to take Kars and Batum, but the strategy was poorly conceived by Enver. After a few initial successes the Turks fell back with heavy losses. In the campaigns of 1915–1916, with the aid of Armenian revolutionaries and irregular forces, the Russians captured Erzerum, Van, Trabzon, Erzinjan, and other lesser cities in the east. In 1916 Mustafa Kemal Pasha in command of the Second Army joined the Third Army on the Caucasus front, but little was accomplished. Transportation was next to impossible; ammunition and supplies of every kind were scarce; and disease was rampant. In the month of February, 1917 forty-two Turkish army surgeons died of spotted typhus alone, and thousands of soldiers died of starvation and general debility.

The revolutions in Russia in 1917 affected the Caucasus front very markedly, especially the Bolshevik Revolution in the autumn. All Russian troops except for the Armenian and Georgian divisions melted away. The Turks advanced rapidly to occupy Kars, Ardahan, and Batum, which the Treaty of Brest-Litovsk gave to Turkey. Georgian and German forces, however, retook Batum and denied Turkish entrance. Later, a Bolshevik-Armenian *coup* in Baku and the massacre of 10,000 Turks produced a concerted Turkish drive which led to the capture of that city in September, 1918 and the killing of many Armenians. Germany deplored the Turkish inroads into the Caucasus and even went so far as to conclude a Bolshevik-German agreement according to which German forces would protect the Caucasus and in particular Baku from attacks by a third party. However, at the end of war in 1918 neither German nor Turkish forces found any support, and the Caucasus area became an Allied problem.

The second ambition of Enver was the conquest of Egypt. Early in August, 1914 Britain took precautionary measures there, and after Turkey's active entry into the war a British protectorate for the duration of the conflict was established (December 18, 1914). Khedive Abbas Hilmi was deposed and Husayn appointed Sultan of Egypt. Jemal Pasha, minister of marine and one of the triumvirate, took command of the Fourth Ottoman Army and assumed responsibility for Syria, including Palestine. Early in February, 1915 his forces made a surprise attack upon the Suez Canal; but possessing inadequate strength to hold the eastern bank, they retired to a line in the Sinai Peninsula with bases at Maan, Beersheba, and Gaza. Throughout 1915 small flying columns raided points of the Suez Canal. These raids compelled the British to maintain a large force there but depressed the morale of the Turkish and Syrian armies because of the inevitable retreats.

An assault in force against the Canal was ordered for February, 1916, but poor transport delayed the attack until the least opportune weather of midsummer. The assault proved a dismal failure; and from that moment until the end of the war Turko-German armies were on the defensive in this theatre of operations. Furthermore, the repressive and harsh policies of Jemal Pasha in Syria turned the diffident Arabs into a hostile population, which began in 1916 to look upon the British as liberators. None the less, in March and April, 1917 at the famous Battles of Gaza Turko-German arms withstood heavy British fire and drove the enemy back to a line in Sinai. Later in that year, a German ordered and directed operation, known as Yilderim and commanded by General von Falkenhayn, attempted to gain a favorable decision in Palestine. Again, failure of transport, sabotage of supplies en route, continuing harassment by Arab desert bands, and a build-up of British forces under General Allenby brought disaster to von Falkenhayn, as von Sanders and Mustafa Kemal had foreseen.

The fourth area of major hostilities in the Middle East was Mesopotamia. British contingents from India seized Basrah even before the Turkish entry into the war and proceeded northward to the confluence of the Tigris and Euphrates. A sizable force under General Townshend captured Kut-al-Amara in 1915; but it was defeated just south of Baghdad in November and fell back to Kut-al-Amara, where the Sixth Turkish Army forced a surrender in April, 1916. However, Halil Pasha, Enver's uncle, failed to pursue his victory and permitted the British and Indian divisions to re-establish their hold on southern Iraq. A railroad was built and superior concentrations of men, artillery, and supplies enabled the British under General Maude to retake Kut-al-Amara and capture Baghdad in March, 1917. Before the year was out the British were halfway between Mosul and Baghdad, but they had not yet reached the former at the time of the Armistice in 1918.

THE ARMENIANS

While the course of World War I was unfolding in the Middle East and shattering the Ottoman Empire, two national groups within the state openly aided the enemy. These were the Arabs and the Armenians. Wealthy representatives of the latter insisted that the Armenian people support the Ottoman government and the war; but the head of the Armenian Orthodox Church, residing in the Russian Caucasus, asseverated that the tsar was the protector of all Armenians. Thus, in Istanbul and the western cities of the empire Armenians complied with war orders, while in eastern Asia Minor the Armenian population, often following Westernized Armenian radicals such as Pasdirmajian, aided

Russia by rebellion and in the region of Van and Erzerum by open warfare. In some districts the entire Muslim population was killed; and in April, 1915 an Armenian government was proclaimed in Van.

These incidents touched off the unfortunate Armenian deportations and massacres of 1915 and 1916. An estimated 1,500,000 Armenians lived in Turkey at the outbreak of war. The great preponderance were in Aleppo and the eight Anatolian vilayets of Erzerum, Van, Bitlis, Kharput, Diyarbakir, Sivas, Adana, and Trabzon. The basic order came in June, 1915. It authorized the transfer of all non-Muslims away from points of military concentration and from lines of communication and required all non-Muslims in the military forces to be relegated to rear service units without arms.

The gravity of the action appeared when actual deportation occurred. Inadequate provisions in Syria, the general destination, led to the death of tens of thousands from exposure, exhaustion, and starvation. It almost seemed as if many were marched off into the desert to die. Everyone suffered, and the prosecution of the war on the Caucasus front was hampered in 1916 and 1917 because of the failure of services in eastern Anatolia which Armenian inhabitants normally provided. Many Armenians were set upon by marauding bands of Kurds and Turks, and unofficial groups such as these perpetrated numerous atrocities. Representatives of neutral governments protested to the Porte, and German officials privately lamented the action. Enver and the government, however, were deaf to all pleas, since a few influential individuals of the Turkish government were actually bent on the extermination of the Armenian population in eastern Turkey. Certainly half a million Armenians perished! No doubt certain deportations were required, but the total action was entirely inconsonant with the need. Many Turks shielded and protected Armenian individuals and groups from the authorities; and in general Turks considered the severity of the Armenian deportations and consequent loss of life as a blot on the Turkish record.

ARAB MOVEMENTS

The other pressing national problem confronting leaders of the Ottoman government was the loyalty and aspirations of the Arabs. No open break occurred until June, 1916, when Sharif Husayn of Mecca proclaimed his personal rule in the Hijaz. Prior to that move, Jemal Pasha as an Ottoman viceroy and commander of the Fourth Army maintained discipline and surface calm in Syria. Jemal supported Pan-Islamism and sought to obtain active support of the Arabs in the war. Documents, however, fell into his hands implicating numerous Muslim and Christian leaders in treasonable activities. In 1915 arrests were made, and eleven persons were hanged in the main square of Beirut. When Enver called upon Jemal for troops for the Gallipoli campaign, an Arab division, including many leaders of *al-Ahd,* was sent in order that more reliable Turkish troops might remain in Beirut and Damascus. A year later (April, 1916) about two hundred Arabs, including many well-known and influential men from the most prominent families, were arrested, tried, and sentenced. Twenty-two were hanged in Beirut and Damascus. This act more than any other precipitated Husayn's declaration of Arab independence.

Before examining the moves for independence made by the western Arabs in Syria and the Hijaz, Arab-British relations should be placed in their proper setting. Petty Arab states existed along the western shore of the Persian Gulf and the southern coasts of Arabia. Almost every one had a treaty of friendship with Great Britain in which the latter exercised power over Arab foreign relations. In effect, protectorates were created. A British minister resident or an agent resided in the shaykhdom or the sultanate, advised on all governmental matters, and doled out gold sovereigns or Maria Theresa silver dollars to keep everybody happy.

When war became imminent, Captain Shakespear of the Royal Navy, then attached to the India Office, visited Abd al-Aziz ibn Saud of the Nejd and entered into a standard Arab-British agreement: Ibn Saud placed his foreign affairs in British hands and accepted a generous subsidy. In regard to the Arabs as a whole and the question of a unified Arab nation, no reference was made and none was implied. Ibn Saud controlled an important segment of the interior of Arabia; and the India Office was merely assuring his neutrality, at least in the struggle between Briton and Turk in Iraq and the Persian Gulf area.

A more significant Arab development involved Husayn, whom the Young Turks sent to the Hijaz as the Prince of Mecca. Early in 1914 Husayn's second son, Abdallah, in passing through Cairo had sounded Lord Kitchener, British agent in Egypt, on the subject of British aid to Husayn, who desired to break with the Turks. After the advent of war, Kitchener recalled the conversation and instructed Ronald Storrs, British Oriental secretary in Egypt, to raise with his favorite chess opponent, Abdallah, the question of an alliance with the British and a declaration against the Turks.

Thus began the celebrated correspondence between Sharif Husayn and the British in Egypt. Husayn found himself in a delicate situation. His third son, Faysal, did not trust the British or French and felt that it would be better policy to co-operate with the Turks and win their gratitude. Abdallah, however, favored independence from the Turks and proposed, in co-operation with Arab secret societies of Damascus

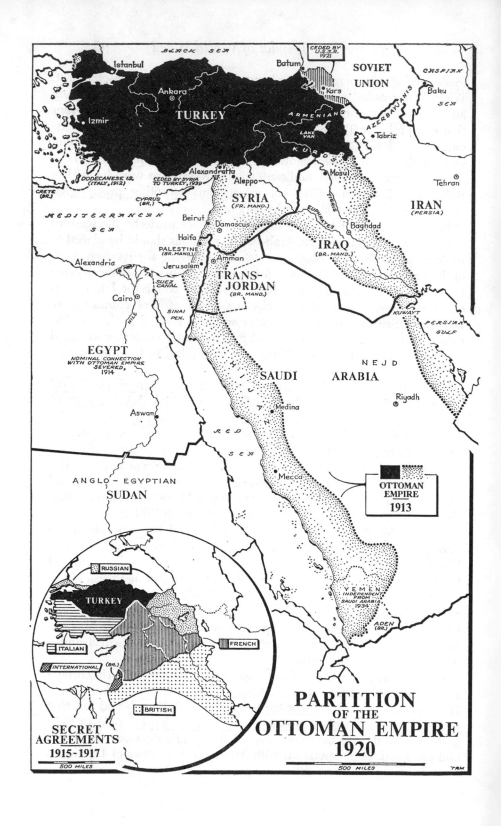

PARTITION
OF THE
OTTOMAN EMPIRE
1920

SECRET
AGREEMENTS
1915-1917

500 MILES

500 MILES

OTTOMAN
EMPIRE
1913

and Beirut, to take advantage of the world struggle to obtain British aid. Husayn postponed the decision until June, 1916. Meanwhile, an exchange of letters between Husayn and Sir Henry McMahon, High Commissioner for Egypt and the Sudan, brought to a head the issue of Arab independence and an Arab state. These negotiations resulted in Britain promising, upon the successful conclusion of the war, an Arab state. The area of the state was to be bounded on the north by a line drawn eastward from Alexandretta to the Iranian frontier and thence southward to the Persian Gulf and was to include the entire Arabian Peninsula. Excepted from this were British Aden and the districts of Syria west of Damascus, Homs, Hama, and Aleppo. The British refused to pledge the latter without the consent of France. Britain promised not to make a peace treaty which did not include this Arab state; and Husayn categorically stated that he would not consent to any part of Arabia becoming the possession of any power, by which he meant France. Also excluded from the United Arab state were the small states such as Kuwayt and Muscat with which Britain had special treaty provisions.

Husayn, however, was not a free agent in dealing with the British. His son Faysal conferred clandestinely in Damascus with leaders of the Arab movement, and in 1915 he presented the secret Damascus Protocol to his father. This document defined the Arab frontiers as Husayn later insisted upon with McMahon, and it demanded abolition of the Capitulations in return for economic preference to Great Britain. Its authors invited Husayn to forward their terms to the British as the basis on which Arabs would revolt. Thus, the Husayn-McMahon correspondence should rightfully be regarded not as a negotiation between two individuals but as a negotiation between representatives of two principals—the British government and the Arab people.

THE SECRET TREATIES

While these negotiations with Husayn were in process, the Allies were engaged in formulating their notorious secret treaties, dividing among themselves both Turkish and Arab parts of the Ottoman Empire. As soon as war broke in 1914, Russia pressed England and France for Istanbul and the Straits and considerable hinterland on each side. After many diplomatic exchanges Russia was reluctantly promised in March, 1915 possession of her age-old quest. In exchange British and French rights in Asiatic Turkey would be defined by special agreement and the neutral zone in Iran included in the British sphere of influence.

A month later the Pact of London was signed to bring Italy into the war. This pact promised Italy sovereignty over the Dodecanese Islands and elimination of all rights of the Ottoman caliph yet remaining in

Libya. Italian interests in Antalya were conceded and that area promised to her; in case Turkey was not dismembered Italy would be given recompense elsewhere.

The most far-reaching of the secret treaties—the Sykes-Picot Agreement of April 26, 1916—allotted to Russia the already promised Straits area, the vilayets of Erzerum, Trabzon, Van, and Bitlis, and Kurdistan. France was granted the coastal strip of Syria northward from Tyre, the vilayet of Adana including Mersin, and a vague area of Cilicia which comprised a triangle of Anatolia marked off by Adana, Sivas, and Mardin. Britain obtained an enclave about Haifa and Acre on the Mediterranean and Mesopotamia from Baghdad to the Persian Gulf. Palestine west of the Jordan River and from Gaza to Tyre was, upon the insistence of Russia, cut from French Syria and promised an international administration because of the Holy Places and numerous Russian Orthodox establishments. The area of Syria from Damascus and Aleppo eastward through Mosul to the Iranian frontier was consigned to French protection, while the region from Kirkuk to Akaba and from the Mediterranean to the Persian Gulf became a British sphere. Alexandretta was designated a free port.

The secret Sykes-Picot Agreement was signed only a few months after agreements embodied in the Husayn-McMahon correspondence were concluded. Husayn did not learn of the perfidy until late in 1917, when the Bolsheviks published the secret agreements found in the imperial archives. Husayn requested an explanation. In February, 1918 he received from Lord Balfour, then the foreign secretary, a statement virtually denying the existence of the Sykes-Picot Agreement and adding a cryptic remark about the consent of the populations concerned. Husayn trusted the British until after the war ended.

The Italians, however, learning of the Sykes-Picot arrangements, insisted upon a further delimitation of their ambitions. Thus, in a railway car on a siding at St. Jean de Maurienne in 1917 the prime ministers of England, France, and Italy agreed that Italy should have the districts of Izmir, Antalya, and Konya and all of southwestern Anatolia. A district north of Izmir also became an Italian prize. At the same time that Italy secured Izmir, Venizelos was promised Cyprus and the territory of western Asia Minor including Izmir as an inducement to bring Greece into the war on the Allied side. Pledges and counterpledges with regard to the future of the Middle East were beginning to mount. But these were only half of them!

THE BALFOUR DECLARATION

Zionism had yet to be heard. Zionism was a socio-political and nationalistic movement developing among European Jews in the last quarter of the nineteenth century. Pogroms in Russia and anti-Semitism in the nationalistic states of Europe fostered political Zionism and provoked Theodor Herzl to establish the World Zionist Organization in Basle in 1897. Concessions were repeatedly sought from the Porte for a Jewish settlement company in Palestine; but the sultan refused, believing it would increase his already diffuse problems of nationalism. And the Zionist Congress declined the British offer of a settlement in Uganda. Zionism without Zion would be paradoxical!

At the outbreak of war in 1914 Zionist activities were centered in Germany. Upon the division of Europe into two camps, however, another center arose in London. There Dr. Chaim Weizmann became the leader. Opposition arose from the Anglo-Jewish Association and the Board of Deputies of British Jews, both of which were anti-Zionist. Weizmann, however, with the support of the *Manchester Guardian*, the Rothschilds, Lloyd George, whose private secretary was Sir Philip Sassoon, and Sir Herbert Samuel, won the favor of Lord Balfour. In the United States a co-operating Zionist committee was organized under the chairmanship of Justice Brandeis and supported by Rabbi Wise, Eugene Meyer, Nathan Strauss, Felix Frankfurter, and others.

The Zionists wanted an Allied commitment to create a Jewish commonwealth in Palestine upon the demise of the Ottoman Empire. Political pressure to this end was exerted, generally in the public presses, and individually upon public and political figures. Slowly a sizable group came to favor such a state, especially when Zionists pledged that the new creation, so strategically placed with respect to Suez, would be in the British sphere of influence. Success came on November 2, 1917, when Lord Balfour wrote to Lord Rothschild:

"His Majesty's Government views with favour the establishment in Palestine of a national home for the Jewish people and will use their best endeavours to facilitate the achievement of this object, it being clearly understood that nothing shall be done which may prejudice the civil and religious rights of existing non-Jewish communities in Palestine or the rights and political status enjoyed by Jews in any other country.

This letter, the famous Balfour Declaration, had the approval of the British Cabinet as well as that of President Wilson, who insisted upon adding the modifying clauses. Later, France and Italy accepted the Declaration, and Wilson publicly acknowledged it in October, 1918. The exact meaning of the Declaration has been much debated in the last decades, but at the time of its writing there was no doubt of its intent. Also it was definitely contrary both to the Sykes-Picot Agreement and to the Husayn-McMahon correspondence. Reasons for its issuance have been advanced by those responsible. It was alleged that its pronouncement was required to gain the support of Jewish circles in Germany and Austria to the Allied side. There may be some basis to this; for in 1918 Germany and Turkey also offered the Zionists a charter for a Jewish settlement company in Palestine. War loans and sales of war bonds have been intimated as contributing factors for the announcement of the Declaration; and statements have asserted that Dr. Weizmann demanded it as payment for his work in the experimentation on acetone. But neither of these has real foundation. Lloyd George had no feeling about the Zionists, but he saw in them a way to keep the "atheistic French" out of the Holy Land. It was constant political pressure and the winning of important men to their cause, for whatever reason, that brought success to the Zionists. They were disappointed, however, that the Declaration did not read "recognizing Palestine as the national home for the Jewish people."

Husayn was dismayed when the news of the Balfour Declaration reached him, and quite naturally he requested an explanation. Profes- sor Hogarth, an Arabic scholar from Oxford, was sent to explain that Jewish settlement in Palestine would not be permitted to compromise "'the political and economic freedom of the Arab population." Again, Husayn accepted the British word.

THE FOURTEEN POINTS

One other Allied promise was made during the war. When Baghdad and Jerusalem fell to British forces, the victorious generals announced that future settlement would be made with the consent of local popula- tions. These utterances foreshadowed the broad concepts of Wilson's Fourteen Points, presented to the American Congress on January 8, 1918. In particular they foreshadowed Wilson's twelfth point, which stated that the Turkish parts of the Ottoman Empire should have a "secure sovereignty" and that other nationalities should be given "an undoubted security of life and an absolute unmolested opportunity of development." Greeks, Armenians, and Arabs felt that this point al- luded to them and built their hopes upon it. Arabs believed that Wil- son's declaration recognized their aspirations as proposed by Husayn and nullified Balfour's Declaration and all secret treaties, agreements, commitments, understandings, and promises made by the powers under the duress of total war.

ALLIED VICTORY

Failure of the German-Turkish campaign, called Yilderim, in the summer of 1917 opened the way for the British build-up in Egypt to move into Palestine. Jerusalem fell to General Allenby in December, 1917; and British forces, accompanied by French detachments, proceeded northward along the coast, taking Tyre, Sidon, Beirut, and Tripoli. The interior lines of communication were continuously harassed by the Arabs under Faysal. The Arab revolution of June, 1916 shattered the Turkish regime in the Hijaz; and Arabs under Faysal east of the Jordan paralleled the actions of Allenby. Under the stimulus and encouragement of such British liaison officers as Colonel T. E. Lawrence, Colonel C. C. Wilson, and Sir Reginald Wingate, and receiving British equipment and gold, the Arabs captured Akaba and Maan and entered Damascus in October, 1918, at the same time as did the British. The Seventh Turkish Army under Mustafa Kemal Pasha held the Arabs before Aleppo, but the armistice signed at Mudros between the Allies and the Turks ended all hostilities.

German failures on the Western Front in the summer of 1918 and the imminent collapse of Germany spelled the end of warfare in the Middle East. Without German matériel and general assistance the Ottoman Empire could not maintain effective resistance. Admiral Gough-Calthorpe, commander of the British Mediterranean Fleet, received representatives of the new Ottoman government of Izzet Pasha aboard the _Agamemnon_ off Mudros on the island of Lemnos and on October 30, 1918, signed an armistice ending the war. It was not an unconditional surrender; but Turkish forces were to be demobilized, and the Allies were to have free access and control of the Straits. Opening the door to total Allied control was Article VII which stated: "The Allies have the right to occupy any strategic points in the event of any situation arising which threatens the security of the Allies." Under such an article any action was allowable.

The war, four years almost to the day, brought many changes to Turkish society. It disintegrated so fully under the terrible conditions of the war that Asquith declared "the Sick Man had really died this time." To describe the miserable conditions in Turkey to those who did not experience them or similar circumstances would require many pages. Suffice it to say that the larger cities were disturbed more than the villages, and Istanbul most of all. Shortages of every kind developed; war profiteers appeared; physical suffering of the masses became widespread; and the general low standard of living deteriorated rapidly, as inflation lifted the prices of everything without much change in wages. Most commodities were scarce. Foreign goods could not be imported, and domestic produce was largely requisitioned by the government. Worse still, the government proved entirely incapable of governing. Inefficiency, mismanagement, and malfeasance dominated every government office. The Capitulations were abolished; the Ottoman Public Debt Administration was terminated; and the war-burdened government assumed control over many unaccustomed activities. The end of the Turkish state seemed obvious, and Asquith completed his declaration on the Sick Man with the pronouncement that "his resurrection was impossible."

Yet, the war generated many new and positive forces in society. As the power of the government waned, Arabs, Greeks, Armenians, and all subject nationalities of the empire gave more open expression to their nationality. For the Armenians, it led to destruction. To the Greeks, it brought a temporary fulfillment of cherished dreams. And among the Arabs, it created the Revolt and new Arab states. For the Turks the rapid decay gave to many liberals and democrats such as Halide Edib and Ahmed Emin and to uncompromising nationals like Mustafa Kemal an opportunity of being heard and of having some heed paid to their demands for governmental leadership which would place the welfare of the nation above self-interest.

Of the other effects of the war, one of the more salutary for the Middle East was the presence of many British, French, Italian, and German soldiers, and their equipment. Thousands of Middle Easterners saw Westerners and their manner of living for the first time. Their machines opened a new world to Arabs and Turks. The impact of the West upon the Middle East in every facet of its living from transportation to religion was more profound and penetrating in these four war years than it had been in several centuries of contact through religious, commercial, and intellectual missions from the West. A new age for the Middle East was born.

REFERENCES: Chapter 28

Volumes cited in Chapters 7, 13, 18, 19, 22, 23, 24, 25, 27, and 35 have value for this chapter.

Michael G. E. Bowman-Manifold, *An Outline of the Egyptian and Palestine Campaigns, 1914 to 1918:* Mackay, Chatham, 1922.

Edmund Dane, *British Campaigns in the Near East, 1914–1918:* Hodder & Stoughton, London, 1917–1919.

Ahmed Djemal Pasha, *Memories of a Turkish Statesman, 1913–1919:* Doran, New York, 1922. The autobiography of one of the triumvirate in Turkey during the war.

Ahmed Emin, *Turkey in the World War:* Yale University Press, New Haven, 1930. A basic and thorough study of political, economic, and social forces developing in Turkey during the war years by the leading editor in Turkey. His name in the 1930's became Ahmed Emin Yalman.

Laurence Evans, *United States Policy and the Partition of Turkey, 1914–1924:* Johns Hopkins Press, Baltimore, 1965. Most thorough.

Harry N. Howard, *The Partition of Turkey; A Diplomatic History, 1913–1923:* Oklahoma University Press, Norman, 1931. The most definitive work on the political, diplomatic, and international aspects of the war in the Middle East.

Robert Rhodes James, *Gallipoli: The History of a Noble Blunder:* Macmillan, New York, 1965. Complete and new interpretation.

T. E. Lawrence, *Seven Pillars of Wisdom:* Jonathan Cape, London, 1935. The full account of the colonel's activities among the Arabs during the war.

Alan Moorehead, *Gallipoli:* Harper, New York, 1956. The story of the famous campaign.

Liman von Sanders, *Five Years in Turkey:* Williams & Wilkins, Baltimore, 1928. The record of the German commanding general stationed in Turkey during the war.

Leonard Stein, *The Balfour Declaration:* Simon and Schuster, New York, 1961. First good complete history.

Ronald Storrs, *Orientations:* Nicholson & Watson, London, 1937. Storrs was the Oriental secretary of the British High Commissioner in Egypt during the war.

Charles V. Townshend, *My Campaign in Mesopotamia:* T. Butterworth, London, 1920. By the commanding general of the British forces.

Arnold T. Wilson, *Loyalties: Mesopotamia, 1914–1917:* Oxford University Press, London, 1930. A detailed record of the military occupation of Iraq.

CHAPTER 29

The Middle East at the Paris Peace Conference

ALLIED CLAIMS AND PROMISES

Less than two weeks after the Mudros Armistice halted World War 1 in the Middle East Germany signed the Armistice with the Allies and war officially ceased. The fate of the Middle East devolved then upon the several armies of occupation and, perhaps even more importantly, upon "the smoke-filled rooms" of Paris, where politicians, diplomats, statesmen, generals, journalists, and representatives of every special interest gathered to make peace. The Middle East, however, was only a small part of the total settlement. Problems with respect to Germany took precedence over all others; and decisions affecting France, Germany, and central Europe frequently compromised the verdict on the Middle East.

The prime conflict concerning the Middle East appeared in the frightful disparity contained in the assorted secret treaties, agreements, and letters exchanged among the Allies, to say nothing of contradictions in numerous pious, platitudinous, and public pronouncements by Allied leaders during the war. A recitation of a few illuminates the confusion at Paris—the London Pact of 1915, the Sykes-Picot Agreement, the Balfour Declaration, the Husayn-McMahon correspondence, the Fourteen Points, the liberation statements at Baghdad and Jerusalem, and the "make the world safe for democracy" slogan. Thus, the hopes of the many who traveled to Paris were high.

Lloyd George went to the conference, professing friendliness and good will for the peoples of the Middle East and clamoring for their welfare and aspirations. But he had every intention of advancing the interest, power, and possessions of the British Empire. Egypt, Mesopotamia, Arabia, Palestine, Iran, Cyprus, and the Caucasus were considered British prizes, and under no circumstances were Istanbul and the Straits to be awarded to France. The entire Middle East, with the possible exception of Syria and parts of Anatolia, was regarded as an economic adjunct of the British Empire. Clemenceau, on the other hand, stood for a French hold upon Syria and southern Anatolia, hoped to acquire or at least dominate the Straits, and dreamed of having a French adviser at the elbow of the sultan of Turkey who would exercise a role similar to that of the British adviser in Egypt. President Wilson, on his trip across the Atlantic aboard the *George Washington,* met daily with his advisers and sincerely discussed plans for peace in the Middle East which would fulfill the pledge made in his Fourteen Points. Since Allied governments concurred in that declaration, he believed it wiped away all previous "sins."

The big three held major decisions in their hands; but hosts of others had greater personal or national interests in the Middle East. Prince Faysal came to Paris to represent the Arabs, his father, and the Kingdom of the Hijaz, which had been a belligerent since June, 1916. Faysal expected England to abide by her pledges given to the Arabs for their national state. Three groups of Armenians presented conflicting claims for their nation, and President Wilson was obliged to send out the Harbord Mission to ascertain the facts. Venizelos, the Prime Minister of Greece, used all of his charm and diplomatic blandishments to obtain the Allied promises with respect to the Greek "Great Idea," i.e., the restoration of the Greek empire to include western Asia Minor, Constantinople, and the Straits. Prime Minister Orlando of Italy intended to receive the Dodecanese Islands, southwestern Asia Minor around Antalya, and an area in and about Izmir.

Bankers, oil men, exporters, bondholders, missionaries, churchmen, shippers, and humanitarians of sundry kinds also converged at Paris to lobby for their respective interests. Amid receptions, gay dinner dances, and week ends at rented chateaux within easy motoring distance of Paris, the future of the Middle East was sought. Everyone was there except the Turks. They did, however, have unofficial agents in Geneva; and Damad Ferid Pasha, the Grand Vizir, was permitted on one occasion to deliver a statement before the supreme council of the conference.

Dr. Weizmann, Judge Brandeis, Rabbi Wise, Professor Frankfurter, and Mr. Sokolov watched over and advanced the cause of Zionism by shepherding the Balfour Declaration through the negotiations to assure its incorporation in all final settlements for the Middle East. Opposing these ardent Zionists stood a few of the Jewish faith such as Edwin Montagu, Claude G. Montefiore, Jacob H. Schiff, Louis Marshall, and Mayer Sulzberger. Henry Morgenthau, Sr., former American ambassador to the Porte and treasurer of the Democratic party's national committee, felt that Zionism endangered the slow process of assimilation of Jews occurring in national states of the West. He also believed that creation of a Zionist state in Palestine would raise the question of dual nationality. With 299 other leading American Jews, therefore, he signed a petition to President Wilson against the establishment of any Jewish state.

Nevertheless, a coterie of active Zionists won the support of Lloyd George, Balfour, Lord Milner, and Lord Robert Cecil as well as the sympathy of President Wilson. The policy of self-determinism, however, seemed to be blocking Zionist aims. Jews constituted not more than fifteen percent of the population of Palestine, and a policy of counting heads would favor Palestine's inclusion in an Arab state as pledged to Sharif Husayn. Lloyd George was unimpressed by Zionist pleas, but he definitely opposed the idea of the Holy Places falling into the hands of "agnostic, atheistic France." More influential with the British was the concept of acquiring Palestine as a stronghold to protect Suez and other British interests in the Middle East. Zionists reinforced this hope by declaring openly that Jews would opt for a British mandate and by talking of eventual home rule for a Jewish Palestine within the British Commonwealth of Nations. Zionist dreams were achieved. A paraphrase of the Balfour Declaration was included in the peace treaties and accepted by the League of Nations.

Out of the welter of claims and counterclaims for the Middle East was born the King-Crane commission. On the suggestion of President Bliss of the American University of Beirut Wilson proposed to the supreme council that a commission of inquiry composed of American, British, French, and Italian representatives go to Syria, Palestine, Mesopotamia, and Armenia. The idea was to obtain the information needed to implement the program of self-determination. At first the French, British, and Italians agreed, but later they refused to co-operate. Therefore, President Henry C. King of Oberlin College and businessman Charles R. Crane, the American appointees, proceeded alone in the spring of 1919 with a staff of experts. They visited Palestine, Syria, and Turkey, receiving petitions and local deputations. Having faith in Western democratic principles, Arabs rejoiced in the coming of the commission. The King-Crane report was submitted in the autumn of 1919 but was suppressed as it ran counter to arrangements already dictated between England and France. Wilson's illness prevented him from pressing the issue.

SAN REMO AGREEMENT

No permanent decisions regarding the Middle East could be reached in Paris in 1919, and the signing of a peace treaty for the area seemed more uncertain than ever. Wilson became gravely ill. The American Senate and people were not favorably disposed to accept a mandate for any territory. Russia was out of the picture. Germany and Austria were broken. And Italy was suffering from internal dissension and disillusionment. Questions of the Middle East, therefore, lay squarely between England and France. Meanwhile, armies of occupation governed the Middle East and the peoples grew restless waiting for peace.

British forces under Allenby controlled Egypt, Palestine, and Lebanon; Faysal and the Arabs held sway over the Hijaz and interior lines of Arabia including Damascus; and Britain was again master in Mesopotamia with an army from Mosul to the Persian Gulf. Official British policy was set to hang on to as much of the occupied area as possible and to make the Middle East a definite part of the British Empire.

But policy was not the chief concern of individual officers or men in the armies of occupation. The British army in 1919 was still the civilian army created during the war; and the aim of the great majority of men was to be demobilized as soon as possible. As officers in the Middle East pulled every string to get out, the turnover in personnel grew serious. Officers newly assigned to the Middle East barely became acclimated before they arranged a transfer home or to some permanent part of the empire. Added to the confusion was the fact that there was little planning or thought for military government or occupation.

In the last months of 1919 British contingents in Beirut and along the Lebanese coast were replaced by French units; and under arrangements concluded in Paris General Gourand became Allied administrator in Syria. These moves gave advance notice to the Arabs that settlement in the Middle East would follow lines drawn in the hated Sykes-Picot Agreement. Anti-Jewish riots in Jerusalem and Jaffa, election of Faysal as king of Syria and of Abdallah as king of Iraq by the Arab National Congress in Damascus, growing tenseness in Baghdad, insurrection in Egypt and the dispatch of the Lord Milner Mission to Cairo drove Britain to realize that a treaty for the Middle East was imperative.

One of the sensitive questions delaying settlement between England and France revolved around the division of Mosul oil. The Turkish Petroleum Company, seventy-five percent British and twenty-five percent

German, obtained in 1914, a few weeks before the outbreak of war, a concession to exploit the oil of Mosul. The Sykes-Picot Agreement, however, assigned Mosul to France. As early as December, 1918, therefore, Britain began pressing the French to allow Mosul to be attached to Mesopotamia. Various oil proposals were discussed, relating Mosul oil to a division of oil in Rumania, Russia, and the British and French colonies. But none of these proposals proved acceptable until the negotiators journeyed to San Remo on the Italian Riviera. There on April 24, 1920 the negotiators came to agree on oil, pipelines, mandates, and united action with respect to the Turks and Arabs.

THE TREATY OF SÈVRES

The San Remo Agreement prepared the way for a peace settlement with the Ottoman Empire, and the Treaty of Sèvres was signed August 10, 1920. By this Treaty the Ottoman sultan recognized the severing of Syria, Mesopotamia, Arabia, and Egypt from his empire. A British protectorate over Egypt was allowed; and independence of the Arab rulers and their states, subject to their treaties of friendship with Britain, was accepted. Provisional independence of Syria and Mesopotamia under the tutelage of some mandatory power was acknowledged. Syria, already assigned to France, included the cities of Alexandretta, Aleppo, Damascus, and Beirut. The vilayet of Mosul was attached to Baghdad and Basrah to form the State of Iraq under British supervision. Palestine, including the lands on each side of the Jordan and extending to the Gulf of Akaba, was given as a mandate to Britain with the Balfour Declaration written into the authorization. Additional understandings were reached. The German shares of the Turkish Petroleum Company were allotted to France. The British were granted oil pipeline transit rights across Syria. And France was given a free hand to deal with Faysal and the Arab Syrian kingdom with force—to crush them if necessary.

The Treaty of Sèvres was obsolete before it was drawn, and because of various exigencies within Turkish portions of the Ottoman Empire it was never fully ratified. Theoretically, then, final arrangements in the Middle East awaited the Treaty of Lausanne in 1923; yet divisions, boundaries, and disposals of non-Turkish parts of the Ottoman Empire of that final Treaty varied only slightly from the transfer of legal authority that was proposed at San Remo and Sèvres. Provisional mandates bargained for at San Remo dictated Arab political and economic life for the following twenty years, and Britain and France immediately took action in their respective spheres. One additional settlement, however, belonged rightfully to this era of treaties and engagements. In March, 1921, Winston Churchill, who was then colonial secretary, held a lengthy conference in Cairo with most of the British Middle Eastern experts, including Sir Herbert Samuel and Sir Percy Cox, high commissioners for Palestine and Iraq, respectively. They hatched a scheme that put Faysal, ousted by the French from Damascus, on the throne of Iraq and carved from the part of Palestine east of the Jordan the state of Transjordan for Prince Abdallah, who originally had been promised Iraq. Since the British did not wish to be under any obligation to the French in getting oil out through Syria, a section of the Syrian desert was claimed for Transjordan. This created a British-controlled route from Mosul to the Mediterranean.

ALLIED OCCUPATION OF TURKEY

In Turkish parts of the Ottoman Empire affairs of the Allies were not faring too well. On November 13, 1918 a combined Allied fleet traversed the Bosphorus and dropped anchor in the Golden Horn. Ten days later an Allied army under a French general entered Istanbul. Soon thereafter, British, French, Italian, and American high commissioners arrived to assume responsibility for the four zones established in the city. Istanbul immediately attracted Western commercial interest, and imports into Turkey to satisfy the lack of goods in the war years gave the city many characteristics of a "boom town," which the occupational forces did not dispel. Greek and Armenian natives welcomed the Allies as liberators, and foreign residents rejoiced that the war was safely over and their fellow Westerners were returning to control the situation. The Allies rolled back the wheels of time to 1914: the Capitulations were restored; the Ottoman Public Debt Administration functioned again; and concession hunting became once more the sport of the day.

Victory was sweet for most. Yet, there was more than the usual share of orphans, refugees, invalids, and general victims of war. At first the Turks were relieved that the fighting had terminated, since they were genuinely weary of war. As the occupation proceeded, however, thoughtful Turks grew dismayed at Allied lack of justice, understanding, and political wisdom. It soon became apparent that Sultan Mehmed VI and his ministers were only convenient Allied puppets. (Following the Armistice successive grand viziers were Izzet Pasha, Tevfik Pasha, and Damad Ferid Pasha.) It also became clear that Anatolia would be carved up, if the Allies could agree on a partition without fighting among themselves.

Britain moved northward from Mosul; France claimed Cilicia as an extension of Syria; and Italian forces landed at Antalya to assure that promises would be fulfilled. One of the tragedies of the time was initiated, when under cover of an Allied fleet Greek troops landed at

Izmir to take possession of what the powers in Paris awarded Venizelos. Supported by Britain and France, Venizelos won Wilson over to the Greek occupation, which began on May 15, 1919. Small incidents of organized Turkish resistance occurred almost immediately; and a few atrocities committed by the Greeks, especially at the village of Menemen near Izmir, made Turkish acceptance of Greek rule in Asia Minor impossible.

TURKISH NATIONALISTS

The day following the Greek landing at Izmir Mustafa Kemal Pasha, appointed as inspector general of the Third Army by the Allied high commissioners and the sultan, sailed for Samsun on the Black Sea coast with orders to commence demobilization and restore law and peace to Anatolia. Before the summer was over Kemal resigned his commission and convened rebellious national congresses at Erzerum and Sivas, calling for all patriotic Turks to join the Association for the Defense of the Rights of Turkey in Europe and Anatolia.

The Greek landing at Izmir produced extensive street demonstrations in Istanbul, and resentment toward the Allies swelled. Ferid Pasha's government was dismissed in October, and a new cabinet was formed under Ali Riza Pasha, who, it was hoped, would reach an accord with Kemal and the Nationalists of the Sivas Congress. As the strength of the Nationalists grew in Istanbul, many members of the Ottoman parliament in Istanbul openly supported the movement. In January, 1920 they drew up a six-point program as the basis on which a lasting peace could be drawn. It proposed self-determination for the Arabs, western Thrace, and the eastern provinces of Kars, Ardahan, and Batum; complete political and economic unity and independence of Turkish areas; international protection of minorities; and internationalization of the Straits, if Istanbul were guaranteed as a secure residence for the sultan-caliph. Increasing popularity of the Nationalists in Istanbul and active collaboration of many leaders with them spurred the British in March, 1920 to occupy the city of Istanbul with a strong military force. Ali Riza was replaced by Salih Pasha. Nationalist leaders and prominent Turks who were unable to hide or flee to Anatolia to Mustafa Kemal were seized and sent to Malta.

Heretofore, the occupation had been nominal. With the British in full control, patriotic Turks flocked to Kemal and his Nationalists. In April, 1920 the Grand National Assembly met at Ankara, adopted the six-point program, and elected Kemal as president of the Assembly. Sultan Mehmed VI dismissed parliament, and Damad Ferid Pasha became grand vizir for the second time. Turkish resistance was fully committed to fight for freedom and independence.

The Allies, however, never imagined that the "sick man" of Europe after the punishment he had taken during World War I could ever rise from his coma. They reasoned that the noises and movements in the interior were only the sounds and twitchings preceding death. The San Remo Conference blithely beckoned the Powers to the Treaty of Sèvres and its unreality. Greece was given western and eastern Thrace, including Edirne and territory up to a line twenty miles from Istanbul. The district and city of Izmir would be administered by Greece for five years, after which a plebiscite would determine its future. Armenia was established as an independent state, whose frontier with Turkey would be arbitrated by President Wilson. Kurdistan, east of the Euphrates River, obtained local autonomy, which might be transferred to independence upon consent of the League of Nations. Although Istanbul remained under Turkish sovereignty, the Straits area was to be controlled by an international commission. Turkey would maintain an army of 50,000 men, all armaments being under Allied supervision. Minority rights were respected. The Capitulations with new humiliating articles were re-established. And the Ottoman Public Debt Administration under British, French, and Italian direction was given almost absolute control over economic, financial, and budgetary matters. Equally galling to the Turks was announcement of the Tripartite Agreement among England, France, and Italy dividing what remained of Turkey into three spheres of influence almost exactly according to lines marked by wartime secret treaties. The Treaty of Sèvres left Turkey prostrate, and no self-respecting Turk could countenance it.

Little wonder that Mustafa Kemal and Nationalists in Ankara were alternately termed bandits and futile wild men and their movement often thought of as a hoax! They faced the British in Istanbul and the Straits, Greeks at Izmir, Italians at Antalya, French at Adana and in Cilicia, British in Kurdistan, and Armenians in the northeastern vilayets. Fortunately for Kemal, the enemy never presented a concerted attack, and he was able to meet them one by one.

MUSTAFA KEMAL

Conceived in the latter part of the nineteenth century and nourished by the poems and polemics of the Young Turk period, modern Turkish nationalism was born in 1919 and 1920. It first saw the light of day on the plateaus of central Anatolia, and its birth pangs were a series of wars for independence against the several enemies cited above. Mustafa Kemal, the military and political midwife, was born in Salonika in 1881. Mustafa belonged to the lower middle class and attended military schools in Monastir and Istanbul, where he distinguished himself in mathematics and oratory. As an officer he served in Damascus and

Monastir and took an active part in the various revolutionary societies that honeycombed the army in the days prior to and after the Young Turk Revolution of 1908. He served in Libya in the war against Italy and participated slightly in the Balkan wars. The outbreak of war in 1914 found him military attaché to Sofia; but he soon effected his transfer and became one of General Liman von Sanders most valued Turkish officers in the Gallipoli campaign. By 1918 he had commanded armies on every Turkish front.

This great leader possessed a brilliant razor-edged mind and a spirit which demanded first-rate performance by himself and those about and beneath him. An early teacher gave him the sobriquet "Perfection" (Kemal), a name which he eventually came to use almost exclusively. Kemal was contemptuous of pomp and hollow ceremony and sometimes gave the appearance of being vicious. Although a devoted nationalist with an indomitable will, an energy, and an incorruptibility that was frightening to many, he was completely wild and licentious in his private life—usually to the total consternation of foreign statesmen and political analysts.

At Ankara in 1920 this tough and uncompromising Mustafa Kemal stood as a Turkish Nationalist hopelessly defying the victors of World War I. At his command he had the scanty resources of a dozen poor upland provinces of central Asia Minor, bedraggled veterans of several scattered armies, and an enthusiastic band of patriots trailing in from Istanbul. However, the crack undefeated Turkish Ninth Army, which had operated in the Caucasus and marched to the Caspian Sea, served as a fine nucleus; and Kemal organized an undaunted force. In the spring of 1920 he drove the French back to Aleppo and removed them from the war by an armistice in May. Then turning toward the Armenians the Turks under Kiazim Kara Bekir Pasha captured Kars and with the help of the Bolsheviks crushed the Armenian forces. The Treaty of Gümrü in December, 1920 ceded Batum to Russia in exchange for the provinces of Kars and Ardahan. A few months later the Treaty of Moscow confirmed this new frontier and pledged Russian aid against imperialists' aims in Turkey. Furthermore, in March, 1921 Kemal reached an agreement whereby the Italians, for certain well-defined economic concessions, evacuated Antalya and Scala Nuova, south of Izmir. Consequently, by the opening of the summer of 1921 Kemal was faced only by weak British occupational contingents on the Straits and the Greek army.

TURKISH GREEK WAR

Since June, 1920 the Allies, through British insistence, had assigned to the Greeks the task of protecting the Allied position in Turkey, "liberating" the country from the Kemalists, and enforcing the peace terms upon the Turks. Beginning immediately, Greek armies advanced in Thrace and Anatolia. Over the following fourteen months they had remarkable success, taking Edirne in Europe and Afyon-Karahisar, Kutahya, Eskishehr, and Izmit in Asia Minor. The only victories Kemal could show were the two tactical battles of Inönü, where Colonel Ismet won lasting fame in January and March, 1921.

Time, however, was on Kemal's side. Britain and France quarreled over German reparations, the question of the Rhineland, and a host of other problems. These quarrels finally caused a break over Turkish policies. Franklin-Bouillon was sent to Ankara, where a secret treaty of peace and friendship was concluded in October, 1921 between France and the Nationalist government. Evidently foreseeing Kemal's victory, France recognized him unofficially in order "to get in on the ground floor" in an economic reorganization and the development of the rich resources of Asia Minor. French munitions actually made their way to Ankara.

King Alexander of Greece died from the bite of his pet monkey in October, 1920. He was succeeded by his father, Constantine, who was recalled from exile. The British distrusted Constantine; and when the Greeks refused to heed British advice against such a move, the British decided to let them manage the Anatolian venture on their own. King Constantine called for an advance upon Ankara, while Lord Curzon searched for an honorable way out for England. In February, 1921 Bekir Sami, the foreign minister of the Ankara government, gladly accepted an invitation to a London conference. The Greeks, however, eschewed the conference, since Lloyd George was guardedly encouraging them to press on against the Turks. After the French and Italian reconciliations with Kemal and a second peace failure by Curzon, the Powers officially declared their neutrality. Lloyd George could promise the Greeks only his political assistance. Although arms were denied the Greeks, the Nationalists were obtaining war matériel from France, Italy, and Russia.

Meanwhile, the Greek advance was checked by the three-week Battle of Sakarya, which ended in September, 1921. Stubborn and heroic Turkish resistance and extended Greek lines of communication decided the issue, although the Kemalists needed a whole year to regroup their forces for the victorious rush upon Izmir. The Greek generals recognized their plight and informed the Allies that Greece would be unable to enforce the Treaty of Sèvres upon Turkey unless they could occupy Istanbul. This condition was abhorrent to the British, who hoped to incorporate Istanbul in the empire.

The break-through on the Sakarya lines occurred on August 26, 1922, and the rout became general following the Battle of Dumlupinar on August 30. General Tricoupis and his staff were captured September 2; Mustafa Kemal entered Izmir on September 11; and by September 19 all Greek forces were cleared from Anatolia. The war with Greece had been won, but intense bitterness remained. The Greek army in retreat pursued a burned-earth policy and committed every known outrage against defenseless Turkish villagers in its path. Shortly after the occupation of Izmir fire broke out and destroyed nearly half of the city. Who started the fire has never been determined, but once under way explosions of hidden Greek bombs and ammunition supplies rendered it uncontrollable.

From Izmir the Nationalists turned upon the Straits. French and Italian forces at the Dardanelles crossed to the European side, leaving the British to hold the positions. Lloyd George called in vain upon the Dominions for reinforcements and the fleet stood by. General Harrington in command of the Straits, however, recognized the hopelessness of his position without more troops and arranged an armistice between the Allies and the government of the Grand National Assembly which was signed at Mudanya on October 11, 1922. Eastern Thrace with Edirne was ceded to the Turks, and the proposition for a conference to negotiate peace was accepted. Kemal had won, and the British post-war policy for Turkey collapsed, taking Lloyd George with it.

LAUSANNE CONFERENCE

Invitations to meet at Lausanne were issued on October 27, 1922. Kemal accepted on October 31. A similar invitation to the sultan's government compelled the Grand National Assembly to pass a law on November 1 deposing Mehmed VI and voiding all laws of his government. Refet Pasha took over control of the city for the Nationalists on November 5, and Mehmed VI fled aboard a British cruiser for Malta. On November 18 the Grand National Assembly chose his cousin Abdul Mejid as caliph. The Ottoman Empire had come to its end.

Convening on November 20, 1922, the Lausanne Conference had a stormy course and one adjournment before the final acts were signed on July 24, 1923. England, France, Italy, Russia, Japan, Bulgaria, Rumania, Yugoslavia, Greece, and Turkey participated in the deliberations and signed one or more of the several documents drawn up. The United States sent only unofficial observers, who did, however, from time to time take an active part in discussions. Lord Curzon, British foreign minister, dominated the conference until it broke up; and his imperious figure of six feet four inches cut a sharp contrast to that of the Turkish delegate, Ismet Pasha, who was only five feet four inches

and a trifle deaf. Few people had ever seen or heard of Ismet until
this conference, and all predicted he could hardly be a match for the
foreign minister of Great Britain and the former viceroy of India. But
Ismet proved to be a stubborn, inflexible, and skillful negotiator.
After all, the Turkish people would fight again to obtain independence,
whereas the British had just sacked their prime minister rather than
run the risk of further war. Frequently when Lord Curzon arrogantly
delivered some advice and admonition, he was infuriated almost to
the breaking point by Ismet who would cup his bad ear and say:
"Répétez-vous, s'il vous plaît?"

The problems of the conference soon fell into topics. Eastern Thrace
with Edirne went with full sovereignty to Turkey. Of the Aegean Islands Tenedos and Imbros went to Turkey, the Dodecanese to Italy,
and the remainder to Greece. The settlement with regard to the
Straits, in which the Russian delegate Chicherin participated, gave
Turkey full sovereignty over the area. It was, however, stipulated that
each shore be demilitarized to a depth of fifteen kilometers and that
navigation of the Straits be regulated according to terms of a special
international convention enacted concurrently with the Treaty of
Lausanne. The Mosul frontier was left to be negotiated at a later date
directly between Turkey and Britain, the latter acting for the kingdom
of Iraq. In regard to the Armenian and Greek minorities Turkey accepted articles similar to minority clauses inserted in treaties with
Austria, Hungary, and Bulgaria; and the Greeks agreed to a compulsory exchange of populations, excluding Greeks of Istanbul and Turks
of western Thrace. The Capitulations and privileges of foreigners in
Turkey were abolished entirely. Financial questions were settled by
terminating the Ottoman Public Debt Administration in all of its manifestations and by a proportionate assumption of Ottoman debts by all
succession states. Finally, the Allies accepted cancellation of all prewar
concessions and contracts, and Turkey agreed not to alter her tariff for
five years after the Treaty of Lausanne came into force.

Over the last three points the conference broke in February, 1923.
Before the conference reconvened in April, the Grand National Assembly rejected any compromise on Ismet's stand, Lord Curzon was
replaced, and the Turks threw a real scare into the Allies by granting
a concession for the development of oil, railroads, and other resources
to an American group headed by retired Admiral Chester. The United
States government protested that it was not actively supporting the
Chester group; but when the conference reopened, the new American
listener, Joseph C. Grew, let it be known that the United States expected to share in any development of oil resources in Turkey and the

Middle East. Such a declaration provided a salutary rein upon British and French ambitions and paved the way for a relaxation of demands upon the Turks.

Ismet went home to Ankara in the summer with the knowledge that Turkey was recognized as an independent free nation, except for the demilitarization of the Straits and the undefined border with Iraq. A modified version of the Lausanne Treaty was signed between the United States government and Turkey, but it was rejected by the American Senate in 1927. Since Turkey and the United States had never been at war, a peace treaty was really not necessary and regular diplomatic relations were resumed late in 1927, when Joseph C. Grew was received at Ankara as ambassador.

The exchange of populations between Turkey and Greece began in the summer of 1923 under the aegis of the League of Nations and proceeded over many months. One and a half million Greeks and half a million Turks were moved at considerable hardship and tragedy to the individuals involved, and the impact upon Greece was most serious. Turkey lost a valuable merchant and commercial class of people, but Ismet argued at Lausanne that such a loss would be more than offset by the advantages of a homogeneous and united Turkish nation.

Ratification of the Treaty of Lausanne and its various conventions was obtained during the summer of 1923. On October 29, 1923, just nine years after the Ottoman Empire entered World War I, the Grand National Assembly in Ankara declared Turkey a republic and elected Ghazi Mustafa Kemal Pasha president.

REFERENCES: Chapter 29

Works important to this chapter are cited in Chapters 7, 13, 18, 19, 22, 23, 24, 25, 26, 27, 28, and 35.

Harold Armstrong, *Turkey in Travail: The Birth of a New Nation:* Lane, London, 1925. The story of the Turkish Revolution.

H. H. Cummings, *Franco-British Rivalry in the Post-War Near East:* Oxford University Press, London, 1938. Discusses the decline of French influence after World War I.

Halidé Edib (Adivar), *The Turkish Ordeal:* Century, New York, 1928. Written by a Western-educated Turkish woman who participated in the Turkish struggle for independence.

C. J. Edmonds, *Kurds, Turks and Arabs: Politics, Travel, and Research in North-Eastern Iraq, 1919–1925:* Oxford University Press, London, 1957. A detailed record in the first person of the problems and settlement of the Mosul border region.

Paul L. Hanna, *British Policy in Palestine:* American Council on Public Affairs, Washington, 1942. Presents the activities and interests of the British in the area.

Harry N. Howard, *The King-Crane Commission: An American Inquiry in the Middle East:* Khayats, Beirut, 1963. A definitive work based on an examination and critical study of all sources available.

Philip Willard Ireland, *Iraq: A Study in Political Development:* Jonathan Cape, London, 1935. Especially good for the war years and the peace settlement.

Stephen Hemsley Longrigg, *Syria and Lebanon under the French Mandate:* Oxford University Press, New York, 1958.

Frank E. Manuel, *The Realities of American Palestine Relations:* Public Affairs Press, Washington, 1949. Chapters IV, V, and VI cover the material of Palestine at the Peace Conference in great detail.

Elizabeth Monroe, *Britain's Moment in the Middle East, 1914–1956:* Johns Hopkins Press, Baltimore, 1963. A comprehensive and objective survey.

H. W. V. Temperley, *A History of the Peace Conference of Paris,* Vol. VI: Henry Frowde & Hodder & Stoughton, London, 1924. By one of the British experts and historians at the conference.

Arnold J. Toynbee, *Survey of International Affairs, 1925:* Vol. I, *The Islamic World since the Peace Settlement:* Oxford University Press, London, 1927. A valuable work.

————, *The Western Question in Greece and Turkey:* Constable, London, 1922. An account of the events in Turkey after 1918.

Arnold J. Toynbee and K. P. Kirkwood, *Turkey:* Ernest Benn, London, 1926. A survey of the background of the Turkish Revolution.

CHAPTER 30

The Turkish Republic under
Atatürk

ESTABLISHMENT OF THE REPUBLIC

On October 29, 1923 the Grand National Assembly voted approval of a declaration asserting that "the form of government of the Turkish State is a Republic." The same day it elected Ghazi Mustafa Kemal Pasha president of the Republic. The idea of a republic, however, was not entirely novel and its declaration only revealed an evolution proceeding naturally since the autumn of 1919.

The shift of power and representation of the Turkish nation from the sultan's government to Kemal's occurred in 1919, when the Nationalists proved strong enough to prompt the sultan and his supporters to dismiss the Ferid Pasha cabinet, call for the election of a new parliament, and induce the new cabinet of Ali Riza Pasha to seek an accord with them. Although Kemal failed to persuade the newly elected parliament to sit at Ankara, it adopted so much of his program that the British fully occupied Istanbul "to protect" the sultan. Kemal then called for the convening of an extraordinary assembly which met April 23, 1920 at Ankara. Naming itself the Grand National Assembly, it recognized the prisoner-like status of the sultan and declared that there was "no power superior to the Grand National Assembly." Kemal became its president and the Council of State was elected to serve as the executive arm of the Ankara government, as it was called.

The Grand National Assembly, however, continued to debate whether it was a permanent or provisional government until January 30, 1921, when it passed ten fundamental articles of government as amendments to the Ottoman constitutions of 1876 and 1908. These articles established the assembly as a permanent institution to be elected every two years. They also served as the basis of government until April 20, 1924, when a new Constitution was adopted. Meanwhile, the second assembly was elected in April, 1923, giving Kemal and his cohorts at the reopening of the Lausanne Conference a strong mandate in their uncompromising stand for full financial, economic, and administrative independence. It was this second assembly which proclaimed the Republic and which later adopted the Constitution.

The assembly in Ankara—something akin to a rump parliament—developed step by step into the Grand National Assembly, acting under authority of the Constitution of the Republic. Meanwhile, Kemal's Association for the Defense of the Rights of Turkey in Europe and Anatolia changed into the People's party (*Halk Firkasi*) in 1922 and then in 1923 to the Republican People's party (*Cumhuriyet Halk Firkasi*). Kemal as president of the People's party used frequent party caucuses for debate and formulation of policy; at these meetings, often continuing through the night, actual decisions were made. While the Greek war was in progress goals were easy to determine, but after the Mudanya Armistice Kemal used every wile and force at his command to carry through his points. When Ismet at Lausanne found Lord Curzon intractable, many Anatolian leaders of the party counseled direct military action upon the British in Istanbul as the best solution. This step, which would have been highly successful initially, was skillfully countered by Kemal, who understood how the Allies would eventually react.

Before the Constitution was adopted, a fundamental change had been made in the religio-political structure of the state. When Mehmed VI left Istanbul for Malta in 1922, the Grand National Assembly declared the caliphate vacant and elected to that office Abdul Mejid, who had never masked his sympathy for the Nationalist cause. Certainly, Kemal and his associates were not prepared to shock the conservative majority of Turks by destroying the position precipitously. Moreover, the anomaly of a caliph without temporal power was not clearly understood; for in many Turkish minds he was equated to the pope. However, after the Nationalists realized the power conflict they could not countenance a caliph who was responsible for the enforcement of Sacred Law and yet only a figurehead for certain traditions.

When voices were raised in the Grand National Assembly on the topic of the caliphate, Kemal proposed that it be abolished and ecclesiastical schools be closed. The question was thoroughly debated at a party caucus in March, 1924 and enacted by the Assembly the following day. In addition, the Ottoman family was banished from Turkey, and Sacred Law courts were abolished. Functions of the ministries governing pious foundations were transferred to a newly created presidency of religious affairs under the immediate supervision of the prime minister, who in a veiled sense became caliph.

Until the spring of 1924 the Turkish government followed the provisions of the Ottoman constitutions of 1876 and 1908 except where these were modified. The widely-anticipated Constitution of the Republic was promulgated on April 20, 1924. Drawn up without too much controversy, it stated that sovereignty resided in the Turkish nation, whose representative was the Grand National Assembly. It declared all Turks equal before the law and forbade special privileges for groups or individuals. Freedom of speech, thought, press, and travel were guaranteed; and a Turk was defined as anyone who was a citizen of the Turkish Republic without distinction of race or creed. The religion of the state was declared to be Islam; the language, Turkish; and the seat of government, Ankara.

The government established by the Constitution was in form a democracy but was in fact, at that time and for twenty years to follow, a one-party government controlled by Kemal and his close political associates. The Grand National Assembly was elected for a four-year term by universal suffrage. (Women received the vote in 1934.) The president of the Republic was elected by the Assembly from its membership for a similar term. The president appointed the prime minister, who selected his cabinet from the deputies with approval of the president and consent of the Assembly. But until 1945 machinery of government was almost entirely in the hands of the Republican People's party. Candidates for election as deputies from the various districts to the Grand National Assembly were nominated by that party, and only one slate of names was presented to voters. Party caucuses determined who ran for what office and from which province. Debates in the Grand National Assembly were largely perfunctory. Kemal made the final decisions.

Mustafa Kemal Pasha was correctly labeled a dictator: he determined high policy, selected high officials of state, and forced his will upon the party and nation. But in most matters affecting the nation and the public at large he was careful to prepare the people by skillfully organized speeches before action was taken. Kemal was convinced that he knew what was best for the Turkish people and also the best way to obtain it. His abiding ambition was for the Turkish people, not for himself. In this way he was a benevolent dictator and extremely popular. Had there been free elections in Turkey while he lived there can be little doubt but that he would have been elected and re-elected president of the Republic.

Following acceptance of the new Constitution and regularization of the republican regime, further reforms came at a bewildering tempo. Whenever possible Kemal and other leaders toured throughout Anatolia, explaining the necessity of what was being done and publicizing new reforms about to be introduced. Kemal definitely turned toward the West and its democratic traditions rather than to Soviet experiments then in progress on the northern and eastern frontiers of Turkey. Leaders of the new state had been educated in the West or influenced by teachers who had received much of their training in the West. In this connection one of the more important schools was Galata Saray Lycée in Istanbul, where the language of instruction was French and traditions were definitely French and Western.

Reforms touched every aspect of life and society in Turkey in the 1920's and 1930's. In the earlier period transition was rapid and followed no clear pattern of planned or co-ordinated development. Perhaps sensing the difficulty of keeping in mind the sequence of these reforms, Kemal terminated the unco-ordinated and rather haphazard course of modernization in 1931. Terming the entire program as Kemalism, he defined his reforms along six broad classifications. These six became the Party's campaign platform for the elections of 1935 and were adopted as undying principles of the new Turkish nation by incorporation into the Constitution by amendment in 1937. They were: republicanism, secularism, populism, nationalism, statism, and reformism.

Article 1 of the Constitution reads: *The Turkish State is a Republic*. Kemal could have made himself king or sultan. He insisted upon a republic, because it was more Western and more democratic and because he believed it suited Turkey. But conservative elements, clients of the Ottoman family, the religious hierarchy, and the devout clung to the old order. Kemal ensured the permanence of the Republic by sweeping legal reforms in 1926.

Abolition of the caliphate and closing the *Shariah* courts did not change the basis of law in Turkey. Law reforms in the nineteenth century Westernized the commercial and criminal laws, but civil law and legal procedures were still tied to Sacred Law, which hardly fitted a twentieth-century republic. In the autumn of 1925 a new law school opened in Ankara to instruct lawyers and judges in fundamentals of Western laws. Then early in 1926 the Grand National Assembly adopted: the new Civil Code and Debts Law, based on Swiss law; the new Penal Code, taken from Italian law; and the new Commercial Code, which was a modification of the German Code. These went into effect later in the year, and since 1927 Turkish law has been an outgrowth of the European Napoleonic Code. With these new codes of a Western and secular nature thoroughly installed, the old regime became such an outmoded way of life that any departure from the Republic was unthinkable.

SECULARIZATION

The second most important reform movement was secularization of the state and society. Islam pervaded all aspects of life in Turkey, and Kemal and many leaders subscribed to the theory, learned from their contacts with the West, that Islam's hold upon society retarded development and created the difference between West and East. Friday, the Muslim holy day, was made a compulsory day of rest throughout the land in 1924, in part to give the day another emphasis. In 1925 dervish orders were forbidden, and their tekkes, holy shrines, and mausoleums were closed. Most startling of all in that year was the law forbidding men to wear the fez and ordering all headgear to have a brim or a visor. Earlier, Kemal was photographed in a straw Panama, and the armed services were outfitted in Western-style military caps. The fez was considered a Muslim symbol, although it came from Europe at the time of Mahmud II. The veil was never outlawed, but its use was discouraged in every possible way.

Adoption of the Swiss Civil Code in 1926 brought many secular changes in its wake. The Muslim calendar for legal, official, and everyday use was abandoned and replaced by the Western Gregorian calendar. Everywhere the Muslim year of 1342 became 1926, although the Muslim calendar was still employed in calculating Ramazan, the month of fasting, and all religious holidays.

A far-reaching effect of Western law was the end of polygamy and the new status of women. Since not very many men had been able to afford more than one wife, the prohibition against polygamy was not very drastic; but the altered condition of life for women began to change the whole fabric of Turkish society.

Progress in secularization went so far that in 1928 the Constitution was amended removing the statement that Turkey was an Islamic state and providing that government officials, in being inducted into office, swore on their honor rather than before God to fulfill their duties. Later, in 1935, the day of rest was changed to Sunday, and the *vikend* (week end) was established by law from Saturday at 1:00 P.M. to Sunday midnight.

Kemal probably was an atheist, but many about him were sincerely religious. Yet, all de-emphasized the place of religion in national life. Fewer individuals observed religious days; and in Istanbul and Ankara many persons paid no attention to Ramazan and many children were not taught their prayers. Religious instruction was removed from public and private schools. The faculty of theology at the University of Istan-

bul enrolled so few that it was consolidated in 1933 with the department of literature. By 1939 Turkey was a secular state, as typical in
this respect as France, Germany, or the United States.

POPULISM

In the Ottoman Empire Capitulations and the *millet* system gave
special privileges to foreigners and to many religious minorities of the
state. Moreover, some families and individuals had certain rights and
immunities. In the Republic, however, Article 69 of the Constitution
states that all Turks are equal before the law and that all "privileges
of whatever description claimed by groups, classes, families, and individuals are abolished and forbidden." It was this idea that Kemal incorporated in the word "populism."

Early Turkish society was democratic in character; certain aspects of
ghazi and *akhi* life were almost communal. Peasant villages in Anatolia
still retained many of these traits. The new republic of Turkey and its
freedom were won by these peasants, and to them the new Turkish society was dedicated. Tax burdens upon them had always been inordi-
nately heavy; and Kemal in an early speech promised them relief on
this score in payment for their efforts in the national struggle. The
Grand National Assembly in 1925 abolished the tithe upon their lands,
and taxes upon agriculture were lightened in order to stimulate greater
production.

Free and universal education was established as another expression
of populism, and primary education in government-supervised schools
became obligatory. In conformity to the constitutional law for universal education, schools were built by the thousands during this era
of Turkish history. Emphasis at first was placed upon teacher training
schools, since lack of teachers handicapped the program's success. Each
village was required to have a primary school of five grades. Secondary
schools were constructed in the towns to prepare students for various
vocations and for entrance to *lycées*, which were the equivalent of
American senior high schools and junior colleges. Beyond the *lycée*
was the University of Istanbul and, later, Ankara University and specialized schools.

The illiteracy rate was estimated at eighty percent, and ability to
read became a privilege that Kemal desired for all. The Arabic script
was never satisfactory for the Turkish language, in which vowels play
an important part in word formation. Writing and spelling were arduous exercises, and sometimes to read a specific passage was difficult
unless one had some idea of what had been written. In 1928 the Grand
National Assembly adopted a new Turkish alphabet based on Latin
characters. Strictly phonetic, it became compulsory January 1, 1929,

and thus after that date all public signs, newspapers, books, etc., were in the new script. The work involved in the change-over was staggering. New textbooks were printed for every subject, and in the autumn of 1928 schools opened several weeks late because books were unavailable. The literate had to learn to read and write all over again, and the government erected huge posters to show the new alphabet. Kemal and members of the Grand National Assembly traveled about the country giving public reading lessons in the Latin characters. Changing headgear was relatively easy in comparison to the alphabet transition. But it was effective. Millions learned to read within the next decade, and the illiteracy rate was reduced to approximately fifty percent. Newspapers multiplied, typewriters became less complex, and a modern national life embracing a majority of the population was born. Populism was marching on!

Adult education has been exceedingly popular in republican Turkey. Beginning with the Young Turk movement in 1908 a program of public education was fostered by the government, first by an organization called the Turkish Hearth (*Türk Ocak*) and after 1932 by the Folk House (*Halkevi*). These organizations had public reading rooms and a staff of leaders who organized athletic, dramatic, musical, social, educational, and inspirational programs for the people. Several hundred such houses were opened before Kemal's death, and they proved most valuable in spreading the spirit of the new Turkey throughout the land and among all strata of the population.

NATIONALISM

The fourth point in the Kemalist program was the development of nationalism. The growth of nationalism in the nineteenth century was effected in the Ottoman Empire in diverse ways. Greeks, Serbs, Bulgarians, Armenians, and others were stirred toward autonomy and independence. Nationalist wars of liberation followed, bringing massacres, atrocities, and devastation to Turks as well as to the others. Turkish Ottomans, when they were touched by nationalism, often were waylaid by Pan-Islamism, Pan-Turanism, or a peculiar kind of synthetic Ottoman nationalism. Kemal, almost instinctively, was a fiery Turkish patriot, proud of being a Turk; and his emotions coincided with the ideas of a few purely Turkish nationalists. He set out in his program to make all Turks proud of their race and heritage.

Although all reforms of the Kemalist regime were tinged with nationalism, none was more pointed than the new histories in the Latin alphabet for elementary and secondary schools. The books minimized the history of the Ottoman Turks in order to forget the centuries after Suleiman I, yet built for the Turks a glorious and significant past

Sumerians and Hittites became Turks. Most non-Semites of Middle Eastern antiquity were claimed as Turks; indeed, all peoples who came from central Asia were classified as Turks. Since the Turkish word for man is *adam* and since Adam traditionally was the first man, it was popularly said that Adam was Turkish and, therefore, that all mankind was Turkish. Individuals who viewed these theories critically were berated, and most skeptics remained silent. Many Turks found genuine satisfaction in these theories, and there was no doubt of their value in generating a more dynamic Turkish national feeling.

Many other strong nationalist drives were innovated indirectly in allied programs. For half a century Turkish literature and even newspaper Turkish were filled with a heavy burden of words taken from Arabic. Since these words were not used in conversational Turkish, they made written Turkish unintelligible to the great majority. After the adoption of a new alphabet the drive to free Turkish from an Arabic vocabulary and even to resurrect Turkish words from obsolescence gained great headway. For a period of several years in the mid-1930's the government published every few weeks a list of new Turkish words and their old equivalents. Since all government publications used the new words and since communications to the government containing old words were often ignored, business concerns and foreign organizations frequently employed someone to keep up with the rapid language changes. The end result perhaps lost the richness and variety of the Arabic language, but an immeasurable gain came in giving Turks a written language closely resembling their vernacular.

Undoubtedly, one of the more dramatic and publicized events was the forced adoption and use of family names. Only a few of the old Turkish families had names, and many did not use them. The Grand National Assembly gave to Kemal the name of Atatürk (Father of the Turks); İnönü, to Ismet in honor of his two victories there; and other appropriate names, to party leaders. The head of each family went to precinct police headquarters and selected the family name from a list of approved Turkish words and names, or a combination of these. No one else in that district could take that name. Most names had a meaning, such as Biyiklioğlu (son of the man with a mustache), Üstündağ (mountaintop), and Kirkağaçlioğlu (son of the man with forty trees).

At times, nationalism seemed to engulf the Turks, and certainly it made them extremely sensitive even to objective and friendly criticism. Whether Atatürk believed in all of the theories which he supported was debatable, but he certainly believed in the necessity of not tolerating public debate about them. In any case they were efficacious; and Atatürk's slogan, Turkey for the Turks and the Turks for Turkey, was proudly accepted by the nation.

STATISM

At Lausanne the most bitter wrangling had been over the Capitulations and implications of economic and judicial imperialism. Turkish victory in these presaged the law reforms and establishment of better court procedures. Economic independence was compromised by the promise not to tamper with the tariff for five years. Kemal's advisers desired to develop the economic resources of Turkey and inaugurate an industrialization without too much foreign influence or participation. The unfortunate experience which the Ottoman Empire had suffered from foreign loans, capital, and concessions conditioned Kemal against any repetition for the Republic. His idea was that Turkey would develop her own resources and industrialize behind a strong protective tariff which could become effective in 1929.

In view of the impending tariff merchants imported excessive quantities in 1929, raising the trade deficit for that year to over 100 million Turkish pounds. By November the demand for foreign exchange to pay bills began to force down the price of the Turkish pound. Fear and speculation played such havoc with exchange rates that the government introduced rigorous controls over the exchange and rates that have never been relaxed. Within a short time the Turks discovered that imports and exports could be more easily regulated through exchange control than by tariffs and quotas and that a managed economy could be introduced.

With the depression, Turkey's exports dropped; in consequence there was a tightening on import permits. When, therefore, Herr Schacht proposed an attractive compensation trade agreement with Nazi Germany, the Turks readily accepted. Trade with Germany boomed, and in 1936 over fifty percent of Turkey's exports went to Germany. American tobacco companies found they could buy cheaper in Hamburg than in Turkish markets. Although Turkey rejoiced that Germans paid higher than world prices for many commodities, she quickly learned that many manufactures of heavy industrial goods were either overpriced in the German market or impossible to buy with blocked marks. To counter this impasse Turkey limited the size of the clearing agreement with Germany and offered a premium in exchange rates for exports to the United States and other hard-currency countries. When World War II broke out, Turkey had clearing agreements with twenty countries and had just entered into a reciprocal trade agreement with the United States.

Kemal understood that agriculture was the principal occupation and resource of his nation and strove to increase the output. He established a model farm near Ankara, where the latest techniques, modern machinery, and implements were demonstrated for all to see. Activities of the Bank of Agriculture, founded by the Ottomans in 1889, were greatly expanded; its loan service to small farmers was increased, and credit co-operatives were authorized in 1929. Agricultural prices began to be supported by the government in 1932, and in 1933 the Higher Agricultural School was opened in Ankara, later to become a part of Ankara University. With all these aids Turkish farmers improved their national position greatly under the Kemalists, even in the face of a world-wide depression of agricultural prices. When World War II broke out, they were relatively prosperous.

In contrast to the progress in agriculture, Kemal felt that advances in industry moved too slowly. Too few people had any industrial know-how, and those with capital tended to follow the traditional practice of investing in buildings or land. Private industry lagged. On the other hand, government monopolies in matches, tobacco and cigarettes, alcohol, and salt and the government acquisition and government operation of railroads, harbor facilities, electric utilities, and coastwise steamers were highly successful. Expansion programs were effective, and railroad lines were extended in several areas. From state monopolies and public works Kemal turned to state enterprises. The Bank of Affairs under government direction aided commerce and to a small degree sponsored industry, but its capital and resources were too limited to give the needed stimulus. Thus, in 1933 the government inaugurated a Five-Year Plan for the development of industry, and the Sümer (Sumerian) Bank was created to own and operate such enterprises. A score of factories were built to produce textiles, paper, glass, sugar, and steel. In 1936 the government established and financed the Eti (Hittite) Bank to do for minerals and the metal industry what the Sümer Bank was accomplishing in other lines.

In Turkey this policy of state enterprises, created and managed by the government, was called statism and gave rise to some debate. Some branded the course as a step toward communism and verified their charge by pointing to the two substantial loans from the U.S.S.R. to provide machinery for the Sümer Bank's textile factory at Kayseri. Others claimed it was a kind of autarchy as preached by Hitler and Mussolini and thus linked Atatürk with the two dictators. Still a third group supported it strongly, asserting that it was a type of state capitalism which would develop the nation without creating individuals of great power and wealth such as Rockefeller, Carnegie, Morgan, and Ford. Different views were held even in high places in the Republican People's party. And in 1937 when Ismet Inönü resigned as prime minister and was replaced by Celal Bayar, the minister of economy, a rumor circulated that Atatürk brought in the latter because he was a more enthusiastic believer in statism.

CONTINUING REFORM

The sixth and final arrow on the shield of Kemalism stood for reformism. By this Atatürk meant opposition to blind conservatism and a rigid adherence to the *status quo*. He did not believe in change for change's sake, but he knew all too well how reformers grow old and conservative, especially when they hold responsible government posts. Kemal wanted his revolution to evolve and expand, as a continuing process. The program with respect to women fell into this category. He wished more than just a change in their legal status and costume. He compelled wives of cabinet ministers to learn to dance; he encouraged girls to become airplane pilots; and he opened the way for women to become lawyers, doctors, bankers, and public officials. Out of 399 members elected to the Grand National Assembly in 1935, 17 were women.

Another important change was in regard to sports. Early Ottomans were keen sports enthusiasts and had competitions in archery, polo, horse racing, wrestling, and many other sports. In the eighteenth century there was a complete reversal; physical exertion was looked upon as degrading and sports participation as undignified. Before Atatürk died in 1938 every city had several sports clubs. Turkey sent entries to the Olympics and to the Balkan Games. And soccer (*futbol*) became the new national sport, which boys and girls everywhere played with great enthusiasm.

The old Ottoman government was corrupt in almost every detail. Bribes and tips were universal, and everyone knew that the magnitude of the service or permission governed the size of the baksheesh. Kemal was ruthless in his treatment of this custom; and although it did not disappear entirely, anyone in the government found guilty of it was speedily dismissed and prosecuted. When it was intimated that one of Kemal's secretaries of long service accepted a silver cigarette case for some service rendered, he was suddenly appointed ambassador to a foreign capital and soon thereafter recalled and dismissed.

One of the most fruitful reforms had to do with the idea of the role of destiny in man's affairs. If some unpleasant circumstance developed or an unfortunate event occurred, the natural reaction was to shrug the shoulders and blame it on God and fate. Through persistent education and practical demonstrations in sanitation, orderly government, and mental attitudes, one heard it freely said that a man's destiny rested in his own hands and the responsibility for mishaps should not be blamed on any supernatural force.

TURKISH POLITICS

Even though there was only one political party under Kemal through most of this period and all politicians supported the six points of Kemalism, it should not be assumed that there was no politics in Turkey. Ismet Pasha became prime minister on October 30, 1923, immediately after the proclamation of the Republic and the election of Kemal as president, and remained in office for thirteen months, when he was replaced by Fethi Bey, another member of Kemal's party. At that time the Progressive party was organized by members of the Nationalist movement in opposition to Kemal. They were a motley, disaffected group. Some were ultraconservatives who wished to restore the sultan-caliph; some were personally ambitious; and others were genuine liberal democrats who looked askance upon Kemal's forceful and dictatorial methods and hoped for true democratic procedures.

Fethi proved to be a poor administrator, and Ismet returned to power in March, 1925. Immediately, he pushed through a law for the maintenance of order under which a Tribunal of Independence was set up. A few dissidents were tried as enemies of the state, still fewer executed, and others exiled. Newspapers were closed, and editors such as the illustrious Ahmet Emin were exiled for varying lengths of time. The liberal Halidé Edib and her husband, Dr. Adnan Adivar, left Turkey and lived in various places in Europe until the exile laws were repealed and political amnesty to all, even to Ottoman royalty, was declared in 1938. Needless to say, the Progressive party was disbanded. Disturbances among Kurdish tribes in the southeastern provinces were attributed to these political events.

Elections for the Grand National Assembly took place in 1927, and Kemal was chosen president for his second term. At a nine-day Congress of the Republican People's party just before the meeting of the Assembly, Kemal made an historic six-day speech which reviewed in detail the events of the resurrection of the Turkish nation from its abject defeat and humiliation at the Mudros Armistice in 1918 to the year 1927. Feeling more secure, Kemalists withdrew the laws for the maintenance of order in 1929; and the following spring Kemal invited Fethi Bey, then ambassador to France, to return and form an opposition party. The Liberal party, as it was called, drew to its support many disgruntled persons from Istanbul and Izmir, where worldwide depression and new tariffs were affecting commerce adversely. The Liberals called for more free enterprise and less statism, claiming that the Republicans were too slow in improving the national economy. They were successful enough to frighten the Republicans; and when a few political rallies ended in disorderly fights, Kemal judged the time

402 THE CONTEMPORARY MIDDLE EAST

had not yet arrived when Turkey might have more than one party. Fethi's party was disbanded in 1930. The quadrennial elections held in May, 1931 reaffirmed the Republican Party's hold on the nation and elected Kemal to a third term. A few members were designated as "independents," but almost immediately thereafter new reforms such as the *Halkevi* program and establishment of the Sümer Bank were undertaken to answer the charges advanced by the Liberal party.

Conditions improved; the Republican party went to the polls in 1935 without opposition; and Atatürk entered his fourth term. This time, thirteen "independents" were elected. In October, 1937 Ismet Inönü resigned as prime minister, to be replaced by Celal Bayar. Although Kemal and Ismet had worked together for seventeen years, basically they were of very different temperaments. Their mutual belief in party discipline, strong public authority, and central control kept them together. But differences in foreign affairs relating to Italy in the Mediterranean and France in Syria led to the break.

Atatürk died November 10, 1938. Excessive drinking and a profligate personal life eventually undermined his iron constitution. His death was a shock to the nation, and the emotional wave which it unleashed demonstrated the love and devotion that he had won from the Turkish people. Inönü was elected president the following day, and the Republican People's party carried on with only a slight break. Bayar soon stepped down from the prime ministership, and more conservative steps were taken in government practices and directions. A new Grand National Assembly was elected in 1939, and Inönü became president again for a full four-year term. Europe and the world, however, were entering into the stages preparatory to World War II; and Inönü was faced with other problems, the discussion of which falls into another chapter of Turkish development.

INTERNATIONAL AFFAIRS

The remarkable internal progress of Turkey and the relatively smooth sailing of Kemal's domestic politics were paralleled by success in the foreign field. The Treaty of Lausanne left the undetermined frontier with Iraq to be settled directly with Great Britain as trustee for Iraq. Negotiations dragged on and reached a highly inflammable point in 1925. Kemal became convinced, with considerable justification, that Britain was fomenting Kurdish revolts in the southeast. To stir the Kurdish tribes was not difficult; and the Mosul province, the area in dispute, had a large Kurdish population whose leaders wanted an independent Kurdistan. Moreover, Kurds within Turkey resisted the centralization process and secularization program of the Nationalists. On several occasions war over Mosul was debated in party caucuses in

Ankara, but peace prevailed. In 1926 a treaty was signed and ratified by England and Turkey, giving Mosul to Iraq. The question of Mosul oil was raised, and allegations were hurled that oil was the real bone of contention. British interests controlled the Mosul concession, which under Turkish sovereignty might be lost. For a time American oil interests supported Turkish claims, but when American companies were allocated nearly a quarter of Mosul oil their fervor for Turkish possession cooled. The treaty did, however, give Turkey ten percent of all oil royalties paid by the concessionaire to Iraq for the following twenty-five years. Turkey promptly settled for a cash payment of £500,000 from Iraq.

Relations with Greece after the exchange of populations improved rapidly. Venizelos made a state visit to Turkey and was received with much fanfare in Istanbul and Ankara. In 1930 conferences held in Athens led to friendly understanding among Turkey, Greece, Bulgaria, Rumania, Yugoslavia, and Albania. Such meetings were repeated annually; and in 1934 the Balkan Pact or Entente was signed, guaranteeing all frontiers and pledging collective security for the Balkans. However, Bulgaria and Albania refused to adhere, because other members declined to discuss minority questions or territorial revision.

In July, 1932 Turkey was admitted to membership in the League of Nations, and in 1934 was elected to a seat on the Council. For a small nation Turkey took an active part in League affairs. She co-operated with League efforts to control illicit traffic in narcotics and maintain collective security. She supported Republican Spain and recognized the full implications of Mussolini's policy of regaining the Roman empire for Italy.

Almost immediately after the attack upon Ethiopia Turkey entered into diplomatic action for changing the demilitarized status of the Straits. Undeclared wars and appeasement of military aggression left Turkey insecure at the Dardanelles and the Bosphorus. After much preparation the Lausanne signatories met at Montreux, where on July 20, 1936 Bulgaria, France, Great Britain, Japan, Rumania, Turkey, and the U.S.S.R. signed a convention governing the Straits. Because of Turkey's actions at the League regarding sanctions against Italy in her Ethiopian adventure, Italy refused to sign the convention until 1938.

Britain went to the conference with the intention of giving Turkey the right to fortify the Straits and administer the Straits regime. It was also the British intention, however, to keep the Straits relatively open to warships when Turkey was a nonbelligerent, thus maintaining an open channel for British naval forces to press upon Russia. The U.S.S.R. attended the conference to give Turkey full sovereignty over the Straits with a proviso limiting very markedly the entry of foreign warships *look up Montreux in Howard (Limits on tonnage of non-Black Sea powers)*

into the Black Sea. Through the centuries Russia desired the Straits open when she felt strong and closed when weak; in 1936 she felt weak. At first the Turkish negotiators at Montreux followed the Soviet line, with every intention of swinging more toward British views at the propitious moment as a necessary compromise. In this way she might come out victorious without offending any power too greatly. That Turkish policy succeeded cannot be doubted. Shortly after an international news broadcast announced agreement at Montreux, Atatürk in full dress attire was seen on the sands in front of his villa near the Sea of Marmara doing handsprings and cartwheels in full celebration of his triumph. Turkey thus gained a heightened sense of international security in a period of growing distrust of collective security and non-aggression pacts.

Two other notable achievements in international affairs followed. In 1937 Turkey entered into the Saadabad Pact with Iran, Iraq, and Afghanistan in much the same fashion as she had in the earlier Balkan Pact. It was Turkey's attempt to bridge the gap between Asia and Europe and maintain friendly relations with her neighbors on both continents.

Turkey's most troublesome frontier was that to the south with Syria. Until 1926 there were many border incidents with France, which charged Turkey with condoning and harboring bandits who raided across the border into Syria. And the situation with respect to the province of Alexandretta remained. In obtaining the Mandate for Syria, France promised to give Alexandretta, where more than 90,000 Turks resided, a separate administration. When in 1936 France was apparently preparing to give Syria independence, Turkey was concerned about the future of Turks in Alexandretta. It was rumored that Kemal departed for Alexandretta to solve the matter dramatically and that only Inönü's hurried interception and convincing arguments induced him to stay his hand. In July, 1938 a Turko-French condominium for Alexandretta was established, and later that year the population gave pro-Turks 22 seats out of 40 in the provincial assembly. Voting themselves autonomy, the deputies proclaimed the Republic of Hatay and immediately sought for union with Turkey. France, not without bitter protests from the Arabs of Syria, acquiesced in this action; and Hatay was annexed to Turkey in June, 1939.

In 1939 as maneuvering among the powers in the diplomatic prelude to World War II became more tense, Turkey's international position grew in importance. Hitler sent Franz von Papen as ambassador to Ankara to cement German relations and strengthen the ties that were built on the very sizable trade nourished by the clearing agreements of 1935. Britain and France, however, countered more successfully with a military alliance and nonaggression pact. After the Mosul agreement relations with England improved; and while Edward VIII and Mrs. Simpson were cruising in the Mediterranean on his yacht in the summer of 1936, a rapprochement between Atatürk and England was consummated in the bar of the Park Hotel in Istanbul. Other Turkish leaders were impressed at the coronation of George VI in 1937, and three credit agreements in the spring of 1938 paved the way for closer understanding between the two countries. In May, 1939 a "declaration of mutual guarantee" was made which was generally recognized as a veiled alliance. At the same time military items and heavy industrial goods were validated for purchase through the credit agreements. Meanwhile, in connection with the annexation of Hatay Turkey signed a non-aggression pact with France and obtained an arms credit. Thus, when the von Ribbentrop-Molotov pact of August 23, 1939 touched off World War II, Turkish leaders found themselves in a neutral position between Germany and the West, yet more committed and more friendly to England and France.

REFERENCES: *Chapter 30*

Volumes already cited and valuable for this chapter are found in Chapters 12, 18, 19, 23, 24, 25, 28, and 29. Chapter 35 contains additional references.

Henry E. Allen, *The Turkish Transformation: A Study in Social and Religious Development:* University of Chicago Press, Chicago, 1935.

Harold C. Armstrong, *Grey Wolf, Mustafa Kemal: An Intimate Study of a Dictator:* Barker, London, 1932. Not always flattering, yet sympathetic.

Eleanor Bisbee, *The New Turks: Pioneers of the Republic, 1920–1950:* University of Pennsylvania Press, Philadelphia, 1951. A spirited study of the many changes in Turkey in the latter part of the 1930's and during the 1940's.

Halidé Edib (Adivar), *Conflict of East and West in Turkey,* 2nd ed.: M. Ashraf, Lahore, 1935. A personal account of the Revolution.

———, *Turkey Faces West; A Turkish View of Recent Changes and Their Origin:* Yale University Press, New Haven, 1930. An interesting essay on why Turkey turned toward the West rather than toward Russia, yet explaining some differences that seemed to appear in the 1920's.

Selma Ekrem, *Turkey, Old and New:* Scribner, New York, 1947. An informal yet valuable essay on the changes in Turkey.

George S. Harris, *The Origins of Communism in Turkey:* Hoover Institution on War, Revolution and Peace, Stanford University, Stanford, Calif., 1967. A new view based on original sources and recent memoirs.

Lord Kinross (Patrick Balfour), *Ataturk: A Biography of Mustafa Kemal, Father of Modern Turkey:* Morrow, New York, 1965. Full and well documented from Turkish sources not yet available to the public.

Irfan Orga and Margarete Orga, *Atatürk:* Michael Joseph, London, 1962.

Elaine Diana Smith, *Turkey: Origins of the Kemalist Movement and the Government of the Grand National Assembly (1919–1923):* The author, Washington, 1959. The best account of this period.

Lewis V. Thomas and Richard N. Frye, *The United States and Turkey and Iran:* Harvard University Press, Cambridge, 1951. A concise and accurate analysis of American interests in these two states.

Max Weston Thornburg, Graham Spry, and George Soule, *Turkey: An Economic Appraisal:* Twentieth Century Fund, New York, 1949. A detailed survey and study of Turkey's economic position and potential.

Edward R. Vere-Hodge, *Turkish Foreign Policy, 1918–1948:* Imprimerie France-Suisse, Ambilly-Annemasse, 1950. Summarizes the main streams of foreign policy events without too much comment.

Donald Everett Webster, *The Turkey of Atatürk: Social Process in the Turkish Reformation:* American Academy of Political & Social Science, Philadelphia, 1939. A detailed study of political and sociological developments in Turkey to 1938.

Ahmed Emin Yalman, *Turkey in My Time:* University of Oklahoma Press, Norman, 1956. The autobiography of Turkey's outstanding newspaper editor.

CHAPTER 31

The Fertile Crescent under the Mandate System

FRENCH OCCUPATION OF LEBANON AND SYRIA

When Prince Faysal galloped at the head of his cavalry into Damascus on October 3, 1918, aspirations for a new Arab nation seemed assured of fulfillment. Political and intellectual leaders were deeply stirred by the thought of a modern state in which Arab peoples might work and achieve the regeneration of their culture and society in a modern independent setting. From the sincere-sounding promises and public statements made by Allied officials Arabs anticipated the creation and general recognition of an Arab national state. On the horizon, to be sure, were a few dark clouds like the Balfour Declaration and the Sykes-Picot Agreement but certainly the bright sun of peace would evaporate these wartime mists.

Faysal and his supporters advanced northward taking Homs and Hama and pressing upon Aleppo, while the British proceeded along the coast to Alexandretta. During 1919 the Allies (British) controlled the coastal regions of Syria, and Arabs held the interior. Since the latter inhabited that area they found it rather incongruous that they were supposedly occupying enemy territory.

After two trips to London and Paris with respect to the peace settlement, Faysal belatedly discerned his naïveté in accepting wartime commitments at face value. Learning at first hand the unreliability of Western leaders, he became the personal victim of slippery French diplomacy and astute British imperialism. The Arabs desired independence, and the Powers would not grant it.

Throughout 1919 little headway toward a satisfactory settlement developed. The Anglo-French Agreement in September was a crushing blow, as it cut off Palestine and provided for a French military occupation of Syria. By December General Gouraud and French troops replaced the British in Beirut and along the Syrian littoral. Faysal's Arabs held the interior. The General Syrian Congress, composed of 85 members elected from all parts of Syria, including Palestine, met in Damascus in July and after considerable free discussion passed resolutions which defined Arab aims. Inspired by the newly formed Arab Independence party, the resolutions requested independence for Syria, including Palestine, with Faysal as king, independence for Iraq with Abdallah as king, repudiation of the Sykes-Picot Agreement and the Balfour Declaration, and rejection of the mandate idea. Another resolution called for refusal of assistance from France in any form. In many ways actions of the Syrian Congress resembled and paralleled those of the Kemalist Nationalists, who at that moment were meeting in Ankara.

Obtaining no redress, the General Syrian Congress declared on March 8, 1920 the independence of Syria, including Palestine and Lebanon, as a constitutional monarchy under Faysal. The French declined to recognize the announcement; and a meeting of the Allied supreme council at San Remo answered the Syrian action by acknowledging, informally yet firmly, a French mandate over Syria and Lebanon and separation of Palestine under the British.

Faysal was caught between the superior force of the Allies and the national patriotism of the Arabs. His wavering caused General Gouraud to fear an Arab build-up in Damascus, where the San Remo awards completely blighted faith in British and French integrity. When he obtained Senegalese reinforcements, Gouraud sent Faysal an ultimatum (July 14, 1920), demanding within four days unqualified acceptance of the French mandate, end of Arab conscription, reduction of the Arab army, adoption of the new French-issued currency in Syria, control of Syrian railroads, and arrest of persons guilty of acts hostile to the French. In the face of a French army advancing from Beirut to occupy Damascus, Faysal telegraphed his agreement. Obviously, the French did not foresee that the ultimatum would be accepted, as new conditions were added and the march proceeded. Faysal ordered the disorganization of the Arab army, but isolated groups opened fire on the French. A bloody engagement occurred at Maysalun Pass, and in the train of airplanes, tanks, and the rattle of machine-gun fire General Gouraud captured Damascus on July 25th. Faysal left within a few days, and the French occupied the whole province of Syria in rapid order.

Although full legal title to the mandate did not materialize until the

Treaty of Lausanne in 1923 and although America did not recognize the mandate authority until 1924, the actions of 1920 confirmed French possession. Detailed French administration began at once. General Gouraud, as high commissioner, issued a decree (September 1, 1920) dividing the mandate for Syria and Lebanon into four separate districts: greater Lebanon; Aleppo, including Alexandretta; Latakia; and Damascus. The latter comprised the Jebel Druze area in the south and all remaining interior regions. The plan seemed to be: divide and rule\

MANDATE FOR LEBANON

The day before the mandate was splintered General Gouraud issued a decree which added the city of Beirut, coastal regions to the north and south including Tripoli, Sidon, and Tyre, and the Bika Valley and Baalbek to the old sanjak of Lebanon to form a new greater Lebanon. Since 1861 the sanjak had had an autonomous political existence under an elected central administrative assembly consisting of four Maronites, three Druzes, two Orthodox Christians, and one member each for the Malkhites, Matawilahs, and Sunnis. By extending the area the French changed population proportions, increasing Sunni Muslims so that Christians held only a slight over-all majority and intentionally reduc ing the preponderance of the Maronite sect.

After the high commissioner's decree of September 1, 1920 a provisional administrative commission for Lebanon was appointed to serve until local governmental authority could be created. A number of the commissioners were Lebanese from various religious groups; but the governor was French. A Lebanese governor, it was said, would cause too much jealousy and friction among the religions! The usual departments of government were formed and staffed by Lebanese, where competent and loyal individuals could be found. But, of course, each department had many French officers and advisers.

Above the governor of Lebanon stood the high commissioner, who had a government of his own to assist him. Separated into departments such as security, education, and public works, this administration was manned by Frenchmen and French colonials who served as the authority to which the Lebanese government looked. A most important group under the high commissioner was that of the information officers, who served in every district of Lebanon, reported developments to the high commissioner, exercised unlimited influence over local affairs, and stood as "tutors" to prepare the country and its people for full independence.

Certain functions of government such as customs, posts, telegraph, railways, public utilities, currency, and local troop levies were not divided locally by the four administrative units. And the high commissioner reserved for his own government full supervision of these "Common Interests." Income from the central operations paid common expenses, and the balance was apportioned among the four state units, always with bickering and dissatisfaction.

One bright point in favor of the mandate system was the allowance for two parallel governments: one held and administered by the Mandatory Power; and one of completely local, in this case Lebanese, organization to be instructed by the other. In theory and in principle, the system was excellent. In actual practice, it allowed for a fully determined colonialism to operate more or less unmolested behind a semblance of local self-government.

FRENCH IMPERIALISM IN LEBANON

French imperialism manifested itself in Lebanon in many ways. In a number of districts martial law was established, and throughout the mandate period the French were quick to decree its use. The press was muzzled effectively; and numerous papers accepted French subsidies and published accounts of all events in a version favorable to French interests. French investors largely owned and operated the railways, public utilities, and banks of Lebanon; and the entire fiscal and economic policy was initiated by the French. New concessions and general contracts granted by the Lebanese government went to French concerns or to Lebanese firms with strong French connections.

In 1920 the *Banque de Syrie et du Grand Liban* was founded as the bank of issue. Stable Egyptian currency had been introduced with Allenby's army, but the French found it awkward to buy their monetary needs in Egypt. The new currency was tied to the French franc, one Lebanese pound being exchangeable for twenty francs. However, it had the disadvantage of fluctuating with depreciating French currency—the fall of the franc played an important role in uprisings in Syria and Lebanon in 1925. Headquarters of the bank were in Paris, and over eighty percent of the capital shares were held by Frenchmen.

French imperialists spoke of their "civilizing mission," a phrase which expressed the view that an area, region, or people would be permanently and indissolubly linked to France if French language and culture flourished in their midst. To gain this end French cultural missions visited Beirut and other cities and towns of Lebanon. But the chief work was accomplished through education and use of French as a second language. French schools of primary, secondary, and *lycée* rank were opened in many communities, and these always obtained more funds and aid than schools where Arabic or some other language prevailed. All schools taught French; and textbooks for history, social sciences, literature, and the humanities had a French coloration on every page. French newspapers were encouraged, and French was an official language in the courts, government offices, contracts, and every walk of life.

There were, however, many favorable aspects of French rule, a concrete indication of which was the higher standard of living and growth of population. Schools improved and increased in number; food and clothing became more plentiful; roads were built; motorcars and transport became available; doctors were trained; disease was controlled; and sanitation and health standards were greatly raised. Striking changes came in the city of Beirut, but developments were widespread across the state. Emigration declined, as life in Lebanon grew more attractive. Populations and standards of living were, of course, on the rise around the world and Lebanon shared in this world trend; credit, however, must also be given to French administration, selfish and blind as it may often have been. One could even find an American drugstore in Beirut, where real American chocolate milk shakes could be bought!

LOCAL LEBANESE GOVERNMENT

In Lebanon as conditions of life flourished, local desire for independence and true self-government spread. In March, 1922, a representative council was elected, which began meeting in May. General Weygand, the second high commissioner, instituted a Lebanese council of state and won Lebanese confidence and affection by his intelligent and judicious decisions. His sudden replacement in January, 1925 by General Sarrail altered the peaceful developments almost immediately. The unfortunate move resulted from the electoral victory of the anticlerical Left in France. (Weygand was a "good Catholic.") General Sarrail's arrogant manners, unwise tactics, anticlericalism, inopportune appointments, and brusque officialism fomented quarrels with the Maronite Church, the Druzes, and many Lebanese leaders. He insulted the representative council, abolished the old elective system recognizing religious divisions of the people, appointed an unpopular Frenchman as governor of Lebanon after first stating he intended to name a Lebanese native, offended the Christian patriarchs, and permitted his war with the Druzes of Syria to spread into Lebanon.

When the general uprisings of 1925 which General Sarrail provoked refused to burn themselves out, the general was recalled and replaced in December by Henri de Jouvenel, editor of *Le Matin* and French representative at the League of Nations. Henri de Jouvenel called upon the representative council to draft a constitution which would recognize the mandate and French responsibility for Lebanon's foreign affairs and give the high commissioner veto power and the right to dismiss the executive head of the state and dissolve the legislature.

Beyond those restrictions de Jouvenel readily surrendered to the Lebanese authority over their own affairs. On May 23, 1926 the Lebanese Republic was proclaimed. Charles Dabbas, an Orthodox Christian, was chosen president by the assembly which consisted of the old representative council and a new senate of twelve appointed by the high commissioner in accordance with the constitution.

Although de Jouvenel resigned in July, his successor, August Ponsot, carried on tactfully. No major political problem arose until the acute world economic crisis and its repercussions in trade, unemployment, and finance in Beirut caused Ponsot to suspend the constitution in 1932. The president remained head of the government, and a new cabinet was appointed with instructions to supervise and regularize all expenditures more closely. A new constitution was promulgated in 1934 by a new high commissioner, Count de Martel. The power of the assembly was restricted, and the sectarian basis of election and membership in previous assemblies was ignored. Political life in Lebanon maintained an uneasy calm, until disturbances in 1936 in Syria forced France to reassess her position in her mandates and negotiate a treaty with Lebanon as well as with Syria.

The sheer weight of French military and naval forces in Lebanon kept political agitation under wraps. Moreover, the French insinuated to Maronite and other Christian leaders in Lebanon that their security against a Muslim tidal wave required full trust in France and cooperation with French rule. However, British concessions to nationalism in Iraq and Egypt incited the Syrian uprisings. These in turn enjoined France to initiate the treaty arrangements with Syria and Lebanon in 1936.

Negotiations of the Syrians for a treaty with France forced similar actions in Lebanon. The French could hardly be less generous to a more friendly Lebanon than she was to a recalcitrant Syria. Inhabitants in the Sunni Muslim parts of Lebanon, which the French decreed to Lebanon in 1920, were divided in their sentiments and wishes in 1936. Many belonged to the Syrian National party of Lebanon and agitated for union with Syria. Others preferred the more stable political life and higher standard of living in Lebanon. The latter began openly to fraternize with Christian groups; and Christians reciprocated by emphasizing their common interests, language, and general culture and by making much of the tacit arrangement by which the president of Lebanon was always a Christian and the prime minister always a Muslim. The Maronites wished to avoid the chances of greater Lebanon being dissolved; for they understood that the old mountain Lebanon was too small to be viable in the twentieth century.

Negotiations for the treaty were opened in October, 1936 in Beirut between President Emile Edde and the high commissioner. A twenty-five year Franco-Lebanese Treaty of Friendship and Alliance was signed November 13. Independence of Lebanon was recognized, and France pledged to support Lebanon's admission to the League of Nations within three years. Lebanon agreed to respect French interests and nationals and maintain the established parity of the two currencies. French troops were permitted in Lebanon without restriction. In Beirut the Christians rejoiced; but many Muslims did not, as they inherently hoped to reunite Lebanon with Syria. Conflict resulted and casualties occurred; yet the Lebanese assembly ratified the treaty in four days and independence seemed assured. In January, 1937 the constitution of 1926 was restored, but difficulties loomed ahead. First, negotiations with Syria over economic matters and a settlement of "common interest" affairs dictated by the treaties with France hit a snag. Then, the Blum government fell in Paris; and the insecure international position frightened French conservatives into refusing the treaties, which the conservatives believed would weaken France still further.

Badly disappointed, the Lebanese marked time while World War II was brewing. Local political parties continued their maneuvers, the conflict centering upon local matters and more often than not upon local personalities. The Unionist party, led by Emile Edde, was pledged to separate independence for Lebanon, while the Constitutionalists under Bishara al-Khuri looked with favor upon close and friendly relations with the other Arab states and did not object to some ties to Syria.

MANDATE FOR SYRIA

All other divisions of Syria created by the 1920 decree had a life during this period even more variegated than Lebanon's. When the decree was issued, native governments were ordered for Latakia, Aleppo, Damascus, and the Jebel Druze. With Alexandretta attached to Aleppo as a special province, Damascene Syrians felt that France was deliberately blocking them from the sea and never admitted the legality of the fragmentation. In June, 1922 independence of the Jebel Druze was proclaimed; and the remaining states were grouped into a federation with an Antiochene Turk, Subhi Barakat, as president of the federal council. The following year each territory acquired a representative council "appointed by an indirect election." (Latakia had become the State of the Alawis.) In 1924 just before quitting Beirut, General Weygand laid the foundations for a treaty settlement with the mandate similar to that which the British gave Iraq. At the same time he terminated the federation by recognizing a separate government for the Alawis and amalgamating Aleppo into the state of Damascus, which then became Syria. Alexandretta, though a part of Syria, had its own administration.

Every action taken by General Sarrail seemed to be wrong. He antagonized the Christians in Lebanon by pursuing the line of domestic French political anti-clericalism in a state that had been organized on a religious basis for centuries. In the Jebel Druze he touched off a bloody uprising by supporting the French delegate, Captain Carbillet. The latter had been doing a splendid job in ramming through new roads, irrigation channels, and reforms of many types; but, ignorant of the Druze character and wholly tactless, the more Carbillet did for them, the more they disliked him. Since the decree of 1920 called for a native governor, Druze leaders petitioned for Carbillet's removal and fulfillment of the promise. General Sarrail replied by inviting the Druze leaders to Damascus, where they were arrested. Revolt flared rapidly across the entire mandate. General Gamelin was given command of the French forces under General Sarrail in September, and severe fighting occurred in the Jebel Druze. In October Druze columns appeared at Damascus, and the bombardment of that city caused damages estimated at several millions of dollars and considerable loss of life.

This tragedy brought Sarrail's immediate recall. Henri de Jouvenel, his successor, called for elections in Latakia and Syria. Subhi Barakat, whom the Damascus faction hated because he wanted to move the capital of a united Syria to Aleppo, resigned the presidency. The presidency was, then, offered to Taj al-Din al-Hasani, chief judge of Damascus; but since his eleven-point program was unacceptable to the French, he refused the proffered post. Every succeeding Syrian request over the following two decades was based on Taj al-Din's platform. He demanded that Latakia and the Jebel Druze be joined to Syria; that areas within Lebanon be allowed to choose between Syria and Lebanon; that a treaty be negotiated and entered into with France; that Syria join the League of Nations; that French troops be evacuated; that a currency reform be enacted; and that Syria be entirely independent in matters of domestic affairs. When the high commissioner refused this program, a Circassian, Damad Ahmed Nami, was appointed president of Syria. Guerrilla warfare continued, and General Gamelin tried to pacify the territory. In May, 1926 Damascus was again shelled. This time fighting was even more destructive and savage than in the previous October. Ponsot replaced de Jouvenel. Both France and the Syrian nationalists began to realize that some compromise was necessary. The latter asked France to forget the past, and Ponsot announced that a constituent assembly would be elected, a constitution drafted by Syrians, a Syrian government inaugurated, and a treaty of alliance with France concluded, in that order.

LOCAL SYRIAN GOVERNMENT

Damad Ahmed Nami resigned in February, 1928, and Ponsot appointed Taj al-Din president of a Syrian council of ministers to form a provisional government and hold elections. This was done in April, the constituent assembly of seventy members meeting in June. Fifty-two of the members were Sunni Muslims; and in this body the nationalist bloc under the leadership of Ibrahim Hananu, Jamil Mardam, Hashim al-Atasi and Faris al-Khuri began to take shape. A more radical independence wing of the bloc was led by Shukri al-Kuwatli, Nabih al-Azmah, Adil Arslan, and Riyadh al-Sulh. The constituent assembly entered into the task of drafting a constitution, which Hananu presented to the assembly in August. It established a Western-type republic with president, prime minister, cabinet, unicameral legislature, and high court. Syria was pronounced to include Lebanon and Palestine; the official religion was to be Islam; and no mention was made of France as a mandatory power. Since several articles violated French international commitments and were contrary to League stipulations, Ponsot found the constitution unacceptable. In a conciliatory speech he urged that five articles be withdrawn and a sixth redrafted. The assembly refused to comply and the quarrels were resumed.

In 1929 the assembly was prorogued, but debate over the constitution continued. In a surprise move in May, 1930 Ponsot unilaterally promulgated new governments for Alexandretta, Latakia, and the Jebel Druze. Simultaneously he established in Syria the constitution, including the five censured articles and the altered sixth. Elections were not decreed, however, until the spring of 1932, and when the chamber of deputies met in June it comprised fifty-four moderates and seventeen nationalists. Muhammad Ali al-Abid, a middle-of-the-road candidate, was elected president of the Republic. Hakki al-Azm, a moderate, accepted the prime ministership and selected his cabinet equally between moderates and nationalists. The latter soon took the lead and pressed for conclusion of a treaty of independence with France.

Throughout 1933 all political conversations centered about a treaty. The French insisted upon exclusion of Lebanon, Latakia, and the Jebel Druze. The nationalists demanded the end of all foreign privileges and dismissal of French armed forces. Unfortunately in May in the midst of the bitter debate Ponsot fell ill, and his successor, Count de Martel, did not arrive until October. When Hakki al-Azm did present the proposed treaty to the chamber in November, such a howl arose that the high commissioner suggested its withdrawal. Parliament was suspended and later dissolved, with the president governing by decrees which were recommended by his cabinet. In 1934 Taj al-Din became prime minister and held on for nearly two years.

However, from January 11 to March 1, 1936 Damascus and most of the towns of Syria became the scene of an organized strike against the French regime. In the midst of the strike Taj al-Din resigned as prime minister and was replaced by Ata al-Ayyubi, a moderate. The French sensed the handwriting on the wall even if they could not see it; and de Martel came to terms with the Nationalist party leaders, Hashim al-Atasi, Jamil Mardam, and Faris al-Khuri. Negotiations for a treaty were resumed in Paris on the basis of Alexandretta being a part of Syria and Lebanon being recognized as a separate state. The long discussions ended only after Yvon Delbos took over for the Blum government and agreed that the Jebel Druze and Latakia be incorporated into Syria. Rejoicing, Syria elected the Nationalists to power in November, 1936. Hashim al-Atasi became president of the Republic, and Jamil Mardam headed the cabinet. The Syrians ratified the treaty which would free them from French imperialism; but, as with the similar Lebanese treaty discussed above, the French government never did ratify it.

In 1939 the cabinet and president resigned, and the high commissioner suspended the chamber of deputies. Syria was back where she was in 1920 when the mandate began. At the outbreak of World War II, Syria was being governed by an appointed council of directors under the immediate control and supervision of High Commissioner Gabriel Puaux, who replaced de Martel in January, 1939.

The bitterest event for the Syrians to swallow was the gift of Alexandretta to Turkey. From the beginning in 1920 the French declared a special administration for Alexandretta in view of the large Turkish population residing there. At first, it was attached to Aleppo but under separate rule. When Aleppo was joined to Damascus to form Syria, Alexandretta retained its own semiautonomous regime as part of Syria but was responsive directly to the will of the French high commissioner in Beirut. When questions over its status were raised by the Turks in 1936 and conversations initiated, Syrians objected. As discussions proceeded to Franco-Turkish responsibility, to an independent Hatay, and to outright annexation to Turkey in 1939, Syrian nationalists protested every step of the way. With considerable justification and legality they declared that the terms of the mandate forbade France from any such action.

For two decades France tried to govern Syria and failed ingloriously. Policies dictated by Paris were high-handed, unwise, and based on an almost complete misunderstanding or disregard of the situation. To cap these mistakes French administrative personnel delegated to Syria were generally either pompous incompetents or officials transferred from North Africa, where they were able to look upon the inhabitants as "natives" without starting a revolt. The Syrians did not want French rule or even French advisers in the first instance; and the French did little to endear themselves to the Syrians.

BRITISH OCCUPATION OF IRAQ

Eastward, the British were having their troubles in Iraq. At the end of the war the British were occupying Basrah, Baghdad, and Mosul and controlling much of the land in between and on the far sides of both the Tigris and the Euphrates. Many British administrators coming in at the end of hostilities brought their families, evidently understanding that this territory was not a temporary acquisition. Sir Arnold Wilson, acting high commissioner, made a virtue of efficient government, irrespective of sentiment, prestige, or local desires. Arab unrest grew from the uncertainties of an Arab state of Iraq. When the news from San Remo arrived, the rebellion burst. From May to October, 1920 a real war, reportedly costing the British nearly £40,000,000, raged in Iraq with resistance forces dominating the whole land except for the three cities of Basrah, Baghdad, and Mosul.

Hurriedly, Sir Percy Z. Cox was recalled from the ambassadorship in Tehran and sent to Iraq as high commissioner. The affection and esteem with which he was held by Iraqis was attested by the welcome showered upon him at his arrival on October 1, 1920 and by the rebellion's termination. Having been British political agent for the Persian Gulf for a number of years and civil commissioner in Iraq during the war years and immediately thereafter, Sir Percy gathered about him a star-studded galaxy of advisers and assistants such as Miss Gertrude Bell, his Oriental secretary, and H. St. J. B. Philby. Quickly he organized a provisional council of state in which Sayyed Abd al-Rahman al-Gailani, Baghdad's *nagib* (official head of the Sunni Arab community), became prime minister. Other portfolios were distributed among influential families and religious sects from different parts of the state. Each minister had a British adviser, and in reality the council was supervised by these advisers. All were under the direction of the high commissioner, and few Iraqis held any illusion that they had a true national government.

THE KINGDOM OF IRAQ

Sir Percy Cox proposed convening a national assembly to draw up electoral laws and establish an Iraqi government; but none was called until 1922 and it did not meet until 1924. The difficulty was the question of a ruler, and the British were fearful lest an assembly choose someone unresponsive to their suggestions. Although the Damascus Congress named Abdallah king of Iraq, the British selected Faysal as king of Iraq in 1920 and Churchill's Cairo Conference nominated him. There were other candidates, but the return to Baghdad of several hundred Arab officers who had served with the British in the Hijaz and Syria gave the necessary weight to the acceptance of Faysal. Abdallah withdrew his name, and Faysal arrived in Baghdad at the end of June, 1921. The council of state invited him to become king; a referendum was held in various districts of the state; and Faysal was enthroned on August 23, 1921. Sir Percy and his associates managed affairs wonderfully!

Until his death twelve years later, Faysal served as king. His charm, tact, and broad tolerance made him an admirable choice; and his knowledge and experience made him acceptable to desert shaykhs, bedouins, and the townsmen of Iraq. At the same time Faysal recognized fully the British position of control and appreciated the fact that without British support he would never have become king. Through the winter and spring of 1922 a treaty was drafted by the British in conjunction with Faysal and al-Gailani. At the last stages the council of state was brought in, and after a serious crisis in August the treaty was ratified in October. It defined the special position of Great Britain in Iraq, actually giving the British military and economic control and, in a veiled manner, granting English nationals many immunities and privileges in the country. British advisers were accepted in all offices. Its many articles justified the objections by the nationalists (of which there were now three political parties: National, Renaissance, and Independent) that the Treaty was only a sugar-coated mandate which, however translated, meant "subjection and colonization."

ANGLO-IRAQI AFFAIRS

Much uncertainty and agitation accompanied the elections for a constituent assembly that convened in March, 1924. King Faysal in his speech from the throne urged the assembly to ratify the treaty with Great Britain, pass upon the constitution, and enact an electoral law for a parliament—all of which was done in 1924. A new treaty with England was signed in 1926 and yet another in 1927. The British pledged under certain qualifications that Iraq would be supported in 1932 for membership in the League of Nations; the qualifications, however, raised such doubt with respect to Britain's sincerity that the treaty of 1927 was never ratified.

Later loopholes as to League support were removed, and the momentous Anglo-Iraqi Treaty of 1930 was achieved. This Treaty, which became the prototype of the Anglo-Egyptian Treaty of 1936 and the treaties of France with Syria and Lebanon in the same year, was an alliance between Iraq and Great Britain for twenty-five years. The two countries agreed to follow a foreign policy not inconsistent with the Treaty, which meant that Iraq assented to "full and frank consultation in all matters" of foreign affairs. Iraq concurred to the presence of British troops in Mosul and other districts for five years and gave a lease on several air bases. In return Britain contracted to defend Iraq in case of war. Attached to the Treaty were annexes giving England considerable power in matters of finance, business, and education and indicating that British advisers were to be employed rather than advisers of other nations. The signing of this treaty by Sir Francis Humphrys, British high commissioner, and Nuri al-Said Pasha, Iraqi prime minister, cleared the way for Iraq's membership in the League of Nations, which voted admission unanimously on October 3, 1932. The high commissioner became British ambassador; the mandate was terminated; and Iraq stood ostensibly as an independent state.

THE GOVERNMENT OF IRAQ

The Constitution placed executive administrative power in the hands of a cabinet headed by a prime minister and composed of at least six other ministers. The cabinet was jointly responsible to the chamber of deputies, which could force the cabinet to resign upon a vote of no confidence. The king, however, could dissolve the chamber. Parliament was bicameral. The chamber of deputies, elected indirectly by universal manhood suffrage, had one representative for every 20,000 male inhabitants with a special provision that four Christians and four Jews were to be elected. (There were eighty-eight in the first chamber.) Maximum life of a chamber was four years. The first was elected in 1925 and elections in 1939 were held for the ninth. The senate was appointed by the king and had a membership of not more than one fourth that of the chamber. Senators were appointed for eight years, and half were appointed every four years. Only the chamber could initiate legislation; and in appearance the chamber, as representative of the people, held the dominant position in the government.

In practical application, however, the cabinet was the powerful body, and none ever fell from a vote of no confidence. The cabinet controlled elections and obtained dismissal of the chamber when necessary. Yet, there were twenty cabinets from 1925, when the Constitution came into force, until the outbreak of World War II in 1939. A cabinet would promise to obtain full independence from Great Britain, and when it failed, it invited the opposition to try its hand. Ministers moved about from post to post in succeeding cabinets. Nuri al-Said Pasha, four times prime minister in that period, appropriately quipped: "With a small pack of cards, you must shuffle them often."

Perhaps the political and ministerial ferris wheel would not have been so pronounced had King Faysal lived longer. In 1933 Faysal became worn with fatigue. His health broke, and he died in Switzerland, where he went for rest and medical care. He was succeeded immediately and without question by his twenty-one-year-old son Ghazi. Young and inexperienced, the new king followed a constitutional policy in the Western tradition. However, Iraq might have been spared some of her political confusion of those years had Ghazi been sufficiently mature and sufficiently concerned with government to play an advisory role in national affairs. Addicted to fast motor cars, he was killed in an accident in 1939. He was succeeded by his four-year-old son, who became the boy-king Faysal II under the regency of Prince Abd al-Illah, the king's maternal uncle and son of Prince Ali, King Faysal I's oldest brother.

MINORITY PROBLEMS IN IRAQ

But Iraq's problems were far from solved by the adoption of constitutional government, technical independence from Great Britain, and admission to the League of Nations. In the northern part of the state Kurdish tribes were preponderant, and with their fellow tribesmen in Turkey and Iran they hoped for the peace settlement to bring forth a Kurdistan. The Kurdish tribes were seminomadic and roamed the mountains and valleys of the eastern highlands, moving freely from country to country and resisting outside authorities. They had no desire to be taxed or organized. The Iraqi government took punitive measures repeatedly against uprisings in the neighborhood of Mosul and Suleimaniyah in the 1920's and early 1930's. Kurds were elected to parliament and served in Baghdad, but settling of the Kurdish tribes was by no means completed in 1939.

During World War I a group of Assyrians (Nestorians living along the upper Euphrates) joined with the British and fought against the Ottomans. Leaving Turkey at the end of the conflict and finding themselves a homeless minority in Iraq, many accepted service in the British army stationed there. In 1933 after Iraq was free and a member of the League, incidents between Assyrians and Arabs led to bloody engagements, massacres in Assyrian villages, and a "pacification" by Iraqi forces commanded by General Bakr Sidki. Britain helped Iraq obtain a generous whitewash of the affair before the League in order not to jeopardize her position in Iraq. Assyrian leadership in this incident was not entirely blameless; for they were working for separate recognition of their community such as was accorded under the old millet system of the Ottoman Empire. Since this was contrary to Iraqi nationalism and unity, Baghdad could not consider it.

The most serious religious problem in Iraq arose from the lasting Islamic schism between Sunnites and Shiites. The latter held a population majority; the former dominated the government and society. As long as Faysal I lived, little trouble developed, for many Shiites were fondly under the delusion that he secretly belonged to their sect. Shiite divines easily stirred their followers; and preachers, entering Iraq from Iran, could easily retire across the frontier when asylum was needed.

SOCIAL PROBLEMS

In addition to minorities and varying religious sects there was a grave social and economic cleavage between townsmen and the tribes. The government of Iraq was definitely in the hands of townsmen; yet the tribes, and particularly their shaykhs, were powerful forces in the Iraqi nation. At least eighty percent of the population won their livelihood from the land, much of which was irrigated. But the science of irrigation had so degenerated over the centuries in Iraq that soils became salty and channels silted rapidly, compelling peasants to move frequently to new land. In the middle Euphrates area the tribes also engaged in stock raising, moving their herds from sparse pasturage as the cover was grazed. Thus the tribes had a constant tie with desert bedouins. The tribal shaykhs were recognized, perforce, by the British in their occupation of Mesopotamia as the responsible heads of the districts, thereby obtaining a quasi-title of ownership of the land. Every assembly and parliament in Iraq always had a goodly number of these shaykhs as members. They were invariably conservative and friendly to the British, in whom they saw a protection from the town-dwelling Iraqi politician. Since the tribesman was a good soldier, the tribes of the middle Euphrates were a force with which to contend until the Iraqi army was equipped with the strength and mobility of more mechanized weapons. General Bakr Sidki again won his spurs of acclaim in 1935 by leading an armed expedition to quell a rising of the tribes of the middle Euphrates.

IRAQI OIL

One of the jarring factors in Iraqi politics, domestic and international, has been the oil resources of the country and their exploitation. Before the war oil rights were granted by the Ottoman government to the Anatolian Railway Company and the Baghdad Railway Company, both German concerns. When the D'Arcy Exploration Company became interested in the Mosul fields, the Turkish Petroleum Company. was formed in 1912 with German, Dutch, and British ownership. The San Remo Conference turned over the German interests to the French; and during the Lausanne Conference the British agreed very reluctantly that half of their holdings, which by this time were owned by the Anglo-Persian Oil Company, would be made available for purchase by the Standard Oil Company of New Jersey and its associates.

The Mosul controversy between England and Turkey was partly over oil; and when in 1925 it appeared likely that Mosul would be awarded to Iraq, that government gave a seventy-five year concession to the Turkish Petroleum Company. The terms granted rights to twenty-four rectangles of land, each of eight square miles, to be selected by the company within four years, after which all remaining areas would be opened to other companies. Several months later the concession was amended, changing royalties from a profit-sharing arrangement to a tonnage basis.

Development, however, moved very slowly. Whereas the oil production by 1930 in Iran had increased to nearly 46,000,000 barrels, in Iraq it was only 909,000 barrels. Iraqi leaders charged that Western oil concerns were holding back in Iraq and exploiting their wells in other parts of the world. Although this might be good business for the companies, to Iraq it seemed entirely negligent; for she was losing revenue when it was sorely needed.

A gigantic gusher was struck at Baba Gurgur near Kirkuk in 1927; but the company did not select all of its plots by 1929, and the government refused to extend the time. After consideration by the League and much negotiating a new concession was made in 1931 to the Iraq Petroleum Company, the company's name having been changed in 1929. The 1931 agreement gave outright concession to lands in the Baghdad and Mosul provinces east of the Tigris, except for a few districts where the Anglo-Persian Company had historic rights. Furthermore, the company pledged to build before 1936 a pipeline system to Haifa and the Syrian coast and to begin annual payments of £400,000 against future royalties. Half of this sum would be nonrecoverable. Royalties were fixed at four gold shillings a ton for a period of twenty years. The pipeline was built from Kirkuk across the Tigris and the Euphrates. There it divided, one branch going to Haifa and one to Tripoli. Both branches began delivering oil in 1934.

Other companies showed an interest in Iraqi oil possibilities, and in 1932 a concession was given to the British Oil Development Company to lands west of the Tigris and north of the 33rd parallel. Payments of £100,000 began in 1933 and steadily mounted. Thus, by the time Iraq attained her independence she was fast becoming independent economically. The concession to the British Oil Development Company just mentioned and another for the district in the south around Basrah have, through holding companies, become affiliated or controlled by the Iraq Petroleum Company. Through further concessions in 1938 the latter company came to hold the oil production of all of Iraq in its hands.

While oil brought Iraq into touch with the great powers, border raids by nomads on the deserts and in the mountains led to interminable negotiations and difficulties with the smaller states upon her frontiers. Boundary settlements with varying degrees of permanence were made with Kuwayt, Saudi Arabia, Transjordan, Syria, Turkey, and Iran. As a further step in regulating the frontiers and relations with Turkey and Iran the Saadabad Pact was signed by the foreign ministers of Iraq, Iran, Turkey, and Afghanistan at the shah's palace near Tehran on July 8, 1937.

POLITICS IN IRAQ

Domestic politics from the very beginning in Iraq were heavily charged with personalities. Each dynamic figure gathered about him a clientele, published a newspaper, and organized a political party. Eagerness for personal power, prestige, and position, however, was sublimated in the struggle for independence from England. Parties emerged, flourished, and died quickly; members and even leaders went from one to another with considerable ease. In the 1920's the three most important and durable parties were the National, the Progressive, and the People's parties. Each pledged to throw off the treaty-mandate subterfuge and obtain real independence. The Progressive party collapsed in 1929, when its leader, Abd al-Muhsin al-Sadun, who had served as prime minister on three separate occasions, committed suicide. The People's party was headed by Yasin al-Hashimi, who in the 1930's led his followers into a collective party known as the National Brotherhood (*Ikha al-Watani*). Prime minister twice, he was active in politics and held various portfolios in a number of ministries until the *coup d'état* of 1936 forced him into exile. Jafar Abu al-Timman, who participated in different ministries, organized the National party. Disillusioned by the acts of his political associates, he moved toward the left. In 1933 he joined the Reform party and took an active part in the 1936 *coup*.

In 1930 when Nuri al-Said Pasha concluded the Anglo-Iraqi Treaty of Alliance, he revived the prewar Covenanters party (*al-Ahd*). But its members were soon swallowed up in the political confusion of independence. Nuri Pasha, an Iraqi who served in the Ottoman army and then joined the Hijaz force supporting the Arab revolt, returned to Baghdad, where he worked for the kingship of Faysal and held office in many cabinets as foreign minister. Prime minister four times before the outbreak of World War II, he was a strong stabilizing force for better government.

Nuri's opponents in 1930 joined together under Yasin al-Hashimi and Rashid Ali al-Gailani to form the National Brotherhood party. This party dominated the government and the cabinets from 1932, when Iraq was admitted to the League of Nations, until it was overthrown by the 1936 *coup*. Meanwhile, another party was created. The Reform party (*Ahali*) resulted from the meetings and discussions of younger Western-educated men who were liberal in their views and desirous of a more democratic and socialistic government. They were disgusted with the shuffling corruption of the conservative governments conducted by their elders. For a few years through their party newspaper they had wide influence; but they soon succumbed to experienced politicians like Hikmat Sulayman and Jafar Abu al-Timman.

Realizing that the power of the National Brotherhood government could not be broken and that the cabinet of Yasin al-Hashimi and Rashid Ali al-Gailani could not be removed without active assistance of the army, Hikmat Sulayman brought about a coalescence of the *Ahali* group with disgruntled army officers who felt that Iraq was not yet ready for full-blown Western democracy and its inefficiencies. The army "hero" proved to be Bakr Sidki.

The plot ripened and in the autumn of 1936 Bakr Sidki Pasha moved on Baghdad. Yasin al-Hashimi, Rashid Ali al-Gailani, and Nuri al-Said escaped into exile; Jafar al-Askari Pasha, perennial minister of defense, was assassinated, and Hikmat Sulayman became the new prime minister. Parliament was dissolved and new elections were so rigged as to return a great number of deputies who had never served in any previous chamber. The socialist predilections of the Ahali group led to quarrels with Bakr Sidki and his army officers. Other officers became jealous of Bakr Sidki, and in August, 1937 he was assassinated. Another army *coup d'état* soon ended the first, and until 1941 one army *coup* followed another most methodically, while politics descended to personal vilification and vulgar invective. Iraq was deeply immersed in this national suffering when World War II began.

REFERENCES: Chapter 31

Important works for this chapter are in Chapters 2, 7, 19, 26, 27, 28, and 29. Chapter 35 contains additional references.

Eugenie Elie Abouchdid, *Thirty Years of Lebanon and Syria* (*1917–1947*): Soder Rihani Printing, Beirut, 1948. Gives a Lebanese point of view.

Alfred Bonne, *State and Economics in the Middle East: A Society in Transition:* Routledge & Kegan Paul, London, 1948. An excellent survey.

Reader Bullard, *Britain and the Middle East:* Longmans, Green, London, 1951. The British point of view.

Hedley V. Cooke, *Challenge and Response in the Middle East: The Quest for Prosperity, 1919–1951:* Harpers, New York, 1952. A good outline of the economic situation and the planning and development.

Helen Miller Davis, *Constitutions, Electoral Laws, Treaties of States in the Near and Middle East:* Duke University Press, Durham, 1947. An indispensable work.

Henry A. Foster, *The Making of Modern Iraq: A Product of World Forces:* University of Oklahoma Press, Norman, 1935. A thorough work on the early period.

Richard N. Frye, ed., *The Near East and the Great Powers:* Harvard University Press, Cambridge, 1951. The chapter "The Scheme of Fertile Crescent Unity: A Study in Inter-Arab Relations" by Majid Khadduri is of special note.

John Gulick, *Social Structure and Culture Change in a Lebanese Village:* Wenner-Gren Foundation for Anthropological Research, New York, 1955. A study of the changes in value systems relating to land, religion, and kinship.

Maurice Hindus, *In Search of a Future:* Doubleday, Garden City, 1949. A study of Iran, Egypt, Iraq, and Palestine.

B. A. Keen, *The Agricultural Development of the Middle East:* H. M. Stationery Office, London, 1946. An outline for the future co-ordination of the resources of the area.

Majid Khadduri, *Independent Iraq: A Study in Iraqi Politics, 1932–1958,* 2nd ed.: Oxford University Press, London, 1960. The best work on this subject.

Seton Lloyd, *Iraq:* Oxford University Press, New York, 1944.

Stephen H. Longrigg, *Four Centuries of Modern Iraq:* Clarendon Press, Oxford, 1925. Gives an excellent background.

————, *Iraq, 1900–1950:* Oxford University Press, London, 1953. A continuation of his earlier work.

————, *Oil in the Middle East:* Oxford University Press, New York, 1954.

Elizabeth P. MacCallum, *The Nationalist Crusade in Syria:* Foreign Policy Association, New York, 1928. The rebellion of 1925 to 1927.

Ernest Main, *Iraq from Mandate to Independence:* George Allen & Unwin, London, 1935. A full study of the early years of Iraq.

Tom J. McFadden, *Daily Journalism in the Arab States:* Ohio State University Press, Columbus, 1953.

R. F. Mikesell and H. B. Chenery, *Arabian Oil: America's Stake in the Middle East:* University of North Carolina Press, Chapel Hill, 1949. Relates Iraqi oil to the whole situation.

Benjamin Shwadran, *The Middle East, Oil, and the Great Powers:* Praeger, New York, 1955. Gives much information about the impact of the oil companies on the peoples of the Middle East.

E. A. Speiser, *The United States and the Near East:* Harvard University Press, Cambridge, 1950. American interests and relations in the area.

United Nations, International Bank for Reconstruction and Development, *The Economic Development of Iraq:* Johns Hopkins University Press, Baltimore, 1952. A complete study of the economic situation in Iraq.

————, *The Economic Development of Syria:* Johns Hopkins University Press, Baltimore, 1955. A complete study of the economic situation in Syria.

Doreen Warriner, *Land and Poverty in the Middle East:* Oxford University Press, New York, 1948. A useful work.

————, *Land Reform and Development in the Middle East:* Oxford University Press, New York, 1957. Excellent chapters on Syria and Iraq.

Nicola A. Ziadeh, *Syria and Lebanon:* Praeger, New York, 1957. A study of the complex political patterns in these states.

CHAPTER 32

Palestine and Transjordan

ZIONISTS, ARABS, AND THE BRITISH

Between the conquest by General Allenby's army in 1917 and July 1, 1920 Palestine, or the Ottoman province of Jerusalem, was occupied and administered by the British army. After the Balfour Declaration but even before the Armistice, the Zionist organization sent a commission to the area headed by Dr. Weizmann, Major Ormsby-Gore, and Major de Rothschild. The purpose of the commission was to establish a link between the military and the Jewish population of Palestine, assist in the return of Jews who fled during the war, and co-ordinate all activities of Jewish organizations and institutions. The future of Palestine hung in the fire, until the San Remo Conference in April, 1920 awarded it to England. Till then, uncertainty nurtured every rumor and fear, and Palestinians experienced a restlessness that later events never did resolve.

At the close of the war the population comprised about 550,000 Muslims, 70,000 Christians, and 50,000 Jews. The Muslims and most Christians were Arabic-speaking natives. Some Jews were cultural Arabs, having lived there for many centuries. The great majority of Jews, however, were newcomers. One group had resided there a generation or two, having immigrated to live and work in agricultural community projects typical of mid-nineteenth-century socialistic utopian societies. The others belonged to *Haluka* communities living on charity from world Jewry. This group included Jews of various nationalities who emigrated to the Jewish Holy Land to pray and die. During the war the Jewish population dropped to an estimated 20,000. Some left Palestine, and a normal percentage of the *Haluka* died without the usual influx of others who wished to die in Palestine.

The Balfour Declaration stated that Great Britain "viewed with favour the establishment in Palestine of a national home for the Jewish people." But the Zionist organization hoped for "Palestine as the national home of the Jewish people, and the right of the Jewish people to build up its national life in Palestine." Active Zionists were confident that with work and time a Jewish national state having all rights and appurtenances of a typical European national state would be created. They worked toward that goal; many acclaimed it openly.

The Arabs of Palestine considered their land as part of Syria and placed their faith in promises made to Sharif Husayn with regard to an Arab state, in Wilson's Fourteen Points, and in the Anglo-French Declaration. The British candidly denied the existence of the Sykes-Picot Agreement and suavely explained away the Balfour Declaration as providing only for a Jewish cultural and religious home. To this the Arabs had no objection, as British Oriental experts well knew. Since Arabs enjoyed a majority of eighty-five to ninety percent of the population, they hoped to become an integral part of the Arab national state; and arrival of the King-Crane commission encouraged them to believe that the Arab view would prevail. The Zionist commission, however, disturbed them; and the return of Jews who fled during the war and the immediate postwar agitation for Jewish immigration into Palestine raised a multitude of fears in their hearts.

The British wanted to incorporate Palestine into their empire because of its proximity to Suez, its suitability as an outlet for Mosul oil, and its strategic position with respect to Arabia. The British army was occupying Palestine, and there seemed to be no good reason for leaving. A Zionist alliance might serve Britain's imperial interests and prevent the French from holding the entire Levantine coast and from approaching this close to Suez.

Obviously, had these British views been clearly focused by the cabinet, the military administration in Palestine would never have been slighted to the extent of having a succession of three chief administrators in 1919. Procrastination, intrigue, war weariness, faction, and strife plagued the British military administration and intensified public unrest throughout Palestine.

BRITISH MANDATE

Reprisals and bloodshed first occured in April, 1920, when many Arab villagers flocked to Jerusalem to the Nabi Musa celebrations. Rumors turned into riots; Arabs who inflamed the villagers and Zionists with caches of arms were seized and sentenced by British military courts to penal servitude. That same month the Powers, meeting at San Remo, affirmed the British mandate over Palestine; and on July 1, 1920 Sir

Herbert Samuel, the first high commissioner for Palestine, including
Transjordan, relieved the military authorities of their burden.

During the five years of Sir Herbert's civil administration four separate, yet parallel, governments were formed. Most important was the
British executive government, composed of various administrative departments over each of which the high commissioner appointed a British director or secretary. These officials formed a cabinet, whose first
chief secretary was Wyndham Deedes. Departments were established
for public works, education, immigration, customs, excise and trade, an-
tiquities, treasury, revenue, attorney-general, police, health, agriculture
and forests, posts and telegraphs, lands, and audit. An advisory council
consisting of ten British officials, four Muslims, three Christians, and
three Jews was appointed. An elective legislative council was projected,
but it never came into existence because of disagreement over the ratio
of representation between Arabs and Jews.

The Jewish community inaugurated the second government. In the
fall of 1920 a Jewish national assembly was elected. It, in turn, appointed a Jewish national council (*Vaad Leumi*), which the high commissioner recognized as representative of the Jewish community in Palestine. The national council governed the Jews of Palestine in personal,
communal, and religious affairs and recommended actions to British
authorities concerning matters affecting the Jewish community. Certain
Jews of prewar Palestinian residence, however, clung to a theocratic
concept of Jewish life and refused to be governed by the national council. Supported by *Agudath Israel*, they disclaimed all connections with
political and nationalistic Zionism, but proved too small a minority for
the British Palestine administration to recognize in any formal way.

The third government was the international Zionist organization with
headquarters in London. It represented more than thirty Zionist groups
in many parts of the world and had sponsored the drive which obtained
the Balfour Declaration. A number of its executives lived and worked
in Palestine; and between 1921 and 1929 they were known as the Palestine Zionist executive. Each member was responsible for some department of work: political, immigration, education, industry, health, and
public works. Sometimes referred to as a quasi-government, the Zionist
executive followed the policies established by the Zionist organization
in London and augmented the administration of the mandatory administration in Palestine. Frequently when the high commissioner's government and the Zionist executive were at odds, the Zionist organization
proved more effective in persuading the British cabinet and House of
Commons to follow the Zionist course than the foreign or colonial secretary was in obtaining support for policies of the high commissioner.

These three "governments" represented imperialism, Jewish settlers, and world Jewry, respectively. The fourth government tried to represent the great majority of the people of Palestine—Muslim and Christian Arabs. Arab notables—of which the two most prominent families were the al-Husaynis and the Nashashibis—at first voiced the opinion that Arab Palestine was and should continue to be a part of Syria. But they had no love for the French and, therefore, dropped that contention after Faysal's defeat at Damascus. Following a large Arab congress at Haifa in December, 1920 the Arab executive was born. Musa Kazim al-Husayni, former mayor of Jerusalem, was its chairman until 1934. Although the Arab executive attempted to parallel the activities of the Zionist executive, it never had the latter's extensive financial resources or wealth of personnel at its call.

In addition to the Arab executive the British created the supreme Muslim council in 1921 to deal with Muslim religious affairs, especially custody of religious endowments and administration of Muslim courts. Fines, fees, and patronage gave the supreme Muslim council real power; and its president, Hajj Amin al-Husayni, became the leading political Muslim figure in Palestine in the 1930's. Commonly known as the Mufti, Hajj Amin was elected, with Sir Herbert Samuel's connivance, to that office in 1921. A position held for life, the mufti of Jerusalem, like muftis in other cities, gave legal opinions on Sacred Law for citizens and the courts.

With four governments in Palestine, each with several parties or groups, and with the eyes of the world upon the Holy Land of three religions, Sir Herbert found the task of governing the mandate a challenge to human ingenuity. He had to remember Britain's imperial concern for Palestine and the entire Middle East. He had to govern the mandate economically and peacefully. He had to fulfill the mission of the mandatory power in instructing the people, eighty-five percent of whom were Arabs, and preparing the way for self-government and independence. And he had to follow the instructions of the cabinet in London, which was persistently dogged by political pressure to honor not only the letter of the Balfour Declaration but also its spirit as interpreted by the Zionists who were already building the foundations for a national state of Israel. The dilemmas posed kept the political scene in Palestine shifting, as first one faction and then another played the leading role.

IMMIGRATION POLICIES

No problem weighed more heavily upon Palestine than that of immigration and population. Zionist leaders, who wished to obtain a Jewish majority as quickly as possible, encouraged mass immigration. When a majority was achieved, Great Britain would be asked to relinquish her mandate, and Palestine would become an independent Jewish national state. Justice Brandeis dissented from this policy, believing that immigration should proceed slowly and only as rapidly as a secure economic basis for the immigrant's livelihood could be assured.

Sir Herbert Samuel upon assuming office in 1920 announced that Jewish immigrants would be permitted to enter Palestine at the rate of 1,000 per month; later that same year an annual quota of 16,500 was set. Under this program nearly 10,000 Jewish immigrants entered Palestine up to May 4, 1921, when immigration was suspended because of serious riots in Jaffa. A month later immigration was permitted to continue; and Churchill, then colonial secretary, announced in a famous memorandum of July, 1922 in answer to Samuel's demand for a policy statement that Britain intended to honor the Balfour Declaration and fulfill the pledge of allowing the Jewish community to increase its numbers through immigration. The pledge with respect to immigration, however, would be interpreted and regulated so that the volume of immigration should not exceed the economic capacity of Palestine to absorb new arrivals.

In actual practice middle-class families or anyone who had $2,500 could obtain an entry permit, and a skilled workman needed only half that sum. In addition the Zionist organization through various funds collected in Europe and America provided the necessary funds for carefully selected immigrants. Immigration increased rapidly, and nearly 35,000 Jews entered in the year of 1925. From 1927 until 1933 the number arriving in Palestine did not always offset those leaving; but beginning in 1933 entries rose sharply and in several years reached 40,000. Moreover, many Jewish visitors remained in Palestine illegally so that the precise number "ingathered" between 1920 and 1939 was unknown, but it was well over 300,000. The total Jewish population rose to 445,000 in 1939, not quite thirty percent of the total population.

Arab influx and natural growth were high, but did not keep pace with the Jews. There were 620,000 Arabs in 1918, and in 1939 the estimate tallied some 1,044,000. The high Arab birth rate accounted for natural growth of about 20,000 a year. Jews with a figure of 6,000 had to find 14,000 immigrants a year to keep pace in their desperate population race.

Whenever immigration reached high figures, riots between Arabs and Jews resulted. The gates would be barred for a few months. Then, political pressure in London resulted in the order's being rescinded. Principles of economic absorptive capacity were constantly discussed, but how to apply them and by what standard they could be judged were never determined. To the Zionist organization any limitation upon "in-gathering" smacked of heresy and appeared fatal to the whole nationalist movement.

LAND POLICIES

A large majority of Jews settling in Palestine came from urban centers in Europe. Yet one of the underlying philosophies of Zionism called for an agricultural society in Palestine, and workers on the land enjoyed a most honored position in Zionist society. Zionists pledged that Arab tenant farmers would not be driven from lands purchased by their Jewish National Fund, but this guarantee proved impossible to fulfill. Some of the very best lands in Palestine were purchased at inflated prices from absentee landlords living in Damascus and Beirut. For centuries a regular land market existed for investment purposes, and transactions rarely affected the tenant cultivator. However, land bought by the National Fund became the inalienable property of the Jewish community with express provisos that only Jews might work the land or be employed upon it. Tenant families which had lived in a village and tilled the land about it for a thousand years were evicted, sometimes summarily. Since rumors fly in the Middle East, each tenant farmer feared he would be the next and reacted vigorously against any Jewish immigration.

Land was expensive in Palestine, because the population was relatively dense already and because expansion of the cultivable area required considerable outlay of funds for irrigation, fertilizers, draining, flushing to counteract salinity, removing stones, etc. In the 1930's farm land cost on an average about four times what it did in the United States, and wages of farm labor were so high that general agriculture on a commercial basis was not feasible. The Jewish National Fund purchased most of the farm land and rented it at nominal fees to farmers who lived in a private village or colony (*Moshavah*), a co-operative village (*Moshav Ovdim*), or a collective village (*Kibbutz*). Cultivation of citrus fruits was encouraged, and in the years before 1939 annual exports reached 10,000,000 cases. These exports provided Palestine with almost all of her earned foreign exchange.

The trend of agricultural development had a marked effect upon the Arab rural community. Living alongside the Jewish agricultural establishments, Arab farmers learned and followed the practices of their neighbors. This was attested by the fact that in 1936 at least half of the citrus production came from Arab lands. Hill-country land that could not be farmed by mechanized equipment and would not easily submit to intensified cultivation was shunned by the Zionist organization and left to Arab peasants. It was marginal farming at best, but the tax structure of the administration bore heavily upon the peasants who worked these lands, and their poverty was sharply depicted against the higher Jewish standard of living.

INDUSTRIAL PROGRESS

Although Zionist groups spent over $75,000,000 in land for all types of farms and although society highly regarded work on the land, the majority of Jews settled in urban communities, the greatest of which became Tel Aviv. Other centers were Jaffa, Haifa, and Jerusalem. The over-all Jewish urban population amounted to seventy-five percent of the Jewish community. At the end of World War I Tel Aviv was a small dingy town of two thousand inhabitants on the outskirts of Jaffa; in 1939 it contained over 150,000 inhabitants and was called "the only purely Jewish city in the world." Much of the industry was located there, and it became the center of artistic and cultural life in Jewish Palestine. The Zionist organization had continual difficulties in persuading immigrants from European cities to settle in rural agricultural villages after they had been sheltered in Tel Aviv.

A relatively large amount of industry developed in Palestine; but up to 1939 it was directed to supplying the local market. Exports from Dead Sea potash and chemical industries were just beginning to show in the trade statistics. In 1935 the pipeline from Iraq began to discharge oil at its terminus in Haifa, but only a negligible amount was refined locally. Palestinians had visions of supplying the industrial needs of a wide area in the Middle East, but at that time they could not meet local requirements.

The industrial and labor picture in Palestine was dominated by the General Federation of Jewish Labor (*Histadruth*). Owning and operating a number of industries, *Histadruth* represented about three fourths of the Jewish workers, whose wages were higher than those of non-members. Arab laborers were unorganized; and the obvious wage disparity and discrimination in favor of Jewish workers incited bitter feelings. Yet unemployment figures were low, and many regulations against hiring Arabs were ignored. For example, by 1935 only twenty-eight percent of the labor on Jewish orange plantations was Jewish. Wages for Arab workmen were higher in Palestine than in neighboring states, but the higher cost of living held any increase in real wages to a minimum.

SOCIAL DEVELOPMENTS

On social and cultural endeavors the Zionist organization and many individuals and groups, such as *Histadruth* and *Hadassah* (American Zionist Women's Organization), expended much time, effort, and money. From the outset, education was deemed most important. The cornerstone of Hebrew University in Jerusalem on Mt. Scopus was laid July 24, 1918, even before the end of the war! Schools of every description—primary, secondary, teacher training, vocational, agricultural—came into existence; and before 1939 every Jewish child received at least a primary education. Hospitals, clinics, maternity and infant care, medical-research laboratories, and public-health campaigns also received much attention. Since public funds from the Palestine government for such uses were insignificant, needs of the Arab population were unfulfilled. But contributions from abroad, particularly America, enabled the Jewish community to maintain a level of public services more comparable to those of Western society.

FINANCES

Activities of the Zionist organization in purchasing land, supporting new immigrants, building schools and hospitals, starting industries, and financing its myriad of projects were made possible by contributions from world Jewry. Estimates show that about $400,000,000 was the cost of the Zionist development in Palestine between 1919 and 1939. Annual exports in the last years before World War II reached $4,000,000, most of which were receipts from the citrus industry. Annual imports rose to about $18,000,000. Other expenses came from the outlay for new land and its rehabilitation—$55,000,000 in 1935—building materials, machinery, and arms and ammunition. A significant number of settlers brought capital with them in the form of foreign exchange, enabling Palestine to make purchases of machinery, capital goods of all sorts, and consumption goods necessary to maintain life. The Palestine Economic Corporation, an American concern, invested in ventures that had a sound economic outlook. Some of these were the King David Hotel in Jerusalem, the Palestine Electric Corporation, and the Palestine Potash Company. Even these, however, would not have been economically sound if world Jewry donations had not generated a good market in Palestine.

Without the steady flow of money and resources into Palestine the Zionist achievement could not have been recorded. At any time after its inception the faltering of Jewish charity would have been disastrous. At no time in that period did Palestine ever approach a self-supporting status, and the bountiful gifts stabilized society at a standard of living far above what any reasonable expectation of the exploitation of the country's resources could produce. To that degree the entire economy of Palestine was false. After the end of the first great surge of immigration, which came to 33,000 in 1925, the fall in the value of Polish currency, slackening of interest in the West, and then world-wide depression brought emigration from Palestine and severe economic crisis. Only the advent of Hitler and the accompanying sympathy toward the Jews saved the Zionist program for Palestine.

BRITISH ADMINISTRATION

Sir Herbert Samuel served as high commissioner for five years. Only one serious outbreak (1921) between Jews and Arabs occurred during his term, and perhaps a recurrence of the riots was averted by the Churchill memorandum of 1922 which promised the Arab community that nothing would be done to jeopardize Arab rights. Outward peace reigned, and prosperity and activity dominated the Palestine scene. The Hebrew University in Jerusalem opened its doors; commerce and agriculture advanced; and political passions seemed to have cooled.

After considerable political controversy and following the Churchill Memorandum and his White Paper of 1922, the council of the League of Nations on July 24, 1922 approved the mandate for Palestine. In entrusting the state to Great Britain the League incorporated the Balfour Declaration in the preamble and recognized the historic association of the Jewish people with Palestine. The terms of conveyance instructed Great Britain to recognize the Zionist organization and in co-operation with it to facilitate Jewish immigration and "close settlement by Jews on the land" without prejudicing the "rights and position of other sections of the population." The mandatory instrument gave Great Britain authority with regard to all Holy Places and Muslim Foundations with the express injunction that they be administered according to religious law, existing rights, and public order. Free access to Holy Places, and free exercise of worship was guaranteed. English, Arabic, and Hebrew were designated as official languages; and all public inscriptions had to be written in Arabic and Hebrew. Article 25 of the mandate exempted all land of Palestine east of the Jordan River from the execution of such provisions of the mandate as Great Britain deemed inapplicable to that area.

To say the least, the terms of the mandate were not easy to fulfill. Every high commissioner from 1920 to 1939 tried to comply with the instructions. But each one discovered how difficult—almost impossible—it was to follow the dictates of the colonial office in London, to "co-operate" with the Zionists, and to maintain the Arab rights and position. Sir Herbert attempted to have a constitution adopted and a legislature elected and convened, but found Arab leaders unwilling to co-operate. Through political boycott and use of threats to riot the Arabs hoped to obtain British recognition that their preponderant majority entitled them to control the institutions of self-government.

Field Marshal Lord Plumer, who came as high commissioner in July,

1925, had been administrator of Malta and a distinguished soldier in World War I. He set out to inform everybody that he intended to pursue the instructions of the Mandate, resisting pressure and threats from any and all sources. His three years were peaceful ones, and British armed forces were reduced as an unnecessary financial burden.

THE JEWISH AGENCY

In 1929 the Zionist organization in its work in Palestine was transformed into the Jewish Agency. This step followed the suggestion put forth in Article 4 of the mandate urging the Zionist organization "to secure the co-operation of all Jews who are willing to assist in the establishment of the Jewish national home." In 1925 Dr. Weizmann advanced the formation of an enlarged Jewish Agency to consist of an equal number of Zionists and non-Zionists and thus obtain support of all Jews for the development of Palestine. But differences over fund raising in America between Rabbi Wise and non-Zionists headed by Louis Marshall and Felix Warburg retarded its approval.

However, in 1929 at Zurich the sixteenth Zionist congress voted the enlarged Jewish Agency. The precarious world economic situation made it imperative for Zionists to win support from whatever source, and the announced objectives of the new Jewish Agency were: assist Jewish immigration to Palestine; foster the Hebrew language and culture; acquire land by the Jewish National Fund as inalienable property of the Jewish people; promote agriculture and colonization based on the principle of Jewish labor; and provide for religious needs of Jewish people. The president of the Zionist organization automatically served as president of the Jewish Agency, Dr. Weizmann becoming its first president. Zionists were hesitant about uniting with non-Zionists for fear that the program would be diluted and compromised. In actual practice the Jewish Agency drew in more and more Jews to support its ambitions, finally committing most Jews to the full program.

In addition to the non-Zionist Jews of the Western world who desired full integration into Western society in Western nation states, two groups were opposed to the policies of the Jewish Agency. The more numerous was composed of the rigidly orthodox in Palestine and elsewhere, who felt that the Zionist program, being nationalistic, destroyed the religious basis of Judaism. The other group, led by Vladimir Jabotinsky, rebelled against the acquiescence of the Zionist organization to the Churchill White Paper of 1922. Calling themselves revisionists, they demanded immediate fulfillment of the National Home by the Palestinian government and condemned inclusion of non-Zionists, whom they regarded as Jewish traitors.

THE PASSFIELD WHITE PAPER

The vocal outbursts of these rabid revisionists, along with disturbances in 1928 near the Wailing Wall, frightened the Arabs and actuated them to be more concerned with Muslim rights along the Wall, which was part of the enclosure of the Dome of the Rock. They irritated worshippers and aroused Jewish ire by disturbing prayers and various religious services. Custom and precedent have always been powerful claims in religious law in the Middle East; and Arab acts, which to Jews and Westerners seemed intentional aggravations, were efforts to maintain legal rights and prohibit new rights from developing.

Tension broke wide open in August, 1929. A group of young Zionists from Tel Aviv, in open defiance of orders from the acting high commissioner, sang the Zionist anthem and raised their flag at the Wailing Wall. The next day a Muslim ceremony took place at the same spot, with minor disturbances occurring. In Jerusalem a Jewish boy kicked his football into an Arab tomato patch, and a fight ensued in which the boy was stabbed. British police arrested the Arab, but were then mobbed by the Jewish throng. Rioting continued for several days, with a dozen assaults upon Arabs and seven on Jews. On August 23 Muslims attacked Jews in Jerusalem, and serious incidents followed in Hebron and Safed. Troops were called from Egypt and Transjordan. On August 26 Jews invaded a mosque in Jerusalem, killing the imam. Later the same day a Muslim shrine was damaged and tombs of the prophets desecrated.

Sir John Chancellor, the high commissioner since 1928, returned on August 29; and order was restored. He condemned Arab leadership for the outrages. Over 130 Jews were killed and 339 wounded; 116 Arabs were killed and an unknown number wounded. Trials were held for over 1000 persons—ninety percent Arabs, ten percent Jews—and 25 Arabs and 1 Jew were condemned to death.

Meanwhile, Whitehall sent out Sir Walter Shaw as head of a commission "to inquire into the immediate causes which led to the recent outbreak in Palestine and to make recommendations as to the steps necessary to avoid recurrence." The League of Nations also sent its own Wailing Wall commission to find some "solution of the problems relating to the question of the Holy Places of Palestine." Furthermore, the British government sent Sir John Hope Simpson to study and report on land settlement, immigration, and development in Palestine. Certainly information would not be lacking!

All reports were submitted; and in October, 1930 Lord Passfield (Sidney Webb), the colonial secretary, issued his famous White Paper outlining British policy on Palestine. The Passfield White Paper repeated the same general view presented in 1922 by the Churchill White Paper and emphasized the equal responsibility of the Palestine government to the Jewish and non-Jewish populations. Attention was drawn to the "economic absorptive capacity" of Palestine, and again the statement differentiated between a Jewish national home and a Jewish nationalist state.

In a constructive vein, Lord Passfield indicated that additional armed forces would be stationed in Palestine to add greater security, especially for the more exposed Jewish settlements. He condemned the Arabs for nonco-operation in establishing a legislative council and promised that steps would be taken to give some self-government to Palestine with or without the help of any particular group in Palestine. The White Paper stressed the poor condition of Arab peasants and pointed out the need for Arab land development. It stated that the immediate task of the Palestine administration would be to assist agricultural progress of the Arabs and to close Jewish immigration if it prevented any Arab from obtaining employment.

The storm of protest which arose from the Zionist camp was serious. The words of the Passfield White Paper could not be assailed, but the tone and interpretation of British intentions crushed the leaders of the Jewish Agency. Weizmann, Warburg, and Melchett resigned their positions. Because of Dr. Weizmann's policy of co-operation with Great Britain and his acceptance of the Churchill White Paper of 1922, he had been under constant pressure from radicals and revisionists, led by Jabotinsky, Rabbi Wise, Rabbi Nahum Goldman, and Ussishkin. In view of their attacks, the Passfield White Paper made Weizmann's position untenable among extreme Zionists.

Pressure upon the British government moved Prime Minister MacDonald in November to announce misgivings over the White Paper and to write a public letter in February, 1931 to Dr. Weizmann, emasculating the White Paper on almost every position it had taken. Then, the Arabs were up in arms, and the Palestine Arab executive denounced MacDonald's letter as a breach of faith. British indecision and wavering invited the Middle East to reason that the Passfield White Paper resulted from the outbreak of August, 1929 and that the MacDonald letter stemmed from Jewish agitation against the White Paper. British prestige suffered; the rewards of violence and threats appeared consequential. Under such conditions a peaceful future for Palestine looked rather bleak.

ECONOMIC ADVANCES

Although the political situation remained unsettled through the next several years and British attempts at inducing some form of self-government proved as fruitless as the first overtures of Sir Herbert Samuel, the economic boom into which Palestine entered gave optimists an opportunity to assert that all was well. Lieutenant-General Sir Arthur Wauchope became high commissioner in November, 1931, just when the boom was first accelerating. Immigration picked up; agricultural and industrial production jumped; government revenue trebled and quadrupled; citrus cultivation spread; and new capital investments gave greater opportunities for labor, which in turn kept wages at a high level. After 1932 arrival of German artisans and capitalists provided greater stimulus to the boom. Genuine international capitalists provided more optimism by discussing the role Palestine might assume as an entrepôt between East and West. Successful transportation routes between Baghdad and Damascus encouraged others to link Basrah and Haifa. The Anglo-Persian Oil Company proposed a pipeline to the Palestinian coast, and air lines planned to use Palestine as a major stop between Europe and India and the Far East.

Legal and illegal immigration swelled, and irresponsible Zionist spokesmen (ignoring the high Arab birth rate) predicted a majority of Jews in Palestine within a decade. In consequence, the Arab executive provoked a series of armed attacks upon the British during the month of October, 1933. Meanwhile, the revisionist Zionists continued to inveigh against the mild course of the Jewish Agency and its collaboration with the British. Dr. Arlosoroff, a leader of the Zionist Labor party and chairman of the political department of the Jewish Agency in Palestine, was murdered by revisionists, and the British suppressed their demonstrations. Commentators, in reviewing these outbursts, noted that the attacks were not by Jews or Arabs against the other and assumed unjustifiably that the two peoples were learning to live together.

The amazing growth of the Jewish community in the years between 1933 and 1936 affected even remote Arab villages in the hill country of Palestine. The great influx encouraged Zionist leaders of the Jewish Agency to predict publicly that at the current rate of "ingathering" Jews would comprise a majority of the population by 1947. Arab political efforts and leadership coalesced into one united group, which called itself the Arab Higher Committee. Evidence of Zionist acquisition of arms through smuggling came to light when a shipment of cement inadvertently was discovered to be 359 drums of firearms and 400,000 rounds of ammunition. A double standard of wage rates developed in Haifa, Jaffa, and Jerusalem, much to the displeasure of Arab labor; and discrimination in hiring became obvious to all. Italian successes in East Africa and appeasement of Mussolini lowered British prestige in the Middle East. The future appeared uncertain.

PEEL REPORT

In the face of these ominous developments Arabs in November, 1935 petitioned the high commissioner, among other things, to establish "democratic government in accordance with the Covenant of the League of Nations and Article 2 of the Palestine Mandate." A month later Sir Arthur Wauchope presented details of a legislative council to be composed of 11 Muslims, 7 Jews, 3 Christians, 2 business representatives, and 5 British officials. Accompanying the announcement was the statement that the high commissioner would proceed with the establishment of the council whether or not any community refused to participate in the elections. The Arabs announced they would co-operate; the Jews declared they would not. The outcry against the move was sharp. Far better to delay self-government for a few years more until a Jewish majority was achieved! The Zionist cause was supported by the English House of Commons; and in April 1936 the high commissioner acknowledged that plans for self-government were postponed.

Hebrew newspapers in Palestine rejoiced over the Jewish victory in the English Parliament, and Arab leaders were dismayed. At a time when Arab strikes and disorders in Iraq, Syria, Lebanon, and Egypt forced England and France to grant self-government, peaceful persuasion in Palestine failed dismally to bring similar concessions.

The stage in Palestine was favorably set for violence. Yet the rising in Palestine came first from the population; only later was it directed by the Arab Higher Committee. Arab highwaymen held up a caravan of cars near Nablus, shooting two Jews. During the following days numerous Arabs in Tel Aviv and Jaffa were attacked by Jews. Then, Arab rioting began and continued in a sporadic way for many months. Strikes ensued; many groups refused to pay taxes; and before the end of April, 1936 a general Arab strike spread to all Palestine. The Arab Higher Committee declared the strike would continue until the British agreed to grant self-government, halt Jewish immigration, and prohibit transfer of Arab lands to Jews. A peaceful strike was contemplated, but feeling ran so high among the Arab population that bombings and property destruction were frequent. There were as many attacks directed against the British as against the Zionists.

In May Great Britain sought to pacify Palestine by sending Earl Peel as head of a commission of inquiry. But an impasse developed: the Peel Commission would not leave England until the strike ended; the Arab Higher Committee would not end the strike until Jewish immigration was suspended; and the British refused to cancel the immigration schedules. Palestine had grown important to the British Empire with regard to air routes to Asia and Africa, sea lanes through Suez and the Mediterranean, and oil deliveries from Iraq. The security of these interests was presented to the British public as dependent upon the success of Zionism in Palestine. British difficulties and embarrassment mounted. Sentiment and pronouncements in Turkey, Iraq, Egypt, and India sided with the Arabs; Poland and the United States, each with large Jewish groups, pressed England to favor the Zionists.

In October, 1936 upon pleas from the kings of Iraq and Saudi Arabia —both of whom were at that time subservient to Britain and British pressure—the Higher Committee called off the strike without obtaining its demands. Zionism and Britain won, but only by giving neighboring Arab governments an active hand in Palestinian Arab affairs (undoubtedly at British invitation). In November Lord Peel and his colleagues arrived in Palestine, made their survey, and in July, 1937 published their report. Without too much difficulty the Peel Report concluded that an "irrepressible conflict" had arisen over the question: "Who, ultimately, would rule the country?" The Report recommended division of Palestine and proceeded to suggest frontiers and conditions of partition. Simultaneously, a White Paper was issued by the cabinet supporting the Peel Report as official policy.

The partition scheme was bitterly assailed by Zionists, non-Zionists, and Arabs. Non-Zionists ruled out a national state of any kind, and the partition plan established one. Zionists, while not entirely shutting the door on the idea of partition, argued that partition had already been enacted when Transjordan was cut off and that further decrease of the national home was contrary to the letter and the spirit of the mandate. The Arab Higher Committee and Arab National Defense party denounced the principle of partition and noted that this particular scheme gave seven eighths of the Arab citrus-groves to Jewish Palestine while seventy-seven percent of the land in that state would be Arab owned. The Arab state could never be solvent and would be dependent upon the Jewish state. Moreover, with unlimited immigration the Jewish state would become overpopulated and demand more space from the Arabs, who would be subject "to perpetual encroachments, political and economic." To Arabs partition was unreasonable and in violation of the mandate and the Covenant of the League of Nations.

assailed ★ by all sides

Pursuing the suggestions given in the Peel Report and White Paper, the Palestine administration took more positive action. Immigration was curtailed, and a firmer hand was directed against Arabs. Jerusalem offices of the Arab Higher Committee were searched. And in September, 1937, after the murder of a British official, Hajj Amin al-Husayn was removed from the presidency of the supreme Muslim council and five of the Higher Committee were deported to the Seychelles Islands. (Hajj Amin escaped to Lebanon.) These acts touched off an Arab rebellion and guerrilla warfare against the British although numerous attacks upon the Jewish community also occurred. The latter, with full approval of the authorities, greatly expanded its illegal self-defense force, the *Haganah,* which totaled over 10,000 men, well trained and well armed by the Jewish Agency.

Into this maelstrom was sent the Woodhead Commission in April, 1938 to reinvestigate the partition scheme and to report on detailed frontiers for the two states. Published in October, 1938, the Woodhead Report outlined three different possibilities. Plan A was the Peel Partition. Plan B left much of Galilee to the British permanent mandate and reduced the Jewish enclave south of Jaffa. Plan C suggested only small Jewish and Arab states, retaining most of Palestine in a mandated territory.

CIVIL WAR

But the plans fell on deaf ears. Palestine was in open revolt. Bands of Arab rebels attacked police stations, driving officials from town to town; and by October, 1938 even the Old City of Jerusalem was occupied by the rebels. *Irgun,* the illegal and secret national military organization of the revisionists, perpetrated many attacks upon the Arabs; and *Haganah* increased its membership and obtained many "opportunities for broader experience." Palestine was on the verge of civil war and rebellion.

The open revolt in Palestine coincided with the pressure of Hitler upon Czechoslovakia, the Munich accord, and the nadir of British prestige. Germany and Italy showered propaganda and courtesies upon the Arabs of Palestine, and England quickly realized how vulnerable her position with the Arab states had become. A new high commissioner, Sir Harold MacMichael, arrived in 1938; and the new colonial secretary, Malcolm MacDonald, declared that plans for partition were being dropped and invited Arabs and Jews to a conference in London.

Representatives of Egypt, Iraq, Transjordan, Saudi Arabia, Yemen, and Palestine Arabs—Husaynis and Nashashibis—came from the Arab side. Representatives of the Jewish Agency and Zionist and non-Zionist Jewish groups from Great Britain, the United States, France, Germany, Belgium, Poland, eastern Europe, and South Africa filled out the roster. The conference opened on February 7, 1939. In essence the British proposed (first to Arabs and then to Jews, since the former would not sit down with the latter) considerable reduction in Jewish immigration and land purchases and establishment of a single self-governing Pal-

The Arabs' last chance lost.

estine after ten years. The Jews refused to discuss the question further and left, since the terms ruled that Arabs would comprise two thirds of the population and Jews would forever be a minority in Palestine. Although definitely more favorable, the Arabs declined to accept the proposals because they did not go far enough.

Rebuffed on both sides and with time running out in Europe, Great Britain issued a White Paper on May 17, 1939, declaring her unilateral solution of the Palestine impasse. Proposals followed the earlier scheme. About 75,000 immigrants would be allowed to enter over the next five years, after which the doors would be open only upon Arab consent. Land sales from Arabs to Jews would be strictly regulated. After ten years self-rule would be established on lines similar to those already prevailing in Iraq.

The Arab Higher Committee rejected this solution, asking for independence at the beginning rather than the end of the ten-year period. Remembering distinctly how the Churchill and Passfield White Papers were quickly disowned by British governments when Jewish pressure was applied, the Arabs could not believe that this White Paper would have a different ending. Jews in Palestine and Zionists throughout the world denounced the White Paper as a treacherous document, and no sacrifice was deemed too great "to frustrate and defeat" it. In Jerusalem there were shouts: "Down with Weizmann!" and "Up with Jabotinsky!" A British policeman was shot in Jerusalem; and Ben-Gurion, chairman of the Jewish Agency executive, announced that this murder "marked the beginning of Jewish resistance" to the new British policy. At the twenty-first Zionist congress at Geneva in August, 1939 Ben-Gurion urged that Jews defy Britain and act in Palestine as though the Jewish Agency were the state. Rabbi Silver of the United States supported Weizmann and pointed out how foolish it would be to side with England in the coming war against the Nazis and at the same time embarrass her in Palestine.

To what extent Great Britain would have moved to implement the White Paper of 1939 cannot be judged. In the summer of that year she was too weak and the crisis in central Europe too serious for any action to be initiated. When World War II broke out Zionists and Arabs recognized that the ultimate outcome of the struggle among the great powers would probably be the determining factor in the future of Palestine. The decision might be made on the battlefields of Europe.

Résumé

The history of Palestine in the two decades between the World Wars had three component parts. The Zionist society worked hard with great faith, courage, and determination to build the national home in Palestine. Any compromise from that goal was dishonorable. The diligence, the improvement of agriculture and land, and the spirit of society were laudable. Zionists were blind, however, to the fact that they were intruders in another people's home and insensitive to the distrust, dislike, and fear that they generated in Arab hearts. Arab society believed that an Arab independent state had been promised and that any infringement of that pledge was dishonorable. The lesser organized Arabs in central Arabia, Kuwayt, the Hijaz, Yemen, Iraq, and Transjordan were independent; and the more developed Arabs of Egypt, Syria, and Lebanon had representative legislatures and considerable independence. Was it not strange that they, the Arabs of Palestine, did not have similar freedom? No society, country, and peoples from distant places gave them hundreds of millions of dollars to develop their country. They felt the indictment that they did not utilize their land was disproved by the uncontestable facts that their citrus groves were as productive as those of the Zionists and that they were better grain farmers than the Jews. The Arabs, however, suffered from benighted leadership, which erroneously judged that violence would intimidate Jew and Briton to give the Arabs independence. The British acted administratively as though Palestine were a colony, but economically as though the land belonged to someone else. British businessmen saw little profit in investing or settling in Palestine when the question of permanence within the empire was doubtful. Through those years Great Britain tried, usually unsuccessfully, to balance her budget; consequently, the idea of spending sums to raise standards of living in Palestine or increase productivity of the land for the benefit of native inhabitants had few supporters. Thus, England just muddled along, gaining enmity on all sides.

TRANSJORDAN

East of the Jordan River, however, British policy fell more into traditional patterns of empire behavior. Since the area east of the river was promised definitely to the Arabs and Sharif Husayn, the British found it good policy as well as convenient to grant administration of that land to Prince Abdallah as a reward for not attacking the French in Damascus. Accordingly Transjordan was given to Abdallah in 1921; and in 1922 the League council exempted it from many provisions of the mandate for Palestine, particularly those referring to Holy Places and implementation of the Balfour Declaration. The following year in Amman, capital of Transjordan, Sir Herbert Samuel announced the independence of Transjordan, which was also proclaimed simultaneously by Abdallah. England, nevertheless, remained in control until an understanding was concluded between the two governments. In actual practice from 1921 onwards Britain gave financial grants to Abdallah, and his administration was assisted by British officials.

In 1926 Abdallah convened a group of Arab notables to prepare the way for an elective legislative assembly. In 1927 petitions were submitted to him demanding a national representative council and freedom from British rule. To meet this pressure upon Abdallah, a treaty was concluded in February, 1928 at Jerusalem between Great Britain and Transjordan, placing their relations on a firm basis. Legislation and administration of Transjordan was exercised by the Prince under authority of the British high commissioner through the British resident stationed in Amman. The British were to control the budget, finances, army, economic development, and foreign affairs. Shortly thereafter, Abdallah issued a constitution providing for a legislative council; but Transjordanian notables refused to co-operate because of excessive control by the British.

Great Britain continued to dominate Transjordan between World Wars I and II, largely through annual financial support to Abdallah, support which increased from about $500,000 a year in the 1920's to $1,000,000 in 1939. Britain had two military forces in Transjordan. First, there was the Arab Legion organized in 1921 by Captain Peake of the Egyptian Camel Corps. It was planned as a police force, but it defended the frontiers from bedouin infiltration. Originally, it had no desert section and no airplanes; but after 1930 it expanded and blossomed into one of the most significant military forces in the Middle East. Although under the command of the Prince of Transjordan, it received five sixths of its financial requirements direct from the British treasury. In the treaty of 1928 provision was made for formation of the Transjordan Frontier Force under direct control of the high commissioner, since he was responsible for Transjordanian foreign affairs and protection of her frontiers.

Both armies were instruments of British government in the Middle East. They served to protect the frontiers of Palestine, Transjordan, and Iraq from raids by Ibn Saud and to maintain and police the corridor between Iraq and Transjordan through which ran the oil pipeline from Kirkuk to Haifa. Transjordan not only was an anchor for the British position in the Middle East but also stood as an important link in her empire. Prince Abdallah performed well for the British and they sustained him in a dignified manner.

REFERENCES: Chapter 32

Almost every volume discussing affairs of the Middle East in modern times bears some relationship to the events and movements presented in this chapter. Of special note, however, are those found in Chapters 7, 19, 27, 28, 29, and 31. Chapter 35 contains additional references.

Meir Ben-Horin, *Max Nordau: Philosopher of Solidarity:* Conference on Jewish Social Studies Inc., New York, 1956.

Norman Bentwich, *England in Palestine:* Kegan Paul, Trench, Trubner, London, 1932. Written by the mildly Zionist British official who served as head of the Department of Justice in Palestine until 1930.

John Bowle, *Viscount Samuel: A Biography:* Gollancz, London, 1957. An objective study of the life of the first High Commissioner.

Israel Cohen, *Theodor Herzl, Founder of Political Zionism:* Thomas Yoseloff, New York, 1959.

Esco Foundation for Palestine, Inc., *Palestine: A Study of Jewish, Arab, and British Policies,* 2 vols.: Yale University Press, New Haven, 1947. A vast work including all kinds of important information on the period of the mandate. Almost a sourcebook.

John Bagot Glubb, *The Story of the Arab Legion:* Hodder & Stoughton, London, 1948. Glubb was the commanding officer.

Philip P. Graves, ed., *Memoirs of King Abdullah of Transjordan:* Philosophical Library, New York, 1950. Covers the important events of the king's earlier life.

Ben Halpern, *The Idea of the Jewish State:* Harvard University Press, Cambridge, 1961. The most profound book on this subject.

J. C. Hurewitz, *The Struggle for Palestine:* Norton, New York, 1950. A first-rate book by a careful scholar.

Albert M. Hyamson, *Palestine under the Mandate, 1920–1948:* Methuen, London, 1950. Follows the Zionist line.

Claude Scudamore Jarvis, *Arab Command: The Biography of Lt. Col. F. G. Peake Pasha:* Hutchinson, London, 1942. Col. Peake organized the British forces in Transjordan.

Bernard Joseph, *British Rule in Palestine:* Public Affairs Press, Washington, 1948. Surveys the mandate period.

Walter C. Lowdermilk, *Palestine, Land of Promise:* Harper, New York, 1944. Outlines and discusses irrigation possibilities in Palestine in glowing terms.

Harry C. Luke and Edward Keith-Roach, *The Handbook of Palestine and Trans-Jordan:* Macmillan, London, 1930. Semiofficial.

Ernest Main, *Palestine at the Crossroads:* George Allen, London, 1937. Discusses the questions of partition and the future.

John Marlowe, *The Seat of Pilate: An Account of the Palestine Mandate:* Cresset Press, London, 1959. A British view.

Joseph B. Schechtman, *The Mufti and the Fuehrer, The Rise and Fall of Haj Amin el-Hesseini:* Thomas Yoseloff, New York, 1965. Unfriendly account of the activities of the Grand Mufti.

Alan R. Taylor, *Prelude to Israel: An Analysis of Jewish Diplomacy, 1897–1947:* Philosophical Library, New York, 1959. Somewhat critical.

Chaim Weizmann, *Trial and Error: The Autobiography of Chaim Weizmann:* Harper, New York, 1949. The life of the leader of Zionism during the mandatory period.

CHAPTER 33

Egypt and the Sudan

THE BRITISH PROTECTORATE

On December 18, 1914 Great Britain unilaterally declared the establishment of a protectorate over Egypt. Although the announcement carried a pledge of ultimate self-government, a protectorate was humiliating to Egyptians. Its Arabic translation was the word used to refer to dependence of certain Christian minorities on European powers. The Egyptian ministry of foreign affairs was abolished; and its functions appropriated by the British agent and consul general, who under the protectorate became high commissioner. Khedive Abbas Hilmi II, pro-Turkish and violently anti-British, had not returned from his summer palace on the Bosphorus when hostilities broke. He was deposed; and his uncle, Prince Husayn Kamal, was proclaimed sultan of Egypt. Already the legislative assembly was prorogued, so the British could expect little opposition during the war. Rushdi Pasha remained as prime minister and concurred readily with British demands; in the face of troops and the disposition of the British government, he had no alternative.

The average educated Egyptian was not overly concerned with these political developments. Egypt had been occupied by England for over a generation, and it appeared natural that in a world struggle Egypt should be aligned with her actual master rather than with any technical or legal overlord such as Turkey. The price of cotton, the question of marketing a new crop, importation of foodstuffs, and issuance of legal tender notes by the national bank seemed matters of far greater importance than national politics.

For nearly four years, therefore, Egypt served as a military base for British forces. At one time there were three independent British commands located there. Prices of cotton more than trebled, and wheat became scarce and high-priced. Troops requisitioned supplies, taking camels and donkeys from the peasants; and Egyptians were drafted into an army which fought alongside the British, although Britain promised to recognize Egyptian neutrality. Inflation was rampant, and fortunes were made by corrupt and illegal practices. The personnel of the British civil service deteriorated in quality, and the military ignored Egyptian sensibilies. The stationing of so many troops in Egypt naturally caused many awkward situations and numerous unfortunate incidents. The public blamed the British for every ill that befell Egypt in the war years.

Rushdi Pasha bravely co-operated with Lord Kitchener, Sir Milne Cheetham, Sir Henry McMahon, and Sir Reginald Wingate. He did not openly press for commitments on the termination of Capitulations or for the steps toward self government which were cited in the protectorate declaration. Secretly, however, Rushdi instructed his judicial adviser, an Englishman, to prepare recommendations on these points. Drafted in the form of constitutional reform, the proposals called for a bicameral legislature, the dominant upper house to be composed of Egyptian ministers, British advisers, and representatives of the foreign communities of Cairo and Alexandria. As soon as its contents leaked to the public, no Egyptian leader could possibly support the document.

Apparently, British officials were out of touch with sentiment in Egypt. Their reports to London did not enlighten the Foreign Office with a true description of trends, but followed the traditional imperialistic philosophy of Lord Curzon, the foreign secretary. The presence of so many Westerners in Egypt, public declarations of Allied politicians, and the coming of age of a new generation hurried Egyptian nationalism forward with great strides in the years between 1914 and 1918.

EGYPTIAN NATIONALISM AND THE WAFD

Two days after the end of the war in Europe Saad Zaghlul Pasha, ardent nationalist and minister of education under Lord Cromer, presented the high commissioner with a list of demands. If allowed, these demands would have given Egypt independence. Informed that London would reply, Zaghlul asked permission to proceed with his delegation (*Wafd*) to London to discuss his independence program. Wingate urged London to grant the wish; but the Foreign Office refused, because Zaghlul had no organized party and in no sense represented the government of Egypt. Upon the approval of Sultan Fuad Rushdi sought an invitation immediately to go to London to discuss the future status of Egypt. (Sultan Husayn died in 1917 and was succeeded by his brother.) Again Wingate urged that an invitation be tendered; but Downing

Street, busy with preparations for the Paris conference, declined and thus encouraged political conditions in Egypt to go from bad to worse. Zaghlul and his delegation avidly organized committees throughout the country and stimulated vigorous nationalistic feeling against the British. Rushdi and his chief associate, Adli Yakan Pasha, resigned after their rebuff; and Zaghlul threatened dire consequences should the sultan appoint a successor. At this juncture (March 8, 1919) Zaghlul and three other leading *Wafd* party members were arrested with Foreign Office approval by the British military (Egypt being under martial law) and deported to Malta. Egyptian reaction was spontaneous; insurrection and violence spread to all districts within ten days. Military forces rushed to Egypt crushed the revolt by the end of the month.

Lloyd George suddenly awoke to the fact that something needed to be done. General Allenby was appointed high commissioner; and Lord Milner was designated head of a commission of inquiry to investigate the situation and report on the nature of a constitution that would be best for Egypt under the protectorate. Zaghlul and his fellow internees in Malta were freed to lay their demands before the Peace Conference. They were bitterly disappointed, however, when the American delegation announced its recognition of the protectorate over Egypt.

In Egypt Wafd leadership was stirring the populace to impress the Milner mission with the strength of the national movement. It did its task so well that any Egyptian seen talking to the mission was branded as a traitor. Various acts of violence occurred against Englishmen. In March, 1920 Lord Milner returned to London uncertain what the next course should be. Still in Europe, Zaghlul visited England to discuss the Egyptian question with Lord Milner. Zaghlul's prestige and nationalist standing were considered impeccable; and his following was so devoted that any solution or compromise he proposed would have been acceptable to the Wafd and all nationalists in Egypt.

A memorandum containing the principles on which a treaty of alliance between Egypt and England might be drawn was composed in August, 1920. It recognized Egypt as a sovereign independent constitutional monarchy with representative institutions. Britain would undertake to defend Egypt, and Egypt would offer all assistance within her borders to England. Egypt would have diplomatic representation abroad, but would co-ordinate her policies with those of Britain. Egypt would appoint British judicial and financial advisers and would permit Britain to maintain a military force in Egypt. The Capitulations would be abolished but England would have the right to prevent adoption of laws inconsistent with legislation under the previous regime. The final point pledged Egypt to call a constituent assembly to ratify the treaty and adopt a constitution.

Lord Milner signed the document as the basis for a treaty which he would be willing to recommend to the cabinet; but Zaghlul temporized, asserting that the memorandum would have to be approved by the people of Egypt before he could go ahead. Several of his party returned to Egypt, where the memorandum was published and Egyptian sentiment tested. The response was lukewarm, largely because Zaghlul gave out public declarations quite noncommittal in tone. At this point he informed Lord Milner that the memorandum was not clear on several points. The British, however, would bargain no further, and conversations were broken off completely.

Zaghlul returned to Egypt in April, 1921, ready to prevent anyone from obtaining a treaty from the British. Adli Pasha, the new prime minister, spent the summer in England trying his hand at treaty-making; but with Zaghlul agitating at full force against him any treaty which was not preceded by termination of the protectorate and martial law was foredoomed.

EGYPTIAN INDEPENDENCE

In December, 1921 Adli resigned. Sarwat Pasha, acting prime minister, formed a new cabinet on the premise that Great Britain would immediately recognize Egypt as an independent sovereign state. Zaghlul's activities were redoubled. Allenby, appreciating that no treaty would be acceptable to Zaghlul, deported him to the Seychelles. Still the British cabinet did not agree to recognition of independence; it took a personal trip to London for Allenby to impress upon England the necessity of accepting the quasi-commitments made in the Milner-Zaghlul memorandum and to Sarwat. On February 28, 1922, the day of Allenby's return to Egypt, he gave out the unilateral British declaration ending the protectorate and elevating Egypt to the rank of an independent sovereign state. Martial law, proclaimed on November 2, 1914, was to be terminated as soon as the sultan's government passed an act of indemnity; and until Egypt and England could conclude an agreement England reserved to herself security of communications, defense, protection of foreign interests and minorities, and affairs of the Sudan. Egyptian nationalists were annoyed that their country's independence was declared by another state. Yet, England assumed the protectorate by unilateral action and might relinquish it in like manner.

The price of cotton fell in Egypt from $187 a cantar to $18 during the world-wide collapse of prices in 1920. Had the depressed situation persisted for any length of time, political anarchy in Egypt might have been attributable to economic difficulties. As it was, the fall from exorbitant heights had beneficial effects upon the fellaheen. Pressure to grow cotton was lessened, and more foodstuffs were raised. In 1922 price recovery allowed the government under the British declaration of independence to develop in a more favorable economic climate. Sultan Fuad became king of Egypt, and a succession of men passed through the chambers of the prime minister. Politics became a three-way embroilment among nationalists, the king, and the residency (as the British high commissioner's office was termed).

THE CONSTITUTION OF 1923

The residency pressed Fuad to appoint a prime minister who would present a constitution for the new sovereign state. Egyptian leaders feared such a step, lest it ruin them politically; and the king insisted upon an article naming him king of Egypt and the Sudan, thus taking a stand which he knew the British would not tolerate. Finally, a constitution was drawn up and promulgated on April 21, 1923; martial law was withdrawn in July; elections for parliament were held in September; and agreement was reached in October concerning service of Britishers in the Egyptian government.

The constitution gave to the king considerable powers. He could dissolve or adjourn parliament. He called parliament, and he could veto acts of parliament. (A two-thirds majority of the membership of each house could, however, override his veto.) The king appointed and dismissed ministers, and could issue decrees in absence of parliament. The king was commander-in-chief of the armed forces; and in reality a determined king could be chief executive of the state. Ministers were responsible to parliament; but since they held office at the pleasure of the king, they found it difficult to serve two masters. Two fifths of the senators were appointed by the king; three fifths were elected. Senators held office for ten years, and membership was restricted to men of considerable property or to persons who had held office or a prominent position in the state. Members of the chamber of deputies held office for five years, and one deputy was elected for every 60,000 inhabitants. The chamber of deputies alone had the right to dismiss the cabinet or a minister by a vote of no confidence; and they could try ministers for malfeasance in office. Nowhere in the constitution was Great Britain mentioned. But with British troops and many British advisers in Egypt and with an Englishman as *Sirdar* (commander-in-chief) of the Egyptian army Egyptians were fully justified in doubting that independence was attained.

EGYPTAIN POLITICS

Zaghlul was released from Gibraltar in March. (He had been transferred from the Seychelles for reasons of health.) And he, together with other Wafd leaders who had also been freed, returned to Egypt in

September in time for elections. They gained 188 seats out of 215 in the chamber of deputies. When parliament convened the next January, Zaghlul promptly accepted Fuad's invitation to form a ministry upon condition that as prime minister he would not compromise the program of the Wafd, of which he remained president.

Assumption of office changed Zaghlul's political life almost completely. Heretofore he had devoted his energies to oust the British and thereby maintain his leadership of the Egyptian people. But under his leadership the Wafd had been a party of agitators, and seemingly it could not change its tactics. His Wafd program had not been completed: British troops and advisers must go; the Sudan must be "returned" to Egypt; and any British claim to share in protecting the Suez Canal abandoned. These goals called for the continuation of intimidation by demonstrations against the British and veiled invitations to violence. Similar stirrings, to which the British reacted strongly, were "encouraged" in the Sudan. The situation was anomalous. As prime minister Zaghlul was responsible for maintenance of law and order in Egypt; but as head of the Wafd, he was in open defiance of law and order.

In the summer of 1924 at Ramsay MacDonald's invitation Zaghlul went to London, ostensibly to negotiate a treaty of alliance. What he did was to present his entire program as unequivocal demands. No treaty was signed; yet Zaghlul returned triumphantly to Cairo. He made a pretense of resigning; but, of course, his resignation was refused. Four days later, November 19, 1924, Sir Lee Stack, governor-general of the Sudan and commander-in-chief of the Egyptian army, was assassinated on the streets of Cairo. Zaghlul immediately, officially, and publicly, expressed his horror at the crime and pledged swift and thorough action to bring the culprits to trial; nevertheless, the deed was the logical and indirect result of open invitations to violence agitated by Zaghlul and the Wafd. Subsequent judicial proceedings demonstrated that leading Wafdists, including two members of Zaghlul's cabinet, were implicated.

The British cabinet decided to take vigorous action. On the afternoon of November 22, escorted by a regiment of British cavalry and in full military attire, Lord Allenby called at the offices of the council of ministers, read in English two communications to Zaghlul, handed him copies in French, and departed. Allenby was angry, and he took every opportunity to display force and humiliate Zaghlul. The note placed blame for Sir Lee Stack's murder upon Zaghlul's "campaign of hostility to British rights and British subjects in Egypt and the Sudan" and asserted that the Egyptian government was held in contempt by all civilized peoples. Egypt was given about thirty hours to meet the following demands: apologize for the crime; punish the criminals; forbid and suppress public political demonstrations; pay a fine of £500,-000; recall all Egyptian officers and army units from the Sudan; notify the competent departments that the Sudan would increase irrigated areas of the Gezira to an unlimited figure; and withdraw all opposition to British wishes in regard to protection of foreign interests in Egypt.

The demands were stiff. Zaghlul discussed them with the cabinet and Fuad and laid them before the chamber of deputies that evening in secret session. Compliance was voted for the first four demands. Upon refusal of the last three, Allenby notified the Sudan government to take necessary actions and ordered the British army to occupy Alexandrian customs offices. Zaghlul resigned; and Fuad appointed Ziwar Pasha, who speedily came to terms with the British concerning the role of British advisers in the Egyptian government.

Parliament was dissolved in December, and new elections were held. The Liberal party, led by elder politicians who were descended from Ottoman Turkish families long resident in Egypt, and a new Unionist party, made up of the king's friends, combined with numerous independents from the provinces to defeat the Wafd. Nevertheless, the chamber of deputies elected Zaghlul its president in March, 1925. This act led the king to dismiss parliament immediately; for he was now determined to crush Zaghlul who seemed to be growing more prominent than the king.

New elections were not held until May, 1926. In the meantime Fuad appointed several new ministers from among his friends, so that the cabinet was controlled by Nashat Pasha and the Unionist party. Allenby retired, and Lord Lloyd, formerly governor of Bombay, became high commissioner. He made common cause with the Wafd to force the king to call for elections, in which the Wafd again obtained a sweeping victory. Despite the victory Lord Lloyd persuaded Zaghlul to step aside; and Adli Pasha of the Liberal party headed a ministry of three Liberals, six Wafdists, and one Independent.

The three-cornered struggle among Wafd, palace, and residency eventually exhausted Adli's strength; and in April, 1927 he resigned, to be replaced by Sarwat Pasha, another Liberal. During that summer negotiations for a treaty of alliance were opened again in London, this time between Sarwat and Sir Austen Chamberlain; but the former did not expect to persuade the Wafd to accept the treaty. In August Zaghlul died and was succeeded as Wafd leader by Nahas Pasha, who at that time was hardly more than a figurehead. Discussions regarding the treaty broke down in March, 1928 over the question of British troops in Egypt. Nahas refused to compromise on that issue, and Chamberlain stated that Britain could make no further concessions than those contained in the draft treaty.

Upon failure of the discussions Sarwat resigned, and Nahas formed a ministry. But Fuad, always eager to discredit possible rivals, forced Nahas to resign by publishing a questionable document disclosing that Nahas and two of his associates received £130,000 for agreeing to transfer certain estates from the king's hands to other management. The next prime minister was Muhammad Mahmud Pasha, an original Wafdist exiled to Malta with Zaghlul but in 1928 supported by residency and palace. Mahmud dissolved parliament and suspended the constitution for three years, thereafter governing as a mild dictator with bitter opposition from the Wafd. Mahmud reached agreement with the British over Nile waters, the old Ottoman debt, and other financial matters. But desire for a treaty with Great Britain remained paramount; and in 1929 while on a holiday in England Mahmud judged the right moment had arrived.

The Labourites replaced the Conservatives, and Arthur Henderson took over the Foreign Office. Lord Lloyd was publicly dismissed for being too autocratic and out of step with the times. In June, 1929 negotiations began, and the Labour cabinet made sweeping concessions with respect to Egyptian national feelings. British troops would remain only around the Canal, Capitulations would be abolished, England would relinquish her right to protect foreigners, and the Sudan question would be considered a subject for further negotiations. However, England would only recognize a treaty ratified by a freely elected Egyptian parliament. The draft treaty was a great victory for Mahmud, but upon return to Egypt his position became untenable. Since the Wafd refused to accept his treaty and since the British insisted upon elections, Mahmud resigned.

Elections returned the Wafdists to power, and Nahas Pasha again came to power as prime minister—as protégé of the British Labour party. But his position was impossible. He had denounced the draft treaty obtained by Mahmud, and the British declared that they had reached the "high-water mark" of concessions. Treaty negotiations were dropped temporarily. And Fuad, fearing the apparent alliance of Wafd and residency led by Sir Percy Loraine, the new high commissioner, engineered the resignation of Nahas and appointed Ismail Sidki Pasha as prime minister.

THE CONSTITUTION OF 1930

Parliament was prorogued; Nahas incited riots; the British sent warships; and Sidki, protesting against foreign intervention, restored order.

In this *coup d'état* of June, 1930 Sidki appeared as the strong man. The constitution of 1923 was abrogated; and a new constitution with a new electoral law rigged to keep Wafdists out of office was quickly adopted. Sidki organized a new political party: the People's party. In coalition with Unionists and Independents the People's party defeated a Wafdist-Liberal united front, which boycotted the election. Sidki was able to establish his dictatorship only through the ineptitude of the British Labour government, which maneuvered both Liberals and Wafdists into indefensible positions. Sidki sent the students back to their studies; politicians muttered rather meekly; and the wealthy landowners gladly supported the new rule for they were surfeited with petty quibbling, jealous vindictiveness, and political arrogance of the nationalistic Wafd lawyers whom they had largely created. No treaty with England was attempted; prime ministers who tried always fell from office, and both Sidki and Fuad preferred British troops in Egypt to the Wafd. Furthermore, Sidki must have understood that the British government would not interfere in Egyptian domestic politics as long as British imperial interests were not directly jeopardized.

Fuad did not intend to permit a potential rival to remain in office very long; and Sidki fell from power in September, 1933 on the issue of a minor scandal, although a paralytic stroke had loosened his grip on affairs several months earlier. A procession of ineffectual prime ministers followed, some of them being the same weak figures who occupied the post ten years earlier after the crisis provoked by the British declaration of Egyptian independence. Power rapidly gravitated to the king, who was also amassing a great fortune. The controller of the royal estates, al-Ibrashi, also grew in influence, as Fuad's ill health rendered him less able to handle his own affairs.

THE ANGLO-EGYPTIAN TREATY OF 1936

Deterioration of domestic affairs prompted the residency in 1934 to advise the dismissal of al-Ibrashi, whom most Egyptians detested. Even the nationalist furor which this intervention incited did not stem the popular tide against palace government; and in November, 1934 the 1930 constitution was abrogated in favor of the 1923 constitution. The latter was not, however reissued, because the British secretly vetoed it.

At this juncture a crisis of an entirely different order appeared in the Italian adventure in Ethiopia. Britain increased her military establishment in Egypt—in Alexandria, Cairo, Suez, and Port Said—with knowledge and consent of Nessim Pasha, prime minister. An election campaign speech in England in October, 1935, however, gave Egyptians their first inkling that British naval headquarters in the Mediterranean were to be transferred from Malta to Alexandria. This startling information had the instantaneous effect of throwing Nahas, Sidki, and Mahmud into a united front and laying Nessim open to the charge of being subservient to the British. A few days later Sir Samuel Hoare, British foreign secretary, heaped more coals on the fire by publicly stating that the Egyptian constitutions of 1923 and 1930 were ill-adapted documents; and government-inspired London editorials advised Egyptians not to manipulate the Ethiopian crisis by blackmailing England into promises which were "manifestly inopportune."

Anti-British riots were spontaneous; and November 21, 1935 was declared an official day of mourning. In an attempt to soothe Egyptian feelings Sir Samuel delivered a public speech a month later. But this speech brought tempers to a white heat by stating that at some future time Egyptian wishes and freedom would be considered but that at the moment Great Britain was too busy with other matters. Fortunately, Anthony Eden soon took over the reins of the Foreign Office; and communications and advice from Sir Miles Lampson, high commissioner, were given some heed. Strangely enough, the last of Hoare's ineptitudes goaded the united front to declare that its leaders would support the negotiation of a treaty with England on the basis of the draft treaty that Egypt rejected in 1930. Also the constitution of 1923 was reissued, elections were set for late spring, and the return to more responsible parliamentary government was envisaged.

In April, 1936 King Fuad died; and his only son, Faruk, ascended the throne. Since the constitution provided that parliament should meet within ten days of the king's death, elections were moved up to make compliance possible. The Wafd party won 166 seats out of 232 in the chamber of deputies and obtained a majority in the senate. With such a solid backing Nahas became prime minister with a Wafd cabinet. Since he named the regency, the power of the Wafd was supreme. Already for several months, he had been chairman of the all-party delegation negotiating the treaty with England. Without fear of recrimination or charges of treason, Nahas consummated the Anglo-Egyptian treaty on August 26, 1936. A landmark had been achieved.

Beyond the malice of internal Egyptian politics the chief stumbling-blocks to such a treaty had been: the Sudan, British armed forces, and the Capitulations. In 1930 negotiations foundered on the Sudan question; and in 1936 all predicted failure when Britain announced that disposition of her forces in Egypt needed reconsideration. Between 1930 and 1936, however, the military evolution became obvious to politician and public alike. When, therefore, the British asked for a wider area in the Canal Zone and more facilities on land, sea, and air, Egyptian objection was only nominal. The occupation was changed to a twenty-year military alliance. Sir Miles Lampson won over the British cabinet and the British public to an appreciation that defense of the Canal and imperial communications could never be solved by British "unilateral action except at an utterly prohibitive cost and in the teeth of bitter resentment." The Sudan settlement permitted again unlimited Egyptian immigration to the Sudan and use of Egyptian troops in the Sudan. The end of the Capitulations, actually arranged by the Montreux Convention of 1937, proved of the utmost consequence to Egypt. Abolition of mixed tribunals and curtailment of consular courts were not abrupt, but the end was set for 1949. Henceforth, foreigners and foreign companies would be subject to Egyptian laws, especially taxation and financial legislation.

The treaty was immensely popular in Egypt. Parliament ratified it by a vote of 202 to 11, and the unprecedented happened when British troops were cheered on the streets of Cairo. But Nahas Pasha's popularity waned when Faruk reached his majority in 1937 and the palace again became a political force. Even the treaty was no longer popular, probably because the Italian conquest in East Africa was legitimized and threat of war in the Mediterranean subsided. Nahas resigned at the end of 1937, and Mahmud headed a coalition cabinet of Liberals, Saadists (a new party of disaffected Wafdists) and Independents. A new election, arranged in 1938, defeated the Wafdists of Nahas; and palace government gained ascendancy. Just before World War II broke out Mahmud stepped down, and Ali Maher Pasha, Saadist leader, became prime minister of a cabinet from which both Liberals and Wafdists were excluded. The wheel turned; Faruk and palace officials won full power.

SOCIAL AND ECONOMIC PROBLEMS

Internal politics and the problem of getting rid of the British consumed the energies and attention of Egyptian leaders between World Wars I and II, and these were the topics eternally discussed in Egypt. However, other problems, certainly basic and significant for the Egyptian nation and perhaps even more difficult to solve, did exist. Foremost was the increasing population pressure. The population increased from 12,718,000 in 1917 to 15,721,000 in 1937, although the cultivated area remained constant. Increased agricultural yields, improved irrigation techniques, and intensive cultivation—three crops per year instead of two—met the situation in part; but there was a general lowering of the standard of living among Egyptian peasantry. Sanitation and health conditions were poor, and the death rate was very high. Yet, the birth rate was higher. These factors, coupled with a lack of coal and industrial development, gave the waters of the Nile an importance which other national societies found difficult to appreciate and explained the critical blow to Egypt intended by Allenby's ultimatum to Zaghlul regarding unlimited irrigation in the Sudan. Although heightening of the Aswan Dam and construction of dams in the Sudan and Uganda augmented water supplies in Egypt, such developments barely kept pace with the growing population (which at the end of the period was increasing at the rate of 1.73 percent per annum).

Tied to this pressure of population were many economic, financial, and commercial problems. Cotton was king, and the government and landowners subverted the entire economy for the benefit of cotton culture. Agricultural experimentation, types of irrigation, industrialization, trade practices, tariffs, bank loans, tenant farm policies, and land reform —all were considered in the light of their relationship to the production of cotton. Taxation in general rested lightly on agriculture and landowners and bore heavily upon imports, industry, and commerce. Abolition of the Capitulations following the Anglo-Egyptian treaty of 1936 and the Montreux Convention in 1937 altered the commercial world of Cairo and Alexandria. General exemption from taxation had given British, French, Italians, Greeks, Armenians, Levantines, Jews, and even Syrians and Lebanese with passports in their pockets advantages which enabled them to dominate Egyptian finance and commerce. If Egyptians and their Ottoman-descended compatriots wished to participate in business in their own country, they found it almost necessary to form a partnership with a foreigner. Furthermore, native businessmen evaded taxes because their foreign counterparts did not pay taxes. After 1936 the situation was rapidly reversed. Foreigners suddenly found it advantageous to have Egyptians as partners, and more corporations engaged in business in Egypt were registered there. "For the first time since the age of the Pharaohs, Egyptian nationality ceased to be a badge of inferiority."

EDUCATION

A third big development in the period between the two wars was in the field of education. In 1914 with a budget of slightly more than half a million pounds the ministry of education had 15,000 students in primary, secondary, and higher schools in all of Egypt. By 1939 the budget rose to four and a half million, the number of students, to 232,000. But there was still much to do. Illiteracy was high, and the size of the task ahead was staggering. Planning and direction were often ill conceived. The stress was upon literature, language, and the humanities. The needs of Egypt at the lower levels of sciences, shop work,

simple foundries, forges, and vocational training as well as at the higher
levels of doctors, engineers, scientists, and industrial managers were
ignored.

Since the constitution of Egypt declared that free education must be
provided for children between the ages of seven and twelve, elementary schools to teach the four R's—reading, writing, arithmetic, and religion—were organized in many villages. By 1939 nearly 1,000,000
children were enrolled. Unfortunately, after a child had finished village school he was not prepared to enter a vocational or secondary
school. Elementary schools attempted only to stamp out illiteracy. However, two parallel systems grew in the 1920's and 1930's and were
preparing Egypt for a fuller national life beyond anything imaginable
by the average British colonial official of the period prior to 1930. The
educational system was slowly creating a national consciousness among
the masses, as the Wafd was doing among the middle and upper
classes. Education was helping to ready the masses for the national determination and political democracy for which Wafd leaders were
striving.

THE ANGLO-EGYPTIAN SUDAN

Whenever Egyptians considered severing British ties, the Sudan
loomed impressively in their thinking. In the nineteenth century the
Sudan had been important to Egypt because of the border warfare and
slave raids that so frequently disturbed their relationship. In the
twentieth century fitting solutions to controversies over Nile water,
dams, barrages, irrigation projects, and immigration became most vital
for Egypt and her burgeoning population.

Shortly after the close of World War I the interrelationship of the
Sudan and Egypt came to the fore with the setting up of the Gezira
project, operation of which began in 1925. The scheme went back at
least to 1900 and Kitchener, who envisaged the irrigation of the triangular stretch of land south of Khartoum between the Blue and White Niles.
Much preliminary work was done in pilot projects, soil testing, and
general planning. World War I delayed the building of the Sennar Dam
on the Blue Nile, and its completion did not come until 1925. Under
Allenby's direction the Gezira commission recommended irrigating
300,000 acres of the possible 2,000,000 acres by gravity flow, with management in the hands of the Sudan Plantations Syndicate, a British
organization. Land tenancies were established at forty acres each, two
thirds of which could be planted to vegetables, grains, and fodders,
which would be tax-free property of the tenant. The remaining one
third had to be planted to cotton, of which the tenant, the Syndicate,
and the Sudan government received 40 percent, 25 percent, and 35

percent, respectively. The government rented land at about fifty cents an acre from the original owners and then assigned forty-acre tracts to applicants. By 1939 the tenants were on the average receiving about $250 as their share from the sale of the cotton crop.

The Gezira scheme was highly successful, and in the last years before World War II the area had reached an annual production of 60,000 tons of cotton and 75,000 tons of cotton seed. Since, however, almost the entire cotton crop was exported to Great Britain and since Sudan cotton was giving the British textile industry a greater independence from Egyptian staples, Egypt grew sensitive to any expansion of irrigated tracts in the Gezira.

Egyptian leaders never abandoned their claim that Sudan and Egypt were indissoluble, chiefly because of the water and the expectation that the undeveloped Sudan would serve as an escape valve for growing population pressures in Egypt. Fears and tensions were, however, diminished by the treaty arranged in 1929 between Lord Lloyd and Mahmud Pasha to govern and allocate the water of the Nile. Instead of being able to irrigate only 300,000 acres of land from the water of the Blue Nile, the Sudan was allotted nearly one billion cubic meters of water by the agreement. The Nile projects commission, which was examining the entire Nile with a view toward building dams and reservoir basins and regulating drainage, siltage, and annual flow, estimated that this Nile water agreement would leave for Egypt a guaranteed annual irrigation water supply of about twenty-two billion cubic meters. After 1929 Egypt seemed assured of all the water she could use; and control of the Sudan ceased, at least for the moment, to be a major political matter.

In the months and years immediately preceding 1939 the Egyptian nation looked with pride upon the accomplishments of the previous two decades. The Anglo-Egyptian treaty of 1936 gave political freedom and sovereignty; the constitution assured political democracy and responsible government; the Montreux Convention of 1937 removed the bonds of economic servitude and set the stage for industrial, commercial, and financial independence; and the Nile water agreement of 1929 allayed the fears of the Egyptians, rich and poor alike, that a foreign power would be able to force a thirsty Egypt into submission. The native Egyptian believed that he now controlled his own life and destiny for the first time in over three thousand years. The wealth of his country would be his own. Great days lay ahead.

REFERENCES: Chapter 33

Numerous volumes already cited contain material of value to this chapter, especially those in Chapters 7, 19, 22, 23, 24, 26, 27, 28, 29, and 31. Chapter 35 contains additional references.

Mekki Abbas, *The Sudan Question: The Dispute over the Anglo-Egyptian Condominium, 1884–1951:* Faber, London, 1952. Written by a Sudanese, it is neither pro-British nor pro-Egyptian.

Jamal Mohammed Ahmed, *The Intellectual Origins of Egyptian Nationalism:* Oxford University Press, London, 1960.

Reginald Davies, *The Camel's Back:* Transatlantic Arts, Hollywood, Fla., 1958. Service in rural Sudan.

Gerold Frank, *The Deed: The Assassination of Lord Moyne:* Jonathan Cape, London, 1964.

Anthony M. Galatoli, *Egypt in Midpassage:* Urwand & Sons, Cairo, 1950. Important discussion of Anglo-Egyptian affairs and political development in Egypt.

Richard Gray, *A History of the Southern Sudan, 1839–1889:* Oxford University Press, New York, 1961.

Christina Phelps Harris, *Nationalism and Revolution in Egypt:* Mouton, The Hague, 1964. The story of the Muslim Brotherhood.

James Heyworth-Dunne, *Religious and Political Trends in Modern Egypt:* The author, Washington, 1950. Particularly good on the Muslim Brotherhood.

Richard Hill, *Slatin Pasha:* Oxford University Press, London, 1965. An account of one of the adventurers in the Sudan.

P. M. Holt, *The Mahdist State in the Sudan, 1881–98. A Study of Its Origins, Development, and Overthrow:* Clarendon Press, Oxford, 1958. Thorough and detailed.

Charles Issawi, *Egypt: An Economic and Social Analysis:* Oxford University Press, London, 1947. A competent economic study by a British-trained Syrian.

————, *Egypt at Mid-Century: An Economic Survey:* Oxford University Press, New York, 1954. A revised edition with later material of the above.

H. C. Jackson, *Sudan Days and Ways:* St. Martin's Press, New York, 1954. Written by a British official in the Sudan from 1907 to 1931.

————, *Behind the Modern Sudan:* St. Martin's Press, New York, 1956. A continuation of the previous entry.

Jacob M. Landau, *Parliaments and Parties in Egypt:* Israel Oriental Society, Tel Aviv, 1953.

Harold MacMichael, *The Sudan:* Benn, London, 1954. Emphasizes development under British rule.

Mohammed Rifaat, *The Awakening of Modern Egypt:* Longmans, Green, London, 1947. Excellent background.

Mary Rowlatt, *Founders of Modern Egypt:* Asia Publishing House, New York, 1962.

Royal Institute of International Affairs, *Great Britain and Egypt, 1914–1951:* Oxford University Press, London, 1952. A thorough survey of the facts.

Ronald Wingate, *Wingate of the Sudan:* J. Murray, London, 1955. An important work.

CHAPTER 34

Shah Reza's Iran

IMPERIALISM IN IRAN

When World War I burst out upon the Middle East, Iran was experiencing chaotic problems involving internal political and constitutional developments, financial and economic turmoil, and intense imperial rivalry among Russia, Great Britain, and Germany. Throughout the nineteenth century Russia and Britain clashed repeatedly in Iran, and each engaged in petty warfare in several sections of the state to obtain imperial privileges of one sort or another. Concession-hunting for railroads, banks, tobacco monopolies, and various public works in Iran paralleled the activities of Europeans in the Ottoman Empire for the same period. Competition came to a head in 1906, when the middle-class merchants and democratic element in Tehran, supported by England, forced the conservative aristocrats and Shah Mohammed Ali Qajar to grant a constitution. The constitution limited royal power and authorized the formation of a cabinet and a bicameral legislature composed of an appointed senate and an elected assembly.

Conflict between the two powers was temporarily halted by the Anglo-Russian settlement of 1907, whereby England was recognized as having dominant consideration in the southern provinces and Russian hegemony in the north was tacitly conceded. Since Tehran was in the Russian zone, Russia evidently felt entitled to sway the reactionary forces to engineer a *coup d'état* in 1908 and discard the constitution. However, Bakhtiyari tribal chieftains from Britain's southern sphere marched on Tehran in 1909, ousted the Shah, restored the constitution, and elevated Shah Ahmed Qajar to the throne.

Once in power the Democrats veered from the British camp and adopted an independent course by inviting Dr. Morgan Shuster, an American, to disentangle the financial aspects of government. Both Russia and England exerted such pressures that Shuster was compelled to leave. "The Strangling of Persia," as he termed the process, continued unabated, and Iranian Democrats turned to Germany in hopes of neutralizing the drive of European imperialism. In the few years prior to 1914 German activities in Iran were fruitful; and during the first months of the war Prince von Reuss concluded a secret treaty with the Iranian government promising arms, ammunition, money, and independence in return for co-operation with Germany.

Britain and Russia, aware of these agreements, acted to hold Iran in their power. Russian troops moved from Qazwin to the outskirts of Tehran and intimidated supporters of the Central Powers to flee to Kermanshah, where an anti-Allied Iranian government was formed. Shah Ahmed remained in his capital with his cabinet, and technically Iran maintained her neutrality. The German consul, Wassmuss, stirred the Qashqai and Bakhtiyari tribes in southern Iran and threatened British oil operations in Khuzistan. To counter this danger and protect the wells, the British weakened their Mesopotamian drive and eventually sent Sir Percy Sykes to organize the South Persian Rifles. In 1917, in co-operation with Russian cossacks from the north, they occupied Kerman, Isfahan, Shiraz, and most of Fars. Russia's collapse, however, left the northern provinces open; and for a time German and Ottoman troops held Azerbayjan, but they were recalled at the end of the war and the British remained dominant in Iran.

POSTWAR PROBLEMS

Lord Curzon had dreams of a British Empire from the Mediterranean to Singapore. With Iraq and Palestine already pledged, Iran was the missing link. Sir Percy Cox was, therefore, sent from Baghdad, where he was sorely missed, to Tehran to escort Iran into the British Empire. An Iran delegation went to Paris; but, being anti-British, it was not permitted to attend the peace conference or to state Iran's case, though Iran did secure an invitation to join the League of Nations. A less hostile delegation negotiated and signed on August 9, 1919 an Anglo-Iranian treaty. Though the words were friendly, it virtually transformed Iran into a dependency of the British Empire; and public opinion throughout the world rightly judged it in that light. Iranian government departments, finances, public services, and the army would be in British hands. Iran received a seven percent loan of £2,000,000; and her tariffs would be adjusted and customs controlled by the British as collateral against the loan.

The Iranian Assembly (*Majlis*) refused to ratify the treaty; and general world-wide British military retrenchment effected a withdrawal of British forces and demobilization of the South Persian Rifles. Bolshevik Russia, on the other hand, pursued a more beguiling course by denouncing tsarist treaties with Iran. In pursuing General Denikin, Soviet forces landed troops in 1920 at Pahlevi on the Caspian, occupied Iranian territory north of the Elburz Mountains, and refused to depart until all British military were evacuated. A Soviet Republic of Gilan was established at Resht under nominal leadership of Kuchuk Khan, over whom, Moscow alleged, she had no authority.

Iran protested and took her plea to Geneva. There she was given quantities of sympathy but informed that better results could be obtained by direct negotiations with the Bolsheviks. Taking these words to heart, she concluded at Moscow on February 26, 1921 a treaty of friendship. The frontiers and independence of each were respected; Iranian debts to Russia were canceled; all concessions were relinquished except the Caspian Sea fisheries, since even Communists had to have caviar; neither would harbor enemies of the other; and if a third power menaced or occupied any part of Iran, Russia might send troops to Iran. Also, Iran promised not to cede to any other power or national thereof any privilege or concession being relinquished by Russia. Shortly thereafter, Russia withdrew her troops and support of the Soviet Republic of Gilan, which promptly succumbed to an Iranian military expedition.

Thus, rejection by parliament of the Anglo-Iranian treaty of 1919, the subsequent withdrawal of British troops, and the Soviet-Iranian treaty of 1921 confirmed the independence of Iran. However, she did not possess sufficient leadership for political democracy and was torn with strife and economic disorder. Disease, poverty, corruption, and debased public morality prevailed everywhere throughout the land. The areas encompassing installations of the Anglo-Persian Oil Company were the only flourishing districts of the country, and they were fully under the thumb of the British government. World War I left Iran in a seemingly hopeless state with little outside interest able and willing to lend a helping hand.

REZA KHAN

Five days before the signing of the Russo-Iranian treaty in Moscow, Reza Khan, an officer of the Iranian cossacks, led his men into Tehran and with a *coup d'état* took over the reins of government. A self-educated trooper with a keen nationalist feeling, Reza rose from the ranks of the Russian-officered Iranian cossacks and became one of its leaders when the Russian officers were ousted in 1920. On his march on Tehran he was advised in part by British officers; and consequently opponents charged, though quite incorrectly, that Reza was a pawn in British imperialistic ambitions.

For the following two decades Reza Khan and his army were the powers that controlled the Iranian government, although following the *coup d'état* a fiery crusading journalist, Sayyid Ziya al-Din Tabatabai, became prime minister. Several others succeeded to that post, until Reza assumed office in 1923 and invited Shah Ahmed to take "an extended and prolonged tour" of Europe. Republican sentiment was astir as Reza looked Westward to pattern his state after Kemal's Turkey. But in 1924 when the stage was virtually set for a republican declaration, the Turkish assembly abolished the caliphate and advanced along its progressive secular path. Frightened Iranian divines raised such a storm that Reza met with a group of religious leaders at Kum. Thereafter public mention of a republic was forbidden. In 1925 Reza Khan Pahlevi became shah, and the throne was vested in male members of the Pahlevi family born of Iranian mothers.

The problems facing Reza Shah in Iran were similar to those before Kemal in Turkey, only far more difficult. The two most pressing were re-establishment of a recognized central governmental authority and reform of national finances. The former was largely a matter for Reza and the army to resolve; the latter remained the work of an American, Dr. Arthur C. Millspaugh, formerly economic adviser to the secretary of state. Employed by the Iranian government in 1922 as administrator general of finances, he held the power and authority of a cabinet minister. By his contract, which ran for five years, no commercial or industrial grant could be made without his consent, no financial decision could be taken without his approval, and no expenditure or contracting of any financial obligation could be assumed without his agreement. With such vast powers and the staunch support of Reza's military force Dr. Millspaugh balanced the budget by reorganizing the tax structure and enforcing the collection of taxes, both current and those in arrears. State enterprises were inaugurated, and economic conditions improved gradually. However, Dr. Millspaugh was frequently tactless and too rigid in his manners for a proud and sensitive people in whom through centuries of personal government pliability had become deeply ingrained. In 1927 he and his American staff departed upon his refusal to renew the contract except on the same terms of power and authority.

One stipulation between Reza and Dr. Millspaugh provided that the budget of the ministry of war would always be met; for Reza understood the source of his power. By 1926, when Reza crowned himself Shah of Shahs of Royal Iran, he had personally led his army to end rebellions in Azerbayjan and Khurasan and had partially tamed the nomadic tribes. His greatest success was achieved in ending the independent rule of Shaykh Khazal of Mohammerah, with whom the British had a "working agreement" with respect to operations of the Anglo-Persian Oil Company. The fixation of Reza's authority over the distant provinces, peoples, and governors of Iran upped state revenues and made Dr. Millspaugh's policies more effective and widespread. This in turn assured a more certain execution of royal government.

According to the constitution of 1906, which was still in force, the power of the nation was vested in the shah, the senate, and the assembly, which by 1926 was filled with Reza's supporters. The senate was appointive, but Reza never called it and never made any appointments to it. The assembly nominated a prime minister who was appointed by the shah. In addition to the prime minister and a few ministers without portfolio, the cabinet comprised ministers of foreign affairs, war, finance, interior, justice, education, agriculture, communications, health (1935), and posts, telephone, and telegraph. Reza Shah's greatest work, perhaps, was the instilling of an enthusiastic attitude toward work among the personnel of these ministries. Sometimes he would appear at a government office early in the morning to see if the officials were on duty and on time.

REFORMS

Public veneration given to religious leaders had proved a stumbling block to many Iranian governments. Reza, therefore, attempted to relegate religion and its institutions to a less important position in national life, particularly after the Shiite divines raised such an effective furor over republicanism in 1924. Dervishes were forbidden to appear on the streets or along the roads of the countryside. Public parades and presentations of the passion play in memory of the deaths of Ali, Hasan, and Husayn were prohibited. Other overt acts showed the supremacy of Reza over the clergy. In 1928 when a religious leader in the mosque at Kum digressed from his sermon to admonish the queen for unveiling her face, Reza hurried there with two armored cars, entered the mosque without removing his boots, and publicly whipped the offending preacher. Veils were outlawed in 1935; at the same time the shah and other officials took to removing their hats and caps in public buildings.

Equally significant and more pointed was the confiscation of religious property, the income from which went to the support of schools, hospitals, state industries, and other state enterprises. No longer were religious teachers and leaders (*mullahs*) independent, and their schools were closed. Their livelihood henceforth came from the state, and their hold over the population through education was shattered. Furthermore, secularization of the law was speeded. The French judicial system was introduced in 1927, and decisions affected by opinions rendered by *mullahs* were declared void and without force. Even religious law over marital status was limited. In 1929 religious courts exercised jurisdiction only over domestic relations, personal status, and notarial acts. Many new laws were promulgated. In 1928 the Capitulations which granted rights to foreigners concerning courts, trials, and legal privileges were abolished. Theological students were subjected to military conscription, and education became a public responsibility under the supervision and regulation of the central government.

One of Reza Shah's most permanent contributions stemmed from his need of better communications to bring the more distant parts of his realm within his power. There may have been 2,000 miles of roads in Iran on the day of his *coup d'état;* at the outbreak of World War II the road system had been extended to over 17,000 miles. In view of Iran's role in the supply line to Russia in World War II, perhaps Reza's most far-reaching achievement was the construction of the Trans-Iranian railway from Bandarshapur on the Persian Gulf to Bandarshah on the Caspian Sea, a distance of 865 miles. Completed in 1938, it was an engineering marvel, consisting of 224 tunnels and passing from sea level to an altitude of nearly 9,000 feet and then down to below sea level. The route pleased neither Russia nor Britain; from their points of view it began nowhere, passed through Tehran, and again ended nowhere. But as the Iranians saw it, the railroad connected the northern fertile provinces with the south and by passing through nomad country facilitated the movement of the Shah's military strength.

Like Kemal in Turkey, Reza felt the need of industrialization and economic development. Fundamentally, Iran had an agricultural economy, and thoroughgoing reforms should have been undertaken in that direction. Improved systems and means of irrigation were proposed, and better agricultural methods were studied. Some beneficial results were obtained. Yet, progress fell far short of the envisaged goals, largely because two thirds of the arable land was held by absentee landlords who were satisfied with the old devises and who demanded an immediate high return on their investment.

Industries were built for refining sugar; spinning and weaving cotton, silk, and wool; canning fish, meat, fruit, and vegetables; soap and vegetable oil processing; manufacturing cigarettes and cigar and pipe tobacco; and making bricks, cement, steel products, and various chemicals. Most of these were state enterprises and varied widely in efficiency and capacity. Prices for the goods produced were high; but a state monopoly over most frontier trade rendered competition with imported goods negligible. None the less, since Iranian industry suffered from lack of technicians and plant managers, the industrial development under Reza proved unsatisfactory. In part because of Russian trade practices, Reza created a state trading mechanism under which much of the foreign trade was managed by the government. Various other monopolies were instituted for special purposes; monopolies on sugar and tea, for instance, helped finance the building of the Trans-Iranian railway.

OIL DEVELOPMENTS

By far the most important industrial enterprise in Iran during the period of Reza Shah's rule was the Anglo-Persian Oil Company. Mr. W. K. D'Arcy, an Australian, obtained in 1901 a concession for the exploitation, sale, and export of oil from all but five northern provinces of Iran. Oil was discovered in commercial quantities in 1908, and the Anglo-Persian Oil Company in the following year acquired the D'Arcy concession. By agreement, Iran received sixteen percent of the profits of any and all companies formed to work the concession. In May, 1914 the British admiralty purchased about fifty-five percent of the company's stock to insure a continuous oil supply for the navy.

After World War I the question of what profits to include while calculating the Iranian government's sixteen percent was bitterly debated, until a settlement was proposed in 1920 by Sir Sydney Armitage-Smith, the Iranian government's financial adviser. The basis for computing profits was described, and in lieu of past royalties and claims a payment of £1,000,000 was made by the company. The agreement was never ratified by the assembly, although the £1,000,000 was accepted; and in 1932 Iran canceled the concession.

The difficulty originated from the fact that Iran had no control over the quantity of oil produced and no guaranteed annual income from the concession. With the complexity of oil operations and the multiplicity of companies, Iran lost confidence in the integrity of the company's bookkeeping practices. Fluctuations in the amounts received by Iran— £411,000 in 1923; £1,400,000 in 1926; £502,000 in 1927; £1,437,000 in 1929; and £307,000 in 1931—left the finances and the budget of the government completely at the mercy of the company, which could shut off the oil wells in Iran at will and obtain the necessary crude oil for its markets in other fields. Furthermore, in 1931 Great Britain went off the gold standard, and Iran's sterling balances were depreciated. The rumor spread that oil products were sold to the British navy at cost. If true, this meant that there would be no percentage of profits for Iran on those sales. Finally, a new concession was negotiated in 1931 by the Iraq Petroleum Company giving more favorable terms to Iraq. Since Anglo-Persian was one of the principal owners in Iraq, the Iranian government felt it should have as favorable treatment.

After bitter wrangling, sharp notes, and the dispatch of British warships to the Persian Gulf England took the case to the League council and tried to submit it to the Permanent Court of International Justice at The Hague. Neither body took action; for Iran protested that neither had jurisdiction, the case being between a private company and the Iranian government. Iran did, however, inform the company that she was agreeable to the granting of a new concession, providing that its terms were more favorable to Iran than those in the previous concession.

The new concession, which was signed in Tehran in April, 1933, included the following provisions: The area covered was immediately reduced by half, and after 1938 to 100,000 square miles, to be selected by the company. The company relinquished its exclusive right to build and operate pipelines in Iran. Iran would receive four shillings per ton on all oil sold in Iran or exported. Iran would be paid twenty percent on all dividends over £671,250, and the company guaranteed that total annual payments to Iran would never be under £750,000. Iran would be secured against any depreciation of sterling. The company was exempt from taxation, but in lieu of such charges the company agreed to pay nine pence per ton on the first 6,000,000 tons exported and six pence per ton above that, the minimum annual payment to be £225,-000. The Iranian government oil commissioner was to be paid £2,000 annually by the company, and he had the right to examine the books and attend directors' meetings. Gulf of Mexico or Rumanian oil prices, whichever was lower, should be the price used in calculating the price of oil in Iran, such public price in Iran to be ten percent lower than the basic price and twenty-five percent lower to the government. Finally, the concession could not be transferred without Iran's consent, and in 1993 all properties within Iran would revert to the Iranian government.

Undoubtedly, the winning of this agreement by Reza Shah was his finest economic and diplomatic victory; and some observers at the time believed that Iran, by this stroke, obtained her independence. Certainly her oil income was placed on a more sustaining basis, even though it seemed clear that the British admiralty was still able to purchase Iranian oil more cheaply than the Iranian government.

INTERNATIONAL AFFAIRS

Shah Reza in his foreign affairs maintained friendly relations with his neighboring powers. Visits were exchanged; and in 1934 he was entertained in Ankara. The crowning achievement was the signing of the Saadabad pact in 1937 with Turkey, Iraq, and Afghanistan at Reza's

Garden Palace in the mountains near Tehran. The pact provided for mutual co-operation, consultations, and nonaggression.

In addition to the concession of the Anglo-Persian Oil Company, which became the Anglo-Iranian Oil Company in 1935 when Reza insisted on the use of the word "Iran" to denote his country, the Anglo-Iranian treaty of 1928 also helped to settle affairs with England. Imperial Airways was allowed to fly planes over Iran; Britain recognized the end of the Capitulations; British support for Shaykh Khazal of Mohammerah was terminated, and Reza took over the Shaykh's role in protecting the oil pipelines; British consuls and agents were still permitted to deal directly with tribes such as the Lurs, Bakhtiyaris, and the Qashqais; and Iran recognized British rule in Iraq. Except for Iran's claim to the Bahrayn Islands all outstanding matters were considered, and the anti-British feelings in Iran were temporarily quiescent. Such feelings could, however, easily be brought to the surface since twisting the British lion's tail was a sporting event for all Iranian nationalists.

Shah Reza's relations with Soviet Russia were more complicated, especially since Iran and Russia had a long common frontier. Iran was traversed by Soviet agents of all kinds, and rebellions occurred in Azerbayjan and Khurasan. When the rebellions were suppressed, all Communist activities went underground. In the Russo-Iranian treaty of 1921, Russia formally renounced all concessions and Iran was forbidden to grant these concessions to other foreigners. Thus, in the 1920's and again in the 1930's, Russia protested vehemently when Iran granted oil concessions in her northern provinces. Since northern Iran's export market was almost exclusively Russian, Russia could and frequently did exert great pressure on Iran by closing her frontiers to Iranian goods. This weapon was invoked in 1926 to obtain a fishing agreement for the Caspian Sea. For political ends Russia dumped goods on Iran and by 1931 had all but ruined Iranian exporters. Sensing the inability of private traders in Iran to challenge the Soviet state trading companies, Reza placed all foreign trade in Iran under state monopoly and control. This device and Germany's return to the Iranian scene with the advent of Hitler gave Iran more freedom from economic domination by the colossus to the north.

Caught between the British in the south and the Soviets in the north, Iran turned to Germany as a counterpoise. German technicians were invited in great numbers, advising the various ministries and aiding in scientific agriculture, communications, engineering works, and industrial enterprises. Compensation and bank clearing agreements were concluded after Dr. Hjalmar Schacht's visit in 1935; and the volume of trade between the two countries jumped. In 1939 over forty percent of Iran's foreign trade was with Germany. In the cultural fields Iranian schools hired German professors, and numerous Iranians took advanced degrees in German universities. Modern Iranian architecture showed strong German influences. Large numbers of Germans visited Iran for various reasons and on diverse pretexts. Nearly a thousand a year came in the period before 1940, and many remained in Iran. Germany was making a valiant bid for Iran; and had peace continued for a few more years beyond 1939, Iran might well have been closely tied to Germany. The rapid events, however, after 1939 quickly changed the picture. Within two years Soviet Russia and Great Britain were partners to destroy Germany, and Iran was forced to co-operate. The entire focus of government and life in Iran was reoriented, and a new era was ushered in.

SHAH REZA PAHLEVI

There can be no debate over the fact that Iran between the two World Wars was the Iran of Shah Reza Pahlevi. But argument still goes on in Iran as to his personality and contributions. An evaluation is not easy, and he has suffered greatly through attempts to compare him and his work with Kemal and the nationalist program in Turkey. The situations facing each were so different in so many ways that comparisons have confused the whole issue.

Reza was an uneducated soldier of Iran who rose to the top because of a burning nationalism and a boundless energy for action. He had a soldier's respect for authority and expected his will to be followed implicitly. The subterfuges of traditional Iranian officialdom frustrated him into direct and ruthless conduct. Discovering that details of governing frequently were not accomplished when his back was turned, he consumed too much of his time with the details. There was a vast amount of work that needed to be done in Iran and too few to do it; and Reza became immersed in a welter of programs too numerous for him to carry through alone. Taking so much responsibility on his own shoulders discouraged initiative in those about him; and the promising projects for agricultural reform, educational and secular development, and state industrial enterprise fell far short of their goals.

In the end Reza became interested in acquiring a great personal fortune in estates and funds in foreign accounts. He grew tired, his temper rose, sensitivity to criticism mounted, and his power became more absolute. Ignorance lured him into many traps and unfortunate decisions regarding policies and men. Probably, his forced abdication in 1941 and the Allied intervention in Iranian affairs saved much of the Westernization program begun by Reza in his early days on the throne. Lack of education did, however, make it possible for him to cut many traditions of Iranian society which a man trained in the niceties and subtleties of Iranian culture and its long history would have been incapable of ignoring. Westernization in Iran had a stout ally in Reza Shah, and certainly at times he carried the movement almost singlehanded. His resolute will and toughness, despite the religion, the great landowners, and the traditional dissimulation of the Iranian people, would not let the regeneration of Iran and her people fail. Successes more than outweighed mistakes.

REFERENCES: Chapter 34

See works already cited in Chapters 4, 6, 7, 8, 9, 19, 20, 22, 23, 27, 28, 29, 30, and 31. Chapter 35 contains additional references.

Peter Avery, *Modern Iran:* Praeger, New York, 1965.

Amin Banani, *The Modernization of Iran, 1921–1941:* Stanford University Press, Stanford, 1961.

Leonard Binder, *Iran: Political Development in a Changing Society:* University of California Press, Berkeley, 1962.

Edward G. Browne, *Persian Revolution of 1905–9:* Cambridge University Press, Cambridge, 1910. The best account of this episode.

Richard W. Cottam, *Nationalism in Iran:* University of Pittsburgh Press, Pittsburgh, 1964.

Lawrence P. Elwell-Sutton, *A Guide to Iranian Area Study:* J. W. Edwards, Ann Arbor, 1952. An important bibliography.

———, *Modern Iran:* Routledge & Kegan Paul, London, 1941. A good survey.

Nasrollah S. Fatemi, *Diplomatic History of Persia, 1917–1923: Anglo-Russian Power Politics in Iran:* R. F. Moore, New York, 1952. Not entirely objective.

Elgin Groseclose, *Introduction to Iran:* Oxford University Press, New York, 1947. A good survey.

William S. Haas, *Iran:* Columbia University Press, New York, 1946. A good survey.

Hassan Kamshad, *Modern Persian Prose Literature:* The University Press, Cambridge, 1966.

George Lenczowski, *Russia and the West in Iran, 1918–1948, A Study in Big Power Rivalry:* Cornell University Press, Ithaca, N.Y., 1949. A first-rate study.

Arthur C. Millspaugh, *The American Task in Persia:* Century, New York, 1925. An account of his first tour of duty in Iran.

———, *Americans in Persia:* The Brookings Institution, Washington, 1946. A personal account by the American adviser to the Shah.

Rouhollah K. Ramazani, *The Foreign Policy of Iran, 1500–1941:* University Press of Virginia, Charlottesville, 1966.

William M. Shuster, *The Strangling of Persia:* Century, New York, 1912. An account of the work and frustrations of an American financial adviser in Iran before World War I and the imperial activities of England and Russia.

Christopher Sykes, *Wassmuss, "the German Lawrence":* Longmans, Green, London, 1936. The story of the German agent in Iran during World War I.

Donald N. Wilber, *Iran: Past and Present:* Princeton University Press, Princeton, 1948.

Arnold T. Wilson, *Persia:* Scribner, New York, 1933. A good survey.

CHAPTER 35

World War II
and the Middle East

TURKISH NEUTRALITY

U pon the outbreak of World War II Turkey declared her neutrality. Yet, her position was not clear-cut. In the fifteen months before the actual rupture of peace and even as early as 1936, Turkish foreign policy had been veering toward Britain and France. In September, 1939 Turkey was joined to England and France by several pacts regarding credits, chrome, and nonaggression. On the other hand, almost fifty percent of her trade was with Germany. Furthermore, the Nazi-Soviet pact of August, 1939 gave Turkish leadership every reason for caution, since Russian power and objectives in the Black Sea area and eastern Asia Minor were difficult to assess.

In such a situation Turkish relations with Russia appeared of paramount importance. Shukru Saracoğlu, Turkish foreign minister, spent nearly a month in Moscow in an attempt to formulate a mutual assistance pact with the U.S.S.R. Molotov set the price: a proviso that the Straits be closed to the British and French and a proviso that Turkey under no circumstances become involved in hostilities with the Nazis. The Turks would not agree. On October 19, therefore, they signed a formal fifteen-year treaty of alliance with France and the United Kingdom. Its terms held that in the event of an act of aggression upon Turkey her allies would come to her assistance, that Turkey on her part would enter the war should it come to the Mediterranean, but that under no circumstances would Turkey be drawn into a conflict against the

U.S.S.R. At the same time loans and credits of £43,500,000 were made to Turkey to bolster her financial position and speed the flow of arms. Britain also had an all-important agreement, which ran until January 1, 1943, whereby she could, if she so desired, purchase and export the entire output of Turkish chrome ore.

Upon the fall of France, the entry of Mussolini into the war, and the loss of British armor at Dunkirk, the Turkish government quickly reassessed its international position. It was suspected that Russia, surely having been awarded Istanbul and the Straits by Hitler, might soon move to seize the prize, as she was already doing in Finland, the Baltic, and Bessarabia. In 1938 and 1939 Turkey had bravely cast her lot with Britain and France; but the likelihood of a German defeat was far removed in the summer of 1940 and the winter of 1940–41. War came to the Mediterranean upon Italy's declaration, but Turkey maintained her neutrality and continued in that course through the Italian campaign against Greece, the German conquest of Yugoslavia and Greece, and the occupation of Bulgaria.

British naval and air personnel in civilian garb were numerous in Turkey, and the British urged Turkish entry into the war at the time of the debacle in Greece. Steadfastly, the Turkish leaders refused. They pointed out that Britain was no more prepared to give planes and heavy armor to Turkey than to Greece and that recklessness on Turkey's part would invite German retaliation. Furthermore, if Turkey could main tain a neutral role, she would serve as a land barrier to Syria, Suez, and the Persian Gulf.

Hitler's invasion of Russia acutely disturbed the orientation of Turkish neutrality. The Turks clearly foresaw that a German defeat would leave Soviet Russia the dominant continental power of Europe. Since the British had promised Russia the Straits in World War I and since the appeasers had been so free with other nations' territories, England might easily concede the Straits to Russia to seal the sudden alliance. Moreover the Straits might be safe from German aggression as long as German arms were engaged deeply in Russia. As American lend-lease began to rebuild British strength, it became possible for the Turks to envisage a negotiated peace without victory which might eventually safeguard Turkish frontiers and leave the Straits in their hands.

The might of Germany from the middle of 1941 to the spring of 1943 awed Turkish leaders; and Franz von Papen, the crafty German ambassador in Ankara, played on the fears and suspicions of Saracoğlu, who as a loyal Turk could only rejoice at the prospect of the crushing of Russia. A ten-year nonaggression pact was, therefore, signed in June, 1941, although Turkey insisted on a statement that this pact did not contravene any previous Turkish commitments. In October a trade agreement was concluded, providing for shipment of various raw materials to Germany, among which would be chrome ore. After January 1, 1943, when the chrome agreement with Great Britain would expire, Germany would be enabled to purchase 90,000 tons of ore in exchange for war equipment valued at L.T. 100,000,000, most of which would have to be delivered to Turkey before the chrome ore could be exported. Although it was a hollow German victory, the Turkish press played it up as a concrete evidence of Turkish neutrality to parallel the argument of Menemencioğlu, who took over the foreign ministry when Saracoğlu became prime minister, that Turkish neutrality benefited the Axis since it kept "British shipping out of the Black Sea!"

Toward the end of 1942 a wavering became noticeable in the Turkish position. German casualties in Russia weakened the contentions of von Papen; and the flow of many millions in American lend-lease goods to Turkey permitted her to give some evidence of her natural sympathy for England and the United States. Although Sir Hughe Knatchbull-Hugessen and Laurence A. Steinhardt, British and American ambassadors, worked hard to bring about friendly relations between Turkey and Russia, President Inönü and others entertained serious doubts about the future good will of Stalin with regard to the Straits.

Throughout 1943 the great discussion centered on opening a second front and the possibility of Turkish co-operation and open participation. The topic was raised early in 1942 in a general way; and in 1943 it was again considered and debated at Casablanca, Adana, Quebec, Moscow, Cairo, Tehran, and Cairo. Churchill repeatedly pressed the case for Turkish entry and a concerted attack upon Germany through the Balkans as the best way to defeat Germany and save central Europe and the Balkans from the Bolsheviks. Russia, on the other hand, believed that Turkey should declare her position against the Axis and shoulder some of the real burdens of war. But Turkey steadfastly refused to abandon her neutrality, recognizing that German bombers from bases in Bulgaria, only twenty minutes from Istanbul, could pulverize that fair city almost at will. The decisive veto on Churchill's plan was exercised by General Marshall. No arms would be spared from the cross-channel attack upon Europe; for unmindful of the future of Europe, Americans at that moment were demanding a frontal attack upon Germany. Without aid, Turkey would not enter the war. She did, however, permit British and American officers to circulate quite freely "incognito." And American airmen, downed in Turkey on the return from bombing Rumanian oil installations and other Balkan targets, were frequently allowed to escape from their internment.

In April, 1944 chrome shipments to Germany were halted; and in

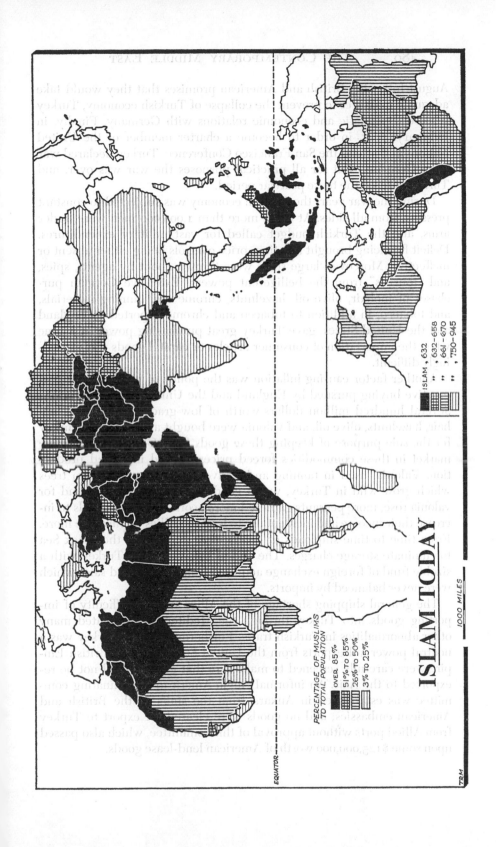

August following British and American promises that they would take adequate measures to prevent the collapse of Turkish economy, Turkey severed diplomatic and economic relations with Germany. Finally, in February, 1945, in order to become a charter member of the United Nations and attend the San Francisco Conference, Turkey declared war upon Germany. But for all practical purposes the war was over, and Turkey entered the tense postwar period.

During the war years the Turkish economy was subjected to constant pressure from all sides. At times more than 1,000,000 men were under arms, and the Turkish budget called for vast military expenditures. Deficit financing brought inflation, price controls being either absent or ineffective. Moreover, large sums were thrown about by agents, spies, and "tourists" from the belligerent powers. Extensive German purchases of mohair, olive oil, hazelnuts, chrome ore, tanning materials, and tobacco, in addition to tobacco and chrome exported to England and the United States, gave Turkey great purchasing power at a time when the importation of consumer articles or capital goods was exceedingly difficult.

Another factor causing inflation was the policy of preclusive or preemptive buying pursued by England and the United States in Turkey. Several hundred million dollars-worth of low-grade chrome ore, mohair, hazelnuts, olive oil, and valonia were bought and stored in Turkey for the sole purpose of keeping these goods from Germany. An active market in these commodities forced prices up and increased production. Valonia, used in tanning and derived from an acorn from trees which grow wild in Turkey, was a good example. As the demand for valonia rose, more peasants gathered more acorns from the woods to increase their income and incidentally to lead the Allies to purchase more. From time to time shiploads of goods were dumped in the Black Sea to eliminate storage charges. The end of the war found Turkey with a sizable fund of foreign exchange acquired from exports and sales which were never balanced by imports.

The general shipping shortage of the Allies and the difficulty of importing goods into Turkey through the Mediterranean created many other abnormalities in Turkish trade. Furthermore, since Turkey was a neutral power, all exports from the United States and the British Empire were carefully screened to make sure that goods would not be reexported to the Axis. An informal Anglo-American co-ordinating committee was established in Ankara from the staffs of the British and American embassies; and no goods were cleared for export to Turkey from Allied ports without approval of this committee, which also passed upon some $125,000,000 worth of American lend-lease goods.

Inflation and mounting deficits induced Inönü in 1942 to experiment with a capital levy tax in hope of lowering prices, balancing the budget, and absorbing some of the abundance of money. A law (*Varlik Vergisi*) authorized the creation of a special committee in each province to levy a tax on all persons according to their capital and in varying percentages on the assumption that they were evading their proper income taxes. Particularly in Istanbul, gross inequalities developed. Greeks, Armenians, Jews, and foreigners were hard pressed, some being assessed sums nearly equal to their total capital. Those who did not pay were sentenced to hard labor on railroads in eastern Anatolia. Representatives of the Allied governments protested to Inönü, but the situation with regard to Turkish neutrality was so delicate that all news of the capital tax was censored in Western presses until the spring of 1943. Upon official pressure at the highest levels in wartime conferences in 1943 the tax was abolished and those who had not paid were released. The experience, however, left an unpleasant residue of insecurity on the part of non-Turkish citizens, who regarded the tax as an expression of unbridled nationalism.

When Turkey broke with Germany in August, 1944, it was feared that a sudden termination of preclusive buying and cessation of German purchases of strategic raw materials along with comestibles such as figs, raisins, and fish would be a ruinous shock to the Turkish economy. However, no break occurred. Shipping became more plentiful; Turkish ports were opened; and Turkish products found a ready market in a world apparently short of almost everything.

For Turkey the period of the war from September 1, 1939 to February 23, 1945 had marked a difficult course of neutrality. Turkey wished to live in peace with the victorious powers; but during the course of the war it was not always clear who would win. Furthermore, at first Russia and Germany were opposed to England and France; but then at one stroke in 1941 Russia and England were combined to crush Germany. Those five and one half years must have seemed endless to President Inönü and the leaders of Turkey!

EGYPT AND THE WAR

In other areas of the Middle East World War II brought armies, shortages, inflation, political strain, economic opportunities, and a variety of social and intellectual upheavals. At the very outset Egypt held a pivotal position. Ali Maher, the prime minister and a person with great influence over King Faruk, induced the government to sever diplomatic and economic relations with Germany as soon as Britain declared war. Martial law was declared; ports were placed under the authority of the

British navy; and censorship of posts and telegraph was established. When parliament convened in November the speech from the throne indicated that Egypt would give active and willing co-operation to England in defense of Egypt. Some concern arose over the price and market for cotton, particularly since nearly twenty percent of Egyptian cotton exports had gone in the previous year to Germany and countries under her control. Demand, however, was brisk; and open-market prices climbed higher than those guaranteed by the government. When Mussolini entered the war, Egypt broke off relations with Italy, but notified him that war would not be declared unless Italy attacked Egypt. As a result of British pressure, Ali Maher, recognized as anti-British, was replaced by Hasan Sabri, an Independent. The latter formed a broad national government, including Ahmad Hasanayn, a pro-Britisher, in the very influential post of chief of the royal cabinet.

The Italian declaration brought the war to Egypt's doorstep. In September, 1940 Italian forces advanced some fifty miles into Egypt toward Alexandria, resting at Sidi Barrani until December, when General Sir Archibald Wavell drove them west of Benghazi. Then, in April, 1941, after contributing heavily to the support of Greece, British forces reeled toward the Egyptian frontier, although the fortress of Tobruk held. From then until May, 1942, General Rommel and his *Afrika Korps* fought a seesaw battle against the British pushing the front to al-Alamayn, only seventy miles west of Alexandria. In October, 1942 a two-week battle at al-Alamayn broke the German army, which continued to fall back with General Bernard Montgomery at the head of the Eighth Army in full pursuit. British and American forces, which landed in Morocco and Algeria on November 8, 1942 under the command of General Dwight D. Eisenhower, met General Montgomery in Tunisia at the end of March, 1943; and the war in North Africa came to its end.

As war raged in the western desert, life in Egypt changed rapidly. Although a few British continued their afternoon cricket matches at the famed Gezira Sporting Club, most found the tensions of war pressing upon them. When the Mediterranean was virtually closed to shipping, a glut of cotton loomed ominously; but Britain solved the problem by agreeing to buy the entire crop at a price which all Egyptians admitted was generous. Husayn Sirri, a nonparty civil engineer, succeeded to the prime ministership upon the death of Hasan Sabri in November, 1940; and policies continued a similar course. Wafdists and Saadists refused to participate in the cabinet. And the following spring when the general situation appeared very black a number of seditious or suspect individuals, such as Ali Maher, General Aziz Ali-al-Masri, and Hasan al-Banna, leader of the extreme Muslim Brotherhood, were confined to residence in rural areas.

Shortages of cereals, inadequate price regulations, and lack of import and export controls created hardships upon the population of Cairo and Alexandria. These developments furthered political disintegration and made the intrigues of King Faruk and the palace clique more effective. The German capture of Benghazi and Japanese victories in south Asia emboldened Faruk and his cronies. The students were called out, and Husayn Sirri resigned February 2, 1942. The following day the British ambassador, in an audience with the king, complained that Sirri's co-operation with the British had been thwarted at every step, urged that a new government commanding the support of a majority of the country be formed without delay, and suggested that Nahas Pasha and the Wafd be called to head the government. On the 4th an ultimatum, supported by the American minister, demanded that Faruk make the appointment or accept the consequences. On the advice of the palace clique, Faruk refused. That evening the British ambassador accompanied by General Stone and a tank force, called upon Faruk at Abdin Palace and offered him the alternative of appointing Nahas Pasha or boarding a British warship at Suez and spending the remainder of the war period on the Seychelles or Mauritius. Faruk chose the former course, and Egypt remained fully loyal to the war effort. Corruption and inefficiency increased; patronage to "deserving" Wafdists became rife; but the Allies no longer had a troublesome, unco-operative, and weak Egyptian government with which to cope.

Nahas held office until October, 1944. In the meantime corruption and favoritism grew, and the hatred between Nahas and Faruk became notorious. Nahas weakened his position and his party by succumbing to unabated nepotism, especially with respect to his wife's family. He quarreled with prominent supporters, many of whom left the Wafd and formed a new party, the *Kutla*. His dismissal was a foregone conclusion. As soon as the theatres of the war were removed to a distance far from Egypt, British insistence upon retention of the Nahas government could no longer be valid. Pledging co-operation with Britain against Germany and Japan, Saadist Ahmad Maher formed a government composed of Saadists, Liberals, and members of the Kutla. On February 24, 1945 he informed the chamber of deputies of the intention to declare war upon Germany in order that Egypt might become a charter member of the United Nations. As he left, he was assassinated by a young fascist Egyptian. Al-Nukrashi, the second in command of the Saadist party, assumed the prime ministership; and a formal declaration of a defensive war against Germany and Japan was issued on February 26. Strangely enough, Egyptian entry into the war opened the postwar period and its many problems for Egypt.

INDEPENDENCE OF LEBANON AND SYRIA

Probability of war in Europe stiffened the French government's attitude toward Syria and Lebanon, and appropriate measures were taken by Gabriel Puaux, the high commissioner. His delegate in Damascus took over control of the police from the minister of the interior. In July, 1939 Hashim al-Atasi, president of Syria, resigned in protest over the gift of Alexandretta to Turkey. Puaux thereupon dissolved the chamber of deputies, suspended the constitution, placed foreign affairs and defense directly in French hands, established a council of five to govern Syria, and again formed separate regimes for Jebel Druze and Latakia.

Upon the outbreak of war General Weygand was sent from France as commander-in-chief of French forces in the Levant. The appointment cheered the Syrians and Lebanese, since Weygand had been exceedingly popular as high commissioner. In September the Lebanese constitution was suspended and the powers of the cabinet transferred to a Lebanese secretary of state, assisted by French advisers. However, the fall of France left the situation uncertain. General Weygand had been recalled, and General Mittelhauser elected to remain loyal to General Pétain and the Vichy government.

In August, 1940 Italian officers arrived in Beirut to supervise the armistice for the Axis, but were frustrated by Puaux and General Fougeres. Many French officers found it possible to slip away to Palestine, where they proceeded to join the Free French forces of General de Gaulle. Others were arrested and imprisoned in Syria and Lebanon. When General Dentz appeared in November as high commissioner, collaboration with Vichy and the Axis became even more open. From the Hotel Metropole in Beirut German agents who flocked into the French mandate began to prepare the states for German control. Economic difficulties and collapse of the French franc, to which Syrian and Lebanese currencies were tied, led to strikes and political demonstrations. General Dentz attempted to soothe local feelings by establishing new governments under Khalid al-Azm in Syria and Alfred Naccache in Lebanon.

The new arrangements only partially settled the atmosphere, because the leaders of Syria and Lebanon were plotting to acquire complete independence at this moment of French embarrassment and did not relish the thought of falling into the orbit of Germany or Italy. In the spring of 1941 infiltration of German "tourists" and use of Syrian airfields for German aid to Iraq posed a serious threat to the British position in the Middle East. The French states were blockaded, and

England declared that use of Syria or Lebanon as a base by any hostile power would not be tolerated. Because of incipient dangers in Lebanon and Syria, British and Free French forces under General Sir Henry Maitland Wilson and General Catroux entered the French mandate from Palestine and Transjordan in June. Resistance by General Dentz was unexpectedly strong, and the Allied forces battled their way into Beirut and Damascus. An armistice was signed in July at Acre. French who wished to be repatriated were permitted to leave; but many remained at their posts, since French cultural institutions were respected and their work was unimpaired.

On the first day of the invasion of the French Levant, General de Gaulle designated General Catroux delegate general and plenipotentiary of Free France in the Levant. He appointed Alfred Naccache president of Lebanon and Taj al-Din president of Syria, and recognized these two states as independent and free republics. Meanwhile, Britain sent General Sir Edward Spears as head of a British mission to the Levant, incorporated the "republics" into the sterling bloc, and brought the supplying of their requirements under the machinery of the Middle East Supply Center in Cairo.

These provisions did not satisfy the nationalists, who complained that the people had no hand in these decisions. Under such pressures the suspended constitutions were re-established in 1943 and elections held for legislative bodies. In Syria the leader of the National Bloc, Shukri al-Kuwatli, became president of the republic. In Lebanon Bishara al-Khuri was chosen president and Riyadh al-Sulh prime minister; the newly elected Chamber had 30 Christian and 25 Muslim members. The French, however, found it extremely difficult to relinquish prerogatives such as issuing decrees and maintaining special troops and agents in the states. Lebanese and Syrians objected to the continuation of these forms of colonialism and adopted resolutions dropping all references to France from the constitutions. When Bishara al-Khuri and the Lebanese cabinet were arrested, a general strike and spontaneous anti-French riots forced the French to give in. When the National Bloc in Syria also demanded withdrawal of French controls, General Catroux agreed (December, 1943). In 1944 the U.S.S.R. and the United States gave full diplomatic recognition of the independence of the two states, which declared war upon the Axis on February 27, 1945 and thereby became charter members of the United Nations. The actions of the Russians and Americans compelled the reluctant British and the weakened French to accept Syrian and Lebanese delegates at the San Francisco Conference and to respect the free position of these two republics of the Levant.

UNREST IN IRAQ

World War II found Iraq in a weak economic condition and a highly charged political atmosphere. In 1939 Britain loaned Iraq nearly £4,000,000 for armaments and railroads, and the Iraq Petroleum Company advanced £3,000,000 to cover ordinary governmental expenses. Nuri al-Said, the prime minister, broke relations with Germany, took over German property, and interned all Germans who remained in Iraq. Although the government declared it would live up to its treaty obligations with Britain, most leaders quietly rejoiced over the embarrassment of England and France and expected that their fellow Arabs in Palestine, Syria, and Lebanon would secure independence during the struggle. Hajj Amin al-Husayni, the Jerusalem mufti, took up residence in Baghdad in October, 1939 and from there directed his campaign to obtain an Arab state in Palestine.

Early in 1940 because of local politics Nuri al-Said resigned his office in favor of Rashid Ali al-Gailani, who was a "hard worker, a persuasive speaker, a passionate nationalist, ambitious and reckless." Unfortunately Rashid Ali had little knowledge of the world outside of Iraq and thus judged the results of his actions in a narrow local perspective. In July, 1940 he offered to join the war openly on the side of Great Britain, if Palestine would be established as a state immediately. At that time an Arab state would have resulted, since Jews comprised only one third of its population. Churchill's refusal split the Iraqi government right down the middle. Nuri led the moderates; and Rashid Ali championed the uncompromising nationalists, who succumbed easily to Axis flattery and thought to use German and Italian arms and money to achieve their nationalist goals.

In November the British ambassador suggested to the regent that a more amicable prime minister be found, an overture which prompted Rashid Ali to look to the Axis for material aid. In December, after refusing the regent's request to resign, he publicly stated that Iraq's foreign affairs were being strengthened with "friendly states" other than Britain. As clandestine relations with the Axis developed, Nuri, Taha al-Hashimi, minister of defense, and three other ministers resigned. When a parliamentary vote of no confidence loomed before Rashid Ali, his plea for the dissolution of parliament was denied by the regent, who then left Baghdad to be free from pressures. In the face of such opposition Rashid Ali resigned, and the regent appointed Taha al-Hashimi upon the insistence of Rashid Ali's army friends who were known as the Golden Square.

Taking office February 3, 1941, Taha al-Hashimi failed to curb the power of the Golden Square. Rashid Ali grew desperate and worked incessantly to return to power. On the night of April 1, 1941, supported by the army, Rashid Ali returned to power in a kind of *coup d'état.* The regent was smuggled out of the country by the American minister; and the British, fearing the worst, landed an Indian army brigade at Basrah to protect an important air assembling base. Discussions between Rashid Ali and Sir Kinahan Cornwallis, British ambassador, did not improve matters. And when more forces were landed at Basrah, the Iraqi army threatened the meager British units stationed at the air base at Habbaniyah in the vicinity of Baghdad. Bombings and artillery attacks lasted from May 2 until May 30, when the British and the Arab Legion from Transjordan relieved Habbaniyah and occupied Baghdad. Rashid Ali and his allies fled to Iran and Turkey; German planes which had just arrived escaped to Syria; the regent returned; and Nuri al-Said eventually became prime minister at the head of a new government.

For the remainder of World War II relative political peace reigned in Iraq, and Nuri al-Said devoted much time and energy to building the Arab League and kindling Arab unity. Iraq declared war on the Axis in January, 1943 and signed the United Nations Declaration the same month. It was the first Middle Eastern state to qualify for membership in the United Nations.

Iraq became greatly involved in the process of supplying goods to the U.S.S.R., and vast numbers of British and American troops were stationed there. In 1942 Iraq was made eligible to receive lend-lease aid, and quantities of military and necessary civilian goods were dispatched. Inflation disrupted her economy in many ways, as British and American expenditures introduced great purchasing power over a wide segment of the population without a concomitant importation or production of consumers' goods. Iraq's economic requirements were screened by the Middle East Supply Center in Cairo; and since she was a member of the sterling bloc, Britain also had an effective instrument in controlling and channeling Iraq's foreign trade to British Empire sources, often to the great discomfiture of American and Iraqi business interests. As World War II came to an end Iraq attempted to break the economic domination which London had effectively maintained since the end of World War I.

OCCUPATION OF IRAN

At the outbreak of World War II Iran under Shah Reza was deeply involved economically with Germany. Large percentages of imports and exports were German, and German technicians were assisting in the development of the industry and the natural resources of Iran other than oil. Although Iran declared her neutrality, official Iranian attitudes were pro-German until the Nazi invasion of Russia in 1941. Shah Reza was decidedly anti-Russian and anti-British, largely because of the time-worn imperialism of those powers in Iran. The British closed the sea routes to Germany and did not permit Iranian goods to pass to Germany through neutral states. The Soviet Union opened her ports, and a treaty of March, 1940 allowed Iranian goods transit through the U.S.S.R. to states having treaty relations with Russia.

Iran swarmed with Axis officials and agents of every sort. S.S. *Oberfuhrer* Ettel became German minister in Tehran, and his Legation served as headquarters for German agents operating in Iraq. Although Russian hands were partially tied because of the Soviet-Nazi agreement, Communist activities flourished in the northern provinces in expectation of taking over Iraq and Iran in accordance with the understanding with Germany.

Hitler's invasion of Russia in June, 1941 changed the situation in Iran almost overnight. On June 26 Soviet Russia informed Shah Reza that Germans planned a *coup d'état* in Iran and that the U.S.S.R. could not ignore the presence and unfriendly activities of Germans there. In July after the Anglo-Soviet agreement for mutual assistance, the two governments initiated joint pressure on Iran to force the unusually large number of Germans in Iran to depart. Shah Reza was furious at such requests, and no action was taken.

Arrangements were rapidly developing whereby Russia would be supplied from Britain and the United States through Iran. Of necessity, Iran could not be permitted to become a tool of Germany. British and Soviet troops, therefore, began their occupation of Iran on August 25, 1941. Token resistance was offered for two days, until a new government under Muhammad Ali Furuki ordered submission and British-Soviet contacts were made at two different points northwest of Tehran. Since Shah Reza was still defiant, Allied forces approached Tehran with the intention of occupying the capital. Instead, the shah abdicated on September 17 because of "failing health"; and his twenty-one-year-old son, Mohammad Reza, was proclaimed shah. Reza was taken first to Mauritius and then to South Africa, where he died in 1944. A round-up of Axis agents and friends bagged several hundred, but the mufti of Jerusalem, Iraqi rebels, and notorious agents such as Franz Mayr and Roman Gamotta escaped the net.

For the remainder of the war Iran co-operated with the Allies; and at the famous Tehran Conference the Big Three, at Roosevelt's suggestion, complimented Iran on her service in the supplying of Russia. The quantities of goods that passed to Russia over the Trans-Iranian railway and by motor truck through Iran were so vast the figures of tonnage are incomprehensible. The operations influenced life in the country very markedly. In time more than 30,000 American troops were stationed there along with many British and Russians. Their expenditures brought quantities of foreign exchange. But the Iranians found little to purchase with these sums, as imports were held to a minimum by the Middle East Supply Center, which controlled Iranian foreign trade. Inflation became very serious with prices for scarce items soaring to such an extent that truck tires sold for £450 each and one aspirin tablet for $2.50. Before the end of the war the general price level had increased 1000 percent over that of 1939, and the dislocation of the Iranian economy became general.

As was so frequently the case, the Allied ousting of Shah Reza also removed the strong hand at the helm of internal governmental affairs. The various elements in Iranian society that Reza ruthlessly controlled immediately reared their heads, weakened the government, and played havoc with the centralizing and nationalizing processes that Reza had engendered. Nomads secured rifles and arms; Shiite divines returned to do battle against a secular state; wealthy landowners ignored taxation; and Communist agitators were released from jails. Dr. Millspaugh was invited again to administer Iran's finances; Colonel Norman Schwarzkopf, another American, reorganized the police; and an American military mission advised the army. German undercover activities continued for many months after the forced reversal of Iranian policy. The German penetration of Russia and the British retreat to al-Alamayn 'encouraged a restlessness among Iranian leaders. Franz Mayr came out of hiding and helped organize a group called Nationalists of Iran. General Zahedi joined the movement and aided in the revolt of the Kurds and the southern tribes. All these activities faded quickly, however, when the Germans faltered at Stalingrad.

In 1942 a tripartite treaty of alliance was signed by Iran, Great Britain, and the U.S.S.R. Iran recognized the foreign troops as in no sense an occupying force, while the other two parties to the treaty acknowledged the independence of Iran and agreed to a withdrawal of their forces not later than six months after the end of the war with the Axis. The supply route to Russia was the major concern. Russia, nevertheless, utilized this golden opportunity to further her imperialistic and Communistic interests in Iran. She aided the Tudeh (Masses) Party, protected their rallies with Soviet tanks, published Communist newspapers, intrigued with Armenians and Kurds, and finally in 1944 demanded an oil concession. Britain tried to counter such moves with her own propaganda, but it was only partially successful. The United States did little at all, although lend-lease was made available in 1942. Iran declared war on Germany in September, 1943, thus qualifying at an early date for membership in the United Nations.

THE MIDDLE EAST SUPPLY CENTER

World War II brought many innovations and organizational devices to the Middle East. None was more encompassing than the Middle East Supply Center. As the volume of supplies for General Wavell poured in, tonnage for civilian use did not abate. Ports and docks were so choked with goods, many of them luxuries, that at times it seemed certain the war would be lost for want of anchorage and unloading space. Out of this chaos was born in April, 1941, this executive agency, which grew and spread its effective control everywhere in the Middle East except Turkey. It allocated available shipping for the several areas; it ascertained the types and quantity of goods to be imported and passed upon import permits; it determined from which country imported goods should come; it guaranteed the Middle East at least minimum requirements of scarce and rationed articles and commodities; and it maintained in the Middle East common stocks of wheat and other bulk items for emergency use.

In the beginning the Middle East Supply Center was operated entirely by the British; but in 1942, when lend-lease goods went to the Middle East and more and more shipments originated in the United States, American officials participated in the direction of policy at the Cairo headquarters and an operational office was established in Washington. However, representatives of Middle Eastern governments did not sit on any of the boards or have any voice in determining policy. Officers of the Middle East Supply Center grew to regard their work and the functions being performed not only as an indispensable contribution to the war effort but also as a benevolent tutelage in techniques of economic planning, area co-ordination, and development of resources. Middle Easterners questioned the advantages and benefits of the Middle East Supply Center, and as the war drew to a close its original justification disappeared.

As early as 1944 it became manifest that Britain, through control of imports, use of the sterling area pool, and denial of dollar exchange, was employing the Center as a restraint of trade and as an instrument for maintaining the economic colonialism of the British Empire. Since such acts were contrary to American foreign trade policies, the United States withdrew from the operations in 1945 and the Center wound up its affairs. Undoubtedly, many of its regional activities would have been advantageous to perpetuate; but nothing had been done to bring in Middle Eastern governments or train local personnel to maintain the work. Thus, when the Center was abandoned, its possible peacetime usefulness did not materialize, and the Middle East returned to divisive and national economic policies. For many states of the Middle East the demise of the Middle East Supply Center more accurately announced the termination of World War II than did armistices, treaties, or the birth of the United Nations.

REFERENCES: *Chapter 35*

Reference items in Chapters 19, 22, 27, 30, 31, 32, 33, and 34 are useful for this chapter.

Cecil Beaton, *Near East:* Bateford, London, 1943.

William Eagleton, Jr., *The Kurdish Republic of 1946:* Oxford University Press, New York, 1963. The story of the Soviet attempt to penetrate this area in World War II.

J. C. Hurewitz, *Diplomacy in the Near and Middle East: A Documentary Record: 1914–1956,* Vol. II: Van Nostrand, New York, 1956. The second volume of an item cited in Chapter 19. Indispensable.

George Kirk, *The Middle East in the War, Survey of International Affairs, 1939–1946,* Vol. II: Oxford University Press, London, 1953. A standard work by an outstanding author. Objective.

———, *The Middle East 1945–1950, Survey of International Affairs, 1939–1946:* Oxford University Press, London, 1954. Indispensable.

Hughe Knatchbull-Hugessen, *Diplomat in Peace and War:* J. Murray, London, 1949. By the British ambassador in Ankara during much of the war.

L. C. Moyzisch, *Operation Cicero,* "Postscript," Franz von Papen (Constantine Fitzgibbon and Heinrich Fraenkel, trans.): Bantam Books, New York, 1950.

Paiforce: *The Official Story of the Persia and Iraq Command, 1941–1946:* H. M. Stationery Office, London, 1948.

M. N. Seton-Williams, *Britain and the Arab States: A Survey of Anglo-Arab Relations, 1920–1948:* Luzac, London, 1948. Pro-British.

Desmond Young, *Rommel, The Desert Fox:* Harper, New York, 1950.

CHAPTER 36

Turkey Becomes a Democracy

THE POWERS AND THE STRAITS

In 1938 when Kemal Atatürk died, his great prime minister and the negotiator of the Lausanne Treaty, Ismet Inönü, was elected president by the deputies of the Grand National Assembly. At the same time and in part due to this election, he acquired the leadership of the Republican party, the one legal political party in Turkey. Almost immediately upon Inönü's assumption of office, Turkey was caught in the maelstrom of World War II. Though he preserved the neutrality of his country until 1945, Turkey found the pursuit of a fully independent policy exceedingly difficult and at times of somewhat doubtful value.

Turkey's diplomatic relations during the war have been discussed in some detail in a previous chapter. Russia tried in vain in the winter of 1939–40 to gain an advantage in eastern Anatolia and at the Straits; and throughout the war she repeatedly indicated dissatisfaction with Turkey's inactive role. Thus, in March, 1945 Russia terminated the Turkish-Soviet treaty of neutrality and nonaggression, stating that it was obsolete. Then in June, when war ended in Europe and the United States and the United Kingdom still faced Japan, with the expected prospect of bitter and large-scale engagements for another eighteen months, Russia demanded the cession of Kars and Ardahan and the granting of Soviet bases on the Straits. Courageously the Turks replied with a categorical "No."

At the Potsdam Conference the three powers agreed that the Montreux Convention of 1936 governing the Straits should be revised and that each of the three powers should discuss the question directly with Turkey. On this basis, the United States presented a note to

Turkey in November, 1945, stating that the United States would participate in a conference to revise the Montreux Convention. Four principles were declared worthy of consideration: that the Straits be open to merchant ships of all nations at all times; that the Straits be open to transit of warships of Black Sea powers at all times; that the Straits be closed to the passage of warships of non-Black Sea powers at all times, except for an agreed limited tonnage, except for the consent of the Black Sea powers, and except when acting for the United Nations; and that certain changes be made to bring the Montreux Convention up to date.

Great Britain supported the American view, and Foreign Minister Bevin and President Truman publicly announced their adherence to such a course. Not until August, 1946, did Russia reveal her views in a note to Turkey. Of the five points declared, the first three were essentially identical to the first three of the American note. Point four, however, called for a regime for the Straits controlled only by Turkey and other Black Sea powers; and point five invited Turkey to organize with Russia a joint defense of the Straits to prevent their use by other countries having aims hostile to Black Sea powers.

Within two weeks Britain and America reacted strongly against the last two points and repeated their willingness to consider a revision at an international gathering. Turkey replied in like vein, stating that the Russian points four and five were "not compatible with the inalienable rights of sovereignty of Turkey" and could not be considered. The Soviets presented another note in September; and England, the United States, and Turkey replied in October, this second round of notes showing no fundamental change in any government's policy. Following these exchanges of views the subject was dropped, and no revision or alteration of the Straits regime or control was effected.

THE TRUMAN DOCTRINE

The Soviets maintained strong pressure upon Turkey by deploying sizable army groups in areas from which attacks upon Turkey could be launched. In the face of any possible development Turkey considered it expedient to keep under arms nearly 1,000,000 men, even though recognizing that such a force could only delay by a few weeks a Russian conquest. The United States showed interest by sending the S. S. *Missouri* to Istanbul in March, 1946 on the pretext of carrying the body of the Turkish ambassador, who had died in Washington in 1944.

The continued Soviet pressure upon Turkey in the immediate postwar period had an adverse effect upon Turkish economy. Government leaders understood Russia could maintain the pressure almost indefinitely and sought a way out of their dilemma. The solution was found in the Truman Doctrine, proclaimed to the American Congress on March 12, 1947; $100,000,000 was requested, along with $300,000,000 for neighboring Greece, to bolster Turkey to become more self-sustaining in her long-range resistance to Russia.

The plan was conceived and worked out by Turkish and American military, economic, and political leaders. It entailed two primary objectives. The first was to mechanize and modernize the Turkish army, so that the effectiveness and firepower potential of each unit would be doubled; this would allow a proportionate cut in the size of the army without reduction in strength. The other objective called for an improvement in the systems of communication and transportation in Turkey to give the army greater maneuverability. A large portion of the first grant to Turkey appeared in the form of military equipment, but a most significant five million was set aside for a public road-building program.

In the two decades following 1947, between four and five billion dollars was expended by the United States on the program for Turkey. The army was reorganized from top to bottom; and tanks, trucks, new artillery, and equipment of every description were brought into Turkey accompanied by teacher-technicians. Ports were enlarged, and hard-surface all-weather roads connecting the major cities were built. Iskenderum (Alexandretta) became a major terminus in the south, from which new roads extending northward and eastward toward the Russian frontier were constructed. Airfields in eastern Anatolia were laid, and American military missions were everywhere. Hydroelectric projects were undertaken; railroads became more efficient; irrigation was advanced; and internal national strength grew by leaps and bounds.

When war broke out in Korea in June, 1950, Turkey declared her position almost immediately and sent a brigade of 5,000 men to support the United Nations position. In the ensuing battles the Turkish forces distinguished themselves with great honor and received world acclaim. Simultaneously, Turkey applied for membership in the North Atlantic Treaty Organization and in September, 1951, along with Greece, was admitted. Izmir became NATO headquarters for the eastern Mediterranean and developed into an important naval base for the NATO powers.

GREECE AND THE MIDDLE EAST

Turkey sought to be not only a land bridge but a military, political, and friendly link between Europe and the Middle East. In February, 1953, therefore, the treaty of Ankara was signed by Turkey, Greece, and Yugoslavia, drawing those three into a co-operative alliance. In 1954 the three agreed upon a twenty-year military pact; and in March, 1955 they formed a Balkan consultative assembly in which representatives of the three would discuss all common problems.

The value of these pacts was sorely tried in 1955 and 1956 by violent emotions roused between Turkey and Greece. A bomb exploded in Salonika near Atatürk's birthplace and slight damages resulted to that shrine, so important to all Turks. Shortly thereafter, a demonstration against Greeks staged in Istanbul and Izmir got out of hand. Before authorities could restore order, several hundred millions of dollars in damages were committed on Greek shops and churches, and faint signs of xenophobia and even of a social and economic upheaval were displayed. Troubles also developed on the Island of Cyprus between Britain and Greece, the latter working in conjunction with the Greek Cypriots to effect union of Cyprus and Greece. Since twenty percent of the population was Turkish and since Cyprus was close to the southern Turkish shore, the Turkish government took a firm stand in opposition to the proposed union. Turkey argued that the island had been given to England to administer in 1878 by the Turks and that if England relinquished control the island should be returned to Turkey. Believing that Cyprus held a strong strategic importance for the Turkish ports of Antalya, Mersin, and Iskenderum, Turkish spokesmen threatened that Turks would fight to prevent Cyprus from joining Greece. As civil strife between Turkish and Greek Cypriots on the island continued, the British in 1957 broached partitioning as the only possible peaceful solution. Ankara accepted this course reluctantly, but Athens rejected the proposal, thus burying the Balkan alliance. Greece also weakened the eastern bastion of NATO by recalling Greek officers from Izmir and declining to discuss NATO affairs with the Turks.

In March, 1959 as the only apparent recourse to the impasse, the three involved powers, Greece, Turkey, and Britain, signed three treaties in London establishing and guaranteeing a Republic of Cyprus which came into being in August, 1960, becoming the ninety-fifth member of the United Nations. Archbishop Makarios, head of the Greek Orthodox Church in Cyprus and leader of the Greek Cypriot community, and Dr. Fazil Küchük, leader of the Turkish Cypriot community, accepted this settlement. According to the constitution, partition or union (*enosis*) with Greece was barred. The Greek Cypriots would elect the president and the Turkish Cypriots the vice president, and both officials would have to sign acts to make them law. There was provision for a council of ministers and a house of representatives, with the stipulation of membership set at a 70-30 ratio of Greeks to Turks. In addition separate Turkish and Greek Cypriot communal chambers were set up to control education, religion, social welfare, and personal affairs, almost like the millets of the Ottoman Empire. The above ratio was also to hold in the membership of the civil service and the police, whereas in the army a ratio of 60-40 was to prevail. In the ensuing elections in 1960, Archbishop Makarios became president, defeating his leftist rival two to one, and Dr. Küchük was elected vice president. Britain retained two bases comprising 99 square miles and 19 other posts including an airfield and radar stations. Greece was allowed a military force of 950 and Turkey one of 650 on the island with the right of periodic rotation of personnel.

But many of the leaders in Cyprus were not prepared for the compromises necessary for the smooth functioning of such a republic. Cypriot nationalism hardly existed, whereas Greek and Turkish nationalism flourished, the former actively espousing union with Greece. In 1963, Archbishop–President Makarios touched off a new crisis by decreeing the end of separate Turkish and Greek municipalities in the cities and proposing thirteen constitutional changes which the Turkish minority feared would endanger its security and the guarantee of specific civil and political rights. Above all, one point would terminate the necessity of all measures having the approval of the vice president, which in popular language meant the end of any Turkish veto power. Makarios asserted that the present constitution was unworkable, but his opponents declared he had never intended that it succeed.

Bloodshed occurred between the communities in December, 1963, and Greece and Turkey supported their respective nationality groups. Terrorism developed and for a time a widening of the conflict seemed imminent. A British proposed cease-fire failed, and the issue went to the United Nations where a mediator was appointed and the Security Council sent a peace-keeping force. Greece and Turkey privately arrived at various compromise solutions for federation and canton-like structures but Makarios vetoed them. He also rejected a settlement formulated by a United Nations sponsored negotiation team at Geneva in July, 1964. Prime Ministers Inönü of Turkey and Papandreou of Greece restrained the hotheads from leading their countries into war. At one time when it appeared Turkey would intervene militarily on the island, United States President Johnson sent a stiff note to Inönü warning him of the dire consequences of such an act. Later that summer both Inönü and Papandreou visited Washington.

By August, the situation in the Eastern Mediterranean was grave. So-called Greek security forces on the island jumped from 20,000 to 40,000 with volunteers and irregulars from Greece. Egypt sent war matériel to Makarios although on one occasion the United States Sixth

Fleet compelled a ship carrying tanks to return to Alexandria without unloading. Other supplies came from the U.S.S.R. which looked with favor on Makarios' stand for independence immediately and *enosis* later. Greek Cypriot forces began to attack ports on the north side of the island where supplies were being landed from Turkey. At this juncture the Turkish Air Force strafed Greek Cypriot positions, and Turkey threatened to invade the island. Apparently at this point the Greek government became disenchanted with the usefulness of Makarios. There was too much flirting with Moscow and too much independence of action. General George Grivas, the hero of the guerrilla bands against the British in the 1950's and the advocate of instant *enosis,* was allowed to return to Cyprus to control the irregulars, and Athens openly criticized Makarios for his military operations. The U.S.S.R. refused to support him and a stalemate developed. Shortly thereafter, a domestic political crisis shook the Greek government, bringing on a military coup whose leaders arrested the cabinet, abolished the parliament, and abrogated the constitution. Although in the autumn of 1967, leaders of the new military regime met face to face at the frontiers in Thrace with negotiators from Turkey, neither side was ready to make adequate compromises to achieve any progress in the Cyprus affair. Meanwhile the United Nations peace-keeping force remained, and the government of Cyprus continued on its rocky course.

In April, 1954 Turkey signed a pact of mutual co-operation with Pakistan—a pact which was hailed as the nucleus for the building of a defense line against the Soviet bloc. And on February 24, 1955 Turkey and Iraq joined in a five-year pact in Baghdad to co-operate and consult each other in all matters of defense. In an exchange of letters on the same day between the two prime ministers the countries agreed to co-operate "in resisting any aggression directed against either of them." The Baghdad pact provided that other nations of the Arab League and any other nation concerned with the Middle East might join. In April the United Kingdom signed; and in September and October Pakistan and Iran became the fourth and fifth members. The Turks believed that these treaties bolstered their flanks and enabled them to play an important role in the Middle East as a link to NATO and the West.

The Turkish commitments drew the concentrated wrath of the Russians and the Arabs. The Turks avowed that they as allies of the British and French would never engage in war against Arabs, but tension mounted along the Syrian border in the autumn of 1957. Syria complained bitterly of Turkish aggressive pressures, and Khrushchev in support of the Arabs warned that the Turks would not last even one day in battle with the Russians. When the United States announced stoutly that her NATO obligations to Turkey would be honored and King Saud offered to mediate the dispute, Russian concern evaporated and Syria dropped her charges (which were never substantiated).

The Iraqi revolution and withdrawal from the Baghdad pact in July, 1958 led to its reorganization as the Central Treaty Organization (CENTO), and the enhancement of Turkey's position in it. Airfields at Adana facilitated the airlift of American troops and supplies in their occupation of Lebanon, thereby committing Turkey more overtly to power struggles in the Middle East. The Turks, however, garnered no small satisfaction in witnessing the speed, might, and decisiveness of their powerful ally. Warnings from Russia that Turkey must not permit bases to be built or used for American nuclear and missile warfare were not nearly so frightening after the American demonstration in Lebanon in 1958. At the time of the U-2 debacle in 1960 Turkey was only indirectly involved, and in 1962 after the Cuban missile confrontation the Turks informed Khrushchev that the missile bases in Turkey were NATO establishments and neither Turkey nor the United States could remove them without full NATO consultations.

POLITICS AND ELECTIONS

The Turkish Constitution always contained statements that Turkey was a democracy, and references to this were made frequently in speeches and in schoolbooks. However, only one political party existed, and various electoral and press laws were adopted which could hardly be classed as democratic in principle or in practice. In 1945, in discussing the charter of the United Nations, a number of deputies in the Grand National Assembly pointed out that by subscribing to the charter and joining the United Nations Turkey would be obligated to practice "genuine democracy." Although a motion to modify all laws of a dictatorial and unconstitutional nature failed to pass, violent discussion ensued.

President Inönü in opening the Grand National Assembly in November, 1945 suggested the repeal of all repressive laws and recommended a change in the electoral law (in effect since 1876) to provide for direct election of deputies. Although the laws were not changed until the following spring, Inönü's speech indicated the way. Articles in the press appeared immediately criticizing the government on many issues; and leaders of a new group, the Democratic party, began to formulate a program and organize. The four principal advocates were: Celal Bayar, the last prime minister under Atatürk; Adnan Menderes, Republican deputy for Aydin; Refik Koraltan, deputy and one-time governor of Artvin; and Fuad Köprülü, scion of the famous family of seventeenth-century Ottoman grand vizirs, deputy, internationally known historian, and professor at the University of Istanbul.

The Democratic party subscribed to the six points of the Republican party—after all they were incorporated into the Constitution. But emphasis was placed upon practice rather than upon policy. The war years had brought many economic dislocations producing inflation, shortages, wealth, hardship, and corruption. The Democrats capitalized on these and attracted to their banner all who had any grievance with the government. In particular they attacked the economic situation. They asserted that the government under the Republicans sacrificed private enterprise in the interest of government ownership and promised that they, if elected, would undertake to turn state industries over to private ownership and operate the government more efficiently on all lines.

The election for membership of the Grand National Assembly was scheduled for the spring of 1947, and the Democratic party favored that date. The Republican leaders, however, became worried over the obvious successes of the opposition and called the election for July, 1946. When the results were announced the Republicans held 391 seats, Democrats 65, and Independents 5. The Democrats questioned the election of 300 Republicans, claiming stuffing of ballot boxes, faulty counting of ballots or no counting at all, and all manner of irregularities. Nevertheless, the election stood as announced and the Democrats began to plan for 1950.

After 1946 several other parties were formed by disgruntled deputies, and the Democrats proclaimed they would not participate in another election until concrete election reforms were introduced. Several times they walked out of the Grand National Assembly but each time President Inönü induced them to return, presumably with promises of new practices. Election booths were adopted, and regulations for nonpartisan election boards were passed. The Democratic leaders toured the country many times and gathered into their party young, energetic men and women from the provincial towns and cities. In the elections in May, 1950 the Democratic party presented in each district local candidates who had prestige and a local following and won a resounding victory. Totals in the new Grand National Assembly were: Democrats 408; Republicans 69; Nationalists 1; and Independents 9. Almost ninety percent of the electorate went to the polls; and in popular balloting Democrats obtained fifty-three percent against forty percent for the Republicans. On May 22, 1950 Celal Bayar was elected president of the Republic to succeed Ismet Inönü, who gracefully relinquished the office and power which he had held for nearly twelve years. Refik Koraltan became president of the Grand

National Assembly. Adnan Menderes assumed the office of prime minister and formed a new cabinet of fourteen ministers, including Fuad Köprülü as foreign minister. The triumph was complete. Of the former leading Republicans, only Inönü and Gunaltay, the last prime minister, won election to the new Grand National Assembly.

During the following four years the first effects of the American aid programs were felt in Turkey, and Turkish economy surged forward in every direction. The Democratic party reaped the benefits of that prosperity period; and although there were numerous cabinet shifts and two new cabinets, Adnan Menderes retained his position of prime minister under Bayar's presidency. In the elections of May, 1954 more than eighty percent of the registered electorate returned 503 Democrats, 31 Republicans, 5 Nationalists, and 2 Independents with fifty-eight percent of the popular vote going to the Democrats and thirty-five percent to the Republicans. The four principal founders of the Democratic party retained their respective positions in the government and looked forward to another four years of leadership.

Almost immediately, however, cracks in Turkish economic conditions appeared with severe reflections upon the political scene. The Democratic leadership reacted vigorously. Radio stations were not allowed to broadcast criticisms of government policies, and newspaper editors were imprisoned for "inciting" public opinion or for "insulting" the prime minister. In 1955 the Republican party refused to take part in local elections, charging that the Democrats would not allow free elections. Kasim Gulek, the secretary general of the Republican party, was arrested when he claimed that the Democrats had stolen the election in 1954.

Restrictive press laws were passed; and at one time in September, 1955 five of the leading newspapers of Istanbul were suspended by government order. Also, a number of the Democratic deputies of the Grand National Assembly were expelled from the party for criticizing the new press laws. At this juncture a further number of deputies resigned from the party to form a new Freedom party which in 1956 gathered greater strength and more illustrious names such as that of the son of Fuad Köprülü, the Democratic foreign minister. Worsening economic conditions brought the downfall of the cabinet in November, 1955, and Adnan Menderes in his new cabinet omitted many old members of his party and included ten new faces. Popularity of the Democratic party in Turkish cities sank in 1956 to a low point; and Republican leaders began to take heart that a victory might be won in 1958, if greater support could be gained in the rural areas. To this end Kasim Gulek visited the Black Sea coastal region in the summer of 1956. However, he found his activities curtailed at every turn by government action; and many began to fear that the "prized" democracy of the Turkish Republic was withering on the vine.

In the winter Kasim Gulek was taken into custody and fined for publishing a speech critical of Menderes, and Ismet Inönü accused the government of political totalitarianism. In 1957 the People's Republican party, the Freedom party, and the Republican Nationals discussed the feasibility of presenting a united-front opposition at the next national election. However, in September Menderes disallowed such an exigency and moved up the elections seven months to October. Campaigning was vigorous; but the Democrats won 424 seats in the Grand National Assembly to 178 for the People's Republicans and four each for the other two parties. Menderes inaugurated a new cabinet in November; and in January, 1958 twenty members of the Freedom party were jailed for holding an illegal meeting, an indication of the confidence and strength of the Democratic administration. Victory gave Menderes a new lease on the prime ministership. He hoped that his dreams for a balanced economy through industrialization and agricultural resurgence would have been achieved sufficiently to safeguard his party from defeat in 1961.

MILITARY COUP OF MAY 27, 1960

Droughts, beginning in the middle of the 1950's, turned wheat surpluses into shortages, further crippled the balance of payments, and undermined the entire economy. Internal and external governmental debts mounted, and though Menderes still refused to adhere to any planning, he vigorously and heedlessly pursued developments in every sector of the national economy. With returns from most of these investments many years away, inflation and its attendant ills were aggravated and went unchecked. Foreign aid, largely American, seemed wasted. Ineffective, sporadic, and stopgap measures were adopted. Futile efforts attempted to curtail luxury imports, black-market activities, and rising prices. In the summer of 1958, in order to obtain a new loan of $359 million from the International Monetary Fund and the United States, Menderes agreed to the Stabilization Program which included official devaluation of the lira to eleven cents, rigorous import controls, investment regulations, an end of deficit financing, and the curtailment of domestic credit. The shock to the urban economy was intense. By the spring of 1959, unemployment, business failures, and shortages had developed everywhere, but still there was no planning. Vocal opposition to the Democratic regime became commonplace among the educated and articulate urban classes who were most affected by the economic dislocation. The more they complained, the more they looked for and found inequities in the enforcement of the controls. It was rumored that the loan of the previous year had already been dissipated.

General carping at governmental actions and ineptitudes turned to outright criticism. In those years politics between the Democratic and the People's Republican parties was passionate and angry. Legal actions against libel were almost unknown, and the party in power usually exercised control over the press and radio to suppress the opposition. In the spring of 1959, while on a speaking tour in southwestern Turkey, Inönü was set upon by a rough pro-Democratic crowd and fell to the ground when a stone hit his head. A few days later a group of soldiers threw a cordon around him in Istanbul to protect him from violence. Blank columns in the newspapers enforced official silence but stimulated inquiry. Rumors flew that President Bayar had ordered house arrest for his bitter opponent. Furious accusations were hurled about the National Assembly in Ankara and Republican leaders interpreted from a few of Menderes' remarks that new elections might be called in 1960.

Such speculations induced Inönü and his party to step up the pressure and to be prepared should the call be suddenly announced. Menderes reportedly had said that he was indifferent to the attitudes of the urban elite as long as he retained the support of the villagers who comprised 70 percent of the electorate. In March, 1959 on an airplane trip to London to sign the treaties regarding Cyprus, he had quite miraculously walked away unscathed from a crash that killed most of the passengers. From that moment Menderes' followers loudly proclaimed that he had been saved by an Act of God in order to lead his country, and many Republicans began to despair of ever defeating him. Early in 1960 several sessions of the National Assembly ended in fistfights. Menderes and Inönü continued to make speeches about the country, and the political tension mounted.

There was a Turkish law forbidding political campaigning except for forty-five days preceding an election. No election had been called, but the leaders were acting as if it had. In April Inönü and some of his party deputies were on their way to Kayseri to participate in a political meeting, when their train was stopped by the army acting on orders from the government. Inönü refused to give way, claiming that the Constitution guaranteed freedom of travel to Turkish citizens and that the Penal Code prohibited interference with a deputy carrying out his duties, and he was allowed to proceed to Kayseri. The uproar from this action and the involvement of the army had not abated when the National Assembly, on the motion of two Democrats, voted to establish the extralegal Committee of Fifteen to Investigate the Activities of the People's Republican party and a Section of the Press. Violent speeches personally attacking Inönü were followed by more fistfights and even pistols appeared. References to the Committee were banned in the press, all fifteen members were chosen from the most partisan of the Democrats, political activity in the nation was suspended, and Inönü was expelled from the Assembly for the next twelve sessions. Within a few days, on April 28 and April 29, university students in Istanbul and Ankara marched on the streets until they were suppressed by military action and gunfire. Daily demands for Menderes' resignation were shouted at him whenever he appeared. On May 21 one thousand cadets of the Military College in Ankara marched on the presidential residence to sing martial songs. On May 25 the National Assembly recessed, and Menderes announced that the investigating committee had finished its work and would soon report its findings. Then, on May 27, 1960 at 4:00 A.M. the army struck. President Bayar, Prime Minister Menderes, the entire cabinet, and most of the Democratic deputies of the National Assembly were arrested, the government offices were seized, and within four hours a bloodless revolution had been accomplished. The military curfew was lifted that afternoon and joyously wild celebrations occurred in Ankara and Istanbul.

THE NATIONAL UNITY COMMITTEE

The day of the coup, the army flew General Cemal Gürsel to Ankara where he was installed as Head of the Provisional Government. Earlier that month General Gürsel, Chief of the Land Forces, had publicly criticized the investigating committee and retired. A father figure at the age of sixty-six, he was a necessary link between the senior officers, the older politicians, and the public on the one hand, and the colonels, majors, and captains who had instigated the coup. The military body formed to govern the nation was known as the National Unity Committee, but for several days the identity of its members, other than General Gürsel, was not revealed nor was it ever stated how the Committee came to be formed. Within a week, however, an official list of the thirty-eight officers of the NUC was published. At a public ceremony on June 24 in Ankara at the National Assembly hall each of the thirty-eight stepped forward, and one by one, over a nationwide radio broadcast, pledged to be loyal, to serve the Turkish nation, and to "work for nothing else than the welfare of the nation and its sovereignty," as well as for the creation of a "new Constitution, and transferring power to the new Parliament."

Who were these thirty-eight officers? Five held the rank of general, six were captains, and the rest were colonels and majors; twenty-two were born after the end of World War I. Most had been educated in the 1920's and 1930's during the heyday of Kemalism, and in various public interviews each one declared that he had participated in the revolution to put the reforms of Atatürk back on the tracks. Most of them at the time of the coup held key posts: martial law commander in Istanbul; commander of the division controlling Ankara; commandant of the Ankara Military Academy; commander of the co-ordination section of the NATO armed forces; commander of the regiment guarding the president, the prime minister, and the cabinet; chief of the staff branch assigning generals and staff officers to their posts; and commanders of the armored forces in Ankara and Istanbul. None came from a prominent family. Each one represented himself, and as the weeks and months passed their unity of action was fractured. Each spoke his own mind in public addresses and differences of opinion were allowed. The longer these officers held political power, the more they were forced to depend upon other soldiers behind them for their real power. By the summer of 1961 the council of the army, a secret group of about 200 officers including General Cevdet Sunay, Chief of the General Staff, was most influential with the NUC and General Sunay even met regularly with the NUC.

The day after the coup the NUC appointed an eighteen-man cabinet, fifteen of whom had not been identified with any political party. Another general was subsequently added and a reshuffling occurred three months later, but only four army officers were included. In June, a Provisional Constitution was promulgated. In addition to providing for a head of state, commander-in-chief, and the cabinet, it empowered the NUC to supervise cabinet ministers at all times or to fire them. Laws were proposed by the cabinet or by members of the NUC, approved by the NUC, and decreed by the Head of State within ten days; a four-fifths vote of the NUC would override a veto. In July, 1960 after the cabinet had singled out many affairs which needed attention, the NUC announced the government's program to balance the budget and end inflation, to free imports and exports of all controls, to devise a constitution on a democratic basis following the United Nations Charter, to reorganize state enterprises and gain entry into the European Common Market, to improve education and health, to undertake land reform, to restrict public works to need only, and to establish a nonpartisan administrative force in government. There was something for everyone in this program.

To reorient the government was a large order, but to reform the armed services was a task more understandable. On August 3, 235 generals and admirals were retired; the next day between 3,000 and 5,000 colonels and majors were retired with two years' severance pay and a full pension. One NUC general, who was sixty-two, put himself on the list as an example of the rejuvenation of the army, certainly a prime motive in the mass retirement. However, it was also apparent that a great many conservative and pro-Menderes officers had been specifically included. There was no public pressure to have this order rescinded, but in October when 147 university professors were ousted there was a loud outcry. How this list was prepared has remained a mystery. A few were fired because they were politically reactionary; some, because they had had violent arguments with those in power; others, because someone disliked them; many, because they were classed as unfit to hold their positions; and all, because the NUC voted them out. In time the various university senates reviewed each case and many were reinstated.

These two actions of mass dismissal were symptomatic of organic changes within the NUC. There was a division arising with one group under the leadership of Colonel Alpaslan Türkeş who for the first four months of the NUC regime was chief secretary to General Gürsel. Türkeş advocated pushing through the entire program of the revolution forcefully and quickly. It was asserted that he was behind the firing of the 147 university professors. Heated quarrels within the NUC in order to reach any decision were the rule, and in November wrangling ended in physical attacks over the establishment of a governmental Cultural Union to oversee all intellectual life in Turkey. Coupled with the known desire of the Türkeş radicals to postpone indefinitely the elections and the return of the government to civilian rule, this proposal raised the specter of dictatorship. In the pre-dawn hours of November 13, 1960 fourteen members of the NUC received messages of their dismissal and were ordered not to leave their homes. In a few days all fourteen were sent abroad as counselors of embassies; Türkeş was sent to New Delhi. Since one member of the NUC had been killed in an accident, there remained twenty-three.

Seven Istanbul University professors, headed by university president Onar, professor of administrative law, who had been injured by the police during the student demonstrations, were flown to Ankara the morning of the coup and at noon were commissioned by Gürsel to draft a new constitution within a few weeks' time. Later three younger professors from the Ankara University Faculty of Political Sciences and Faculty of Law were added. Not until October was the Onar constitution submitted to the NUC and by that time fights within the commission, considerable public debate, and a remarkable series of constitution seminars, organized by the Ankara faculty and attended by politicians, journalists, and many members of the NUC, had produced feelings that a Constituent Assembly was needed. On January 6, 1961 this Assembly was convened in two houses: the Senate, made up of the NUC; and a 272-member House of Representatives elected from the provinces, the People's Republican and the Republican Nation parties, and such groups as university faculties, the press, the judiciary, teachers, trade associations, labor groups, and forty-four appointed by General Gürsel and the NUC. Members of the People's Republican party dominated the Assembly. The Onar constitution was shelved as too legalistic and detailed in nature, and a twenty-man committee of the House was selected to draft a new constitution. Under the able chairmanship of Enver Ziya Karal, professor of the history of Turkish revolution at Ankara University, a more political document was produced. The Karal Constitution was accepted by the Constituent Assembly on May 27, 1961, the anniversary of the coup. In July a national referendum approved it by a sixty-two percent vote, with eighty-three percent of the electorate participating. That such a large number cast a negative ballot was fair warning that many voters still gave their devotion to Menderes.

From the autumn of 1960 until the end of the summer of 1961, the attention of the nation was in large part focused on Yassi Island in the Sea of Marmara where Bayar, Menderes, the cabinet, governors, police officers, and the Democrat members of the Grand National Assembly, 592 defendants in all, were being tried. The NUC chose a 31-member High Investigation Commission, a nine-judge tribunal, and a team of prosecutors. Chief Judge Salim Başol showed considerable fairness and moved much too slowly for many perpetrators of the coup. Fat dossiers were compiled for each case, and the prosecutors strove to show violations of law and the Constitution, personal use of state funds, acts bordering on treason, and a great variety of peccadilloes in an attempt to obtain convictions or at least to destroy these politicians in the eyes of the nation. The trials were not very successful, as the vote on the Constitution showed. The trials were filmed and broadcast, the Yassi Hour became popular, and Menderes was not permitted to be forgotten. Many came to believe the tale that each night he mounted his white horse and rode over the water to pray at a famous mosque on the Golden Horn! Most of those who had voted Democratic in the past three parliamental elections were unconvinced by these trials, regarded the charges as trumped up, and the evidence as fraudulent. The trials closed in September, 1961 with 15 receiving the death sentence, 31 were given life imprisonment, and 133 were acquitted. Prime Minister Menderes, Foreign Minister Zorlu, and Finance Minister Polatkan were hanged, but President Bayar's death sentence, because of his age and poor health, was commuted to life imprisonment.

On October 15, 1961, about a month after the hangings, the electorate went to the polls to choose 150 senators and 450 members of the assembly. The Constitution provided for a two-house parliament—in addition to the elected senators, the president of the Republic could appoint fifteen and the remaining 22 (one refused) members of the NUC were given life membership. The two houses meeting together as the Grand National Assembly would elect a president for a seven-year term. Upon the successful referendum on the Constitution political parties expanded their activities. Ismet Inönü, as the respected leader of the People's Republican party, expected to win a majority in each house and thus to become the new Prime Minister of the nation. Since the Democrat party had been outlawed two new parties were formed with the hope of attracting former Bayar-Menderes followers. The Justice party under General Ragib Gümüşpala selected its name to signify the need to assure justice to the former national political leaders and openly asked for Democrat votes. The New Turkey party under Ekrem Alican pitched its campaign to attract intellectuals who had been Democrats in 1950 but who had withdrawn from the party after the election of 1954. The fourth party to contest the election was the Republican Peasants' Nation party which had been a minor conservative party since 1946; in 1961 under the new direction of Osman Bölükbaşi it hoped to profit from the military turn of events. The election was orderly, perhaps because the NUC had insisted that it should be conducted without incident.

Over eighty-one percent of the electorate voted. In the Senate the division by majority vote was: Justice, 70 seats; People's Republican, 36; New Turkey, 28; and the Nation, 16. For the Assembly where there was proportional representation the count was: People's Republican, 173 seats; Justice, 158; New Turkey, 65; and the Nation, 54. In the popular vote, the People's Republican party won about the same number of votes it had in the elections of 1950, 1954, and 1957, and no one could deny that the Justice party had inherited most of Menderes' votes. His trial lawyer at Yassi Island was elected to the Assembly as a Justice party candidate as was the widow of the last Democrat Minister of the Interior who had committed suicide while awaiting trial. No party held a majority in either house so that there was no question over the election of Cemal Gürsel as president on October 26, 1961, by the Grand National Assembly. He promptly resigned from the army and was sworn in as fourth president of the Turkish Republic.

THE SECOND TURKISH REPUBLIC

President Gürsel's first obligation was to appoint the Prime Minister, but a corollary to this task was to find someone who could form a cabinet that would obtain the support of the House of Representatives (Assembly). The election showed that a coalition was the only choice.

Gürsel picked Inönü as the most likely to succeed as prime minister under such conditions. The situation insured that no drastic policies or measures would be adopted but also made any action difficult. After political maneuvering for two weeks Inönü induced the Justice party to join with his People's Republicans in forming a coalition cabinet in which each party held eleven posts, although the major ones were occupied by his party. In the Justice party program one of its major attractions was an implied pledge to obtain amnesty and release of Democrat political figures held since the day of the coup in 1960. Inönü discovered that an amnesty for Bayar and all of the others was a daily plea of Justice leaders, making extremely difficult the formation of a progressive and positive program by the cabinet or the Assembly to which it was responsible. In the first months little was accomplished, and critics openly challenged Inönü's regime to act or resign. In February, 1962 nearly seventy officers led by Colonel Talat Aydemir, Commandant of the Ankara Military Academy, staged a revolt to overthrow Inönü but it was easily suppressed. The officers were gently retired from the forces and placed under house arrest. In May, when a bill granting amnesty to these officers was passed by the Assembly, the Justice party demanded that the bill be expanded to include imprisoned Democrats. They withdrew from the coalition, but Inönü was able to form a new cabinet with the support of the New Turkey and Republican Peasants' Nation parties.

Early in 1963 a law was approved granting amnesty to many Democrats, and Bayar was freed for six months for medical treatments. Massive demonstrations against his release occurred in Istanbul, Ankara, and Izmir so that Bayar was placed under protective custody in a hospital. Justice leaders accused the Republicans of having fomented these protests, and the tension touched off another attempted army coup in May, again led by Colonel Aydemir. This was more serious than that of the previous year; he and six others were sentenced to death, and about 1,500 War College cadets and 150 officers were implicated. These incidents, coupled with a general economic stagnation that extended well into 1963, brought a reaction favorable to the Justice party which then won 65 percent of the popular vote in local elections in November and carried victories in 42 of Turkey's 67 provinces. Consequently, Inönü was deserted by his allies in the coalition and resigned. President Gürsel invited Ragib Gümüşpala, the Justice leader, to form a cabinet. But, on the latter's inability to find a majority, Inönü put together a third cabinet by obtaining the support of the independents in the Assembly, and a vote of confidence of 225 to 175.

Massive loans from the United States and other NATO nations, from a Consortium for Aid to Turkey which was composed of her eleven major European trading partners, from the European Investment Bank, and from the International Monetary Fund created a forward surge in Turkish economic conditions in 1963 and fine harvests of wheat, cotton, and tobacco gave Inönü a base on which to hope for a successful administration. During and after the Cuban crisis of October, 1962 Turkey had rejected proposals that NATO missile bases be dismantled. How real those refusals were cannot be determined for in April, 1963 Turkey announced the abandoning of her Jupiter missile bases and the return of all nuclear warheads to the United States. Relations with the U.S.S.R. eased and in July Khrushchev informed Turkey that there was no need to change the regulations governing the Straits as Stalin had wrongly demanded in 1946.

Turkey's policies, nevertheless, continued to look westward and declarations for American friendship persisted. The new and extensive five-year development plan was enacted in 1963 and called for governmental expenditures of two billion dollars and private investments of more than four billion dollars to increase the gross national product by 40 percent. Whatever chances Inönü had to continue maintaining the People's Republican party in office were ruined by the affairs in Cyprus in 1964. Grievances of the Turkish Cypriot minority incensed the Turkish nation; many Turks felt that their government had the right to intervene overtly and blamed Inönü for being soft and too subservient to American exactions. He was condemned for going to Washington when Johnson called; his support in the Assembly on Cyprus was a narrow 200 to 194 with several abstentions. In the opening weeks of 1965 Süleyman Demirel, who had become the new Justice leader on the death of Gümüşpala, announced a campaign to take over the government. On February 13, 1965 the budget bill was defeated 225 to 197, the cabinet resigned, and President Gürsel invited Senator Suat Hayri Ürgüplü to become prime minister and form a cabinet. He was an independent and was to serve as the head of a caretaker government until the October 10 elections for the Assembly. However, Demirel was appointed his deputy and ten Justice men were in the cabinet. Demirel declared the Justice party wanted to prove to the military and to the voters that it could govern peacefully and successfully.

According to the Electoral Law, primaries in eligible parties for the 450 Assembly seats are held forty-two days before the election; official campaigning among the parties is not allowed until two weeks before the election and lasts for only ten days, permitting a four-day respite until the day of balloting. Elections for the six-year Senate seats are staggered by having one-third elected every two years; the first Senate election was held in 1964 at which time Süleyman Demirel was too young to run for office, the minimum age requirement being 40 years. All through the spring and summer the campaigning accelerated and six distinct parties were engaged. Great interest was aroused and keen competition developed in the primaries for places on the party tickets. Over 1,100 candidates in the Justice party contested for the 450 places. Demirel pledged support of the May 27, 1960 coup and its six-point program and advocated continued alliance with the United States and NATO, an understanding of Russia, and an honorable settlement of the Cyprus problem. He emphasized questions concerning domestic affairs, and called for an orderly and progressive advance in industry, agriculture, and education. Cleverly, he adopted a gray horse as the party symbol, plainly bidding for those still loyal to Menderes and his "white horse." Inönü, as the People's Republican leader and eighty-one years old, appealed to those in governmental circles, the older established families, dedicated Kemalists, army officers, and many intellectuals to return his party to office. As the campaign progressed, he turned more toward the U.S.S.R. and asserted that his party was neither an American stooge nor a capitalistic pawn and was, in fact, somewhat left of center. Ekrem Alican and the New Turkey party struggled to find a middle course between socialism and capitalism but his suggestions for a mixed economy fell on sterile soil. Former Colonel Alpaslan Türkeş and some of his army friends took over the Republican Peasants' Nation party at a party caucus early in 1965; in the campaign he stressed the need for scientific planning for the most effective development of the nation's resources and stated that private enterprise should be clearly limited in its activities. That party's former leader, Osman Bölükbaşi, formed a new Nation party, opposing all leftist tendencies and maintaining all of the more conservative traditions of Turkish society. On the left of all these, Mehmet Ali Aybar established the Labor party which contended that land reform should be immediate; that foreign trade, banking, and insurance be nationalized; and that all industry be conducted solely by the state.

In spite of acute differences, the election was held in an orderly manner. Only 60 percent of the electorate exercised their rights, and as the returns came in it was apparent that perhaps a million of Inönü's party had remained at home rather than vote left of center. The Justice party won 240 seats and a clear majority; the People's Republicans garnered 134; and the new Labor party won only 15. President Gürsel invited Demirel to form a new government; within a few days an entire Justice cabinet was announced and was given a vote of confidence by the Assembly.

The dire predictions concerning the advent to power of the Justice party were unfounded. Prime Minister Demirel steered a middle course between East and West. Soviet Premier Kosygin visited Turkey in 1966, and his call for the withdrawal of all foreign troops from Cyprus was well received. Many nationals from Western Europe and the United States entered into industrial and economic ventures in Turkey, and Demirel initiated the construction of the Keban Dam, 670 feet high, on the Euphrates River, to be completed by 1970. In March, 1966 President Gürsel, who had been in a coma for some weeks, was declared incapable of carrying out his duties. In his place, General Cevdet Sunay, conveniently appointed to the Senate, was elected as the fifth president of Turkey. Senate elections in June, 1966 brought the Justice party 56 percent of the popular vote, indicating general approval of Demirel's conduct. The People's Republican party had not given up hope, as was shown in its partial rejuvenation by the election of Bulent Ecevit, a vigorous young member of the Assembly who had been minister of labor from 1961 to 1964, as secretary general and leader of the party. Since Ecevit and Demirel were American-educated, the vocal anti-American forces may gravitate to the other parties.

ECONOMIC PROGRESS

In 1944 Turkey severed economic relations with Germany on the understanding that the Western Allies would not permit her economy to founder. She based her fears of economic collapse on the knowledge that she would no longer sell quantities of goods to Germany and that the Allies would cease their preclusive buying programs. However, no decline was apparent; and inflation forced prices upward. The continued unbalanced budget over the next years maintained economic activity at a high level. With the vast American aid that began to flow in 1947 the economic development of Turkey progressed rapidly.

As soon as the curbs on the press were relaxed in 1945 discussion of private enterprise and criticism of the state monopolies and business appeared. The new Democratic party seized upon this discontent, and the Republican administration took steps to further private enterprise in many ways. One of the most important of these steps was support for the Industrial Development Bank of Turkey. This private bank, approved and aided by the government, set out to make funds available for private business and serve as a bridge between the needs of businessmen and the conservatively held savings of the ordinary Turk.

In the years after 1946 Turkish industry grew by leaps and bounds. The purchasing power of the peasants, who constituted the great majority of Turks, was sustained by the government at a high level, and suddenly the wants of the peasant burgeoned to an unprecedented degree. The total population of Turkey climbed to over 24 million by 1955, an increase of over 3 million from the 1950 census. New industries, in part founded by foreign capital in partnership with Turkish capital, were sprouting in all regions of the country. Yet, the expansion was not entirely healthy. Many accused Menderes of wasteful activities and found fault with his rapid rebuilding of parts of Istanbul; in fact when a building or house was summarily torn down, it was said to have been "Menderized." Still he forged ahead, planning a wondrous high-level bridge across the Bosphorus to link the highways of European and Asiatic Turkey. New dams were designed and opened; a plant to manufacture soda was accepted from the Soviet bloc; and a 1000-mile oil pipeline from Iran to Iskenderum was projected. His energies and ambition were indefatigable.

On the other hand, the Democratic party did not find it easy to dispose of state-owned enterprises, and long-range planning did not take into account many short-range problems. By the beginning of the second term of President Bayar in 1954 Turkish economy was in serious jeopardy. Foreign exchange was scarce; commercial payments abroad were months in arrears; and business obligations were mounting. The American government refused to grant a sizable loan on the basis that the Menderes cabinet ignored economic principles of sensible growth. Imports of many commodities such as coffee were strictly limited, and their scarcity created unfriendly attitudes toward the government. The Turkish pound, whose official rate was eighteen cents, fell to seven cents on the black market with repeated rumors of devaluation and repeated official denials. World oil companies threatened to discontinue petroleum shipments, unless past due bills were paid more promptly. Menderes appeared oblivious to difficulties and faced mounting inflation with increased activities. The national budget in 1957 reached $1,400,000,000 and passed $1,650,000,000 in 1958. A forty percent duty was levied on most imports; and thirty percent of the budget went for capital development, twenty-five percent for defense. Sizable trade agreements were negotiated with Yugoslavia, Czechoslovakia, and other Soviet bloc states which were particularly interested in Turkish tobacco. New sugar factories were built, and in 1957 the Krupp interests of West Germany agreed to invest over a billion marks in a new blast furnace which would add 800,000 tons of steel to Turkish production. Menderes' confidence in Turkey's future was boundless, even though the economy was passing through the kind of "growing pains" that Western economies experienced repeatedly in the nineteenth century. Perhaps his audacity sprang from the assurance that the United States would bail him out if conditions became serious. In 1958 grants and loans were obtained from the United States and Western Europe to prevent a collapse which would have injured NATO immeasurably and damaged American interests. As already indicated, however, the shock of the stabilization program was so severe that it was an important factor in bringing on the coup of 1960. Such a firm policy might have produced the desired results in a better developed economy, but in Turkey an expansion and growth of unlimited dimensions seemed both warranted and needed. Menderes found an increasing majority of Turks clamoring for "an ever larger share of the national product for immediate consumption," and after he was gone the NUC and the leaders of the Second Republic experienced the same public pressures. When the coup occurred the policies of credit restriction had been loosened and credit eased again in 1962 with the re-establishment of civilian rule. The great difficulty with Menderes, however, was his inability to oppose any project for development or improvement. He refused to plan since that might prohibit the inclusion of a new unplanned project, and budgets for him thwarted his freedom for economic activity. Consequently the stabilization program was unselective and constantly side-stepped.

When the NUC took over, the Menderes regime was branded as economically incompetent and dishonest. The highly-touted balanced budgets from 1950 to 1960 were shown to have resulted from legerdemain, and the total deficit for those years amounted to $236 million. Although this was quite modest in comparison to most governments in the world, it seemed enormous to the average Turk. At the same time it was revealed that the total public debt was over $1 billion and the nation's foreign debt stood at $965 million, a sum so vast that it crushed any hope for solvency and posed an intolerable burden on future foreign exchange earnings. These findings led many businessmen, even those who had profited from and strongly supported Democrat policies, to acquiesce to the NUC restrictions and to appreciate the attempts of Inönü and Demirel to proceed with economic plans and an orderly development.

Nevertheless, the foreign debt continued to grow and by 1966 stood at approximately $2,414,000,000, taking about forty percent of foreign earnings to service the debt. The gross national product, however, increased markedly during these years, from $6 billion at the time of the coup to over $9 billion by 1967. The list of new enterprises was never ending. By the end of 1962 all domestic needs for refined petroleum could be met by Turkish refineries and prospecting for oil in various sections of the country and off shore had brought in new producing areas to the point where it was expected that Turkey within a few years might become self-sufficient in regard to power. In 1965 a second steel plant went into operation with a large yearly saving in foreign-exchange expenditures. Hopes of joining with the European Economic Community were satisfied in 1964 when Turkey became an associate member with the prospect of forming a full customs union with members within seventeen years. Turkey began earnestly in 1964 to seek European tourists to visit her beaches, to view her treasure of antiquities, to explore her cities and countryside, and to bring in large amounts of foreign exchange. To attract these tourists, roads, hotels, transportation, and numerous other services had to be furnished, facilities which in the end would also transform the Turkish economy and social fabric. Similarly, 200,000 Turkish workers in Western Europe in 1965 remitted more than $100,000,000 in foreign exchange to their families at home. The money contributed greatly to the Turkish economy but the skills and ways-of-life which were acquired and eventually returned to Turkey were even more important than were French francs or German marks. The Turkish economy was showing signs by the mid-1960's of reaching a take-off point where it might sustain itself. Many felt that this fact alone justified the 1960 coup, while Menderes' apologists contended that the extraordinary economic activities and innovations of the controversial 1950's were only now bearing their promised and expected fruition. Since Turkey remained an agricultural country, the solution of her financial problems rested upon the production of wheat, cotton, tobacco, fruits, and nuts in exportable quantities perhaps more than upon the development of natural resources and industrial advance.

AGRICULTURE

The answer rested upon the attitude of the Turkish farmers. In the days of Atatürk the government patronized the peasants and never imposed taxes on farm income. The fact that no change was made was largely responsible for the unbalanced budget and to some degree for the ills of the economy. The government established a soil office, which bought grain, tobacco, and other farm produce at established prices, frequently above world prices. Production was stimulated; and after the road-building program opened up many new areas in Anatolia and greatly reduced the costs of transportation, the quantities of wheat delivered to the soil office soared. This program, coupled with bountiful rains and the importation of tractors, plows, and harvesters, led in 1952 to an exportable surplus of one and one half million tons of wheat. Cotton culture advanced in the Adana plain; markets were excellent for tobacco; and new areas were opened for the growing of sugar beets to supply Turkey's fifteen sugar refineries. In the six years from 1951 to 1956 Turkey exported over sixteen million tons of grain for an income of $550,000,000, whereas thirty years earlier with a considerably smaller population Turkey was forced to import grain and flour. Part of this surge in agricultural production may have resulted from the land-distribution programs which, though approved earlier, were first implemented in 1945 and pushed only after 1950. Almost five million acres of land were distributed among 200,000 peasant families. Unfortunately, droughts in 1956 and 1957 were instrumental in changing the wheat surpluses to deficits, and in each of these years over 600,000 tons of wheat were obtained through American aid grants. To stimulate greater production higher prices were set for wheat in 1957, although a scarcity of consumer goods and other price controls deterred the farmer from bringing his crops to market. However, as long as rates of exchange between Turkish pounds and hard currencies of the world remained unrealistic in regard to purchasing power, the extent of exportable farm surpluses in Turkey depended upon the amount of governmental price supports. The devaluation in 1958 sought to offset the effect of Turkish inflation which had forced the American tobacco companies to curtail their purchases in Turkish markets.

The well-being of the agricultural society in Anatolia and its staunch support of the Democratic party were significant factors in the strength of Adnan Menderes after 1954. Although crises in foreign trade and in finance shook the faith of the larger cities in his leadership, his following in the rural provinces enabled him to enact restrictive press laws silencing his urban critics without offending his peasant friends, who re-elected him in 1954 and again in 1957. Thus, the leaders of the coup in 1960 had to treat the agricultural sector of the economy most carefully. A policy of land reform was included in the initial program proposed by the NUC and agricultural investments have held a high priority, especially under Justice party rule. For the first time an income tax was levied on agricultural incomes in 1961, but this touched the wealthier farmers and the largest producers whose tax-free incomes under Menderes had been under attack by economists and merchants. Improved conditions lifted annual exports of cotton and tobacco to $100,000,000 each in 1965, and agriculture accounted for eighty-five percent of total exports and about forty percent of the gross national product. New dams and irrigation systems with expanded production of fertilizers and farm machinery continue to increase the total output and enable agriculture to maintain its position in relation to both the earnings of foreign exchange and the gross national product.

RELIGION AND EDUCATION

One of the greatest changes in Turkey related to the advance of democracy could be seen in fields of religion and education. The rural population never really subscribed to Atatürk's program on the de-emphasis of Islam. As soon as the peasant had a voice in affairs, he insisted that religion be restored to some semblance of its former position in society, although he did not insist that the separation of state and religion be undone. Many serious-minded leaders regarded that much of value would be gained by reinstating the spiritual and ethical values of Islam, and religious instruction in schools was permitted by lay teachers. In 1949 the College of Theology, which had been closed at the University of Istanbul by Atatürk, was reopened as a part of Ankara University and a new Institute of Islamic Studies was founded at the University of Istanbul. The study of the old script became possible; mausoleums of holy men and the caliphs were once again open to the public; a few new mosques were built; religious days of fasting and feasting were more widely observed; and the muezzin's call to prayer was again sounded in the traditional Arabic. Radio Ankara programed reading from the Koran, and attendance at the mosques increased noticeably. Likewise, in the schools a real awakening in the study of Ottoman history occurred. Atatürk, in order to escape the unhappy seventeenth- and eighteenth-century Ottoman history and strengthen Turkish nationalism, had hurdled all of Ottoman history and found glory for the Turks in earlier epochs. In Turkey after World War II the writings on early Ottoman history by Fuad Köprülü were rediscovered, and a more systematic and scholarly investigation into the origins of Ottoman institutions and the foundations of Turkish life in Asia Minor began. Higher education was advanced by the opening of Atatürk University in 1958 at Erzerum in the eastern section of Asia Minor and by the founding of the Middle East Technical University in Ankara. The flood of articles and monographs from the pens of Turkish students of science, social subjects, and the humanities presaged a flourishing intellectual development and the attainment of a more stable and balanced society.

It has been pointed out that traditional Islam entered politics when Inönü permitted a multiparty system in 1946. The Democratic party of Bayar and Menderes included in its program strong attractions for the conservative and simple Islam of the Anatolian villagers and was successful to a degree never possible for the heirs of Atatürk. The People's Republican party was never able to erase from the villagers' minds the formerly incessant Kemalist line that "they were primitive and nasty and superstitious" and that to participate in modern Turkey they would have to abandon their ancestral ways and become civilized. The Democrats built 15,000 mosques for them in ten years and subsidized Koran reciters for mosques in every village. On the other hand, of the 60,000 "men of religion" in the country barely eight percent had as much as a primary school education (five grades).

The educated and Westernized Turks, especially Republicans, deplored this "abuse of religion in order to win votes," and officers of the NUC cited this tactic as one of the most significant in moving them to revolt. They were particularly furious and at the same time ashamed of the Democratic use of Menderes' escape from the airplane crash in England in 1959. Every radio in the land blared forth the view that God had saved him to lead his country and henceforth a vote against Menderes was a vote against God. Moreover, when he returned to Istanbul over 100,000 loyal followers were at the airport to greet him; as he stepped from the craft a score of sheep had their throats cut so that the evil force that had sought Menderes' blood would be satiated. This ceremony was repeated twice before he reached his hotel, and reports and pictures of these demonstrations and rites were circulated to every village to the dismay of secularized Turks. With this kind of religio-politico campaigning, opponents felt helpless in front of the ballot box and abetted the coup.

Although the leaders of the People's Republican party and the NUC delivered scathing rebukes to Menderes for pursuing this policy, they were following a like practice within a short time—6,000 mosques were built between 1960 and 1964, and the NUC gave sizable sums to religious training schools. Contrarily, the NUC advocated the advancement of village education and sought to meet the ever difficult problem of teachers for the villages by changing the obligatory two-year military service as reserve officers for all *lycée* graduates to a like service as teachers in village elementary schools. In the 1965 elections the villagers voted for the Justice party candidates recognizing in them the heirs of the Democrats. When Inönü introduced the concept of left of center for his party, Justice campaigners equated this with atheistic Russian Communism. Turkish peasants have hated Russians for generations and to this has been added the word *Communist* which has replaced the word *infidel* as the common insult to hurl at opponents. The Justice party led them to believe "it would bring them peace and quiet and an end of nagging."

Modern Turks have looked upon their country as the bridge between the West and the Middle East and frequently objected to the inclusion of Turkey in the concept of the term "Middle East." Turkish leaders in 1953, at the time of the celebrations of the five-hundredth anniversary of the Turkish capture of Constantinople, presented the thesis that the Ottoman occupation of the Balkans and the holding of the Straits, at a time when the peoples of Western Europe were disorganized and weak, had preserved Western Europe, the entire Mediterranean area, and Western civilization from the inroads and destruction from the barbarians of the East. In the minds of Turkish leaders NATO and CENTO were the logical continuations of this age-old role of Western Turks.

REFERENCES: Chapter 36

Additional references for this chapter are found in Chapters 7, 12, 23, 30, 31, 35, and 41.

Firouz Bahrampour, *Turkey: Political and Social Transformation:* Theo. Gaus' Sons, Brooklyn, 1967.

Nuri Eren, *Turkey Today—and Tomorrow: An Experiment in Westernization:* Praeger, New York, 1963. An interesting analysis by a Turkish diplomat.

Sydney Nettleton Fisher, ed., *The Military in the Middle East: Problems in Society and Government:* Ohio State University Press, Columbus, 1963. Six main essays by different authors on six countries.

Frederick W. Frey, *The Turkish Political Elite:* Massachusetts Institute of Technology Press, Cambridge, 1965.

George M. Haddad, *Revolutions and Military Rule in the Middle East: The Northern Tier:* Robert Speller & Sons, New York, 1965.

Kemal Karpat, *Turkey's Politics, The Transition to a Multi-Party System:* Princeton University Press, Princeton, 1959. A very solid and scholarly work.

Lord Kinross (Patrick Balfour), *Within the Taurus:* J. Murray, London, 1955. A trip across Asia Minor.

Bernard Lewis, *The Emergence of Modern Turkey:* Oxford University Press, London, 1961. A first-rate account of the development of Turkey in the nineteenth century under Kemal, and an analysis of the decade of the 1950's.

Geoffrey Lewis, *Turkey:* Praeger, New York, 1960. A standard work.

Mahmut Makal, *A Village in Anatolia* (Wyndham Deedes, trans.): Valentine, Mitchell, London, 1954. An important insight into village life in Asia Minor by one who grew up in such a village.

Richard D. Robinson, *The First Turkish Republic: A Case Study in National Development:* Harvard University Press, Cambridge, 1963. A judicious apologia for the Menderes regime.

Arthur Paul Stirling, *Turkish Village:* Weidenfeld and Nicolson, London, 1965.

Walter F. Weiker, *The Turkish Revolution, 1960–1961: Aspects of Military Politics:* The Brookings Institution, Washington, 1963. A detailed account of the military government, and a discussion of the participants, their policies, and aspirations.

CHAPTER 37

Iran—Nationalism Versus Imperialism

U.S.S.R. AND AZERBAYJAN

The treaty of alliance signed on January 29, 1942 by Great Britain, the U.S.S.R., and Iran provided that Allied forces would be withdrawn from Iran within six months after an armistice with Germany and her associates. Again in 1943 at the Tehran Conference, Roosevelt, Stalin, and Churchill signed on behalf of their governments a statement, suggested by Loy Henderson, United States ambassador to Iran, that they desired to maintain "the independence, sovereignty, and territorial integrity of Iran" and that Iran's economic problems would receive their full consideration.

Signature of the armistice with Japan on September 2, 1945 inaugurated the six-month period and encouraged Iranian nationalists to look forward to March, 1946 as a month when all foreign troops would be evacuated. Their high hopes were soon dashed; for in December the Soviets engineered and supported a Communist revolution in Tabriz. Although the Communist Tudeh party had been dissolved in Azerbayjan, a new Azerbayjan Democrat party under the leadership of Comintern agent Jafar Pishavari established the autonomous Republic of Azerbayjan. During the war this province was under complete Russian control, and Tehran officials of the Iranian government were even denied entry there. Taxes could not be collected, and local officials usually discovered that orders from Tudeh party leaders carried more authority than their own.

Almost immediately government troops were sent from Tehran to quell the rebellion, but Soviet troops blocked the roads with Sherman tanks. Open interference by the U.S.S.R. was charged by Iran, and in January, 1946 an appeal was made to the United Nations. Russia pursued delaying tactics there, evidently hoping to bring additional troops into Iran and in the end present the West with an accomplished deed. A week later the Iranian parliament by a margin of only one vote chose Ahmad Qavam as the new prime minister; and the Western press assumed that Iran was on her way behind the Iron Curtain, since Qavam had befriended the Tudeh party in 1943. In February, however, Qavam visited Moscow and returned with the announcement that his mission had been fruitless.

March 2, 1946 passed without any sign of the withdrawal of Soviet troops. The American troops had gone before January 1 and the British left in February. But additional strength for the Russians entered Iran in March, and the cold war began.

The shrewd and patriotic Qavam proved too skillful for the Soviets to manage. He simulated Communist sympathies and held out great hopes for steering Iran into the Soviet bloc, but always escaped at the last minute from the Russian embrace.

Qavam's first task was to cajole the Russians into removing their troops. He played into the hands of Tudeh party leaders in Tehran, giving their newspapers free rein and encouraging them to hold mass demonstrations in front of the parliament building to prevent parliament from meeting and thus ensure its automatic and legal termination. This allowed Qavam to rule by decree until a new parliament would be elected. Qavam closed down anti-Soviet newspapers and arrested rightist political and army leaders. Meanwhile the Iranian ambassador to the United States, Husayn Ala, laid a complaint before the Security Council of the United Nations and pursued a vigorous policy to secure Soviet withdrawal.

At the Security Council Gromyko walked out as a stalling device to gain time for a bilateral settlement in Tehran. Stalin evidently decided, in the face of strong British and American statements in support of Iran's case and the new world publicity flowing from the United Nations' first large problem, not to use force in Iran. On March 24 Russia announced that evacuation would begin immediately and be completed in five or six weeks. As a part of the bargain Qavam agreed to allow an autonomous regime in Azerbayjan and to form a Soviet-Iranian Oil Company, fifty-one percent Soviet-owned, to exploit oil in northern Iran. Since Stalin did not favor public discussion of his bargain, Qavam pressed for Security Council consideration and thereby obtained an admission from Russia that Azerbayjan was an internal Iranian problem with which the Tehran government would deal "benevolently." Qavam received Azerbayjani Communist leaders in Tehran and appointed one who had been educated in Russia as Iranian governor-general in Tabriz.

Feeling that Iran was in the bag, Russian troops departed on May 6, 1946. Qavam played his cards well. The Tudeh party and Azerbayjan Democrats held monstrous demonstrations in Tehran, and a vociferous attack was launched against the Anglo-Iranian Oil Company. Three Tudeh members and a notorious fellow-traveler were included in August in a new Qavam coalition cabinet, composed of Qavam's new Iran Democrats, the Tudeh party, Azerbayjan Democrats, the Socialist party, and two other left-wing groups. The Soviet position reached its high point; and to the world at large it appeared that Iran had been won by Russia, since the process that proved so successful in eastern Europe and the Balkans seemed well advanced in Iran.

However, Qavam may have been cautiously leading the Russians into a trap. He talked of reform, undoubtedly quite sincerely. Yet Russians and the Tudeh party could hardly work against the rapid growth and popularity of a reforming Iran Democrat party, which by the end of the summer had political control and could dominate any forthcoming election for parliament.

At this point Qavam may have overplayed his hand; for the young Shah called him in and demanded his resignation, informing him that the army agreed to support the Shah if trouble occurred. Qavam pledged his loyalty to the Shah and was reinstated on promises to fire the three Tudeh members of the cabinet (commerce, education, and health), liquidate the autonomous Azerbayjan province, and organize a real party to face Tudeh. Parades and demonstrations of Qavam's Iran Democrats suddenly outshone those of the Tudeh party, and Qavam won the shah's support. He also won a majority for his party in the parliamentary elections which began in December.

Since he declared that elections in all provinces, including Fars and Azerbayjan, would be held under the supervision of government forces, the Soviets were presented with a difficult choice. Only if Qavam's Iran Democrats won the election could the new parliament be expected to vote an oil concession to the Soviet-controlled company. Only if an election were held could an oil concession be submitted to an Iranian parliament. But no national elections could be held so long as the Soviet-supported autonomous province of Azerbayjan existed. Tehran troops entered Azerbayjan in November, and fighting developed. United States Ambassador George V. Allen quickly declared that his government favored Iranian sovereignty and territorial integrity as provided for in the United Nations Charter and adhered to the principle that it was entirely normal and proper for the Iranian government to send its security forces into the provinces to preserve order during elections. Since Russia did not wish to send in troops, she stood by and witnessed the collapse of the Communist regime in Azerbayjan, the leaders of which fled to the U.S.S.R. The Tudeh party in Tehran disintegrated and refused to participate in parliamentary elections.

Elections were held in a leisurely fashion throughout the country during the winter months. Qavam's coalition, without the Tudeh or the Azerbayjan Democrat party, won handily, although another coalition of opposing parties and 36 independent candidates led by Mohammad Mosaddeq protested Qavam's method of conducting the election. The shah opened the new parliament in July, 1947; and a few weeks later it gave to Qavam a vote of confidence (78 to 38). Almost immediately upon the convening of parliament the Soviets pressed for ratification of the oil concession to the Soviet-Iranian Oil Company which Qavam had initialed in the spring of 1946. Qavam, at this juncture, informed the Soviet ambassador that the oil agreement was unsatisfactory and that parliament could not be forced to adopt it in its present form. Russian reaction was sharp, and Qavam was accused of treacherously violating his agreement and returning to the policy of hostility and discrimination practiced by Shah Reza and previous reactionary governments.

The Iranian government took heart from the decisive stand and support of the United States. The Truman Doctrine with respect to Greece and Turkey was announced in March, 1947; and in the reorganization of the Department of State it was noted that a new division linked Iran with Greece and Turkey. Qavam's new cabinet included three graduates of the American College of Tehran, and the United States extended a military credit of $25,000,000. Princess Ashraf, the shah's twin sister, visited the United States; and General Norman Schwarzkopf, American adviser to the Iranian gendarmery, assisted in the establishment of order and governmental control in Azerbayjan.

As it became more apparent that parliament would rebuff the Soviets, the British became fearful that a categorical refusal would lead very naturally to difficulties over the Anglo-Iranian Oil Company concessions and possible nationalization. The English ambassador advised Qavam not to slam the door in the face of the Russians but to leave it somewhat ajar. However, Qavam had no real choice. Sentiment in parliament was inflamed; and Mosaddeq reminded Qavam of the law of 1944, sponsored by that fiery nationalist, forbidding an Iranian government from granting or even negotiating an oil concession with a foreign state without parliament's consent. In September,

Ambassador Allen, speaking before the Iranian-American Cultural Relations Society, reiterated American respect for Iranian sovereignty and said: "Iran's resources belong to Iran. Iran can give them away free of charge, or refuse to dispose of them at any price, if it so desires . . . The American people will support fully their [Iranians] freedom to make their own choice." With this public support and an agreement of the United States to send a military mission to raise the efficiency of the Iranian army, parliament on October 22, 1947 voted 102 to 2 to void Qavam's agreement with the U.S.S.R., exempt him from penalties of the 1944 law, and authorize the government to enter into negotiations to regain the national rights with respect to oil in areas where the British held concessions.

The U.S.S.R. fumed, hurled charges at Qavam, and stated that Russia would consider Iran a bitter blood enemy. But the crisis passed. Iranian leaders breathed easier; and Iranian politics returned to normal. At the same time Qavam's coalition evaporated. In December he failed on a vote of confidence; and within two weeks his parliamentary opponents accused him of embezzlement, ordering improper arrests, suppressing opposition newspapers, and governing by decree without parliamentary approval. He was arrested and allowed to go to Paris for "his health."

DEVELOPMENT PROGRAMS

Qavam's successor was his immediate predecessor, Ibrahim Hakimi. The new period was one of countless problems of reform and national organization.

Extreme nationalism aroused by the Soviet conflict stirred the urban populace of Iran, especially in Tehran. And the enthusiasm generated by discussion of oil concessions to the U.S.S.R. and the ringing Iranian patriotism expressed by the American ambassador boded ill for the Anglo-Iranian Oil Company.

Shortly after returning from the Tehran Conference, Roosevelt argued that Iran would be the ideal place to show the world what an unselfish American policy in the way of economic and technical assistance could do for a less favored friendly nation. When America supported Iran so staunchly in her stand against the Soviets, American prestige soared and Iranian leaders anticipated all manner of benefits and assistance. The needs were titanic and endless. Irrigation, agricultural methods, improved seeds and stock, tools, plows, machinery, land ownership, health and sanitation, education, industry, dams, electric power, and many other items were all recognized by thoughtful Iranians as pressing problems. American assistance in providing capital and technical and managerial know-how was most acceptable, because the United States seemed less imperialistic than other powers and was not associated with past struggles of Iran against Russia or England. Furthermore, many Iranians were impressed during World War II by American power and productive capacity.

In the 1930's Reza Shah developed plans for modernizing Iran. The war disrupted these plans completely; but they were not abandoned, and in 1946 Qavam gathered about fifty notables and experts to draw up at the shah's insistence a seven-year development plan for Iran. A commission with a planning board came forward with sketches for programs requiring nearly two billion dollars. Unhappily, the projects were hopelessly vague, extravagant, and unrealistic.

To reduce the plans to a scope practical for Iran's economy and stage of development the American Morrison-Knudsen International Company was given a contract in December, 1946. Its job was to survey the resources, needs, and possibilities and to propose a new plan. Its report of 320 pages was ready in 1947, and Qavam applied for a loan of $250 million from the International Bank. The new plan would cost $650 million, but was designed eventually to be self-sustaining. The bank asked for more data on the self-amortization of some projects, and an investigation by a consortium of engineering firms began in 1948. At the time American interest was centered upon Greece, Turkey, and western Europe; and Iran seemed remote. Moreover, an American grant of $25 million credit for military surplus purchases in 1947 was acted upon most dilatorily in Iran, and parliament did not approve it until February, 1948. Then, in July, the grant was reduced to $10,000,000 ($120,000,000 original cost); and no arms reached Iran until 1949.

Nevertheless, many Iranian leaders hoped to reform their country and in 1949 the engineering consortium (Overseas Consultants, Inc.) presented its final five-volume survey, whose projects parliament had already begun to implement by authorizing the seven-year development plan. This plan called for development of agriculture, industry, mines, oilfields, communications, transportation, education, health facilities, municipal reform, housing, and other operations for developing the country and improving living conditions of the people. The cost was set at $651,000,000, a sum to be realized from oil royalties and an International Bank loan.

FAILURE OF AMERICAN AID

Time passed, and nothing happened. Truman launched the Point Four Program in 1949, and there was considerable talk in Iran about aid from the United States under that project and in arms credits and grants under the Mutual Defense Assistance Act. Although American leaders were sympathetic to Iranian needs, there was a very general feeling that Iranian politics were unstable and that funds, either loans or gifts, would be largely wasted and lost. Cabinets came and went in Tehran. Hakimi, who had followed Qavam, was out in June, 1948. His successor, Abd al-Husayn Hazhir, resigned in November; Mohammad Said Maraghay lasted until March, 1950. Ali Mansur remained in office until June, when the shah appointed General Ali Razmara. Upon the latter's assassination in March, 1951, Husayn Ala held the prime ministership for a month. On April 28, 1951 Mohammad Mosaddeq ushered in a new period of Iranian development.

In 1949 the shah decided to take a hand in obtaining aid and accepted an invitation to visit the United States. For six weeks he observed, talked, and listened. When he left in December, a joint statement was issued by the shah and President Truman that the United States would support the Iranian application for an International Bank loan and would aid Iran under the Point Four Program. The shah, on his part, stated that Iran would welcome such assistance and that he hoped for increased investment of private capital in the Iranian economy. He promised that appropriate measures would be taken to encourage such investment.

Upon the shah's return he gave enthusiastic support to reform. A new American ambassador, Henry F. Grady, arrived in June and gave Iranians great hope for transforming the continual promises and statements about aid into reality. An anticorruption commission was appointed to ferret out, publicize, and punish corruption in government, but conditions grew even worse. Then, the outbreak of the Korean War ended any hope in Iran of obtaining American aid; and a deputy in parliament formally asked the government to explain why Iran should "bother" anymore with the United States. At this point $500,000 was made available for Point Four work in Iran and the Export-Import Bank authorized a $25,000,000 loan. The shah announced that a program of land reform in Iran was being inaugurated by splitting up his royal estates into small farms which would be sold to peasant operators on long-term installment payments. But developments moved slowly, and other landowners failed to follow suit. Also, it became obvious that the seven-year development plan was dead.

The economic situation in Iran floundered seriously, and only a powerful remedy could avert a crisis. The end of World War II and evacuation of foreign troops had halted a sizable influx of foreign exchange, and a general decline in world trade in 1948 and 1949 depressed Iranian economy still further. Receipts from oil payments slumped under the administration of the British Labour party because of its general restrictions upon dividend payments. In the first three

months of 1950 Tehran reported thirty-five major bankruptcies; and
Husayn Ala, the foreign minister, declared that American assistance
was most urgent. Although the deterioration threatened a collapse of
the government and likely victory for a resurging Tudeh force, the
governing upper class appeared supremely indifferent. Corruption
continued unabated; land reform was quietly opposed; the wealthy
and influential ignored their income taxes; and prestige politics remained the sport of the great landowners. Pressures, however, developed to reconsider the concessions held by the Anglo-Iranian Oil
Company as commanded by parliament in 1947.

OIL PROBLEMS

Ever since 1940 voices were raised over the question of oil concessions and in particular with respect to royalties. In 1944 Mosaddeq,
almost singlehanded, pushed through parliament the law forbidding
further oil concessions or even their discussion with foreigners. Following the resolution of 1947, cabinet leaders started to consider the
position of the Anglo-Iranian Oil Company and the income from oil.
The income was never enough and did not compare favorably with
receipts of certain Latin American countries. As finances grew desperate and American aid did not materialize, eyes turned more and more
toward the prospering Anglo-Iranian Oil Company which had every
appearance of possessing greater wealth and income than the Iranian
government.

For the public the oil crisis began June 1, 1948, when the Company
announced that payments would remain the same as in 1947, even
though the Company's net profit after taxation jumped from $26,880,000
in 1947 to $52,080,000 in 1948. In 1947 the Iranian government
received $19,880,000 in royalties and taxation, whereas the British
government received $56,000,000 directly in dividends and taxation.
When these figures were presented to the Iranian public, the outcry
was sharp. Then the announcement followed that the British government was limiting dividends, which according to the royalty formula
would keep payments at the 1947 level.

Another galling feature of the old 1933 agreement was a stipulation
that petroleum would be sold in Iran at ten percent below world
prices. Since such prices were computed by adding to Gulf of Mexico
oil prices the costs of transportation from Texas to the Persian Gulf,
the Iranian public felt that, even with ten percent discount, schedules
were unreasonable, particularly since the Company sold oil to the
British navy at a still lower price. In addition to the benefits received
by the British navy, the Iranian public believed that substantial profits
were concealed by the practice of selling petroleum products cheaply

to affiliated concerns. In this way higher profits would flow to stockholders, but would not be reflected in higher royalties to Iran.

In view of the dissatisfaction in Iran, officials of the Anglo-Iranian Oil Company visited Tehran in the summer of 1948 and received a twenty-five-point memorandum from Prime Minister Hazhir asking for an agreement similar to that which Venezuela had with American companies. In particular, this meant fifty percent of the Company's profits. Furthermore, employment of fewer foreigners and training more Iranians for technical and managerial positions in the Company were demanded. Prime Minister Maraghay pursued the same policy and informed the Company negotiators that a fifty-fifty sharing of profits was being discussed at that moment in Saudi Arabia by the Arabian-American Oil Company.

After considerable delay an agreement was signed in 1949 by the Company and the Iranian government. This Gass-Golshayan agreement, better known as the supplementary agreement, increased the discount on oil sales in Iran to the same figure given to the British navy and arranged the payments to double those stipulated in the old 1933 schedules. However, for prosperous years such as 1947, 1948, and 1949 the payments fell short of fifty percent. In lean years, as the Company pointed out, they might be better than that. Just at that time the Company's 1948 report was published, showing that Britain received $79,240,000 in taxes and Iran $37,800,000 in royalties. The uproar was deafening. One of Mosaddeq's henchmen in the parliament filibustered, and the parliament ended without any action being taken upon the agreement.

When the new parliament met in 1950 the question of the agreement fell to a newly created oil committee of the parliament. Headed by Mosaddeq, who now led a National Front party with eight members in parliament, the committee refused to act. Prime Minister Mansur was unable to induce the Company to consider a fifty-fifty split, although in this plea he had the support of the American ambassador. General Razmara, upon becoming prime minister in June, 1950, urged the Company to make some concessions in the way of greater discounts to Iran and the employment of more Iranians. Razmara argued that such a conciliation would permit him to support the agreement; but the Company was obdurate, pointing out that had Iran accepted the agreement in 1949 she would have received over $64,000,000 instead of $37,800,000 for that year.

The United States warned Great Britain that some appeasement would be necessary. Since the Company refused to take any action until Razmara brought the agreement to parliament, debates were held in December, 1950 and the oil committee rejected the agreement because it did not satisfactorily safeguard Iranian rights and interests. Almost immediately the Company urged Razmara to reopen negotiations to seek a fifty-fifty split of the profits. But it was now too late! Mosaddeq had presented a resolution demanding nationalization of the oil industry and calling upon Razmara to find out whether such a step was feasible. After consultation he reported publicly on March 3, 1951 that nationalization was impractical; he was assassinated four days later.

NATIONALIZATION OF OIL

Within a week parliament passed a bill nationalizing the oil industry, although it was not signed by the shah until May. Britain objected, and Prime Minister Husayn Ala rejected the protest. Riots, strikes, and wild demonstrations affected the area of the oil installations. British cruisers appeared in the Persian Gulf, and refineries at Abadan shut down. When Husayn Ala did not move to take over the properties of the Anglo-Iranian Oil Company, parliament forced his resignation; and Mohammad Mosaddeq, hero and chairman of the oil committee, became prime minister on April 28, 1951. The following day a law was passed to evict the Company, and Mosaddeq ousted it on October 1, 1951.

In May, as soon as the Mosaddeq government took steps to implement the nationalization law, the Company and the British government proposed arbitration. Upon Mosaddeq's refusal they applied to the International Court of Justice at The Hague for a decision. Mosaddeq declared the Court had no jurisdiction over the case, which was a dispute between a private company and the sovereign state of Iran. When British Foreign Minister Morrison complained that the Iranian government had not responded to requests of negotiation and admitted that Britain was prepared to consider a settlement which would involve some form of nationalization, Mosaddeq supposed that the main battle had been won and was ready to begin negotiations with the Company.

But any and all negotiations proved arduous. Each side believed it possessed the stronger bargaining weapons to back up its legal position. In addition, each had certain psychological, political, and economic internal forces which it was disastrous to disregard. Finally, each side either ignored or was misinformed about the views, intentions, and strength of its opponent.

As early as June the Company revealed one aspect of its strength by discussing publicly technical, financial, and marketing realities of the oil industry. It was asserted that only the Company could operate the intricate industry and the Abadan refinery; that only the Company could provide the great outlay of capital needed; that production in Kuwayt could within one year be stepped up to replace any loss in Iran if the Company were dispossessed; that the output of the Abadan refinery could be supplied within three years from new refineries; and that the tanker fleet could be easily shifted to other routes, thus leaving to the National Iranian Oil Company only the small domestic market in Iran.

The Company believed that the desperate plight of Iranian economy and finances could not withstand the added shock from loss of royalties and that political leaders who had to a considerable degree received the financial benefits of the oil income would quickly force Mosaddeq to come to terms. Also, the Company held that the action of the Iranian government was illegal, since it contravened several articles of the 1933 agreement.

On the other hand, the Company and the British government failed to read the signs of the times in Tehran or comprehend that nationalization of the Anglo-Iranian Oil Company united the various divergent classes in Iran as nothing had done for two generations. Nationalization suddenly meant independence and Mosaddeq not only had twisted the British lion's tail—something all Iranians had secretly been longing to do for a long time—but had pitted the Iranian lion against the British lion and had won. Razmara faltered on that point and was murdered. Mosaddeq always understood a like fate could be his.

Mosaddeq, on his part, encouraged the Iranian populace to assume that income from the oil industry would enable them to live in ease and comfort. But he did not realize the complexities of the international oil industry or the difficulties involved in selling Iranian oil without world co-operation. Furthermore, he did not take into account that neighboring countries such as Iraq, Kuwayt, and Saudi Arabia might object if oil companies restricted production in their fields to provide a market for Iranian oil.

Mosaddeq believed that Britain and western Europe required Iranian oil for continuance of their economies and thus would be forced to come to his terms. He also expected that the United States would support Iran in her struggle with the Company, because American ambassadors were friendly and had warned Britain of the serious consequences of the loss of Iranian oil. Moreover, he fully anticipated that the United States would give aid to Iran for fear that Iran would drift behind the Iron Curtain if her economic position became more chaotic than it was already.

Iranians perhaps misjudged British tempers and failed to understand that neither Labourites nor Conservatives wanted to liquidate the empire. Thus, the roles played in World War II by Iranian oil for the British navy and high-octane gasoline for the Royal Air Force were overlooked entirely; and the relationship of Anglo-Iranian oil to British dollar earnings and sterling oil was ignored. Because Iranian leaders had studied the process and legality of nationalization of industry in Great Britain enacted by the Attlee government, they assumed that England would recognize the legality in Iran. However, they failed to perceive that such acceptance would invite nationalization in Iraq, Saudi Arabia, Bahrayn, and Kuwayt—a thought which gave nightmares to oil officials the world over.

In the ensuing debate between the Company and Iran the position of Prime Minister Mosaddeq was exceedingly strong. Although his National Front party had a delegation of only 8 out of 136 in parliament when he became leader of the government, his following and influence was widespread in all classes. One of his staunchest supporters was a leader of the Shiite divines, Ayatollah Sayyid Abd al-Kasim Kashani. He hated the British, who had interned him as a German agent during World War II. In 1949 after an unsuccessful attempt upon the life of the shah, Mullah Kashani was suspected of inciting Devotees of Islam (*Fidaiyan-i Islam*) to commit such assassinations and was exiled. Elected to parliament in 1950, he returned to take his seat and was no doubt implicated in the death of Razmara in 1951. As long as Mosaddeq was uncompromising with the British, Kashani worked with the government and used his position to excite popular religious fervor as a strong prop for Mosaddeq.

OIL STALEMATE

Almost from the moment of Mosaddeq's entry into office and the beginning of the drive to eject the Anglo-Iranian Oil Company until his unsuccessful *coup d'état* in August, 1953, the drama of the nationalization of oil in Iran had many scenes, a large cast of players, and a constant shift of location. There were five proposals made by the British, the United States, or international groups to effect a settlement; and all failed. In June, 1951 the Company agreed to the principle of nationalization and proposed formation of a new company with British and Iranian directors to handle production and distribution of petroleum products for Iran. A sum of $28,000,000 would be paid immediately to Iran; and $8,400,000 would be paid monthly until an agreement on payments was reached. In July Truman entered the controversy and sent his personal ambassador, W. Averell Harriman, to reopen negotiations and reach a settlement. Joining with Stokes, the representative from Great Britain, Harriman supported the British proposal which Mosaddeq refused on the basis that some understanding on compensation to be paid for the oil properties should first be reached.

By the end of the summer of 1951 the oil industry in Iran was shut down; the tanks were full; and no oil was being loaded. British personnel left the area; and British naval contingents and paratroopers were brought up to more advanced posts. Attempts at arbitration and use of the International Court foundered. Iran contended that the matter was an internal affair and that any outside interference or consideration infringed upon Iranian sovereignty. When the Security Council of the United Nations considered the question at the request of Great Britain, Mosaddeq came to New York to state again the case that this was not a subject for United Nations concern since the Charter forbade acts which impaired the sovereignty of any member. While in the United States Mosaddeq discussed the question with high American officials, but no meeting of minds occurred. The United States government and American oil men reassured the British that America would not take on the job of running the oil business for the Iranian government. At the same time the American government made available over $300,000,000 in dollar grants to England to enable her to buy oil in the Western Hemisphere. With this aid and encouragement the British position with Iran remained obdurate. Still further, the United States refused to grant loans to Iran to offset losses from royalties, although $24,000,000 was granted in 1952 for Point Four projects.

Production was hurriedly upped in other Persian Gulf oil-producing states, since the situation appeared to be critical. Meanwhile, the International Bank submitted an offer to operate the oil industry without prejudice to either party of the controversy; but the endeavor tripped on the price of oil, the employment of British technicians, and the role and authority of the Bank of Iran in the conduct of the business.

After these failures, the issue was reduced to the amount of compensation. In August, 1952 Truman and Churchill sent a joint proposal that the question be submitted to the International Court. Initiation of such a step would start the flow of oil to world markets; and the United States would advance $10,000,000 to Iran. Mosaddeq countered with the demand of $137,200,000 from the Company, the sum which would have been due to Iran up to that time if he had not filibustered the supplementary agreement of 1949 to death in the Iranian parliament. He also suggested that compensation be based only on the physical property of the Company in Iran. His counterproposals were rejected by the British.

In October, Iran severed diplomatic relations with Great Britain; but

Mosaddeq said he would agree to an International Court adjudication of compensation, if the bases used were those employed by the British government when it nationalized properties in the United Kingdom. Thus, in February, 1953 a revised proposal, supported by the Eisenhower administration, was forwarded to Mosaddeq. At the same time the United States promised an advance payment of $100,000,000 against future oil deliveries. This proposal was also declined with the statement that Britain must first state her claim.

Each time that exchanges were made tempers became worse; and charges and countercharges, repeated in all of the presses of the world, grew bitter and exaggerated. Mosaddeq asserted that the British were asking compensation for future expected profits now to be lost and that he would, therefore, demand payment by the Company of all royalties that Iran should have, but had not, received in the past.

As the controversy dragged on, Britain and the West adjusted to the loss of Iranian oil. By the spring of 1953 many oil men were actually worrying about what they would do with Iranian oil and where they could market it if it suddenly became available again. There was a glut of oil on the world market without Iranian oil.

GOVERNMENTAL CRISIS

But in Iran affairs were descending rapidly to a state of chaos. Loss of royalties was beginning to pinch. Thousands of Iranian oil workers were transferred to the public payroll. And scarcity of foreign exchange and absence of any great earning power destroyed Iran's foreign credit. Since the great mass of Iranians, however, were not dependent upon or affected by royalty payments or lack of foreign exchange, life did go on. Nevertheless, Mosaddeq was not nearing any solution, and nationalists were becoming frustrated. The army was short on supplies; and the wealthy landowners who governed the country soon discovered that loss of the royalty revenues on which their corrupt governmental practices battened was forcing them to change their ways.

Accusations of various types were hurled at Mosaddeq in parliament. A crisis developed in July, 1952 upon the opening of the newly-elected seventeenth parliament. Before he would accept the prime ministership, Mosaddeq demanded a vote of absolute power and rule by personal decree for six months to inaugurate governmental, economic, and social reforms. Many members of his own party objected. So did the shah, when he was asked to allow Mosaddeq to become minister of war as well as prime minister. Thereupon Mosaddeq resigned, and the shah appointed Ahmad Qavam to form a cabinet. Qavam publicly branded Mosaddeq as a demagogue and Kashani as a hypocrite and stated that he would settle with the British. Quite understandably he was forced to resign. But first there were four days of bloody rioting led in Tehran by Mosaddeq, Kashani, and a resurgent Tudeh party.

To avoid civil war the shah sent for Mosaddeq, whereupon Kashani through his influence over the Devotees of Islam halted the violence in Tehran. Kashani was elected speaker of parliament; and in August Mosaddeq became minister of war and was granted unlimited powers. He had reached the pinnacle of his career; soon the cracks in his structure began to appear. Quarrels within his own party arose over appointments; and in January, 1953, when he obtained a continuation of his personal rule for another year, Kashani deserted him. Tight press-censorship laws were promulgated, along with prohibitions against strikes by government workers and against the importation, manufacture, sale, and use of alcoholic beverages. In February demonstrators attacked Mosaddeq's home, forcing him to flee for safety to the United States Point Four office. In July Kashani failed to be reelected Speaker; and thereafter many members of Mosaddeq's National Front party resigned their seats in parliament. Mosaddeq was gathering more and more power of the government into his own hands, and even those of his party who were members of the oil committee deserted. Events began to move with a rising crescendo.

In July General Fazullah Zahedi, one of the popular strong men in the army and Mosaddeq's open opponent, left the parliament building where he had been taking sanctuary for ten weeks, having been guaranteed personal safety. When Mosaddeq announced a popular referendum would be held on the question of the dissolution of parliament, the storm began to break. Only the shah could dissolve parliament; any other step was unconstitutional. Kashani placed a religious boycott on the referendum; but voting proceeded, separate polling places being provided for those voting for and those voting against the measure! Mosaddeq won with 99.93 percent of the vote and on August 12, 1953 announced his intention to dissolve parliament.

MOSADDEQ'S FALL

By this time the government of Mosaddeq had lost the support of every political and social group in Iran except a small number of bazaar merchants of Tehran and the Communists, who throve on the disorders. The mobs of Tehran could be swayed easily to demonstrate for almost anyone. Mosaddeq had tried to make political capital from his nationalization of oil over too long a period without adding any new funds to this original capital; and now he faced political bankruptcy. He did not understand the world ramifications of the oil industry. He did not have the personality, organization, or real courage to become a dictator. His playing with fire with the Communists failed to smoke out any assistance or sympathy from the United States. Lacking any solid support from Iranian nationalists, the army, landowners, religious groups, or the shah, Mosaddeq lost out completely when the chips were down.

Many Iranians believed that Mosaddeq would be able to obtain aid from the United States, and encouragement for this view was fostered by promises of President Truman. In the spring of 1953 Secretary of State Dulles changed the American tune and helped to pull out the rug from under Mosaddeq. In May Dulles visited every capital in the Middle East from New Delhi to Athens with the exception of Tehran, ostensibly because time did not permit; but all Iran understood. In July much publicity was given to Eisenhower's letter to Mosaddeq declaring that aid would not be given to Iran unless the oil dispute with Britain was settled or arbitrated. A few weeks later Dulles stated that aid would be withheld from Iran because Mosaddeq openly countenanced and apparently co-operated with the illegal Tudeh party.

Allen Dulles, the secretary's brother, and Princess Ashraf, the shah's twin sister, visited each other in Switzerland; and General Schwarzkopf, who had organized the Iranian gendarmery and was a friend of the shah and General Zahedi, visited Iran as a tourist in August. On August 13, after Mosaddeq had usurped the shah's power by deciding to dissolve parliament, the shah dismissed Mosaddeq and appointed General Zahedi as prime minister. Mosaddeq refused to be dismissed and remained in office through the use of troops. On August 16 the shah fled by plane to Baghdad and Rome, and Zahedi escaped to the provinces. But on August 19 crowds in the streets of Tehran began to shout: "Long live the Shah." Zahedi's men precipitated the attack upon Mosaddeq. A minor tank battle decided the issue in favor of the shah and Zahedi, who appeared before nightfall. The shah returned on August 22; Mosaddeq was caught and arrested; a new cabinet under Zahedi was approved; and on September 5, Eisenhower granted $45,000,000 to Iran on an emergency basis.

The new government began to ferret out Communists and crack down on opponents. Mosaddeq was found guilty of attempted rebellion and sentenced to three years' imprisonment. Husayn Fatemi, his foreign minister, was tried and shot for inciting rebellion. In October ninety-five percent of the shops in the bazaar closed in protest against vocal attacks upon Mosaddeq. Several merchants were arrested; and when a second attempt at closing was tried in November, government workmen demolished the vaulted roofs over the alleys in four areas of the bazaar—an action which brought the merchants quickly to support Zahedi.

THE OIL SETTLEMENT

The grant from the United States was made on the condition that the oil dispute be terminated. Herbert Hoover, Jr. spent two weeks in Tehran in October discussing a settlement, which still could not be effective in Iran if it appeared to revive any aspect of colonialism. In February, 1954 a consortium of eight major world oil companies met in London to debate the complex problem of getting Iranian oil swirling into world markets and royalties flowing into the desperate Iranian treasury. On August 5, 1954 Iran signed an agreement with an oil consortium incorporated in the Netherlands, whereby the consortium would extract, refine, and market petroleum for the National Iranian Oil Company (NIOC). The Iranian company would receive half of the profits and pay $70,000,000 a year for ten years as compensation for nationalization. Parliament ratified the agreement in October, and oil began to gush immediately. The pivotal problem was solved. After that date the world demand for oil products expanded rapidly, enabling the sale of Iran's oil without market dislocations, and yearly payments to Iran rose sharply to approximate $300,000,000.

In 1956, NIOC took over the Russian oil concession east of Tehran, thus controlling the oil resources of the entire nation. In August a team of consortium engineers brought in a prodigious gusher in a new field near Kum. Capacity production for this single well was estimated at 150,000 barrels daily, three times greater than the most productive well in Iran heretofore. Bidding for exploitation of the Kum strike was intense. Ente Nazionale Idrocarburi of Italy initiated discussions for a concession; and in April, 1957 agreement was reached between NIOC and the Italian firm AGIP Mineraria by which Iran would receive seventy-five percent of the profits.

Exploration for other oil fields continued apace, and in 1958 concessions were granted for $25 million to Pan-American International Oil (PAIO), a subsidiary of the Standard Oil Company of Indiana, and to AGIP, both as partners of NIOC to explore off-shore fields in the Persian Gulf. The Island of Kharg in the gulf was chosen in 1959 as a convenient base for oil operations, including those of the consortium, and pipelines were laid between Kharg and the mainland in 1960. NIOC acquired tankers and began to find markets for its oil in Argentina, India, and Japan. In 1965 an additional port for refined petroleum products with pipelines, refineries, and docks was under construction at Bandar Mashut, some 550 miles south of Abadan, and in August, 1966 NIOC signed an oil agreement with Entreprise Française des Recherches et d'Activitées Petrolières (ERAP), whereby ERAP is neither partner nor concessionaire but only a contractor to NIOC. Two other significant developments also occurred. Schemes for the piping and utilization of the seemingly limitless quantities of natural gas in the southern oil fields, burned-off and wasted for decades, turned into a reality in 1965 with the founding of the National Iranian Gas Corporation (NIGC). A mill was shipped from the United States to roll pipe for the line, Great Britain agreed to help finance it, and the U.S.S.R. signed an arrangement to aid in the engineering and construction of the line to the Caspian Sea area in the U.S.S.R., and to receive payment in natural gas deliveries. The other innovation has been the launching of a petrochemical industry under the control of the National Iranian Petrochemical Corporation (NIPC), with a $170 million complex appearing at Bandar Shapur in partnership with Allied Chemicals of New York, and a $21 million petrochemical plant at Abadan with B. F. Goodrich Company participating. Natural gas will be a profitable export but of greater import will be its boon to industry in overpopulated Tehran and its power for developing the vast natural resources of Iran that have remained unexploited and almost unknown. In 1966 royalties and income from oil stood at approximately $500 million, but add to this the income to be generated from natural gas and a modern petrochemical industry and within a few years, under favorable conditions, some of Mosaddeq's dreams will not seem so impossible.

AFFAIRS OF GOVERNMENT

The second compelling situation after Mosaddeq's downfall was the restoration of constitutional government. In December, 1953 the shah dismissed parliament and called for elections to begin that month. Zahedi's followers and the shah's friends won in the elections and dominated the new parliament. In April, 1955 Zahedi retired as prime minister and the shah appointed Husayn Ala to the post. Husayn Ala had been prime minister, foreign minister, minister of the court, and ambassador in Washington and was recognized as friendly to the West. An attempt was made on his life in November, 1955; but he forged ahead in strict control of governmental processes and political order. Elections were held again in 1956. This time the lists of candidates and the manner of the elections insured a victory for conservatives, landowners, and friends of the shah. Former members of the National Front party protested; and Allah-Yar Saleh, Mosaddeq's ambassador in Washington, sought refuge in the parliament building and went on a hunger strike to call attention to the injustice and mockery of the election. In September the Majlis convened and the supreme court was reformed with nine new appointments. Early in 1957, following the capture and murder of some American officials in a southern province, Ala resigned to become minister of the court; and the shah appointed Manouchehr Eghbal as prime minister of a new cabinet. Manouchehr Eghbal had been chancellor of Tehran University, and he set out to revise the constitution by amendment. He organized a Nation party to support his policies and combat a new opposition party (People's), led by the shah's friend, Assadollah Alam, who had coalesced groups interested in agricultural reform, the division of large estates, labor, and equality for women. Though both parties began to direct their energies toward the 1960 election for the twentieth Majlis, there was relative political calm in the two years preceding the election. The shah divorced Queen Soraya in 1958 because she had not borne him a son and the following year married Farah Diba, who presented him with a son and heir to the throne in October, 1960. A second son was born in April, 1966.

Beginning in 1960 Mohammed Reza Shah appeared to show greater concern for progressive administrations and to exercise his influence and power for what came to be termed the "White Revolution," or "Revolution from the Throne." The birth of an heir may have prompted him to act more vigorously for the needs of the nation and may have given him a long-range view of his position. In any case, shortly after the Majlis election in 1960 and even though Prime Minister Eghbal's Nation party had won two-thirds of the 200 seats, the shah publicly complained about voting irregularities. Eghbal, of course, resigned and the shah appointed Jafar Sharif-Emami, whereupon all the members of the Majlis resigned, since the shah had impugned their right to hold their seats. New elections for the twentieth Majlis were held early in 1961, and the new Majlis gave Sharif-Emami a vote of confidence. Because the two contesting parties held an almost equal number of seats, power rested on the shoulders of the independents. In May the shah appointed an independent, Dr. Ali Amini, as prime minister and he formed a completely independent cabinet. Income from oil was on the increase but the state coffers were empty. Dr. Amini was a sensitive, well-educated, and honest aristocrat with a keen feeling for social responsibility and the welfare of the masses. Within a few days the Majlis was dismissed and the shah and Dr. Amini set out to reform the nation from the top down. Five generals were arrested on charges of corruption and embezzlement, and many civilian officials were investigated and discharged. The cabinet issued a land law decree requiring all landowners to sell to the government all land holdings in excess of one village and stating that the government would sell such land to landless villlagers. In March, 1962 the shah presided at such a distribution in Azerbayjan. In Tehran the students rioted when scholastic requirements were raised and tightened. Dr. Amini was unmoved and the demonstrations were suppressed.

In July, 1962 Dr. Amini's health failed and, disappointed in not getting the grants-in-aid he expected from the United States, he resigned. The shah appointed his friend Assadollah Alam, the leader of the People's party, who pledged to continue the reforms. At a meeting of 5,000 village representatives in Tehran the shah unfurled a six-point revolutionary program: (1) The break-up of large estates held by religious foundations and individuals and the distribution of these to landless peasants; (2) The nationalization of forest areas; (3) The sale of some 200 government industries to privately owned companies to obtain funds to compensate the landlords and to establish agricultural co-operatives; (4) The compulsory payment of twenty percent of industrial and business enterprise profits to the employees; (5) The forming of literacy corps from those in military service to go into the villages to teach the illiterate; and (6) The enacting of new electoral laws to eliminate corruption in the elections. Alam supported this program wholeheartedly and in January, 1963 a referendum approved it by a vote of over 5.5 million to 4,000. Shiite religious leaders protested vehemently but most had expected this because their support came largely from the landed estates of their foundations.

The promised elections came in September, 1963 not only for the Majlis but for the thirty elective seats of the Senate. The old parties (Nation and People's) and the National Front were not permitted to present candidates. The New Iran party (Congress of Free Women and Free Men) was organized by forty-year-old Ali Mansur particularly to support the shah's six-point program. He won 181 of the 200 seats in the Majlis which now was dominated by agrarian reformers and the urban class rather than the great landowners as had been true in the past. The shah appointed thirty new members of the Senate, including two women. For the first time in Iranian history women voted, and in the cities they went to the polls in great numbers. In the referendum earlier that year, women had gone to the polls and put ballots in the boxes but these were not counted! With the backing of the Congress group the shah appointed Mansur prime minister in March, 1964; he won a unanimous vote of confidence in the Majlis and 51 out of 60 in the Senate. Mansur agreed to dissolve the state sugar monopoly and submitted a new bill limiting land holding from 75 to 300 acres, depending upon the type and use of the land. Unfortunately, Mansur was assassinated in January, 1965; in his place, the shah put the former finance minister, Amir Abbas Hoveida, a member of the Congress group, who declared he would fulfill Mansur's programs. The land reform measures did not progress as rapidly as many had hoped, and by the end of 1965 some 14,000 peasants had received titles to their lands. Lack of knowledge and finances and the limited number of co-operatives hampered its forward thrust. Hoveida organized an Agricultural Extension and Development Corps, similar to the Literacy Corps and the Health Corps, to help the villagers learn how to manage the lands coming into their possession. More and more it was understood in government circles that oil and industry might be important and impressive in moving Iran into the modern world but the modernization of agriculture and the income and production from it would be the salvation of the future.

BETWEEN EAST AND WEST

Soon after Zahedi assumed power, relations improved with the U.S.S.R. A trade agreement doubling the amount of goods previously exchanged was signed, and the Soviets indicated a desire to settle outstanding boundary and financial controversies. In June, 1954 a new commercial protocol was concluded with the U.S.S.R., whereby Iranian imports of machinery were permitted, and in July Russia agreed to return to Iran eleven tons of gold and $8,000,000 in goods held for safekeeping in Russia since the early days of World War II. At the same time the Soviets warned Iran not to join in any of the American military measures being taken in the Near and Middle East. At the time that the transfer of the gold was made in July, 1955 the shah and his new queen, Soraya, were invited to visit Moscow; and it became apparent that the Kremlin had decided to win Iran by a more friendly attitude. It was nearly a year, however, before the visit was made. Meanwhile, Iran joined the Baghdad pact on October 11, 1955. This move brought two notes from the U.S.S.R., declaring that adherence to the pact violated Iran's treaty obligations to the U.S.S.R. These notes were viewed as thinly veiled threats to implement clauses in the treaties giving Russia the right to intervene or enter into the northern provinces of Iran if the latter's independence were threatened.

Friendly relations with the United States were continued by Zahedi, Ala, Eghbal, and the prime ministers who followed. An American military mission was established to train the Iranian army and sizable quantities of military equipment were received under mutual defense arrangements until 1966, when the United States declared that the Iranian economy had become strong enough to support its army. In addition to equipment $30 million was expended annually to subsidize the army; in the two decades from 1946 to 1966 over $700 million in military aid and matériel had been given by the United States. Grants for technical aid, loans from the Export-Import Bank and the International Bank for Reconstruction and Development, other loans, and outright gifts from the United States, all totaled over $550 million in non-military aid by 1966. Until 1956 much of the foreign-aid program had been controlled and directed by American advisers but at that time the Ala government assumed responsibility and direction for development.

The shah's trip was planned to improve relations between Iran and the U.S.S.R. in line with settlements in 1954 and 1955 of a number of irritating problems. The signing of the Baghdad pact and the favorable reception of the Eisenhower Doctrine in certain government circles did not help. The Kremlin protested but no break occurred and the many friendly gestures of the U.S.S.R. toward Iran continued. Direct rail service was opened between Moscow and Tehran in 1958 and negotiations were under way for a nonaggression pact. After the revolution in Iraq in 1958 and the transformation of the Baghdad pact into CENTO, Iran suddenly seemed to have greater strategic value for the United States, and in 1959 Iran signed a bilateral agreement with the United States, the latter to render aid in case of any aggression upon the former. Khrushchev was furious and broke off all negotiations with Tehran but shortly realized he should not write off Iran without another attempt to neutralize the Caspian area. In 1960 Moscow suggested that aid for the development of oil, natural gas, and heavy industry, specifically a steel industry, would be available from the U.S.S.R. in exchange for a nonaggression pact and a pledge that Iran would not allow foreign bases or rocket launching sites to be established on her soil. Discussions on this proposal went back and forth until 1962, when Iran agreed that no rocket bases would be permitted. This cleared the way for friendlier relations and the next year President Brezhnev visited Iran and was warmly applauded when he addressed the Majlis. Definite aid projects moved slowly but a number came to be fulfilled in 1966 when the U.S.S.R. agreed to help in several significant ways toward the building of a natural gas pipeline from the oil fields of southern Iran to Astara, a U.S.S.R. port on the Caspian sea, and to take natural gas as payment. Credits were advanced for $286 million for development of the iron mines at Baft, the coal mines at Kerman, and for building several machine-tool plants and a steel mill at Isfahan. At the same time it was announced that the United States was terminating aid programs and grants and that technical assistance would end in 1968, all on the grounds that the Iranian economy had reached the level where it could progress on its own. Without great military assistance from the United States, Iran began to obtain her needs as best she could, and in February, 1967 announced the purchase of $110 million in Soviet arms to be paid for within eight years by the delivery of natural gas and other commodities. In 1966 industrial development and trade talks took place between Iran and Japan, India, Ceylon, Pakistan, Israel, Sudan, France, Germany, Italy, Denmark, Great Britain, the U.S.S.R., Bulgaria, Poland, Hungary, Rumania, Yugoslavia, Czechoslovakia, and the United States, among others. It was apparent for all to see that the Iranian economy was a world attraction and the possibilities were multifold. New enterprises ranged from aluminum plants to fish-meal factories.

DAMS AND PLAN ORGANIZATIONS

During World War II and immediately at its termination there had been great hopes that the generally known natural resources of Iran, in addition to that of oil and gas, could be developed. The shah and his ministers had initiated plans, and experts had been hired to survey the country and to suggest five- and seven-year plans to implement these findings. It seemed to many that there were surveys of surveys but Qavam and Mosaddeq never had the freedom to give much support to these. As soon as the oil crisis was settled, Zahedi announced the inauguration of a five-year development plan to be financed by oil revenues and, if possible, by the International Bank. The plan concentrated on building dams, hydroelectric power plants, irrigation systems in arid regions, and drainage of land in swampy areas. Recognizing that the vast majority of Iranians were agriculturists and that the well-being of the nation would be served best by improving their property and increasing their productivity, the Bank loaned $75,000,000 in 1957 to finance agricultural transportation, industries, social services, and electric-power development. In April, 1956 the five-year plan was extended to seven years; projects costing $1,000,000,000 were outlined. Others moved to aid the programs. In 1957 the oil consortium announced that it intended to spend $140,000,000 in general developments in the various oil centers. Many West German scientists were invited to Iran, and Americans aided in founding the Abadan College of Engineering. A five-year contract under the seven-year plan to develop the resources of Khuzistan in southern Iran was signed in March, 1956 by the American Development and Resources Corporation, which agreed to start construction on a 660-foot high dam on the Dez River in March, 1958.

Beginning in 1960, the many aspects of planning affected every strata of Iranian society. Over all of the planning was the Plan Organization, a type of governmental corporate structure to devise the plans, to obtain and control finances, to supervise implementation, and to operate various completed enterprises. Sixty percent of oil revenues had been earmarked for Zahedi's five-seven year plan, and much had been poured into the building of dams, which eventually would go a long way through irrigation, flood control, and electric-power generation in changing the economy of Iran. In 1961 the great Karaj Dam, northwest of Tehran, was completed. In 1962 the 352-foot high Manjil Dam on the Sefid Rud River in Gilan was opened. Built at a cost of more than $100 million by French contractors, it would irrigate about 375,000 acres and produce 132,000 kilowatts of electric power. The new Mohammed Reza Dam on the Dez River was dedicated in 1963, and the contract with the Development and Resources Corporation was renewed for an additional $140 million. It was intended that this dam would irrigate 360,000 acres in the province of Khuzistan in southwestern Iran, provide 520,000 kilowatts of electricity, and serve as the key project of a Dez River Authority that would transform Khuzistan into a rich agricultural producing area as it has been in several eras of the past. In 1962 the formula of sixty percent of the oil revenues was changed to a flat $130 million per year, to which was added for that year new loans from the International Bank for Reconstruction and Development and the United States Development Loan Fund. The Plan Organization owned or controlled fifty-two manufacturing enterprises, and these had been turned over to the Ministry of Industry and Mines to sell to private companies to obtain funds to purchase lands for the peasants. Tight financial conditions in Iran from 1960 to 1963 forced the government to hold this scheme in abeyance, and in later years the land reform moved slowly so that disposing of the industries, which became more profitable, was not as pressing. Tea, textiles, cement, and sugar production increased greatly, and in 1961 the cane-sugar plant of Khuzistan first came into operation.

The greatest interest developed in 1961 and 1962 in the third seven-year Development Plan to run from 1962 through 1968. As originally drawn in 1962, the plan carried a budget of $1,870 million, five-sevenths of which was to be financed within Iran. It called for an annual growth rate of six and one-half percent in productivity—ten percent in fact, but the lower figure was adjusted to the increase in population. Hardly under way, the Plan's budget and scope were expanded to $2,720 million, to cover new communications systems and extended agricultural programs. Many pessimists saw their fears justified when there was only a three percent increase in 1965 and a welter of faltering half-finished projects. Many of these were completed, however, and a boom generated great optimism in 1966. The gross national product increased by twelve and one-half percent and a per capita national growth of ten percent. There was good weather for agriculture and overachievement in many industries. The Plan Organization advertised a large budget of $844 million for the year, and industrial and development activity was so promising that capital began to flow into Iran from every direction. The shah and all of his people were confident that Iran was on her way toward a position no longer dependent on either East or West but free to make her choices and to maintain the dignity of independence. So certain was the shah of the future of his country that he agreed to hold a coronation ceremony, long postponed, which was performed and celebrated in a brilliant and traditional manner on October 26, 1967. The shah placed the crown upon his own head and then crowned the queen, the first woman to wear the crown in Iran. Mohammed Reza Shah previously had declared he would not have the ceremony until he had a male heir and until the poverty and hardship in his country had been attacked and progress could be seen.

REFERENCES: Chapter 37

Important readings for this chapter are also found in Chapters 30, 31, 34, and 35.

Lawrence P. Elwell-Sutton, Persian Oil. A Study in Power Politics: Lawrence & Wishart, London, 1955. A discussion of the oil dispute in Iran.

Nasrollah S. Fatemi, Oil Diplomacy: Powderkeg in Iran: Whittier Books, New York, 1954. Written by the brother of Mosaddeq's foreign minister.

Alan W. Ford, The Anglo-Iranian Oil Dispute of 1951–1952: University of California Press, Berkeley, 1954. Thorough and detailed review of the events.

Richard N. Frye, Iran: Henry Holt, New York, 1953. A survey.

A. H. Hamzavi, Persia and the Powers: An Account of Diplomatic Relations: 1941–1946: Hutchinson, London, 1946.

Pollock Irwin, A Tar Heel in Iran: Heritage House, Charlotte, 1957.

Norman Kemp, Abadan. A First-Hand Account of the Persian Oil Crisis: Allan Wingate, London, 1953.

A. K. S. Lambton, *Landlord and Peasant in Persia:* Oxford University Press, New York, 1953. Scholarly and valuable.

Walter Z. Laqueur, *Soviet Russia and the Middle East:* Praeger, New York, 1959. A penetrating description of many aspects of communist activity in the Middle East, and the Soviet dilemma over a desire to help Communists in the area versus the policy of aiding governments that persecute Communists.

T. H. Vail Motter, *The Persian Corridor and Aid to Russia:* Department of the Army, Washington, 1952.

Norman S. Roberts, *Iran, Economic and Commercial Conditions:* H. M. Stationery Office, London, 1948.

Clarmont Percival Skrine, *World War in Iran:* Constable, London, 1962.

Anthony Smith, *Blind White Fish in Persia.* E. P. Dutton, New York, 1953. The title is misleading: it is an excellent study of village life in Iran.

Joseph M. Upton, *The History of Modern Iran: An Interpretation:* Harvard University Press, Cambridge, 1960. A fine thought-provoking essay.

William E. Warne, *Mission for Peace: Point 4 in Iran:* Bobbs-Merrill, New York, 1956.

Donald N. Wilber, *Contemporary Iran:* Praeger, New York, 1963.

CHAPTER 38

Oil and Arabia

The collapse of the Ottoman Empire and the withdrawal of Turkish forces from the Arab provinces following the Mudros armistice in 1918 created in the Arabian peninsula a partial political and power vacuum. Within two years the French took over Syria and the British Palestine, Transjordan, and Iraq in accordance with their prearranged agreements. For the remainder of the peninsula the situation was quite different. London did not doubt that it was to be a British sphere of influence.

Even before World War I the Persian Gulf had become an English lake; official British residents and agents controlled the foreign affairs and advised the rulers of the petty states on the eastern Arabian shore from Kuwayt to Muscat. On the southern shore Britain held her colony of Aden and protected or had treaty rights with the various sultans and amirs. And even Abd al-Aziz ibn Saud, ruler of the Nejd, admired the British. But along the western coast communications from Istanbul by sea via Suez, by land routes from Damascus, and by the Hijaz railway enabled the Ottoman Empire to maintain more than a shadow of control. From this coast and from Syria and Iraq the Porte found it profitable and possible to keep a hand on the precarious balance among the marauding Arab tribes of the interior deserts and sway decisions favorable to Turkish allies.

SHARIF HUSAYN OF MECCA

In essence the British inherited the Turkish role, beginning in actual practice in 1916 when they subsidized Sharif Husayn of the Hijaz on the western coast and recognized and subsidized Abd al-Aziz ibn Saud in central and eastern Arabia. Sharif Husayn was given nearly $1,000,-

ooo in gold each month and supplied with arms to captain the Arab rebellion against the Turks. Husayn proclaimed himself King of the Arab Peoples and was promised a united Arab state at the end of the war. When the mandate system was established and Syria, Palestine, and Iraq were taken by France and England, he was disillusioned and provoked. In 1921 after the Cairo Conference the British proposed a treaty which recognized Husayn as the sovereign of the Hijaz, and continued his subsidy indefinitely. Yet, he refused; for his pride and honor would not permit him to accept the clauses which mentioned Britain's "special position" in Iraq and Palestine. The payments of gold ceased and Husayn was on his own, although negotiations were attempted in 1923 and again in 1924.

Without special British protection and assistance Sharif Husayn of the Hijaz, even though he styled himself King of the Arabs, reverted to being only one of five independent Arab rulers, and not the strongest of these. His position was not enviable. He had taken the lead in the discussions with the British regarding Syria and Iraq; now, the onus of failure was his, even though he always acted as if his sons Abdallah and Faysal in Transjordan and Iraq were only his viceroys in those "Arab provinces." Unfortunately for his son Ali, heir in the Hijaz, his viceroys had taken with them most of the veteran army built up during the war.

Husayn was not, however, an Arab of the tribes or the desert. He had lived in Istanbul at the court of Abdul Hamid II for fifteen years and looked down upon such individuals as Abd al-Aziz ibn Saud as uneducated bedouins, and certainly he did not know how to talk with them. They, for their part, considered Husayn an effeminate town-dwelling Europeanized Arab who had lost genuine Arab characteristics. Husayn offended the Arabs of Arabia at every turn and insulted their chiefs in unforgivable language. During the war when he was trying to get the co-operation of all Arabs against the Turks, he rejected a draft agreement proffered by Abd al-Aziz ibn Saud with the remark that it must have been "penned by a madman or a man in his cups."

In addition, Husayn was a miserable administrator. Almost the sole income of the Hijaz was derived from the annual pilgrimage. Husayn mismanaged it, offended the Egyptians over ceremonials, and permitted pilgrims to be fleeced by the merchants until it became a scandal throughout the Muslim world. His final mistake was the assumption of the title of caliph in 1924 after the Turkish Republic abolished the Ottoman caliphate and exiled the last caliph.

Indian Muslims objected to this act; and Abd al-Aziz ibn Saud boiled in rage that that "sinful man" should so desecrate the position held by Abu Bakr and Umar. Moreover, Ibn Saud had several old scores to settle with Husayn and he needed the income from the pilgrimage. Most important of all, however, was the natural inclination to unite the Arabian peninsula under one rule—his rule!

IBN SAUD

Abd al-Aziz ibn Abd al-Rahman ibn Saud Al Faysal, but better known in the West as Ibn Saud, was born in 1880 to the Saud family of Riyadh in the Nedj. Since the middle of the eighteenth century his family had been the political mainstay of the puritanical sect of Islam originated by Muhammad ibn Abd al-Wahhab, and the Saudis aided in the propagation of Wahhabism throughout Arabia. Ibn Saud's ancestors battled Muhammad Ali and Ibrahim, who invaded Arabia from Egypt. The most serious and persistent rivals and enemies, however, were the Ibn Rashid family of the Shammar tribe to the north, centered upon the town of Hail. Ibn Saud's uncles lost out in the constant warring, and at an early age Ibn Saud lived in exile in Kuwayt and other Arab towns. His father renounced any right to rule, but the son was of a different character. In 1902, against seemingly impossible odds, Ibn Saud led forty young Arab bloods up tilted palm trunks over the walls and roof tops of Riyadh in a typical derring-do, so much loved and admired by the Arabs, and recaptured the city for himself and family.

In the years that followed he was able to ward off the blows of the declining Bani Rashid and in 1913 captured from the Turks the valuable province of al-Hasa on the Persian Gulf, not knowing then that al-Hasa was practically floating on oil. When World War I descended upon the Middle East, Ibn Saud was visited by British officers and finally came to terms with Captain Shakespear, sent there by Sir Percy Cox, who for years had been chief British resident in the Persian Gulf. Ibn Saud agreed to accept $25,000 a month, not join with the Turks against the British, and not make any foreign commitments without informing the British.

Upon the defeat of the Turks in Arabia during the war and with the knowledge of the provisions of the Mudros armistice as well as the Sykes-Picot agreement, Ibn Saud was as anxious to extend his rule as any other Arabian potentate. Though each of the Arab lords might speak of Arab unity and the Arab nation whose modern destiny would be fulfilled under his specific leadership, each lord was thinking more realistically in terms of personal power, prestige, and wealth. Each was jealous of the others and intensely sensitive lest one trespass on his territory.

In 1911 Husayn captured Ibn Saud's brother and forced Ibn Saud to acknowledge Turkish overlordship to obtain his brother's release. No Arab chieftain could have done otherwise and retained his honor; yet the humiliation rankled in Ibn Saud's breast. In 1916 Ibn Saud agreed to follow Husayn's leadership in the resistance movement against the Turks, but he thought of the Arab grouping as an alliance of equals. Ibn Saud held as preposterous and vainglorious Husayn's claim to be King of the Arabs.

The first blow was struck in 1919. Abdallah, Husayn's second son, led a column of armed men to seize the oasis of Khurma. Ibn Saud held Khurma, but the British Foreign Office ill-advisedly awarded it to Husayn. Ibn Saud fell upon Abdallah at Turaba and annihilated his army; Abdallah barely escaped with his life, and the British informed Ibn Saud he could keep his conquests but must not invade the Hijaz.

When in 1920 and 1921 Britain installed Abdallah in Transjordan and Faysal in Iraq, Ibn Saud felt that he was being surrounded by Husayn and the Hashimite clan. The apparent encirclement spurred Ibn Saud to move outward. He sent his son Faysal in 1920 with a force of 5,000 men across 700 miles of difficult trails to attack the highlands of Asir and the realm of the Idrisi family, which was being squeezed by the tactics of Husayn and Imam Yahya of Yemen.

Forging a stronger bond of friendship with the Idrisi and obtaining their allegiance, Ibn Saud sensed that this was the moment to settle his family feud with the Bani Rashid. The Bani Rashid were still discredited for having sided with the Turks during the war, but the Hashimites in Amman and Baghdad had not yet found an opportunity to obtain their subservience. In a series of swift and daring expeditions Ibn Saud captured Hail in the autumn of 1921 and incorporated the land of the Shammar tribes into his Kingdom of Nejd. A number of the Bani Rashid resided as his "guests" at Riyadh, and Ibn Saud became the sole power in the interior expanses of Arabia. A provisional settlement was made with the British with regard to their "protected" areas. Sir Percy Cox in 1922 drew up with Ibn Saud the protocol of Ukair, loosely defining areas and districts. At this time two neutral zones were set up on the boundaries of Ibn Saud's kingdom—one facing Iraq and the other next to Kuwayt. These neutral zones served as buffer regions, so that wandering tribes would not create incidents.

The extension of his realm, however, led to serious economic problems. The annual income of the kingdom (in other words, Ibn Saud's income) at the time was about $750,000, to which was added $30,000 subsidy from the British. For a state which had just doubled its responsibilities, however, the income was patently insufficient and to augment it in Arabia seemed exceedingly difficult. In the winter of 1923 Ibn Saud went again to Ukair to meet with agents of the Anglo-

Persian Oil Company and the Eastern General Syndicate. They bid against each other for an oil concession in Ibn Saud's lands. He was not much impressed but needing money desperately he gave the concession to the latter for a rental of $10,000 a year. Interestingly enough, only two years' rental was paid; and then, upon the advice of geologists who explored the al-Hasa desert, the concession was abandoned!

KING OF SAUDI ARABIA

In the autumn of 1923 Great Britain held a conference at Kuwayt of all Arab amirs, shaykhs, and sultans under their subsidy. They were told that payments would stop at the end of March, 1924; a lump-sum full payment was handed them forthwith. From that moment they became free agents. But at the same conference the British delineated the frontiers among the several Arab states, insisting among other points that Ibn Saud must relinquish Khurma and Turaba to Husayn. Ibn Saud left the conference refusing to accept the frontier decision.

Ibn Saud had hardly reached Riyadh when Husayn arranged to be proclaimed caliph. The announcement shocked Ibn Saud, who felt that the Holy Places of Islam were being defiled by a presumptuous person. At the same time it undoubtedly revealed to him a sure escape from his poverty. Drive Husayn from the Hijaz and obtain the pilgrimage income for himself! In August the blow was struck. The first battle was at al-Taif, and in October Ibn Saud occupied Mecca. Husayn fled to Jidda and abdicated in favor of his eldest son, Ali. He, then, took up residence in Akaba until June, 1925, when the British conveyed him to Cyprus. There he suffered a stroke and lived on, a broken man, until he died in 1930 in Amman at the court of his son. Ibn Saud could have pressed on easily and defeated Ali at Jidda, but he realized that this might involve the powers. Ali recognized his hopeless position without aid from England. He, therefore, surrendered to Ibn Saud in 1925 and went to Baghdad to live at his brother's court.

Ibn Saud was now master of all Arabia except for Aden, Yemen, Asir, and the various shaykhdoms of the Persian Gulf area. The people of the Hijaz declared him King of the Hijaz, a title which he added to that of Sultan of Nejd. The Wahhabis in taking Mecca destroyed a number of the shrines which they considered the works of the devil, and Ibn Saud refurbished the Holy Places which Husayn had permitted to fall into a sad state of repair. In 1926 he held an Islamic congress in the Hijaz. This congress had a double role: to bring Islamic leaders of all schools of thought from all parts of the Muslim world to see him and the administration he was inaugurating in the Hijaz; and to allow his own Wahhabi theologians to rub elbows with

Muslim divines of other training and experience. Incidentally, the Congress might popularize the pilgrimage, which now became his greatest source of income, and bring in a larger revenue.

Abd al-Aziz ibn Saud was one of those individuals whom people refer to as a born leader. He inspired confidence. He was just and honorable in his administration and prompt in his decisions and actions. He observed the Wahhabi code; yet social innovations were not blindly obstructed just because they were novel, but carefully appraised and judged accordingly. The introduction of the telephone and the radio into Arabia, for instance, was bitterly opposed by the arch-conservatists among his Wahhabis, who argued that these instruments must be agents of the devil since they could carry the voice so far. Ibn Saud neatly disputed that contention by pointing out that these instruments would bring the word of God and that one would be able to hear worthy divines of the al-Azhar read the Koran. The telephone and the radio came to Arabia.

Life around Ibn Saud, whether he was at al-Taif, Mecca, Medina, or Riyadh, was simple, democratic, and direct. He lent a sympathetic ear to the troubles of the poorest of his subjects, and arrogance was foreign to his character. The business of government was dispatched with simplicity and efficiency. A trusted friend of long standing, Abdallah Sulaiman, served as finance minister, treasurer, and paymaster and on most occasions kept the state's money in his bedroom at the palace in Riyadh. At one time he commented on his anxiety over the risk involved when the balance rose to $50,000 in cash.

The military power of Ibn Saud rested on a combination of factors, the chief of which was the organization of the *Ikhwan* (Brotherhood). In Muslim history such groups were important in Morocco, the Sudan, Iran, Turkey, and many other places; and Ibn Saud's founding of these communities in 1912 proved most significant in his rise to power. The first brotherhood was established around the desert wells of Artawiya, where the fighting bedouin were partially settled. Its motive was partly economic; and Ibn Saud provided funds for a mosque, religious establishments for reading and writing, wells, agricultural irrigation, arms, and ammunition. The settlement was a religio-socio-military camp and became the prototype of several hundred such towns. From the brotherhoods Ibn Saud received his most devoted soldiers and the necessary stiffening for the regular bedouin levies and volunteers that made his army and expeditions to Yemen, Asir, and "the frontiers" of Iraq and Transjordan so feared and so successful.

Of equal significance was the extension of Ibn Saud's power, law, and order over the bedouin tribes of the Hijaz and other provinces coming under his rule. Traditionally independent and subject only to their own tribal customs, they rebelled against Ibn Saud's justice, military conscription, peace, and taxation. When Ibn Saud learned of a particularly serious raid committed by the Bani Harb, he fell upon their encampment and subdued them completely. He tied other tribes to his rule by the holding of suitable hostages at his court and by judicious marriages for himself and his sons. In 1932 the official name of the state was changed from the Kingdom of the Hijaz and of the Nejd and its Dependencies to the Kingdom of Saudi Arabia. At that time it comprised most of Arabia.

After the occupation of Jidda Ibn Saud in 1925 arranged with Sir Gilbert Clayton the treaties of Bahra and of Hadda, which defined on paper the frontiers with Iraq and Transjordan. However, no mention was made of Maan and Akaba, which Ibn Saud claimed since they had heretofore been incorporated in the Hijaz, but which the British occupied in July and joined to Transjordan. In 1927 Sir Gilbert returned to Arabia and the treaty of Jidda was signed. Great Britain recognized Ibn Saud as a sovereign and independent ruler. No mention was made of Britain's "special interest" in Palestine or Iraq. (It will be recalled that recognition of special interest in these areas had been demanded a few years earlier from Husayn.) And Ibn Saud pledged "to maintain friendly and peaceful relations" with Kuwayt, Bahrayn, Qatar, and the Oman Coast—all of which were under the protection of Great Britain. The Treaty of Jidda set a precedent, and within a few years Ibn Saud was recognized by and had similar treaties with Italy, France, Russia, Turkey, Iran, and other states which had Muslim subjects.

The problem of Asir troubled Ibn Saud for many years. After the death of Muhammad Idrisi in 1923 his heirs mismanaged affairs and quarreled continually among themselves. Already Ibn Saud had won victories in the highlands of Asir; and when Imam Yahya of Yemen took the port of Hodeida and the southern coastal region of Tihama, the Idrisi called upon Ibn Saud for help. Becoming in 1930 a protectorate and virtually an integral part of Ibn Saud's Arabia, Asir was divided. Imam Yahya failed to halt his aggressions in Asir, although Ibn Saud offered peace on the basis of the *status quo*. Yemen's refusal brought hostilities in 1934 and a quick and crushing victory for Ibn Saud. In the treaty of al-Taif peace was established magnanimously on the basis proposed before the victories. Imam Yahya retained the plain of Tihama and the valuable port of Hodeida; and there were no reparations, indemnities, or payments. Ibn Saud had shown his authority and his power; he had also proved to the Arabs his leniency, his honor, his generosity, and his wisdom. He now had stature among the Arabs.

DISCOVERY OF OIL

Life in Arabia might have gone along smoothly and comfortably almost indefinitely, had not the world-wide depression of the early 1930's upset Ibn Saud's economy. The scale of government operations and Ibn Saud's personal expenditures depended upon the pilgrimage traffic, which in the late 1920's had amounted to over 100,000 visitors each year. In 1931, however, the traffic dropped to 80,000; in 1932, to 40,000. The Kingdom of Saudi Arabia could no longer meet its bills.

Through the advice of H. St. John B. Philby, an English Arabist, a convert to Islam, and after 1930 a member of Ibn Saud's privy council, Karl S. Twitchell, an American mining engineer who had been exploring in Yemen, was employed to search for oil and other mineral resources in Saudi Arabia. His expenses were paid by the American philanthropist Charles R. Crane, of World War I King-Crane Commission fame. First visiting Jidda in 1931, Twitchell examined the Hijaz for water resources and returned a pessimistic report. At the same interview, however, he suggested the possibilities of oil and minerals. While Twitchell was exploring the breadth of the country in 1933, Ibn Saud gave a concession to the Standard Oil Company of California and received an advance of 30,000 gold sovereigns. The concession ran for sixty years, and a royalty of four gold shillings per ton would be paid to Saudi Arabia.

Almost immediately the California Arabian Standard Oil Company (CASOC), owned equally by Standard Oil of California and the Texas Company, was formed. Mapping, geologic surveying, and drilling in al-Hasa province were initiated by engineers who came across to the mainland from Bahrayn, where oil was found in 1932. It was a long and discouraging process. No oil in commercial quantities was found at the depth at which oil had been discovered in Bahrayn. However, with the deepening of well number seven at Dhahran in 1938 oil was found in quantity. The first oil was shipped in November to Bahrayn. In accordance with the concession Ibn Saud received another £50,000 in gold. Piers were quickly constructed; and the first tanker was filled directly at Ras Tanura in May, 1939, Ibn Saud turning the first valve. Exploration spread. Before World War II other producing wells were located north of Dhahran and another forty miles west of Abqaiq.

When the war came 12,000 barrels were going daily to Bahrayn, and Saudi Arabia was considered as a future important oil-producing state. In 1940 the Italians bombed Bahrayn and Dhahran, breaking one pipeline. However, oil production was not expanded in Saudi Arabia during the war for lack of men and equipment. Moreover, the American government believed that the increased needs of gasoline could be obtained more easily from efforts in other fields.

At the time Twitchell was looking for oil he had, as a good mining engineer, his eye out for minerals, especially gold. After trials and disappointments gold was found between Mecca and Medina at Mahab Dhahab. A company was established in 1934 to work the mine, probably one of King Solomon's. Called the Saudi Arabian Mining Company, it was owned by the American Smelting and Refining Company, the American Cyanamid Corporation, several Britishers, and by Saudi nationals. (The Saudi nationals owned fifteen percent.) The government received as royalties five percent of the gross value of all metals recovered. At the outbreak of the war Ibn Saud was receiving several hundred thousand dollars a year from the gold mines.

WORLD WAR II

With the outbreak of World War II and the fall of the pilgrimage trade after Italy entered the war Ibn Saud was precipitously reduced to desperate financial straits. In 1940 CASOC advanced several million dollars against future royalties; and in 1941 Ibn Saud requested a further advance of $6,000,000, declaring that without that sum the state he had built would disintegrate. Since the future of CASOC was obviously at stake, a proposal was made to the American government to grant the sum against future oil deliveries. President Roosevelt directed the bid to the British government, which began advancing sizable sums to Saudi Arabia in 1941. By the spring of 1944 Ibn Saud was over $50,000,000 in debt to London, and the end was not in sight. After a great deal of debate and study in Washington American lend-lease to an amount of $34,000,000 was made available to Saudi Arabia, several millions of which were in the form of newly minted silver coins. In 1944 the American army requested the building of a refinery at Ras Tanura; compliance strained the finances of the company, which had changed its name to Arabian American Oil Company (Aramco). In 1945 an underwater pipeline was built to Bahrayn, enabling the flow of oil in Saudi Arabia to be increased. Royalties paid by Aramco to Ibn Saud began to obviate the subsidies from the West.

The bounty which Saudi Arabia received during the war had a most deleterious effect upon Arab society. Shipping was exceedingly scarce; technical services were impossible to obtain at almost any price; and machinery and capital goods were allocated by the Middle East Supply Center to Saudi Arabia in infinitesimal quantities, if at all. Because of Wahhabi views on loans and inadequate banking facilities much of the cash journeyed to Cairo, where it was turned into luxury articles of small bulk that could be easily shipped by small dhows to the Arabian coast. Lavish living and excessive incomes for the family of Ibn Saud and his friends became the custom, and a great part of the income of the state was squandered in a fashion reminiscent of the palaces and their entourages in Istanbul and Cairo during the 1860's and 1870's. The total income of the government jumped from about $7,000,000 in 1939 to over $200,000,000 by 1953. Even so, balancing accounts and keeping debts from growing were feats too difficult and too restraining to find sympathetic support in high places.

EXPANSION OF OIL PRODUCTION

In the postwar era in Saudi Arabia society became entirely dependent upon oil royalties. Consequently, the production of oil and all of its ramifications were of the utmost importance to the government. Toward the end of the war the demand for petroleum products in the Mediterranean became staggering, and the need of a pipeline from Dhahran to the Levant coast prompted the American government to suggest that it buy into Aramco and finance the pipeline. Private oil companies raised a violent storm; but it appeared that the European market for oil in the recovery period would be insatiable, and it was imperative that more pipelines be built from the oilfields to the Mediterranean. Aramco was compelled to seek additional capital for the construction; and in 1946 arrangements were made for Standard Oil of New Jersey and Socony-Vacuum to acquire thirty and ten percent, respectively, of Aramco stock.

French petroleum interests brought suit against this action. They alleged that it violated the Red Line agreement of 1928, which stipulated that oil companies participating in the Iraq Petroleum Company would not engage separately in oil production in Arabia. Work on the pipeline, nevertheless, was started, and steel pipe began to be shipped in 1947. All work on the line ceased during the Palestine War. Syria, Lebanon, and Jordan declared that the lines would not be permitted as long as the United States supported the partition of Palestine and the creation of Israel. Ibn Saud, however, announced that he would not revoke the American oil concessions because of the American stand on Palestine; and work was resumed in February, 1949. The oil companies reached a settlement with the French, and thereupon organized the Trans-Arabian Pipe Line Company. Over half a billion dollars was expended between 1948 and 1953 in constructing the TAP-line and developing new fields and facilities for Aramco. In December, 1950 the 1,068 mile TAP-line was completed, and 300,000 to 500,000 barrels a day began to flow from Dhahran to Sidon. New production was brought in every year, and after 1955 oil was being produced at a daily rate exceeding one million barrels. In 1943 the daily rate had been 15,000 barrels; in 1946, 165,000 barrels; and in 1950, 500,000 barrels.

The original concession to Aramco provided for royalties of four gold shillings, or the equivalent in dollars or sterling, per ton of oil produced. During the war and in the years immediately following gold sovereigns commanded a high premium in the Middle East, and the question of the equivalent of four gold shillings was hotly debated. At the official exchange rate a gold sovereign was worth about $8.25, which made the royalty about $1.66 per ton (22 cents per barrel). But sovereigns were bought and sold in the open markets in the Middle East at twice the official rate. In 1948 Aramco agreed to value the gold sovereign at $12.00, which raised the royalties to $2.40 per ton (32 cents per barrel).

As production increased and Aramco profits began to swell, Ibn Saud pressed for greater returns for his government. At the end of 1950 a new concession was signed which gave Saudi Arabia: four gold shillings, at the official $8.25 rate per ton; a twenty percent tax on Aramco profits before United States taxes; and certain customs duties and taxes or fifty percent of Aramco profits after United States taxes, whichever sum was the greater. Made retroactive to January 1, 1950, the new formula increased the 1950 royalties from $60,000,000 to $90,000,000. By 1956 the payments were topping $250,000,000 annually, and a decade later all revenues from oil, including royalties and taxes, tripled that sum. The negotiation and announcement of these terms led to the breakdown of discussions in Iran and a change in the rates in Iraq. In fact, the Aramco–Saudi Arabia concession terms in 1950 established the general pattern of royalties throughout the Middle East for the next several years.

Although Aramco held the concession for the exploitation of oil in Saudi Arabia as well as in her half of the neutral zone adjoining Iraq, the Paul Getty Oil Company possessed rights for the neutral zone facing Kuwayt, where operations produced significant quantities of oil and royalties for Saudi Arabia. In order not to give Americans a full monopoly of oil interests, King Saud granted in 1957 to the Arabian Oil Company of Japan the right to explore for oil in the waters of the Persian Gulf off the shores of the neutral zone, with the agreement giving Saudi Arabia fifty-six percent of the profits. This concession raised serious questions because the states bordering on the Gulf had no understanding with respect to territorial limits and offshore claims. Furthermore, Aramco was anxious about its fifty-fifty profit-sharing arrangement. King Saud declared that the Aramco rates would not be affected, and in 1965 the several Persian Gulf states accepted the idea that offshore rights could be extended to the middle of the Gulf.

Each year after 1956 the production of oil increased beyond all predictions. At first a daily average of one million barrels was a yearly goal frequently reached, but in 1962 it soared to one and one-half million barrels daily, and in 1966, including Saudi Arabia's share of neutral zone production, topped two and one-half million barrels a day, placing Saudi Arabia as the fourth world producer, after the United States, the U.S.S.R., and Venezuela. Offshore discoveries, added to continuous exploration and new finds in the neutral zone and by Aramco, more than maintained the quantities of proven oil reserves which were fifty billion barrels in 1960, seventy billion in 1966, and eighty-one billion by 1967. In the 1950's Aramco surrendered its claims to the western half of the country and again in 1963 gave up additional areas at the request of the government which desired to be freer in negotiating with other interests. In this vein, a combination of French companies obtained a concession to drill in the Red Sea in 1965.

One of the difficult problems for Saudi Arabia and the oil companies is supply and demand, modified by the discoveries of oil in many new regions such as Libya, the desires of each nation to be self-sufficient in petroleum products and, if possible, to become an exporter to earn foreign exchange. Increases in world consumption did not always keep pace with production but any reduction of exports hurt Saudi Arabia's budget since it was dependent on oil exports (often eighty percent), and larger exports from one country too frequently meant that the international oil company curtailed production in another country. To meet this challenge Abdallah al-Tariqi, director of petroleum and mineral affairs of Saudi Arabia, initiated in 1960 at Baghdad the Organization of Petroleum Exporting Countries (OPEC), composed of Iran, Iraq, Kuwayt, Saudi Arabia, and Venezuela. OPEC sought to stabilize world prices, obtain reasonable profits for oil companies, assure a voice in all oil decisions, guarantee that consumers would not be cut off from supplies, and boycott companies not co-operating with OPEC. Since its formation Libya has joined, and frequent meetings are held to discuss problems and to arrive at common policies. The fact of its existence compels the oil companies to ameliorate policies and decisions unfavorable to the individual states belonging to OPEC in which Saudi Arabia has taken a leading role.

DEVELOPMENTS IN SAUDI ARABIA

The vast influx of money generated many plans for the improvement of Saudi Arabia. In 1947 a four-year plan to cost $270,000,000 was outlined in general terms. It called for the building of railroads, highways, ports, airfields, schools, hospitals, electric-power plants, irrigation systems, and conduits and canals for supplying water to Jidda,

Mecca, and other cities. Aramco proved an interested ally in these programs and loaned or helped to locate able engineers for many of the projects. In 1951 the railway between Dammam and Riyadh was completed, and in 1955 work was begun on the line to connect Riyadh and Jidda by way of Medina. In 1954 conferences were held with representatives of Syria and Jordan to rehabilitate the Hijaz railway, which ran from Damascus to Medina; and in 1956 an American firm was employed to draw plans for its rebuilding to link Riyadh and Dammam with Syria and Asia Minor. Plans for an asphalt highway from Jidda to Dammam by way of Mecca, al-Taif, Riyadh, and al-Hasa materialized in 1955; and in following years other highways were restored to facilitate pilgrimage routes from Iraq. The port of Dammam was reconstructed, and three small ports on the Red Sea improved. To serve as a gateway to Medina and for pilgrims the port of Yanbu was developed in 1961 on the Red Sea. Clearing the reef-strewn harbor at Jidda was considered, although difficulties seemed insurmountable. In 1957 King Saud University in Riyadh was opened, and former palaces in Jidda, Medina, and Riyadh were converted into schools. The Islamic Sharia College was opened in Medina in 1961, and the Petroleum and Mining College in Dhahran was founded in 1965. With the assistance of $5 million from UNESCO in 1966 a College of Education was begun in Riyadh. Elementary schools appeared in all parts of the kingdom in great numbers; in 1963 alone there were 100 new schools for boys and 62 for girls. Hospitals were built in numerous places, and new construction in Riyadh turned the capital into a bustling city. The spectacular Nasriya Palace was inaugurated in 1957, and all offices of the government were moved from Jidda. Each succeeding year found transportation and communications vastly improved, thereby extending the power of the central government more resolutely over all sections of the state and linking Saudi Arabia more closely to other areas of the Middle East.

When Prince Faysal was in power and after he became king in 1964 economic development had the highest priority. Mounting oil revenues helped him implement these ideas upon which he felt the only possible salvation of the Saudi family rested. For a number of years surveys by air and land had revealed sizable and commercially valuable deposits of iron, copper, and silver, and the amounts of sulphur obtained from oil were vast. A steel-rolling mill was projected in 1964 not far from Jidda, contracts were given to a British firm, and it was opened in 1966. Over forty percent of the budget was set aside for development and in the years of 1965 and 1966 a glass industry was established at Riyadh, and plants for producing sulphur, paint, ammonia and its derivatives, petrochemicals, fertilizers, carbon black, and other products were built in Dammam by British, Italian, and American firms. Everywhere one turned new activity, hardly dreamed of five or six years before, was at hand. Engineers were studying the laying of natural-gas pipelines to deliver the wasted trillions of cubic feet of gas from the oil fields of al-Hasa to every part of the land.

One of the most significant developments of the early 1950's was the al-Kharj agricultural program. At al-Kharj deep wells were cleaned; pumps were installed; and more than 8,000 acres of land, almost miraculously, produced fine alfalfa, vegetables, melons, and fruits in great abundance. Begun in wartime under American stimulus, the al-Kharj project served as an example of what could be done to increase the local food supply. The scarcity of water hampered agriculture, except in some of the great free-flowing oases in al-Hasa, and its lack began to pinch the industrial plans of King Faysal. Schemes for bringing water from the Euphrates to Riyadh were not too far-fetched, and Saudi Arabia engaged in several desalinization pilot projects. In 1962 it was noted that there was more drilling for water than for oil. Each water find was widely celebrated. Realizing the significance of water, the government divided the country into eight areas for the purpose of mapping water resources and retained American, British, Italian, and French companies to carry out intensive hydrological surveys in several of these areas. In 1965 Aramco announced the discovery of a reserve of fresh subsoil water, estimated at twenty trillion gallons, and struck another extensive fresh-water reserve sixty miles east of Riyadh. However, the supply of water in the capital became more and more critical, and in 1966 a Finnish concern won a contract to build and deliver water-purification equipment for the city. The availability of fresh water was perhaps more crucial than the presence of oil for the future of Saudi Arabia.

MILITARY FORCES

For all of Ibn Saud's character and personality, he never for a moment dropped his guard or forgot that his position rested on military power. In 1947 a British army mission came to train his forces in the use of more modern weapons. And in 1951 Saudi Arabia signed a mutual-defense assistance agreement with the United States, which in 1956 shipped various types of equipment, including eighteen tanks. Also in 1956, several jet fighter-planes were obtained from Egypt. The most powerful military base in that part of the Middle East was located at Dhahran. Here, toward the close of the war the United States constructed a mighty airfield and installations from which planes could control much of the Middle East and bomb strategic spots in the U.S.S.R. American rights to the base were discussed in

1949 and extended from month to month until June, 1951, when a five-year lease was signed. When in 1956 Saudi Arabia requested that the United States pay an annual rental of $50,000,000 for Dhahran, the United States conducted a study to determine if new developments in missiles and air power had not rendered Dhahran unnecessary. For several months the lease was extended on a contingency basis. Then, in 1957 upon King Saud's visit in Washington a five-year renewal was authorized. In exchange the United States promised to train a small Saudi navy, provide for instruction of an air force at Dhahran, and expand the army school at al-Kharj. Some training jets were also delivered as part of the program. However, in 1961 King Saud informed the United States that the lease for the base would not be renewed again. Prince Faysal evidently had promised Nasser that he would take this stand, and in April, 1962 the Dhahran base was relinquished to Saudi Arabia and another vestige of World War II was removed.

The outbreak of civil war in Yemen in the autumn of 1962 re-emphasized the military aspects of life in Saudi Arabia as the United Arab Republic was supporting the Yemeni republican forces under al-Sallal while Imam Muhammad al-Badr and the royalists sought protection from Saudi Arabia. At the same time that military threats arose in the southwest, Kuwayt in the northeast looked to Saudi Arabia to help ward off the danger of invasion from Iraq. Jet fighters were quietly invited back from the United States in 1963, and American paratroopers participated in the training of the Saudi Paratrooper Corps. Although settlement of the Buraimi oasis dispute with Great Britain had not been reached, a British military mission arrived to advise the Saudi army, and, in 1964, 300 antitank missiles were purchased in England. Arms were secured in France, and over $100,000,-000 was spent on a modern air defense system complex. More arms were purchased from the United States in 1965, and large sums were annually expended to maintain a strong defense and to give aid to al-Badr. Surface-to-air missiles were bought from Great Britain in 1966, and more than $100,000,000 was allocated to provide the army with land transportation and maintenance facilities from the United States. The military seriousness of the civil war in Yemen and Nasser's involvement there and in Aden and the South Arabian Federation were impressed upon King Faysal, not only by the frequent bombing of Saudi towns near Yemen but also by such actions as the warm reception accorded publicly to ex-King Saud when he visited Cairo and Saud's statements favoring al-Sallal and the Yemeni republicans and accusing King Faysal of supporting the royalists and a reactionary regime.

FINANCIAL PROBLEMS

One of the vexing problems in Saudi Arabia was that of finance and currency. Since there was no paper money, the medium of exchange had been foreign gold coins and local silver coins and Ibn Saud failed to establish any stable ratio of value between the two. Gold coins were almost exclusively English George V sovereigns, which were the generally recognized standard of value in Saudi Arabia. Silver riyals were first circulated in 1933, and a concerted attempt was made to maintain a parity between gold and silver. However, the world decline of silver prices and the abandonment of the gold standard by England and the United States played havoc with the exchange rates. World War II raised black-market rates of gold from $35 to over $85 an ounce.

In 1952 an American financial mission, arranged under the American Point Four program, reorganized the currency situation at the request of Ibn Saud. New Saudi gold sovereigns of $8.24 value were issued, a monetary agency was established, and an exchange rate of forty silver riyals to a Saudi sovereign was fixed. The great value of the monetary agency rested upon its ability to stabilize the value of the currency by buying and selling riyals and foreign exchange on the money markets in Jidda and Dammam. Furthermore, after the new royalty rates were fixed in 1950 more of Saudi Arabian income was received in sterling and other soft currencies, the disposal of which was more easily arranged by the agency.

The agency was also able to assist in the preparation of a budget. The first budget, of about $55,000,000, was drawn up for the fiscal year of 1948; but Ibn Saud ignored it, and no budget was published again until 1952. Budgets have been presented each year since. In 1956 the budget approximated $300,000,000; but there was no certainty that the government adhered to it, since a distinction between the public treasury and the private purse of the king and the royal family had not been finely drawn. The accounts of the government were usually balanced by the following year's royalties and normally ran a deficit in the neighborhood of $50,000,000. Finances continued to deteriorate, and the complexities of the modern commercial and financial world appeared almost too much for King Saud. In 1957 Saudi Arabia joined the International Monetary Fund and the International Bank for Reconstruction and Development, but deficits and irresponsible spending habits of the royal family brought matters to a climax in March, 1958. At a full family council Prince Faysal, nominal first minister, was handed complete authority over internal, foreign, and financial policies of the state. The international aspects of this denouement were high-lighted in the world presses, but the financial angles were probably more important. Spending was curbed, and national budgets were expected to have more significance in the future.

Faysal ran the state along tight financial lines. He felt that his first task was to observe the balanced budget and retire the debt. Luxury imports including automobiles were forbidden and the civil list for the royal family was greatly reduced. Princes complained and King Saud, unable to curb his style of living or proverbial generosity, saw his personal debts rise in 1959 from $8,400,000 to $31,600,000. At the end of 1960 the king, prodded by many courtiers and even some of the tribal shaykhs, rejected Faysal's budget and reassumed full powers of per-sonal rule. There were changes in the cabinet, and Saud appointed his son as minister of defense to insure the personal loyalty of the military. Again budgets were ignored and debts mounted. How long this situation could have prevailed is difficult to guess, for the civil war in Yemen brought many of the princes and the tribal leaders to their senses. On top of civil turmoil, bankruptcy was intolerable and a strong hand was demanded. Faysal was forced upon Saud again in October, 1962 as prime minister, a new cabinet was formed, and King Saud's sons were omitted from the list. Faysal set the 1963 budget at $550,000,000 and promised to have the public debt fully discharged by the end of that year. Each year his budget remained in balance; in 1964 it stood at $700,000,000 and in 1966 at $1,100,000,000. Nearly forty percent was apportioned for economic development. Currency in circulation reached unprecedented levels—over a billion riyals in 1964, a figure which had doubled in five years. Still the gold and foreign exchange cover was maintained and the value of the riyal held firm on world exchanges at four and one-half to the United States dollar. The monetary depression and chaos under King Saud gave way to in-dustrial growth, financial stability, and general optimism under King Faysal.

SAUDI RELATIONS IN THE MIDDLE EAST

The position of Saudi Arabia with regard to control of the Muslim Holy Places and her wealth guaranteed respect from the other Middle Eastern states. That esteem was promoted even more widely by Ibn Saud's remission of taxes and special charges upon those making the pilgrimage to Mecca. This had a profound effect and encouraged the yearly visitors. In 1953 the number of visitors rose to 120,000. There had been a time, not too remote, when the fees of these pilgrims kept the state solvent. What a change the oil made!

Saudi Arabia was one of the first members of the Arab League and steadfastly participated in its deliberations, although she never took the leading role which her wealth, prestige, and position as custodian of the Holy Places might warrant. During the Palestine war, Saudi Arabia, not having a frontier contiguous with Palestine, did not send troops or take an active part. She co-operated in the boycott of Israel, however; and does not permit Jews to land at the Dhahran airport. In 1946 Ibn Saud protested to President Truman against the American position on the partition of Palestine, and the President tried to assuage the Saudi Arabians by awarding the Legion of Merit to Ibn Saud and Crown Prince Saud. In 1948 Ibn Saud became so incensed over the American recognition of Israel and the dishonoring of the pledge given him that he refused a $15,000,000 Export-Import Bank loan.

In 1953 a serious dispute arose with Great Britain over the possession of the Buraimi oasis. In 1952 a "standstill" agreement with Britain had been reached concerning the Persian Gulf Arab shaykhdoms under British protection, but with the steady advance of oilfields southward in eastern Arabia no ill-defined frontier was safe. Britain contended that the Buraimi oasis was a part of Trucial Oman; but Ibn Saud also claimed it, and Saudi forces held the oasis. The United States encouraged a settlement by arbitration. The court in Geneva broke up, however, charging Saudi Arabia with bribery and coercion; and the question still remained unsettled.

As the strife between the Soviet and Western blocs grew tense, the position of Saudi Arabia became uncertain. The West proposed the creation of a Middle Eastern defense pact to strengthen the lines of the Middle East against the advances of the Soviet bloc. In 1954 Saudi Arabia followed the lead of Egypt and declared her opposition to such a pact.

After the Baghdad pact was signed in 1955 Saudi Arabia joined with Syria and Egypt in a Damascus pact; with Yemen and Egypt in 1956, in a Jidda pact; and with Egypt, Jordan, and Syria in 1957, just preceding King Saud's visit to the United States, in the Arab solidarity agreement. These agreements provided for joint military forces and declared that an attack upon any one member would be regarded as an attack upon all signatories. That Saudi Arabia had a fundamental interest in assuming such a role was seriously questioned; it appeared more likely that Saudi Arabia was being used by Syria and Egypt in the desperate plight confronting those two states. Saudi Arabia supported Egypt in her nationalization of the Suez Canal Company, although halting the flow of Saudi oil through the Canal was a serious blow to Saudi finances. Later, in 1956, when Israel, England, and France invaded Egypt, Saudi Arabia ordered general mobilization and called on all Arabs to oppose the attack. Diplomatic relations with the aggressors were severed, and King Saud took a strong stand in favor of Arab nationalism. Yet, through the entire Suez affair King Saud was vexed that Egypt had seized the Canal without consultations with other Arab states. He feared, however, to take a position in opposition to Nasser since a growing number of Arab nationalists in Saudi Arabia equated Arab nationalism and Nasserism.

Throughout the period of the union of Egypt and Syria in the United Arab Republic and the vagaries of Nasserism in Iraq, Jordan, and Syria, Saudi Arabia pursued a course of Arab neutralism, supporting the Arab League and adhering to the principle that one Arab state must not interfere in the internal affairs of another. In the light of this policy King Saud protested to Iraq over her threats against Kuwayt in 1961 and dispatched troops there to safeguard the latter's newly declared sovereignty. Likewise in 1962 Saud and Faysal condemned United Arab Republic intervention in Yemen on the side of the republican regime and broke diplomatic relations with Nasser. Aid and sanctuary on several occasions were given to al-Badr, and Faysal rejected President Kennedy's proposals for a settlement in Yemen as not sufficiently recognizing the royalist claims and more importantly as foreign interference in Arab affairs. Faysal stoutly believed that the republican regime in Yemen would collapse within a few hours if Egyptian forces were withdrawn and insisted, therefore, that President al-Sallal's power in Yemen was artificial. Egyptian bombs fell on Saudi border towns all too frequently, and, despite the Buraimi question, in 1963 Faysal resumed diplomatic relations with Great Britain and took costly and decisive steps to strengthen his own military forces to show Nasser that he could not be cowed into abandoning his neighboring Arab state. A military stalemate soon resulted in Yemen with al-Sallal and the Egyptian soldiers possessing the plains and the capital while al-Badr and the royalist tribes were secure in the highlands. Faysal met twice with Nasser in 1964 and again in 1965, but agreed-upon cease-fires, conferences in the Sudan, at Jidda, and in Yemen itself between the rival parties, and arbitration and peacemaking efforts by the Amir of Kuwayt were unsuccessful. When Great Britain announced in 1966 that her withdrawal from Aden was fixed for 1968, Nasser could not bring himself to pull out his troops from nearby Yemen. Faysal maintained that the settlement in Yemen should be so arranged that the Yemeni people could determine their own future. No immediate compromise from these two positions seemed possible until the aftermath of the Israeli-Arab War of June, 1967 forced Nasser to agree to withdraw his forces and permit a third force to commence the long process of binding up wounds and achieving a compromise. The decision for this policy was reached at the Arab summit meeting at Khartoum in August, 1967.

KING SAUD AND KING FAYSAL

Whether or not these positions would have been taken had Ibn Saud been living is difficult to say. Abd al-Aziz ibn Abd al-Rahman ibn Saud Al Faysal died November 9, 1953 and was immediately succeeded by the eldest of his thirty-five living sons: Saud ibn Abd al-Aziz al-Saud. For a number of years the aged Ibn Saud had been afflicted with arthritis and was approaching blindness. In 1933 Prince Saud was declared heir apparent and participated in governmental activities. Other sons shared duties of administration; the most prominent of these was the second living son, Prince Faysal. In the king's last years definite ministries of government were established, and in October a formal cabinet was organized, although the first cabinet meeting was not held until the following March. Prince Saud served as prime minister. Other ministries created from time to time were: foreign affairs, finance, defense, agriculture, interior, commerce, health, education, and information. Prince Faysal was declared heir to the throne and continued his work in foreign affairs. Various developments slowly showed that a new man was king. In 1954 Abdallah Sulaiman resigned. He had been Ibn Saud's closest adviser for a quarter of a century on all matters, but especially those concerned with finance. As finance minister he channeled income of the state into capital developments whenever possible and restricted expenditures of the princes. Shortly thereafter, H. St. John B. Philby, an adviser of Ibn Saud since 1930 and a special friend of Prince Faysal, was expelled from Saudi Arabia for "unfriendly" acts. Corruption spread rapidly, especially in the techniques of awarding contracts, government officials being handsomely "rewarded." Many Saudi officials were able to buy estates in Egypt or apartment houses in Beirut, and the construction of palaces in al-Taif and other spots in Arabia proceeded apace.

Even more significant, however, was the presence of numerous Arab political exiles. The most notable of these were Adib al-Shishakli and Fawzi Silu of Syria, both of whom were dedicated in their opposition to Shukri al-Kuwatli and Nasser. Suddenly in March, 1958 as a result of a family conference in Riyadh, King Saud assumed the role of a "constitutional" monarch. The reins of government were awarded to Prince Faysal, who was generally acknowledged as a firmer and more talented administrator than his brother. Problems of finance, bitter Arab rivalry, intense Arab nationalism, internal social upheaval, international politics, traditional nepotism, and the impact of modern living produced such dire conflicts that King Saud was unequal to the task of governing. In the face of these forces King Saud publicly stated in the middle of 1957 that no Arab state should interfere in internal affairs of another Arab state and asked pointedly that Cairo and Damascus newscasts withhold their vilification of King Husayn of Jordan. Later Saud declared complete solidarity with King Faysal of Iraq and then in 1958 congratulated all sides upon the formation of the United Arab Republic and the Arab Federation. The final straw appeared to be his failure to disprove complicity in an alleged plot to assassinate influential personages in Syria.

Prince Faysal, once in power, dismissed the new minister of finance; removed Prince Fahd, the King's son, who was minister of defense; and fired five of the King's foreign advisers. A stronger hand was at the helm, and significantly his mother belonged to the powerful and highly revered Wahhab family. Momentarily, at least, a course of neutrality between Arab factions seemed the best political path for Saudi Arabia; and Prince Faysal was judged the one suited for leadership.

The social impact of the oil wealth in Saudi Arabia has been beyond calculation. Aramco established numerous schools for workers and their children in oil-producing areas in addition to providing many types of technical and mechanical instruction and training for the workers themselves. Their wants and demands expanded rapidly. In 1953, 13,000 out of 15,000 Arab workers for Aramco in Dhahran went out on strike for better living conditions, increased wages, and many other items usually presented in a typical Western industrial strike. A peaceful settlement was arranged, but shortly thereafter King Saud issued a decree prohibiting strikes. The affair pointed to future problems not only for Aramco but even more for the royal family and the officials who had squandered the wealth of the nation. Saudi Arabian officials considered the question of oil nationalization; but the case of Iran did not encourage precipitate action. In June, 1954 the Saudi Arabian Tanker Corporation with an independent tanker fleet owned by A. S. Onassis, a Greek of Argentine citizenship, was formed and granted special rights. This was an indication of the ideas current at the court at Riyadh. Aramco was most generous in its relations with the Saudi government and behaved in a most benevolent manner in Arabia; yet there could be no question that many people in Saudi Arabia contemplated nationalization.

The question of highest priority, however, was how to cope with the ineptness and prodigality of King Saud in a government where his wish was law. As already indicated, a conclave of the royal princes in the spring of 1958 insisted that Prince Faysal rule the state. Having promised his father many years before that he would never raise a hand against his older brother, Faysal refused the proffered kingship but became prime minister with a council of ministers whom he could appoint or dismiss. This arrangement lasted until December, 1960 when King Saud reasserted his authority, and Faysal dutifully stepped aside. The drastic measures adopted by Faysal to end corruption and waste, to institute efficiency and tighten authority, and to modernize the state and society had irritated too many influential figures and depressed the economy. Within a short time, however, the downward trend prevailed. King Saud was not well and went to the United States in November, 1961 for an operation and the removal of cataracts from his eyes. Faysal was still popular with many of the princes and shaykhs and was left in charge of the government in the king's absence.

The government struggled along and King Saud's return did not ameliorate the situation. Numerous pro-Nasser groups were coalescing into substantial factions, and in August, 1962 Prince Talal and three other brothers left for Beirut publicly censuring their brother for idleness and mismanagement. The revolt in Yemen in September opened the eyes of even the most conservative elements as to what could happen at home and they automatically called for Prince Faysal. Refusing to be king, he again took over on October 17, 1962 as prime minister, forming a new cabinet, and removing from office all of King Saud's sons. Prince Faysal in an address to the nation outlined a new ten-point program which called for: the drafting of a constitution or a body of fundamental law; the organization of a legislative body or consultative council; the establishment of a ministry of justice; the abolition of slavery (over $1,000,000 was appropriated to compensate slave owners); and a rapid economic and social development. Prince Faysal began to establish a more progressive regime, and Prince Talal and the others returned to Riyadh in 1963, forgiven for their defection. In March, 1964 King Saud failed miserably in his bid to regain his powers when a majority of the princes objected, and the ulema pronounced that Faysal had a right to rule as a regent for the king. Saud became a figurehead again and found his annual allowance cut from $40,000,000 to $20,000,000. Finally on November 2, 1964 Saud renounced his right to the throne, left Saudi Arabia, and Faysal was recognized as king. Twelve of Saud's sons pledged their allegiance to Faysal, and in January, 1965 the popular fifty-two-year-old Prince Khalid, another son of Ibn Saud, was named deputy prime minister, crown prince, and first heir to the throne. Saud lived in Vienna, Paris, and other favorite spots, continually in need of medical attention. Reported to have very large sums on deposit in Swiss banks, Saud lived extravagantly and never fully accepted his dethronement. In

1967 he visited Cairo, asserted that he was still king of Saudi Arabia, and posed as he had done so often in the past as the champion of the liberals. It appeared that he was asking for the support of the pro-Nasser elements in Saudi Arabia, and undoubtedly Nasser was using him to gain his own ends in the Arab world. Saud went one step further by favoring al-Sallal and the republicans in Yemen over al-Badr and the royalists. King Faysal properly ignored these claims and proceeded diligently with the difficult task of developing and modernizing his state with the hope that Saudi Arabia would evolve rapidly and take her place in the modern world.

Of the other political states in Arabia, the five principalities of note are Bahrayn, Kuwayt, Oman, Qatar, and Yemen; in addition, there are two groups of states to be considered, Aden and the Federation of South Arabia, and the Trucial States along the coast of the Gulf of Oman.

BAHRAYN

Bahrayn is a shaykhdom composed of several islands totaling 200 square miles and standing off about twenty miles from the coast of Saudi Arabia and the Qatar Peninsula in the Persian Gulf. Inhabited largely by Arabs and ruled by Iran for more than a century, Bahrayn was taken by Arabs from Qatar and became a British dependency through naval action in 1820. Except for pearl fishing, smuggling, slave trade, and the breeding of white donkeys, Bahrayn was quite unimportant until the presence of oil was suspected in the 1920's.

In 1930 after three other concerns had held oil concessions, Standard Oil of California and The Texas Company formed the Bahrayn Petroleum Company (Bapco), a Canadian corporation, and obtained the concession. Oil in commercial quantities was discovered in 1932, and Bahrayn oil entered the world markets in 1934. A refinery was constructed to handle the output of 30,000 barrels a day in Bahrayn and an additional 125,000 barrels coming from Saudi Arabia by an underwater pipeline. Originally the royalty amounted to ¾ Indian rupees per ton, but in 1952 Bapco entered into an equal profit-sharing agreement with the ruler who at that time derived about $8,000,000 in royalties to add to his $3,000,000 income from customs and other taxes. Oil reserves were thought to be limited, but better prices and offshore exploitation doubled royalty income by 1959. The shaykh visited King Saud in 1958 and agreed to divide oil royalties from disputed underwater areas between the two states. In 1965 a forty-five-year concession was granted to Continental Oil Company for the exploration and production rights in two offshore areas. Although other state income increased proportionately, Bahrayn's economic and financial condition was quite stationary in comparison to neighboring oil-rich states. Great Britain under pressure agreed in 1966 to give Bahrayn £ 1,000,000 for the use of military facilities on the islands and to pay an annual rental of £ 500,000 beginning in 1968. Bahrayn authorities, pointing out that there were no currency restrictions or income taxes, tried to attract foreign firms to invest in Bahrayn and to participate in the development of fishing, shipping, and industrial enterprises.

Bahrayn has been ruled by the al-Khalifah family for more than a century, the ruler in 1967 being Shaykh Isa ibn Salman al-Khalifah. A treaty with Great Britain places the foreign relations of the shaykhdom in British hands. From 1926 until 1956 the principal adviser of the shaykh was Sir Charles Belgrave, who assisted the shaykh in giving good municipal government. With a heterogeneous population of about 110,000 largely located in two cities, the problems were those of schools, water supply, sewers, streets, and hospitals. Arab nationalism spread among the younger groups on the island, and in 1956 during the first Suez Canal crisis Arab nationalists threatened to destroy the refinery and the pipelines if armed might were used by the West against Egypt. During the invasion of Egypt by Israel, England, and France, the British sent armed reinforcements to Bahrayn; and the Arab nationalist National Union committee was dissolved. Three of its leaders were sentenced to St. Helena for plotting to kill the shaykh and Sir Charles Belgrave. Inexorable Arab nationalism confronted the shaykh; and in 1958, at the time of the creation of the United Arab Republic and the Arab Federation, the shaykh visited Riyadh to explore the possibilities of some type of union among Saudi Arabia, Kuwayt, and Bahrayn.

These peculiar dangers passed and the Arab nationalist movement concentrated less on Nasser and the United Arab Republic and more on Arab socialism in Bahrayn. Most salutary was the freeing of the three nationalist leaders in 1961 from St. Helena on writs of habeas corpus and their compensation in the amount of $42,000 each. From time to time there were strikes and student demonstrations, and members of the Arab Nationalist Movement were arrested in 1963 for creating strife and instigating disorders; two years later the National Progressive Front led a strike against Bapco that was short lived. The nationalists were confronted with a most remarkable, just, and generous labor code that had been operative in Bahrayn since the 1950's. The al-Khalifah family was noted for its leniency, life on the islands was secure and not too harsh, and the appeal of agitators was always temporary.

KUWAYT

North of Bahrayn on the mainland of Arabia near the head of the
Persian Gulf lies the Amirate of Kuwayt. Long a port and the seat of a
profitable shipping trade from Basrah to Zanzibar, Kuwayt first came
to world attention during the Berlin to Baghdad railroad epic. Lord
Curzon brought it under British protection in 1899 to prevent the
German imperialists from obtaining a suitable terminus for their road
to the east. Thereafter, it lapsed into oblivion, except for the British
agents of the colonial office, until the end of World War I. Ibn Saud
tried to seize it for his growing kingdom, but British guns turned him
away.

When oil was struck on Bahrayn in 1932, world oil companies
sought concessions in Kuwayt. The final settlement was a compromise
between British imperial control of Kuwayti foreign relations and
American energy. The Kuwayt Oil Company, Ltd. (KOC), a British
corporation owned equally by the British Petroleum Company and the
Gulf Oil Company, received a concession in 1934 for the entire 5,800
square miles of the state. Oil was not found until 1938, when the
Burghan field was tapped and proved to be the largest known pool of
oil in the entire world. Commercial production, however, was stalled
during World War II and did not begin until 1946. Even then operations went slowly. But in 1950, as troubles loomed in Iran, production
was increased rapidly and further exploration brought in new fields.
The original concession called for a royalty payment of seven cents a
barrel, but a new agreement in 1951 called for an equal sharing of
company profits. In 1955 production soared over a daily mark of
1,000,000 barrels; and royalty payments to Shaykh Sir Abdallah al-
Salim al-Sabah exceeded $250,000,000. In addition, the shaykh gave a
concession for his half of the neutral zone bordering Saudi Arabia to
the American Independent Oil Company and the Paul Getty Oil Company for a down payment of $7,000,000 and a guarantee of thirty-five
cents a barrel royalty. Exploration and production continued to increase rapidly. In 1961 concessions were given to the Arabian Oil
Company of Japan for the neutral zone offshore rights at a 57–43 break
of the profits favoring Kuwayt and to the Royal Dutch Shell Company
for the Kuwayt offshore areas. At the same time the Kuwayt National
Petroleum Corporation (KNPC) was founded with sixty percent held
by the government and the remainder by Kuwayti nationals; KNPC
held an option to buy twenty percent of Shell's concession. Oil production passed the 2,000,000 barrels per day mark in 1960; royalties stood
at $600,000,000 and petroleum exports, crude and refined, at well over
$1,000,000,000. KNPC opened a new refinery in 1966, and a wholly

owned subsidiary set plans to market its products directly to the consumer in Denmark. Many observers wondered what Kuwayt would do when her oil resources were gone but exploration, both onshore and offshore, kept expanding the proven reserves. In 1966 reserves were estimated at sixty-eight billion barrels and one year later at seventy-five billion barrels.

With a population of less than 200,000 before 1950 and only 467,000 recorded in the census of 1965, less than half of whom were native born, the wealth pouring in changed the life of the people rapidly. Shaykh Sir Abdallah invested nearly half of his royalties in foreign securities as a saving for future needs of his people. The other half has been used to build schools, roads, hospitals, electrical plants, and other requirements of a modern community. In November, 1966 the ruler opened Kuwayt University with faculties in arts, sciences, and education. Because water was almost negligible, a large sea-water conversion plant was built, and contracts were given in 1958 to an American concern to expand the facilites. Three of five projected desalinization plants had been completed by 1965. Another scheme was the planning of a channel across the desert to bring fresh water from the Shatt al-Arab to Kuwayt, but strained relations with Iraq delayed its completion. KOC constructed three oil refineries, and in 1958 two American firms began work on a $23,000,000 contract to construct modern port terminals. A modest development program had been drawn up in 1950, revised in 1954, and largely completed in 1960. By that time the general statement bandied about was that everything needed had been completed and the city and state had been constructed. But when new building slowed down and government land purchases stopped, everyone complained of a financial and commercial recession. Although per capita income reached $3,500 in 1962 and national exports totaled $1,110,000,000 and imports only $324,000,000, government leaders realized that continued expansion had to be ordered. A petrochemical fertilizer plant was built in 1965, a cement plant was scheduled, and a massive new five-year plan with goals for 1970 was devised to bring the per capita income for that year to $4,580.

The city of al-Kuwayt, with the highest per capita income in the world, became a modern town within a decade with more automobiles and more hard-surfaced roads per capita and more air conditioners per habitation than any other city in the world. Its wealth attracted people from many parts of the world, especially from other Arab areas. The influx of Egyptians and Palestinians was relatively high, a factor which sensitized most Kuwaytis to the virus of Arab nationalism. In 1956 during the first Suez crisis shops and offices in Kuwayt closed in protest of the London Conference, and the government informed the oil companies that public opinion in Kuwayt would stop the flow of oil should the West attack Egypt. Later, when Israel, England, and France attacked Egypt, public meetings and demonstrations were banned. However, schools were closed, and shops refused to serve British and French customers. The threat to block oil shipments was not executed, but precautionary measures were enforced around the oil installations. In 1958 the chief of police in Kuwayt declared publicly that the United Arab Republic answered Kuwayt's national aspirations; and at the time of the Iraq Revolution Shaykh Sir Abdallah announced his sympathies for the new regime, even though he remained in constant telephone communications with the British commander on Bahrayn. Within a few days the shaykh conferred with Nasser in Damascus; for he sensed full well the confusing and contradictory dynamics of the Middle Eastern situation and knew how fraught with uncertainties was his own future.

Within a few months Shaykh Sir Abdallah saw that rivalries among Saudi Arabia, Iraq, and the United Arab Republic would permit him to retain his position, and in 1959 he forbade the demonstrations for Nasser. Shortly, discussions with Great Britain led to a peaceful termination of the treaty of protection and the Amirate of Kuwayt was declared free and independent on June 19, 1961. In less than a week Amir Abdallah was threatened by Iraq, and President Kassim announced that he would annex Kuwayt, claiming that it had been a part of the province of Basrah in the Ottoman Empire and now should return to Iraq. Kuwayt called upon Great Britain for protection; three warships and marines arrived on July 1 to stay until August when troops offered by Saudi Arabia, Jordan, and the United Arab Republic gave security. Kuwayt joined the Arab League but the U.S.S.R. delayed her entry into the United Nations until 1963. Amir Abdallah promulgated a provisional constitution in December, 1961 and set in motion elections for a constituent assembly, which met and drafted a constitution calling for an elected National Assembly of fifty members, five from each of ten elected districts. In January, 1963 there were 204 candidates for the fifty seats. The majority supported the rule of the al-Sabah family but ten belonged to an Arab Nationalist party. The amir's brother, Sabah al-Salim al-Sabah, was chosen prime minister and named heir to the throne, and when Abdallah died on November 27, 1965 he became the new ruler. The amirate remained under al-Sabah's control, and the family occupied eleven of the sixteen places in the cabinet. Amir Sabah named his cousin Jaber al-Ahmad al-Jaber prime minister and in 1966 named him heir to the throne.

Kuwayt had been fortunate in 1961 to find protection in Arab rivalries, but her tremendous wealth and oil resources proved a constant invitation for aggression. To counterbalance this menace the Kuwayt rulers and government initiated a policy of granting and loaning significant sums to other Arab states. In 1962 the Kuwayt Fund for Arab Economic Development (KFAED) was established with capital amounting to $140,000,000. It was increased from time to time and by 1966 had expended nearly $600,000,000 to Sudan, Algeria, Jordan, Iraq, the United Arab Republic, Tunisia, Lebanon, Morocco, and the Persian Gulf states for railways, phosphate plants, the Suez Canal, agricultural development, highways, hospitals, schools, communications systems, and many industrial enterprises. To support the United Arab Republic after the loss of Suez Canal earnings in 1967, Kuwayt, joining with Saudi Arabia and Libya, contributed over $100,000,000 to maintain some semblance of solvency for Nasser. The wealth of Kuwayt, at the same time, was a world force. Even after her own separate currency was adopted in 1961, Kuwayt dinars were closely associated with British pounds, and it was reported that more than ten percent of British foreign earnings and holdings came from Kuwayt. Any sudden movements of Kuwayt funds decidedly weakened sterling and it was suggested that large withdrawals of Kuwayt deposits forced the closing of the Intra Bank in Beirut in 1966.

In Kuwayt education is free from the elementary school through the university; medical attention and hospital care are free; there are no taxes; there is no poverty; and there are more millionaires per thousand of population than anywhere. Yet in December, 1965 eight members of the National Assembly resigned in protest against the government, asserting that restrictions were being placed on civil freedoms. A trace of Kuwayti nationalism was arising, and the government began to deport non-Kuwayti Arabs and to enact more stringent laws regarding the obtainment of Kuwayti citizenship. The continued existence of small states has always been fraught with danger and this is especially so when sitting atop the world's largest proved oil reserve, large enough to produce oil at the present rate for more than a hundred years.

OMAN

The Sultanate of Oman, sometimes referred to as Muscat and Oman from the official residential town of the sultan, is situated at the southeastern corner of the Arabian Peninsula. Inhabited since antiquity, Oman was of little importance after the advent of the use of steam and drew attention only in recent years. By the Treaty of Sib in 1920, the sultan recognized that the interior of the country would be governed by an elected imam who would have political and religious authority. No great difficulties or problems arose until 1954 when Ghalib ibn Ali was elected imam against the strong wishes of Sultan Said ibn Taymur ibn Faysal who had held this power since his accession in 1932. Warfare broke out between the two in 1955 with Imam Ghalib supported by the Arab League including both Egypt and Saudi Arabia, and Sultan Said aided by British troops. For many years the sultan's foreign relations had been managed unofficially by Great Britain, a practice which obtained tacit recognition through treaties of commerce and navigation in 1939 and 1951. The United Nations Security Council refused to place the Omani problem on its agenda in 1957; by 1959 the imam and his followers had been routed from their mountain strongholds and fled into neighboring Saudi Arabia, and from there had made their way from one Arab capital to another receiving red-carpet treatment but no substantial help for their return to Oman. In 1963 a United Nations official visited Oman and reported that local governors and shaykhs were not sympathetic to Imam Ghalib and that the country was peaceful and under control of the sultan's government.

In 1963 oil in commercial quantities was discovered by Petroleum Development (Oman) Ltd., owned jointly by Shell Petroleum Ltd. and the Gulbenkian interests. Pipelines and installations were started to bring oil into production in 1967.

QATAR

Only a few specialists had ever heard of Qatar before the discovery of oil there in 1950. Under a treaty of 1916 with the British the shaykh pledged to prevent piracy along his coasts and recognized a perpetual truce with Great Britain that virtually controlled all of Qatar's foreign relations. Occupying a barren peninsula of 4,000 square miles jutting eastward into the Persian Gulf, the shaykhdom had one principal town, Doha, and was ruled absolutely by the al-Thani family. The Qatar Petroleum Company, a subsidiary of the Iraq Petroleum Company, holds the mainland concession and exploits its major well at Dukhan, about sixty miles from Doha. Offshore rights are held by Overseas Exploration Company, a Shell subsidiary, and its first well began producing in 1961. A small refinery was built at Umm Said on the south shore, and by 1966 Qatar was receiving over $100,000,000 annually in royalties and production stood at 276,000 barrels daily. In this same period the population tripled, reaching 70,000, with about half the total residing in Doha.

The shaykh gave half of the royalties to his family, used one-fourth to cover the expenses of government and the development of services, and kept the remaining one-fourth for himself. Shaykh Ali ibn Abdallah ibn Qasim al-Thani acceded to the rule in 1949 and found the problems of oil development and the resulting riches so vexing and tiring that he retired in 1960 to his villa in Switzerland and abdicated in favor of his son Shaykh Ahmad ibn Ali al-Thani. At the time of unrest in Bahrayn in 1963 there were pro-Nasser demonstrations and some disorder in Doha. A state of emergency was invoked in April, 1964 after which Shaykh Ahmad outlined a program for improving communications systems, developing a water and sewage system, and providing housing for indigent families. The oil bounty continued to pour in and the ruler's problem was how to use the wealth wisely for all the people without generating an uncontrolled social and political revolution that would undermine society too rapidly and surely end in chaos.

YEMEN

Another corner of Arabia presented to the modern world the Imam-ate of Yemen, which in 1948 was one of the most remote and isolated spots in the world. In 1934 Ibn Saud forced peace upon the ruler of Yemen, Sayef al-Islam Yahya Hamid al-Din. The latter, however, kept his country closed to foreign influence. Charles R. Crane visited the country in the 1930's; and Karl Twitchell built bridges there to connect Sana, the capital, with the ports on the Red Sea. The British had a running quarrel with Imam Yahya over the frontier between Yemen and the Aden protectorate, which was never very clearly defined. A British-Yemen treaty of friendship was signed in Sana in 1934, largely to establish the frontier on a basis of the *status quo*. Relations with England, however, were never very cordial because of the friction over boundaries and because of the sizable colony of Yemenis in Aden who did not look very kindly upon the government and policies of Imam Yahya.

In the period between the two great wars the imam turned to Italy for support. A ten-year treaty was signed in 1926, and in 1927 a Yemeni mission visited Mussolini and obtained arms and munitions in Italy. In 1937 the treaty was renewed for twenty-five years, and Italian doctors and technical people appeared in Yemen. During the war Yemen remained neutral, but after the Nazi defeats in North Africa ousted Germans and Italians from her territory. Diplomatic missions were received, and Colonel William Eddy in 1946 negotiated a treaty of friendship and commerce with Imam Yahya for the United States. In May, 1947 the United States extended a credit of $1,000,000 to Yemen for the purchase of surplus war materials. Yemen joined the Arab League in 1945 and was admitted to the United Nations on September 30, 1947.

Society changed slowly in Yemen; and Imam Yahya remained the despot, attempting to hold the line as he had done for forty-three years. Many of the younger generation and leaders of the rival princely family of Yemen—the al-Wazir family—plotted to remove the old imam. The former group became known as "Free Yemenis." They were led by Imam Yahya's sixth son, Prince Sayef al-Islam Ibrahim, who settled in Aden in 1947. In February, 1948 Imam Yahya and several of his ministers and sons were assassinated. Prince Ibrahim flew in from Aden, and al-Sayyed Abdallah ibn Ahmad al-Wazir became imam. To counter this *coup d'état* Yahya's eldest son, Sayef al-Islam Ahmad Hamid al-Din, received aid from Ibn Saud and gathered loyal forces in the area. He overthrew the insurgents in March. Over thirty rebels were beheaded, and Prince Ibrahim died in prison from a "heart attack."

In 1951 Imam Ahmad requested that Yemen be included in the American Point Four program, and a medical mission visited the country. An agricultural school was opened at Taizz; French engineers were commissioned to build a new pier at Hodeida; and a radio station, a printing press, and a woolen and cotton weaving factory were imported. Yet, development of Yemen proceeded at a snail's pace.

Forces for change attempted a *coup d'état* against Imam Ahmad in April, 1955. The revolt was led by his brother, Prince Sayef al-Islam Abdallah, who had traveled in the West and represented Yemen at the United Nations. It was crushed by the quick action of the imam's eldest son, Prince Sayef al-Islam Muhammad al-Badr, who led his troops to Taizz to free his father. Prince Abdallah and another brother, Prince Abbas, were hanged; six other conspirators were beheaded; and Prime Minister Prince Hasan, who was at the moment in Cairo, was ordered to remain abroad.

The attempted *coup,* however, did stir up action in Yemen. Imam Ahmad took over the post of prime minister himself; he appointed his son, al-Badr, deputy prime minister, minister of foreign affairs, and minister of defense; and formed a cabinet including fourteen other ministers. In November, 1955 a thirty-year concession was granted to the American Yemen Development Corporation to prospect and exploit the mineral resources of Yemen on a fifty-fifty basis. Several American engineers visited Yemen to begin a more thorough mineral survey. Iron deposits of commercial value were found in 1956, but transport difficulties precluded mining operations for several years.

The interests of the U.S.S.R. in the Middle East in 1956 included Yemen. Four Soviet economic experts flew from Cairo to discuss development proposals. A trade mission from the Soviet bloc arrived in Taizz, the imam's favorite residence and thus the capital, and negotiated trade agreements for the U.S.S.R. and East Germany, a treaty of friendship with Czechoslovakia, and recognition of Communist China. Arrangements were also made to send Yemeni students free of charge to Czechoslovakia for six-year courses in medicine and engineering. Prince al-Badr, upon formal invitation, made a state visit to Moscow in the summer of 1956, and other state visits in 1957 to London, Belgrade, Bucharest, and Moscow. From the U.S.S.R. he received a loan of $60,000,000 and from Communist China he obtained a five-year trade agreement and credits of $16,000,000 to build a three-hundred-mile road from Hodeida to Sana and to set up a number of factories. During the war in Sinai Yemen offered to permit volunteers to go to Egypt, and Soviet-bloc arms shipments arrived in Yemeni ports in 1957. The pressures upon the borders of the Aden protectorate continued and the raids grew more numerous, even though Imam Ahmad declared in 1957 that he had no intention of denouncing the 1934 and 1950 treaties with Great Britain. He protested against the British granting of an oil concession for the Kamaran Islands and pursued the traditional Yemeni policy of forming alliances and signing treaties with British opponents. Yemen complained of the Baghdad pact, and in 1956 signed with Egypt and Saudi Arabia the Jidda pact which established a five-year military alliance. After the formation of the United Arab Republic in 1958 Crown Prince al-Badr visited Cairo and Damascus; and upon authority from his father he signed a pact creating the United Arab States, which was a loose and vague federation of Yemen and the United Arab Republic. The head of each state, however, held veto power for his own state with respect to acts of the union, and it appeared that the United Arab States was only a paper affair.

The moves of Imam Ahmad and Crown Prince al-Badr in the direction of the Soviet bloc were not interpreted as an indication of sympathy for the Communists. Yemen pictured the West in terms of Great Britain, and the British-American sponsored Baghdad pact was regarded as anti-Yemeni. Therefore, the Jidda pact, the United Arab States, and the amicable posture toward the Soviet bloc were demonstrations of independence. In this respect they were similar to the treaties and friendly gestures of the 1920's and 1930's between Yemen and Italy.

As the years went by Imam Ahmad's rugged frame was beset by many ills and he decided after much hesitation to go to Italy for treatment in the summer of 1959. In his absence he left his son and crown prince Muhammad al-Badr as regent. Seizing the opportunity, al-Badr immediately liberalized the rule, abrogated the absolute authority of the imam, removed many tyrannical officials, and instituted an eight-man advisory legislature. Imam Ahmad hurried home, placed al-Badr under house arrest, and beheaded, mutilated, or imprisoned al-Badr's closest partners. Although there were several attempts to assassinate Imam Ahmad, Yemen remained frozen until his death on September 19, 1962 whereupon his son became the new ruler as Imam Sayef al-Islam Muhammad al-Badr. He appointed Soviet-trained Colonel Abdallah al-Sallal army chief of staff, and there was promise that Yemen under the young imam would begin to move into the twentieth century. A week later al-Sallal and a military junta beseiged and bombarded the royal palace at Sana, declared that Imam al-Badr had been killed, and they were forming a Republic of Yemen. Ten high-ranking officials were executed by a firing squad. However, al-Badr was not dead and about ten days later he held a large news conference in the mountains of northern Yemen.

A state of civil war between royalists and republicans continued to exist, and there was no indication of a settlement as of 1967. Serious fighting tapered off in 1965, and several arranged ceasefires were broken by raids or bombings. At the very outset al-Sallal arranged a five-year military defense pact with Cairo; between 20,000 and 70,000 Egyptian troops were sent to Yemen. Their presence insured the position of al-Sallal and control by Nasser over republican Yemen. The modernized Egyptian army found fighting successful campaigns an impossibility in the mountain areas, and therefore largely restricted their activities to the plains and the larger towns. The royalists were supplied with arms and ammunition that Saudi Arabia had purchased for them in various markets of the world, but the fighting forces were almost entirely made up of hill tribesmen who fought willingly against the Egyptian forces as foreign invaders. Furthermore, they were always eager to capture automatic weapons, machine guns, fine rifles, and stores of ammunition. No one doubted that they would conquer the plains within hours after the departure of Egyptian troops. Nasser seriously weighed this fact in 1965 as the war dragged on, costing him more than $500,000 a day and pinning down the best of his army. Some formula for a negotiated compromise was most appealing until the British announced in February, 1966 that they would be leaving Aden in 1968. At the news, Nasser ceased considering the removal of his troops from Yemen, because from Yemen he could occupy the vacuum in Aden and thus hold both ends of the Red Sea. However, the debacle of the Israeli-Arab War in June, 1967 so weakened the political, financial, and military posture of the United Arab Republic that their position in Yemen could not be maintained. Withdrawal began slowly in the autumn of 1967.

Toward the end of 1962, after the Republic of Yemen had been recognized by the U.S.S.R., the United Arab Republic, and a number of other states, the United States proposed the withdrawal of all foreign troops from Yemen. On this basis the United States recognized the republican regime, at which time the United Nations admitted the republican official as the representative of Yemen. But withdrawal was not effected and Ralph Bunche was sent by the United Nations to try his hand at negotiations. When he proved unsuccessful a two-hundred-man mission designated by the Security Council arrived in June, 1963 to supervise a disengagement. In 1964 Nasser and Prince Faysal, meeting in Cairo, discussed the situation and arranged a truce-meeting in the Sudan between the factions but it never took place. Meeting again in Jidda in 1965, the two reached a compromise whereby a peace conference would convene in November at Haradh, Yemen, to draft provisions for an interim government, schedule the departure of foreign troops, and plan for a plebiscite to be held within one year. It was expected that a coalition government would rule with neither al-Sallal nor al-Badr participating. Following a month of fruitless sessions, the conference ended when the royalists proposed the provisional government be called the Government of the State of Yemen while the republicans insisted the word "Republican" be included. Moderates on each side began moving into positions of responsibility and willingness to compromise was beginning to appear in 1966 when England made the declaration on Aden. After that Nasser's stand hardened and he would not tolerate any Yemeni official who openly opposed the Egyptian "occupation" of Yemen. However, in 1967, after the June fiasco, Nasser gave his word to King Faysal at the Khartoum meeting that Egyptian troops would depart from Yemen and that support for al-Sallal and his intractable position would not be maintained.

Royalist Yemen was under the rule of Imam al-Badr and the leading members of the ruling family. Government structure remained as it had, but as the struggle wore on, modernized and moderate individuals of talent influenced and shaped al-Badr's decisions. In 1965 he agreed to limit his authority, to accept a constitution and a state council, and to create a modern legislature. Republican Yemen had more difficulty. President al-Sallal served as his own prime minister until the spring of 1964 when al-Jayifi was named to the post. Shortly after the coup in 1962 al-Baydani had been deputy prime minister and foreign minister, but early in 1963 he had left the country and was under house arrest in Cairo. The president, however, was a hard man to please in addition to being in poor health, and he was forced to remain in Cairo for medical treatments for protracted periods. With jealousy and distrust between the Shafii and Zaydi branches of Islam rampant in republican circles the wheel of political fortune turned easily. President al-Sallal appointed al-Amri as prime minister early in 1965 when al-Jayifi and three others resigned. In April, al-Amri was out and Shaykh Ahmad Muhammad Numan was in. He had fled to Aden in 1948 when he had taken part in the revolution against Imam Yahya, but the British deported him in 1960 for his activities there in the Free Yemeni Movement. Because Numan attempted to set the stage for peace talks with royalist moderates he was replaced in June by the returning al-Amri. In 1966 al-Amri moved into the camp of the Yemeni First party and in July announced a forthcoming election for a one-hundred-and-one-man consultative council. Events moved rapidly and on August 11, 1966 he launched a coup by trying to seize the capital's airport and radio station. He was foiled, however, by the United Arab Republic ambassador who arrived just in time with superior forces. President al-Sallal, sent back to Yemen from Cairo, was met at the airport by a heavy guard of Egyptian tanks. He assumed the post of prime minister and al-Amri and forty of his associates, including Numan, went to Cairo under arrest. President al-Sallal re-established his absolute authority by cleansing the services of all compromisers and Yemeni Firsters; seven former high officials faced a firing squad and over one hundred senior army officers were purged. As Nasser's puppet, al-Sallal, if his health permitted, would hold Yemen safe, it was assumed, until the British departed from Aden. However, after Nasser's agreement with King Faysal at Khartoum to countenance a settlement between republicans and royalists, al-Sallal vowed to fight on alone. In November, 1967, while he was on his way to Moscow to attend the fiftieth anniversary of the Russian Revolution, he was overthrown by a bloodless coup, obviously with the approval of Cairo. A triumvirate of moderate republicans, Numan, Abd al-Rahman Iryani, and Muhammad Ali Uthman, called for an immediate conference of major republican tribes to organize a group to discuss with the royalists steps to end the five-year civil war. A new republican government was formed, with Iryani as president and Muhsin Aini as prime minister.

ADEN AND THE FEDERATION OF SOUTH ARABIA

The port of Aden is located on a rocky peninsula jutting out from the south coast of Arabia into the Indian Ocean about one hundred miles east of Bab al-Mandeb, the narrow strait controlling the southern entrance to the Red Sea. Aden, the sole port in the entire area, has been important for trade between East and West, including Africa, since antiquity. The Ottomans took it in 1538 but gave it to the imam of Yemen in the seventeenth century. A local shaykh seized Aden in 1735 and occupied it until the British came in 1839. After the opening of the Suez Canal, Aden grew rapidly into one of the great British coaling stations, a submarine cable center, and, as a free port, a trading entrepôt. From the Crown Colony of Aden the British spread their influence along the entire southern Arabian coast and by individual treaties with local rulers established what came to be known as the Eastern Aden and the Western Aden protectorates. The former comprised five independent sultanates and two shaykhdoms; the two largest sultanates together were usually called the Hadhramaut from which originated many of the prosperous Arab merchants of Indonesia. After gaining a comfortable fortune in the Indies many of these merchants returned home to retire in pleasant highland villas looking out to sea. In Western Aden, which surrounded Aden and bordered on Yemen, there were seven sultanates, six shaykhdoms, two amirates, and one confederation of tribes.

After World War II social and political attitudes in Aden and the protectorates changed markedly. During the war, campaigns in East Africa, oil shipments from the Persian Gulf, the fleets of Allied ships carrying cargo to the U.S.S.R., and the mountains of war supplies and civilian goods on their way to Middle East theaters of war raised Aden to the third-ranking port, after London and Liverpool, in the British Empire. Labor union actions and strikes always seemed to turn into Arab nationalist demonstrations. In 1954 the Anglo-Iranian Oil Company erected a $150,000,000 refinery there and almost overnight created a new city, Little Aden, to support it. The contrast in living conditions, public conveniences, and services with Aden proper brought many of the residents of Aden out of their lethargy, wondering why if improvements could be made so easily they did not enjoy them too. In the states of the protectorates a new generation of rulers was emerging. They wanted improved conditions but even more they wanted additional independence. Formerly they had been governed through New Delhi but after Indian independence in 1950 Aden governors were dependent directly upon London, and the individual princes longed for more power and home rule.

Talks in London in the summer of 1958 led to the creation on February 11, 1959 of the Federation of the Arab Amirates of the South, comprising six of the states of the Western Aden Protectorate. Later that year another was admitted, and over the subsequent years others, even some from the Eastern Protectorate, joined to make a total of seventeen in 1966. The name was changed in 1962 to the Federation of South Arabia and Aden became a member in 1963. A new capital, al-Ittihad, at Bir Ahmad and not far from Aden, was completed and occupied in 1961. The Federation was governed by a seven-member Supreme Council elected by a Federal Council composed of six members from each state except Aden, which had twenty-four. Yemen refused to recognize the Federation because she had laid claim to the territory ever since it was lost in 1735. In Aden especially there have been many Yemeni workers and refugees who have mounted a Free Yemeni Movement. As long as Imam Ahmad ruled in Sana they did not wish to return or form a union, but with the revolution of 1962 and the birth of the Republic of Yemen conditions altered immediately. President al-Sallal claimed Aden and the Federation of South Arabia, strongly supported in this demand by Nasser. Labor unrest, strikes, bombings, and general anti-British terrorism multiplied, and leaders of the various states who co-operated with the British or participated in Federation matters were subjected constantly and inevitably to threats of violence and assassination. The magnitude of terrorism had so risen by 1965 that public meetings of Britishers in Aden invited hand grenade tossing, and bomb packages came regularly with the mail. Great Britain promised independence for 1968, and on February 22, 1966 it was announced in the House of Commons that troops would be withdrawn at that time. Agitation grew worse and competition developed in Aden and the Federation states among Arab nationals for the role of the successor to British political power. One of the most important was the National Front for the Liberation of Occupied South Yemen (FLOSY), sponsored by the United Arab Republic. Others were the Organization for the Liberation of the Occupied South, the People's Socialist party, the People's Congress party, the South Arabian league, the Aden National Liberation Front, and the Arab Socialist party. Each was aiming at 1968 but each had its eyes on all of the others. Meanwhile terrorism mounted to a point near war. A peace mission from the United Nations was rebuffed and not able to leave its hotel. In the spring and summer of 1967, with the help of strategic coups and kidnappings in the several shaykhdoms and sultanates comprising the Federation, the National Liberation Front (NLF) emerged as the chief rival to FLOSY. By the end of the summer NLF controlled all of the states of the Federation; Federation officials thereupon recognized their impotence and declared that the union ceased to exist. With Nasser's need to cut his commitments abroad, NLF showed that it had more muscle of its own than did FLOSY. The position of the British grew more untenable and the date of withdrawal was moved up to November, 1967. For a time it was uncertain if a force or a group could be found to receive the symbol of authority from the British but NLF appeared to have the upper hand when the remnant of the Federation army threw in its lot with NLF. Qahtan al-Shaabi, NLF's leader, formed a group which assumed office when the British left.

TRUCIAL STATES OF OMAN

Lying along a four-hundred-mile strip of the coast of Arabia on the Persian Gulf south from the Qatar Peninsula to the Straits of Hormuz and along the Gulf of Oman to the territory of the Sultan of Oman are seven Arab shaykhdoms. For centuries they won their livelihood and existence from the sea in pearl diving and piracy and in between times raided each other. In 1820 a British naval expedition from India in collaboration with a land force from Muscat caught them in a vise and forced a treaty upon each of the seven rulers by which they agreed not to make war on each other, not to raid shipping, not to permit or traffic in slavery, and not to make treaties with other powers. Great Britain in return agreed to protect them from outside aggression. It proved difficult for England to enforce the treaty and equally distasteful for the seven shaykhs or their successors to abide by a rule so contrary to habits and patterns of life established over centuries of fighting. In 1853 a Perpetual Maritime Truce was signed, giving the name to the group. These seven are: Abu Dhabi, Dubai, Sharjah, Ajman, Umm al-Qaywayn, Ras al-Khaymah, and Fujairah. Each is hardly more than a small coastal town with a desert hinterland, although Abu Dhabi holds several of the settlements in the inland Buraimi oases. Dubai has the largest town; Sharjah has been the location of the British political resident agent, a small military force, and an airstrip; Abu Dhabi is the largest. In 1960 the total population of all seven states was estimated at 86,000. The seven shaykhs meet twice a year in a kind of council, but no formal organization has developed by which one could think of the states as being a federation.

When piracy and slave trading were no longer possible or profitable, the Trucial shaykhs turned to smuggling and shipping gold to India. Pearling became the mainstay of the economy and reached its peak about 1925, at which time the revenue in the pearl trade for all of the Persian Gulf area including Kuwayt and Bahrayn was about $10,000,-000. Less than a tenth of this came to the seven rulers of the Trucial States. The marketing of cultured pearls hurt the trade, and then the development of even less expensive synthetic pearls, followed by the depression, finished it off so that real pearls were no longer coveted gems, largely because only experts could tell the real from the cultured and often then only by using a microscope. In the years after World War II the total value of the pearling industry in the Persian Gulf was estimated at $250,000. As life in Saudi Arabia, Kuwayt, Bahrayn, and even Qatar quickened from the impact of oil wealth, the towns of the Trucial States were in the doldrums and their shaykhs seemed to be enjoying idleness. Gold smuggling into Iran and India sparked the trade of Dubai and al-Khaymah, and the British presence in Sharjah furnished an income there. For Abu Dhabi, the possession of part of the Buraimi oases region and its partial occupation by Saudi Arabia brought support, interest, troops, and money from the British, and gave to that inland area of Abu Dhabi the greatest activity in the Trucial States. Yet, Abu Dhabi in 1961 was still insignificant with a population of about 15,000 and a total revenue of a little under $150,000 for its ruler Shaykh Shakhbut ibn Sultan ibn Zayd who had acceded to his position in 1928 at the outset of depressed economic conditions.

In the summer of 1961, however, Shaykh Shakhbut and his neighbor Shaykh Rashid ibn Said al-Makhtum of Dubai visited London, as the oil companies wished to make sure that the oil deal with them would be on the generally accepted basis of a fifty-fifty split of the profits. For more than a decade Petroleum Development (Trucial Coast) Ltd., later named Abu Dhabi Petroleum Company, a subsidiary of Iraq Petroleum Company, held the concessions for the seven shaykhdoms. Some oil had been located in 1950 but oil had been struck in 1960 in commercial quantities at Murban and Umm Shaif, both in Abu Dhabi. Offshore concessions had been given by Abu Dhabi and Dubai to Abu Dhabi Marine Areas Ltd., two-thirds owned by British Petroleum Company and one-third by Compagnie Française de Petroles, and a strike had been made in 1958 near Das Island offshore from Umm Shaif. In 1962 Shaykh Shakhbut received $20,000,000 in royalties, and each year it increased so that in 1966 it was $84,000,000 and in 1967 $100,000,000. Production jumped rapidly to reach 367,000 barrels daily, more than in Qatar or Rumania. Proven crude reserves were estimated on January 1, 1967 to be about twelve and one-half billion barrels.

What to do with all this money! That was a heavy problem for Shaykh Shakhbut for he had no experience or training to help him find an answer. His wants were simple and his pleasures of hawking were inexpensive. He stored rupee notes in trunks in his fort and had them inspected periodically by a secretary because on one occasion he found a trunkful had disintegrated when moths got inside and fed on the notes. It was a small calamity when the Bank of India refused reimbursement as the value of the notes was beyond estimation. At other times he voiced the wish that the oil companies would take their half and leave his half in the ground where it would be secure and less bothersome. He baffled the British oil company executives by declining to make any new contract with them until in September, 1965 he succumbed to their entreaties to take more and accept the fifty-fifty split of profits. Immigrants brought diseases unknown to the local

Arabs; there was an emphasis on speed and education; prices soared; visitors came and went without his knowledge; and changes were everywhere and very disconcerting. He was not convinced that it was for the betterment of his people.

Changes and "improvements" could not be denied. A new twenty-five-room air-conditioned hotel appeared in 1962, and a 25,000-gallon water distillation plant became operative in 1963. In 1965 plans were drawn for some new roads, an international airport, and a bridge across the Muqtaa Channel to connect the chief island with the mainland. In 1966 more distillation plants came into use, and new piers and loading berths for crude-oil tankers were built at Das Island. Developments were too slow and too difficult to wheedle from Shaykh Shakhbut. A family council deposed him and sent him to Bahrayn on August 6, 1966 and placed his youngest brother, Shaykh Zayd ibn Sultan ibn Zayd, in control. Shaykh Zayd, who had been the governor for the Buraimi district, announced in October, 1966 a $42,000,000 development plan with Arabicon, a British consortium, to build a covered market for Abu Dhabi, a seawall, sewage works, one hundred miles of dual highway from Buraimi to Abu Dhabi, sixty miles of urban roads, seventy miles of water pipelines, and to undertake a land reclamation project. He also met with the other shaykhs of the Trucial States to discuss a true federation and economic union. It appeared that Abu Dhabi would soon take her place with the more progressive oil states of the Persian Gulf.

REFERENCES: *Chapter 38*

Significant works for this chapter are also found in Chapters 4, 7, 19, 22, 23, 24, 27, 28, 29, 31, 32, and 35.

Fereydoun Adamiyat, *Bahrein Islands:* Praeger, New York, 1955. Geographical and historical.

Richard Aldington, *Lawrence of Arabia: A Biographical Enquiry:* Collins, London, 1955. An assessment of this controversial figure.

Harold C. Armstrong, *Lord of Arabia, Ibn Saud: An Intimate Study of a King:* Barker, London, 1934. An early and friendly biography.

Charles Belgrave, *Personal Column, An Autobiography:* Hutchinson, London, 1960. Belgrave was adviser to the Shaykh of Bahrayn.

Jacques Benoist-Mechin, *Arabian Destiny:* Essential Books, Fairlawn, 1958.

Erich W. Bethmann, *Yemen on the Threshold:* American Friends of the Middle East, Washington, 1960.

Edward Hoagland Brown, *The Saudi Arabia-Kuwait Neutral Zone:* Middle East Research and Publishing Center, Beirut, 1963.

Eleanor F. Calverly, *My Arabian Days and Nights:* Thomas Y. Crowell, New York, 1958. Medical work in Kuwayt, 1909–1929.

H. R. P. Dickson, *The Arab of the Desert:* Macmillan, New York, 1949. A sociological study of the nomads of Arabia.

———, *Kuwait and Her Neighbors:* George Allen & Unwin, London, 1956. A lengthy survey of statistics, history, travel, and life over a long period of time in this corner of the Persian Gulf.

Abbas Faroughy, *Introducing Yemen:* Orientalia, New York, 1947. A good survey.

Claudie Fayein, *A French Doctor in the Yemen* (Douglas McKee, trans.): Robert Hale, London, 1957. An excellent travel book.

David H. Finnie, *Desert Enterprise: The Middle East Oil Industry in Its Local Environment:* Harvard University Press, Cambridge, 1958.

Robert Graves, *Lawrence and the Arabian Adventure:* Doubleday, New York, 1928.

Charles W. Hamilton, *Americans and Oil in the Middle East:* Gulf Publishing, Houston, 1963.

Rupert Hay, *The Persian Gulf States:* Middle East Institute, Washington, 1959.

David Howarth, *The Desert King: Ibn Saud and His Arabia:* McGraw-Hill, New York, 1964.

William Harold Ingrams, *Arabia and the Isles:* J. Murray, London, 1942. A study of the Aden protectorate.

———, *The Yemen: Imams, Rulers, and Revolutions:* Praeger, New York, 1964.

Robert Geran Landen, *Oman since 1856: Disruptive Modernization in a Traditional Arab Society:* Princeton University Press, Princeton, 1967. An outstanding work in diplomacy, imperialism, and political development in the Persian Gulf area.

Roy Lebkicher, George Rentz, and Max Steineke, *The Arabia of Ibn Saud:* Russell F. Moore, New York, 1952. Excellent study.

Wayne A. Leeman, *The Price of Middle East Oil: An Essay in Political Economy:* Cornell University Press, Ithaca, 1962.

George Lenczowski, *Oil and State in the Middle East:* Cornell University Press, Ithaca, 1960.

George A. Lipsky *et al., Saudi Arabia: Its People, Its Society, Its Culture:* Human Relations Affairs Press, New Haven, 1959.

Clarence Mann, *Abu Dhabi: Birth of an Oil Sheikhdom:* Khayats, Beirut, 1964. A revealing description of the impact of the discovery of oil in an undeveloped state.

James Morris, *Sultan in Oman:* Faber & Faber, London, 1957. Travel story by a correspondent of *The Times.*

Muhamad Mughraby, *Permanent Sovereignty over Oil Resources: A Study of Middle East Oil Concessions and Legal Change.* Middle East Research and Publishing Center, Beirut, 1966.

H. St. John B. Philby, *Arabia:* Scribner, New York, 1930. Philby was a British Muslim who served as adviser to Ibn Saud for several decades and was one of the outstanding Arab scholars of his day. A good survey.

———, *Arabia of the Wahhabis:* Constable, London, 1928. Tells of Ibn Saud's conflicts with the Rashids.

———, *Arabian Days:* Robert Hale, London, 1951. An excellent account of the life of Ibn Saud.

———, *Arabian Highlands:* Cornell University Press, Ithaca, 1952. Travels in Arabia and particularly in Asir.

———, *Arabian Jubilee:* Robert Hale, London, 1951. An excellent story of the life of Ibn Saud and his dynasty.

———, *Arabian Oil Ventures:* The Middle East Institute, Washington, 1964.

————, *The Empty Quarter:* Constable, London, 1933. Account of a travel through southern Arabia.

————, *Forty Years in the Wilderness:* Robert Hale, London, 1957.

————, *The Heart of Arabia*, 2 vols.: G. P. Putnam, London, 1923. Of great geographical value.

————, *The Land of Midian:* Ernest Benn, London, 1957.

————, *A Pilgrim in Arabia:* Robert Hale, London, 1942. A description of the pilgrimage to Mecca.

————, *Saudi Arabia:* Benn, London, 1955. A history of the state.

————, *Sheba's Daughters:* Methuen, London, 1939. An account of trips in the interior of Arabia and to Hadhramaut.

Wendell Phillips, *Unknown Oman:* David McKay, New York, 1966. A friendly account by an adviser to the sultan.

Ameen Rihani, *Around the Coasts of Arabia:* Houghton Mifflin, London, 1930. A description of the Arab states in the Persian Gulf region.

————, *Makers of Modern Arabia:* Houghton Mifflin, New York, 1928. An older work, but still useful.

Richard H. Sanger, *The Arabian Peninsula:* Cornell University Press, Ithaca, 1954. A good survey of the whole area.

Hugh Scott, *In the High Yemen:* J. Murray, London, 1942.

Freya Stark, *The Southern Gates of Arabia:* Penguin Books, New York, 1945.

Bertram Thomas, *Alarms and Excursions in Arabia:* Bobbs-Merrill, Indianapolis, 1931. Travels in south Arabia and Oman.

Lowell Thomas, *With Lawrence in Arabia:* Grossett, New York, 1955.

Arthur S. Tritton, *Rise of the Imams of Sanaa:* Oxford University Press, London, 1925. An excellent study.

Karl Twitchell, *Saudi Arabia:* Princeton University Press, Princeton, 1953. A fundamental work by a mining and hydraulic engineer.

Daniel van der Meulen, *Aden to the Hadramaut: A Journey in South Arabia:* J. Murray, London, 1947.

————, *The Wells of Ibn Sa'ud:* Praeger, New York, 1957. Rise of Saudi family and the development of the state.

F. S. Vidal, *The Oasis of al-Hasa:* Arabian American Oil Company, New York, 1955. A discussion of the geography and economy of this province of Saudi Arabia.

R. Bayly Winder, *Saudi Arabia in the Nineteenth Century:* St. Martin's Press, New York, 1966. A most valuable and comprehensive study.

CHAPTER 39

The Arab Crescent and the Arab League

FRENCH EVACUATION

Undoubtedly with quite different motives, the U.S.S.R., China, and the United States recognized the unconditional independence of Syria and Lebanon in 1944. Shortly thereafter, both declared war against Germany in accordance with the Yalta program and joined the United Nations as charter members. Immediately, the question of the presence of British and French troops occupied all Syrian and Lebanese minds. British troops antagonized only the more uncompromising, but the French symbolized the previous mandate-colonial status. Fear of the permanence of French control governed emotions in Beirut and Damascus.

General de Gaulle understood that the troops would have to be withdrawn, but he evidently hoped to retain a strong French influence in the Levant by means of treaties with Syria and Lebanon which would be at least as favorable as the British treaties with Iraq and Egypt. He particularly desired that the French language be accepted and taught in the schools and that the French schools be entirely free from Lebanese and Syrian control. Naval, military, and air bases for the French would be held indefinitely, and assurances would be given that the Levant remain a French sphere in economic matters.

Syria and Lebanon indicated a willingness to discuss these points and negotiate treaties, but only after departure of the troops. The landing of additional French soldiers in Beirut was interpreted as military pressure. Open resistance to the French was staged, and the

French shelled Damascus in May, 1945. This goaded Churchill into serving an ultimatum upon de Gaulle to cease fire and detain his troops in their barracks while British forces restored order. Thereafter, the only question remaining was when and how would the troops be withdrawn. The British and French discussed the evacuation at great length and in great detail throughout 1945 and into 1946. The Syrians came to believe that British troops were concentrated there to prevent disorders resulting from the presence of French troops and that French troops were being kept there because the British troops would not leave. The Security Council of the United Nations, prodded by the U.S.S.R. and the United States, recommended that foreign troops leave Syria and Lebanon as soon as practicable. The last French troops departed from Syria in April, 1946, but remained in Lebanon until December. The two countries of the Levant had achieved independence!

REPUBLIC OF LEBANON

In Lebanon the nationalist-minded leaders who had controlled the quasi-independent regime since 1943 remained unchanged. The confessional aspect of the state was upheld, as was the tradition that the president be a Maronite Christian and the prime minister a Sunni Muslim. At that time the Lebanese chamber of deputies included 30 Christians and 25 Muslims; and during the month of the final departure of the French, Riyadh al-Sulh formed a coalition cabinet at the invitation of President Bishara al-Khuri.

New elections for the chamber were held in 1947. The Constitutional party, the one in power, succeeded easily to manage the elections and continue in office. Beirut newspapers protested; and Kamal Jumblat, a young Druze socialist, resigned from the cabinet. But the leaders were unmoved. The problem of Palestine, the economic detonations resulting from independence, the postwar relaxations, and the East-West crisis gave Lebanese politicians ample opportunity for disagreement. Perhaps the smallness of the country, the paucity of its natural resources, and the obvious diversity of religious affiliations—the customary attribute of national distinction in the Middle East—bound together all political leaders except the extremists. Among themselves they quarreled over favors, prestige, position, and power, but they usually closed ranks on foreign crises. Cabinets changed frequently, but the leaders shuffled the various ministerial posts among themselves. In the years following the departure of the French troops prime ministers succeeded one after another. Between 1946 and 1966 twelve different men occupied the position, many of them on several occasions. But most of them were in the cabinet when not holding the

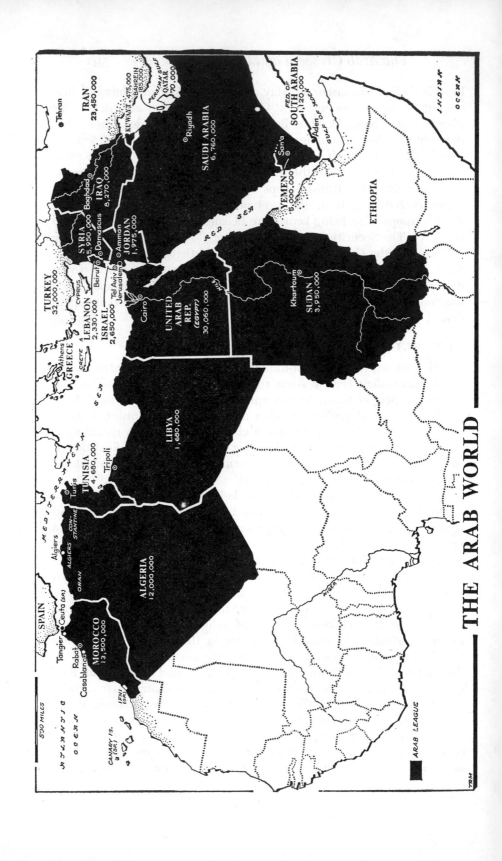

THE ARAB WORLD

500 MILES

SPAIN

Tangier
Ceuta (SP.)
Rabat
Casablanca
MOROCCO
13,500,000

IFNI
(SP.)

CANARY IS.
(SP.)

ATLANTIC OCEAN

Algiers
CON-
STANTINE
ALGIERS (SP.)
ORAN

ALGERIA
12,000,000

Tunis
TUNISIA
4,680,000
Tripoli

LIBYA
1,680,000

MEDITERRANEAN SEA

GREECE
Athens

CRETE

CYPRUS
LEBANON
2,330,000
Beirut
ISRAEL
2,650,000
Tel Aviv
Jerusalem

TURKEY
32,000,000

SYRIA
5,950,000
Damascus
JORDAN
1,975,000
Amman

Cairo

UNITED
ARAB
REP.
(EGYPT)
30,060,000

RED SEA

IRAQ
8,270,000
Baghdad

IRAN
23,450,000
Tehran

PERSIAN GULF
KUWAIT 475,000
BAHREIN 150,000
QATAR
70,000

SAUDI ARABIA
6,760,000
Riyadh

YEMEN
5,000,000
San'a

Aden
GULF OF ADEN
FED. OF
SOUTH ARABIA
1,120,000

INDIAN OCEAN

Khartoum
SUDAN
3,950,000

ETHIOPIA

NIGER

ARAB LEAGUE

prime ministership. Bishara al-Khuri was overthrown in September, 1952 by a bloodless public strike and demonstration which resembled a vote of no confidence. Since General Fuad Shihab refused to call out the army, al-Khuri's only recourse was to resign. Mismanagement, corruption, and arrogance were the charges against him. Kamal (Camille) Shamun, leader of the Progressive Socialist party, was elected president; and Khalid Shihab, as the new prime minister, asked for and was granted full powers for six months. Elections in July, 1953 showed little change, since membership in the chamber of deputies was to a large extent predetermined by its proportional representation according to religious affiliation. The electoral law of 1952 decreed the chamber to be composed of 13 Maronites, 9 Sunnites, 8 Shiites, 5 Greek Orthodox, 3 Druzes, 3 Greek Catholics, 2 Armenian Orthodox, and 1 collectively to the minor groups such as Protestants, Jews, and Roman Catholics. Abdallah al-Yafi, a Beirut lawyer, became prime minister again and also held for a time the portfolios for interior, defense, and information.

Lesser and fringe parties did not succeed in winning many supporters, but they did have considerable nuisance value and kept the leaders in office more alert to their responsibilities. The largest of these parties—the Nationalist Bloc, at one time led by Raymond Edde—believed that Lebanon's destiny, and certainly her independence, rested upon close relations with France. Of course, this party declined after the French departed. Kamal Jumblat pursued a utopian socialist doctrine, whereas Mustafa al-Aris and Khalid Bakdash professed Marxist dogmas and served as Soviet agents. Antun Saada denied the partition of Syria and formed his Syrian National party, a pro-fascist group which strove incessantly and often violently for the reunion of Lebanon with Syria.

The fundamental political problem in Lebanon after 1945 revolved around her geographic location. A narrow populous strip along the coast, Lebanon is an Arab state of many religions tied strongly to Arab culture and Arab traditions. Yet, the wealth of the state and many of its people depended upon the sea and commerce with the outside world, mainly the West. As a result, Lebanese political leaders attempted to pursue two courses.

Beirut and the other Lebanese towns on the coast prospered greatly during the mandate period, mainly from commerce. Beirut became Westernized to a remarkable degree, and during the war served as a port and base for operations in the Levant. National independence gave Beirut the opportunity to become one of the great markets in the Middle East. Her merchants proved equal to the responsibility, and Beirut evolved rapidly into a great Middle Eastern commercial and financial center. Shortly after 1948 Lebanon established a free money market which attracted Middle Eastern moneys to her banks. Officials and favorites of Middle Eastern potentates transferred their funds to Beirut banks or invested in apartment houses and businesses of many types. Beirut developed into a busy port, and the airport, which welcomed international jet airplanes, was served by over thirty different airlines.

Although the Lebanese rejoiced over the departure of the French, they were not bitterly anti-French. The many business connections precluded a complete break. And Lebanese-Syrian currency remained tied to the French franc until 1948, when France devalued the franc by forty-four percent without increasing the cover for the Syrian-Lebanese pound as had been agreed in 1944. France offered to make up the balance in properties claimed by France in Lebanon, in European currencies, in credit for purchases in France, and in additional French francs. Lebanese leaders protested vigorously but in the end accepted the offer, fearing a breakdown in trade. Lebanon obtained a ten-year guarantee of her currency against French devaluation and a liquidation of all French government property claims in Lebanon. The financial settlement, rearranged and improved upon again in 1959, smoothed relations with France, and trade between the two countries was maintained at its customary level. In 1955 France extended a credit of $15,000,000 for the purchase of French goods and in later years acted to facilitate trade. In 1964 the charter of the French-owned Banque de Syrie et du Liban expired and the new state Bank of Lebanon was established to take over the issuing of currency and to conduct banking for the government. French control and the mandate period were fully concluded by the termination of this last visible instrument of power.

Every year after World War II Lebanon had a sizable unfavorable balance of trade that was more than redressed by commercial services, tourism, remittances from Lebanese emigrants and those living abroad, and investments of foreign capital. In 1958 just a day or two before the formation of the United Arab Republic, large capital sums flowed to Beirut from Syria. Wealthy individuals in Arab countries and from many other parts of the world have found Lebanon a suitable haven for their funds. In 1965, for example, it was estimated that $150,000,000 from Syria, Saudi Arabia, and Kuwayt was deposited in Lebanese banks. When such moneys were invested in local apartment houses or in new industry, the balance of payments was aided, but it endangered the liquidity of these accounts. High interest rates attracted floating capital and "hot" money always has had an affinity for numbered banking accounts. The closing of the doors on October 15,

1966 of the Intra Bank of Beirut was a rude shock to the Middle East. With liabilities of over $230,000,000 it could not cover some rather large withdrawals. Its funds were tied up in the ownership of airlines, real estate properties in many countries, and other frozen assets. A three-day bank holiday was declared, and the Bank of Lebanon guaranteed the solvency of all other banks in the country.

For some years business and political leaders in Lebanon deplored the nation's dependence on commerce and banking as too uncertain in times of world recession or tension and advocated that measures should be found to direct the economy toward industry with greater emphasis on scientific and specialized agriculture. Difficult as this was where consumer prices were high and natural resources few, considerable progress was achieved. Five-year plans were enacted in 1962, 1964, and 1965 for $150,000,000, $325,000,000, and $975,000,000 respectively, for highways, irrigation and water resources, electric power installations, education, harbor and transportation facilities, and industry. Beirut River was realigned and land reclamation salvaged 250,000 abandoned acres. A project to develop irrigation and electric power along the Litani River was adopted in 1954 but it moved slowly so that the first stage, in part financed by Kuwayt through KFAED and in part by an International Bank loan of $27,000,000, was not completed until 1965 when a ten-mile tunnel through the mountains diverted much of the flow to irrigate the western slopes. Although industry was left to the private sector of the economy, progress was stimulated by favorable consideration from the government. The recession of 1961 faded, and each year thereafter seemed more prosperous and auspicious. In the first half of 1966 eighty new factories with an investment of about $4,000,000 went up in Lebanon. A three-year agreement on trade and technical co-operation was signed in 1965 with the European Economic Community whose member countries granted "most favored nation treatment" to Lebanon. In time, Lebanon hoped for associate membership in the European Common Market.

Since Syria refused in 1948 to accept the French offer to offset, in part, the losses to the backing of the Lebanese-Syrian pound resulting from the sudden devaluation of the franc, a new and separate Lebanese currency was established. Within a few weeks the currency break with Syria presented difficulties of payments, exchange rates, and trade balances. An agreement extended the economic unity of the two countries for an additional three years and arranged that forty-four percent of the aggregate customs receipts at all frontiers would be credited to Lebanon. However, divergent economic interests of the two countries caused one storm after another and in 1950 precipitated an economic break and the closing of the frontier for nine months.

Syria exported grain and livestock and aspired to industrial development. Lebanon lived by foreign trade and her industry had not reached the point where a protective tariff, such as Syria desired, appealed to the majority. In 1952 an economic agreement with Syria was signed at Shtoura, providing that royalties from oil lines of the Iraq Petroleum Company and the Trans-Arabian Pipe Line Company would be divided equally and that no duties between the two countries would be levied on agricultural produce or livestock. Tariffs on industrial products would be protective for certain categories of goods in which Syria and Lebanon had manufacturing interests.

Relations between Lebanon and the United States were most cordial during this period. Dr. Charles Malik, Lebanon's representative to the United Nations and ambassador to the United States, carried a message of good will and understanding to the American people. Dr. Bayard Dodge and Dr. Stephen Penrose, Jr., presidents of the American University of Beirut, served as unofficial yet very effective ambassadors of the American people; and several official American ambassadors of exceptional imagination and tact furthered the warm relations between the two nations. The very considerable emigration from Lebanon to the United States in the past also played an active role in maintaining interest and understanding between the two countries.

The Trans-Arabian pipeline to carry oil from the Saudi Arabian fields to the Mediterranean had its terminus near Sidon in southern Lebanon. In 1947 Lebanon forced work to cease on the line because of the American position on the partition of Palestine. Construction, however, was resumed in 1949; and oil began to flow in 1950. A refinery was built in Sidon to process petroleum, and a second was erected in 1955. On the coast north of Beirut the Iraq Petroleum Company's pipeline touched the sea at Tripoli, and after World War II two new parallel lines were laid to offset the disuse of the Haifa line and market the increased Iraqi production. The lines and refineries brought a very welcome income. But in 1956 a new law was passed, imposing heavy taxes retroactively to 1952 on foreign oil companies having pipelines in Lebanon. Aimed at Iraq Petroleum Company and TAP-line, the law was sponsored by Prime Minister Abdallah al-Yafi and Minister of State Saib Salam, who was also chairman of the ministers' oil committee. The latter was negotiating with TAP-line officials and representatives of Syria, Jordan, and Saudi Arabia, who suggested that the usual fifty percent of the profits be divided equally among the four Arab states. Lebanese ministers, however, wanted fifty percent of the profits on oil passing through pipelines in Lebanon. IPC immediately objected, dropped its plans for an additional pipeline to Tripoli, and discharged employees in the Tripoli area. Lebanese opposition attacked the government for its ineptitude in the retroactive tax law. Not until 1958 was agreement reached to pay Lebanon $16,000,000 in back transit fees and to raise the rate so that yearly royalties jumped from $1,000,000 to $3,500,000. Then in 1962 IPC built a modern refinery at Tripoli and agreed to make available to Lebanon all of her domestic needs in local currency. At the same time a similar settlement was concluded with TAP-line whereby $12,500,000 was received for "payments in arrears" and a new rate was set that moved the yearly rate from $1,250,000 up to $4,500,000. Although Lebanon had no oil of her own, she began to benefit from Middle Eastern oil resources to some small degree. Even this was lost for a time in 1966 and 1967 when Iraq turned off the flow at the time of bitter negotiations with IPC over royalties and policies and again with the shutoff of all oil deliveries to the West, especially to the United States and Great Britain, during and after the Israeli-Arab War.

Although the U.S.S.R. recognized Lebanon in 1944, the Soviets gave only passing interest to Lebanon and Communist groups there. In Beirut the Communists were extremely active in the trade-union movement, led by Mustafa al-Aris. Street demonstrations were so frequent that they bored the public; but Communists enjoyed such success among the students at the American University in organizing parades and protests that government officials closed it temporarily in 1954. Yet, in the 1953 elections all Communists failed miserably at the polls, and their sympathizers were defeated.

After 1954 the U.S.S.R. changed her earlier indifference. Lebanon signed an economic agreement with Russia in April; and a similar trade pact was initialed in 1955 with East Germany. Russian technicians surveyed Lebanon in 1956 for various economic and industrial possibilities, and trade agreements were negotiated with Communist China and Bulgaria in 1957. Rapidly expanding population, limited land resources, and unemployment offered fertile fields for Soviet activities. Lebanese officials recognized the challenge and initiated various projects, the most promising being the Litani River irrigation and hydroelectric power plan. Beginning in 1960, leaders of all groups adopted a policy of nonalignment and used this term repeatedly in public pronouncements. Officials too closely identified with American or French circles had to step aside and non-Lebanese Arab Communists were deported. Trade was encouraged with the Soviet bloc; nevertheless, Lebanon in the main remained a Western-oriented nation. She could not deny her position on the Mediterranean, her past history, and her cultural associations.

By far the most pressing event for Lebanon to consider after World War II arose from the partition of Palestine and the birth of Israel.

Lebanon showed her Arab character by joining the Arab League at its inception and participating in its decisions and actions. She argued in the United Nations against partition and revealed her attitude by halting work at Sidon on the pipeline. However, Lebanon's part in the Palestine war was very small, and she suffered only a handful of casualties (ten killed, twenty wounded). Fawzi al-Kawukji, a native of Tripoli and an old soldier from the days of Ottoman army service, led a group of irregular soldiers, some of them Lebanese, into Palestine before the end of the mandate to try to prevent the formation of the state of Israel. Whenever he visited Lebanon, he was always honored by public demonstrations which definitely indicated Lebanese sympathy for the Palestinian Arabs. Furthermore, Lebanon lodged no protest when he based the operations of his National Liberation army in Lebanon.

Lebanon found no difficulty in subscribing to the various truces declared in the Palestine war and easily entered into armistice negotiations. Israeli forces withdrew from four Lebanese villages which they had occupied; and on March 23, 1949 an armistice was signed, recognizing the previous Palestine-Lebanon frontier with demilitarized zones on each side. Lebanon refused to recognize Israel, however, and adopted the boycott practices of the Arab League. Since unemployment was widespread in Lebanon, the influx of over 100,000 Arab refugees, equal to almost ten percent of the total population of Lebanon, injected an explosive factor into the Palestine settlement. The refugees were located in fifteen camps scattered from Tripoli to Tyre and were supported by United Nations grants; but their continued presence and natural increase to 130,000 by 1959 and to 150,000 by 1967 graphically illustrated to Lebanese citizens that Israel was a disturbing factor in Middle Eastern society. The Arab boycott of Israel was supported by the government which also approved of the denial of Suez passage to Israeli shipping.

The relative calm in Lebanon was shattered in 1956 by the Suez crises. President Shamun supported Egypt in her nationalization move, and mass rallies and strikes condemning Western pressures on Egypt were permitted in Beirut and other cities. When the Sinai war began, Lebanon declared a state of emergency and Shamun invited the heads of all Arab governments to Beirut to determine what action should be taken. Lebanese leaders spoke vigorously in the United Nations and in many forums, lamenting the aggression upon Egypt and urging the speedy withdrawal of Israeli forces from Gaza and the Straits of Tiran.

As soon as the most irritating aspects of the Sinai war were soothed, Lebanese leaders engaged in a bitter parliamentary election. Abdallah al-Yafi fell from office in November, 1956 and was replaced by Sami al-

Sulh. In April, 1957 a new electoral law was adopted, enlarging the membership of the chamber of deputies to 66 and calling for four-year terms. Campaigning soon began in earnest, and a National Union Front announced its opposition to Sami al-Sulh and President Shamun.

Collecting around several disgruntled former prime ministers such as Saib Salam, Abdallah al-Yafi, and Husayn Uwayni, the Front presented a five-point platform: no amendment to the constitution allowing Shamun to succeed himself; absolute neutrality; rejection of foreign military bases and pacts like the Baghdad pact; refusal of any aid which would compromise Lebanon's sovereignty; and a close and impartial co-operation with other Arab states. Election clashes occurred, and on one occasion Saib Salam was beaten by the police and arrested. General Shihab declared the elections would be conducted fairly; and in July the government won 50 seats, the National Union Front 8, and the Independents 8. Significantly, Saib Salam, Abdallah al-Yafi, Kamal Jumblat, Rashid Karami, and other prominent politicians failed to win election and, in August Sami al-Sulh reshuffled his cabinet.

The politicians who found themselves frozen out of office commenced a battle to regain power and discovered eager allies in Syria and Egypt. Arms smuggling from Syria became commonplace, and Lebanese frontier police were shot in attempts to halt the illicit traffic. Terrorists bombed the Parliament building and the Government House. Lebanon's public acceptance of the Eisenhower Doctrine became a prime target of the opposition. Foreign Minister Charles Malik reiterated that Lebanon would side with Arabs in any dispute with the West involving legitimate Arab rights and aspirations. (He warned, however, that Middle Eastern conflicts could not be solved by alliances with Communists.) When the Syrian fuss arose with Turkey in 1957, any aggression against Syria was acknowledged as an attack upon Lebanon. Nevertheless, acts of terrorism persisted, and it was necessary to deport numerous Syrians and Jordanians.

The achievement of the United Arab Republic increased pressures and tensions surrounding Lebanon. Leaders announced immediately that Lebanon would not join the United Arab Republic or the Arab Federation; and infiltration of arms and men from Syria and Egypt mounted. Malik confirmed a report that he had received a promise of unlimited military and economic aid from the United States to maintain Lebanon's independence, although in the fiscal year beginning in July, 1957 direct American aid was programed at only $15,000,000.

In March, 1958 a reorganized cabinet under Sami al-Sulh won a vote of confidence of 38 to 15 with 13 abstaining. But at the same time 82 Lebanese leaders, including the heads of several of the religious communities, signed a statement warning President Shamun against amending the constitution and seeking re-election when his term expired in September. Political agitation grew pernicious, and in May a pseudo civil war was inaugurated by outbreaks and demonstrations in Tripoli and Beirut. Soon designated as rebels, politicians out of office extended independently their sway over specific areas: Saib Salam in the Basta quarter of Beirut; Kamal Jumblat in the Druze mountain area; Rashid Karami in the sector north of Tripoli; and others in two or three isolated regions. Syrian and Egyptian nationalists, commandos, and arms, with the silent connivance of Damascus and Cairo, helped the rebels; but the fracas reached a stalemate, as General Fuad Shihab refused to commit the army to either political camp and acted only to maintain public order.

Civil strife languished after President Shamun passed out the word he would not try for re-election, after a team of United Nations investigators and a trip to the Middle East by Dag Hammarskjöld whitewashed the complicity of the United Arab Republic, and after General Shihab acquiesced to a quiet demand that he accept the presidency at the election in July. At this juncture, the Iraq Revolution erupted and the possibility of sizable intervention from Syria became so real that President Shamun called upon President Eisenhower for urgent relief. The immediate landing of American marines in Beirut upped the quarrel of local politicians to the level of the cold war between East and West. Many blustered, and Nasser flew to Khrushchev in Moscow; but it was soon evident that no one would seriously challenge the American position. The Americans asserted that the marines would be withdrawn as soon as a peaceful solution of Lebanese politics could be devised. As was expected, the presidential election resulted in the choice of General Fuad Shihab; and the rebels declared general satisfaction, if and when the American troops would leave. The expressed desire of most Lebanese political leaders resolved itself around the widespread hope in Lebanon and in many quarters of the Middle East that genuine neutrality would descend upon Lebanon so she could become "the Switzerland of the Middle East."

President Shihab was inaugurated September 23, 1958, three days after Sami al-Sulh had left for France and self-imposed exile; American troops departed October 25th; and the four hundred United Nations observers were gone by November. The president designated Rashid Karami as prime minister of a cabinet that in a few days was reduced to four members, the others being Husayn Uwayni, Raymond Edde, and Pierre Gemayel. The Chamber voted in November to give Karami authority to rule by decree for six months. Some of the more open wounds of the battles began to heal and calmer relations with the

United Arab Republic alleviated much of the bitterness. Shihab and Nasser met for a warm exchange at the Lebanese–Syrian border, and in Cairo Karami signed a beneficial Lebanese-United Arab Republic economic pact. Transit trade through Lebanon to Saudi Arabia, Jordan, and the new United Arab Republic was normalized by a revised traffic accord. Karami skillfully avoided involvement in the heated quarrels between Nasser and General Kassim of Iraq and so satisfied domestic and foreign policy inclinations of Lebanese factions that he remained at the helm until the spring of 1960. Then he stepped aside for the formation of a caretaker cabinet in preparation for the summer elections for a new Chamber whose number had recently been increased to ninety-nine. It should be noted that the number of members in Lebanon's Chamber is usually divisible by eleven so that the accepted ratio of six Christians to five Muslims can be easily maintained. No official census has been taken since 1932 as few wish to disturb this proportion. The new division in 1960 consisted of 30 Maronites, 20 Sunnites, 19 Shiites, 11 Greek Orthodox, 6 Druzes, 6 Greek Catholics, 4 Armenian Orthodox, 1 Armenian Catholic, 1 Protestant, and 1 other Christian.

The elections of June and July were most orderly. Fourteen parties participated and Karami's party won eleven seats. Forty-one independents were elected. With such a peaceful situation President Shihab announced his resignation, saying that he had taken the position during a period of tenseness and it might be better for him now to step down. When ninety members of the new Chamber urged him to reconsider he acceded to their pleas. Saib Salam whose relations with Nasser were most cordial formed a cabinet of eighteen, intending to unite all parties and shades of opinion. It proved so unwieldy that Salam reduced the number to eight, but in October, 1961 after a public quarrel with Kamal Jumblat and the secession of Syria from the United Arab Republic Karami formed a new cabinet that remained in office until the preparations for new elections in 1964. In those years Karami skillfully steered a neutral course among the Arab states. Each of the successive coups in Syria sent seismic waves across Lebanon. In December, 1961 the National Socialist party attempted a coup with the intent of joining Syria, Iraq, Jordan, and Lebanon into one state that would oppose pan-Arab nationalism and the Arab socialism of the United Arab Republic. Over 1,500 were seized in thwarting the coup, 700 of whom were resident aliens from Palestine and Syria. In general during Karami's administration Syria regarded Lebanon as a center of Nasserite conspiracy. Upon Karami's resignation prior to elections in April and May, 1964 Husayn Uwayni formed a caretaker government that continued on with the new Chamber. Shihab refused to consider the suggestion that the constitution be amended to allow him a second term, and fifty-one-year-old Charles Hilu, minister of education, was elected fourth president of Lebanon and took office in September. President Hilu joined hands late in 1965 with Karami to purge public life and the government of gross inefficiency and corruption. Uwayni had been ousted in July, attacking Karami so severely that the leading political figures refused to serve in the cabinet with Uwayni. Filling his cabinet, however, with experts and technicians, Karami proceeded with his program, removing from office thirteen judges, sixteen diplomats, seventeen national security police, and ninety-nine other civil servants. With no patronage at their disposal, party leaders, especially Saib Salam, were so piqued that Karami was forced out and was replaced in April, 1966 by Abdallah al-Yafi and a ten-member cabinet of politicians. After the failure of the Intra Bank in October and a series of charges that the cabinet had been negligent in handling the affair, and that the Bank of Lebanon, whose governor was Philip Taqla, on leave as foreign minister in al-Yafi's cabinet, had not supported Intra Bank adequately in the crisis, Karami and his technicians were back in control in December.

In Arab affairs Karami and most of the political parties adhered to Arab League policies. Although Lebanon did not join in 1965 in an Arab Common Market with Syria, Jordan, Iraq, Kuwayt, and the United Arab Republic, pleading her special trading position and connections with the European Economic Community, Lebanon joined in 1964 with Syria, Jordan, and the United Arab Republic in establishing the authority for the use of the Jordan River and its tributaries for the benefit of its Arab riparian states. Approval was given in 1965 for a pumping station at the Wazzani Springs to divert water to the Banyas River in Syria whence it would flow into the Yarmuk River in Jordan. Palestinian refugees in Lebanon, organized in a society, al-Fatah, conducted a number of raids in 1965 into Israel; she retaliated by attacking two Lebanese border villages. Even so, Lebanon sought not to provoke Israel but the cabinet did receive authority to permit troops from other Arab countries to enter Lebanon to protect the Wazzani Springs against any Israeli attack. In May, 1967 at the outset of the crisis between Israel and Syria, Lebanese officials requested that the United States Sixth Fleet in the eastern Mediterranean not make its scheduled call in Beirut, because they feared that such a visit might be interpreted as Lebanese bowing to non-Arab pressures. All Lebanese leaders upheld Arab causes and positions against Israel but tried to remain aloof from inter-Arab quarrels and combinations in the same degree that they avoided too close an alignment in other conflicts in the world.

REPUBLIC OF SYRIA

When World War II ended, Syrian political leaders who had battled for complete independence in the mandatory period were in control and had the satisfaction of forming the first fully sovereign Syrian republic. Shukri al-Kuwatli held the presidency; Saadallah al-Jabri was prime minister; and Jamil Mardam, Faris al-Khuri, Hashim al-Atasi, and Khalid al-Azm were prominent political figures, who held other important posts. A new chamber of deputies, elected in the summer of 1947, confirmed the position of the government leaders; and Jamil Mardam, who had become prime minister in December, 1946 remained in office for two years.

National feeling in Syria ran high. The actions of the French had been more drastic in Damascus and the interior provinces of Syria than in Beirut. Three times in recent memory they had wantonly shelled Damascus, which had been the site of the Arab congresses as well as the capital of Faysal's short-lived Arab kingdom in 1920. All French schools in Syria were closed in 1945; and when France devalued the franc in 1948, Syria issued her own separate Syrian pounds immediately. In April French offers of reconciliation were refused, and any official who appeared friendly or compromising toward the French was digging his own political grave.

The dream of a united Arab state to include Lebanon, Syria, Transjordan, Palestine, and Iraq never died in Syria. As Syria emerged independent upon the close of the war, the value of union appeared greater than ever; many Syrians regarded it as almost a necessity. Each state separately was weak; together they would have strength. Yet, an arrangement to accomplish even partial federation required political genius of a high order. Fertile Crescent unity was not a new idea, but after the area had been divided between England and France unification had been impossible.

The fall of France in 1940 whetted Abdallah's ambitions to join Syria to Transjordan; but in 1947 President al-Kuwatli of Syria publicly stated that in any uniting Transjordan would be annexed by Syria. Syrian political leaders had no intention of being governed by Abdallah or his greater Syria from Amman. Indeed, they did not relish the thought of surrendering position and power in Syria to any group or person. Others within Syria looked forward to the merger of Iraq and Transjordan, the two Hashimite kingdoms, and the eventual inclusion of Syria and Lebanon. Leaders in Iraq and Syria discussed the union of their two states into a Fertile Crescent union. The Syrians believed that they possessed a more advanced population and that though slightly smaller, they would dominate Iraq. On the other hand Iraqis recognized that their country contained greater wealth, both developed and potential, and felt certain that Iraq would lead the combined state. The drawing together of Iraq and Transjordan threw Egypt and Saudi Arabia into each other's arms. Egyptian leaders could not contemplate other leadership than theirs in the Middle Eastern Arab states; and Ibn Saud, an enemy of the Hashimites since the days of World War I, was apprehensive about an enlarged Hashimite state on his northern confines from the Red Sea to the Persian Gulf.

Syria played an active part in the formation of the Arab League, attended its conferences, agreed to all Arab League declarations of united Arab opposition to the partition of Palestine, and promised to co-operate militarily against the formation of a Zionist state. In 1947 the Palestine liberation committee obtained over 27,000 volunteers in Syria for commando units, and Druze chiefs notified the government they could furnish 10,000 men for the fight. In the spring of 1948 various high Syrian army officers, including Colonel Adib al-Shishakli, participated in operations in the Palestine war; but in the actual fighting Syrian forces proved to be ineffective. Three small villages in the Hulah marsh area were occupied, but there was no great enthusiasm to shed Syrian blood so that Abdallah in Transjordan or Faruk in Egypt might have more territory to rule.

On March 30, 1949 Chief of Staff Husni al-Zaim carried out a bloodless *coup d'état*. Learning that President al-Kuwatli was planning his dismissal, al-Zaim arrested the president, the prime minister, and many leading political figures. The public approved for a number of reasons: the Palestine war was a failure; corruption was not reduced; the constitution had been amended to permit the president to succeed himself; and al-Kuwatli opposed the Fertile Crescent unity plan. The politicians in their governmental techniques had failed to bring to Syria the "promised day" after ousting French and foreign influences. A new cabinet was formed; al-Zaim as prime minister also held the portfolios of defense and interior. Political parties were outlawed, and a new constitution was planned. In June "The Leader" was elected president; but on August 14 General Sami al-Hinnawi arrested al-Zaim, who was immediately shot.

Husni al-Zaim had started out marvelously, arranging a cease-fire agreement with Israel in April and obtaining assurances from Nuri al-Said that Iraq would come to the assistance of Syria if attacked by Israel. Husni proposed unity with Iraq "on the basis of a full autonomous state for each country," and military figures journeyed between Damascus and Baghdad. Fearing Hashimite rule in Syria, Egypt and Saudi Arabia rushed diplomatic and financial support to al-Zaim. At this point al-Zaim abandoned unionist policies, and became president of a new Syrian republic. Worst of all, he showed an inclination to restore to France some aspects of her cultural influence. French, for instance, became an official language, along with Arabic.

Upon the execution of al-Zaim, General al-Hinnawi called upon Hashim al-Atasi, an elder statesman, to form a new government. A constituent assembly was elected in November, and al-Atasi was chosen head of the state. (Women voted for the first time.) Meanwhile, discussions wih Iraqi officials proceeded to a point of drafting the framework of a common regime; Syria and Iraq would have a common army, a supreme cabinet including foreign affairs, defense, finance, and economy, and a customs and monetary union. But the Republican Bloc, enemy of union, stirred the army to move. On December 19, 1949 Colonel Adib al-Shishakli arrested al-Hinnawi, who was charged with treason and conspiracy with a foreign power (Iraq).

Colonel al-Shishakli did not at first rule directly. The constituent assembly declared Syria to be a republic; Hashim al-Atasi was elected president and Khalid al-Azm became prime minister. No one, however, doubted who was the real power in the government. Early in 1950 al-Shishakli visited Cairo and Riyadh. In the former he was welcomed; and in the latter he obtained a loan of $6,000,000, which was to be repaid by shipments of Syrian goods over a three-year period commencing in 1955. It seemed more natural geographically and in most ways for Syria to be drawn toward Iraq; yet the diplomacy and wealth of Egypt and Saudi Arabia repeatedly proved irresistible to Syrian leaders. The prime minister, Khalid al-Azm, voiced the opinion of many when he declared that "he resented finding Syria like a 'commodity' offered for sale by contending parties." In June Nazim al-Kudsi of the People's party, the largest single party in the assembly, became prime minister. Unity with Iraq and Transjordan had been defeated, since the People's party stood for an Arab union of all Arab states and peoples—a posture which in 1950 meant victory for the Egypto-Saudi bloc over the Hashimites.

Colonel al-Shishakli desired sincerely to return Syria to civilian government; and al-Kudsi's cabinet reflected that intention except for Colonel Fawzi Silu, al-Shishakli's close friend in the ministry of defense who kept the army's hand on political affairs. A liberal constitution adopted in September contained detailed and specific articles with respect to education, labor, land ownership, and the rights of the citizen.

The new constitution and the new government, however, did not alter the fundamental weakness of Syria or usher in a new flourishing economic order. Syrian frustration led to a refusal of United States Point Four aid and a pronouncement that Syria would "go it alone."

However, Syria began to look to the Soviet bloc. Maaruf al-Dawalibi, one-time minister of economy and a leader of the Islamic Socialist Front, concentrated on an anti-Western campaign; attacks were made upon American activities, and Syria was urged to sign a nonaggression pact with the U.S.S.R.

One cabinet succeeded another in 1951; and in November a prolonged cabinet crisis ended with Maaruf al-Dawalibi as prime minister. In Berlin during World War II he had been political secretary to the ex-Mufti, had been hunted in Paris by the West, and was now a leader of the Islamic Socialist Front. The philosophy of this group, as one member described it, was "a Marxist drink in a Muslim cup."

Colonel Adib al-Shishakli acted swiftly. Most of the cabinet was jailed. President Hashim al-Atasi resigned and Colonel Fawzi Silu became prime minister. Political parties were outlawed, and plans for a new government and a new constitution were initiated. The new constitution was not presented until July, 1953, at which time al-Shishakli became president and prime minister. He organized an Arab Liberation party which won seventy-two of the eighty-two seats in the parliamentary elections in October, since the other three major parties boycotted the election.

Colonel al-Shishakli overreached himself, and his time was running out. He arrested many leading political figures, including al-Atasi, and declared martial law in Damascus and Aleppo. But the army revolted in the latter city, forcing al-Shishakli to flee in February, 1954. Hashim al-Atasi became president again; the 1950 constitution was reinstated; and the 1949 chamber of deputies was recalled. Elections for a new parliament were held in October, returning eighty-one independents out of a total membership of one hundred and forty-two. Khalid Bakdash, leader of the Communist party, became the first Arab Communist duly elected to an Arab parliament on a Communist ticket. Ex-president Shukri al-Kuwatli returned from five years of exile in Egypt and was elected president in August, 1955. A succession of prime ministers battled with the complex economic, social, and political problems of Syria after the overthrow of al-Shishakli. But none found a constructive program, largely because of virulent nationalism and the submergence of Syrian interests to those of Egypt and Saudi Arabia.

The political instability in Syria in the decade after World War II was extremely detrimental to economic planning and development. Excellent plans for the division and distribution of large tracts of land among poor and landless peasants were enacted into law, but were not implemented to any great extent. Intentions in that direction antagonized the large landowners and led in part to the demise of the al-

Shishakli regime in 1954. After the breakdown of economic relations with Lebanon, Syria took active steps to improve the port facilities of Latakia and channel more of Syria's foreign trade through that point. A port authority was established under the able direction of Nur al-Din Kahalah, an American-trained Syrian engineer; but Latakia did not have the geographical advantages of Tripoli, Beirut, Sidon, and other Lebanese ports.

Oil pipelines from Saudi Arabia and Iraq pass through Syria, and Syria obtained generous royalties for oil flowing through the pipes. In 1949 a concession for oil in Syria was granted to the Syrian-American Oil and Gas Company, but no significant resources have been located. Other plans with Jordan for the development of electric-power stations and irrigation projects on the Yarmuk River were advanced, but political uncertainties and jealousies prevented their implementation.

Frequent raids and counterraids on the border of Israel kept Syrian insistence on nonrecognition of Israel alive. The greatest of these raids was committed in December, 1955, when Israeli forces attacked Syria from the shores of Lake Tiberias. Since the Western powers, and particularly the United States, were identified with the foundation of the Zionist state, the West bore the onus of the Syrian defeat and frustration. Not until 1955, however, did the Syrian political leaders turn more directly to the Soviet bloc and begin to put into effect the old axiom that my enemies' enemies are my friends.

The signing of the Baghdad pact in March, 1955 galvanized Syrian policies and directed Syrian politicians into the Egypto-Saudi camp. The Syrians were already suspicious of the series of treaties of friendship among Turkey, Iraq, and Transjordan in 1946; but the Baghdad pact, especially after the ready adherence given to it by Britain, was anathema to Syrian nationalists and incited most of them to join the Egyptian camp. The earlier Arab League collective-security pact had been an Egyptian political move to forestall an Iraqi-Syrian union rather than to provide defense against Israel. Rejection of the Middle East defense organization, likewise, had been vigorously pleaded in order to assure that no increase of power would accrue to the Hashimites of Iraq and Jordan.

Syria quickly closed ranks with Egypt and Saudi Arabia, declaring that Syrian armed forces would be joined with those of her friends under a unified Egyptian command. In October, 1955 the Damascus pact was signed, pledging mutual assistance and establishing an alliance among the three states. In January, 1956 the pact was consummated by a $10,000,000 loan to Syria by Saudi Arabia and by the arrival of Soviet war matériel from Egypt. Syria signed trade agreements with the U.S.S.R. and Red China in November, 1955 and with

Rumania in January, 1956. Syria also joined in denouncing all acts of the United States, and the pronouncements of the Syrian representative to the United Nations became more bitter and more fiery.

Shukri al-Kuwatli, who was elected president in 1955, lived in exile in Egypt from 1949 to 1954. There he drank the waters of the Nile and witnessed the exciting successes of Colonel Nasser. In Damascus any role other than that of a friend to Egypt was unpardonable and impossible, since the new and young army staff officers were ardent supporters of Colonel Nasser and his revolution. Thus, when Nasser nationalized the Canal, Syrian demonstrations were more open and enthusiastic than those of other Middle Eastern states. Syrian spokesmen swore that the oil pipelines would be sabotaged should the West be guilty of aggression against Egypt. And in November, when the invasion occurred, they made good on their threat. After the fighting in Sinai ceased, Syria did not permit the repair of the pipelines until Israeli forces withdrew from the Gaza Strip.

In June, 1956 Sabri al-Asali became prime minister again. He reshuffled his cabinet in December, and again in January, 1957, when he received a vote of confidence of 69 to 4, with 49 of the Constitutional Bloc abstaining. He had organized several discordant political cliques into a loosely knit coalition, freely supported and influenced by liberal donations and pertinent broadcasts from Saudi Arabia and Egypt. Opposition to the Baghdad pact acted as the mortar binding them together against the Constitutional Bloc, most of whose members represented Aleppo and were receptive to the older idea of union of Syria and Iraq.

To distract attention of the masses from political sniping a running series of plots, accusations of treason, scandals, and political witchhunts were offered in Damascus. Israel, the United States, Iraqi royalty, Turkey, and al-Shishakli were the most convenient whipping boys. At one time forty-seven prominent politicians were court-martialed on charges of fomenting a revolution. Most were tried *in absentia*, but many who appeared confessed meekly to the charge. Incidents such as these abetted the drift toward the left; and trials with regard to the 1955 assassination of leftist Chief of Staff Colonel Adnan Malki added fuel to the fire. These affairs, however, were not entirely effective; for serious "anticonspiracy-trials" riots occurred in Aleppo, where the government of Sabri al-Asali, supported by such wily and skillful politicians as Akram Hurani, Michel Aflaq, Khalid al-Azm, and Salah al-Bitar, was unpopular.

The regime needed arms to prevent an internal *coup* by the dissidents, to strengthen Syria's position vis-à-vis Israel and Iraq, and to wield important influence upon the affairs of Jordan. Furthermore, the army was moving rapidly into the political arena; and officers had a natural desire for more improved weapons in greater quantities. Following Nasser's example, Syria applied to Moscow and received about $60,000,000 in tanks and other matériel in 1956. President al-Kuwatli visited the U.S.S.R., and a dozen MIG-17 jet fighters appeared in Syria. Soviet-bloc ships unloaded their cargoes at Latakia. In 1957 Soviet activities in Syria gave Western leaders and sympathizers pause for thought. Khalid al-Azm on his return from Moscow and Prague announced a loan of $150,000,000 on very favorable interest rates and repayment terms; and projects totaling $570,000,000 to be financed by the Soviet bloc were revealed along with an economic and technical assistance agreement with the U.S.S.R. Many observers believed that Syria was almost irretrievably on her way behind the Iron Curtain.

Concomitantly with these anti-Western developments, Syrian concern for Jordan was marked by the sending of heavy arms to assure Jordanian resistance to Iraq and the West. Early in 1957 Syria signed the Arab solidarity pact, agreeing to contribute about $7,000,000 to support Jordan in her break with Great Britain. When the April crisis arose in Jordan, Syria moved an armored regiment into Jordan to bolster General Ali Abu Nuwar in his bid to throw Jordan into the Nasser camp. After Husayn personally quelled the rebellion, Syria acceded to his demands and unwillingly withdrew her army. Although Syrian leaders fulminated and plotted against Husayn's regime, they were again foiled by the airlifting of American arms into Amman in September.

Each frustration drove the Syrians further to the left, strengthened Soviet bargaining, and emboldened the Pan-Arabists in Aflaq's Arab Renaissance party, the Baath party. It also brought to a head an acute rivalry brewing in the army for a decade. Young army graduates of the Homs Staff College were fiery Arab nationalists who pointed to the defeats in Palestine and the weakness of Syrian policies as positive proof of the senior officers' incompetence. Lt. Col. Abd al-Hamid Sarraj, chief of army intelligence, emerged as the leader of the junior officers; and in March, 1957, the issue was joined when the older officers tried to isolate him by sending him to a post in Cairo. He refused to go; and General Afif Bizri, new chief of staff, was surrounded by Sarraj's friends.

NORTHERN REGION OF THE UNITED ARAB REPUBLIC

Meanwhile the plot to unite Syria and Egypt germinated. As early as July, 1956 the Syrian chamber approved appointment of a committee to negotiate a federal union with Egypt. President al-Kuwatli proved to be a willing tool, and the schedule for the union's consummation and the various steps toward it were outlined. The danger to the intriguers lay in the resistance expected in Aleppo from officers opposed to the youthful clique. To drown all possible opposition in a bath of emotional nationalism conspiracies jeopardizing national integrity were unearthed and ordinary frontier incidents involving opium smugglers and cattle rustlers along the Turkish border were magnified into a frightening crisis. Turkish acts of aggression were imputed to machinations of Western imperialists.

The resulting tension not only silenced internal opposition, but also served as a screen for the arrival of Egyptian troops to forestall a likely *coup d'état* of the 1949 variety. The shallowness of the Turkish crisis was disclosed, when King Saud offered to investigate the charges. Syria refused, and Khrushchev quickly dropped the issue. But the Egyptian regiments remained in Syria. In November, the idea of union was approved in principle; and in February, 1958 the union was officially declared by the Syrian government and Nasser. The latter, however, was somewhat cool to the haste in which the union was effected. A few days following the announcement, Khalid Bakdash, leader of the Arab Communist party, enplaned from Damascus with his family for Moscow; and there was a very considerable flight of capital to Beirut. Nasser became president and al-Kuwatli vice-president of the United Arab Republic, which was divided into two regions; Egypt and Syria. A plebiscite was held, and al-Kuwatli invited all Arab states to join.

To effect the union of two sovereign states has always been a most difficult, perplexing, and sometimes painful experience. In the case of Egypt and Syria, who had no common frontier, were nearly 600 miles apart, and had such disparate economies and social customs, it was a daring but rigorously enforced step. In a few weeks Syrian foreign affairs and defense were thoroughly submerged by Egyptian policies that were paramount everywhere. Nasser as president of the United Arab Republic directed all activities and made all appointments of officials. Unity in other matters moved more deliberately. Budgets, finances, and currency were to remain separate for five years, at least, but trade and economic measures were to conform as soon as possible, and in each case Egyptian patterns were to be imposed upon Syria. Egypt's austere economy of the post-Sinai War period was placed on Syria and all imports were rigidly licensed. Merchants grumbled and permits for expensive luxury goods were denied. Egyptian land reform ideas were extended to Syria and all holdings over 740 acres were to be distributed to landless peasants. The separate tribal law for the eastern nomads that had been practiced and maintained for centuries was abolished, and 250,000 Bedouins suddenly had to conform to Syrian law. Still, all might have become acceptable had there not been severe drought and crop failures in 1958, 1959, and 1960. The barley crop was wiped out in 1958, and there was only a forty percent yield of wheat in 1959. Famine was avoided by shipments of $9,600,000 of grain from the United States in 1959 and $17,000,000 worth in 1960, all for nontransferable Syrian pounds. Export trade with Lebanon, Syria's best customer, was shattered in part by the difficulties and border closing of 1958, in part by the shift to Soviet orientation and Egyptian controls, and in large part by the scarcity of commodities. The day was saved by Egyptian budgetary support, by aid from the United States, by a $7,500,000 credit from the International Monetary Fund, by development loans from the U.S.S.R., and by relatively normal cotton crops.

Politically it was not possible to govern Syria like an Egyptian province. Nasser announced the appointment of the first United Arab Republic cabinet in March, 1958 and four vice presidents, the two from Syria being Akram Hurani and Sabri al-Asali. Salah al-Bitar became a minister of state in the cabinet and most regular cabinet posts had two heads, one for Syria and one for Egypt. Significant Syrian appointments were Colonel Abd al-Hamid Sarraj as minister of the interior and Nur al-Din Kahalah as minister of public works. A few days later General Afif Bizri was named commander of the United Arab Republic First Army (Syria). All political parties in Syria were dissolved. The importance of this latter action became more apparent as the summer wore on, for political figures such as Hurani, al-Asali, and al-Bitar lost the base of their power and found themselves isolated in Cairo or eased out of position, sometimes not so gently. Within two weeks General Bizri resigned from his command, fleeing the country several months later. With political parties and leaders gone and the Syrian army immobilized and demoralized by control from Cairo, real power in Syria fell to Colonel Sarraj and his loyal intelligence forces. The task of governing and administering Syria fell to an executive council of eleven, later eighteen, and a moribund legislative council, both hand-picked by Nasser. Under the chairmanship of Kahalah, a nonpolitical technician and an engineer, the executive council prepared Syrian budgets, planned industrial development and irrigation projects, and carried on the usual administrative functions of government.

The major weakness of this arrangement stemmed from the lack of sufficient authority to crack heads together and get things done. To mend this tendency of cross-purposes Nasser in the autumn of 1959 sent Field Marshall Abd al-Hakim Amer to Damascus as chief of government to bolster the might of the executive committee. The

Syrian military resented his presence and looked to Colonel Sarraj as the leader of Syrian factions. A year later Sarraj assumed the chairmanship of the executive committee at which time Kahalah took over the direction of planning and administering a new five-year plan for industrial and public works. As head of the executive, the police, and military intelligence Sarraj's position in Syria rivaled that of Nasser in Egypt. The union, on the other hand, freed Syria from a great deal of petty politics and feuding and provided a kind of leadership and strength from Egypt. The ten-year development plan drawn up in the early 1950's moved forward. The Rastan Dam on the Orontes, irrigating 62,500 acres, was completed in 1961, and the great Euphrates Valley Project to cost nearly $300,000,000 was initialed. Under the supervision of Kahalah a dam was to be built to add 1,500,000 acres to cultivation, avert disastrous floods, and produce enough electric power to satisfy the needs of the country for the foreseeable future. In 1960 a Syrian delegation in Moscow signed twenty economic development projects totaling another $300,000,000. Industries of many kinds began to hum and production of textiles, cement, and glass increased remarkably. At the new petroleum refinery at Homs a problem arose over marketing the surplus gasoline.

These new social and economic forces at work in Syria engendered bustle and creativity and unchained the imaginations of Syrians who had been suppressed and shrouded by politics since the end of World War I. However, the better established groups and families involved in land, trade, finance, politics, and the army discovered that the union relegated them to less prominent positions and infringed upon too many of their accustomed prerogatives. Land reform sapped their privileges and power; trade quotas, import licenses, and nationalization hampered their business opportunities; banks were nationalized or Arabized (thorough control as to ownership, loans, and types of assets held); political parties were outlawed and leaders suddenly found themselves without followers or organization; and the army officers were frustrated and divided by their loyalties to the uncertain power of Field Marshall Amer and the clandestine intelligence apparatus of Colonel Sarraj.

Acute rivalry and controversy between these two quietly waxed through 1961. In Damascus Sarraj called together all governors and important officials to outline for them future steps in the growth of Syria and to receive their loyalty to him. Amer objected violently and on September 21 Nasser called them to Cairo to settle the dispute. Sarraj evidently got the worse of it for he resigned his vice-presidency on the twenty-sixth and returned to Damascus. However, with both Amer and Sarraj absent for nearly a week, the army recognized its opportunity; banding together with all of the dissident groups, including the mufti of Damascus whom Amer had summarily dismissed a few weeks before, they staged a successful coup early on the morning of September 28, 1961. Nasser's first reaction was to order purely Egyptian cadres of the army to seize the rebels, naval units to occupy Latakia, and paratroopers to drop on Damascus. Informed that these would be unsuccessful, he declared the next day that Arab should not fight Arab and recognized the *fait accompli*. On October 28, 1961, the Syrian Arab Republic was by unanimous vote readmitted to the Arab League.

THE SYRIAN ARAB REPUBLIC

Perhaps if Nasser had granted regional autonomy to Syria within the United Arab Republic, Syrian nationalism and pride would not have been so outraged at being ruled by Egyptians. Syrian officers resented their second-rate positions and the stifling of political activity was more than the Baath party leaders thought they had bargained for. The military council placed Mahmun Kuzbari and a civilian group at the head of the government. He pledged to reverse the nationalization process which had been launched that spring and to re-establish a free economy although he declared that the land reform measures would stand and also the law requiring that twenty-five percent of the profits in an industry be distributed to the employees. Activity on the part of political parties was prohibited. Marshall Amer escaped to Egypt the morning of the coup; Colonel Sarraj was arrested and imprisoned four days later; and Kahalah was appointed head of the Euphrates Valley Project. Syria was readmitted to the United Nations on October 13, and all of the major powers recognized the new state prior to the action by the Arab League. National elections were held on December 1 and December 2 for a Constituent Assembly that would serve as a parliamentary body until the constitution was readied. Moderate conservatives held a majority in this body that elected Kuzbari as its speaker and Nazim al-Kudsi as president of the state. Maaruf al-Dawalibi was appointed prime minister of a civilian cabinet. He asserted that his government would pursue a policy of nonalignment in foreign affairs and at home a course of "constructive socialism." A short-term loan of $16,000,000 was obtained from West Germany to tide them over and al-Dawalibi led a delegation to the U.S.S.R. and Czechoslovakia for economic assistance and military supplies. Early in March, 1962 a new agreement was reached with TAP-line raising the annual revenue to $3,000,000 and receiving $10,000,000 in retroactive payments. Parliament voted to cancel all nationalization effected under the United Arab Republic but did retain some control over big business. In five months Syria appeared to have adjusted to the new order and one could marvel at the flexibility and ingenuity of Syrian politicians and the sophistication of her army officers.

However, everyone was not satisfied. Officers of the army and air force overthrew the government in Damascus on March 28, 1962 and four days later there was a countercoup in Aleppo by "free" officers who appealed to Nasser for intervention. He refused to be drawn into the Syrian dispute and within a week General Abd al-Karim Zahr al-Din, commander in chief of the army, resolved the impasse at a conference in Homs. President al-Kudsi was requested to resume his office and the rebellious officers left Syria. Ahmad Bashir al-Azmah headed a new cabinet that promised to hold a national referendum on the question of rejoining the United Arab Republic. He ordered the renationalization of al-Khumassia, a large business-holding company controlling sizable sections of Syrian industry, especially in textiles, cement, and detergents. All foreign banks were nationalized and a stabilization fund of $41,600,000 was obtained from the United States, West Germany, Italy, and the International Monetary Fund, a loan that, along with a bumper crop said to have been the best since 1932, made it possible to liberalize foreign exchange controls. Internal dissension proved more than al-Azmah could handle, and in September Khalid al-Azm, sometimes called "the Red millionaire," became prime minister and ruled by decree after dissolving the Constituent Assembly.

Every successive coup made the government weaker and more imperious and deepened the rifts within the body politic. The Baath party with each change profited from its better organization and from its well defined and articulated objectives. Baath, or Renaissance, was developed during World War II by Michel Aflaq, a French-educated Arab from a Christian family, who stressed nationalism, unity, and socialism as the three forces that Arab society should pursue and implement in order to rejuvenate the Arab world and to restore its once-famed brilliance and affluence in commerce, industry, and culture—a full-flowered Arab renaissance. The Baath's main opposition was lodged in the pro-Nasser elements of the army and among those who believed that only under Nasser's leadership could the cherished dream of Arab unity be achieved. Nasserite and Baathist ministers in al-Azm's cabinet quarreled repeatedly and when a Baathist coup in Baghdad on February 8, 1963 overturned and executed Kassem a similar blow was expected in Damascus. It came on March 8.

Led by young officers, the National Council of the Revolutionary Command seized the government and placed the Baathists in control. Salah al-Bitar became prime minister and seventy-four business, political, and military leaders were deprived of their civil rights. Included among these were Kuzbari, Hurani, al-Kudsi, al-Azm, al-Azmah, al-Asali, and al-Dawalibi. Colonel Sarraj had already escaped from prison and fled to Cairo. On March 14 al-Bitar announced that steps were being taken to form a tripartite union with Iraq and the United Arab Republic. Conferences were held in Cairo and on April 17 with much fanfare a charter uniting the three states was proclaimed. It was dead, however, before it was published because Syria and Iraq insisted upon equal votes whereas Nasser demanded that voting should depend upon population, probably because Egypt's population was greater than that of the other two combined. As it became public knowledge in May that union talks had failed, Nasserites staged demonstrations and riots in Aleppo and Damascus to exert mob pressure on the Baathists. Two hundred and fifty were arrested and General Amin al-Hafiz, a staunch moderate Baathist, assumed the post of deputy prime minister. At the end of June he was pushed aside by pro-Nasser General Muhammad Ziyah al-Hariri who became chief of staff and minister of defense. He lasted ten days at which time the Baathists seized full power again, sent him off to Vienna, and re-established General al-Hafiz who retained command of the Syrian government from one position or another until he was ousted on February 23, 1966 by a radical left-wing branch of the Baathists.

While al-Hafiz ruled, al-Bitar served as prime minister part of the time and al-Hafiz held the position himself at other times. As long as the Baathists dominated the government in Iraq the two states co-operated in many affairs and the pan-Arab executive of the Baathist party directed policies. Syria sent 5,000 soldiers to help Iraq in quelling Kurdish revolts and in October, 1963 an Iraqi–Syrian Supreme Defense Council was created. This was abrogated after Arif eased the Baathists from power in Iraq. Relations with the United Arab Republic were normalized and al-Hafiz represented Syria in 1964 at the Arab summit meetings in Cairo and Alexandria, and Syria joined with Lebanon, Jordan, and the United Arab Republic in the plans for diverting water from the Banyas River to the Yarmuk and thence to Jordan. Throughout this period there were numerous clashes, some most serious, along the 45-mile Israeli frontier with each side sending or allowing raids and shooting incidents upon the other, always maintaining tension at a high pitch. At home nationalization, industrialization, and development proceeded rapidly. After five large textile factories were taken in 1964 businessmen ordered a general strike that al-Hafiz broke by threatening to nationalize all retail businesses in Hama and Damascus. In 1965 he nationalized all major manufacturing and processing plants, public utilities, domestic and foreign oil companies, and many export–import firms. Owners were paid in three percent government bonds redeemable in fifteen years. A French group received a contract to build an international jet airport in Damascus and a West German consortium was the successful bidder on the Euphrates Dam. But al-Hafiz was too conservative for some, too radical for others, too cool toward Nasser, or too friendly.

During 1965 an extreme left-wing pro-Chinese group among the Baathists reached for power. General Salah Jadid became chief of staff and in September what was billed as a minor shuffle of the cabinet brought in Yusuf Zuayyin as prime minister, Dr. Ibrahim Makhus as his deputy, and General Hamad Ubayd as minister of defense. Their plot came to a head in December, 1965 when General al-Hafiz noticed that some of the loyal officers on his staff were being reassigned by General Ubayd to distant posts. Key army units were brought in line, each declaring loyalty to al-Hafiz. The Syrian executive of the Baath party that had fallen into the hands of these dissidents and radicals was dissolved and its offices and functions taken over by the more moderate pan-Arab executive body controlled by al-Hafiz, Salah al-Bitar, Michel Aflaq, and Munif al-Razzaz, its chief executive. Yusuf Zuayyin and all of his cohorts were removed from the cabinet, and al-Bitar formed a new twenty-man cabinet of moderates on January 1, 1966. It lasted fifty-four days. General Jadid and the extreme army wing of the Baath party arrested and imprisoned al-Hafiz, al-Bitar, Michel Aflaq, and al-Razzaz. General Jadid became the chief executive of the Baath party and chairman of the National Revolutionary Council; Nur al-Din al-Atasi, chief of state; Yusuf Zuayyin, prime minister; Hamad Ubayd, chief of staff; General Hafiz Asad, minister of defense; and Dr. Ibrahim Makhus, deputy prime minister and foreign minister.

This extreme faction declared that it wanted to maintain a "permanent struggle" on all fronts and aimed shafts at Nasser by coupling him with "traitors in the Arab world" who compromised with "imperialism" and reaction. It assailed him for abandoning the Yemenite Republic to the "jaws of reaction" at the Jidda agreement with Saudi Arabia and for the unfulfillment of his obligations to Palestine. It complained that the U.S.S.R. talked but did nothing, whereas Communist China understood the needs of the Arabs and was prepared to help them. Some even spoke of Syria becoming a "second Albania." At home, Dr. Makhus, the chief ideologist of the group, called for a "developing and deepening social experience" for everyone. Another consideration in evaluating the Jadid government was that Generals Jadid and Asad and Dr. Makhus were members of the Alawi minority group of north Syria and General Ubayd was from the Druze minority.

Not belonging to the main stream of Syrian religious and social groups, they found satisfaction in pressing their Arab nationalism and socialism.

Throughout 1966 and into 1967 many delegations from the new regime visited the Soviet bloc countries, seeking trade pacts, cultural missions, industrial aids, and major development loans. The arrangement with West Germany for the Euphrates Dam was dropped and in April, 1966 the U.S.S.R. granted $157,000,000 for the first stage of the dam that would double the cultivable area of Syria. When requests for greater royalties from the transit oil of the Iraq Petroleum Company failed, the IPC pipelines were closed in December, not to be reopened until Syrian demands were met in the spring of 1967. Border incidents on the Israeli frontier increased in number and seriousness in 1966, especially as action on the water-diversion plans commenced. In July Israel attacked in considerable force the earth-moving machinery employed and some of the foundations of the project. In January, 1967 acts of violence became so numerous that the United Nations brought about a temporary ceasefire. Raids with mine explosions and shooting of Israeli soldiers and police were frequently carried out by members of al-Fatah, a society of Arabs dedicated to the regaining of Palestine for the Arabs. Many units of this society were based in Syria but raids often came from Lebanon or Jordan. In November, 1966 Israel attacked and destroyed the village of al-Samu in Jordan to warn that al-Fatah raids should be stopped. Syria called for the deposing of King Husayn of Jordan for not having prevented the raid or retaliating in like measure. A crisis flared in May, 1967 when Syria believed that she had evidence that Israel was preparing an attack in such depth that even Damascus might fall. Sensing that this might be similar to the Israeli war on Suez in 1956, Syrian leaders called on Egypt and the other Arab states to make good on their pledges to come to her assistance and protection.

When the Israeli-Arab War broke out on June 5th, the main fighting occurred in Sinai and Jordan, and not until the fourth day did Syria feel the full brunt of the Israeli forces. By the time the ceasefire became effective Syria had lost the Golan Heights above the Sea of Galilee and the Israeli army had occupied the city of al-Quneitra. It was rumored that the road from the latter into Damascus was wide open and only the ceasefire kept the Israelis from attacking the Syrian capital. President al-Atasi and Dr. Makhus attended the meetings of the United Nations Security Council and the General Assembly and repeated their nation's stand that no direct negotiations with Israeli leaders were possible until the Israeli forces had fully withdrawn from Arab lands occupied since June 4th. Syria refused to attend the Arab summit meetings at Khartoum in August, although Dr. Makhus had participated in the sessions of the Arab Foreign Ministers Conference that had preceded the summit meetings and had remained on in Khartoum throughout the entire period, conferring regularly with the other Arab leaders. In the autumn, while King Husayn was in Washington, Syrian leaders publicly stated that he did not speak for them. Of all the Arab states, it appeared that Syria was the most willing to continue the struggle against Israel.

KINGDOM OF IRAQ

From the declaration of war against the Axis by Iraq in January, 1943 until the Revolution of 1958 there were twenty-one changes of prime minister, comprising thirteen different men. On six different occasions Nuri al-Said Pasha occupied that position; and at all times he was the most powerful political leader in Iraq. When he was not prime minister, he served as minister of defense or from his seat in the senate pulled the strings and directed the policies followed by others.

Elections for the chamber of deputies were usually well managed by Nuri al-Said. In the second election of 1954 his Constitutional Union party received 94 seats, and Independents, all of whom were his supporters, won 29 seats. This left 12 seats, which were divided among the Umma, Istiklal, and Popular Front parties, all of which professed left-wing socio-nationalist ideas. All political parties were dissolved in November, 1952, and again in 1954. These moves were instigated to force parties to reorganize or to reapply for party licenses, some of which might be denied. The Communist party remained underground and worked assiduously through other groups and parties. Istiklal, which had been fascist, collaborated with the Communists, whose leader was Yusuf Salman Yusuf, better known as Fahd. In Iraq the Communists found their following in the educated youth of the lower middle class in Baghdad, Basrah, and other large cities and in the fascists who adhered to the Rashid Ali movement from 1935 to 1941.

In 1939 when King Ghazi was killed at the age of twenty-seven in an automobile accident, the throne passed to his four-year-old son Faysal II. King Ghazi's cousin Abd al-Illah, the son of Ali and dispossessed king of the Hijaz, became regent and heir to the throne. The authority of the palace was prescribed by the constitution; yet the regent's influence was felt in all quarters through these most difficult years of World War II, the Palestine war, and the end of imperialism. On May 2, 1953 King Faysal II reached his eighteenth year and assumed full power.

The experience of the British with the Rashid Ali episode during the war opened their eyes to the necessity of revamping their attitude toward Iraq. Iraqi leaders, indirectly encouraged by growing American interest in the area, pressed for a new treaty to replace the one of 1930. Negotiations led to the signing of an Anglo-Iraqi treaty at Portsmouth, England on January 15, 1948. Britain agreed to withdraw her forces from two air bases but retained the right to send troops in the case of war or threat of war. Almost immediately students who were incited by the opposition parties for political reasons rioted in Baghdad; and the regent declared publicly that the new treaty did not "realize the national aims of Iraq." The day after Prime Minister Salih Jabr reached Baghdad from London he fled for safety to Transjordan. The treaty was never ratified, and the 1930 treaty remained in force until Britain joined the Baghdad pact in 1955.

In 1947 Salih Jabr, who was serving as a convenient screen for Senator Nuri al-Said, tried to bring about a union with Transjordan. In the end he settled for a treaty of friendship and brotherhood which stated that each party must consult the other in matters of foreign affairs and announced an intention to establish security, co-operation, and complete mutual understanding. Although criticized in parliament, it was ratified in June and served as the basis for joint operations in the Palestine war. The treaty of friendship with Turkey, ratified in July, brought an even stronger protest, since it implicitly recognized the Turkish possession of the Sanjak of Alexandretta and aligned Iraq with powers opposed to the Soviet Union. More significantly, the Egypto-Saudi camp within the Arab League viewed the Turkish treaties as strengthening the Hashimites, and therefore, detrimental to interests of the Arab League. (Transjordan signed one with Turkey, too.)

Iraq, however, did not consider her actions as violating the letter or the spirit of the Arab League. Actually, the movement for the formation of the league had some of its roots in Baghdad; and Iraq leaders heartily supported actions of the league except in cases directed against Iraq. In 1947 Iraq protested against the partition of Palestine; and between 15,000 and 20,000 soldiers were at the front alongside the Arab Legion of Transjordan in the Palestine war. These forces were the most successful of any Arab army; at one time they were in sight of the Mediterranean coast and were only eight miles from the coast when armistice negotiations began in 1949. Since Syrian and Egyptian forces had been defeated and since Iraqi troops were obviously unable to risk facing the entire Israeli army alone, the troops withdrew. And Iraqi leaders agreed to accept, pursuant to the Iraqi-Transjordan treaty of friendship and brotherhood, whatever armistice arrangements Transjordan could make. When these were made in April, Iraq's unpaid and ragged army sold its equipment and went home.

Although the geographical position of Iraq precluded any appreciable number of Arab refugees locating there, sympathy for them ran high. Responsible officials declared they would not open any negotiations with Israel until the plight of the refugees was relieved. Ill feeling toward Jews in Iraq mounted in proportion to the misery of the refugees and the general disillusionment over the war's outcome. In October, Nuri al-Said made the suggestion that Iraq would welcome 100,000 refugees if she could send 100,000 Iraqi Jews to Israel. Public acts against Jews in Iraq multiplied. In March, 1950 a law was passed permitting Jews to renounce their Iraqi citizenship and leave the country; and in the following months thousands left. In May over 50,000 were flown to Israel; and before the year was out almost all Jews had left Iraq.

Frustration and unrest mushroomed in Iraq. This was especially true in Baghdad, whose population was expanding rapidly. Lack of full independence from Britain, the Palestine war fiasco, political corruption, nationalization of oil in Iran and the new fifty-fifty profit-sharing arrangement in Saudi Arabia, the high cost of living, ownership of land, and the disastrous annual flooding of sections of Baghdad were the concern of many Iraqis. Since the political structure in Iraq hardly touched the ordinary person, "grass roots" stability in government was quite absent. An explosion occurred in November, 1952 over some examinations given by the dean of the School of Pharmacy. Demonstrations turned to general riots, which were exploited by the Communists. The regent declared martial law, called upon the army, and appointed Chief of Staff General Nur al-Din Mahmud as prime minister. The latter abolished political parties, jailed right- and left-wing party leaders, closed the schools and all but one newspaper, and placed a curfew on Baghdad.

The lid was clamped on just in time, but professional politicians were frightened and realized that reforms of many kinds had to be initiated. Fortunately new financial resources were at hand. Oil production, because of the close-down at Abadan, had been expanded; and a new 30-inch pipeline from Kirkuk to Banyas on the Mediterranean had just been opened. More important, the Iraq Petroleum Company agreed in 1952 to a new schedule of royalties, increasing them to fifty percent of the profits before taxes. The treaty was retroactive to 1951; and as world requirements of petroleum spurted, royalties mounted until in 1955 they were estimated at $250,000,000.

By a law passed in 1950 seventy percent of all oil royalties were devoted to economic development of a permanent nature. The most outstanding were flood control and irrigation projects on the Euphrates, the Tigris, and the Diyala rivers. Aided by a loan of $12,800,-

ooo in 1950 from the International Bank, the development board began flood control and irrigation works at Samarra on the Tigris and at Ramadi on the Euphrates. Completed in 1956, the Samarra barrage diverts excess water to the Wadi Tharthar, a dry depression the size of the Dead Sea. It prevented serious flooding of Baghdad in 1956, and the waters from the lake created in the Tharthar depression have made it possible to reclaim valuable land by irrigation. Another project at Musaiyb, about forty miles south of Baghdad, was completed in 1957; the land irrigated and drained provided plots for 5,000 peasant families. Since a survey made in 1950 revealed that nearly eighty percent of cultivable land in Iraq was state-owned and unoccupied, the development board through the Musaiyb project and similar actions under the Homestead Act (Dujaylah) of 1945 made concrete developments to improve the lot of poverty-ridden sharecroppers.

Other developments cleared vast slum areas in Baghdad and launched public-housing projects. Schools were extended to push down illiteracy rates. The state aided the Date Growers Association in processing, storing, and marketing its dates. A large government-owned oil refinery was opened in Basrah in 1952; and the Baghdad Light and Power Company was nationalized in 1955, with compensation of $5,600,000 going to the owners. In Mosul in 1957 a cotton-spinning factory was opened; when fully completed, it would supply one third of Iraq's requirements. A five-year development plan was outlined to run from 1956 to 1960 to expend $1,100,000,000 for flood control, irrigation, industry, mining, electric power, roads, public buildings including schools, hospitals, sanitation, public housing, and bridges. In 1957, $40,000,000 was added for a social-development program. Even the great reduction of oil production for several months in 1956–1957 during the Sinai war did not curtail the program of the development board, which announced that it held over $280,000,000 in unspent funds. Many Iraqi leaders looked into the future to see a great and prosperous Iraq, provided there was internal peace and no attacks from the Soviet bloc. Others were extremely impatient and believed that the government of Nuri al-Said moved too slowly, too inefficiently, and too indifferently to achieve a better life for the Iraqi populace.

Because of the proximity of the U.S.S.R. and because of the two Soviet states in Kurdistan and Azerbayjan in 1946–1947, Iraqi leaders had a more discerning respect and fear of Russian power than did other Arab leaders. Consequently, it was natural and expedient to favor cordial relations with Turkey, Great Britain, and the United States. Although the public attacked these three foreign states from time to time, the concerted policy of the government advanced friendly relationships with each. The treaty with Turkey was concluded in 1947. In 1951 Iraq requested Point Four aid from the United States; and in that same year military aid in the form of arms was arranged.

In 1955, however, the situation changed rapidly. The U.S.S.R. entered the Middle East diplomatically, and Iraq reacted by signing on February 24 the so-called Baghdad pact with Turkey. In general, this pact repeated the terms of the treaty of friendship, but it added military co-operation and co-ordination. In April Britain adhered to the pact by signing an exceedingly important agreement with Iraq. Among other things, this agreement wiped out the treaty of 1930, provided for Britain to evacuate her troops and air force from the Habbaniya and Shuayba airfields, and gave fuller sovereignty and independence to Iraq. An improvement over the draft treaty of 1947, this instrument brought Britain into the Baghdad pact and gave Iraq her desires. It was similar to those granted earlier by Britain to Egypt and by France to Syria. Soon Iran and Pakistan joined the Baghdad pact, making an alliance of a chain of states separating the Soviet bloc from the strategic areas of the Middle East. Although the United States did not join the pact, she sent military missions to the area, provided military equipment for member states, and affiliated officially with the pact's military and economic committees. Iraq received twelve Centurion tanks in 1956 and twenty-eight more in 1957.

Egypt viewed the Baghdad pact as a threat to her control over the Arab League and her leadership in the Arab world. Nuri al-Said was accused of being the tool of Great Britain and restoring colonial status to Iraq. Syria at first tried to mend the quarrel between Cairo and Baghdad, but in the end succumbed to Egyptian oratory and Saudi money and participated in the Damascus pact in opposition to the one of Baghdad. Calling Nasser a dictator and declaring that the Baghdad pact was Iraq's concern, Nuri al-Said held firm to his course. He was confident that peace and security from fears of Russia, economic development and an increased standard of living, and a cultural and social renaissance would create in Iraq a life and society to parallel the modern rejuvenation of Turkey as well as the medieval splendor and wealth of the days of Harun al-Rashid.

Although Nasser was regarded as a genuine rival for leadership in the Arab world, Nuri al-Said always defended Arab feelings against the West and vehemently adjured that Western threats of force when Nasser nationalized the Canal violated the United Nations Charter. When Israel, France, and England invaded Egypt in 1956, Iraq was in an embarrassing position. Her army, poised on the Jordanian border because of the apprehension which months of Israeli military build-up had engendered, entered Jordan; and she broke diplomatic relations with France. The clamor against Great Britain was fiery in Baghdad; and Iraqi officials boycotted all meetings of the Baghdad pact from November, 1956 to March, 1957 whenever Britain was represented. Parliament was suspended in December; five opposition leaders were arrested; and numerous non-Iraqi Arabs were deported. When parliament was reconvened in February, Nuri received a vote of confidence of 79 to 14. Syria complained so insistently over the presence of Iraqi troops in Jordan that they were recalled in December, world opinion having halted further military action in the Palestine-Sinai region and assured a containment of the war. Any semblance of normalcy was not attained until March, 1957, when the pipelines in Syria were repaired. At the time oil production was resumed, reports indicated Iraq stood to lose about $90,000,000 in royalties because of the break.

With the coming of spring, the return to relative peace, and the flow of oil, Nuri al-Said resigned, at which time Ali Jawdat assumed the office, to be followed a few months later by Nuri's close friend, Abd al-Wahhab Marjan. The government ceased to jam the wave lengths from Cairo and Damascus, and Nuri al-Said visited several European capitals and Washington to discuss wider support of the Baghdad pact and a solution to the Israeli problem. As the process of the United Arab Republic's formation unfolded, political tension in Baghdad mounted. The possibility of union between Iraq and Jordan had been discussed for many years, and the annexing of Jordan had been openly proposed in December, 1956. The union of Syria and Egypt forced the issue in Jordan, where the government of King Husayn could not endure as a solitary force. In February, 1958 King Faysal went to Amman; and after visits there by Nuri al-Said and Crown Prince Abd al-Illah, often called the real power in Iraq, an Arab federation of Iraq and Jordan was proclaimed. King Faysal was recognized as chief of state and King Husayn as second in leadership and successor to the headship should his cousin die or be removed. Defense, foreign affairs, finance, and education for the whole state were consolidated; but treaties, laws, budgets, and local administrations of each state of the federation retained their validity and were not binding upon the other. In March a federal council composed of fifteen members from each state was named, and a constitution was drafted and proclaimed. In Iraq Nuri al-Said resumed the post of prime minister; parliament was dissolved; and a call went out for elections for a new parliament to ratify the constitution.

Upon hearing the news Nasser congratulated the two kings for completing the federation; but in a few weeks the friendly remarks turned into violent condemnations and open invitations to Arab nationalists in each state to remove the kings, by assassination if necessary. The May elections turned out as expected. Nuri al-Said's supporters were returned. In most districts there was no contest; and in some not even a vote was taken. On May 10, 1958 parliament ratified the constitution of the federation; and King Husayn supposed that he had found someone who would protect him. Precisely at that moment, however, rebellious disturbances in Lebanon shook the Arab world.

REPUBLIC OF IRAQ

Iraqi troops were ordered in July to march into Jordan to be ready to safeguard the Shamun administration if needed. But their commander, General Abd al-Karim Kassim, refused to fight against other Arabs; turned upon Baghdad; and in an easy and swift *coup d'état* on July 14, 1958 overthrew the king and Nuri al-Said, both of whom lost their lives in the revolution. The Baghdad mob became delirious with excitement, sacked the British Embassy, and seized a few Europeans and Jordanians. Order, however, was quickly attained. The reverberations from this successful blow were felt around the world, and secondary reactions to it were more pertinent elsewhere than in Iraq.

General Kassim proclaimed the Republic of Iraq and became prime minister of the state. Oil production did not stop; the pipelines were undamaged; and neutrality was pronounced as the policy of the state. Within less than a month the new government was recognized by the United Arab Republic, the U.S.S.R., the states of the Baghdad pact, and the United States. Kassim declared that the Republic would honor Iraq's international obligations and did not formally resign from the Baghdad pact. When King Husayn announced he was assuming the position of chief of state of the Arab federation, Kassim renounced the union and Jordan acknowledged the demise of the federation.

The completeness of the revolution and its full acceptance by the general populace throughout the state amazed only those not familiar with social and national conditions. Nuri al-Said was thoroughly disliked in Iraq, and the crown prince was hated. The same government had been in power too long and had failed to satisfy the aspiration of the majority. Land reform, poverty and the low standard of living, Israel, social advances for the urban masses, sanitation and health, and the depressed state of the educated middle class were but a few of the problems which the people of Iraq felt pressing upon them and the belief was widespread that Nuri al-Said and the Hashimites had not tried to cope with them adequately.

In the minds of the populace the old regime had built too many palaces and had allocated too much of the oil royalties (seventy percent) to dams and less useful capital works. Many of these were still in the construction stage and their returns were yet to be enjoyed by the public. General Kassim dismissed the Development Board and reorganized its functions in a cabinet committee directly under the prime minister. He announced that the new board would receive fifty percent of the royalties and would work to establish Iraq as a welfare state based on practical socialism. Under a new five-year agricultural program holdings larger than 500 acres of nonirrigated lands or 250 acres of irrigated lands would be expropriated and distributed to land-less peasants in plots from 7½ to 30 acres. The new board would set up government-owned basic industries in steel, machinery, and petro-chemicals and in 1959, after a great many prerevolutionary contracts were canceled, the U.S.S.R. agreed to furnish credits of $140,000,000 for technical assistance in constructing and operating plants for steel, tractors, textiles, nitrates, and hydroelectric power.

Coming so soon after the birth of the United Arab Republic, General Kassim's revolution whetted the enthusiasm and expectations for an immediate fulfillment of Arab unity with the United Arab Republic. Colonel Abd al-Salam Muhammad Arif, second in rank among the revolutionaries and assistant commander in chief of the armed forces led the group that soon came to be called Nasserites. Watching the trend in Syria, Kassim and others had no desire to be puppets of Cairo or hold sinecures of some sort, and the fundamental Iraqi nationalism of these leaders eliminated Colonel Arif. At the end of September, 1958 Kassim dismissed him as deputy prime minister and minister of the interior and designated him as ambassador to West Germany. A revolt by his regiment was crushed and in November, along with many Nasserites, he was arrested and held for trial on the charge of having attempted to murder Kassim. A trial in 1959 found him guilty and sentenced him to death; at a later date the death sentence was lifted.

On the last day of 1959 Kassim revealed a four-year economic plan, totaling $1,100,000,000, to change the face of the nation. A steel mill was planned near Khadhimaya and large sums were allocated for other industry, housing, public welfare, land reclamation, transporta-tion, and communications. Although crops still were poor in 1960, as they were in many parts of the Middle East, Iraq pushed ahead with oil royalties in these programs, and in 1961 a new five-year develop-ment plan to cost $1,590,000,000 was unveiled. The U.S.S.R. pledged aid for dams, new railroads, and sulfur and phosphate explorations; West Germany agreed to build bridges and river regulators; Sweden would improve and deepen ports; and Great Britain, Austria, Czecho-slovakia, Hungary, Yugoslavia, Poland, and Japan or their nationals became involved in Iraqi economic affairs. There were over 150 new agricultural and industrial projects initiated in 1961, and by that date over sixty percent of the cultivated lands had been broken up into smaller plots. But there was no real peace in Iraq.

Until General Kassim was overthrown and executed by a coup on February 8, 1963 his regime was constantly beset by a three-way struggle among Communists and pro-Communists on one side, pan-Arab nationalists, usually Nasserites, on another, and Iraqi nationalists on the third. There was street fighting in Baghdad at the slightest incident. In March, 1959 a revolt broke out in Mosul led by the tribes and pan-Arabists, but blaming the United Arab Republic for plotting it, the army loyal to Kassim crushed it with the aid of Kurdish forces. Then, in July, riots supposedly instigated by Communists in Kirkuk between Turks and Kurds were quelled. However, Iraq returned in 1960 to Arab League meetings, political parties were allowed again, and tension with other Arab states had been dissipated to the extent of having a meeting of the Arab League Council in Baghdad, but on June 25, 1961 Kassim laid claim to Kuwayt. Because of the return of British forces and the quick reaction by the other Arab states, especially Saudi Arabia and the United Arab Republic, Kassim did not press his diplomatic blunder. Iraq walked out of the Arab League meeting that admitted Kuwayt to membership and broke relations with states recognizing her independence. Except for improved relations with Syria after the downfall of the United Arab Republic, Kassim, in general, remained isolated from the other Arab states throughout 1962.

Since the end of World War I and the Paris and Lausanne conferences the question of the Kurds in northern Iraq has been constant. The British and Nuri al-Said discussed, negotiated, fought, and left the Kurdish problem unsolved. Kassim's attitude seemed to have changed but this was only a temporary lull. Under the leadership of Mulla Mustafa Barzani, Kurdish resistance arose in 1961. Although temporarily subdued, it exploded in 1962 into a full-scaled revolt so that all of northeastern Iraq except for the cities and towns was entirely in Kurdish hands. Barzani and the Kurdish tribes wanted independence or at least autonomy in a federalized or decentralized Iraq. Because the major oil resources of the state were in this region the government was unwilling to tolerate secession or totally local control. The army had been committed to subdue the Kurdish provinces but had never succeeded. Each time a government in Baghdad hinted at some accommodation with Barzani the generals showed their disaffection. The people in Basrah and Baghdad, on the other hand, chafed at the continuing conflict and the percentage of the national budget consumed in the struggle.

The Kurdish dilemma on top of the divisive political pulls of Nasserism, Communism, and Iraqi nationalism set the stage for the successful coup of the Baath party on February 8, 1963 against Kassim who had been unable to articulate an appealing ideology. He lacked charisma. The Iraq executive dominated by the pan-Arab executive of the Baath party, mostly from Damascus, engineered the coup in collaboration with the army and immediately organized a National Council of the Revolutionary Command. Colonel Abd al-Salam Muhammad Arif was appointed president and General Ahmad Hassan Bakr became prime minister. Overnight a roundup of Communists indicated the nationalist orientation of the Baathists who preached Arab unity; through President Arif, at that moment hardly more than a puppet and a useful name for the less known Baathists, bids were issued for union with the United Arab Republic. The Baath revolution the following month in Syria prompted the futile meetings in Cairo in April and hollow declarations of Arab solidarity. Barzani from his redoubt in the north welcomed the Baath coup and accepted the olive branch. Conferences in June foundered again on the basic points; the new regime pressed by the soldiers resumed Kassim's campaigns. At odds with the Kurds, the Communists, and Nasser, political affairs hardly seemed to consume the full energies of the Baath leaders; they canceled the ambitious five-year development plan of 1961 as being ineffective and replaced it with one of their own, although projects already initiated went unchanged.

The U.S.S.R. protested vigorously to Prime Minister Bakr about the treatment that Kurds and Communists were receiving from the Baathists, and Nasser began to assail the Baghdad regime for treachery to the Arab cause. In May most of the non-Baathists were ejected from the cabinet and a small Nasserite revolt was broken ruthlessly while talks for complete economic union with Syria were in progress. All of the problems facing Baghdad and the continuous discussion within the Baath hierarchy failed to bring unanimity of purpose or direction. By autumn abeyant Iraqi nationalists in Baathist circles resented the domination by the international or Syrian Baathists in every dispute concerning Baghdad policy; on November 18, 1963 all non-Iraqis were forced out of positions of influence, and President Arif assumed full power, appointing General Tahir Yahya as prime minister. Two months later Arif showed his hand by removing all extreme Baathists from office and went on to form his own Iraqi Arab Socialist Union. A Baathist coup in September, 1964 was foiled and its leaders imprisoned. Later cabinet shifts added more of the pro-Nasser coterie.

From the day in 1963 that President Arif moved to exercise his position, a rule of personal authority prevailed in Iraq well into 1967.

It faltered for a few days after April 13, 1966 when Arif lost his life in a helicopter crash in southern Iraq. His elder brother, General Abd al-Rahman Arif hurried home from a military mission in Moscow, was elected president, and carried on with the same fundamental program and political orientation. Beginning with the establishment of the Baathists in Baghdad, Barzani refused to bargain for anything short of Kurdish autonomy and a statement in the constitution that "Iraq is a federative state of Arabs and Kurds." With the inability of the first Arif to meet this condition Barzani asserted *de facto* autonomy for Iraqi Kurdistan and established a parliament and a legislative supreme revolutionary council of forty-three members. The fighting continued and in May, 1966 the second Arif launched an offensive with 65,000 troops and co-ordinated heavy bombing by the air force, in the hope of settling the issue once and for all. The offensive failed in its objectives, and the Kurdish forces scored some notable victories over the Iraqi armies. For many months the civilian prime minister, Dr. Abd al-Rahman Bazzaz, had been advocating a moderate stand on Kurdish rights; when the military approach failed again as he had predicted, he announced that the government was prepared to recognize "Kurdish nationality, language, and tradition." Kurdish delegates were received in Baghdad and Dr. Bazzaz publicly outlined on June 29, 1966 a twelve-point program for the Kurds. Among other things, Dr. Bazzaz promised general amnesty for Kurdish rebels; recognition of Kurdish cultural and political autonomy; decentralization of the government; proportionate Kurdish representation in the cabinet, the army command, and the diplomatic corps; economic redevelopment in the north; and the appointment of Kurdish officials in Kurdish areas. Barzani accepted these proposals but pan-Arabs and the army did not. The following day an attempted coup by General Arif Abd al-Razzak, former prime minister, a Nasserite, and commander of the air force, failed in overthrowing Dr. Bazzaz but the army was so incensed at the implied surrender to the Kurds that President Arif was pressed into appointing General Najih Talib as prime minister. In May, 1967 affairs became so tense that Arif took over the office himself. Meanwhile there was no solution of the Kurdish problem.

From the time of Kassim's demise until the summer of 1964 when the first Arif had consolidated his authority, few new steps were taken in agricultural and industrial progress. In July, 1964 Arif nationalized banks, insurance companies, and thirty industrial and commercial firms; by mid-1965 it was estimated that fifty-five percent of foreign commerce and seventy-five percent of manufacturing was in government hands. A budget of $2,300,000,000 was set aside for an ambitious five-year economic plan to add eight percent to the national income each year through 1970. The Soviets provided $134,000,000 and technical assistance in 1966 to begin the Haditha Dam on the Euphrates and a Finnish concern won a contract for $28,000,000 to heighten the Diyala River Dam. Except for the U.S.S.R. loan, one from the Kuwayt Fund, small loans from the United States Export–Import Bank, and the International Bank for Reconstruction and Development, Iraq expected to finance the five-year plan through oil royalties. In December, 1966 Syria blocked the pipelines to the Mediterranean as a weapon in her negotiations over transit fees with IPC. Such measures materially reduced the revenue accruing to the government and, although sympathetic to the needs of Syria, President Arif evinced relief when a settlement was reached in the spring of 1967 and oil royalties began to flow into the treasury again.

When Colonel Arif had been the first in command under General Kassim in 1958, he had been ousted for being too pro-Nasser. As a figurehead under the Baathists in 1963, President Arif showed no public inclination toward Cairo. When he became president in fact, he approached Nasser in 1964 to try for a reconciliation and cabinet shifts were made to bring in more Nasserites. Most of these resigned in July, 1965 charging Arif and General Yahya had been intentionally dilatory in implementing Arab socialism and union with the United Arab Republic. Pressure brought to the prime ministership on September 2 General Arif Abd al-Razzak, an ardent Nasserite and commander of the air force. A fortnight later while President Arif was attending the Arab summit meeting in Casablanca, al-Razzak tried to seize power for himself but the coup was frustrated by action of General Abd al-Rahman Arif, the president's brother. Thereupon, a new cabinet under the moderate Dr. Abd al-Rahman Bazzaz was set up and he continued on after the first Arif was killed and into the presidency of the second Arif. In June, 1966 al-Razzak tried a second coup, as has already been described, when Dr. Bazzaz attempted conciliation with the Kurds, and General Najih Talib announced at the time he took the reins of office in August that he believed in "a society of self-sufficiency on the basis of a fair Arab socialism." In the spring of 1967 at the onset of the Israeli crisis President Arif took over the post of prime minister and sent Iraqi troops into Syria to bolster their position and to demonstrate his opposition to the state of Israel. When the Israeli-Arab War erupted in June, Arif sent his troops to the west; 30,000 entered Jordan, remaining there as a kind of reinforcement to King Husayn and as encouragement for him to take a firmer posture toward Israel and the Western powers. Dr. Adnan Pachachi, the foreign minister, spoke eloquently at the various meetings of the United Nations. President Arif maintained a middle course in the debates of the Arab summit meetings at Khartoum. It is interesting to note how similar were the problems of Nuri al-Said, Kassim, and the two Arifs in the period after the close of World War II.

THE ARAB LEAGUE

Through these pages numerous references to the Arab League have appeared. The idea of the unity of Arabs, co-operation of Arab states, and one federated or national Arab country were not novel when Anthony Eden, British foreign minister, in his famous Mansion House speech of May 29, 1941 said in reference to Arab desires for unity that Britain would give "full support to any scheme that commands general approval." Arab leaders took the statement to mean that henceforth the British would drop their policy of "divide and rule" and that it would be safe to suggest ways to unite the Arabs. In 1942 Nuri al-Said circulated his "Blue Book" which suggested the "reuniting" of Syria, Lebanon, Palestine, and Transjordan into one state (Syria) and the formation of an Arab League to include any Arab states which might desire to join. Egypt and Saudi Arabia were lukewarm, fearing the Greater Syria embodied in his idea. After Eden commented again that the initiative of an Arab League "would have to come from the Arabs themselves," Nahas Pasha put forth in 1943 other suggestions and discussed them with the Arab prime ministers. In 1944 a committee representing the Arab states, including Palestine, presented the Alexandria Protocol to the governments of the Arab states. In essence it was the draft charter of the Arab League. Following discussions within each Arab government, official representatives of Iraq, Syria, Lebanon, Transjordan, Saudi Arabia, and Egypt signed on March 22, 1945 at Cairo the Arab League pact. Other members joined later: Yemen (May 11, 1945), Libya (March 28, 1953), Sudan (January 19, 1956), Morocco (October 1, 1958), Tunisia (October 1, 1958), Kuwayt (July 20, 1961), and Algeria (August 16, 1962). The pact provided for a council, composed of a representative of each member state and a secretariat-general whose permanent seat was to be in Cairo. The council was to hold two ordinary sessions each year in March and in October and extraordinary sessions whenever two members made a request.

The purpose of the League was to seek co-operation of member states in economic, cultural, social, and health affairs, in communications, and in matters affecting nationality. It embodied a guarantee of the sovereignty of each member and a promise to respect the systems of government established in other member states and to abstain from any interference in internal affairs of other member states. No collective-security or mutual-defense articles were included in the pact; and

no separate arrangement developed until 1950, when a loosely constructed security pact was accepted.

Although Great Britain had called the Arab League into being in
hopes of obtaining greater security in the Middle East, the Arab states
found in the League a promise of co-operation against the partition of
Palestine and the birth of a Zionist state. In this connection six Arab
rulers, at the invitation of King Faruk, met at Inshas, Egypt in 1946
and pledged their co-operation in opposing Zionist claims to Palestine.
To implement the promise, the Arab League council in extraordinary
session at Bludan, Syria voted to send notes to Great Britain and the
United States protesting the recommendations of the Anglo-American
committee of inquiry. If notes proved unsuccessful, the council agreed
to meet again to discuss diplomatic and economic (oil) measures
which might be taken.

Egypt, Saudi Arabia, and Iraq each considered how the center of
the Arab League might be located in her country and acted accordingly. From its inception, however, Egypt had the upper hand and its
second secretary-general was Abd al-Khalik Hassunah, former Egyptian foreign minister. When partition of Palestine became certain, the
League admonished its members to resist and later urged them to go
to war against Israel. Saudi Arabia and Yemen, however, gave only
token aid; Syria and Lebanon proved ineffective; and the Egyptian
army was poorly equipped and mismanaged. Only Abdallah's forces of
Transjordan, the Arab Legion, and the Iraqi troops showed any
capacity for the fight; and only on their center front was there success.
Egyptian forces aimed at Jerusalem with the intention of having the
honor of capturing the Holy City and incidentally getting there before
Abdallah did. Furthermore, Egyptian plans were to hold back until the
Arab Legion and the Hashimite forces had been bled white and then
come in for the victory and possession of Palestine. Although in urging
the war in Palestine each state signed the accord that no part of
Palestine would be annexed to another Arab state, none intended to
uphold that agreement. Agents of the Arab League refused arms to
other Arabs in Palestine if they were supporters of Arab families
known to be inimical to Hajj Amin al-Husayni, the ex-mufti who looked
upon himself as the future ruler of Arab Palestine.

As defeat was experienced in Palestine, the Arab League declared
that any member which made peace with Israel would be expelled and
voted to oust Jordan, which annexed the remaining Arab portions of
Palestine. The weakness of Syria in the face of a vigorous and
victorious Israel frightened the Syrian leaders and almost drove them
into the arms of stronger Iraq. The Egypto-Saudi axis forestalled that
rapprochement by inaugurating in 1950 a treaty of joint defense and

economic co-operation which obligated all to take up arms if any one
of them became the victim of agression. Actually designed to prevent
the Fertile Crescent unity program but purporting to strengthen the
Arab states against Israel and satisfy clamors of Arab nationalists in
the streets, the treaty was signed by five states. Iraq and Jordan
acceded to it in 1951 and 1952 respectively.

Beginning in 1950 the Arab League expanded its activities in many
directions. An economic council was created to co-ordinate and unify
economic policies, commerce, trade, and financial developments of the
Arab states. In 1959 the council proposed a common market for Arab
states and called for an Arab Navigation Company, an Arab Airline
Company, and an Organization for Arab Economic Development that
had a capital of about $70,000,000 by 1964. These companies were
approved by the League Council in 1961 at which time an Arab
Tankers Company was included. The economic council sought to consolidate Arab policies with regard to world trends and in 1964 set up
an office in Brussels to serve as a liaison for the European Economic
Community. Similarly, suggestions were made for common approaches
and policies to be taken by member states of the Arab League at the
GATT negotiations in Geneva. Councils for education, science, communications, and aviation were also established to serve similar and
parallel purposes in those fields. Conferences and congresses were
sponsored on medicine, the press, Islam, Arab history, oil concessions,
the petroleum industry, banking, chemistry, pharmacy, law, dentistry,
industrial development, tourism, engineering, and many other subjects
and professional fields. These meetings were valid steps in the direction of real unity and effective means of drawing leaders in Arab
society together for the exchange of ideas and the comparison of
problems. These meetings were profitable and are continuing; it is
significant to note for example that in April, 1966 these were held in
various Arab cities—the fifth Arab Medical Conference, the fifth Arab
Chemistry Conference, the tenth Arab Pharmaceutical Conference, a
meeting of the Arab Engineers' Association, and a conference of Arab
Education and Economic Planning Ministers. Over five hundred people attended the second Arab Dental Conference in 1960 and fifty-
seven oil companies had representatives at the Arab Oil Congress in
1961. Yet resistance of individual states to the many suggestions often
proved strong, as each state found it difficult to surrender national
interests and special advantages.

International diplomacy and politics, however, stood supreme. The
Arab League declared its sympathy for Arab struggles in Morocco and
Algeria, supplied funds to nationalists there, granted asylum to the
leaders, and urged that economic measures be taken against France.

Indonesian acts to nationalize Dutch properties were approved, as was the Greek stand in regard to Cyprus, although after Cyprus gained her independence Arab states having diplomatic relations with Cyprus were warned to watch Israeli activities there. Egypt was supported in her struggle with Britain over Suez Canal bases; Yemen and Saudi Arabia were aided in their disputes with Britain over Aden and the Buraimi oasis; and West Germany was invited to reconsider her reparations agreement with Israel. In 1965 all Arab states were asked to recall their ambassadors from Bonn upon West German exchange of ambassadors with Israel, and some Arab states threatened to recognize East Germany. After Iran's recognition of Israel in 1960 the Foreign Ministers' Conference of the League requested Iraq in the name of the League to persuade Iran to "appreciate her relations" with the Arab states when dealing with Israel. Oman and Kuwayt were asked to join the League. The latter replied that she would become a member "as soon as she completed her internal renaissance"; Britain answered for the former, stating simply that Oman was under the sultan of Muscat and thereby was not an independent state. A request went to the United Nations in September, 1960 to place the question of Oman on its agenda. Later that year the United Nations officially recognized the Arab League as a regional organization, a move that facilitated agreements between the Arab League and WHO (1961) and other United Nations bodies. Furthermore, it made possible the opening of Arab League offices with full diplomatic status in such non-Arab capitals as New Delhi and Katmandu in 1965.

Early in 1955 when Iraq announced her intention of entering into a military arrangement with Turkey, the Arab League broke wide open. Egypt threatened to resign from the "Collective Security Pact" the day Iraq would sign the treaty with Turkey; and Saudi Arabia and Yemen promised to follow Egypt into a new pact which would exclude Iraq. After the signing of the Baghdad pact, however, Egypt did not walk out. Instead she moved quickly to form the Damascus pact and attract to her banner all other Arab states. It seemed that the old Egypto-Saudi rivalry with the Hashimites had returned. Not feeling the threat of Russian aggression as did Iraq, Egypt was concerned lest Iraq, with her potential wealth and significant military and economic aid from the West, become suddenly as strong as Turkey and therefore the natural leader and respected military force among the Arab states.

In this struggle Lebanon refused to commit herself; and Jordan, torn with internal strife by the partisans of the two camps, also remained unpledged. The crisis over the Egyptian nationalization of the Suez Canal Company tended to restore unity to the Arab League; for Iraq, Lebanon, and Jordan declared their concurrence in Egypt's actions.

Once more, a temporary accord was attained for the sessions of the Arab League. However, the basic struggle for hegemony in the Arab world was reflected in the discussions of the Arab League councils. Plans for an Arab Investment Bank were drawn and suggestions that all pipelines in the future should be financed, owned, and operated by Arabs fell on receptive ears. The League censored Great Britain for actions in Aden and the formation of the Federation of South Arabia as being inimical to Yemen and for arming the sultan of Muscat in his military operations against the imam of Oman.

The Arab League in internal political affairs proved ineffective, and its domination by Egypt and the United Arab Republic robbed it of complete usefulness. Egypt, Syria, Yemen, and Iraq often but not always stood firmly together; Jordan, Libya, Tunisia, and sometimes Iraq looked nervously at Nasser's commanding position; Sudan remained neutral and uncommitted; Lebanon and Kuwayt hoped to play roles of compromisers for the several factions; Saudi Arabia faced many internal problems and played an independent game, joining one group and then another; and Algeria and Morocco had border problems and fought against each other. The establishment of the rival United Arab Republic and Arab Federation in 1958 was looked upon as the death knell of the Arab League; and its inability to reach any helpful conclusion upon Lebanon's petition during her civil rebellion seemed to prove its weakness and subservience to Egyptian policy. The friendly hand extended by Nasser to Kassim in Iraq in the latter's first days of rule was a move to revitalize the force of the Arab League under the direction of Egypt.

During those days of strain it was important and propitious that the Arab League Council continued to hold its regular meetings at which foreign ministers or even prime ministers exchanged courtesies, had opportunities to size up their colleagues, and discussed the wide range of affairs confronting one another. They supported Syria in her border clashes with Israel; rejected a United Nations plan to give Arab refugees jobs in Arab countries; outlined steps to counter Israeli activities in African countries; moved to open information centers in Asia, Africa, and Latin America; entreated members of the European Economic Community not to admit Israel to associate membership; and appealed to India and Pakistan to halt their military actions. Many intra-Arab questions were so portentous and overriding that only heads of state could make commitments and decisions. Such an Arab summit meeting was held in Alexandria in September, 1964 and another was convened at Casablanca in September, 1965. Although one was called for Algiers in 1966, it was indefinitely postponed because the issues and differences were too explosive. Israeli plans to divert the waters of the Jordan for industrial uses in the Tel Aviv area and for irrigation to the south always found a fiery reception among the Arabs. At Alexandria schemes for Arab utilization of Jordan basin waters were reviewed and plans were adopted to divert some of the headwater rivers of the Jordan such as the Hasbani and Banyas rivers to the Yarmuk where the Mukheiba Dam would regulate the use of the water in Syria and Jordan. At Casablanca further support was adjured and the initiation of its first stages at al-Adasiah, eighty miles from Amman, was examined. Promises were given to provide air cover for the building of all aspects of this scheme from attack that Israel had threatened. Other agenda items dealt with the civil war in Yemen and unsuccessful mediation attempts by Egypt, Saudi Arabia, and Kuwayt, and with inter-Arab propaganda. At Casablanca, a solidarity pact was signed in which each state forswore all radio, newspaper, and oratorical attacks, political or personal, on other Arab states or leaders. It was hoped that this would "heal strained relations" among the members of the League, a necessity if the central and most unifying question of Palestine were to be met. Agreements were reached and extended at all of the summit meetings as well as at council meetings concerning the boycott of Israel. Each country was pledged to cease trade and all dealings with firms and individuals in all countries that had financial, business, or personal connections with Israel. Pressure was applied, sometimes most effectively, to obtain a change in policy of foreign firms and a regular "blacklist" was maintained. In 1963, for example, with the rising markets in the Trucial States after the exploitation of oil, boycott offices were opened in Abu Dhabi, Dubai, and Sharjah. A Palestine Liberation Organization, although not supported or recognized officially, was openly tolerated and its strength and development under Ahmad al-Shuqayri were favorably noted. Such attacks as the Israeli raid in Jordan on the village of al-Samu in November, 1966 conditioned all Arab League states to realize the necessity of union in face of Israeli attacks and retaliation. In the May, 1967 crisis arising over the Syrian fear of Israeli attack in depth, each Arab League state voiced its support of Arab solidarity and acted to support Syria, even to the extent of agreeing that troops of one Arab state might be tolerated on the soil of another. Following the Six-Day War and the unsatisfactory results at the United Nations the Sudanese Prime Minister, Muhammad Ahmad Mahjub, with much difficulty and a great deal of preliminary negotiations, was able to convene an Arab summit meeting at Khartoum in August. Every head of state was there, or was represented by his prime minister, except for Syria whose foreign minister, Dr. Makhus, attended. A seven-point resolution, passed by the meeting, recognized the need for greater solidarity among the signatories in concerted efforts to eliminate all traces of aggression and the need to unify diplomatic and political actions "to ensure the withdrawal of Israeli forces from the occupied Arab territory." Included also was a recommendation to speed the liquidation of foreign bases, to consolidate military preparedness, and to employ oil policies as a weapon to achieve goals. At the conference, Saudi Arabia, Kuwayt, and Libya agreed to give financial aid to the United Arab Republic and Jordan because of their losses from the war. In addition an agreement was reached between Saudi Arabia and the United Arab Republic to withdraw aid to warring sides in Yemen, and a committee of Iraq, Morocco, and Sudan was formed to supervise the implementation of the agreement and to work for unity and stability in Yemen and full sovereignty and independence for her people.

Such demonstrations of Arab unity can be fleeting, however. Once a common danger has passed, the permanent question of an Arab federation or a federal union and its leadership or domination remains.

REFERENCES: Chapter 39

Important references for this chapter are also found in Chapters 27, 31, 32, 35, and 38.

Kamel S. Abu Jaber, *The Arab Ba'th Socialist Party: History, Ideology, and Organization:* Syracuse University Press, Syracuse, 1966.

Doris Goodrich Adams, *Iraq's People and Resources:* University of California Press, Berkeley, 1958.

M. S. Agwani, ed., *The Lebanon Crisis, 1958: A Documentary Study:* Asia Publishing House, New York, 1965.

H. B. Allen, *Rural Reconstruction in Action: Experience in the Near and Middle East:* Cornell University Press, Ithaca, 1953. A review of a number of cases worked upon in several states of the area.

Morroe Berger, *The Arab World Today:* Doubleday, New York, 1962.

Lord Birdwood, *Nuri as-Said: A Study in Arab Leadership:* Cassell, London, 1959.

B. Y. Boutros-Ghali, *The Arab League, 1945–1955:* Carnegie Endowment for International Peace, New York, 1955.

Emile Bustani, *Doubts and Dynamite: The Middle East Today:* Allan Wingate, London, 1958.

Erskine B. Childers, *Common Sense about the Arab World:* Macmillan, New York, 1960.

Charles W. Churchill *et al., The City of Beirut: A Socio-Economic Survey:* Dar el-Kitab, Beirut, 1954.

Sydney N. Fisher, ed., *Social Forces in the Middle East:* Cornell University Press, Ithaca, 1955. A collection of essays on various occupational groups in the Middle East and their points of view.

John B. Glubb, *A Soldier with the Arabs:* Harper, New York, 1958.

————, *War in the Desert:* W. W. Norton, New York, 1961.

Halford L. Hoskins, *The Middle East: Problem Area in World Politics:* Macmillan, New York, 1954. A survey of the major areas of tension.

Arslan Humbaraci, *Middle East Indictment:* Robert Hale, London, 1958.

J. C. Hurewitz, *Middle East Dilemmas:* Harper, New York, 1953. The difficulties before the United States entered.

Michael Ionides, *Divide and Lose, The Arab Revolt, 1955–1958:* Geoffrey Bles, London, 1960. By an hydraulic engineer interested in the waters of the Jordan.

Malcolm Kerr, *The Arab Cold War, 1958–1964: A Study of Ideology in Politics:* Oxford University Press, London, 1965.

Muhammad Khalil, *The Arab States and the Arab League: A Documentary Record;* Vol. I, *Constitutional Developments;* Vol. II, *International Affairs:* Khayats, Beirut, 1962.

George E. Kirk, *Contemporary Arab Politics:* Praeger, New York, 1961.

Alec Seath Kirkbride, *A Crackle of Thorns: Experiences in the Middle East:* John Murray, London, 1956.

Kathleen M. Langley, *The Industrialization of Iraq:* Harvard University Press, Cambridge, 1961.

Walter Z. Laqueur, *Communism and Nationalism in the Middle East:* Praeger, New York, 1956. An encyclopedic treatment of Communists and their fronts and endeavors in the Middle East. Excellent.

Robert W. Macdonald, *The League of Arab States:* Princeton University Press, Princeton, 1965.

Abid A. al-Marayti, *A Diplomatic History of Modern Iraq:* Robert Speller, New York, 1961.

Gavin Maxwell, *People of the Reeds:* Harper, New York, 1958. The marsh Arabs in Iraq.

A. J. Meyer, *Middle East Capitalism:* Harvard University Press, Cambridge, 1959. A standard work.

Arthur E. Mills, *Private Enterprise in Lebanon:* American University of Beirut Press, Beirut, 1959.

Hazem Saki Nuseibeh, *The Ideas of Arab Nationalism:* Cornell University Press, Ithaca, 1956. The growth and development of nationalism in the Middle East.

William R. Polk, *The United States and the Arab World:* Harvard University Press, Cambridge, 1965. A challenging analysis.

Fahim I. Qubain, *Crisis in Lebanon:* Middle East Institute, Washington, 1961.

———, *The Reconstruction of Iraq:* Praeger, New York, 1958.

Fayez A. Sayegh, *Arab Unity: Hope and Fulfillment:* Devin-Adair, New York, 1958.

Yusif A. Sayegh, *Entrepreneurs of Lebanon: The Role of the Business Leader in the Middle East:* Harvard University Press, Cambridge, 1962.

Patrick Seale, *The Struggle for Syria: A Study in Post-War Arab Politics, 1945–1958:* Oxford University Press, London, 1965.

Benjamin Shwadran, *The Power Struggle in Iraq:* Council for Middle Eastern Affairs Press, New York, 1960.

Wilfred Cantwell Smith, *Islam in Modern History:* Princeton University Press, Princeton, 1957. A thoughtful and philosophical study of the position of religion in the present-day Middle East.

Desmond Stewart, *Trouble in Beirut:* Wingate, London, 1959.

Michael W. Suleiman, *Political Parties in Lebanon: The Challenge of a Fragmented Political Culture:* Cornell University Press, Ithaca, 1967.

Jack H. Thompson and Robert D. Reischauer, eds., *Modernization of the Arab World:* D. Van Nostrand, Princeton, 1966.

Gordon H. Torrey, *Syrian Politics and the Military, 1945–1958:* Ohio State University, Columbus, 1964.

United Nations, *Economic Developments in the Middle East, 1945 to 1954:* United Nations, New York, 1955. A thorough survey of economic developments in Egypt, Iran, Iraq, Israel, Lebanon, Syria, and Turkey.

Dorothy Van Ess, *Fatima and Her Sisters:* John Day, New York, 1961. Reminiscences of fifty years in Iraq.

Labib Suwiyya Yamak, *The Syrian Social Nationalist Party: An Ideological Analysis:* Harvard University Press, Cambridge, 1966.

David Yaukey, *Fertility Differences in a Modernizing Country:* Princeton University Press, Princeton, 1961.

CHAPTER 40

The Partition of Palestine: Israel and Hashimite Jordan

THE JEWISH REFUGEES

The British White Paper of 1939 supposedly placed the future of Palestine on ice for the duration of World War II. Land transfers from Arabs to Jews were halted, and total immigration for the next five years was set at 75,000. The Jewish Agency and the Arab Committee acquiesced to these terms, but few believed that the Palestine problem would not demand a solution immediately at the end of the war. Each party to the dispute girded its loins for the eventual struggle.

The official Zionist position was outlined in a program drawn up in 1942 by American Zionists at the Biltmore Hotel in New York City. Ratified in Jerusalem by the inner general council of the Jewish Agency, the Biltmore program called for the establishment of a Jewish commonwealth, including all of Palestine, and for unlimited immigration under the control of the Jewish Agency.

As the war in Europe drew to a close, the drive to obtain fulfillment of the Biltmore program was intensified by pressures from all sides. Jews from Germany, Poland, and eastern Europe fled from their homes behind the Iron Curtain and found temporary refuge in German and Italian displaced-persons camps. World Jewry in the West, in memory of the Jews massacred by the Nazis, felt a "divine impatience" over the procrastination in finding homes for these displaced persons. Illegal entries into Palestine multiplied, and thousands filtered through the lines held by the Jewish brigade in Italy. Others came by ships of every description. Crises arose when British authorities would not permit them to land, turned them back, or interned them in Cyprus or Mauritius. The *S.S. Patria,* crowded with visaless refugees, was sunk off Haifa; and passengers were allowed to land and remain. On the other hand, passengers on an old cattle boat, S.S. *Struma,* were denied visas, and all lives but one were lost when she sank in the Black Sea. Incidents such as these heightened the irritation at the delay in opening the gates of Palestine to the homeless.

To the new leader of the Jewish Agency, David Ben-Gurion, the refugees, if settled in Palestine, would provide the needed majority and pressure to assure a dominant position for the Zionists. The Jewish Agency, therefore, insisted that the refugees come to Palestine and urged maintenance of the quota system in the United States to prevent their departure for America, the destiny which most preferred.

Any influx of Jews into Palestine found ready opposition from the Arab governments. Britain, in the midst of war, had her hands full with internal security in the Arab states. There was rebellion in Iraq. Pressure on the government was required in Egypt. Thus, Zionist policies for Palestine had to remain quiescent in order not to incite an Arab uprising, which the British believed to be certain if Jewish immigration stood at a high level. The speeches of Anthony Eden relative to Arab unity were wartime statements to insure passive Arab collaboration and mitigate distrust of the British. Since Zionists feared that time might be against them, they urged the attainment of their program in 1945 and rejoiced at the Labour victory at the polls, because irresponsible promises of Labour leaders, in opposition and out of power, were exceedingly favorable to Zionist aspirations.

Ben-Gurion had already warned that the reply to the British government, should it return to the 1939 White Paper, would be "bloody terror" and "constant and brutal force" in Palestine. Likewise, Rabbi Silver, president of the Zionist Organization of America, condemned the moderate diplomacy used by Weizmann as old-fashioned and inspired the Jewish masses to maintain their fighting spirit and prepare for any emergency. Sir Stafford Cripps and Ernest Bevin learned, however, that there was an Arab as well as a Jewish question. All ministries of the government concerned with the Middle East "sang the same refrain. . . . nothing should be done that would further antagonize the Arabs." The Labour government, therefore, postponed any new departure and left the 1939 White Paper in effect. President Truman, who bore no responsibility for problems of the Middle East, supported the immediate granting of 100,000 immigration certificates requested by Ben-Gurion and entreated Attlee to act quickly in the matter. To this the British declared that no radical change in policy toward Palestine could be made unless the United States would share in the maintenance of security in Palestine. Attlee knew Truman would refuse to consider this move.

ZIONIST RESISTANCE MOVEMENT

Delay brought terror to Palestine. Weizmann, Ben-Gurion, and Moshe Shertok (Sharrett), head of the political department of the Jewish Agency, were in London. None the less, Ben-Gurion gave his approval of overt actions by the three illegal Zionist armed forces in Palestine: Haganah (Defense), Irgun Zvai Leumi (Zionist National Military Organization), and the Stern Gang (Fighters for the Freedom of Israel). Haganah with a membership of about 60,000 had been organized in the early days to defend isolated Jewish settlements from Arab attacks and in the 1930's spread, with winks from the British, to every Jewish community in Palestine. During World War II it acquired by various illegal means weapons of every description from small side arms to tanks! In 1945 the "brilliant and biting" Moshe Sneh, aged thirty-seven, assumed command of Haganah and worked out arrangements to co-ordinate efforts with Manachem Begin, leader of Irgun, and Nathan Friedman-Yellin, leader of the Sternists. All three of these men had been fellow-residents together at the Jewish Academicians House at the University of Warsaw. Irgun and the Stern group were right-wing semi-military organizations with an activist leadership dedicated to obtaining a Zionist political state which would include all of Palestine. They fought against the Arabs in the 1930's and were fascist in character, in sharp contrast to Zionists of the Jewish Agency and Haganah who were more likely to be socialists.

The British were caught between urgent Zionist and American demands and a categorical refusal of the Arabs to countenance any relaxation of the 1939 White Paper. Upon the stalling of the Labour government Sneh suggested to the Jewish Agency executive that the military organizations cause "one serious incident" to be publicized as a warning of what would erupt unless Zionist policies obtained. Ben-Gurion gave his approval; and on October 10, 1945 the Palmah (Haganah commandos) raided a British camp at Athlit and freed 208 illegal immigrants detained there. On the night of October 31, the Palmah sank three small British naval ships and tore up the tracks of the Palestine railway in 153 places; Irgun attacked the Lydda railway station; and Sternists sabotaged the Haifa oil refineries. Two weeks later government buildings in Jerusalem and Tel Aviv were fired and troops and police were attacked. Ten days later two coast-guard stations were blown up. Late in December Irgun raided a military arms depot in Tel Aviv, killing nine men of the security forces. Although conferences were held between leaders of Irgun and the Jewish Agency every fortnight, Ben-Gurion and Shertok denied all cognizance of these affairs and feigned helplessness in preventing them when hailed before the British high commissioner.

These activities launched the Jewish resistance movement directed against British authority. Its organization and its operations were typical of the guerrillas which the British had aided, only months previously, in Nazi-occupied countries of Europe. In Palestine, however, the shoe was on the other foot and not at all comfortable. Upon rumors that British delays would continue until further investigations were made, Zionist leaders declared: "Six million Jews died in Europe while we waited for the democratic powers to act. Thousands more of the remnant will die if we sit here with hands folded during the winter, while they investigate again." The situation in DP camps in West Germany was being aggravated intentionally by clandestine operations of Haganah in bringing Jews from central Europe—notwithstanding public accusations by Weizmann, Walter Winchell, and Eddie Cantor that all who made such charges were anti-Semitic or the remark by Rabbi Wise that such statements reminded him of the forged Protocols of the Elders of Zion.

ANGLO-AMERICAN COMMITTEE OF INQUIRY

Since Britain hesitated to act because of Arab pressures and since the United States was insisting on action without any willingness to shoulder responsibility, an Anglo-American committee of inquiry of six Britains and six Americans was appointed to study the question. The committee was to meet in Washington, London, Europe, Palestine, and the Arab states and recommend proper and possible steps to achieve a solution. In the early months of 1946 while the committee questioned individuals in Palestine, terrorist deeds continued. Haganah publicly boasted of its participation, although Ben-Gurion disgusted most of the committee in his quibbling testimony about the existence of Haganah. The report of the committee recommended granting immediately 100,000 immigration certificates to European Jews. It recognized, however, that hostility between Jews and Arabs made the establishment of an independent Palestine impossible at the moment, and therefore advised that Britain retain the mandate until a trusteeship agreement under the United Nations could be arranged, that steps be taken to raise the Arab standard of living in Palestine, and that all laws discriminating against Arabs be removed.

British leaders were provoked when President Truman suggested 100,000 visas be given at once. The Labour government was faced with a dilemma. Approval of the British loan was before the American Congress where Zionists had many friends; negotiations were in process for a treaty with Egypt; Soviet pressures upon Turkey, Iran, Kurdistan, and northern Iraq were increasing day by day. The cost of maintaining a sizable force—at least 100,000 men—in Palestine was a heavy charge on a tight budget for a state on the verge of bankruptcy. Furthermore, if Britain were to evacuate from Egypt as seemed likely, the need of a strong base in Palestine became imperative.

As the British cabinet weighed the dilemma, violence spread in Palestine. Munitions thefts, explosions, sabotage, bank robberies, killings of English soldiers, and destruction of bridges served as an open declaration of war by the Jewish resistance movement. Since Jewish leaders in Palestine believed British temporizing was based on fear of Arab revolt, they reasoned that outrages would obtain concessions from a fearful England. British reactions proved to be typical. Jewish Agency leaders were arrested and their offices occupied; members of the Palmah were rounded up; and great caches of arms were seized. In retaliation Irgun, with the connivance of Haganah, blew up the King David Hotel in Jerusalem, British military headquarters, killing ninety-one people and wounding forty-five others. Obviously the Anglo-American committee of inquiry failed to solve the Palestine issue.

Arab meetings at Inshas and Bludan apparently demonstrated the unity of the Arab states in opposition to any increase of Jewish immigration and a willingness to co-operate against British and American military and economic interests in the Middle East if Palestine were not settled to their liking. Jamal al-Husayni returned to Jerusalem from exile in Rhodesia and Hajj Amin al-Husayni arrived in Cairo.

To resolve the impasse a new Anglo-American suggestion, called the Morrison-Grady plan, was presented. This plan advocated the creation of separate Arab and Jewish autonomous provinces under a central government which would control Jerusalem and the Negev. Similar provincial autonomy plans had been rejected by the Anglo-American committee of inquiry and even before that had gathered dust in the colonial office for several years. Its presentation at this time was an open admission of the sterility of the thinking on Palestine. Rejected by both Arabs and Zionists as unsatisfactory, the plan was modified by leaders of the Jewish Agency, who at this time abandoned the Biltmore program and indicated a readiness to accept a viable state in Palestine. It was insisted, however, that under all circumstances the state include the Negev.

The possibility of a solution was in the air, and Weizmann's moderation gained ascendancy—only to be shattered beyond repair by President Truman's announcement in October, 1946, just before the congressional and the New York gubernatorial elections, that the United States strongly supported immediate entry of 100,000 Jews into Palestine. Furthermore, at the world Zionist congress at Basle in December Weizmann was elected president by only fifty-one percent of the vote and the activism of Ben-Gurion and Rabbi Silver carried political resolutions against the moderation of Weizmann, Shertok, and Rabbi Wise. Rabbi Silver's prescience assured the congress of American support, politically and financially, for establishment of an independent state of Israel. At the same time he predicted that an independent state could never be achieved by a policy of "gradualism."

Any hope for continuation of the talks in London was completely dashed, even though Azzam Pasha, secretary-general of the Arab League, declared that, as never before, he felt that a real solution had been imminent. Terrorism revived in Palestine. The pattern followed a sequence: crime, arrest, punishment, and reprisal; or armed robbery of a bank, a youthful extremist caught and whipped by the authorities, and a British officer and three sergeants seized by Irgun and flogged. In January, 1947 a Jew was sentenced to death for his part in an attack upon a police office where a policeman was killed. Irgun abducted a British judge and a civilian from the Tel Aviv district court and did not release them until a stay of execution of the condemned man was signed.

PALESTINE BEFORE THE UNITED NATIONS

In February, 1947 the British made one last desperate offer, but each side refused it. Shertok stated that not enough of Palestine was allotted to the Jewish part; Arab delegations were opposed to the Jewish immigration quota of 4,000 per month or any partition of Palestine. Consequently, Foreign Minister Bevin decided to refer the question to the United Nations. In the House of Commons debate it was intimated that England would give up her mandate shortly and in the meantime would take no action to prejudice the eventual United Nations decision and disposal.

At British request a special session of the General Assembly of the United Nations was called to consider Palestine. The United Nations Special Committee on Palestine (UNSCOP), composed of representatives of eleven states (Austria, Canada, Czechoslovakia, Guatemala, India, Iran, the Netherlands, Peru, Sweden, Uruguay, and Yugoslavia), was authorized to investigate any question relevant to Palestine and report to the United Nations by September 1. UNSCOP visited Palestine in June and July, during which time Zionist terrorists demonstrated their techniques. An attack made on the prison in Acre resulted in the freeing of many prisoners, and two British sergeants

were hanged by Irgun as a reprisal for hanging three Jews appre-
hended in the Acre prison delivery. Another incident timed for the
benefit of UNSCOP involved the voyage of the S.S. *Exodus 1947,*
purchased in the United States and boarded at Marseilles by 4,554
Jewish passengers with passports and visas for Colombia. British
authorities seized the ship at Haifa and turned her back to France.
Later most of the passengers were sent to DP camps in the British
zone of West Germany.

The situation remained tense as all awaited the UNSCOP report
being drafted at Geneva. Of the eleven members, all agreed that the
mandate had proved unworkable. Iran, India, and Yugoslavia approved a bi-national federal state; and the other eight favored a
partition plan envisaging an economic union. Partition lines formed
three sections of territory for Jews and three for Arabs with northern
and southern points of intersection and communication. Jerusalem and
Bethlehem were internationalized. The Arab and Jewish states would
become independent only when they signed a ten-year economic union
compelling the stronger Jewish state to assist the poorer Arab one. As
proposed, forty-five to fifty percent of the population in the Jewish
state would be Arab, and one percent would be Jewish in the Arab
state. Referred to as "death by a thousand cuts," the partition plan was
as improbable and impractical as the signing of a ten-year economic
union between the two was unthinkable. Moreover, the British announced they would not "participate in the execution of a settlement"
unless both parties accepted it willingly—an unlikely prospect.
UNSCOP called for establishment of the states before October 1, 1948;
and Britain declared the mandate would be terminated May 15 and
her troops evacuated before August 1.

The General Assembly reached a vote on the UNSCOP report on
November 29, 1947, approval being obtained by a vote of thirty-three
to thirteen, with eleven abstentions. Several days before the vote was
taken it appeared that the partition plan might not obtain the necessary two thirds majority of those voting; but several postponements
gave Zionists and sympathizers among United States officialdom opportunity to put pressure on China, Ethiopia, Greece, Haiti, Liberia,
and the Philippines, all of which intended to vote against partition.
Greece, alone, withstood the pressure.

THE PALESTINE WAR

The partition plan of the United Nations touched off a civil war in
Palestine which had been in process of formation for several months.
Thereafter, Haganah, Irgun, and Sternists openly attacked the British
when in need of arms, and Arab forces grew in numbers with

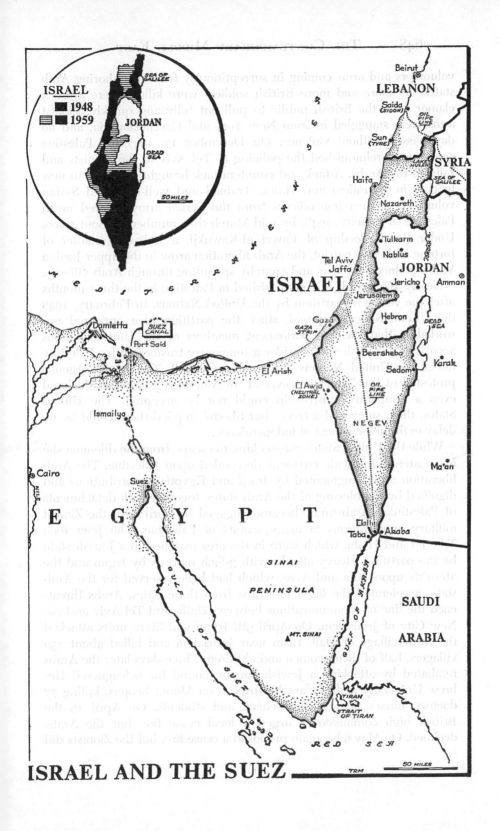

ISRAEL
■ 1948
⊞ 1959

SEA OF GALILEE

ISRAEL

JORDAN

DEAD SEA

50 MILES

Beirut

LEBANON

Saida (SIDON)

OIL PIPE LINE

Sun (TYRE)

HULEH

SYRIA

SEA OF GALILEE

Haifa

Nazareth

Tulkarm

Nablus

JORDAN

Tel Aviv
Jaffa

Jericho

Amman

ISRAEL

Jerusalem

Damietta

Port Said

SUEZ CANAL

El Arish

El Awja
(NEUTRAL ZONE)

Ismailya

Gaza

GAZA STRIP

Hebron

Beersheba

Sedom

DEAD SEA

Karak

OIL PIPE LINE

NEGEV

Ma'an

Cairo

Suez

E G Y P T

NILE

Elath
Taba   Akaba

SINAI

PENINSULA

SAUDI

MT. SINAI

ARABIA

GULF OF SUEZ

GULF OF AKABA

TIRAN

STRAIT OF TIRAN

RED   SEA

ISRAEL AND THE SUEZ

TRM

50 MILES

volunteers and arms coming in surreptitiously from neighboring Arab states. As more and more British soldiers were killed, there arose a clamor from the British public to pull out fully and quickly. Zionist arms were smuggled in from New York and Czechoslovakia, and no day passed without violence. On December 15, 1947 the Palestine government relinquished the policing of Tel Aviv to the Zionists and Jaffa to the Arabs. Attack and counterattack brought savagery to new heights in Jerusalem and Haifa. Trained and well-equipped Syrian volunteers with a few officers from the Syrian army entered north Palestine in January, 1948; by mid-March they numbered about 5,000. Under the leadership of Fawzi al-Kawukji, a Lebanese soldier of fortune and Arab patriot, the Arab liberation army in the upper Jordan Valley reduced the fear and anarchy spreading through Arab villages.

Nearly 100 British soldiers perished in Palestine in the three months after the voting of partition by the United Nations. In February, 1948 the United States proposed, since the partition plan appeared un-workable, that the five permanent members of the United Nations Security Council should consider a temporary trusteeship for Palestine under the United Nations Trusteeship Council. The Jewish Agency protested at this "shocking reversal" of American policy and declared even a temporary trusteeship could not be accepted. The United States, then, suggested a truce; but Shertok replied there could be no delay in the achievement of independence.

While the United States was seeking to escape from the dilemma she had fostered, full-scale civil war descended upon Palestine. The Arab liberation army, augmented by Iraqi and Egyptian contributions and dignified by the blessing of the Arab states, together with detachments of Palestinian Arab units, became engaged in April with the Zionist military organizations in many sectors of Palestine. The Jews took Tiberias and Haifa, which were in the area assigned to a Jewish state by the partition. Heavy attacks with 3-inch mortars by Irgun and the Sternists upon Jaffa and Acre, which had been reserved for the Arab state, accelerated the flight of Arabs from those cities. Arabs threat-ened the line of communications between Haifa and Tel Aviv and the New City of Jerusalem. On April 9th Irgun and Stern units attacked the Arab village of Dair Yasin near Jerusalem and killed about 250 villagers, half of them women and children. Three days later the Arabs retaliated by attacking a Jewish convoy bound for beleaguered He-brew University and Hadassah Hospital on Mount Scopus, killing 77 doctors, nurses, university teachers, and students. On April 18 the British high commissioner urged a local cease fire, but the Arabs declined. On May 9 he again proposed a cease fire, but the Zionists did not reply. As war spread and its outrages multiplied, civilians tried to escape. Zionist authorities were vigilant and allowed no Jew to leave without an exemption from military service issued by Haganah and a receipt for taxes paid for military financing. Arab refugees did not find such barriers; and it was estimated that by the middle of May, 1948 Arab civilian refugees from thirty exposed villages and from Tiberias, Haifa, Jaffa, and other occupied cities totaled about 150,000.

In the midst of such anarchy Ben-Gurion, flanked by his twelve fellow ministers of the national council of the Jewish state, proclaimed on May 14, 1948 at Tel Aviv the establishment of the Jewish state in Palestine, to be called Israel. President Truman announced *de facto* recognition of Israel by the United States sixteen minutes after Ben-Gurion's proclamation in Tel Aviv.

The Arab League had previously declared that it would not recognize the State of Israel and that League members would be encouraged to intervene in Palestine. On May 15, 1948 the Palestine war began. Two Egyptian forces entered Palestine. One proceeded along the coast (in the area assigned to an Arab state) to Isdud, twenty miles south of Tel Aviv, where it was halted by an Israeli force; the other crossed the Negev, through Beersheba, to Bethlehem and the southern suburbs of Jerusalem. A Palestinian Arab force held the Lydda airfield, and an Iraqi force crossed the Jordan and advanced to Tul Karm, ten miles from the Mediterranean. A small Lebanese token force crossed into Palestine from southern Lebanon, and an army of a few thousand Syrians served to pin down a few Israeli forces in the north. The Arab Legion of Transjordan held the center of the line, occupied areas in the Arab portion of Palestine, and defeated Israeli attacks upon Jerusalem.

Although the Arab radio and press claimed victory after victory and called excursions through Arab-held areas as triumphant advances in Palestine, the Arab leaders knew their lines were overextended and that success had not been theirs. Arab soldiers found their equipment obsolete, inadequate, or defective; officers were inexperienced and incompetent in staff work; the zeal of the Arab soldier was cool. Moreover, the Arab Legion was under orders not to move into territory awarded to the Jews by the United Nations partition plan. On the other hand, Israeli activity and ardor were highly stimulated. In the early days of the war Ben-Gurion clashed with Israel Galili, the army commander, over the organization of the army and bitter controversy developed between Haganah and extremist groups. But Ben-Gurion became official commander-in-chief of the army, and direct leadership was given to Yigal Yadin and Yigal Alon.

The Palestine war distressed the powers, and on May 20 the Security Council appointed Count Folke Bernadotte of Sweden United Nations mediator for Palestine, giving him quite a free hand to bring about an end to hostilities. A truce was arranged that ran from June 11 to July 8, and a second truce began on July 19. In October Israeli forces drove the Egyptians from most of their positions in the Negev, including Beersheba; cleared northern Palestine; drove Fawzi al-Kawukji and his Arab liberation army into Lebanon and Syria; and occupied fifteen Lebanese villages. In December Israeli mechanzied forces, supported by a cover of planes, drove the Egyptians into a narrow corridor at Gaza and invaded Egyptian territory in the Sinai Peninsula, compelling the Egyptian government to sue for a cease-fire arrangement on the promise of agreement to an armistice.

Without question the Israeli army won the Palestine war. To a very marked degree during those months Israel was a nation in arms fighting for her independence and her very existence; and this spirit pervaded the fighting units. Pride in the courage and derring-do of the Jewish soldier and his feats in the face of great danger aroused soldiers to extraordinary accomplishment. This singleness of purpose permeated all levels of society and eliminated most problems of discipline. Early in the struggle independence of the Sternists and Irgun was largely curbed, even with force on several occasions. In contrast, diversity of aims, personal jealousies, and national self-interest of the Arab states and their leaders deprived the Arab armies of the cooperation and coordination necessary for victory.

Moreover, the Israeli army and the individual Israeli soldier were much more efficient than the Arab counterparts. A majority of the fighting men of Israel were Westerners and Western-trained, giving them a decided advantage in handling the weapons of war and particularly in the marshaling of men and materials. Although many Arab volunteers flocked to fight under the banner of Fawzi al-Kawukji and Arab state armies gave Arabs a numerical superiority, Jewish volunteers from the United States, Great Britain, and European states were usually war veterans with highly trained skills in the use of the tanks, mortars, airplanes, and mechanized equipment which in the end gave the Israeli forces a decided edge.

In the spring of 1948 the Arab states, taken as a whole, were better supplied than the Zionists; Iraq, Transjordan, and Egypt had arms treaties with England. But by the autumn of 1948 the situation was fully reversed. Numerous shipments of smuggled arms from the United States arrived in Israel; and generous dollar gifts collected in the United States purchased quantities of first-class arms from Czechoslovakia. Bombers were obtained in the United States and England;

and the British forces, still evacuating Palestine, illegally disposed of all types of supplies. Two staff sergeants received £20,000 from Haganah for several tanks. Frequently officials from the United Nations mediators' team stood by helpless in Haifa and watched Jewish stevedores unload crates of arms and ammunition. The arms embargo to the area hindered the Israeli effort very little; but it proved a real hardship to the Arabs, who were not so successful in circumventing it.

Then, too, truces worked to the disadvantage of the Arabs. Delays gave greater opportunity for ambitions and jealousies of leaders and factions to produce friction and open feuds at the expense of the Arab effort. The Arab soldier by training and experience was a good fighter when aroused, but equally ready to return home when the fighting was over. To kindle their ardor a second and a third time proved difficult, and to explain to the Arab soldier the reason for a truce was a fruitless task.

ARMISTICE

During the first truce Count Bernadotte made several suggestions to the Israelis and Arabs for a basis on which peace could rest. A new and fundamental point incorporated the Arab portion of Palestine into the state of Transjordan, a development which Israelis rightfully recognized would alter the balance of power in Palestine. As the end of the month of truce approached, Israel rejected the mediator's offers, but went along with Lebanon, Transjordan, Iraq, and Saudi Arabia to have the truce prolonged. But not Syria and Egypt! They, with Iraq, were so involved in a press build-up to destroy Israel, that the governments hardly dared to postpone the battle. The second truce was never well observed; and the Israelis, who conquered three times more Arab territory in the second stage of the war than they had in the first, were difficult to contain. Count Bernadotte continued to search for a peaceful solution and in one suggestion placed Jerusalem in the Arab sector. But Israel without Jerusalem was an emotional impossibility to Zionists; and the head of the Sternists in his newssheet wrote: "The task of the moment is to oust Bernadotte and his observers. Blessed be the hand that does it." A few days later Bernadotte was murdered by a Sternist soldier, who was allowed to escape.

In the autumn of 1948 several cease-fire agreements were arranged after engagements between Israel and Egypt and Syria. Ralph Bunche, the acting mediator, continued to press for the signing of armistices between Israel and the Arab states; and at his headquarters on the Island of Rhodes, he obtained in February, 1949 an armistice between Israel and Egypt. The important article pertained to the temporary frontier between the two states: the Gaza strip was left to Egypt, but the line was so drawn that many Arab villages were separated from their farm lands; the al-Awja area was demilitarized on the Israeli side, and Egyptian forces on their side were withdrawn fourteen to seventeen miles.

An armistice between Israel and Lebanon was signed in March, and the old frontier was recognized and demilitarized on each side. The question of a settlement with Syria was delayed by the *coup d'état* of Husni al-Zaim; but Ralph Bunche obtained agreement and an armistice in July. The frontiers remained as they were drawn in 1920; the upper Jordan River and the Sea of Galilee were wholly in Israel except for a small part of the Lake Hulah marsh area, which was recognized as a demilitarized zone.

With Transjordan the settlement was far more complex. Debates at the United Nations in the autumn of 1948 revealed that the Western powers agreed that King Abdallah of Transjordan might take over what was left of Arab Palestine, an annexation perfectly agreeable to him. Although such a step was definitely in opposition to the ex-mufti's government-of-all-Palestine plan proclaimed at Gaza, the main area left to Arab control was occupied by the Arab Legion of Transjordan. Israel refused to consider surrendering her award of the Negev in the partition plan for western Galilee, which she had conquered in recent months. Israeli forces ignored cease-fire agreements in Jerusalem and later the armistice with Egypt and pushed south, hoping to establish themselves on the Gulf of Akaba, open a route to the Orient for the new state, and bypass Suez. British troops occupied the port of Akaba to prevent its fall to Israeli forces, but Israeli troops reached the Gulf at a small port, renamed Elath.

In central Palestine the position of the Arab Legion grew precarious after the Iraqi army returned home. Israeli commanders told King Abdallah to withdraw to a depth of two miles on a fifty-five mile front, or Israel would resume hostilities. Such an expansion was necessary to the state of Israel, as the Arab lines blocked the main road connecting Tel Aviv with Galilee; but for Transjordan it left many villagers destitute since their lands were on the other side of the line. With these concessions the armistice was signed in April between Israel and the new state of Jordan, which had been announced in December, 1948. Iraq came under this armistice, since she had declared she would recognize any armistice entered into by her fellow Hashimite ruler.

ARAB REFUGEES

After the several armistices defined the temporary boundaries of Israel, the greatest question remaining was that of the Arab refugees. The number of Palestinian Arabs from the area incorporated in Israel gathered in camps in surrounding Arab states totaled some 700,000 in 1949. The camps were located in the Gaza strip held by Egypt, and in Jordan, Syria, and Lebanon. Egypt and Lebanon had serious over-population problems; east Jordan was quite barren; and west Jordan, the portion of Palestine annexed to Transjordan, did not have the resources to support a large influx of destitute people. Also many inhabitants of Jordan were without means of support, because the new frontier line put their lands in Israel.

The refugees had left their homes for a variety of reasons. In Haifa blaring loud-speakers manned by Jews circulated through the city building up fear in the minds of Arab residents until they broke and fled. In other cities Arabs were expelled when the Israelis took over, and in a number of Arab villages Israeli forces demolished the houses so the Arabs could not return. The massacre at Dair Yasin and the numerous outrages and reprisals of previous years frightened the Arabs. Hearing over the radio optimistic broadcasts and news reports that Arab armies from Egypt, Syria, Iraq, and Transjordan would be victorious in a week or two, many Arabs in towns and villages turned the key in their doors, pocketed them, and walked away, fully expecting to return with the victorious armies in a few days.

The refugee question was also a main stumbling block to any peace settlement. Most refugees believed that they wished to return, although very few would have felt at home had they been allowed to go. Conditions and even the surroundings had changed. But lands, buildings, and bank accounts required compensation, if refugees stayed away. Arab leaders had not the political courage to tell the refugees they could not return; and Israel agreed to discuss compensation and aids to resettlement only in an all-over peace arrangement with the Arab states.

Late in 1948 the United Nations set up a disaster-relief operation to care for refugees, but their numbers grew so rapidly that the United Nations Relief for Palestine Refugees (UNRPR) was organized January 1, 1949 to operate for nine months until the next harvest. Extended until May, 1950 UNRPR worked through the Red Cross and the American Friends' service committee. When refugee work appeared to be a long-range rehabilitation task as well as straight relief the United Nations Relief and Works Agency for Palestine Refugees in the Near East (UNRWA) was created. Work-relief projects and reintegration schemes were developed, but refugee camps continued to aggravate the settlement of peace in the Middle East and acted as breeding grounds for frustration and social revolution. Israel remained adamant with regard to taking back any of the refugees and in 1957 declared that even to mention the subject was illogical since there was so much land available in Syria and Iraq. One positive step to alleviate tension, however, was taken in October, 1956 by releasing eighty percent of the funds in blocked accounts of the refugees.

Another issue in settling the war was the status of Jerusalem. The partition plan of 1947 called for internationalization of the Holy City. The armistice between Israel and Jordan left Jerusalem divided with barbed wire cutting across it. (The eastern part and most of the Old City were given to Jordan.) Although the United Nations declared that Jerusalem must remain an international zone, it became two cities. Israel refused to demilitarize her sector, asserting that it was surrounded by Arab territory on three sides. In 1949 a number of the ministries were moved from Tel Aviv to Jerusalem, and in December the *Kneset* (Parliament) met there. In January, 1950 it was proclaimed that Jerusalem had been the capital of Israel since her founding. All government offices moved there except the ministry of foreign affairs, which remained in Tel Aviv to keep in touch with foreign diplomats. (Many governments, including the United States, forbade their diplomats to move to Jerusalem and refused to recognize it as the capital.) Over the years the Kneset met in seven different makeshift buildings but in August, 1966 moved into a luxurious palace, constructed as a permanent home for the Kneset by gifts from the Rothschilds. Many Israelis complained that it was too costly and so remote that the Kneset "would no longer function in public view in downtown Jerusalem." In 1958 the chief military parade commemorating the founding of the state was held in Jerusalem. Although its proximity to Jordan caused much apprehension in many capitals, Ben-Gurion insisted upon the demonstration, and over 250,000 people flocked to Jerusalem to participate in the joyous occasion.

Meanwhile, King Abdallah proceeded formally to incorporate the Arab portion of Palestine into his state, renaming it the Hashimite Kingdom of Jordan. An election was held in April, 1950; and a new cabinet was formed composed of six ministers from Transjordan and five from Palestine. Israel refused to recognize the incorporation; but the Arab League states grudgingly permitted King Abdallah his expansion, even though they threatened to expel from the League any state which took any part of Palestine.

By 1950 the situation in Palestine reached a state of uneasy equilibrium which commanded some notice from the powers. Consequently, the American, British, and French foreign ministers, meeting in London, signed a tripartite agreement affirming that their states would take action to prevent any violation of frontiers or armistice lines. They also declared that they were prepared to forestall an arms race between the

Arab states and Israel. This meant lifting the arms embargo and acceptance by the powers of the armistice lines and the *status quo* in the Middle East.

THE STATE OF ISRAEL

When the state of Israel was proclaimed in 1948 by Ben-Gurion, a provisional government was organized. The ministers were leaders of the former semi-official departments of the Jewish community and their tasks were co-ordinated to the war effort. In January, 1949 elections were held for a national parliament and constituent assembly (*Kneset*). *Mapai* (Workers party) received almost thirty-six percent of the vote and obtained the largest bloc of seats in the Kneset. Although a committee was directed in 1950 to bring in a written constitution for the state, Ben-Gurion, the prime minister, was predisposed to an unwritten constitution in the British manner and desired that the constitution be built up law by law. One of the very first laws (the Law of Return) provided for unlimited ingathering of Jewish people, the immigrants automatically becoming Israeli citizens upon their entry.

The Kneset was composed of 120 members elected by proportional representation. Elections were held in 1951, 1955, 1959, 1961, and 1965. Thirteen parties were represented in the Kneset elected in 1951. Ben-Gurion's Mapai won 45 seats; General Zionists (a center bourgeoisie party), 20; Mapam (Social Democrats), 15; Herut (Irgun and right-wing), 8; and Maki (Communists), 5. The other seats were scattered among the remaining parties. The election of 1955 showed gains for the extremes and losses for Mapai and the General Zionists. In 1959 some of the religious parties gathered in a National Religious Front and obtained twelve seats. Mapai more than recovered its losses of 1955 with Mapam and the General Zionists declining badly. In 1961 Ben-Gurion resigned over the Lavon affair and called for a new election when he could not fashion a coalition to form a government. The party line-up in the new Kneset remained about as it had in 1959 except for a new Liberal party under the leadership of Nahum Goldmann, a former American citizen who became an Israeli. Merging the General Zionist and Progressive parties, the Liberals won seventeen seats, equaling that of the right-wing Herut party and being second to Mapai's forty-two seats. Ben-Gurion, with difficulty, put together a shaky coalition and held on until 1963 to resign in favor of Levi Eshkol, declaring he planned to return to his kibbutz and write his memoirs. When Eshkol refused to reopen the Lavon affair and appeared weak in handling Arab and domestic problems, Ben-Gurion called for his resignation. Disputes within Mapai ended in Ben-Gurion and six of his associates leaving the party in 1965. They established a new party, *Rafi* (Israeli Workers' List), and entered the election contests of that year. Herut and the Liberals coalesced for the election as did Mapai and a few minor parties. Seventeen parties presented candidates and with Ben-Gurion in the fray heading Rafi, it was a spirited election with eighty-three percent of the electorate casting ballots. Eshkol and his Mapai and associates gained some 45 seats; Herut–Liberals, 26; National Religious Front, 11; Rafi, 10; Mapam, 8; and Independent Liberals, 5. Following the election, Ben-Gurion declined an invitation to rejoin Mapai and asserted he would continue fighting the "stupid and corrupt regime of Eshkol."

Chaim Weizmann was elected to the presidency, a five-year term, in 1948 and served until his death in 1952. After Albert Einstein refused the offer, the honor of the presidency went to Itzhak Ben-Zvi, who was re-elected in 1957 and again in 1962. Upon Ben-Zvi's death in 1963, Zalman Shazar was elected president. Ben-Gurion served as prime minister from 1948 until January, 1954, when he retired to a kibbutz in the Negev. His successor, Moshe Sharrett (Shertok), was a leader of Mapai, head of the political department of the Jewish Agency, and minister of foreign affairs. However, as the situation within and around Israel became more serious, Ben-Gurion returned to the cabinet as minister of defense in February, 1955, and as prime minister, in November. In 1956 Sharrett was relieved of the foreign ministry because he did not favor the use of reprisal attacks upon Egypt, Syria, and Jordan. Mrs. Golda Meir, minister of labor, took his place. After the Sinai war Ben-Gurion remained as prime minister until he resigned in June, 1963, undoubtedly tired from compromising with coalitions. As a successor he chose Levi Eshkol, his minister of finance and prominent member of the powerful Histadruth, the Israeli Federation of Labor. Eshkol's cabinet was approved by a 64 to 43 vote in the Kneset.

The handling of the Lavon affair still rankled Ben-Gurion and he demanded that it be reopened. In 1954 bombs planted in books in the United States Information Agency library in Cairo exploded killing several persons. Egyptian investigations traced the act to Israeli agents who were caught and tried. Egypt claimed that the plot had been an Israeli attempt to anger Americans against Egypt and to effect the cutoff of all American aid in food, arms, and support for the Aswan Dam. Lavon as minister of defense at the time was blamed for the act and forced to resign in 1955. Lavon, Secretary General of Histadruth, refused to be the "goat" and in December, 1960 he was exonerated by the cabinet, which accepted the evidence that Lavon's signature to the documents and orders had been forged. Although Ben-Gurion had not been prime minister when many of these arrangements were said to have been made but had been closely associated with Moshe Dayan, army chief of staff at that time, and other individuals involved, he felt the blame was being shifted to him. In December, 1964 Eshkol resigned over the issue. Ben-Gurion, at this point, split with Mapai. With the support of Moshe Dayan he formed his own party, Rafi, and presented a slate of candidates for the election of 1965. The majority of Mapai supported Eshkol, for the Israeli public had grown weary of all the wrangling and gossip over the Lavon affair. Both Ben-Gurion and Dayan were elected but their party received only nine percent of the popular vote, placing ten members in the Kneset. In January, 1966 Eshkol formd a new coalition cabinet, made up of members of Mapai, the National Religious Front, Mapam, and Independent Liberals. The most important change was in the foreign ministry where Abba Eban replaced Mrs. Meir. When the crisis developed in late May, 1967 over the Straits of Tiran and war was imminent, Eshkol gave the portfolio of the defense ministry to General Moshe Dayan who remained in the cabinet after the fighting had ceased. For a time some speculated that General Dayan might replace Eshkol, but by September, 1967 it appeared that Eshkol had become stronger than ever; he was able on several occasions to reprimand Dayan publicly for policy statements which the cabinet evidently had not approved.

Real authority rests in the hands of the prime minister, who is the chief executive. Ben-Gurion usually held the post of defense minister as well as prime minister; the concentration of power was considerable, especially because there was no effective committee in the Kneset to review affairs of the ministry of defense. Sharrett was foreign minister and prime minister, whereas Eshkol followed the custom of Ben-Gurion and headed the defense ministry along with the prime ministry. Every cabinet after the first election of the Kneset was a coalition centered around the Mapai party of which Ben-Gurion and Eshkol have been president. Various parties have joined with Mapai, and these have changed through the years with the exception of Mapam. The National Religious Front consisting of middle-of-the-road parties with a religious basis supported Mapai after 1959. Several cabinet crises occurred over Jewish dietary beliefs and the question of women serving in the armed forces. There were important discussions over the question of who was a Jew. In 1960 it was decided that a Jew is a person born of a Jewish mother who does not belong to another religion or is a convert according to law; in 1962 it was further ruled that a Jew who becomes a Christian convert is not called a Jew and is not entitled to claim Israeli citizenship. In 1963 the National Religious

Front, as its price for support for Eshkol against Ben-Gurion, demanded the elimination of a nonkosher kitchen in the new S.S. *Shalom*, a luxury passenger ship then being built for the New York run.

Free immigration into Israel had been the goal of Zionist leaders from the beginning of the mandate, and the great debate over the 100,000 quota in the years after World War II made it imperative that unlimited immigration should be a cardinal principle of the new state. In the first decade after independence at least 800,000 entered Israel, swelling its population rapidly; 700,000 came in the first four years. Since fifty-five percent of these postindependence immigrants were Sephardi Jews of Oriental origin, their assimilation presented new problems for Israel. Furthermore, because the birth rate in this group was much higher than in other groups, there was a possibility that in the decades to come Sephardi Jews might outnumber the dominant Ashkenazi. The most serious problem continued to be that of Westernizing these Oriental Jews as soon as possible after their entry, so that their presence did not strain the economy of the state to the breaking point. Yet, the appeal went forth for greater immigration; and in May, 1958, at the time of the tenth-anniversary celebrations, Ben-Gurion announced that the population of Israel had attained the two-million mark. In 1957 there were 71,000 immigrants (including 30,000 from Poland, 13,000 from Egypt, and 12,000 from North Africa); and a plea was sounded for two million immigrants in the next five years to insure the security of the state. The response, however, was poor and in the second decade of the state the numbers of immigrants fell to a yearly average of 25,000. In some years there was a spurt; such as the case when Rumania temporarily lifted her ban on Jewish emigration. By 1967 the population of the state had risen to an estimated 2,650,000. Economic difficulties in Israel, resulting from great minuses in the balance of payments, a widening gap of imports over exports, greater military expenditures at the expense of development, and a sharp dropping off of capital investments, reparations, bond sales, and charitable gifts, brought unemployment, devaluation, and belt-tightening pressures. Furthermore, more than 40,000 Oriental immigrants were held in makeshift camps with no occupation of any sort, and riots occurred in Haifa, Beersheba, and other cities over discriminatory practices of the government in housing, jobs, and education for the Oriental Jews. Consequently, immigrants did not come and many Israelis began to emigrate in worrisome numbers. On August 2, 1966 the Law of Return was amended by the Kneset to curb the practice of returning and residing in Israel long enough to acquire citizenship and a passport and then departing. In 1967 at the time of the Israeli-Arab

War several thousand foreign Jews came suddenly to aid in the emergency but in the summer and autumn it became apparent that not many of these would stay and that not many new immigrants had arrived.

ISRAELI ECONOMY

The economy of Israel has been exceedingly precarious ever since her birth in 1948 and will so continue in the future unless some unforeseen developments occur. Most inhabitants expect and obtain a standard of living comparable to that of central Europe, although Israel is a small, poor, and underdeveloped country of the Middle East. This has been made possible by gifts and loans from foreign governments and individual Jews in many countries. The United Jewish Appeal each year sets a goal of approximately $250,000,000, which is the main source of maintaining a balance in Israeli finances.

Imports for several years ranged from four to five times the value of exports. In 1953, for example, imports were $335,000,000 as against exports of $86,000,000, leaving an unfavorable balance of trade at $249,000,000. Although the Israeli pound was devalued in February, 1962 from $0.55 to $0.33 and Draconian measures were taken to cut consumer spending from ninety percent of national production to sixty-four percent, the situation deteriorated. In five years, 1961–1965, the average yearly unfavorable balance was $371,000,000, and in 1964 it stood at $454,000,000. Early in 1958 pride was evidenced in statistics showing that expenditures for 1957 exceeded income from foreign trade by only 300 percent. Histadruth owns and operates nearly seventy-five percent of industrial production in Israel and is the main strength of the Mapai party. High wages have kept production costs high and made many types of work unprofitable, and troublesome inflation has forced round after round of wage increases. Israel has applied for a link with the European Economic Community. Associate membership was denied, but in 1964 a three-year tariff agreement was signed, cutting rates on twenty-five items but not oranges, which are a major export item for Israel. At the end of the three-year period in 1966 Israel was left with a deficit of $100,000,000 in trade with the European Economic Community. In 1966 Israel had an unfavorable balance of payments of over $600,000,000. A new economic policy had to be found, and critical reports were forthcoming on the inefficiencies of the kibbutz, the question of agriculture versus industry, luxurious living, high wages, and the general standard of living. Because Histadruth, the Israeli Federation of Labor, controlled Mapai, and Mapai dominated the government, there was considerable doubt as to how strong a check Eshkol could maintain on wages, prices, and the standard of living. In 1967 wages and prices continued to rise at their usual rates until the Israeli-Arab War in June when the entire economy was disrupted for several weeks. Trade losses were large but wages were maintained for all workers throughout the crisis. Contributions from world Jewry, especially from the United States, for and because of the war, plus a significant increase in the sales of Israeli bonds totalled several hundred million dollars and literally amazed the leaders of Israel and the world Jewish community. Yet, the expenses of the war and its aftermath of occupation of the west bank of the Jordan left Israeli finances in a weak position. In November, 1967, when Great Britain devalued the pound sterling from $2.80 to $2.40, Israel followed by devaluing the Israeli pound from $0.33 to $0.28½. This meant that prices of Israeli exports to England would remain as before but exports to the United States and other economies not devaluing would have an advantage of fourteen percent.

The burden of the immigrants upon the economy hampered capital development in many ways. New houses were built by the tens of thousands, and the newcomers were fed and clothed for many months before they were integrated and absorbed into Israeli society. Some Israeli economists suggested that immigration be limited, but such a policy was anathema to leaders who had heard British and Arabs mouth such proposals for a quarter of a century. In 1950, in anticipation of 600,000 additional immigrants in the following three years, Israel organized a drive to raise one and one half billion dollars (one billion of which was to come from the United States) to settle the new people. After the Sinai war as the number of new immigrants dropped off, the building trades in Israel suffered a slump with mass dismissals. The conclusion of German reparations in 1965 and the serious decline in charitable gifts from world Jewry made the crisis more acute. One cause of the crisis was frequently attributed to the great mass of immigrants over the previous twenty years, the rapidity of their integration into the economic life of the state, and the lack of any critical evaluation of the productiveness of these immigrants, the usefulness of the work in which they were engaged, and the general criterion used in planning their employment.

The need of capital funds for irrigation projects, industry, communications, and exploration for natural resources exceeded most expectations. Too often a new project of development was not considered from any economic point of view, and frequently the cost was thought unimportant. World Jewry's gifts declined after independence was achieved. In January, 1951 a half-billion bond issue for capital development was launched in the United States, but sales were disappointing. Moreover, the economic plight of Israel became so grave and consumption goods so scarce that proceeds of the bond sales were used to buy food and other essential imports. In August, 1952 relief came in the form of an agreement with West Germany, whereby Israel received $822,000,000 in reparations to be paid in goods over the next fourteen years. A claim was made for $500,000,000 from East Germany, but it was unsuccessful because the U.S.S.R. did not press the payment as the United States had in the case of West Germany. Drives continued in the United States, and Israeli spokesmen in 1957 acknowledged that financial aid from bond sales facilitated the military build-up in Israel by allowing certain dollar earnings to be diverted for arms purchases. France extended credits of $45,000,000 in 1957, and loans were obtained from the Export-Import Bank and the International Bank for Reconstruction and Development. During its first ten years Israel received more than $2,550,000,000 as imports of capital. Much of the foreign exchange generated by this influx had been spent for consumer goods, creating inflation and some luxury living, and producing an artificial standard of living that demanded a continuation of this stream of foreign capital and "spending money." The shock of the termination of West German reparations was so great that a loan of $40,000,000 was arranged in 1966, and considerable dismay was shown in Tel Aviv when there was no indication that it would be repeated in subsequent years. Each year sizable loans and grants-in-aid for nonconvertible funds were made by the United States, but the pinch became painful in 1966. As industry advanced, many Western firms set up branches and subsidiaries in Israel that brought in considerable capital. However, all understood there was a limit to this type of growth, given the political and economic isolation of Israel in the Middle East.

One of the gravest burdens upon the Israeli economy was imposed by the economic boycott by the Arab states. The more natural proclivity of Israelis was for industry or mechanized and specialized production, which would complement the raw materials and agricultural produce of Arab countries. Iraq shut off the flow of oil in the pipeline to Haifa, forcing Israel to buy higher-priced petroleum from the Gulf of Mexico. This pressure stimulated a drive to become more independent of the Arab states in matters of transport as well as in oil. Explorations proceeded; and the Heletz oilfield was developed, the seventeenth well spouting in 1957. Elath on the Gulf of Akaba was pushed as the gateway to the east: a railroad connecting Elath with the national network in the Negev was begun in 1956; an oil pipeline from Elath to Haifa was completed as far as Beersheba in 1957; and the highway from Elath to Beersheba was opened in 1958. After exploratory talks with Asians and Africans Israeli leaders felt that their industry and commerce had a propitious future in those continents; and Elath was the key as long as free passage through Suez was denied to them.

Interest in Elath, however, did not blind the Israeli planners to their dependence upon the West and Mediterranean contacts. In 1960 a loan from the International Bank for Reconstruction and Development for $27,500,000 was negotiated for the construction of a deep-water port at Ashdod, eighteen miles south of Tel Aviv. When the port was completed in 1965 the ports of Jaffa and Tel Aviv were closed, and Ashdod and Haifa were the only two Mediterranean ports. In the 1967 crisis it soon became apparent that the closing of the Straits of Tiran by the United Arab Republic to Israeli shipping and other flags carrying strategic goods to or from Elath on the Gulf of Akaba was for Israel the most vital issue immediately at stake. As the war flared it became apparent that Israel intended to occupy the east bank of the Suez Canal before agreeing to any ceasefire. After the war came to a halt Israel would not consider a pullback or any negotiations that did not guarantee free use of the Suez Canal as well as her control of the Straits of Tiran.

Irrigation of the Negev and utilization of its land inspired Israeli engineers and planners to build gigantic canals from the north, circumventing Jordan, to the barren southlands. Syria and Jordan protested this unilateral use of Jordan waters, but no international plan or division of the water was accepted. Israel engaged in the drainage of the Lake Hulah swamps to provide land for new immigrants and channel the excess water to other areas, particularly the growing industrial districts around Tel Aviv. Since part of the Lake Hulah area was in the demilitarized zone, Syria protested the building of a water canal from that area. In 1953 the United Nations Mixed Armistice Commission admonished Israel to cease the work, and the United States temporarily withheld funds from Israel, hoping to force her to comply with the United Nations order. Political pressure exerted upon Washington was so effective that the curtailment was dropped and engineers resumed work upon the projects, and in 1957 final stages of the work were begun. Settlement and irrigation in the Negev remained the most promising and exciting development in Israel. The potential of the area are discussed so frequently that no politician could possibly subscribe to any deal whereby the Negev would be separated from the state. In 1958 a loan of $24,200,000 was obtained from the Export-Import Bank for irrigation and water-supply development, largely in the Negev. May 5, 1964 when water from the Jordan began to flow southward through the channels and pipes was a day of great celebration. By 1967 two other water intakes from the Sea of Galilee were in operation.

THE EICHMANN TRIAL

On May 23, 1960 Ben-Gurion startled the world by announcing that Adolf Eichmann, head of the German Gestapo Jewish Affairs Bureau during World War II, had been captured and was in Israel where he would be tried for his war crimes against the Jewish people. Located in Argentina and abducted by Israeli agents, he had been flown directly to Israel in an Israeli plane used to transport an Israeli official to a conference in Buenos Aires. The trial opened before three distinguished Israeli judges on April 11, 1961, and Eichmann was ably defended by Robert Servatius of West Germany. He declared that the kidnapping of the prisoner in Argentina made the trial illegal, that Israel and Israeli law did not exist during World War II, and that no Israeli court could be objective in this case. Gideon Hausner, Israeli Attorney General, as the chief prosecutor, stated that the manner of bringing the prisoner to trial was irrelevant to the legality of the trial; that no court could be objective in view of the enormity of his crimes; and that there was no international or other national tribunal available for the trial. Eichmann entered a plea of not guilty and a fifteen-count indictment was pressed against him. The trial ended August 14, 1961 after an almost daily procession of gruesome photographs, letters, diaries, and witnesses portrayed the dreadful events perpetrated against the Jews for which Eichmann was held responsible, either directly or indirectly. He was judged guilty by the court on December 11, 1961, sentenced to death by hanging on December 15, and executed on May 31, 1962 after the president had denied his plea for mercy.

The extensive publicity given to the trial and the horrible details contained in the evidence and accusations served to remind the world of the terrible suffering experienced by Jews and to bolster flagging sympathy and support for Israel in terms of gifts, loans, bond sales, and diplomacy. Within Israel, the trial spurred comfortable and lagging spirits to make greater efforts to build the state.

FOREIGN AFFAIRS

Israel looked to the United States for political and financial support. Each year Israel sought grants and loans from the American government and the minister of finance always submitted a large budget to the Kneset. In 1958 he asked for $640,000,000; in 1966 it was set at $1,100,000,000. But these figures did not give a true picture of the state, for various other expenditures and receipts from United Jewish Appeal and other sources were not included in the regular budget. In the face of mounting armament in Egypt, Syria, and other Arab states Israel turned to the United States, England, and France for arms of the most recent manufacture and type. In 1958 she obtained Mystère jets from France and a submarine from Great Britain; in 1962 the United States supplied Hawk missiles worth $25,000,000; and in 1966 strictly offensive weapons such as Skyhawk bombers with a sufficient range to be able to bomb the Aswan High Dam on the Nile were delivered from the United States. Since the cost of such weapons if purchased in an open market was prohibitive, Israel urged that arms be supplied at prices more commensurate with her ability to pay. Israeli leaders believed that their favorable press and many sympathetic coreligionists in the United States would make it difficult for any American administration to act for long in a manner unfriendly to Israel. It was largely this support and confidence that gave the Israeli government its courage in the face of the surrounding hostile Arab states. This trust was not misplaced for the United States government and people openly supported and favored Israel during and after the Israeli-Arab War in June, 1967 at the many meetings of the United Nations Security Council and General Assembly, even to the extent of abstaining from voting to demand that Israel desist from incorporating the Arab part of Jerusalem into the Israeli sector and into the State of Israel.

After the British evacuated their army and officials from Palestine in 1948 the Israeli attitude toward England grew less tense and more friendly. Britain unfroze most of the Jewish sterling balances, and trade between the two countries improved. From time to time criticism was leveled at the supplying of arms to the Arab states, and British withdrawal from Suez Canal zone bases was recognized as increasing Egyptian power and Israeli insecurity.

In the early days of the state of Israel relations with the Soviet bloc were cordial, and sizable shipments of arms from Czechoslovakia in 1948 were instrumental in winning the Palestine war. Maki (the Communist party) was active, and Mapam subscribed to Marxist philosophy. Mapai, the largest party, followed a left-wing political ideology and was not antagonistic to advanced socialist concepts. However, most Israelis were fiery nationalists and found it difficult to subvert their aims to those of the U.S.S.R. Moreover, there was evidence that Stalin in his last years became anti-Semitic. And after publicity over the trial of the Jewish doctors and attacks upon representatives of Mapam in Russia, a serious bomb explosion occurred in February, 1953 at the Soviet Legation in Tel Aviv, and diplomatic relations were severed. Following Stalin's death, however, anti-Semitism was dropped, and relations were resumed in July. In 1955 when the Soviet bloc began cultivating the Arabs more sedulously and "arms deals" were made, Israeli feelings toward the U.S.S.R. took a sharp turn for the worse. Nonetheless, since the Arab states did not permit their oil to be delivered to Israel, arrangements were concluded in July, 1956 to import over a two year period about $20,000,000 in oil from the U.S.S.R., the price being considerably less than dollar oil from the Western Hemisphere. Trade agreements with Soviet-bloc states were maintained, and one with Poland was renewed. After the Sinai war the Arab states complained so bitterly to the U.S.S.R. over the oil affair that deliveries were discontinued. Sharp words were exchanged during the period of the Sinai war and the diplomatic struggle over evacuation of the Gaza Strip, but no break occurred.

Relations remained cool and in the 1960's as Israel looked more to the West for trade and support and sent her technicians to aid developing African and Asian countries, thus competing with Soviet engineers and agents, the U.S.S.R. grew more critical of Israel. In 1964 all outstanding commercial agreements with Israel were canceled, and Israel on her part complained of the treatment of Jews in the U.S.S.R. and the limitations placed on their cultural development as Jews. Usually the Soviet delegate to the Security Council of the United Nations sided with Syria in disputes between Israel and Syria and used his veto on one occasion in 1966 to block condemnation of Syria. In the crisis of 1967 the Soviet delegate in the Security Council meetings attacked Israel bitterly and severely as an imperialist and a tool of the imperialists.

After the armistice agreements came into effect in 1949, hopes for peace remained unsatisfied; and the growth of Arab nationalism, particularly in Egypt and Syria, gave Israeli leaders cause to look to the defenses of the state. The most common expression of Arab leaders in this respect was contained in the idea of a "second round" in which the Israelis would be driven into the sea. On the other hand, some political leaders in Israel, frequently of the Herut party, spoke of the need to expand and to take Akaba to the south and to incorporate all of Palestine, even Transjordan, into the state of Israel. To many Arabs across the frontier the likelihood of expansion being forced upon Israel by the swarms of immigrants seemed very real. Border incidents occurred every few days. Israel was not always blameless in these affairs and was censured or reprimanded for several: in October, 1953, when about 250 well-trained Israeli troops attacked the Jordanese village of Kibya, destroying the houses and one school and killing fifty-three people; in February, 1955, when an Israeli force killed a large number of Egyptians in the Gaza area; and in December, 1955, when an army group attacked Syria in the Lake Galilee region. The United Nations Mixed Armistice Commission under General Van Bennike and General Burns tried to watch over the frontiers and observe the truce, but never had sufficient force to police the entire frontier.

Until 1956 Israel felt considerable security because of the support of the United States and world Jewry. Her military posture with respect to her neighbors was excellent; and jealousies and rivalries among the Arab states, notwithstanding the Arab League, appeared to be her salvation. In 1956, however, there seemed some danger that the balance might be changing in favor of Egypt. The Soviet-bloc arms deals of 1955, the inability of the West to act in the face of Nasser's nationalization of Suez, and Nasser's success in aligning Syria, Jordan, and Egypt in a military pact under one command tightening the noose around Israel led Ben-Gurion to undertake a military build-up in 1956. To allay obvious fears in Damascus, Amman, and Cairo, as well as in Washington and perhaps in Moscow, Ben-Gurion declared in June that Israel would refrain from war even if provoked. Reprisal raids fell under a different category; a punitive drive went into Jordan on October 10, so worrisome in fact that the British warned Tel Aviv that aggression against Jordan would activate the Anglo-Jordan security treaty. And, later in October, Israeli delegates at the United Nations asserted a preventive war would never be launched against their Arab neighbors.

THE SINAI WAR

Three days after the statement at the United Nations, Israel mobilized and the following morning, October 29, invaded Egypt. The army moved quickly, and by November 7 most of the Sinai Peninsula had been occupied. Sharm al-Shaykh, guarding the Straits of Tiran and the entrance to the Gulf of Akaba, was taken. Seizure of the Suez Canal by heavy bombing, joint invasion, and capture of Port Said and the northern half of the Canal by British and French troops in an action on October 31 was initiated as an intervention to keep the two antagonists apart, to secure the Canal, and to stop the war. Announced Israeli war objectives were: to weaken the Arab positions and destroy their arms; unseat Nasser by administering a swift military defeat; open the Suez Canal to Israeli use; control the passage of ships into the Gulf of Akaba; and free the port of Elath.

From the very beginning world opinion was so shocked by the action that achievement of the war aims was doubtful. Eisenhower telephoned Eden some days before the outbreak to dissuade him from engaging in such measures. The day preceding the attack Eisenhower had warned Ben-Gurion against taking any overt measures; and immediately after the attack an emergency meeting of the United Nations Security Council denounced the invasion and demanded a cease-fire. England and France entered the fray with the avowed purpose of keeping the Canal open for traffic. Egypt, however, found it easy to block the Canal by sinking ships in the channel. With the United States, the U.S.S.R., Canada, India, and most of the world ranged against the three invaders, the cease-fire was accepted on November 7. Withdrawal from Suez by the English and French and from Sinai by the Israelis started within a few days. United Nations forces were gathered and came in to prevent incidents. But Israel refused to surrender the Gaza Strip and Sharm al-Shaykh. Ambassador Eban in Washington and Mrs. Meir at the United Nations tried by every means to hold on to these two key points and offered to yield only if guaranteed freedom from Egyptian raids and open use of the Straits of Tiran. Eisenhower denounced any such promise and castigated the idea of permitting gain from aggression. Finally, in March, 1957 Ben-Gurion, in the teeth of violent opprobrium from the Herut and other activist elements in the Kneset, agreed to withdraw from both points on the "assumption" that border incidents would halt and that the Gulf of Akaba would be open to Israeli shipping. The troops pulled back, Egyptian civil administrators took over in the Gaza Strip, and the United Nations Emergency Force (UNEF) patrolled only the Egyptian side of the frontier, including Sharm al-Shaykh. In many observers' eyes the situation returned fully to the conditions prevailing upon the outbreak of the incident.

Almost immediately after the British and French invasion of Port Said, Hugh Gaitskell in the House of Commons questioned his government about its collusion in planning the Sinai war. In reply Selwyn Lloyd, the Foreign Secretary, said, "There was no prior agreement between us about it," and Prime Minister Eden a few weeks later added, "There was not foreknowledge that Israel would attack Egypt —there was not." Finally, after a decade, with the publication of Israeli General Moshe Dayan's diary and other studies as well as interviews with some of the principals involved in 1956 such as French Foreign Minister Christian Pineau, and Selwyn Lloyd, Gaitskell's suspicions have been vindicated.

Throughout the summer of 1956 the plot thickened. The nationalization of the Suez Canal, the denial of its use to Israeli shipping, the Egyptian possession of the Straits of Tiran, and its closure to the

Israelis almost strangled Israeli trade with Japan, Asia, and East Africa. Oil from the Persian Gulf was cut off. A direct attack upon Egypt seemed the only way out, but Ben-Gurion held that such a unilateral move would be exceedingly dangerous and would open Israeli cities to bombing by Egypt's Ilyushins against which he had little defense. General Dayan wrote that if they did not succeed at the very outset in surprising the Egyptians and knocking out their planes while still on the ground, the Israeli plan would fail. Israel needed the collaboration of the British and the French, especially the former and their Canberra bombers based on Cyprus. Britain was seriously provoked by the nationalization of the Canal, and France was furious over the help Egypt was affording to the rebels in Algeria. At first England and France wanted to make the assault without Israeli participation, but Israel declared they were engaging in the enterprise willy-nilly. On October 10 France and Israel were in agreement over the plans for French naval support and air cover as well as air-dropped supplies when Israel started her attack on Egypt. On October 16 Eden and Lloyd went to Paris and held top-secret meetings with Premier Mollet and Pineau at which time the British pledged to participate and a French telegram (picked up by American intelligence) alerted Ben-Gurion: "You can depend absolutely on the British." Then, on October 24 or October 25 at Sèvres, outside of Paris, Ben-Gurion with General Dayan at his side, Mollet, and Patrick Dean, British Foreign Office official, signed an Anglo-French-Israeli agreement to attack Suez.

The plan was for Israel to start the attack on October 29, 1956 as though it were a typical border-reprisal raid, and for two days her air force with immediate undercover French assistance would confine itself to protecting Israeli skies and ground forces. This ruse was set so that Egypt would consider it a raid and not bomb Israeli cities. Then, two days later, England and France would enter the war, bomb Egyptian air fields, seize the Canal, and cut off Egyptian forces in the Sinai Peninsula where they could be utterly destroyed. It all went as planned except that the Anglo–French force did not act quickly enough, perhaps in an attempt to conceal the collusion. It gave time for world opinion, and the actions of the U.S.S.R. and the United States to force the ceasefire and eventual evacuation.

The aggressive nationalism of Zionism was disclosed by the Sinai War, and many Zionist sympathizers the world over were keenly chagrined by the revelation. The Arab states experienced defeat again and, amazed at the deftness of England and France and the might of Israel, felt the urgent need for more military equipment, organization, and co-operation. The Gulf of Akaba with UNEF occupying Sharm al-

Shaykh remained open, and though Egypt and Saudi Arabia protested its use, they made no move to block the Straits of Tiran. Border attacks ceased elsewhere for a time; and large-scale or scheduled raids were halted, as no Arab leader wished to tempt the fate Nasser had so narrowly escaped.

That Egypt would not some day seek revenge for this humiliation no one could gainsay, but Nasser's first reaction was to seek greater influence throughout the Arab world and to disregard Israel. When turmoil developed in Jordan later in 1957, Israel warned against Iraqi or Syrian troops occupying Jordan. It was an open secret that Israel felt compelled to seize all of Palestine west of the Jordan River if Jordan were annexed to another Arab state. The Israeli victory in Sinai hastened the formation of the United Arab Republic. Ben-Gurion declared that this posed no danger to Israel. However, when the revolution in Iraq in 1958 shook confidence in the future of Jordan, Israeli leaders again warned that Israel would move to the west bank of the river if Syrian or Iraqi troops entered Jordan. Since world-wide tremors would follow in the wake of such a move a special session of the General Assembly of the United Nations was hurriedly called in hopes of finding a more permanent solution to Israel's position in the Middle East. In any case, the future of Israel seemed assured. But questions of permanent frontiers, relations with her Arab neighbors, and her influence with the world powers remained to be settled.

ISRAEL AND HER ARAB NEIGHBORS AFTER SINAI

Following the Sinai war, Israel proceeded with her plans to build a natural uranium nuclear reactor in the Negev to develop rockets and missiles and perhaps an atom bomb, although she insisted that all such scientific activity was for peaceful purposes. The United States complained in 1960 but did not press the issue and in 1963 shipped four tons of heavy water to be used in this research. At the same time, Israel was concerned about a similar Egyptian enterprise in the western desert where German scientists were at work. In 1963 two Israeli agents were arrested in Switzerland for threatening the families of German scientists working in Egypt. Israel formally requested the West German government to take steps to prevent its scientists from working in Egypt. Bonn did make announcements opposed to such German engagements but no effective bars were imposed.

With UNEF and the United Nations Egypt-Israel Mixed Armistice Commission (UNEIMAC) stationed on the Egyptian side of the frontier, clashes after 1957 were rare there. Israel would not permit either of these groups on Israeli soil so that the United Nations groups were unable to control Israeli movements. In 1959 there was some action over Egypt between MIG-17's and French Mystère jets, and Israel was condemned for this by UNEIMAC. For the most part, Israeli clashes with her Arab neighbors turned to Syria. The border existing there was not drawn but had come into being at the end of the fighting in 1948. A neutral demilitarized zone was established and both sides asserted the rights of its owners to cultivate it. Israel claimed the ownership of the zone and thus organized the cultivation of the land. Each spring there were raids by Arabs upon Israelis who were cultivating land in the demilitarized zone, to which Israel frequently answered with reprisals. In 1960 Arabs tried to cultivate some of the area, and Israel wiped out a Syrian base at Tawafik in a large operation for which she was condemned by the United Nations Syria-Israel Mixed Armistice Commission (UNSIMAC). In 1962 there was another near Nuqaib north of the Sea of Galilee for which Israel was censured by the United Nations Security Council. These were followed by other Israeli attacks in Syria, Lebanon, and Jordan, usually with artillery and airplanes and sometimes tanks. In July, 1966 Israel made an air attack upon Syria at the beginning of the water-diversion scheme because it would lessen the flow of the Jordan in Israel. Syria took the case to the Security Council, which did not pass any resolutions against Israel. The most serious Israeli reprisal of 1966 occurred on November 13 against the village of al-Samu, Jordan. The Security Council censured Israel for the deed on November 25 and there were reverberations from this aggression in many quarters. King Husayn of Jordan was bitterly criticized by the Arab League and by large numbers of his own subjects for not having replied to the Israeli forces, and some feared he might lose his throne as a result of the incident. Israel was worried over this possibility, for any new group in Amman would be less friendly to Israel than Husayn had been. Within Israel there was grave concern lest Eshkol's government had gone too far and been too provocative. Many Israelis wondered publicly whether or not the idea that the Arabs only understood force was the proper assessment of the situation. But the problem of the infiltration of the Israeli frontier by Arab individuals, Arab groups, and Arab terrorist societies such as al-Fatah, the planting of mines, arson, and the shootings of soldiers, police, and farmers continued and grew in rates of incidence, the amount of destruction, and loss of life. The solution seemed as far away as ever but a number of Israelis doubted that reprisals were the answer. In the spring of 1967 incidents again occurred, and in April a serious one showed five Syrian villages shattered by bombs dropped from airplanes; investigations by UNSIMAC blamed Israel for violating the armistice.

THE SIX-DAY WAR, JUNE 5-10, 1967

Tensions multiplied and Israeli cabinet members, under great pressure from the public for action against mines, bombs, and killings, spoke out on the possibilities of a penetration in depth in Syria, which was regarded as the base of the al-Fatah operations. Syria believed they had evidence that an Israeli move was scheduled for May 17, 1967. Alarmed, they called upon the United Arab Republic to make good on her mutual-defense pact. This led Nasser to request U Thant, Secretary General of the United Nations, to remove UNEF from the United Arab Republic. This he promptly did, some thought too promptly, and since Israel had refused in 1957 to accept any UNEF groups on her soil the frontier was suddenly alive with military forces on each side. With UNEF leaving Sharm al-Shaykh, the United Arab Republic took over the guns there and announced the closing of the Straits of Tiran to Israeli shipping. Because Egypt had never renounced her claim that these Straits were territorial waters, and had never recognized the Israeli possession of Elath, Nasser's position was strong. The loss of free navigation to and from Elath through the Gulf of Akaba and the Red Sea to the markets of Japan and the East, and to the oil fields of the Persian Gulf was so menacing that Israel declared she would fight rather than acquiesce in this closure. This was the difficult problem immediately facing the Security Council in 1967.

When it became apparent that neither the United States nor the United Nations was able to effect an immediate opening of the Straits of Tiran, Israel launched an attack upon the United Arab Republic in order to seize the Straits and to control the Sinai Peninsula. Although Jordan and Syria had joined with the United Arab Republic to form a united front, Israel believed that the most serious challenge would come from the United Arab Republic. Furthermore, Nasser had begun to mobilize his troops in Sinai even before the United Nations Emergency Force withdrew. Coupled with his bellicose public speeches and the tone of Cairo Radio, the concentration of Egyptian forces east of the Suez Canal compelled Israel to act. General Moshe Dayan, the hero of the Sinai Campaign of 1956 and a co-founder of the Rafi party, entered the cabinet as Minister of Defense. On June 5, Israel, in a series of surprise attacks, destroyed the air capabilities of the United Arab Republic, Jordan, and Syria. With complete mastery of the skies and superb coordination of all branches of the service, Israeli forces within six days occupied all of the Sinai Peninsula to the east bank of the Suez Canal, all of Jordan west of the Jordan River, and the Golan Heights and the city of al-Quneitra in Syria. They then agreed to a cease-fire called for by the United Nations Security Council.

Throughout the summer and autumn of 1967 there were many sessions of the Security Council and the General Assembly to attempt some settlement of the issues at stake between Israel and her Arab neighbors and to bring peace to the Middle East. Abba Eban presented the basic requirements of Israel exceedingly well. Repeatedly, Israel stated that there could be no peace until the Arab states sat down and negotiated directly with Israel, although it was apparent that no Arab leader felt sufficiently secure to do this. Israeli demands, in addition to recognition by the Arabs, were the establishment of definite boundaries, the guaranteed use of the Suez Canal and the Straits of Tiran, and the end of raids and terrorism. Within a few days of the cease-fire, the Arab part of Jerusalem was legally incorporated into the Israeli sector and General Dayan and others categorically stated that this act was permanent and not negotiable. Structures before the Wailing Wall were bulldozed away so that the many thousands who came there to pray could be accommodated. As the summer passed and it became less certain that the Arab leaders would negotiate, especially after the Arab summit meeting at Khartoum at the end of August, the Israeli government was faced with the problem of a solution to the occupied territories. Some thought of establishing an Arab state envisioned by the 1947 decision of the United Nations in partitioning Palestine and others proposed an autonomous Arab state federated with Israel, but neither was advanced as an official proposal. In the autumn of 1967 the Israeli destroyer *Eilat* was sunk off Port Said by sophisticated seek-and-destroy missiles from a United Arab Republic ship; a few days later the oil installations at Port Suez were destroyed in retaliation by Israeli gunfire. These acts strengthened the hands of those in Israel who demanded a hard line against the Arabs. Some additional difficulties arose from the Israeli victory. The problem of the new refugees augmented the existing refugee problem, and former trade patterns across the Jordan river were hampered and upset as a result of the Six-Day War. Each day that no settlement was achieved the *status quo* became more difficult to dislodge. The United Nations seemed helpless. The General Assembly passed by an overwhelming vote a resolution calling upon Israel not to unify Jerusalem, but Israel disregarded it completely. On November 22, 1967 the Security Council passed unanimously a British-sponsored measure authorizing U Thant to send to the Middle East a special personal representative to negotiate a peace between Israel and her Arab neighbors based upon Arab recognition of Israel and the establishment of permanent borders, withdrawal of Israeli occupying troops, Israeli use of the Suez Canal and the Straits of Tiran, and a just settlement for the Arab refugees. Gunnar Jarring of Sweden was appointed for this mission but his chances for success were uncertain because Nasser subsequently declared that the Suez Canal would not be opened to Israeli ships and that he could not recognize Israel. At the same time, Israel declared that there could be no substitute for direct negotiations with the Arab states. Israeli leaders were not sure that the Israeli public would condone any withdrawal from lands won in the Six-Day War.

TRANSJORDAN

East of the Jordan River Prince Abdallah ruled his semidesert domain and seminomadic people under the tutelage of Great Britain. The strength of his position was anchored to the financial and diplomatic contributions of the British and was buoyed up by the Arab Legion and the Transjordan frontier force, the strongest Arab armies in the Middle East. The British found them useful in Iraq and Syria during World War II, and Abdallah was the staunchest friend of the British in the Middle East.

Abdallah's rule and his governmental machinery were uncomplicated until 1949. He succeeded in settling some of the nomads, who were quite happy until a dry year came along. When crops were poor and pasturage inadequate, the customary raiding of neighbors who fared better was forbidden. Without relief from the government in such years settled existence was impossible.

A new treaty was drafted and signed in 1946, recognizing Abdallah as king of Transjordan and giving him greater independence from Great Britain, which was permitted to keep a military mission and various training facilities in the country. A constitution was promulgated and became effective in 1947, providing for a chamber of deputies to be elected for a five-year term and consisting of 20 members: 12 Muslims, 4 Christians, 2 bedouins, and 2 to represent the Circassian and Shishan communities. The other house of parliament was a council of notables composed of ten members appointed by the king.

King Abdallah was strongly criticized in the Arab League for agreeing to such a subservient position as the treaty established, and Transjordan's application for membership in the United Nations was blocked by the U.S.S.R. on the grounds that Transjordan was not independent. Consequently, another treaty was signed in March, 1948, specifying "co-operation and mutual assistance" between Transjordan and Great Britain. Prime Minister Samir Rifai Pasha called for elections in October, 1947, and only one political party (the Government Revival party) presented candidates for the chamber of deputies, although a few independents were returned. A new cabinet was organized under the direction of Tawfik Abu al-Huda, who had held office under Abdallah since 1938.

Aside from Abdallah's relations with the British and the annual subvention received from them, his main attention politically centered upon the Arab League. Because of Abdallah's everlasting dream of a greater Syria over which he would rule, Egypt and Saudi Arabia were always unfriendly. The latter was especially incensed when in 1947 Abdallah summoned a congress to support the free Hijaz movement.

During the Palestine war the Arab Legion defended Jerusalem and successfully held the fortress of Latrun from a desperate Israeli attack. Together with Iraqi troops, Abdallah's forces held the lines from the Gulf of Akaba to north central Palestine near Janin and bore the main brunt of Israeli drives. Abdallah favored the Nashashibi, Tukan, and other Palestinian Arab families as opposed to the al-Husayni family and the ex-mufti Hajj Amin. When the defeat of the Arabs could no longer be denied, Abdallah acted to incorporate what remained of Palestine into his state and in June, 1949 renamed it the Hashimite Kingdom of Jordan.

HASHIMITE KINGDOM OF JORDAN

Almost overnight King Abdallah's problems became exceedingly complex. The small state of an estimated 400,000 inhabitants suddenly burgeoned into a kingdom of 1,360,000 people. More than half of the Arab refugees flocked into Jordan. Those who had means of support, an education, or a skill either integrated themselves into Jordanian life or migrated to other Arab lands or to the far corners of the earth; nearly 500,000 did not and continued to live in refugee camps. A serious problem arose in those villages of Arab Palestine whose lands and support were cut off by the armistice lines of 1949.

Grave as the refugee situation was for Abdallah, the Arabs, and the world, the most significant aspect of this influx and the annexation of Arab Palestine to Transjordan sprang from a transformation in the character of the state. West Jordanians and refugees after 1950 comprised more than half of the population. On the average they were better educated, more politically minded, more ardent in their Arab nationalism, and more unremitting in their desire to have a "second round" with Israel and regain mastery in their own state.

In 1949 Abu al-Huda reorganized the cabinet. Previously, three of the nine members were west-bank Jordanians; now many other Palestinians received important government posts. The new cabinet formed under Said al-Mufti, a Circassian, was responsible to parliament rather than to the king. In 1950 the size of the chamber of deputies was doubled, and half of the members were elected to represent each side of the Jordan. The council of notables was also increased to a membership of twenty, seven of who were Palestinian.

The Palestinian Arabs, accustomed to blaming their woes on the Jews and the British, turned their venom on King Abdallah and the Amman government. Although Abdallah was not greatly interested in economics, an irrigation project to provide arable land for refugee families was inaugurated near Shunah on the Wadi al-Arab. Musa Alami founded an Arab development society which built several model villages near Jericho; and UNRWA contributed to a number of programs, which incidentally were productive and beneficial to the state. But none was enough, and the king bore the brunt of the attack. Abdallah was sane and shrewd, as well as moderate and realistic. For these attributes he was despised and murdered on July 20, 1951 in Jerusalem by an adherent of the ex-mufti Hajj Amin al-Husayni.

KING HUSAYN

The king's eldest son, Talal, was in Switzerland but returned and was proclaimed king in September. His mental stability was highly questionable; and in 1952 he departed for Europe, leaving the kingdom to his son Husayn. The latter became king on his eighteenth birthday, May 2, 1953. The post of prime minister became more important, but until 1956 the position shifted from one old-time political friend of Abdallah to another: Samir al-Rifai, Tawfik Abu al-Huda, Fawzi al-Mulky, Said al-Mufti, Haza al-Majali, and Ibrahim Hashim. A new star arose in 1956 in Colonel Ali Abu Nuwar, who had been military aide and companion of King Husayn for many years. He became chief of staff, head of the Arab Legion, and contender for complete power in Jordan.

All authorities agreed to the need for development in Jordan, and recognition of the potential of Jordan waters led to many schemes. The difficulty of achievement stemmed from the conflicting interests of Lebanon, Syria, Jordan, and Israel and from the absence of peace in the Middle East. Division of the water proved a stumbling block, and the natural storage reservoir, Lake Tiberias, was wholly located in Israel. In spite of failure to come to terms on a regional system Syria and Jordan drew up a pact to build a hydroelectric-irrigation-dam project on the Yarmuk River. Other plans were made to construct roads, reforest considerable areas, and build a cement factory. United Nations Technical Assistance Administration allocated sizable sums for Jordan; and in 1954 the United States Foreign Operations Administration gave $8,000,000 for development work, while Point Four programmed over $4,000,000 for Jordan. Britain continued her support of the Arab Legion (£ 12,500,000) and subsidized the government to the extent of several million pounds annually. In 1956 the sum was £3,-350,000.

The signing of the Baghdad and Damascus pacts in 1955 and the formation of power rivalries in the Middle East placed Jordan in a critical position. Her dynasty belonged to the same family as that of Iraq, and her financial ties to England favored a closer relationship to the Baghdad pact. But the bitter denunciations of the pact from the other Arab League states, led by Egypt and Syria, warned Jordan of the dangers in allying herself with Britain, Turkey, and Iraq. Furthermore, Palestinian Arabs, in their eternal campaign to regain possession of the whole of Palestine, were very skeptical of a pact which included or was under the patronage of any Western state; for it was generally understood that the West would not easily permit the destruction of Israel.

Thus, in December, 1955 when pressure was exerted upon Jordan to join the Baghdad pact, Prime Minister Haza al-Majali, who was amenable to such a move, was forced out of office after five tumultuous days of riots, attacks upon British and American diplomatic offices, and a final declaration of neutrality. Saudi Arabia announced her willingness to contribute to the support of Jordan's government and the Arab Legion on condition that the British were ousted. John Bagot Glubb Pasha, English head of the Arab Legion, was dismissed summarily in March, 1956 and was replaced shortly by Colonel Ali Abu Nuwar. Britain continued financial support, but sympathizers of President Nasser rapidly gained in strength and position. King Husayn was young and inexperienced. Colonel Abu Nuwar, young and exceedingly ambitious, looked upon himself as the Nasser of Jordan and gathered together a band of young and ardent nationalistic officers seeking power.

JORDANIAN CRISES

In June, 1956 Prime Minister Said al-Mufti admitted that he planned to negotiate a revision of the treaty with Britain, but parliament was dissolved the day before it was to debate the subject. A caretaker government under Ibrahim Hashim was appointed to serve until the elections in October. Meanwhile, nationalization of Suez, Nasser's rages, and the West's menacing maneuvers to control or internationalize the canal played into the hands of the young Palestinians. Ali Abu Nuwar flitted from Beirut to Damascus to Cairo to Riyadh and back again, receiving assurances of military assistance from Syria, Iraq,

Egypt, and Saudi Arabia in case Jordan were attacked. All were cognizant of the gradual Israeli mobilization and fully expected that Israel planned to occupy all of Palestine west of the Jordan, as Ben-Gurion and other Israeli leaders had so often threatened. In case of war it was agreed that an Egyptian would command a unified Arab army.

Such a backdrop for an election campaign assured a pro-Egyptian victory. About fifty percent of the qualified voters cast their ballots, and the National Socialists under Sulayman Nabulsi won eleven seats in the 40-member chamber. Nabulsi formed a new cabinet to include six others from his own party, two independents, one Nationalist, and one from the Pan-Arab Renaissance party. Nabulsi's cabinet was installed the day Israel invaded Egypt. Nabulsi broke relations with France; and Syrian and Iraqi troops moved in to safeguard Jordan from Israel and, incidentally, from one another.

During the winter Nabulsi wished to recognize the U.S.S.R. and Communist China and frequently suggested that Jordan should ask for arms and aid from the Soviet bloc. Passionately anti-British, he reminded Syria, Egypt, and Saudi Arabia of their offer to assume the annual subvention Jordan received from Great Britain and declared that as soon as they implemented their proposal Jordan was ready to terminate her treaty with Great Britain. Fulfillment came with the Arab solidarity pact in January, 1957; Egypt and Saudi Arabia each promised to contribute £5,000,000 and Syria promised £2,500,000 for support of the Jordanian army.

British negotiators arrived in Amman in February, and arrangements for annulment of the treaty and a cash settlement to England for her installations and property were reached in March. Many Jordanians rejoiced as the British troops commenced to depart; and Nabulsi, in collaboration with Ali Abu Nuwar, appeared ready to form a closer political, economic, and military union with Syria and even to permit Russians and foreign Communists entry into Jordan. However, King Husayn dismissed Nabulsi and precipitated a crisis. Three others tried their hands at forming a cabinet before Ibrahim Hashim turned the trick. Ali Abu Nuwar fled to escape arrest; and his successor, Ali Hayari, followed him a few days later. Martial law was declared and a curfew decreed for all principal cities. Syrian troops, however, occupied north Jordan, and the fate of King Husayn hung in the balance for a number of days. Showing real courage, Husayn rallied his bedouin troops about him at Zerka and throughout the spring and summer re-established peace and his authority.

Finances were in serious condition, and there loomed a $20,000,000 deficit in army funds. Saudi Arabia paid her first installment on the Arab solidarity pact in May, but nothing was forthcoming from Egypt or Syria. Husayn, therefore, asked aid from Iraq and the United States; the latter contributed $20,000,000. Arms from the United States were airlifted dramatically and publicly to Amman in September. Feeling more secure, Husayn convened parliament in October and denounced U.S.S.R. sympathizers. The Pan-Arab Renaissance (Baath) and Communist parties were outlawed, and the conspiracy to merge Jordan with Syria was driven underground.

The next crisis arose when Syria and Egypt formed the United Arab Republic. Husayn begged his cousin to visit Amman and protect Jordan by establishing some type of federal union. As a result the Arab Federation was consummated in February, 1958; and its constitution, proclaimed and ratified by parliament in March. Provisions were included to insure separate treaty obligations, as Husayn did not believe Syria would countenance his adherence to the Baghdad pact. King Husayn became an alternate to the chief of state, and procedural steps for closer federation were undertaken. A joint budget was fashioned with Jordan's share being set at twenty percent. An Iraqi was designated chief of staff of the Arab Union Army; and a cabinet with Nuri al-Said as prime minister, Ibrahim Hashim as deputy prime minister, three Iraqis, and two Jordanians was announced. Although Nasser fumed at King Husayn for betraying the Arab nation to imperialists and assailed him as a decadent weight upon Arab nationalism, Husayn believed he had weathered the storm and that union with Iraq would protect him from Syria and strengthen his stand against Nasserism.

But still another and more serious crisis fell on Husayn in July, 1958, with the Revolution in Iraq and the murder of King Faysal, of Arab Federation prime minister Nuri al-Said, and of two Jordanians in the Federation cabinet. Left technical head of the Federation, King Husayn proceeded to assert his authority. But to block any overt action, General Kassim of Iraq abrogated the Union. This abruptly threw Jordan adrift in a turbulent storm of Arab nationalism. Husayn's sworn enemies, Ali Abu Nuwar and Ali Hayari were lodged in Cairo and aided in plotting his overthrow. They might have succeeded had not British paratroopers dropped in from Cyprus. The bedouin troops rallied to Husayn's side, and his throne seemed secure as long as the British troops remained in Jordan. An assassin encouraged by broadcasts from Damascus and Cairo might, however, pierce his tight personal security forces and slay him. This, it will be recalled, was the fate of his grandfather.

Almost within hours after the British occupation in Jordan the question of Jordan and Husayn's future arose. This artificial state needing an annual subsidy of over $50,000,000 could hardly be justified; for it could not perform the services for which it was created in 1920. One English politician aptly phrased the situation when he spoke of "a kept king in a kept country." A "villa in Lausanne" for Husayn was mentioned. The crux of the problem seemed to be peaceful liquidation of the state. But since Israel threatened to seize the lands west of the river if Syria or Iraq took over or partitioned the state, any sudden disappearance of Jordan might touch off a veritable holocaust in the Middle East.

With Egypt and Syria bound together in the United Arab Republic, with General Kassim riding the wave of popularity in Iraq after having ousted the monarchy and destroyed the Hashimite family there, with the Saudi family maintaining its perpetual feud with the Hashimites, with Israeli hotheads talking of annexing all of Palestine west of the Jordan River, with several thousand British soldiers in Jordan causing Arab nationalists everywhere to call King Husayn the tool of the imperialists, and with half of his own subjects wishing for a different state and a different regime, that "villa in Lausanne" must have been tempting. Though total revenue of the state in 1958 amounted to $86,000,000, nearly $64,000,000 came from grants and subsidies from Great Britain and the United States. Imports were more than eleven times the amount of exports. Local capital was virtually nonexistent and exploitable natural resources were unknown. But King Husayn was tough and tenacious. He enjoyed the loyalty of his army, which was regarded as the best trained and equipped force among the Arabs. The British troops left in November, and Husayn in assessing his position set out on a three-pronged drive to keep his throne. His program consisted of internal economic growth and development, hopefully to make Jordan economically self-sufficient by 1970; of democratizing the government, progressing as rapidly as the several elements in Jordan's society could be brought into accord; and of steering an artful course among the jealousies, rivalries, ambitions, and ideologies of his Arab neighbors and retaining his independence from the great powers.

In 1959 the Jordan Development Board was established to co-ordinate and sponsor efforts to increase the productivity of the state. A major project was the East Ghor Canal, which was to channel off water from the Yarmuk River and carry it parallel and east of the Jordan River for more than forty miles toward the Dead Sea to irrigate tens of thousands of acres of dry but fertile lands. The first stage was finished in 1961 and the second in 1962. The total cost was more than $25,000,000 and at that point 40,000 acres were irrigated. The banks of the Canal would be heightened as more water became available; at the two Arab summit meetings in 1964 the plans for diverting water from the Hasbani and Banyas rivers to the Yarmuk and building dams on the Yarmuk were designed to augment the flow into an enlarged East Ghor Canal. King Husayn laid the corner foundation-stone for the Makhiba Dam on the Yarmuk on May 25, 1965. In 1961 agreements were entered into with West German concerns to improve port facilities at Akaba, and a major port there was outlined and approved in 1965. The Jordan Refining Company was built at Zerka and TAP-line promised to make available 300,000 tons of oil annually. The Jordan Phosphate Company received loans from the United States government to enlarge its facilities for exploiting the vast chemical deposits in the Dead Sea. Tourism became a growing industry and the archeological remains and historical sites in Jordan, of which there are an untold number including the unique ruins at Petra, were widely publicized in Europe and America along with improved tourist accommodations. As a further boon to these developments, Jordan joined with Syria, Kuwayt, and the United Arab Republic in 1964 in an Arab Council for Economic Unity and a limited Arab Common Market in 1965. Already in 1962 agreements had been reached with Saudi Arabia for the free movement of people and capital between the two states. To reach the goal in 1970 was optimistic but with peace, good will, and determination, it might be approached.

In 1959 there was relative political calm within Jordan. Internal problems in Saudi Arabia, General Kassim's reorganization in Iraq, and the difficulties of merging Syria and Egypt into the United Arab Republic occupied the full attentions of King Husayn's covetous neighbors. Samir al-Rifai, who had replaced Ibrahim Hashim as prime minister when he took his post in the Arab Union, resigned for reasons of health in May, 1959, and Hazza Majali took his place. Majali was killed when a bomb exploded in his office in August, 1960; the same day King Husayn appointed Bahjat al-Talhuni as prime minister. The radio invectives from Cairo and Baghdad upon Jordan's rulers and government reached such a crescendo that it was recognized that for survival there had to be a greater sharing of responsibility in Jordan. Elections were held in October, 1961 for the Council of Representatives but only ten percent voted, and only twenty of the sixty seats were contested. To counter this discouraging apathy in January, 1962 the king appointed as prime minister Western-educated Wasfi al-Tal who selected an entirely new cabinet, no member of which was in parliament and all who were Western-educated. Parliament was dissolved and new elections were held for the Council in November. This time seventy percent voted, and there were 166 candidates for the sixty seats for which only three had unopposed candidates. In January, 1963 al-Tal and his cabinet received a vote of confidence of forty to eighteen from the new Council. When the Baath revolutions occurred in the next weeks in Iraq and Syria and their leaders made speeches on Arab unity and flew to Cairo for talks with Nasser, Husayn feared al-Tal would not be able to hold the clamors for union in check and appointed veteran Samir al-Rifai to the post. The more modern Council refused to give him its confidence, so Husayn dissolved parliament, appointed his uncle, Husayn ibn Nasser, to head the government and called for new elections. These caused no incident and most who were elected were supporters of the monarchy. In the summer of 1964, Bahjat al-Talhuni was in again and after the Arab summit meetings had settled some of the controversies and initiated the Jordan River diversion scheme, Wasfi al-Tal returned to continue his program of modernizing the administration in Amman. A final move was King Husayn's designation of his youngest brother, Amir Hassan, as heir to the throne in place of his own infant son Abdallah, whose mother had been Antoinette Gardiner, daughter of an English adviser to the government.

An equally difficult task for King Husayn has been to cope with the mercurial fluctuations of Arab world politics. In 1959 Majali restored diplomatic relations with the United Arab Republic, and the Syrian frontiers were opened once more. He declared that the Palestine question was foremost in his policies and that Jordan would make no military alliance outside the Arab League. But the next year he stood fast in opposing the formation of an Arab Palestinian army or state, and nine men were sentenced for conspiring with the United Arab Republic to overturn Husayn's rule in Jordan. Majali was killed shortly after this by a bomb, and his successor, al-Talhuni, held investigations on the bombing that led to a charge against two United Arab Republic secret service agents. Kassim was recognized and in 1961 relations quieted until Husayn supported Kuwayt against Iraq and recognized Syria when she seceded from the United Arab Republic. Again the vilification poured forth from Cairo and Baghdad, and after the revolution in Yemen in 1962 Husayn turned more toward King Faysal in Saudi Arabia. Relations did not mend until 1964, at the Arab summit meetings in Cairo in January and Alexandria in September, where the several Arab states pledged $200,000,000 for the Jordan water diversion to the Yarmuk River. Also at the Cairo gathering it was voted to create an Arab political entity for Palestine and to draft a constitution. Arab refugees from Palestine were to elect delegates to a national assembly, which would meet every two years, alternating between Jerusalem and Gaza. Known as the Palestine Liberation Organization (PLO), it was to raise an army that would have a separate identity but be a part of the army in each of the host Arab states. In 1966 Husayn agreed that PLO might conduct elections in Jordan for the national assembly, but he refused to accept its armed forces or PLO leader Ahmad al-Shuqayri's suggestion that the capital of Jordan should be transferred to Jerusalem. Arab defamations continued, and Damascus suggested that the Syrian army would gladly supply arms to those who wished to overthrow Husayn. Yet, in May, 1967 at the height of the crisis with Israel, Husayn flew to Cairo where Nasser embraced him at the airport and together they signed a five-year mutual defense pact and Jordan pledged its army, should war come with Israel. Husayn believed fully that his throne would be lost and he assassinated if his army did not move promptly and with full vigor on the center front in an Arab-Israeli confrontation.

Within a few hours after the beginning of hostilities on June 5 the Jordanian air force had been destroyed by Israeli actions. Complete mastery of the air over Jordan gave Israel such an advantage that King Husayn's army was ineffective. The entire west bank area was lost and about 200,000 refugees fled eastward across the river. One might easily have assumed that the enormity of the defeat and the loss of territory, especially Jerusalem, would spell the end of King Husayn, but he remained courageous and fearless throughout the fighting and emerged from those days with increased prestige and honor. The most productive part of Husayn's kingdom was gone, his finances were in shambles, and his armed forces were without equipment. Throughout the summer various moves were made to enable the new refugees to return to their homes or to the camps. Israeli officials allowed about 14,000 who had homes to return, but none were accepted back in the camps. King Husayn assumed virtual command of all branches of his government and attended the Khartoum summit meeting. Saudi Arabia, Kuwayt, and Libya agreed to aid him financially and 30,000 Iraqi troops remained in Jordan to protect the king as well as to strengthen his position against Israel. In the autumn Husayn visited Moscow to explain the Arab position and to sound out possibilities for replacing his lost military equipment. In November, 1967 he visited Washington and the United Nations, where he indicated that he and other Arab leaders might be able to find a path that would lead to recognition of Israel.

REFERENCES: Chapter 40

The number of books covering this subject is very large and is growing rapidly. Of special significance are items cited in Chapters 27, 31, 32, 35, and 39.

King Abdallah, *My Memoirs Completed* (Harold Glidden, trans.): American Council of Learned Societies, Washington, 1954. A continuation of reference edited by Philip P. Graves cited in Chapter 32.

Aqil Hyder Hasan Abidi, *Jordan: A Political Study, 1948–1957:* Asia Publishing House, New York, 1965.

Menachem Begin, *The Revolt: Story of the Irgun:* Schuman, New York, 1951. Fascinating story of this organization.

David Ben-Gurion, *Israel: Years of Challenge:* Holt, New York, 1963. An account of the founding of the state and the accomplishments of the first decade.

———, *Rebirth and Destiny of Israel:* Philosophical Library, New York, 1953. The role of the state of Israel as seen by the first prime minister of the state.

Norman Bentwich, *Israel:* McGraw-Hill, New York, 1953. A reasonable account.

———, *Israel Resurgent:* Praeger, New York, 1960.

Earl Berger, *The Covenant and the Sword: Arab-Israeli Relations, 1948–56:* University of Toronto Press, Toronto, 1965.

Folke Bernadotte, *To Jerusalem:* Hodder & Stoughton, London, 1951. By the United Nations representative.

Marver H. Bernstein, *The Politics of Israel—The First Decade of Statehood:* Princeton University Press, Princeton, 1957.

E. L. M. Burns, *Between Arab and Israeli:* Harrap, London, 1962. By the Canadian general at the head of the United Nations Truce Supervision Organization.

Abner Cohen, *Arab Border-Villages in Israel, A Study of Continuity and Change in Social Organization:* Humanities Press, New York, 1965.

Hedley V. Cooke, *Israel: A Blessing and a Curse:* Stevens and Sons, London, 1960.

Moshe Davis, ed., *Israel: Its Role in Civilization:* Harper, New York, 1956. A collection of twenty-one papers that support the thesis that "the Zionist movement is, after all, historically a special form of Messianic expectation."

Moshe Dayan, *Diary of the Sinai Campaign:* Schocken Books, New York, 1967. A first-hand account by the commanding general.

Ann Dearden, *Jordan:* Robert Hale, London ,1958.

Abba Eban, *The Tide of Nationalism:* Horizon Press, New York, 1959.

S. N. Eisenstadt, *The Absorption of Immigrants: A Comparative Study Based Mainly on the Jewish Community in Palestine and the State of Israel:* Routledge & Kegan Paul, London, 1954.

Harry B. Ellis, *Israel and the Middle East:* Ronald Press, New York, 1957. Straightforward account.

Walter Eytan, *The First Ten Years: A Diplomatic History of Israel:* Simon and Schuster, New York, 1958.

Aryei Fishman, ed., *The Religious Kibbutz Movement:* Jewish Agency for Palestine, New York, 1957.

Rony E. Gabbay, *A Political Study of the Arab-Jewish Conflict: The Arab Refugee Problem (A Case Study):* Librairie Minard, Paris, 1959.

A. Granott, *Agrarian Reform and the Record of Israel:* Ayre & Spottiswoode, London, 1956. An important study.

George L. Harris, *Jordan: Its People, Its Society, Its Culture:* Human Relations Area Files Press, New Haven, 1958.

E. H. Hutchison, *Violent Truce:* Devin-Adair, New York, 1956. A story of the border warfare between Israel and the Arab states.

Oscar I. Janowsky, *Foundations of Israel: Emergence of a Welfare State:* D. Van Nostrand, Princeton, 1959.

Jon Kimche, *Seven Fallen Pillars:* Praeger, New York, 1953. An account of the Israeli-Arab War.

Jon Kimche and David Kimche, *A Clash of Destinies: The Arab-Jewish War and the Founding of the State of Israel:* Praeger, New York, 1960.

Barnett Litvinoff, *Ben-Gurion: The Biography of a Statesman:* Praeger, New York, 1954.

James G. McDonald, *My Mission in Israel:* Simon and Schuster, New York, 1951. The experiences of the first American ambassador to Israel.

James Morris, *The Hashimite Kings:* Pantheon Books, New York, 1959.

Martin Noth, *The History of Israel:* Harper, New York, 1958.

Edgar O'Ballance, *The Arab-Israeli War, 1948:* Praeger, New York, 1957. A military study.

Robert David Ottensooser, *The Palestine Pound and the Israel Pound:* E. Droz, Geneva, 1955. Discusses the sterling balances and the effect of dollar receipts as gifts.

Raphael Patai, *Israel between East and West:* Jewish Publication Society of America, Philadelphia, 1953. A thoughtful approach by an eminent sociologist.

————, *The Kingdom of Jordan:* Princeton University Press, Princeton, 1958.

Frederick G. Peake, *History and Tribes of Jordan:* University of Miami Press, Coral Gables, 1958.

Don Peretz, *Israel and the Palestine Arabs:* Middle East Institute, Washington, 1958. A very thorough study of a difficult problem.

Stewart Perowney, *The One Remains:* Hodder & Stoughton, London, 1954. The story of the Arab refugees and especially of the Arabs who did not leave Israel.

Paul G. Phillips, *The Hashimite Kingdom of Jordan: Prolegomena to a Technical Assistance Program:* University of Chicago Press, Chicago, 1954. An economic geography.

William R. Polk, David M. Stamler, and Edmund Asfour, *Backdrop to Tragedy: The Struggle for Palestine:* Beacon Press, Boston, 1957.

Emanuel Rackman, *Israel's Emerging Constitution, 1948–1951:* Columbia University Press, New York, 1955. Since Israel does not have a written constitution complete in a single document, this is an important subject.

Guiseppe Riciotti, *The History of Israel:* Bruce, Milwaukee, 1958.

Bernard A. Rosenblatt, *The American Bridge to the Israeli Commonwealth:* Farrar, Strauss, and Cudahy, New York, 1959.

Alex Rubner, *The Economy of Israeli: A Critical Account of the First Ten Years:* Praeger, New York, 1960.

Harry Sacher, *Israel: The Establishment of a State:* British Book Centre, New York, 1952. A good Zionist presentation.

Nadav Safran, *The United States and Israel:* Harvard University Press, Cambridge, 1963.

Robert St. John, *Ben-Gurion:* Doubleday, New York, 1959.

Richard H. Sanger, *Where the Jordan Flows:* Middle East Institute, Washington, 1964.

Fayez A. Sayegh, *The Palestine Refugees:* Amara Press, Washington, 1952. An Arab view.

Joseph B. Schechtman, *The Arab Refugee Problem:* Philosophical Library, New York, 1952. More Israeli than Arab in viewpoint.

————, *Rebel and Statesman—Early Years:* Thomas Yoseloff, New York, 1956. A biography of Vladimir Jabotinsky, founder of the Revisionist movement in Israel.

Walter Schwarz, *The Arabs in Israel:* Faber and Faber, London, 1959.

Benjamin Shwadran, *Jordan: A State of Tension:* Council for Middle Eastern Affairs Press, New York, 1959.

Moshe Sicron, *Immigration to Israel, 1948–53:* Falk Project for Economic Research in Israel, Jerusalem, 1957.

Gerald Sparrow, *Modern Jordan:* George Allen & Unwin, London, 1961.

Melford E. Spiro, *Kibbutz: Venture in Utopia:* Harvard University Press, Cambridge, 1956. An intimate study of a kibbutz by an American.

Georgiana C. Stevens, ed., *The United States and the Middle East:* Prentice-Hall, Englewood Cliffs, 1964.

S. G. Thicknesse, *Arab Refugees: A Survey of Resettlement Possibilities:* Royal Institute of International Affairs, London, 1949. The outlook when the problem first arose.

Basil J. Vlavianos and Feliks Gross, eds., *Struggle for Tomorrow: Modern Political Ideologies of the Jewish People:* Arts, New York, 1954. A syllabus of the several political parties in Israel and their ideas.

Murray Weingarten, *Life in a Kibbutz:* Reconstructionist Press, New York, 1955. Written by an American who helped found a kibbutz.

Alex Weingrod, *Reluctant Pioneers: Village Development in Israel:* Cornell University Press, Ithaca, 1966.

L. F. Rushbrook Williams, *The State of Israel:* Macmillan, New York, 1958.

CHAPTER 41

The Advent of the Egyptian Republic

ANGLO-EGYPTIAN AFFAIRS

The murder of Ahmad Maher in 1945 raised Mahmud al-Nukrashi, second in the Saadist Party, to the vacant prime ministership and highlighted the varied and long-standing questions that clouded the relations of Egypt and Great Britain. Having declared war against Germany, Egypt entered the United Nations as a charter member and immediately pressed Great Britain that provisions of the Anglo-Egyptian treaty of 1936 infringed upon Egyptian sovereign rights beyond a point tolerable for an independent state.

When Attlee replaced Churchill, the Egyptian populace believed that an enlightened and generous British government had come to power and that the moment was propitious for a thorough renovation of relations with England. Thus, in December, 1945 Nukrashi asked England for a re-examination of the treaty, but did not urge his demands in the face of British preoccupation with Soviet pressure upon Azerbayjan and the Turkish Straits. The Wafd, in opposition, along with the fascist Young Egypt, the Muslim Brotherhood, Communists, and nationalist student groups, rioted in February, 1946, forcing Nukrashi's resignation for his supineness toward the British. Faruk, thereupon, appointed Ismail Sidki, who permitted some demonstrations as salutary but clamped down sternly when they seemed to get out of hand.

Negotiations with the British were now a political necessity. Sidki formed a team of twelve to discuss revision of the 1936 treaty. The Wafd refused to participate unless Nahas Pasha was designated chairman of the delegation, and this Sidki could hardly accept. Through the summer months of 1946 the debate centered on three issues: evacuation, joint defense, and the Sudan. Despite good will and an earnest desire for a trustworthy accord on each side basic desiderata upon which neither could compromise kept the two parties poles apart. Egypt held that the British military occupation must end everywhere in Egypt and that foreign troops must leave. If war broke out or if Egypt felt threatened by war, she would call upon England to come to her aid. With respect to the third issue, the unity of Egypt and the Sudan under the Egyptian crown must be recognized. Attlee confirmed that Britain was willing to withdraw her forces from Egypt after ratification of an alliance specifying terms for the return of troops and use of bases in Egypt. But Soviet demarches against Iran, Turkey, and Greece led political and military figures in London to a careful consideration of the safety of the Suez Canal. Churchill, in opposition, put his finger on the sensitive spot when he warned that if Britain withdrew Egypt would surely refuse permission for British troops to re-enter the Suez Canal zone, even in time of danger.

Nonetheless, there might have been a solution had not public statements about the future of the Sudan provoked a complete breakdown of the discussions. Agreement was reached that the British would leave Cairo, Alexandria, and the Delta in 1947, and the canal zone in 1949, and that joint defense obligations (re-entry of British troops) would become operative if aggression were committed against Egypt or one of her immediate neighbors. If some other Middle Eastern state were the victim of an aggression, discussions would be mandatory. Agreement on the Sudan left the rule as established in 1899, but mentioned "unity between the Sudan and Egypt under the common Crown of Egypt." Sidki publicly claimed success in achieving the desired union, whereas Bevin confided to his opponents in parliament that the *status quo* remained and assured the Sudanese that no step would be taken to prejudice their desire for independence and self-government. Sidki promptly resigned, and treaty revision reached a stalemate. Nukrashi returned to office and took the dispute to the security council of the United Nations. At Lake Success through July and August of 1947 proposals and counterproposals were debated, but none could obtain sufficient votes to pass. The British refused to budge on the Sudan, stating bluntly that they did not intend to appease Egypt by compromising the right of the Sudanese for self-determination. The Egyptians could not give up their contention with respect to the unity and oneness of the people of the Nile Valley. Furthermore, since British troops departed from Cairo and Alexandria, part of the Egyptian protest no longer pertained.

EGYPT AND THE SUDAN

The future of the Sudan loomed large in the minds of Egyptians. The water of the Nile passed through the Sudan, and the possibility of dams and water diversion frightened Egypt. The Sudan was underpopulated and contained vast areas where the expanding population of Egypt might earn a livelihood. Moreover, cotton culture in the Sudan was considered an unnecessary and threatening competition for the cotton of Egypt. In view of these factors Egypt desired to control the Sudan and force Sudanese economy into a role complementary to her own. To foster such a development there was pronounced on every opportunity the cliché: the unity of the Nile Valley and her peoples.

Another underlying consideration for Egypt in the question of the Sudan and "unity of the Nile" was the utilization of the Nile for electric power and wider irrigation in Egypt. A swelling population presented an awesome and relentless specter to Egyptian politicians. Industrialization needed power, which was available if the Nile could be harnessed. Bids for the development of hydroelectric generating stations at Aswan Dam were entertained in 1947. Fertilizer plants to produce more than half of the nitrates so vital for Egyptian high-yield agriculture were specified; and a steel mill to exploit the high iron content of hematite ore deposits in the Aswan vicinity was contemplated. The foundation stone of the Aswan hydroelectric plant was laid in 1948, and contracts for machinery were awarded to a number of European firms. (The estimated cost was $43,500,000.) Work progressed slowly, and in 1952 completion of the project was still estimated to be five years away. Other projects for increasing the water supply were advanced. In 1951 discussions were held to consider a dam at Marawi, and it was agreed that the Sudan might raise by one meter her dam at Sennar. By far the most novel scheme was the project entered into with Uganda for building a dam below Owen Falls and utilizing Lake Victoria as a huge storage reservoir which would be tapped by channel through the Sudan and provide Egypt with a more steady year-around flow of water. Agreements were tentatively made with Great Britain in 1949, but final consummation was delayed by the many controversies with England.

THE PALESTINE WAR

Soon after Prime Minister Nukrashi returned from the United States and his futile attempt at the United Nations, partition of Palestine and war against Israel engulfed the attention of Egypt and dissipated the resources of the nation. Having had an active hand in the creation of the Arab League and aspiring to dominant leadership among Arab states, Egypt sent two forces into Palestine in May, 1948. One advanced through Gaza along the coast, and the other pushed inland to Bethlehem and the outskirts of Jerusalem. In October Egyptian forces suffered several reverses from Israeli surprise attacks in the Negev, incidents which left the Egyptians discredited. When armistice talks were opened on Rhodes in January, 1949, the disposition of Beersheba was debated. In February Egypt signed the armistice, leaving her in possession of the narrow Gaza strip and recognizing the demilitarization of the al-Awja area on the Sinai frontier. The armistice was a humiliation for the leader of the Arab League and an experience her soldiers would not soon forgive the politicians in Cairo whom they were sure were responsible for the defeat. Over 200,000 refugees were huddled into the narrow barren Gaza strip, giving solemn testimony of the defeat of the Arabs and creating a vexatious problem for Egypt.

THE MUSLIM BROTHERHOOD

The inflamed nationalism, rampant during the Palestine war, provided the perfect climate for the growth of *al-Ikhwan al-Muslimin* (the Muslim Brotherhood). Founded in 1929 by Hasan al-Banna, then a youthful teacher in Ismailia in the Suez Canal zone, the Muslim Brotherhood grew under the founder's fiery oratory and positive approach to a personal and social religion. He exhorted his followers to return to the Islam of the Prophet, which meant an acceptance of the Koran as divine revelation and the law of society. He desired to recreate Egypt, as well as other Muslim lands, into an Islamic theocracy and thwart the trend toward a secular state. But the true strength of the Muslim Brotherhood lay not so much in its ideology as in the energy, devotion, fanaticism, ruthlessness, and singleness of purpose of the leaders and in the tightness of its organization.

In its earlier years the Muslim Brotherhood maintained an active program in social welfare and in agricultural co-operatives, but in later years it dedicated its workers in a militant spirit reminiscent of fascism. The goal became the remaking of society into a mystical resemblance of Hasan al-Banna's concept of early Islamic life. No compromise from the "right way" could be tolerated. In the Palestine war the fearlessness of Brotherhood units at the front occasioned many heroic acts, which however in no way changed the outcome of the war. Reprisals, pressure, assassination, and armed gangs gave the Muslim Brotherhood power, and its actions attracted the youth who yearned for a positive course to follow.

Responsible government in Egypt found the Muslim Brotherhood a serious threat and took punitive measures against it. In 1946 fifty-seven members were arrested in Alexandria; in 1948 after the murder of the chief of police thirty-one were arrested in Cairo, and Prime Minister Nukrashi ordered the Brotherhood dissolved. A few days later Nukrashi was assassinated by one of the Brethren. In 1949 when Hasan al-Banna was murdered, the government took no serious steps to ascertain his assailants. In 1951 permission was given to reactivate the Brotherhood on condition that its semimilitary activities be discontinued. Hasan al-Hudaibi, elected supreme guide in 1951, did not have the unrelenting zeal of al-Banna, and the movement began to lose its original drive and spirit.

POSTWAR ECONOMY

Postwar Egypt found herself in a curious economic situation. Price levels were still high; employment, full; and commodities, scarce. But over £E450,000,000 in funds loaned to Britain during the war were held in blocked sterling assets in London. For the first time in the memory of man Egypt became a creditor state—and almost overnight. Egypt clamored for the release of her balances to purchase machinery, machine tools, industrial and capital goods, and the entire gamut of consumption articles. Bankrupt Great Britain could only allow a few purchases and promise the rest in the future. Egypt wanted the sterling balances convertible into dollars; but England found this impossible, and the United States refused to bail her out. Formal negotiations were opened in 1947 over the balances. New Egyptian credits were unblocked, and a schedule for the release of old funds was established. By 1950 the balance had been reduced to £E270,000,-000; and in 1951 a further agreement was reached whereby the balance would be wiped out by 1961.

But sterling balances only spotlighted the economic needs of Egypt. Schools, health facilities, industry, fertilizers, and better markets for her cotton, arms, and communications were required in an increasing volume. Land reform to break up the concentration of arable acreage in the hands of a few was recognized as a necessity by all except some who owned estates. Revision of the tax structure to lighten the inordinate tax burden on commerce and industry and to increase taxes on income and land also became a necessity if Egypt hoped to emerge as a modern state with a healthy economy. No country in the Arab Middle East was better prepared to accomplish these changes than Egypt. She had a progressive society, and an educated group which understood the needs and many of the ways in which they could be solved. But political power remained in the hands of those who were insufficiently concerned to inaugurate the inevitable social and economic revolution in Egypt.

Nevertheless, some positive steps were taken. In 1947 a law was passed with regard to Egyptian companies, requiring forty percent of the directors, seventy-five percent of administrative and clerical employees, ninety percent of the laborers, and fifty-one percent of the capital to be Egyptian. A progressive income tax was enacted in 1949. And in 1951 a social-security program and a new land tax were introduced. A five-year social and economic plan was also drawn up in 1951, providing £E100,000,000 for irrigation schemes, £E20,000,000 for drinking water, £E15,000,000 for an iron and steel mill at Aswan, and £E10,000,000 for a hydroelectric generating station at Aswan. At the same time a five-year arms program to cost £E400,000,000 was initiated. Business activity, industry, and trade were advancing with marked acceleration, and it was foreseen that within a decade or two Egypt might enjoy a developed economic society.

FARUK AND POLITICS

Politics were unstable in Egypt because of the corruptness and vagaries of King Faruk and his palace entourage. With immense wealth in land at his disposal, his political power was vast and no one could foretell where his fancy might stop. For a time he even subsidized Hasan al-Banna and the Muslim Brotherhood. His influence over appointments, government contracts, policies of all kinds, land sales, and every aspect of society smothered the sparks of political responsibility or democratic action and tended to corrupt a number of wealthy landowners, ambitious journalists, lawyers, and politicians. Public morals were at a low ebb.

Following the assassination of Nukrashi, the question of the withdrawal of British troops from the Suez Canal zone dominated the national scene. Since the British strongly intimated that a secure settlement could not be achieved unless Egyptian leaders and negotiators had the solid support of the Egyptian nation, a free election which Wafdists would not boycott was a necessity. Although charges of cooperation with the British during the war and corruption were leveled at Nahas Pasha, the elections held in January, 1950 demonstrated Wafd supremacy and his hold upon Egypt. Returns for the chamber of deputies showed: 228 Wafdists, 28 Saadists, 26 Liberal Constitutionalists, 6 Nationalists, 1 Socialist, and 30 independents. Nahas Pasha assumed the prime ministership again and formed a Wafdist cabinet which remained in power until the riots of January, 1952.

Before considering developments under Nahas Pasha's new administration, one solid accomplishment in 1949, the termination of the mixed courts in October, should be mentioned. Mixed courts were established in 1876 to handle cases involving foreigners, and their demise had been fixed by the 1937 treaty of Montreux. Transfer of cases and jurisdiction to Egyptian courts occasioned no difficulties or strains, mainly because of the excellence of Egyptian courts, the availability of Egyptians who had been sitting as judges in the mixed courts, and the membership and admission of most of their lawyers to the Egyptian bar. Egypt celebrated their ending, but paid tribute to the great public service rendered over the years by the mixed courts and openly recognized the "high tradition of judicial administration" left to Egypt as an invaluable legacy. However, these courts had become an anachronism, and their passing removed another vestige of the hated imperialism of the West.

SUEZ CANAL ZONE

Re-establishment of a Wafdist party government under Nahas Pasha immediately brought the Suez Canal zone and its British control into prominence. In part, the Suez Canal Company had agreed to terms with respect to the law of 1947 regarding companies engaged in business in Egypt. The Suez Canal Company consented to employ Egyptians for eighty percent of the technical positions and ninety percent of the administrative jobs. The number of Egyptian directors of the company was raised from two to seven out of a total membership of thirty-two; and seven percent of company profits, not to be less than £E350,000 annually, were paid to Egypt.

But foreign troops in the Canal Zone still caused a sore spot. Throughout 1950 Nahas Pasha toyed vaguely with the problem. A few conversations were exchanged with the British, but no real discussions were held. Finally, in November Nahas Pasha formally requested the British to leave the Sudan and the Suez Canal zone, but formal talks were not initiated until 1951. Meanwhile, suggestions for a regional-defense pact for the Middle East were informally broached and as quickly denounced as only a substitution of collective for British imperialism.

By October pressure within Egypt and the intractability of the British impelled Nahas, after innumerable warnings, to abrogate unilaterally the Anglo-Egyptian treaty of 1936 and the Anglo-Egyptian agreements of 1899 establishing the condominium over the Sudan. This drastic declaration brought forth within five days the British suggestion and invitation that Egypt become one of the founders, along with England, France, Turkey, and the United States, of a Middle East defense command similar in scope to the North Atlantic Treaty

Organization. Britain announced she was ready, if Egypt would form such a command, to abandon the Anglo-Egyptian treaty of 1936 and her rights therein to military establishments and troop bases in the Suez Canal zone.

Demonstrations, riots, and limited military engagements broke out at several points in the canal zone. Egypt protested that a Middle East defense command could not be accepted, since it would inevitably mean the presence of foreign troops in Egypt. Britain, on her part, stated frankly that troops and officials would remain in the Sudan and in the Suez Canal zone regardless of Egypt's unilateral denunciation of her international commitments. Incidents became more frequent; and on January 25, 1952 an engagement occurred at Ismailia involving 1500 British troops. More than forty Egyptians were killed.

RIOTS AND REVOLUTION

The following day, "Black Saturday," riots and demonstrations in Cairo, protesting the British actions, broke into a savage explosion against the British, foreigners, and authority. Damage ran into the tens of millions; Shepheard's Hotel was destroyed; and subversive elements tried to overturn the government. Martial law was hurriedly declared, and on January 27 King Faruk replaced Nahas Pasha by Ali Maher Pasha with directions to maintain security and order. Ahmad Husayn, the leader of Young Egypt (*Misr al-Fatah*), which had turned from its fascism of the 1930's to socialism, was arrested for plotting the demonstrations and abetting the riots.

After "Black Saturday" the situation remained tense. Ali Maher notified fifteen nations that his government regretted the losses and injuries sustained by their nationals, and a £E5,000,000 fund was created to cover damages to shops and property. He transferred the military-training programs for volunteers in the Muslim Brotherhood and Young Egypt to the ministries of war and navy and initialed a four-year plan to increase irrigation from the Nile. But his actions did not solve the immediate problems and were considered only half measures. In March Ahmad Nagib al-Hilali took his place. Parliament was suspended for thirty days, and later new elections were postponed. Conversations with the British over the Sudan and the canal zone were resumed, but were abandoned when the British declared they would recognize the king of Egypt as king of the Sudan only if the Sudanese likewise recognized him as their king. On June 29 Husayn Sirri became prime minister; and on July 21 al-Hilali returned to that post again, only to be turned out on July 23 by an army *coup d'état*, ostensibly led by Major General Muhammad Nagib.

In a broadcast to the nation General Nagib attacked corruption and bribery as the "main reason for our failure in the Palestine war; they are the main reason for troubles in Egypt's political and economic life." He went on to say that his group of officers sincerely believed that steps "were necessary to inspire the Egyptians with a new spirit and determination to go ahead and work toward fulfilling Egypt's national aspirations." These few words, whether his own or prepared for him, contained the significant principles of the revolution. King Faruk was forced to abdicate on July 26, 1952 in favor of his infant son, Prince Ahmad Fuad.

The army always contended that the defeat in Palestine occurred in Cairo and refused to shoulder the blame. When Cairo labeled the army as the scapegoat, the officers revolted, at the same time subscribing to the popular opinion that the economy and political life of the state had to be cleansed thoroughly before Egypt could become a modern state or hope to stand up against Israel. Revolution would lead to a full reformation of the state. Ali Maher was invited to form a civilian cabinet; all civilian titles were revoked; secret political-police sections of the royal and provincial governments were abolished; political prisoners were released; corrupt officials were dismissed and arrested; and censorship of the press was terminated. Elections for parliament were announced for February, 1953; and a land reform program drawn up by army leaders was submitted to the prime minister.

That measures for land reform came from army sources indicated that the Revolutionary Command Council (RCC), about which little was heard in the first weeks of the revolution, played a powerful role in events of the day. The RCC assumed that the disproportionate size of land holdings by a few was the prime cause of the abject poverty of the masses. The RCC was comprised of less than a score of officers from various branches of the services. Each officer of the council held the support of other officers, and thus the RCC acted as the governing body of the revolution. The most powerful leader of the RCC was Lt. Colonel Gamal Abd al-Nasser. General Nagib did not belong originally to the RCC but was picked by the officers to serve as their "front man." Both right wing (Muslim Brotherhood) and left wing (Communists, Socialists, and the renovated Young Egypt group of Ahmad Husayn) had their supporters among the officers and voices in the RCC.

In September, 1952 Ali Maher resigned as prime minister and Nagib took over, at the same time arresting fifty "former associates" of ex-King Faruk. Almost immediately the new cabinet decreed that all political parties be purged of corrupt leaders and reorganized within a month. At first the Wafd refused to comply, but later arranged to do so by elevating Nahas to honorary president. Four hundred and fifty army officers were dismissed, and a steady house cleaning began in the various ministries and bureaus of the government. Raids were made on homes of "hostile elements" in Cairo and Alexandria, and quantities of documents to use in prosecuting officials for inefficiency or malfeasance were carried off. The rector of al-Azhar University was replaced by a theologian friendly to the revolution. And in November Nagib was voted dictatorial powers until January.

In September, 1952 the cabinet decreed a new agrarian law, restricting land-ownership to 200 acres and stating that the government over the ensuing five years would expropriate excess lands, beginning with the largest estates. Compensation in the form of three percent thirty-year government bonds would be at the rate of ten times the rental value of the land. Until lands were seized by the government, owners would be taxed at a rate of five times their normal rates, although owners might sell lands in five-acre lots to farmers already owning less than ten acres. Land taken by the government was to be sold in two- to five-acre tracts to farmers owning less than five acres. The price was fixed at fifteen percent above the compensation price and was to be paid over a thirty-year period at three percent interest.

THE REPUBLIC OF EGYPT

It soon became obvious that the RCC had no special plans or program outlined when the revolution began. King Faruk had tried to close down the Officers' Club when the royal candidate for its presidency was defeated by the candidate backed by the "Free Officers" (RCC) group. The latter group was publicly noticed first in 1950, when parliament censured its existence. Acting before King Faruk destroyed it, the RCC believed that if it "turned the rascals out" all of Egypt's troubles would be ended and the whole nation would come forward and usher in a glorious regime for a better Egypt. Nasser wrote in his account of the revolution that the RCC soon learned, after waiting briefly for the Egyptian people to unite in such a task, that vigorous leadership was necessary to prevent chaos and accomplish its dream. The RCC revolution in Egypt was three revolutions in one: a "French Revolution," to get rid of a king and form a republic; an "American Revolution," to drive out the British; and a "Kemal Atatürk Revolution," to transform and regenerate the social and economic facets of an old civilization. For purposes of clarity and to avoid a chronological discussion of events on almost a day-to-day basis, each revolution will be examined singly. Yet the interplay of one revolution upon another and the basic complexity of the situation should never be overlooked in assessing the forces at work in Egypt in the period beginning in 1952.

Once the power of the army was established by the *coup d'état,* even though it worked through a civilian government, the influence and authority of the king vanished. The deposing and exile of King Faruk were simple matters of informing him that he had to go. Six weeks later army officers discovered that politicians were relatively unconcerned about the revolution and Nagib became prime minister, receiving supreme powers until January, 1953. Later, his powers were extended for another six months. The RCC, however, still entertained the idea that old-line political leaders were being "reconstructed." Most of these were released from jail; and Nagib and Mustafa Nahas, leader of the Wafd, met and publicly declared their peace. In December, 1952, upon the recommendation of a national committee appointed to consider the constitution, the constitution of 1923 was abolished and the draft of a new constitution requested. In March, 1953 the committee suggested the formation of a republic, which was declared on June 18, 1953. Nagib was acclaimed president and prime minister, and Nasser became deputy prime minister and minister of the interior of the parliamentary Egyptian republic.

The RCC announced that it would rule for a transitional three-year period, when parliamentary government would be established. In Cairo and Alexandria a large group of politically conscious citizens were conditioned by years of national agitation and training to be apprehensive of military dictatorships. They accepted the need of army action to rid the country of Faruk, but feared that soldiers would be loath to step aside once they learned to enjoy political power.

NAGIB AND NASSER

Nagib and Nasser heeded these susceptibilities. The numerous problems pressing for a solution afforded displaced politicians a fine opportunity for criticism. At the time of the *coup d'état* Colonel Rashid Muhanna of the RCC was a member of the Muslim Brotherhood and was selected as one of the regents for the infant king. Shaykh Hasan al-Bakuri of the Brotherhood executive served as minister of religious foundations in Nagib's first and succeeding cabinets. The Muslim Brotherhood was a powerful group. It was capable of organizing "spontaneous" demonstrations, and frequently made common cause with Communists, socialists, fascists, and Wafdists.

Communists were arrested from time to time, and new parties were created to evade the law requiring old parties to reorganize their leadership. In September, 1953 the government instituted a new revolutionary tribunal to try enemies of the state and particularly to crack down on an alliance formed by Communists, Wafdists, Saadists, and confederates of ex-King Faruk. Hasan al-Hudaibi, leader of the

Muslim Brotherhood, disclaimed any conflict with the RCC; but Nahas and his wife, Ibrahim Abd al-Hadi, former Saadist prime minister, Dr. Hafiz Afifi, former chief of the royal cabinet, and others were arrested, arraigned before the tribunal, and sentenced to long prison terms.

Extremists, however, did not surrender so easily. In January, 1954 serious fighting broke out between a group of the Muslim Brotherhood and the Liberation Rally, the youth organization sponsored by the RCC. In a six-day state of emergency which ensued the Muslim Brotherhood was dissolved; and seventy-eight of the members, including Hasan al-Hudaibi, were arrested. More Communists were jailed; and on February 25, 1954 the first showdown occurred between Nagib and Nasser. It appeared that Nagib was willing to make peace with the Brotherhood and some of the old political groupings, proceed immediately with the calling of parliamentary elections, and reinstitute civilian government. Nasser and his followers felt such a course would surely return the old crowd to power, defeat the revolution, and hurry the social and economic principles of the new order to an early grave.

Nasser, for the RCC, announced that Nagib had "resigned" from the presidency and the prime ministership "three days ago" and was confined to his house. Nasser became prime minister; but this development did not please the socialists, the Muslim Brotherhood, the Wafd, or any of the old-line or extreme political forces in Egypt. On February 27 Major Khalid Muhi al-Din, an avowed socialist, member of the RCC, and commander of the tank corps, appeared before Nasser and demanded that Nagib be reinstated. When Nasser ordered his arrest, the major coolly remarked that his officers at the tank park were at that moment preparing to launch an assault upon the RCC headquarters if their major was not back in their midst with an affirmative response within two hours.

Nasser gave in when an officer brought word that Muhi al-Din was not joking. The tanks were manned, the motors were running, and the ammunition was in place! Nagib returned to the presidency, but Nasser remained as prime minister. Sentiment for a civilian government was very strong, even in the army. Students demonstrated against the military regime; and the Egyptian bar, in a memorandum signed by one hundred leading Egyptian lawyers, asked for a return to civil rule. Nagib and Nasser called in Ali Maher, who after proper consultation announced on March 4, 1954 that a constituent assembly to which the military regime would turn over its authority would be called within three months. On March 8 Nagib became prime minister again and chief of the RCC, the office of which declared that power would be transferred to a civilian government on July 23, 1954.

Leaders of the Muslim Brotherhood, Nahas, and other politicians were released from arrest.

At the end of March the RCC threatened to resign, and Nasser and Major Salah Salim absented themselves from RCC meetings. The pressure was on, and Nasser emerged victorious. It was announced that the RCC would not relinquish its power and that elections would not be held until 1956, when the three-year transitional period terminated. In April Major Khalid Muhi al-Din went to Paris "on business for the RCC," and Nasser averred that Nagib had become the tool of dishonest politicians of the old regime. On April 18, 1954 Nasser again became prime minister and brought eight members of the RCC into the cabinet. In June nine officers of the tank corps were sentenced to fifteen-year prison terms; and in September five leaders of the Muslim Brotherhood were stripped of their Egyptian citizenship.

Following the signing of the agreement in October, 1954 with the British with respect to the evacuation of the Suez Canal zone, Nasser narrowly missed being assassinated by a member of the Muslim Brotherhood. The treaty was not tough enough for them! The mob immediately burned the Brotherhood headquarters, and four hundred of them, including Hasan al-Hudaibi, were arrested. President Nagib was relieved of his office on November 14, 1954 and placed under house arrest; it was charged that he co-operated with the Muslim Brotherhood and Communists in their attempt to overthrow Nasser and the RCC. A list of 133 "wanted" members of the Muslim Brotherhood was published, and the faculty at al-Azhar University denounced religious terrorists. Hasan al-Hudaibi and others went on trial, and six were hanged for complicity in the attempt on Nasser's life. The presidency was offered to a former cabinet minister and scholar, eighty-four-year-old Ahmad Lutfi al-Sayad; he declined the honor.

Shortly thereafter Nasser became acting president and in May, 1955 declared that parliamentary government would be restored as promised in 1956. When that time came Prime Minister Nasser introduced a draft constitution, which was submitted to a national plebiscite on June 23, 1956. Following its approval, the national assembly met and elected a president as the constitution provided. The public then voted, on July 7, 1956 its approval of the president, also as outlined in the constitution. These events transpired without any hitches; President Gamal Abd al-Nasser was duly elected and inaugurated as head of the Islamic Arab Republic of Egypt. Containing a full bill of rights and obligations for the individual and guaranteeing the economic, physical, legal, and moral welfare of Egyptian citizens, the constitution provided for a national assembly, elected for a term of five years, and a president who could dissolve the assembly, propose, veto, and promulgate laws, and appoint and dismiss civil, diplomatic, and military officials.

The transition from military rule to constitutional government appeared complete. However, the constitution of 1956 was drawn to place extraordinary power in the hands of the president. Thus, the change altered Nasser's title, but not his power. On the surface the wishes of a large segment of the populace of Cairo and Alexandria for civilian constitutional government were met; and the professed popularity of President Nasser in his heroic acts of the summer of 1956 belied, at least for some time, doubts regarding the success of the transition and its permanence.

THE SUDAN AND SUEZ

The second aspect of the Egyptian revolution was, as one American observer aptly phrased it, "Turning out the Redcoats." Two phases dominated the operation: freeing the Sudan and obtaining full sovereignty over the canal zone. Prime Minister Nagib was especially favored to accomplish the former. His mother was Sudanese, and no one dared accuse him of being negligent in pressing Egyptian interests in the Sudan. In 1952 Nagib held conversations with various Sudanese party leaders and signed an agreement approving the establishment of self-government in the Sudan by the end of 1952. Anthony Eden announced that Great Britain subscribed in principle to Nagib's arrangement, and on February 12, 1953 an Anglo-Egyptian agreement was entered into in Cairo ending the condominium of 1899. Although Nagib gave the Sudan the opportunity of choosing not to become federated with Egypt, the minister of national guidance, Major Salah Salim, included Sudanese affairs in his responsibility and by several excursions to Khartoum endeavored to influence developments there along a course advantageous to Cairo.

The signing of this Anglo-Egyptian agreement served as a step in solving Suez difficulties. Negotiations with the British were reopened in April but were broken off summarily, again over conditions upon which British and Allied troops might return. Talks were resumed but the deadlock seemed impassable. After Nagib returned from a pilgrimage to Mecca, a sixth meeting was held on September 1, 1953, and agreement was reached on four points: an Egyptian would command the bases in the canal zone; his deputy, a technical adviser, would be a Britisher and would receive orders from London as well as from the commander; 4000 British technicians would remain until Egyptians were trained to take over; and the British garrison would depart from the zone eighteen months after full agreement was reached and ratified.

Still, the problem of the technicians' garb and the return of the troops produced a stalemate. Nasser berated Great Britain, accusing her of backtracking in her negotiations and publicly declaring that British troops could have an automatic right of return in the case of an act of aggression against any member of the Arab League security pact (all except Libya). In November he asserted that Egypt could compromise no further on this issue—England was holding out for Turkey, too. In March, 1954 Nasser gave in on the inclusion of Turkey on condition that technicians not wear uniforms. To Egypt, uniforms meant foreign soldiers, and no Egyptian political negotiator could ever convince Egyptian nationalists that British rule was ended if British soldiers remained. To the British uniforms meant that individuals would not be subject to Egyptian law. (The question of retirement pay, army seniority, and other matters of military or civilian status also figured in the discussion.)

In July negotiations moved to high-level discussions. Antony Head, British war secretary, went to Cairo; and President Eisenhower sent a letter to President Nagib stating that "simultaneously" with the signing of an Anglo-Egyptian accord on the Suez Canal zone the United States would enter into "firm agreements" with Egypt for economic assistance to strengthen the Egyptian armed forces. An agreement in principle was made on July 27, 1954, although the formal arrangement, which comprised a thirteen-article document, two annexes, seventeen exchanges of notes, and an agreed minute, was not signed until October. There were five main points: British troops would be withdrawn by June 18, 1956; the Anglo-Egyptian treaty of 1936 was abrogated; Britain or her allies would be afforded facilities for the entry of troops into Egypt in case of an attack upon Arab League states or Turkey; each party pledged to uphold the Constantinople convention of 1888 guaranteeing freedom of navigation of the canal; and the duration of the agreement would be seven years. The American role in bringing a settlement between Cairo and London was generally recognized, and three weeks after the signing of the formal Suez documents Egypt and the United States entered into an arrangement whereby Egypt would receive a grant of $40,000,000 for the modernization of her economy. The United States also consented to consider proposals concerning construction of a high dam at Aswan, an offer which started quite a different chain of events.

The Suez Canal zone treaty was hailed everywhere as a great achievement on the road to general peace throughout the world.

Extremist groups in Egypt deplored the signing of any agreement with Britain and tried to assassinate Nasser for his part in it. More significantly, the departure of the British troops, which occurred on schedule, created a power vacuum in the canal zone. Egypt had grandiose ideas of filling the vacuum herself, but her military strength and industrial potential excluded such a possibility for years to come. At the ceremonies of exaltation on the day of the final departure the principal guest of honor in Egypt was the Soviet minister of foreign affairs, Shepilov, whose presence indicated the Soviet hopes in occupying the place vacated by the British!

ARMS FOR EGYPT

When Egypt entered into the Suez agreement with England, Nasser expected to arm and operate the military establishments in the zone. Modern military machines, however, were so costly that only a nation with a large heavy industrial capacity could afford the matériel unless purchased at a nominal price representing only a fraction of the real cost. Nasser undoubtedly recognized this; for Egyptian officials in conversations in Washington revealed that Eisenhower's letter was interpreted as the prelude to an arrangement between the United States and Egypt similar in character and scope to the American program in Turkey, where nearly a billion dollars had been spent by the American government.

Requests for arms aid, specific and general, were forwarded to Washington. But no action was taken. Prior to the settlement over the Suez Canal zone the United States granted specific sums for land reclamation and small irrigation projects; and after the signing of the agreement an offer of $40,000,000 was made for improving the general economy. But little was forthcoming for the army. Israel and her American friends objected strenuously; and Nasser was unable for internal political reasons to enter into agreements such as Turkey had with the United States.

Thus, receiving little military aid from the West, Colonel Nasser turned to the Soviet bloc. Because of the unsettled frontier with Israel Egypt felt insecure. Moreover, Nasser's power rested on army officers who demanded first-rate equipment. If he could not satisfy them, they would turn to someone else who would promise that kind of arms. Unless Egypt had arms of sufficient quantity and quality she could not expect the Powers to believe that she could maintain and operate the bases along the canal. Egypt would control and man the defenses of the zone; the Powers would furnish the matériel and the finances!

Consequently, Nasser announced on September 27, 1955 that an arrangement had been concluded with Czechoslovakia to obtain arms in exchange for cotton. (Later he admitted that the agreement was with the U.S.S.R.) Subsequently, at least two hundred MIG jet fighters, one hundred tanks, six submarines, and varying amounts of artillery, smaller arms, and ammunition were obtained. The first deliveries came from Europe and the Far East and were unloaded in October at Alexandria and Suez. Egyptian and neighboring Arab nationalists rejoiced over the news, since they interpreted the turn of events to mean that they were more independent of the Western imperialist powers and could at their own convenience attack Israel, the satellite of those same powers. Whether or not Nasser could prevent Egypt from falling into the grip of the Soviet bloc, as he asserted he would, only the passage of several years could tell.

NASSER SEEKS TO DOMINATE THE MIDDLE EAST

The absence of peace between Israel and Egypt remained constant under Nagib and Nasser, as it had under their immediate predecessors. The pattern of infiltrations, border raids, reprisals, bombings, protests, threats, accusations, and denunciations was unchanged. Israeli boats and ships of other nations laden with cargo for Israel were denied passage through the canal on the score that Israel was not at peace with Egypt and that goods which would aid an enemy could legally be denied transit through the canal in so far as it was a part of Egyptian territory.

Perhaps the most serious incident occurred on the night of February 28, 1955, when Israelis at half-battalion strength fell upon Egyptian positions near the outskirts of Gaza, killing 38 and wounding 31. Whatever may have been the reason for the attack, it had the effect of forcing Nasser to obtain arms somewhere, regardless of price or strings. This act above all others drove Egypt to the Soviet arms deal.

With regard to the other states of the Middle East Nagib and Nasser looked upon themselves as natural leaders and sought to augment the dominant role of Egypt. Egypt had the largest population and with the exception of Lebanon, was by far the most Westernized Arab state. Her newspapers, movies, radio, universities, industry, and commerce outstripped those in other Arab countries. Naturally, Arabs turned to Nasser for leadership. "Free Officer" or "RCC" groups sprang up in Syria and Jordan, and Nasser gave their leaders encouragement and assistance.

With Arab League headquarters and staff located in Cairo and most of its council meetings held there, the natural tendency for Arab political leaders to gravitate to Egypt encouraged Nasser's aggressive stand. Although Major Salah Salim conferred with Arab officials at every capital, the Cairo newspapers and radio exercised an influence

portentous in character through the Arabic-speaking world. Nationalism sponsored and disseminated by those media always was Arab in
scope, rarely Egyptian. In fact, Egyptian nationalism and Arab nationalism were equated; a Syrian or an Iraqi national who proposed any
course of action in the interests of his own nation which might run
contrary to the interests of Egypt was immediately branded, even in
his own country, as opposing Arab national interests.

When information leaked out that Iraq was contemplating turning
her Turkish treaty of friendship into an effective military alliance
under the aegis of the West, Nasser urged the rejection of such a step
and in February, 1955 threatened to destroy the Arab League if Nuri
al-Said proceeded with his plans. After the Baghdad pact became a
reality, agreement was reached in March at Damascus among Egypt,
Syria, and Saudi Arabia for an alliance; and in April, 1956 Egypt
engineered the Jidda pact, which allied her to Saudi Arabia and
Yemen.

Meanwhile, in October, 1955 Nasser entered into mutual defense
pacts with Syria and Saudi Arabia, establishing machinery for joint
commands which expectedly would be in Egyptian hands. With Syria
Nasser agreed to bear sixty-five percent of the expenses, while with
Saudi Arabia each would pay the costs to the extent of her own participation. In December, 1955, when Amman was pressed to join the
Baghdad pact, Egyptian radio newscasts warned Jordan of the villainy
of such a move and subsequently aided Colonel Ali Abu Nuwar in the
increase of his political and military stature in Jordan.

Nasser and the Arab League also looked with sympathy upon the
actions and aspirations of Arab nationalists in Morocco, Algeria, and
Tunisia; and funds were collected and sent to help them achieve their
goals. With regard to Cyprus Nasser staunchly supported the idea of
self-determination, since that course obviously would drive the British
from the island. Cypriot terrorists obtained bombs and munitions in
Egypt; and public pronouncements favored union of Cyprus and
Greece. In the Sudan Egyptian policy was less successful. Once the
Sudanese attained self-government and release from Great Britain, the
experience of freedom was so sweet they hesitated to exchange it for
Egyptian control. Political parties favorable to federation with Egypt
cooled their ardor, and political leaders enjoyed the prerogatives of
cabinet offices. In April, 1955 no agreement was reached over division
or use of Nile water for power and irrigation, and in the program
concerning the construction of the high dam at Aswan no discussions
were undertaken over creation of the lake which would inundate a
considerable area in the Sudan. Major Salah Salim, most active in
pursuing Egyptian policies in the Sudan, was relieved of his post in

August, 1955. He was replaced by Fathi Ridwan, an ardent nationalist who in earlier days had been a follower of Ahmad Husayn's fascist Young Egyptian "Green Shirts," a socialist, and a "fellow traveler."

Nasser's most caustic wrath was reserved for Nuri al-Said, his arch-enemy and the architect of the Baghdad pact. More than rivalry between Nuri and Nasser was involved. It was a rivalry between Baghdad and Cairo, and between Iraq and Egypt for leadership in the Arab world—a competition extending back into history to medieval and early Muslim periods and into antiquity as far as records go. The Middle East had become more power conscious than ever before, and all looked with appreciation and understanding to what the American aid program was accomplishing in Turkey. Nasser evidently expected an "Eisenhower-Dulles Doctrine" for Egypt as a reward for signing the treaty with the British in 1954, a treaty which he entered into with great personal risk. His enemies were ready to murder him for signing any treaty with Britain, and they referred to him scathingly as Gamal Abd al-Dulles. Suddenly he feared the tables were turned. Nuri al-Said had aligned with Turkey and the West, and the military aid program would strengthen an Iraq already witnessing the first pleasures of national exhilaration from development programs and oil royalties. Cairo broadcasts vilified Nuri as a British agent and beamed at Baghdad calumnies against his leadership, virtually inviting Iraqis to rejoin the Arab nation, which, of course, meant return to Egyptian leadership. Revolution did not occur in Iraq, although sentiment in favor of the pact and the position of Nuri was greatly shaken.

EGYPTIAN AFFAIRS

In other fields of activity the revolutionary forces were equally engaged. Many leaders of the new government under Nagib and Nasser contemplated establishing a secular government, but discovered that they had to proceed cautiously toward such a goal because of the power of the Muslim Brotherhood. Individuals among them spoke privately of the need for a Muslim reformation, and after curtailment of the Muslim Brotherhood in 1954 a more open policy was pursued. Muslim and non-Muslim religious courts in Egypt were abolished in 1956, and cases pending in those courts and all others of similar nature were heard in secular Egyptian courts. The decree did not repudiate Sacred Law but henceforth precepts of Sacred Law were interpreted by civil judges.

Social developments were not entirely forgotten, and contributions of the revolution in the field of social welfare for the masses may in the long run be the most beneficial aspects of the new regime. A minimum wage for agricultural workers was set, and relief programs for the destitute were inaugurated. Village schools were built, teacher training extended, health services widened, and many projects instituted for agricultural improvement in the way of seeds, breeding stock, and fertilizers. Industrial areas, which have grown in a few localities, were not neglected; and social workers were employed to begin the monumental task of aiding new factory workers to make the adjustment from village life to the strange ways of an urban center.

When Nagib announced his *coup d'état*, he blamed corruption and bribery for the ills that beset Egypt. Dismissal of inefficient and corrupt officials was approved, and a special court was established to try cases of corruption. Trials began in 1953, starting with Fuad Sarag al-Din, former minister of interior and finance in the Wafd government. The graft committee pressed charges against him, alleging that he had manipulated the cotton market for his private profit to the extent of £E22,000,000. Through the summer of 1953 the graft committee ferreted out all kinds of irregularities and arrested ex-prime minister Ibrahim al-Hadi, Nahas's wife, and even Faruk's press officer on the embezzlement of £E14,000. Much publicity was given to these trials and proceedings, mainly to demonstrate the sincerity and fervor of the revolution and reduce the natural tendency toward corrupt governmental practices.

The population in Egypt in 1956 numbered about 22,000,000 and was increasing by 500,000 every year. Without a parallel increase in economic output the standard of living remained in a most precarious state. Thus, the most pressing problems for Nasser were economic. The marketing of cotton, the great cash crop of Egypt, and its world price concerned every government of Egypt since the end of World War II. In 1948 when cotton prices were high, Egypt bartered 38,000 tons of cotton for 211,000 tons of Russian wheat. The Egyptian government supported the cotton market at levels frequently above world prices and thus resorted to the expedient of exchanging cotton for foodstuffs, which were likewise priced above the world market. Rather than grow wheat and other edible crops which peasants might surreptitiously eat absentee landlords preferred to produce cotton, control its marketing, and be easily assured of full delivery of the crops on the part of the peasants. Again in 1952 Egypt bartered $25,000,000 of cotton for $22,000,000 of Russian wheat.

So anxious on the question of land distribution were the leaders that after the departure of King Faruk they brought forth precipitously the land reform measures. Implementation, however, progressed slowly. In December, 1952 a loan of £E200,000,000 at three percent for thirty years was authorized to finance land transfers, but in four years less than 200,000 acres were appropriated by the government and put into the hands of the peasants. Landowner opposition and likelihood of reduced production on broken estates deterred a government already hard pressed by the realities of politics and economics.

In 1953 a five-year development plan was announced, and a newly created permanent national resources development board called for $60,000,000 to irrigate 37,000 acres of new land, distribute better wheat and hybrid corn seeds, and improve roads in the Nile Delta. Plans were also advanced for the reclamation of another 80,000 acres of land at a cost of $25,000,000, of which the United States would contribute $10,000,000. The greatest plan of all, of course, was the great dam at Aswan, which would take years to construct and cost hundreds of millions of pounds, but it would irrigate approximately two million acres. It was obvious to all, however, that the economic situation in Egypt could not wait for the completion of such a project.

Egypt needed power for industry, irrigation pumps, and the machines concomitant with a modern society. Advancement of hydroelectric power development at Aswan was furthered in 1953 by the acceptance of a French bid of £E10,141,000. The exploration and discovery of oil in commercial quantities had long been hoped for in Egypt, but foreign concerns were discouraged by the severe laws in regard to foreign companies. New laws were enacted more favorable for the investment of foreign capital, and in 1954 a thirty-year concession was granted for the exploitation of oil in the western desert to the Coronada Petroleum Corporation of New York, which agreed to spend a minimum of $8,000,000 for exploration within six years. Another concession was awarded to the Egyptian Oil Exploration Company, a subsidiary of the Cities Service Company of New York. Oil was found in 1955 in the Sinai Peninsula, where the National Petroleum Company brought in a well for which it claimed a production of 3,000 barrels a day. Although this amount, if developed, would have an annual output equal to only one day's production in either Saudi Arabia or Kuwayt, it was hoped that wider and continued exploration would locate enough oil to satisfy Egyptian needs.

Reforms, social measures, expanded government services, strengthening of the army, and irrigation and hydroelectric programs increased the size of annual budgets, even when longer-range capital-improvement projects were excluded. The regular budget for expenditures for the year 1955–56 stood at over £E315,000,000. Income from taxes and other sources, though not fully published, obviously fell behind the outgo. Nasser resorted to loans rather than to increased tax collections. Finding opposition from the National Bank of Egypt to extensive borrowing, Nasser issued a decree in 1955 requiring all directors over sixty years of age to be dismissed from the boards of Egyptian companies.

This law was specifically designed to remove from the bank those opposed to his financial policies. Thereafter the government borrowed £E300,000,000 to support the cotton market and incidentally bartered some of the purchased cotton for wheat and arms. Other sums went for various projects and to commence work at Aswan. Money in circulation jumped by thirty percent. A flight of capital from Egypt was the immediate result. Inflation showed its head, gold balances dropped, and wealthy Egyptians turned their cash into any goods that could be purchased. Thus, by 1956 the economy of Egypt had become subject to fluctuations and the vagaries of weakness.

The economic pressures in Egypt, which the old regime largely ignored and which in the absence of any national or moral inspiration brought its downfall, were still present to crowd in upon Nasser and his government. He described himself as a "man in a hurry" and warned that "the longer I take to do things the less time I will have to accomplish them." Many things that Nasser, the RCC, and the dedicated men about them wished to do were long-range affairs requiring twenty or forty years to effect. But peasants and the lower classes of the cities would not wait for the better life unless they could have some concrete assurance that it would come and at least a small down payment on it immediately. Also, the old ex-pasha and wealthy landowner, who found his income diminished, the bulk of his lands seized, the cotton market no longer "rigged" in his favor, his taxes collected, and his name reviled, distrusted the new order as long as he could not see an "obvious and irrefutable national good" resulting immediately from his own discomfiture.

HIGH DAM AT ASWAN

It behooved Nasser to give an earnest demonstration of the "promised future." Construction of the high dam at Aswan was carefully and gloriously pictured as the rational step to revolutionize the Egyptian standard of living. Two million acres of new land would be irrigated and almost limitless kilowatt hours of electricity generated. Upper Egypt would become industrialized and relieve the population pressure. This, joined to a thirty percent increase in arable land, would give Egypt a balanced and healthy economy. At a cost of six, seven, or perhaps even nine hundred million dollars over a period of ten to fifteen years the dam could be built.

The Egyptian economy was too poor to build the dam itself. The extra reserve was not there. A charge of seventy or eighty million dollars a year taken from the living of the people would lower the standards beyond endurance. Furthermore, an estimated two hundred million dollars in foreign exchange would be required in the early stages of construction to import necessary equipment and materials. Dreams of the high dam at Aswan circulated for a number of years, and in 1954 current plans for Nile development included such an undertaking. The United States government admitted an interest, and discussions with regard to its feasibility and financing grew more serious. The possibility of a loan of $200,000,000 from the International Bank was investigated.

Talks on these subjects were held in Washington in 1955. The arms deal with the Soviet bloc had already been announced and consummated by some shipments. These events gave rise to fiery denunciations of the West, and Nasser defiantly warned that his acquisition of arms must not lead to Western shipments of arms to Israel. At the same time Egyptians and the Arab world were treated to bitter harangues against the Western Powers on the creation of the Baghdad pact and the invitation for Jordan to join.

Nasser's government already had trade pacts or barter arrangements with Czechoslovakia, Communist China, East Germany, Hungary, Rumania, and the U.S.S.R. The West looked upon these as economic necessities for Egypt and regarded Nasser's ranting against Great Britain and the United States as bombast for domestic consumption. In spite of these factors, therefore, the United States offered in December, 1955 to grant $56,000,000 to Egypt to strengthen her internal economy on the basis that work on the high dam would begin, and Great Britain agreed to release £5,000,000 for the same purpose. Although the American Congress refused to consider the proposal that the Egyptian grant be made annually for the ensuing ten years, there was an understanding that such a course was more than likely. With the American grant it also became apparent that Egypt's economy would be considered strong enough to warrant a $200,000,000 loan from the International Bank, which approved the Egyptian application in February, 1956.

At this juncture Nasser appeared to have been triumphant. He had obtained from the U.S.S.R. the arms his soldiers were demanding and at the same time was offered approximately $900,000,000 over a ten-year period to build the dream of every educated Egyptian. Egypt stood where Turkey had stood in 1947, and the promise of the future was even brighter.

But Nasser failed to grasp the opportunity. His basic ignorance of the West, his inexperience in politics, economics, and foreign affairs, and the weakness of his advisers led him astray. It was announced that the U.S.S.R. was also offering to finance the building of the high dam at Aswan "with no strings attached." Authority for this notice became uncertain, as the Russians at a later date maintained that they never made such an offer. Nasser continued to deliver emotional diatribes against the West, complaining of the humiliating "strings" demanded by the United States, and consummated new trade pacts with Communist China, Bulgaria, and North Vietnam. To the West it appeared that Nasser was courting the Soviet bloc in order to increase the grants from the West. Public discussion of the high dam financing and the pledge of cotton crops to the Soviet bloc in payment for arms created in the minds of Western leaders doubts as to the wisdom of proceeding with the construction. Political and economic conditions in Egypt deteriorated. News was more rigidly controlled, and a feeling of insecurity spread among Nasser's supporters.

On June 18, 1956 the last contingent of British soldiers departed from Suez in accordance with the treaty of 1954. Foreign Minister Shepilov of the U.S.S.R. was the honored guest of the three-day celebration. In his speeches and those of Nasser opprobrium was heaped upon the West; and Shepilov declared that the U.S.S.R. was happy to see the end of political and military imperialism and encouraged Nasser to work to remove economic colonialism as manifested in the Arab world by the oil companies.

These attacks by Nasser and his open embrace of the Soviet bloc paralleled a further worsening of the Egyptian economic state. In March, 1956 another loan of £E25,000,000 was floated, expenditures continued to exceed income, charges for sustaining the expanding military establishment mounted, and gold balances dropped sharply. The situation in Egypt was growing tense, and Western leaders began to entertain doubts about the ability of Nasser and his close coterie of friends to maintain their authority. Thus, in July, 1956 when the Egyptian ambassador to Washington returned from Cairo with instructions to notify the American government of Egypt's readiness to accept the American offer to build the high dam at Aswan, Secretary of State Dulles abruptly informed him on July 19 that times and conditions had changed and that the United States had withdrawn the offer.

NATIONALIZATION OF THE SUEZ CANAL

The manner in which the notice was given advertised the fact that a calculated rebuff was intended, perhaps to downgrade Nasser's reputation as Washington had downgraded Mosaddeq's in 1953. Immediately the political situation in Egypt and the Middle East became critical. Attacks upon the West were scurrilous in tone, and disappointment in Egypt was very real. Nasser struck back by nationalizing the Suez Canal Company on July 26, 1956. He had raised great expectations in Egypt on the building of the dam. He had overplayed his hand and all Egypt and the Arab world knew it. Without some dramatic coup he was lost. The Suez Canal provided the answer. President Nasser, in his declaration, stated that Egyptian officials had taken over the company offices in Egypt, ordered all employees to stay on the job, asserted that the canal would remain open and operate as usual, and explained nationalization would permit use of the $100,-000,000 annual profit to build the Aswan Dam.

The boldness, excitement, and drama of the action were heady capsules for the Arabs and a much needed tonic for Nasser's prestige. When England and France threatened to use force against Egypt, all of the Arab states, as well as Russia and India, rallied to Nasser's support. Workmen in Iraq, Kuwayt, Jordan, Syria, and Lebanon pledged to cut the oil pipelines if the West attacked Egypt.

Nationalization of the Suez Canal Company had been contemplated in previous years by other Egyptian governments. At the end of World War II Egypt unsuccessfully offered to buy, with some of her blocked sterling, the canal shares held by Britain. The 1949 agreement guaranteed Egypt £E350,000 annually from the company or seven percent of the gross profits, whichever was greater; and many employees were Egyptian nationals. In 1955, although gross revenues in tolls from the canal operations were nearly $100,000,000, the figure cited by Nasser, profits were only $31,000,000 and the Egyptian share was $2,170,000.

According to terms of the concession, ownership of the canal would revert to the Egyptian government in 1968, at which time the government would purchase the assets of the company. The company had begun to arrange its affairs for that eventuality by disposing of unnecessary properties. Some of its profits, however, were held in reserve; and in May, 1956 the company upon pressure from Nasser agreed to invest some $60,000,000 of reserves in Egyptian development projects.

Since the end of World War II the tonnage and ships using the canal increased each year, especially with the phenomenal growth in oil shipments from the Persian Gulf to western Europe. The company drew up plans for widening and deepening the canal to accommodate the larger tankers which shippers were building. Already oil companies had ordered a few 80,000-ton tankers which could transport oil around Africa as cheaply as two smaller ones using the quicker and shorter route through Suez.

The canal was the subject of the international Constantinople convention of 1888 in which free passage of the waterway was guaranteed in peace and war to all ships. Egypt, however, was held to be the custodian of the canal's security; and Article X stated that the provisions of the convention "shall not interfere" with steps Egypt "might find it necessary to take for security . . . the defense of Egypt and the maintenance of public order." Until 1954 it was recognized that Great Britain was the protector of the canal; but Egypt, using Article X of the convention, had acted since 1948 to deny passage of the canal to Israeli shipping, and by inaction on this point the powers condoned the Egyptian interference with Israeli use of the canal.

Reaction in the West, especially in England and France, to the nationalization was precipitous. Naval units were moved to the eastern Mediterranean, troops were readied, and paratroopers were rushed to Cyprus. In London and Paris government leaders pointed out that Nasser by the seizure was assuming a position along the vital artery of world commerce and that he would be able to close the route at his whim and thus subject western Europe to a kind of economic blackmail. The bulk of the oil consumed in western Europe was Middle Eastern oil, sixty percent of which passed through the canal. It was charged that Nasser violated international treaties and ignored the international character of the canal.

The issue resolved itself into four main points. Paramount was the ability of Egypt at some unforeseen moment to close the canal, raise rates, or deny entry to ships of a single state and thus jeopardize the security and well-being of any nation. As Nasser had been able to do that for quite some time, nationalization of the canal hardly changed the status or the international conditions of the waterway or its transit. Secondly, genuine concern was felt in many quarters over the question of whether or not Egypt could manage the intricate operations of the canal and maintain its efficiency. Expert opinion, however, held that Egypt would be able to run the canal with a modicum of co-operation and good will. A third and very significant factor involved prestige. It appeared to the Western public that Nasser had, with support from the Soviet bloc and neutralist India, gained a diplomatic victory. The fourth and most telling component of nationalization arose from its avowed purpose of obtaining a munificent income and the invidious inference that the canal company had reaped exorbitant profits. In 1955 slightly over thirty-one percent of the gross revenues showed as profits, a percentage exceedingly high in relationship to most companies. Two-thirds of the profits, however, were set aside for improvements on the canal. Therefore, unless Nasser could run the canal more economically than the company and was willing to forego capital expenditures, profits from the canal would not go far in building the high dam.

Under nationalization operation of the canal continued and ships passed through as usual. Egyptian funds were frozen in England, France, and the United States; and Egypt permitted British and

French companies to pay tolls for their ships into Suez Canal Company accounts in Paris and London. Hurriedly, a twenty-four nation conference in London devised a plan whereby Egypt would own the canal, but an international body in accordance with an international treaty would operate and control it. Although agreeing to maritime states advising on the operations of the canal, Nasser politely rejected the proposal and insisted on "the sovereign right of Egypt to run the canal." Thereupon, England and France applied further pressure upon canal operations by inducing many British and French pilots to quit their jobs, hoping thereby to prove that Egypt could not run it. Next, the London group, led by Secretary Dulles, formed a Suez Canal Users' Association (SCUA), which would employ its own pilots, navigate its own boats, pay for all upkeep of the canal, and give Egypt a fee for its use. Nasser vehemently declared that imposition of SCUA would mean war.

As time passed, opportunity grew for a reasonable settlement and the boats were still going through the canal. It was illogical to deny that Egypt had the sovereign right to nationalize the Suez Canal Company, and no action was being taken in violation of the Constantinople convention of 1888. Moreover, Nasser became less bold, as Arab opinion cooled. Iraq, Kuwayt, and Saudi Arabia were suspicious of references in his speeches to "Arab oil" as if it belonged to Egypt. They resented the fact that he took this step without conferring with other Arab League states and were apprehensive lest oil production would be curtailed and their royalties reduced. Nasser's coup with regard to the canal appeared less startling and less successful, and it became apparent to all that revenue from the canal would never build the high dam at Aswan, which still appealed to most as the only first-rate project to solve Egypt problems. In October, 1956 each side to the dispute brought the matter to the security council of the United Nations, where agreement was reached on six basic principles for the canal's operation. Accepted by England, France, and Egypt, these six principles were an equitable compromise devised as a "face-saving" program for all.

THE SINAI WAR

Emotionalism aroused by the keen disappointment over the Aswan Dam fiasco and the obvious success in the Suez triumph waned, and diplomats believed that "reason" through these six principles, largely drafted at the United Nations, would prevail. The calm, however, was rudely upset by the Israeli invasion of Sinai on October 29, 1956. Many of the aspects of this event and the British and French plot, using the Israelis as a willing foil, have been discussed in the preceding chapter.

As surprising as was this attack to the world public, many foreign
offices and military intelligences were well aware that forceful pressure
of strength was being mobilized by England, France, and Israel to
apply to Egypt, perhaps with the expectation that Nasser's regime
would collapse and Egyptian sovereignty would again become the
weak reed it had been under Faruk. Britain and France had agreed at
their secret conclave at Sèvres to enter the war in not less than four
days after the Israeli attack, and the ultimatum that they delivered to
Egypt and Israel on October 30 calling for a halt to the war and
insisting that each withdraw from positions ten miles from the canal
was in part a ruse to cloak their collusion and in part to enable them to
occupy the canal area without Egyptian resistance. Aware of the
French air force participation in the war from the start and the build-
up of British contingents in Cyprus, Nasser early in the war ordered
his troops to fall back to positions west of the canal, grounded some of
his planes, and sent the rest to bases in Saudi Arabia. Nasser refused
the ultimatum and the powers entered the fray. Air attacks on November 2 shocked the entire world and precipitated meetings of the
Security Council, which called for an immediate ceasefire. Co-operation by naval forces and paratroopers brought the fall of Port Said,
whereupon the U.S.S.R. warned that she was prepared to use force if
need be to obtain the withdrawal of Western and Israeli troops from
Egypt. In the face of sharp words from the United States and the
U.S.S.R. a ceasefire was ordered on November 7, and United Nations
observers entered the canal area the next day. British and French
evacuation commenced in December upon the arrival of the United
Nations Emergency Force (UNEF), and Israel withdrew from Sinai
in January. Only after severe pressure from the United States in March
did Israel give up her hold on the Gaza Strip and the Straits of Tiran.
United Nations salvage crews cleared the canal, which Egypt had
blocked in several places during the war, and shipping was resumed in
April.

Upon Egypt the effects of this episode were incalculable. A large
part of the arms recently acquired from the Soviets was lost in Sinai,
and the Egyptian army was again said to be weak and unprepared.
The Western world and the Middle East were blanketed with accounts
of the rapidity and apparent ease with which the tough and highly-
trained Israeli army had occupied Sinai and much was made of the
phrase, "one hundred hours to Suez," without examining the role the
expected British and French invasions had upon Egyptian strategy.
The destruction in Port Said, the damages in Sinai, and the loss of
revenue from Suez operations were severe blows to the national
economy. Had not the United States and the U.S.S.R. rescued Egypt,

Nasser would have fallen to the British, French, and Israeli attack, Egyptian and Arab pride would have suffered enormously, Israel would have held Sinai including the Straits of Tiran, England would have returned to her position astride the canal, and armed aggression would have been shown to be profitable.

Curiously, however, Nasser assumed a bold posture and emerged from the disaster stronger than ever. All Arab nations rallied publicly and diplomatically to his side; and in January, 1957 he arranged the Arab solidarity pact, whereby Jordan could throw off her British financial shackles to become the ward of Syria, Saudi Arabia, and Egypt. Interpreted realistically, this meant Nasser's paramountcy in Jordanian affairs. Simultaneously, Nasser decreed the "Egyptianization" of seven banks and seventeen insurance companies owned by British and French interests. Stockholders and directors, henceforth, must be native-born Egyptian citizens. Though he lost out in Jordan in April and King Saud pursued a reserved course after a trip to Washington, Nasser grew more popular with the Arab masses throughout the Middle East.

During the crisis Britain and the United States froze sterling and dollar balances, a step which proved a real hardship on Egyptian trade and industry and drove Nasser more definitely into the Soviet economic orbit. A barter of agricultural products for 500,000 tons of Soviet oil was arranged in March. A credit of £E20,000,000 was secured from Czechoslovakia. In November General Amer revealed in Moscow the receipt of 700,000,000 rubles in economic and military aid to be paid over a five-year period at 2½ percent interest. And in 1958 Nasser made an extensive tour of the U.S.S.R., during which Khrushchev promised him all the aid necessary in uniting the Arab people.

After Israeli troops left Gaza, relations between Egypt and the West improved. Shortly, negotiations for compensation of Suez Canal Company shareholders were initiated in Rome, and after much parleying among the several categories of holders agreement was reached in 1958 for a payment of £E28,300,000. Egyptian authorities operated the canal efficiently, and the International Bank explored the economic feasibility of widening the canal to permit constant two-way traffic. Egyptian bank balances were released, and the question of building the high dam at Aswan was again pondered. The International Bank agreed to reconsider the project, and in 1958 British engineers discussed the complexities of its construction. West Germany advanced credits of 400,000,000 marks to develop Egyptian industry, the first realization of which appeared in the German-constructed steel mill at Helwan. That the numerous Soviet barter deals fettered Egyptian exports to the West was implied in a decree of March, 1958, allowing a discount of twenty-three percent on cotton export prices to hard-currency countries.

Following the Sinai war Egyptian politics remained unsettled. Early in 1957 Doria Shafiq, a zealous feminist, called for an end to the dictatorship in Egypt, but firm control of the state was not relaxed. Yet, pressure for some show of democratic action gave rise to a call for elections to a national assembly having 350 seats. Only one political party, the National Union, was permitted, and Nasser became its head. However, 5,000,000 voted in July and contests were so close in many districts that run-offs were required in about two-thirds of the constituencies.

THE UNITED ARAB REPUBLIC

In Arab politics, however, the year 1958 was one of remarkable developments. Provisions of the various pacts which Egypt had entered into with other Arab governments stipulated that unified military command rested in Egyptian hands. Thus, in 1957 when the Syrian-Turkish crisis unrolled, Egyptian troops were sent to Syria and their three naval transports lingered at Latakia for several weeks. Their presence in Syria insured a peaceful birth of the United Arab Republic. Certain Syrian groups had long favored a merger with Egypt, and Nasser's Radio Cairo carried to every Syrian village a vigorous propaganda for uniting all Arabs. Communist and Soviet inroads into Syrian political life advanced so rapidly that Syrian leaders recognized their only salvation in combining with Egypt. The rush of events carried Nasser pell-mell into the union, obviously more hastily than desired; but he could hardly refuse the fruits of his own propaganda. The United Arab Republic was declared with little deliberation on February 1, 1958, and several days later Nasser presented to a cheering throng in Damascus a seventeen-point program for the new state. He was nominated by the Egyptian assembly as president of the new republic, and before the month was out a plebiscite supported the move almost unanimously. Nasser declared that a new assembly would be appointed. It was composed of 300 Egyptians and 100 Syrians. A cabinet for the UAR was also selected. Significantly, twenty of the thirty-four members were Egyptians; and Egyptians held, among others, the portfolios for defense, foreign affairs, education, and national guidance.

As the months passed, many North Syrians acted displeased over the merger. Nasser revealed that Syria was not as rich as he had supposed and that union would take a number of years to perfect. Nevertheless, its creation upset the balance of power among the Arab states and gave the UAR genuine hegemony in the Middle East. The imam of

Yemen sent his son to Cairo to seal the establishment of the United Arab States. Although only a nominal merger, it gave lip service to the idea of Arab unity, showed the imam's respect for Nasser's position, and permitted the imam internal immunity from the beams of Radio Cairo. Forces similar to Nasserism in Iraq, Saudi Arabia, Kuwayt, and Jordan were encouraged; and after the first surge of Arab emotionalism and joy over the union of Jordan and Iraq coursed through Nasser, he reacted swiftly to the challenge to his dominance and condemned that federation as the evil doings of "imperialists." Elements in every Arab state looked to him for inspiration and sought to attach themselves to his political coattails. Nasser could hardly disappoint them. Radio Cairo invited Arabs in Baghdad, Beirut, and Amman to revolt against their rulers. Syrians found the Lebanese borders easy to infiltrate, and Nasser's agents abetted the civil disturbances that racked Lebanon in 1958 preceding the election of General Shihab. He inspired the men who led the Iraq revolution in July, 1958; and his brand of Arab nationalism conditioned the masses in Iraq to accept the new leaders with open arms. Nasser apparently had no direct hand in the revolution, but he quickly welcomed General Kassim's acquisition of power and successfully gathered considerable credit among Arabs from the coup by rejoicing over the victory. With the death of Nuri al-Said in Iraq and the expected defection of Iraq from the Baghdad pact, Nasserism became the only non-local force in the Arab Middle East. Had not American marines and British paratroopers landed in Lebanon and Jordan, those states might have fallen to his partisans. The shaykh of Kuwayt and Prince Faysal of Saudi Arabia recognized the shift in power and hastened to make their peace with Nasser before their dynasties followed the Hashimites of Iraq into oblivion.

The appointed assembly of four hundred for the United Arab Republic was looked upon as a preliminary body to take some of the first steps in consummating the union. Elections in Syria were too normal a process to ignore, and in Egypt elections were a long tradition. The problem was how to bypass the politicians and get through to the people. Early in 1959 leaders began to publicize a new electoral and parliamentary process. On July 8 local elections were held in the thirty-three provinces of the UAR to select 40,000 committeemen who, in Nasser's words, would inaugurate a kind of "school for democracy." These committeemen met in each province, discussed local and general needs and problems, and elected provincial councils. These councils in turn chose delegates to the National Union, 2,000 in all who met in Cairo on July 9, 1960 to act as the electors of half of the National Assembly. The National Assembly of 600 members—400 from Egypt and 200 from Syria, even though Syria's population was less than a fifth of Egypt's—was formed, half elected by the National Union and half appointed by Nasser from the National Union's membership. The machinery for obtaining the National Assembly had been devised to eliminate political parties and politicians. The Baath leaders in Syria were so opposed to it that Nasser dropped Hurani and al-Bitar as vice presidents; on July 21 when the National Assembly met, he announced the appointment of the Syrian Nur al-Din Kahalah as vice president. Kahalah was an engineer not a politician. President Nasser took his constitutional oath of office, and the fiction was maintained that the people ruled through this hierarchy of committees, councils, unions, and assemblies. A month before, however, an Executive Council of fifteen had been designated as a kind of super-cabinet to make decisions, but even here most questions of any weight were referred to the Supreme Council of three—President Nasser, Field Marshall and Vice President Amer, and Vice President (Syria) Abd al-Latif al Baghdadi. Because the constitution stated that the president had sole authority of appointing and dismissing vice presidents, Nasser's role in the government was supreme. With the skilled Syrian politicians disgruntled and located in Syria, they collaborated with disaffected soldiers, merchants, and landowners to lead Syria out of the union, as has been discussed in a previous chapter. Nasser's immediate reaction was to send the navy and a paratroop contingent to Latakia, but on sober second thought he only complained, and the United Arab Republic was reduced to Egypt.

THE UNITED ARAB REPUBLIC WITHOUT SYRIA

The shock of Syrian secession to the Egyptian region of the United Arab Republic was minimal because most of the adjusting had been on the Syrian side. In the fall President Nasser called for new elections to be held in February, 1962 for the National Union (sometimes called Congress), which would represent "genuine popular forces—peasants, workers, artisans, industrialists, etc."—of the nation. He appointed 250 members and 1,500 were elected. At its first meeting in May, Nasser, with great flourish, presented the National Charter, which provided for an Executive Council of twenty-five to act as the government's cabinet and above it a Presidential Council of twelve, many of whom served as deputy prime ministers with responsibilities for the policies of a specific department such as the foreign ministry, defense, interior, or agriculture.

Ali Sabri, a socialist, was selected as prime minister and promises for a National Assembly, some political activity, and a new constitution were given. The Arab Socialist Union under Nasser's presidency was launched as the sole political party in the UAR to gather into its folds all political activists and would-be leaders from the nation's various social and economic sectors enumerated in the call for elections to the National Union. A great deal of hard work at the grassroots level produced sufficient support and understanding to hold elections for the National Assembly in March, 1964. A Nasser-approved list of 1,748 candidates, all members of the Arab Socialist Union, filed for the 350 seats of the National Assembly. The normal life of the Assembly was set at five years although the president could dissolve it at will and call for new elections in sixty days. The Assembly could give a vote of no confidence in the cabinet as a whole or single out individual ministers for its disapproval. What would happen if a cabinet received a negative vote was not elucidated. Nasser remained president and was elected to a third six-year term in March, 1965. Field Marshall Abd al-Hakim Amer was chosen first vice president, Ali Sabri remained as prime minister of a cabinet of thirty ministers and an inner cabinet of eleven deputy prime ministers. In October, 1965 Vice President Zakariya Muhyi al-Din was sworn in as prime minister with an altered cabinet; Ali Sabri was appointed vice president and was given the post of secretary-general of the Arab Socialist Union. There had been alleged plots against Nasser and the governmnt by the Communists and the Muslim Brotherhood, and Muhyi al-Din was delegated supposedly to clamp down more rigorously on these groups. At the same time economic conditions had worsened and relations with the West were at a low point. The new prime minister was known as a moderate and more adept at solving economic dilemmas. A year later he was replaced by Sidqi Sulayman, one of the seven members of the executive committee of the Arab Socialist Union and previously cabinet minister in charge of all the affairs of the Aswan High Dam. Sulayman continued the more moderate program, holding a tight check on the dissident elements and emphasizing the industrial and economic development of society.

ARAB SOCIALISM

European Communism because of its emphasis on dialectical materialism and its tendency toward atheism had difficulty in making an appeal to any significant number in Egypt. This foreign ideology, supported by one of the great powers of the world, was an easy target for the deep-rooted and almost timeless Egyptian xenophobia. On the other hand, capital enterprises were in the hands of foreigners or the very rich who in their mode of life had largely de-Egyptianized themselves. Governmental control over agriculture and commerce had been traditional in historic times, and in the monolithic structure being devised by Nasser any different pattern was unthinkable. The state held a responsibility for the economic well-being and advancement of its citizens and whether it was called state capitalism, étatism as in Kemalist Turkey, or state socialism really made no difference to the state managers. Arab socialism had all the right connotations, did not conflict with Islam or the past, and with such a name it was an exportable commodity to neighboring states.

Steadily the government increased its hold over commerce, industry, and finance by the process of nationalization of many types of businesses. By 1961 all banks and insurance companies had been nationalized in what was deftly called "Arabization," and all newspapers and periodicals were placed under the control of the National Union and later the National Assembly. In 1962 estimates showed that ninety percent of all major businesses had been "Arabized," including flour mills, transportation firms, and seventy-seven bakeries in Cairo. In 1963 rice production and the ginning and exporting of cotton were nationalized, and foreigners were forbidden to own farmlands in Egypt. Over one billion dollars in property was sequestered when the property of Egypt's richest citizens, "422 millionaires and reactionaries," was confiscated. A highly progressive income tax was enacted and by law twenty-five percent of net profits in all businesses had to be distributed to the employees. Because many businesses were now owned and operated by the state, supposedly without profit, all government employees were given an annual bonus equal to ten days' salary.

The United Arab Republic had development plans too. The second five-year plan, drawn up for 1960 to 1965, called for a total expenditure of about four billion dollars to raise the national income by forty percent. The steel mill at Helwan would operate at full capacity, crude-oil production would increase by thirty percent, from four and one-half million tons, and cotton yield would pass ten billion pounds annually. A thorough survey and search for mineral resources were undertaken, and great satisfaction resulted from extensive deposits of iron, phosphate, manganese, copper, nickel, and gold found in the region of Aswan. The Pan American Oil Company brought in commercially productive wells in the Gulf of Suez and the Red Sea; natural-gas strikes were made in the delta area; and several rich seams of coal were discovered. The greatest single venture was the building of the Aswan High Dam. As already discussed, this project had been temporarily thwarted in 1956, but at the end of 1958 the U.S.S.R. loaned $100,000,000 to get it underway, and many Soviet experts arrived in Egypt to study the various aspects of its construction. In 1959 the Soviet Union agreed to support all three stages of its building, and open construction began in January, 1960. Prime Minister Khrushchev attended the celebrations in May, 1964 when the first stage was completed and again promised to see it through to completion. Water began to be backed up in 1965. The second most dramatic development project was the Suez Canal. In 1958 a record number of ships, 17,842, used the canal, but already the size of oil tankers, nearly half of the ships passing through, was increasing to the point where many were unable to navigate the narrow and shallow course. Once builders reached the tonnage that was too great, the impulse to build much larger tankers for rounding Africa was at hand. In 1959 three American firms had contracts for $18,000,000 to deepen and widen the canal so that ships of 37-foot draft could pass. But this was recognized as only a temporary palliative, and the Nasser Plan was blueprinted to spend $270,000,000 over a ten-year period to enable supertankers of 47-foot draft to navigate the channel. In 1966 the canal earned $197,000,000 on the passage of 20,285 ships. However, tankers of 300,000 to 2,000,000 tons dwarfed the 1959 supertankers of 80,000 tons, so that there was growing concern in the United Arab Republic over the prospects of oil shipments through the canal from the Persian Gulf to Europe.

Through the years industrial development in the United Arab Republic moved rapidly forward. Agreements were reached with Soviet-bloc countries and Communist China for financial and technical aid to industry of every sort. The same was true for Western nations including the United States. West Germany found, for example, that in 1963 she had loaned the United Arab Republic $57.5 million to assist in twenty-five development projects. In this decade the United States gave large amounts of aid to the United Arab Republic, and almost every year shipments of wheat in very great quantities and other foodstuffs for nonconvertible currency arrived from the United States. The continuing problem of the population explosion was a counterbalance to these advances. In 1958 at the time of the formation of the United Arab Republic, Egypt's population was estimated at 24,000,000 and in 1966 at slightly over 30,000,000, or an increase of twenty-five percent in only eight years. The annual increase in population was rapidly approaching the one million mark, and when the impounded waters of the Aswan High Dam became available to expand the irrigated lands in Egypt, they would hardly feed the increasing numbers added after the project was begun. Any improvement in the standard of living had to come from improved agricultural methods and industrial production. Another grave problem facing the United Arab Republic's leadership was the management of the national economy. The incidences of waste and improper utilization of resources were high. The expenditures for the armed forces and the daily cost of the adventure in Yemen were questionable in view of the smallness of the gross national product and the basic need for capital development at home. As signals of these basic ills, the cost of living was on the rise constantly, fourteen percent in 1965. In 1966 a system of forced savings began, and the price of rice to the consumer was doubled by government action in August. One-third of the nation's gold holdings, $25,000,000, was sold abroad. These were attempts to meet the unbalanced situation but were not cures or remedial actions. Arab socialism was being tested.

NASSER AND THE WORLD

Following the Sinai war of 1956 and the Soviet agreement to aid in building the Aswan High Dam, United Arab Republic relations with the U.S.S.R. and the Soviet bloc continued on a friendly government-to-government level. Large quantities of military goods including jet fighters, bombers, tanks, submarines, mortars, and heavy artillery were supplied, ostensibly in exchange for future cotton shipments, but arrangements were shrouded as were the actual military deliveries. Soviet technical assistance, equipment, and machinery which were accepted for a variety of projects and new industries in some years reached a figure of $175,000,000. Leading United Arab Republic political and military figures visited Moscow and other Soviet-bloc capitals to sign trade agreements and obtain support in world affairs. In addition to Khrushchev's visit to the United Arab Republic in 1964, Chou En-lai was in Cairo in 1963, Walter Ulbricht in 1965, and Alexei Kosygin in 1966. In spite of these visits and the massive aid for the Aswan High Dam and other programs, Nasser maintained an active repression of Communists in the United Arab Republic. Several hundred were jailed at various times, and special crackdowns were conducted almost yearly, much to the annoyance and embarrassment of Soviet leaders who admonished Nasser publicly for his treatment of these left-wing agitators. The Soviet Union, nevertheless, upheld its position of general support and made numerous commitments such as the promise to lend nuclear support to the United Arab Republic in the event of war with Israel, should the latter employ nuclear weapons. In the May, 1967 crisis between Israel and the United Arab Republic, the U.S.S.R. strongly supported the latter in discussions at the United Nations Security Council.

Nasser's relations toward the West were always somewhat fragile because of past European imperialism and the difficulty that Europeans and their governments had in throwing off the concepts on which that imperialism had been based. In 1959 a general settlement was reached with Great Britain and diplomatic relations were resumed. England released £50,000,000 in frozen sterling and waved payment of £50,000,000 for installations at Suez; the United Arab Republic waived damages inflicted by the 1956 bombings and invasion of Port Said and the Suez Canal, returned sequestered property, and agreed to pay £27.5 million for nationalized British property. After the settlement Great Britain gave the United Arab Republic credits from year to year for purchases of machinery and manufactures although after 1963, with Nasser's growing involvement in Yemen and his interest in Aden and the Federation of South Arabia, relations became strained with London. Diplomatic relations were severed in June, 1967 over the crisis in the Middle East. In 1958 France agreed to pay the United Arab Republic $57.4 million for the release of French property sequestered during the 1956 episode, but relations remained delicate, and in 1961 a ban was placed on the entry of French citizens into the United Arab Republic over alleged French implications in espionage and assassination plots against Nasser. In 1967 President de Gaulle took a neutralist stand on the Middle East crisis and would not involve France in the meetings of several maritime powers that were considering means of forcing the Straits of Tiran and breaking the blockade of Elath. On this basis the United Arab Republic's regard for France took a turn for the better. West Germany, as has been related already, gave many loans and considerable aid to the United Arab Republic for industrial development, and many West German scientists were employed in missile and rocket endeavors in the western desert. In March after Ulbricht's visit to Cairo and the raising of the United Arab Republic mission in East Berlin to the level of a consulate, Bonn protested and diplomatic relations were broken. Nasser declared these actions resulted from West German arms shipments to Israel.

Relations with the United States fluctuated widely in the period after 1956. Suspicious of the close relations between the United States and Israel and mindful of great American wealth and power, the United Arab Republic was wary in her attitudes toward the United States. The United Arab Republic needed vast amounts of wheat and other farm products, aid for industrial and public-works developments, and from time to time simple loans to sustain her budget. In 1959, $25,000,000 was obtained for wheat, flour, cornmeal, and powdered milk; $12,000,000 through the Export-Import Bank for locomotives and railway equipment; $2,000,000 for newsprint after the U.S.S.R. suddenly cut off the supply; $8,500,000 for technical aid; and $56,500,000 from the International Bank for Reconstruction and Development for widening and deepening the Suez Canal. Every year after that the variations of help and its magnitude were startling. In 1962, for example, about 500,000 tons of wheat were shipped to Egypt; there was a grant of $40,000,000 to construct forty-nine storage silos;

and the United States indicated the likelihood of making $100,000,000 available in various forms each year for the next five years. When the United States strongly requested that the United Arab Republic cease sending arms shipments to the Congo and appeared to tie American aid to her compliance, Nasser's reply was sharp and defiant. The American library in Cairo was sacked and burned. Although the United Arab Republic agreed to make recompense for the damage, the American House of Representatives voted in 1965 to suspend aid to Egypt unless the president declared that shipments were in the American national interest. Later that year $37,000,000 was released for food shipments and $55,000,000 in 1966. However, in the crisis with Israel in 1967 the United Arab Republic was angered by American declarations of guarantee to Israel and by American leadership in trying to organize an international maritime force to break the blockade of Elath. Accusing the United States of participating with Israel in the war against the Arab states, the UAR broke diplomatic relations with the United States on June 6, 1967.

The United Arab Republic tried to establish friendly relations with the new states of Africa, and in 1961 Nasser attended the African Congress at Casablanca after which he recognized the pro-leftist Gizenga as the rightful ruler of the Congo and withdrew Egyptian contingents from the United Nations forces in the Congo. Later that same year he hosted the All-African Peoples Congress in Cairo in the hope of establishing leadership in this movement. He talked of creating an African common market but found little interest among underproducing countries lacking in capital, skills, and production rather than lacking in markets. Nasser had frequent meetings with Nehru of India and Tito of Yugoslavia in which the three hoped to form a third force of uncommitted nations. Many of their problems were the same, but as developing nations they did not attract a following among the other new and underdeveloped nations for they had little concrete aid to offer.

The greatest role and the greatest hope for leadership of the United Arab Republic in the world was in the Middle East and among the Arab nations and peoples. Nasser was cast as the hero of the modern Arabs, and he had a large and devoted following in every Arab country from the southeastern tip of Arabia to Morocco on the Atlantic. They kept the political pot boiling in Syria and Iraq, and those who desired a change in Saudi Arabia, Kuwayt, Yemen, Aden, and Jordan were in his camp. In 1962 at the outset of the revolution in Yemen, the United Arab Republic was the first among the Arab states to recognize the republican regime of al-Sallal; on November 10, 1962 Nasser signed a joint defense agreement with al-Sallal and sent 12,000 soldiers to fight against the forces of al-Badr. Although in December Nasser agreed to withdraw his forces to induce American recognition of the new Yemeni regime, they never left and the United Arab Republic sustained the republicans and controlled them to the point where Cairo dictated policies and the names of officeholders in Sana. Saudi Arabia began to shelter the monarchists and funnel arms and ammunition to them so that a stalemate arose. Estimates were made that the United Arab Republic had expended about one billion dollars on the effort, and Nasser sought a way out to end the cost and cut the casualties. Truce meetings and ceasefire agreements with King Faysal were of no avail. In February, 1966 after England announced her planned withdrawal from Aden in 1968, Nasser not only decided to stick it out in Yemen but also encouraged his supporters to acts of violence and terror in Aden and throughout the Federation of South Arabia so that a regime favorable to the United Arab Republic and her policies would emerge in 1968. The Baathist coups in 1963 in Baghdad and Damascus were supposed to be first steps to the recreation and extension of the United Arab Republic. Conferences to effect these steps proved that Arab peoples might want Arab unity, but Arab leaders were not prepared to sacrifice local interests and personal positions to Egyptian dominance in any United Arab Republic.

Arab leaders recognized that Saudi Arabia, Kuwayt, Iraq, and Libya had wealth in oil royalties and looked to those states for economic leadership but the United Arab Republic as the most populous, the most modernized in such areas as industry, education, and transportation, and the best equipped in modern Soviet weapons was regarded as the natural military leader. Nasser had been the most successful in standing up to the powers in 1956, and the propaganda effort from Cairo had succeeded in making Nasser the outstanding charismatic figure in the Arab world. With Arab summit meetings in Alexandria and Cairo, a busy metropolis of nearly four million people, and the headquarters of the Arab League located there, it was natural and easy for Arab states to follow the lead of the United Arab Republic in general world affairs and in matters of joint military action and defense against Israel. President Arif of Iraq joined in a mutual military command with the United Arab Republic in 1964 and Syria followed in 1966. They were pledged to join with each other in a war against Israel, and each agreed to accept Palestine Liberation Organization armies as adjuncts to their own forces. In May, 1967 Syria called upon Nasser to make good his pledge to come to Syria's assistance should Israel attack. Feeling that he would have a serious problem at the Israeli frontier because of the United Nations Emergency Forces, Nasser requested U Thant to remove these troops from their places along the Gaza Strip, the Sinai Peninsula, and the Straits of Tiran. The United Arab Republic immediately re-instituted the blockade of Elath she had enforced up to 1956. Israel reacted, as the tension mounted, and as each side prepared for war great solidarity appeared among all the Arab states; each one gave its support to the United Arab Republic as the strain existing between Syria and Israel shifted southward toward the Israeli-Egyptian frontier.

AFTER THE SIX-DAY WAR

When war came in June the United Arab Republic bore the main brunt of it, but other fronts were opened between Israel, Syria, and Jordan. At meetings of the United Nations Security Council in New York delegates from Lebanon, Syria, Iraq, and Morocco spoke eloquently for the United Arab Republic; people in most Arab capitals attacked American and British embassies; and Iraq, Syria, Sudan, and Algeria joined with the United Arab Republic in breaking diplomatic relations with Great Britain and the United States on June 6, 1967. The cease-fire of June 10, 1967, called for by the United Nations Security Council and arranged for U Thant by General Odd Bull of Norway, left the Israeli troops in Sinai and virtually the entire east bank of the Suez Canal. In general the line was the center of the canal and for several weeks thereafter occasional spurts of gunfire erupted when one side or the other launched a small boat, apparently to test the vigilance and determination of the other. The United Arab Republic lost most of her air force and a large part of her tanks and other war matériel. Several thousand soldiers, mostly officers, remained as prisoners of war in Israeli hands.

Nasser publicly assumed the blame for the disastrous defeat and resigned his office. The general reaction against his resignation was so insistent that he rescinded his decision and subsequently enjoyed greater popularity and esteem than ever. The quality of the military leadership and the lack of organization and commitment were blamed for the infamy of the moment, and several thousand officers were relieved of their commands. It was reported that many officers had deserted their posts and men in the face of the enemy and that the planning of offense and defense had been exceedingly faulty. It was asserted that only sons of the influential had been accepted for the air force and that this branch of the military had not been as dedicated to the nation as it should have been. Disgruntled officers were kept under close surveillance, and at the time that Nasser went to Khartoum for the summit meetings Field Marshall and Vice President Amer was arrested. Shortly thereafter Amer committed suicide and it was announced that he had been involved in a plot to overthrow Nasser.

Whether or not all the groups in Egypt could allay their differences and remove Nasser seemed problematical.

As soon as the ceasefire became effective, various Arab leaders indicated the need for a conference of leaders of Arab states to define a unified position. Arab foreign ministers and prime ministers met at the United Nations and their speeches at both the Security Council and the General Assembly indicated a singleness of purpose but the course of action needed to achieve their goals was not clear. The prime minister of Sudan arranged to have an Arab summit meeting at Khartoum; on September 1, 1967 he announced its final resolution, which affirmed Arab solidarity and the necessity for joint efforts to eliminate all traces of Israeli aggression. In addition the resolution called for liquidation of all foreign bases in Arab countries, consolidation of military preparedness to face the Israeli victory, consideration of oil as a diplomatic weapon, and upholding of the rights of the Palestinian people to their land. This meant refusal to recognize Israel or to have negotiations with her. At the summit meeting Saudi Arabia, Kuwayt, and Libya promised the equivalent of $100,000,000 to the United Arab Republic to offset loss of revenue from the Suez Canal and thus to enable Nasser to remain firm in not opening the waterway to Israeli ships. In addition Nasser and King Faysal of Saudi Arabia agreed to end their interventions in the Yemeni civil war. Each promised to withdraw forces and financial aid, and a committee representing Iraq, Morocco, and the Sudan was appointed to supervise the withdrawal. This understanding led to the overthrow of al-Sallal in November, 1967 and so weakened the forces of FLOSY in South Arabia that its rival party, NLF, gained the upper hand and received the power and symbols of government when the British evacuated Aden and the surrounding area on the last day of November, 1967.

On the international scene the U.S.S.R. supported the position of the United Arab Republic at the meetings of the United Nations and began to replace much of the military equipment lost or damaged in the Six-Day War. By the end of the summer it was estimated that nearly eighty percent of the air strength had been restored and new additions had been made to the navy. As evidence of the latter, the Israeli destroyer *Eilat* was sunk in late October by four new-type missiles. The port of Alexandria became a base for Soviet ships, enabling Moscow to station more of her fleet in the Mediterranean. The president of the Soviet Union visited Cairo on June 21 and was followed by high ranking military persons. For the first time Nasser surrendered to Russian demands that Soviet military personnel be stationed in Egypt to train United Arab Republic officers in the use and maintenance of

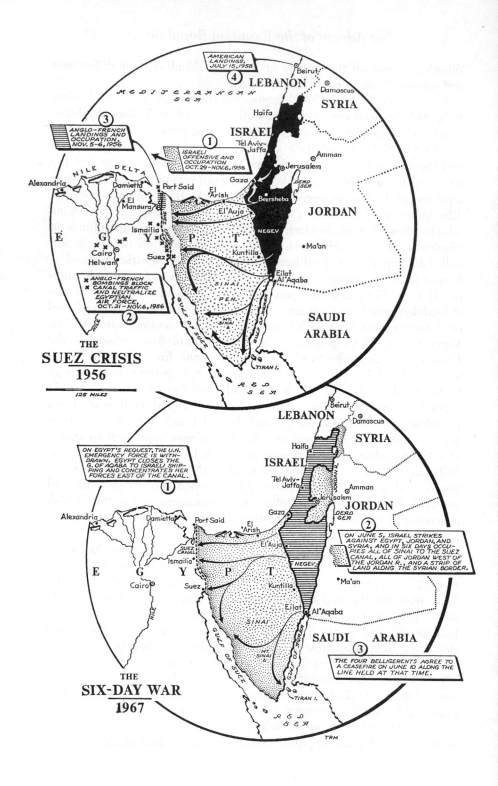

AMERICAN LANDINGS, JULY 15, 1958 (4)

LEBANON

Beirut

Damascus

SYRIA

Haifa

ISRAEL

Tel Aviv-Jaffa

Amman

Jerusalem

(1) **ISRAELI OFFENSIVE AND OCCUPATION OCT. 29–NOV. 6, 1956**

(3) **ANGLO-FRENCH LANDINGS AND OCCUPATION, NOV. 5–6, 1956**

MEDITERRANEAN SEA

NILE DELTA

Alexandria

Damietta

Port Said

El 'Arish

Gaza

DEAD SEA

El Mansura

Beersheba

El 'Auja

JORDAN

E G Y P T

Ismailia

NEGEV

Cairo

Helwan

Suez

Kuntilla

Ma'an

(2) **× ANGLO-FRENCH BOMBINGS BLOCK CANAL TRAFFIC AND NEUTRALIZE EGYPTIAN AIR FORCE OCT. 31–NOV. 6, 1956**

SINAI PEN.

Eilat
Al 'Aqaba

SAUDI ARABIA

MT. SINAI

GULF OF SUEZ

GULF OF AQABA

THE
SUEZ CRISIS
1956

125 MILES

TIRAN I.

RED SEA

LEBANON

Beirut

Damascus

SYRIA

Haifa

ISRAEL

Tel Aviv-Jaffa

Amman

Jerusalem

JORDAN

(1) **ON EGYPT'S REQUEST, THE U.N. EMERGENCY FORCE IS WITHDRAWN. EGYPT CLOSES THE G. OF AQABA TO ISRAELI SHIPPING AND CONCENTRATES HER FORCES EAST OF THE CANAL.**

Alexandria

Damietta

Port Said

El 'Arish

Gaza

DEAD SEA

SUEZ CANAL

El 'Auja

JORDAN R.

Ismailia

NEGEV

E G Y P T

Cairo

Suez

Kuntilla

Ma'an

(2) **ON JUNE 5, ISRAEL STRIKES AGAINST EGYPT, JORDAN, AND SYRIA, AND IN SIX DAYS OCCUPIES ALL OF SINAI TO THE SUEZ CANAL, ALL OF JORDAN WEST OF THE JORDAN R., AND A STRIP OF LAND ALONG THE SYRIAN BORDER.**

NILE

SINAI

Eilat
Al 'Aqaba

SAUDI ARABIA

MT. SINAI

GULF OF SUEZ

GULF OF AQABA

(3) **THE FOUR BELLIGERENTS AGREE TO A CEASEFIRE ON JUNE 10 ALONG THE LINE HELD AT THAT TIME.**

THE
SIX-DAY WAR
1967

TIRAN I.

RED SEA

TRM

Soviet equipment and to aid in the organization of a more effective armed force. The extent to which Soviet pressures upon Nasser in the political and diplomatic fields were successful was not open knowledge but after the Khartoum conferences the United Arab Republic quietly turned to repairing her relations with the United States and Great Britain. The charges that the two powers had aided Israel with air cover during the war were dropped and shipments of oil to Great Britain by other Arab states went unnoticed. Many American diplomats returned to Cairo and the American University was permitted to reopen for the fall term. In November, 1967 King Husayn traveled in the West and saying he spoke for Nasser informed all that Nasser would agree to a recognition of Israel. Shortly thereafter Nasser seemed to disavow such an idea for he publicly denied such a course. When Gunnar Jarring, Swedish Ambassador to Moscow, was appointed special United Nations representative to the Middle East to aid in the negotiation of a settlement as outlined by the British resolution passed unanimously by the Security Council on November 22, 1967, Nasser was careful not to be too enthusiastic over the terms lest he weaken his already insecure position.

INDEPENDENCE OF THE SUDAN

At the end of World War II the growing sentiment in Egypt for the unification of the Nile and the absorption of the Sudan left the British unmoved; but it attracted the support of Ashiqqa party leaders in the Sudan, largely because they sought to play Egypt off against Great Britain. In 1947 the British announced that, even without any agreement or confirmation from Egypt, steps would be pursued to form an elected legislative assembly with an executive council at Khartoum. The new governor-general, Sir Robert Howe, proceeded slowly; and elections did not materialize until November, 1948. The Umma party, which gathered its inspiration from Sir Abd al-Rahman al-Mahdi of the family of the famed nineteenth-century Mahdi, incorporated in its platform a program of independence and won the election. The Ashiqqa party showed friendship for Egypt, boycotted the election, and became split in 1951 between the rivalry of Ismail al-Azhari and Muhammad Nur al-Din. However, all parties in 1950 voiced demands that Great Britain and Egypt grant the Sudan the right of self-government and self-determination as early as 1951.

Within a few months after the revolution in Egypt, General Nagib met with many Sudanese leaders and discussed the future of the Sudan. He reached an agreement with Abdallah al-Fadil al-Mahdi of the Umma party (National party advocating separate independence for the Sudan) approving the establishment of self-government in the

Sudan by the end of 1952. For a three-year period the administration, police, and army were to be Sudanized, after which time the right of self-determination would be exercised by the peoples of the Sudan. Anthony Eden announced that Great Britain subscribed in principle to this arrangement; and on February 12, 1953 an Anglo-Egyptian agreement was entered into in Cairo ending the condominium of 1899 and accepting the self-government statute formulated by the Sudan government in 1952. Following this recognition, three committees were established: for the governor-general, an advisory committee of five, a Pakistani (chairman), a Briton, an Egyptian, and two Sudanese; for the supervision of elections, a committee of seven, an Indian (chairman), a Briton, an Egyptian, an American, and three Sudanese; and a committee of five, a Briton, an Egyptian, and three Sudanese, to proceed with the process of Sudanizing the government. The self-governing statute of the Sudan became official on March 21, 1953; and preparations for the election of a two-chamber parliament were launched.

Two prominent parties opened their campaigns. The Umma party declared that it favored the founding of a republic. Leaders of the party were members of the family of the Mahdi, whose head was Sir Abd al-Rahman al-Mahdi, spiritual leader of the Ansar sect of Muslims. Although "umma" signifies nation and is the label of many national parties throughout the Arab world, "umma" was also used to designate the universal Islamic state proposed by the Mahdi in the nineteenth century and was thus for many modernized and educated Sudanese an anachronistic symbol. Immediately prior to World War II the graduates' general congress split on the issue of a policy to achieve independence for the Sudan. The Umma group favored a slow process under the guidance of Great Britain; by contrast the Ashiqqa party advocated an immediate separation from England and close cooperation with Egypt. Thus, to the ardent nationalists, Umma had been a stronghold of the conservatives and the *status quo*.

The Ashiqqa party abstained from voting in the 1948 elections and in 1953 posed as the sponsor of separation from Great Britain and the end of the condominium. Sir Ali al-Mirghani, head of the Khatmiya sect, served as titular head of the party, which now took the name of National Unionist party (NUP). The active leader was Ismail al-Azhari, graduate of the American University of Beirut and teacher of mathematics at Gordon Memorial College in Khartoum. A rival appeared in Muhammad Nur al-Din, but both espoused a close tie of some kind with Egypt. Elections were held in November, 1953. Of the ninety-two seats for the house of representatives NUP won forty-seven, and Umma nineteen. The other seats were scattered, but one went to a

Communist (Anti-Imperialist Front). In the senate of thirty elected
and twenty appointed members NUP obtained thirty-one places;
Umma, only seven.

Parliament was convened on January 1, 1954 by Sir Robert Howe,
the governor-general. NUP organized the houses. Ismail al-Azhari
became prime minister and minister of interior, and formed a cabinet
of twelve (including ministries of interior, education, agriculture,
irrigation, finance, economic affairs, commerce, defense, justice, public
works, communications, and health). Sudanization proceeded rapidly;
and in August eight Sudanese became provincial governors, replacing
the customary British civil servants.

Early in 1955 the NUP started to splinter over the question of the tie
to Egypt. Three members left the cabinet to establish a new Republican Independence party, which presented a platform of unfettered
sovereignty for the Sudan but pledged cultural and economic co-
operation with Egypt. By June Ismail al-Azhari veered to the same
position and ousted Muhammad Nur al-Din from the cabinet and the
party because of his open advocacy of union with Egypt.

In August leaders of NUP and Umma requested Egypt and Great
Britain to withdraw their troops from the Sudan—which they agreed
to do before November 12, 1955. The self-determination plan called for
an election in the Sudan to determine the future after the troops were
evacuated. A plebiscite was agreed upon by the two parties to
determine the future status, and they also called for the choosing of an
assembly to draw up a constitution. Egypt and Great Britain agreed
on December 3, 1955 to recognize the self-determination procedure
drawn in the Sudanese parliament and appointed a seven-nation
committee to observe the self-determination.

However, Sir Ali al-Mirghani and Sir Abd al-Rahman al-Mahdi met
that same day for the first time since 1946 and effected a compromise.
On December 19, 1955 the Sudan house of representatives declared
Sudan an independent state and requested recognition from Egypt
and Great Britain. The senate passed the same declaration on December 22; Egypt and Great Britain granted their approval and recognition on January 1, 1956; India and the United States accorded their
recognition on January 2. Sudan became the ninth member of the Arab
League on January 19; and on February 6 Sudan was admitted to the
United Nations as the seventy-seventh member.

In February Ismail al-Azhari formed a new coalition cabinet of
sixteen members; and in March a resolution was passed, adopting
"The Republic of the Sudan" as the official name of the state. Supported by all parties, the new government was thrown almost immediately into the choice of support and adherence to the East or the West.

In March a Soviet mission arrived to establish an embassy at Khartoum and offered to give economic aid and technical assistance on terms similar to those proposed to Iran and Syria. Some military equipment arrived from Egypt, and a Czech mission agreed to sell arms to Sudan.

Nearly fifty percent of Sudan's trade had been with Great Britain, less than ten percent with Egypt. Cultural ties with Egypt were strong; and a great number of Sudanese were educated in Cairo and Alexandria, where they came under strong Egyptian influences. The problem of the Nile waters was a vital one for Sudan, but doubly so for Egypt. Negotiations between the two states ended in stalemates and in a general feeling of suspicion and distrust on the part of Sudanese for the high-sounding Egyptian phrases. With these complex and diverse forces at work upon Sudan, a policy of complete independence and an honest neutralism attracted general support. In June, 1956 Sir Ali al-Mirghani and his Khatmiyah followers resigned from NUP and founded the People's Democratic party. They favored continued independence of Sudan, peace, neutralism, support of the Bandung conference resolutions, a better standard of living for all in Sudan, and the convocation of a constituent assembly to draft a permanent legal basis for the state. As twenty-one deputies and fourteen senators were members of the new party, Ismail al-Azhari's cabinet lost its majority. A coalition of Umma and the People's Democratic party (PDP) elected Abdallah Khalil to the prime ministership by a vote of 60 to 32. Hamza al-Mirghani represented PDP in the cabinet as deputy prime minister.

Khalil took office as events in Suez, Egypt, and the Middle East assumed world-wide significance. Sudan was a member of the Arab League and denounced the use of force, declared that SCUA violated international law, and, later, condemned England, France, and Israel for their aggression against Egypt. The blocking of the canal, however, hurt Sudan's trade more than that of any other state. Three times within a year Khalil flew to Cairo for talks with Nasser to discuss the relationship of the two countries and to impress upon Egypt that Sudan's problems were her own and separate from those of Egypt. Khalil believed in true neutralism and notified Nasser that Sudan would obtain economic aid and military equipment wherever she could and that Egypt could do likewise. Furthermore, he proclaimed that Sudan would not join with any other state, Arab or otherwise, in a pact or defensive alliance. Accordingly, Khalil accepted aid from the U.S.S.R., gave contracts to West German firms to construct irrigation canals (at a cost of £5,000,000), and welcomed financial, economic, and agricultural assistance from the United States.

Throughout 1957 the National Unionists called for a general election, but Khalil postponed it because of Middle East tensions. In 1958, nominations produced 637 candidates for the 173 seats in the house and 135 candidates for the 30 seats in the senate. Elections held in February gave 63 seats in the house to Umma, 45 to NUP, 27 to PDP, 20 to Southern Liberals, 16 to uncommitted southerners, 1 to Southern Federalists, and 1 to the Anti-Imperialist (Communist) Front; in the senate 14 seats went to Umma, 5 to NUP, 5 to PDP, and 6 to southern parties. Voting at a time when Egypt was forming the United Arab Republic with Syria, Sudan evidenced no desire to federate in any way with Egypt; for Khalil's coalition had a working majority in each house. A new cabinet was installed with much the same membership as before, and Sudan pursued her course of neutralism in Arab affairs and in the world at large.

Undoubtedly, one of the factors giving Khalil such a generous mandate was the pre-election quarrel with Egypt over the territory north of the twenty-second parallel. Egypt had claimed this land for many years, but it had been occupied and administered by the Anglo-Egyptian Sudan. Egypt objected to Sudanese elections in the area, sent an army detachment up the Nile, and presented Sudan with an ultimatum to withdraw her armed forces from the village of Halaib. Khalil refused and asked the Security Council of the United Nations to order Egypt to halt her aggression. The Arab League could not take action against Nasser, but Haile Selassie intervened quietly. Egypt agreed to postpone the issue until after the election in Sudan; this decision virtually conceded the disputed region to Sudan, since elections for the latter would give a kind of legal sanction to Sudanese sovereignty. Nasser saved face by publicly asserting that there had been no quarrel between Egypt and Sudan and that the entire incident was the machination of evil imperialists.

MILITARY GOVERNMENT

If there were no quarrel over the territory there were differences over the use of the Nile's water. Early in July, 1958 Nasser publicly asserted that Sudan had violated the 1929 Nile Water Agreement by undertaking the new Managil Project, a plan similar and contiguous to the Gezira Scheme, whereby a significant part of Nile water was to be taken without any prior consultations with Egypt. Certainly he contended Sudan could not expect any solution to the flooding of the Nile Valley and the city of Wadi Halfa unless the needs of Managil were included. A week later at the time of the Baghdad coup it was feared that a parallel coup under Egyptian auspices might occur in Khartoum. Rumors began to circulate that PDP was about to withdraw from its coalition with Umma and join with NUP to force Khalil's resignation because they objected to his pro-Western policies and his failure in coming to an agreement with Egypt over the Nile. Fearing that this would move Sudan into the Egyptian camp, General Ibrahim Abboud, commander of the army, in an easy military coup on November 17, 1958 suspended the constitution, turned out the cabinet, dissolved parliament, and declared a state of emergency. A thirteen-member Supreme Council of the Armed Forces proclaimed that it held supreme constitutional authority of the state and that its president, General Abboud, would exercise all legislative, judicial, and executive powers and remain commander-in-chief of the armed forces. He appointed a cabinet responsible to him composed of seven officers and five civilians to carry on the government. But it was not clear sailing for General Abboud. There were three attempted coups against his regime in 1959. The first one in March was initiated by three junior field commanders who demanded faster reforms and modernization of society and government. Abboud met this challenge by reconstituting the Supreme Council to a membership of ten, all new appointees, including the three authors of the ultimatum. In May a coup failed when Abboud arrested fifteen army officers, two members of the Supreme Council, and twenty-four leaders of the outlawed Communist party. A third try in November was equally disastrous for those implicated. Again in July, 1961 disorders in Khartoum led to the arrest of a number of former political and government leaders including Abdallah Khalil of Umma and Ismail al-Azhari of NUP. However, with improved economic conditions and apparent progress in developing resources, political stability induced General Abboud to take the first step toward more responsible government. Khalil, al-Azhari, and others were released, and three more civilians entered in the cabinet shuffle. He announced that in the future a 72-member Central Council of State would be formed, including 54 members to be chosen by elected provincial councils. Six million voters cast their ballots on April 26, 1963 to elect rural and municipal councils, which in turn would choose the provincial councils. This first lesson in democracy occurred without any widespread disorders although the response in the three southern provinces was accompanied by doubts and the continued rumblings of nationalist and separatist movements.

A factor in Khalil's failure in 1958 was the near-economic collapse that summer, largely due to a poor cotton crop and low world prices against higher prices paid by the government to Sudanese producers. In 1956 the Managil Project had been drafted to bring under irrigation 830,000 acres as an extension to the one million acre Gezira Scheme. Costing over $100,000,000, this project was devised in four stages with the first stage being cultivated in 1958 and the second in 1959. Other development plans involving $280,000,000 over the years 1958 to 1962 emphasized the building of railroads, roads, hydroelectric plants, aviation lines, and telegraph services. Almost half was expected to come from the International Bank for Reconstruction and Development, which loaned $39,000,000 in 1958 for extension of railways south and west of Khartoum. There were other assistance agreements with the United States, Great Britain, West Germany, the U.S.S.R., and Yugoslavia. General Abboud made no changes in these policies, and the Managil Project was completed in 1962. Work on other dams was forwarded to finish the Roseires Dam and the Khashm al-Girba Dam. The former would irrigate an additional 870,000 acres in the east-central region of the Sudan, and in part it was being financed by West Germany, the International Bank for Reconstruction and Development, and the International Development Association. The other dam on the Atbara River in the northeast was designed particularly to provide lands for the villagers in the Wadi Halfa region who would be displaced by the waters behind the Aswan High Dam. In 1963 a new Sennar Dam was being constructed to furnish more electric power. General Abboud approved long-range economic development plans in 1961 and had them incorporated in 1962 into a ten-year plan, which would increase the gross national product by sixty-three percent. Old trade and assistance agreements were being renewed and recast, and new ones were negotiated in 1963 with Hungary, Czechoslovakia, the United Arab Republic, and Kuwayt. General Abboud also tackled the long-standing argument with Egypt over the Nile waters and in November, 1959 accepted $43,000,000 from Egypt to help resettle those in the Sudan who would lose their lands and homes from flooding caused by the Aswan High Dam. A general agreement was also reached whereby in the future the Sudan would be authorized to take 18.5 billion cubic meters of water annually from the Nile leaving some 55.5 billion for Egypt. There was genuine satisfaction in the Sudan over this division, for it was far more than she had previously.

RETURN TO CIVILIAN RULE AND THE SOUTHERN PROVINCES

On October 30, 1964 rioting and bloodshed erupted in Khartoum as a result of many frustrations, the greatest of which were the continuing unrest and disorders throughout the southern provinces and their effect on the political life of the entire state. General Abboud was compelled to step aside for a civilian caretaker-government under Sirr al-Khatim al-Khalifah, an independent. A fortnight later Abboud was fully separated from the government, and al-Khalifah appointed a five-man council to assume the presidential function—one chair of the five, reserved for a southern representative, was unfilled. Elections for a Constituent Assembly were called but were held only in the northern provinces between April 21 and May 8, 1965. The assembly was constituted for a membership of 233, but sixty seats for the south were not filled as conditions prevailing there did not permit voting. For the north the returns showed that Umma won 75; NUP won 54; Bija Tribes Congress (formerly with PDP) received 10; Muslim Brotherhood won 3; PDP received 3; and the remainder went to independents. On June 10 an equal coalition government of Umma and NUP members was formed by Muhammad Ahmad Mahjub of Umma and Ismail al-Azhari, the NUP leader, who was elected president of the five-man Supreme Council. In October a cabinet crisis arose over Mahjub's representing Sudan at the African summit meeting at Accra. NUP contended that al-Azhari, as president of the Supreme Council, should have attended as the chief delegate; the coalition was only restored by Mahjub's pledge that at future meetings al-Azhari would be the representative. In June, 1966 the Constituent Assembly voted a censure motion against Mahjub's rule, charging corruption and failure, and elected Saddiq al-Mahdi, new leader of Umma, as prime minister and instructed him to form a new cabinet. It signaled the arrival of a new political force in Umma. In a fifteen-man cabinet, Saddiq al-Mahdi placed eight members of NUP, three independents, and only four from Umma, but these four among themselves held the offices of prime minister, information, defense, interior, labor, and health. When taking office, al-Mahdi was thirty years old, an Oxford-educated economist, and a modernist who had broken with his uncle, the leader of the Ansari sect, over the question of conformity with past religiously oriented and traditionalist governments and society. This great-grandson of the Mahdi advocated neither capitalism nor Communism but a "clear-cut form of socialism" to harmonize the efforts of government capital and individual effort. He said, "We must shape Sudan in accordance with the modern world or perish." In general NUP had been more enthusiastic and understanding about socialism than had Umma, and thus al-Mahdi's line-up in the cabinet can be explained. He set out to restore confidence among the international community in Sudan's stability, position, and responsibility. He declared adherence of commitments to the United Nations, the Arab League, and the Organization of African Unity. He also set out on a tour of the southern provinces to try to end the long rebellions there. He promised, furthermore, to promote the decentralization of government and to appoint a national commission to draft a permanent constitution for the state. At the same time he tightened the strings of the economy, placing a prohibition on imports of nonessential goods and eliminating extravagant borrowing from the central Bank of Sudan, established in 1960. Loans were obtained from the International Monetary Fund, the United Nations Special Fund, the Agency for International Development, Bulgaria, and French and British banks. With no overpopulation and no food shortages, al-Mahdi was optimistic about Sudan's future.

To a considerable degree, however, a greater political tranquility was required, and this would depend on al-Mahdi's skill in solving the southern problem. After the declaration of Sudan's independence and the departure of the British, strife between the southern Negro pagan- and Christian-populated provinces and the northern Arab Muslim regions surfaced in various manifestations. Self-rule, autonomy within a loose federation, secession, and independence had supporters who mistrusted the government of Khartoum and the Arab politicians and generals. To the centuries-old fires of distrust and fear were added the now fagots of African nationalism. In 1964 large-scale fighting broke out at Wau. Government forces were successful, and tens of thousands of rebels and secessionists fled into Uganda, Kenya, Tanzania, Ethiopia, Chad, Niger, the Congo, and other African states. Over three hundred Christian missionaries active in these provinces were deported, and three of the rebel leaders were sentenced to be hanged. Sirr al-Khatim al-Khalifah offered amnesty to all southern leaders and again after quelling race riots in Khartoum repeated amnesty to all. William Deng, the leader of the Sudan African National Union (SANU) from exile in Uganda pleaded the southern cause, but others who believed his organization to be too soft and ineffective organized Anya-Nya, a terrorist society pledged to kill Arabs in Sudan's Equatorial Province. Although al-Khalifah went to Uganda to negotiate with SANU and conferences were held in Khartoum, no solutions were reached; the elections of April, 1965 could not be held in the south, and their sixty seats remained empty in the Constituent Assembly. Later in 1965 SANU leadership passed to Aggrey Jaden but no satisfactory answers to the difficulties were found. A new separatist group, Azania Liberation Front, was born, and the stream of exiles and refugees widened. Kenya, Tanzania, and Ethiopia promised Prime Minister Mahjub that they would no longer permit rebels and insurgents to use their countries as bases of operations, but no such word was forthcoming from Uganda or the Congo. In the decade from 1956 to 1966 poor crops and economic distress were hardships that cabinets in Khartoum were able to weather, but bloodshed in the southern provinces pulled down one government after the other. Saddiq al-Mahdi felt that there was a real basis for "national cohesion" in the Sudan, and southern leaders had more confidence in him than in his predecessors. However, an election in April 1967 in the southern provinces upset the previous balance in the Constituent Assembly. A new cabinet was formed on May 26 under Mahjub, who had been elected prime minister again on May 18.

When the crisis between Israel and the Arab states developed in May, 1967 Sudan supported the United Arab Republic; after war broke out Sudan severed relations with Great Britain and the United States. In order to achieve a firmer union of the Arab states Prime Minister Muhammad Ahmad Mahjub called for an Arab summit meeting in Khartoum. After difficult preliminaries and much jockeying he was able to convene the conference which met for six days. Closing on September 1st, it condemned Israel as an aggressor and reaffirmed Arab solidarity. In an attempt to heal the most disrupting force among the Arab states, Sudan arranged a compromise between Saudi Arabia and the United Arab Republic over Yemen, and together with Iraq and Morocco comprised the committee entrusted with conducting the withdrawal of outside forces from Yemen and helping the Yemeni leaders reach an accord.

REFERENCES: Chapter 41

Important references for this chapter are also found in Chapters 7, 22, 23, 27, 31, 33, 35, and 39.

Michael Adams, *Suez and After: Year of Crisis:* Beacon Press, Boston, 1958.

Robert Loring Allen, *Middle Eastern Economic Relations with the Soviet Union, Eastern Europe, and Mainland China:* University of Virginia Press, Charlottesville, 1958.

Hamed Ammar, *Growing Up in an Egyptian Village:* Grove Press, New York, 1954. A description of the life and culture of the fellahin of an Egyptian village.

Rashed el-Barawy, *The Military Coup in Egypt: An Analytic Study:* Renaissance Book Shop, Cairo, 1952. The first report on the revolution.

A. J. Barker, *Suez: The Seven Day War:* Praeger, New York, 1964.

Willard A. Beling, *Pan-Arabism and Labor:* Harvard University Press, Cambridge, 1960.

Morroe Berger, *Bureaucracy and Society in Modern Egypt: A Study of the Higher Civil Service:* Princeton University Press, Princeton, 1957. A study of the personnel in the Egyptian government and their activities.

L. M. Bloomfield, *Egypt, Israel and the Gulf of Aqaba in International Law:* Carswell, Toronto, 1957.

John C. Campbell, *Defense of the Middle East: Problems of American Policy:* Harper, New York, 1960. A careful, restrained study.

Erskine B. Childers, *The Road to Suez: A Study of Western-Arab Relations:* Macgibbon & Kee, London, 1962. An interesting and provocative study in depth.

John Connell, *The Most Important Country:* Cassell & Co., London, 1957. Background to the Suez crisis.

Charles D. Cremeans, *The Arabs and the World: Nasser's Arab Nationalist Policy:* Praeger, New York, 1963. One of the better surveys, and most understanding.

A. N. Cumberbatch, *Egypt: Economic and Commercial Conditions in Egypt, October, 1951:* H. M. Stationery Office, London, 1952.

Harry B. Ellis, *Challenge in the Middle East: Communist Influence and American Policy:* Ronald Press, New York, 1960.

Leon D. Epstein, *British Politics in the Suez Crisis:* University of Illinois Press, Urbana, 1964.

Saad El Din Fawzi, *The Labor Movement in the Sudan, 1945–1955:* Oxford University Press, New York, 1957. An historical background, the development of the movement, and its role in the new state.

Herman Finer, *Dulles over Suez: The Theory and Practice of His Diplomacy:* Quadrangle Books, Chicago, 1964.

Matthew A. Fitzsimons, *Empire by Treaty, Britain and the Middle East in the Twentieth Century:* University of Notre Dame Press, Notre Dame, 1964.

Richard N. Frye, ed., *Islam and the West: Proceedings of the Harvard Summer School Conference on the Middle East, July 25–27, 1955:* Mouton, The Hague, 1956. Excellent chapters on the development of secularism and the role of Islam in Turkey.

George L. Harris, ed., *Egypt:* Human Relations Area Files, New Haven, 1957. A fine survey.

Charles Issawi, *Egypt in Revolution: An Economic Analysis:* Oxford University Press, New York, 1963.

Jean Lacoutre and Simone Lacoutre, *Egypt in Transition:* Criterion Books, New York, 1958.

J. H. G. Lebon, *Land Use in Sudan:* Geographical Publications Ltd., Bude, England, 1965.

Daniel Lerner, *The Passing of Traditional Society: Modernizing the Middle East:* The Free Press, Glencoe, 1958.

Tom Little, *Egypt:* Praeger, New York, 1958.

Austin L. Moore, *Farewell Farouk:* Scholars Press, Chicago, 1954.

Gamal Abd al-Nasser, *Egypt's Liberation:* Public Affairs Press, Washington, 1955. A kind of blueprint of the revolution. First issued under the title *The Philosophy of the Revolution* in Cairo in 1954.

Mohammed Neguib, *Egypt's Destiny:* Victor Gollancz, London, 1955. The story by the Egyptian general who headed the revolution in 1952.

Anthony Nutting, *I Saw for Myself:* Doubleday, New York, 1958. The Suez crisis.

Patrick O'Brien, *The Revolution in Egypt's Economic System, From Private Enterprise to Socialism, 1952–1965:* Oxford University Press, New York, 1966.

Fahim I. Qubain, *Education and Science in the Arab World:* Johns Hopkins Press, Baltimore, 1966.

Benjamin Rivlin and Joseph S. Szyliowicz, eds., *The Contemporary Middle East: Tradition and Innovation:* Random House, New York, 1965. More than fifty articles and readings by scholars and political figures.

Terrence Robertson, *Crisis: The Inside Story of the Suez Conspiracy:* Atheneum, New York, 1965.

Pierre Rondot, *Changing Patterns of the Middle East:* Praeger, New York, 1961.

Nadav Safran, *Egypt in Search of Political Community:* Harvard University Press, Cambridge, 1961.

Sadek H. Samaan, *Value Reconstruction and Egyptian Education:* Columbia University Press, New York, 1955. A discussion of new forces and ideas in Egypt, especially for the training of teachers.

Hugh J. Schonfield, *The Suez Canal in World Affairs:* Constellation Books, New York, 1952. An updating of his volume, *The Suez Canal,* 1939.

Mekki Shibeika, *The Independent Sudan:* Robert Speller, New York, 1960.

Ivar Spector, *The Soviet Union and the Muslim World:* University of Washington Press, Seattle, 1959.

Julius Stone, *Aggression and World Order:* University of California Press, Berkeley, 1958. Legal case study of the 1956 crisis.

P. J. Vatikiotis, *The Egyptian Army in Politics: Pattern for New Nations:* Indiana University Press, Bloomington, 1961.

Wilton Wynn, *Nasser of Egypt: The Search for Dignity:* Arlington Books, Cambridge, 1959.

Mahmoud Y. Zayid, *Egypt's Struggle for Independence:* Khayats, Beirut, 1965.

CHAPTER 42

World Interest in the Middle East

After World War II the world at large became greatly concerned with affairs of the Middle East. The advent of the state of Israel and the enormous flow of oil focused attention upon the area and emphasized its importance in matters of politics, transportation, communications, religion, culture, markets, military strategy, imperialism, and nationalism. Ships flying the flags of more than fifty different nations passed through the Suez Canal every year. No nation or people could ignore the evolving problems of the Middle East.

From the departure of Napoleon from Egypt in 1799 until the summer of 1956 the British enjoyed the dominant imperial role in the Middle East. Throughout the nineteenth century Russia, France, Austria, Italy, and Germany had interests in the Middle East and from time to time possessed temporary or limited hegemony in all or various parts of the area. But Great Britain held sway more consistently; and her ambassadors, merchants, and navy exerted a profound influence wherever they went. Many pages of the preceding chapters testify to British concern in developments in Iran, rule in Egypt, trade of Aden, navigation of the Straits, and political, social, economic, and military events in all lands lying within a circle touching these four spots on the globe.

British involvements in the Middle East were various and comprehensive. Paramount solicitude, however, revolved around the fact that the Middle East lay astride the route to India, which Britishers regarded as the jewel in the crown of the empire. This route must be protected and kept open at almost any cost. After the construction of the Suez Canal this interest became stronger than ever.

The British used every device to maintain their imperial position in the Middle East. Officials and colonial agents, both in London and the Middle East, regarded the inhabitants as "natives" in the Kipling sense and believed that the best way in which to preserve peaceful and proper relations was to co-operate with the native ruler. Support was given to strengthen him with his people. Where possible, however, a constitution with a house of representatives and a house of notables was introduced. Such a government, created in the image of the British government, was expected to function in a friendly and peaceful manner within the British family of nations.

In any case, the British by economic, financial, military, and ideological means fully intended to retain their dominant position in the Middle East. However, weakened at home by losses in World War II, Great Britain found the retention of the Middle East beyond her means in the face of rising nationalism in the Middle East and growing economic strength and determination among Turks, Arabs, Israelis, and Iranians. Withdrawal of the British, partial though it was in the 1950's, led to a realignment of the power and position of foreign states and internal factions. Readjustment of these forces gave rise to uncertainty and feelings of insecurity, evidences of which were particularly noticeable in the controversies surrounding the issues of oil in Iran, Cyprus, the Suez Canal, the 1958 revolution in Iraq, and the various pacts, unions, and federations among the Arab states.

The eclipse of British power in the Middle East became nearly complete in the 1960's. Except for the Persian Gulf principalities of Bahrayn, Qatar, Oman, the Trucial States and Aden and its dependencies formed into the Federation of South Arabia, the British raj had left. The announcement of their departure from Aden in 1968 gave forewarning of such an impending vacuum that factions multiplied and disorders erupted to a point of such chaos in 1966 and 1967 that the British were induced to arrange a November 30, 1967 date for final evacuation. The weakness of the British voice at the United Nations Security Council debate and its relative ineffectiveness upon national policies in Israel, the Arab states, India, or any other state were apparent to the world during the crisis of 1967, with its short Israeli-Arab war in June. British interest might remain but her power and influence were gone. In 1968, she announced a full withdrawal from the Persian Gulf to be completed by 1971.

French interests in the Middle East go back as far as the Crusades. French merchants prospered in the Levant in early modern times, and

Bourbon monarchs frequently dispatched their most skilled ambassadors to the Porte. In the nineteenth and early twentieth centuries French ambitions for Middle Eastern empire were avidly pursued by Napoleon III and republican foreign ministers, but without much success.

Never able to match the power of England and plagued by miserable governments in Paris, French empire-builders, except for their brief success in Syria and Lebanon between World Wars I and II, devoted their energies to spreading and establishing French culture among the elite of the local peoples. Cabinets and governments might come and go in the Middle East, as they did in France; but if the people were imbued with French culture and spirit and thus wedded to French civilization, a lasting sympathy for France would be generated. Such an understanding would be translated into trade, concessions, successful diplomacy, and allies in international conflict and wars. These were the true sinews of empire. However, the utter defeat of France in World War II and the weakness of her economy dispelled most of the prestige held by France in the Middle East. Admiration for French manufactures and French ways largely vanished in the postwar period, even though the French language remained popular as a means of communication in cultured circles—a fact which over a longer period of time might substantiate the French claim to the permanence of their civilization in the Middle East.

In 1956, greatly agitated by Nasser's aid and encouragement to Algerian leaders in their drive for independence, France, along with Great Britain and Israel, attacked Suez and gave overt aid to the latter with French pilots flying Mystère planes over Sinai. In subsequent years France supported Israel in various ways, but in the 1967 crisis de Gaulle maintained a neutrality, which to the Arabs appeared to be a friendly and sympathetic position in sharp contrast to British and American attitudes. Whether or not France would project this position into political and economic gains remained to be seen, but almost immediately some Arab spokesmen suggested that British and American oil rights and properties be transferred to French, Italian, and Spanish companies. In 1967, therefore, it could no longer be said, as it had been a decade earlier, that French influence and prestige in the Middle East had vanished. Furthermore, as the leader of the European Economic Community, France was a potent force in Middle Eastern affairs, especially since Israel indicated a serious and anxious desire for admittance into the European Common Market.

American merchants and missionaries since early in the nineteenth century were actively engaged in the Middle East. The United States government, however, evinced little direct concern in their affairs and hardly raised a finger over the Middle East until at the Paris Peace Conference Wilson had a fling at effecting an American settlement for the area. Since the American people in general were indifferent toward the Middle East, only a division of Mosul oil aroused Americans to any form of imperialism in that region at the end of World War I.

In the midst of World War II President Roosevelt would have given to the British complete political and economic responsibility for the Middle East, not only in wartime, but also in the postwar period, had not Cordell Hull objected. As the war came to an end American involvement in Middle East affairs became more apparent and, as British power waned, more obligatory. The American public was unprepared for its new duties, as was best indicated by President Truman's conduct and relations with the British regarding the immigration into Palestine and the peace of the mandate.

Neither the American people nor the American government has had any imperial ambitions in the Middle East. American oil investments in the area are very extensive, estimated at more than two billion dollars, but it is doubtful if the United States would exert much pressure on their behalf. The welfare and security of Israel has evoked greater concern in the United States than any other Middle Eastern issue, although American political and financial devotion to Israel noticeably began to ebb in 1952 and suffered further declines after the United Nations vote of censure in 1955 and the aggression in Sinai against Egypt in 1956. Strong popular sentiment for Israel was a latent force, however, and its strength could not be overlooked or underestimated. For aid to the Arab states it was always more difficult to obtain approval of the Congress than it was for Israel. American prestige suffered enormously among the Arabs during the crisis of 1967 from American actions in the United Nations Security Council which were readily translated by the Arabs as moves to favor Israel. Speeches by American leaders discussing steps to be taken to fashion an international maritime association to break the blockade of the Straits of Tiran to Israeli shipping were taken by the Arabs as suggesting aggression against the United Arab Republic. Such moves had a tendency to throw the Arabs into ready and waiting Soviet arms and to augment most aspects of the old East-West competition and conflict in the Middle East.

Americans in and out of government desire peace in the Middle East, friendship with its people, and co-operation with its governments. The great majority of Americans believe that this goal can be attained by educating the people, improving their health, and raising their standards of living. To this end grants-in-aid, Point Four programs, scholarships, exchange professorships, and a variety of similar projects have been initiated by the American government, individuals, and the great philanthropic foundations.

Soviet Russia's aim has been to secure the friendship and sympathy of Middle Eastern peoples for the way of life in the Soviet bloc and to win the co-operation of their governments with that of the U.S.S.R. Attainment of these objectives has been sought by a clever mixture of pressure and inducement upon political figures to pursue Russian policies and by the steady exploitation of every incident and disturbance to keep society in a constant ferment of unrest and uncertainty. Skillfully, Soviet envoys and agents have played upon the fears and aspirations, defeats and disappointments, and the emerging nationalism of the Middle East in order to turn the people, especially the leaders, away from the West and toward the Soviet bloc.

Beginning in 1955 Soviet arms were supplied in ever-increasing quantities to Middle Eastern Arab states as a further move to draw them closer to the Soviet orbit and free them from susceptibilities to Western pressures. Complementing these arms were sizable developmental grants and loans for such important and visible items as the Aswan High Dam, the Euphrates Valley project in Syria, and innumerable factories, roads, harbors, and industrial complexes. Significantly, leaders in Syria and Yemen and to a lesser degree in other states began to look to Peking for an ideology more radical and more revolutionary than that offered by Moscow, even chiding Nasser as being an opportunist and a traitor to the course of reform in the Arab world. Aid in various forms supplemented this ideology. The Israeli-Arab crisis and the Six-Day War in June, 1967 were harsh testing experiences for the Soviets, but the initial results brought them favor among the Arabs. Their stand in the United Nations Security Council sessions, Kosygin's presence and speech at the General Assembly, and the Soviet president's visit to Cairo eleven days after the war were open proofs of Soviet friendship and support. Replacement from the Soviet bloc of the arms lost and expended in the disastrous war was a reassuring gesture giving courage to the Arab military and their leaders. In the summer of 1967 it appeared that the Soviet position in the Arab Middle East was stronger than it has ever been. Alexandria quietly became available as a base for Soviet warships and the age-old Russian dream of a warm water port in the Mediterranean appeared to have been fulfilled.

The Middle East has sometimes been referred to as "the concourse of the continents." Standing at the juncture of Asia, Africa, and Europe, the area links the continents by narrow land routes and by narrow waterways. The Turkish Straits, Suez, the Red Sea, the Bab-al-

Mandeb, the Straits of Ormuz, and the Persian Gulf have through the ages served man in his communications, travels, and trade. Although air travel may seem to have lessened the importance of these old arteries of the world, the commotion aroused in foreign offices of world powers by the stoppage of the Suez Canal in 1956, and again in 1967, amply illustrated that Middle Eastern waterways had not lost their age-old usefulness and value. Each year tonnage and the number of ships transiting through the Suez Canal steadily increased, even in the face of larger and more supertankers to carry oil from the Persian Gulf around Africa to the Western world.

Until the advent of mechanized means of transportation, caravan routes across the deserts of the Middle East played a vital part in the life of the area. Since World War II fewer caravans have used the old trails, but new pipelines transporting oil across the barren wastes have brought added importance to the states and peoples along these routes.

Since the end of World War I the relationship of the Middle East to air routes between Europe, Asia, and South Africa has not been overlooked. By the middle of the century great international airports had developed at Istanbul, Beirut, Tel Aviv, Cairo, Khartoum, and Dhahran; and almost every international air line had scheduled flights to or through the Middle East. Thus, in the twentieth century transportation and communication routes by land, water, and air placed the Middle East in a position as commanding as ever before.

The unprecedented expansion of the oil industry in the Middle East since the close of World War II has drawn the attention of every part of the world to the Middle East. In 1938 the Middle East accounted for 5.7 percent of world production; in 1946, for 9.4 percent; and in 1966, for 28.9 percent. Concentrated in Saudi Arabia, Kuwayt, Iraq, Libya, and Iran, with a rapidly growing development in Qatar and Abu Dhabi, the output for 1966 topped 10,600,000 barrels daily of crude petroleum, about half of which passed through the Suez Canal until its closure in June, 1967. The security and welfare of the West depends upon the flow of Middle East oil. The great bulk is delivered to western Europe, and without the power and heat derived from that oil the free countries of Europe would suffer incalculable losses. Recognition of the role played by Middle East oil in British life was contained in a speech of Prime Minister Eden in the House of Commons in March, 1956, when he said that the British were obliged to remain in Cyprus to protect the flow of oil to Great Britain.

If in the past oil production in the Middle East and the acceleration of its yields had a bearing upon Western economy, the oil reserves of the area are staggering in their relationship to the future. Each year exploration has increased the estimates. In 1920 the potential reserves were set at 5.8 billion barrels; in 1945, at 18 billion; in 1949, at 32 billion; in 1951, at 48 billion; in 1954, at 83 billion; in 1967, at nearly 300 billion; and new discoveries continue to be announced. In relation to the rest of the world the Middle East was estimated in 1949 to hold forty-one percent of total reserves; in 1954, fifty-six percent; and in 1967, more than sixty-five percent. In the face of these facts no Western leader can afford to ignore the Middle East and its destiny.

To transport any appreciable tonnage of Middle East oil to the Soviet bloc would require the laying of an entirely new series of pipelines or the acquisition of a sizable fleet of tankers by the states concerned. Under normal circumstances neither of these would be feasible, and several years would be required for the accomplishment of either. Moreover, the Soviet Union began to export oil in the 1960's and in the crisis in 1967 made offers to sell oil to Western European countries. In any struggle, therefore, between East and West the object of the former would be to deny the latter access to Middle East oil. The Soviet desire to frustrate ready and easy utilization of the oil by the West could be seen in the speeches by Foreign Minister Shepilov on his visits to the Middle East in 1956, and again in Soviet actions in 1967 at the time of the Israeli-Arab conflict.

Considering the important lines of communication through the Middle East, its geographic position at the juncture of three continents, its great oil production, and its almost unbelievable petroleum reserves, the military significance of the Middle East becomes apparent immediately. Some strategists have likened Asia Minor to a huge anchored aircraft carrier invaluable in any military operation approaching central and eastern Europe from the south or attacking Arabia, Africa, and India from the north. Control of the north coast of Africa continues to be a strategic key to the Mediterranean and southern Europe. One of the historic military roads to India passed through Iran, and there is no reason to believe that the route has become obsolete. Finally, there is the manpower of the Middle East. Properly trained, equipped, and officered, the Middle Easterner would undoubtedly become a good soldier. The West usually regards the Middle East as an avenue leading to the East; the East regards it as a window opening out upon the West. Whichever way, it is a rich military prize.

The Middle East contains the Holy Places for the three popular Western religions: Judaism, Christianity, and Islam. These religions have spread wide and far and count their devotees in the millions;

subjects of the great powers have deep and powerful emotions with regard to these Holy Places and to the Middle East as the birthplace of their faiths.

In the Middle East itself religion has played a commanding role in political, economic, and social aspects of life for many centuries and in all probability will continue to be important for a considerable time in the future. A vibrant nationalism, however, has held the center of the stage since World War I. Nationalism has grown virulent and has so seized the bodies of the adolescent states of the Middle East that even their leaders find difficulty in distinguishing "between truth and error, fact and fancy, knowledge and poetry, achievement and wish." Nationalism in this form has often confused the real issues in question and has won boisterous support for glib demagogues, whether they be local leaders, diplomats, or foreign ministers, who promise more than they know can be delivered. In such a race the honest statesman is left at the starting gate.

Position and prestige have been held in high esteem in the Middle East for many ages. In the rivalry for the area each little coup, special favor, or small success is accompanied by much trumpeting, and "face saving" has been elevated to a fine art. The means and manner of accomplishment assume an importance frequently above the end itself; and often obvious, logical, and beneficial courses of action cannot be taken because rivals and opponents have already suggested or pursued those roads.

From one end of the Middle East to the other no word stands lower in the political and national vocabulary or is more reviled than imperialism. Since World War I the chief ingredient of nationalism has been the desire to obtain full and complete independence from the great imperialist powers. Schoolbooks, lectures, newspapers, radio, speeches, conversations, and acts of every kind have, overtly and covertly, carried the important message. Foreign soldiers and officials must go! Economic servitude and colonialism must end! Foreign cultures in the schools must cease! Deeds, speeches, public documents, and international agreements of every political figure are closely scrutinized, almost word for word, for even a vague allusion to something which might be considered submissive to outside domination or influence.

Nevertheless, the process of Westernization has marched relentlessly forward in the Middle East. The Western powers held the Middle East in their empires for several generations and controlled the economy of the Middle East. Consequently, the progress of Westernization had to be denied or lamented by nationalists and politicians. Modernization was a more palatable term.

The exact nature of Westernization defies definition. At best it might be considered as the infiltration of scientific knowledge and its proper application into as many aspects of life as possible. As the penetration spreads, deeply and laterally, the extent of Westernization may be measured.

Machines and mechanization certainly will come to the Middle East in significant magnitude within a decade or two. But there is no certitude that the people will be Westernized. Leaders may cast their lot and those of their peoples with the West, as in Turkey and Israel. Some may decide their interests lie with the Soviet bloc. Others may try to follow a neutralist course. Whichever it may be, military administrators and colonial officials testify that advances of civilization have made it virtually impossible to rule a people against their own wishes. To maintain and operate the Suez Canal against the will of the people of Egypt is practically out of the question. To keep oil flowing through pipelines from Arabia to the Mediterranean in the face of determined Arab resistance could hardly be done.

To win the Middle East, therefore, requires the winning of the Middle Eastern peoples. Like a rich girl, the people of the Middle East do not want to be wooed for wealthy oil possessions or valuable real estate. They wish to be courted for themselves. Their culture, skills, and civilization must be understood and appreciated and their desires respected. The age of being "natives" has passed. Until 1950 the future Westernization of the Middle East could hardly be doubted. By 1968, with the progress of Arab socialism, the activities of pro-Chinese Communists, and the assistance from the Soviet bloc paralleling the development and strength of Israel, strongly supported by the United States, the future of the Middle East had become less certain.

Index

A NOTE ON THE TYPE

The text of this book is set in Caledonia, a Linotype face designed by W. A. Dwiggins (1880–1956), who was responsible for so much that is good in contemporary book design. Though much of his early work was in advertising and he was the author of the standard volume, Layout in Advertising, *Mr. Dwiggins later devoted his prolific talents to book typography and type design, and worked with great distinction in both fields. In addition to his designs for Caledonia, he created the Metro, Electra, and Eldorado series of type faces, as well as a number of experimental cuttings that have never been issued commercially.*

Caledonia belongs to the family of printing types called "modern face" by printers—a term used to mark the change in style of typeletters that occurred at the end of the eighteenth century. It is best evidenced in the letter shapes designed by Baskerville, Martin, Bodoni and the Didots.

This book printed and bound by American Book–Stratford Press.

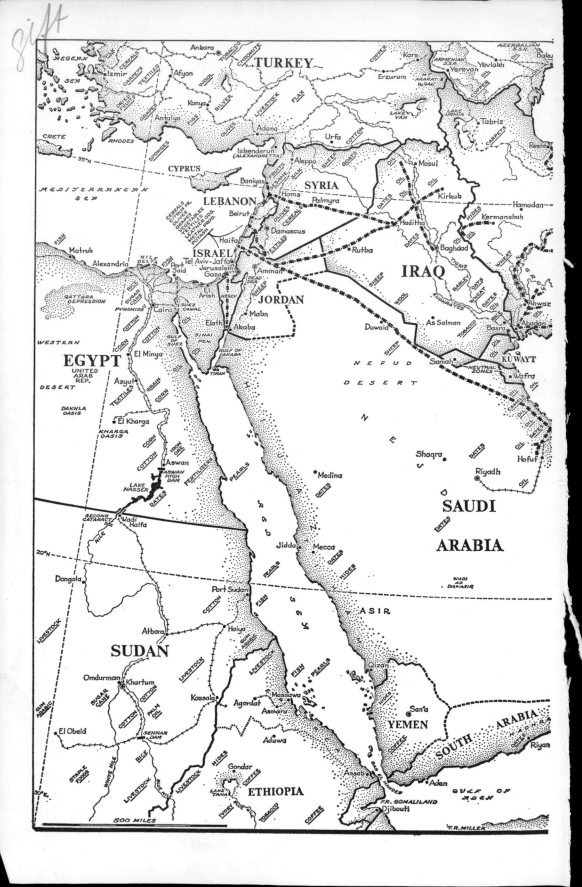